Y0-CBB-136

Professional Accounting In 30 Countries

International Practice Executive Committee
American Institute of Certified Public Accountants

Library of Congress catalog card number: 75-1717

Table of Contents

Preface

This book is an updated and expanded version of *Professional Accounting in 25 Countries* which was published in 1964. The material in the book was assembled and reviewed by the firms of members of the AICPA International Practice Executive Committee.

Each chapter is current as of the date indicated. Significant changes which have occurred after that date are included in the Addenda to the extent that information was available at the time of publication.

The sections on the various countries include descriptions of the accounting profession, auditing and reporting standards and accounting principles, and in some cases illustrative financial statements. They also include brief descriptions of the several forms of business organizations and requirements for stock exchange listing and security offerings. These latter descriptions are neither exhaustive nor legally complete, since they are only intended to indicate, in a general way, the auditing, financial reporting, and disclosure implications which exist in the various corporate laws or commercial codes.

United States principles, standards, and practices have been adopted as a frame of reference—not because they are necessarily more proper or correct than any others, but simply because one set of criteria is needed for purposes of comparison. Information pertaining to all other countries, therefore, is presented in comparison to the situation prevailing in the United States.

A precise summary comparison of professional standards and the reliability of financial statements among the 30 countries included in this publication is impractical, because the factors upon which judgment might be based are both voluminous and diverse.

It should be noted that in some countries the standards expressed through legal or professional channels represent more of a statement of goals than achievements, and the reader must consider whether practice conforms to precept. He should be aware that such conformity does not always exist.

Although this book is a result of the cooperative efforts of many people, particular acknowledgement and appreciation is extended to Robert L. Lutz, CPA, who provided freely of his time and talent for the benefit of the profession in the capacity of technical editor, and to Katharine Coveleski, production editor, and Diane Ganci Bree, production associate.

International Practice Division
American Institute of Certified Public Accountants

Argentina

[illegible]

Argentina

Argentina

As of June 1973

Forms of Business Organization

Business organizations in Argentina are governed by the Commercial Code and by Law No. 19,550, which significantly modified the code and became effective on October 23, 1972.

The principal forms of limited liability organizations are the corporation (sociedad anónima or S.A.), the registered branch of a foreign corporation, and the limited liability company (sociedad de responsabilidad limitada or S.R.L.). Many organizations with local financing are formed as S.R.L. companies because of the limited liability feature, the speed of formation, and relative freedom from government supervision.

Business in Argentina may also be carried on as one of several types of partnership or as a sole proprietorship, all of which generally involve unlimited liability for the owners. The majority of international companies have chosen to operate in Argentina as corporations or branches of foreign corporations.

Sociedad Anónima (S.A.)

The corporate form most closely resembling the typical U.S. corporation is the sociedad anónima. The corporate name must be followed by the words "Sociedad Anónima" or the initials "S.A." and may include an indication of the nature of the business in abbreviated form; for example, Industrial y Comercial (Industrial and Commercial), abbreviated I.yC. The following are the main features of the sociedad anónima as defined by Law No. 19,550:

1. There must be at least two shareholders. Each province, as well as the city of Buenos Aires, which as federal capital constitutes a separate federal district, is empowered to approve the formation of a sociedad anónima.
2. Corporations, foreign or domestic, may be shareholders as well as may natural persons.
3. No minimum capital is required.
4. Capital is required to be divided into shares of equal par value which can be either bearer or nominative (registered) shares. Until the shares are fully paid, however, they must be registered. Bearer shares are freely transferable, whereas negotiability of registered shares can be restricted by the company's bylaws.
5. The issuance of stock for less than par or nominal value is not permitted except for certain companies quoted on the stock exchange.
6. Capital must be fully subscribed at the time the sociedad anónima is created. At least 25 percent of subscribed capital must be paid in at the time of incorporation and the balance fully paid within two years. If the payment is made in assets rather than cash, the subscribed capital must be fully paid upon organization.
7. Administrative and supervisory bodies include a board of directors, executive committee, vigilance committee, and the syndics (statutory examiners).
    a. The board of directors, whose number may vary from one (three, in the case of companies referred to in paragraph 8 below) to a maximum fixed by the shareholders, are elected by the shareholders or by the vigilance committee as the bylaws may prescribe.
    b. The executive committee, if the bylaws provide for one, is composed of directors and is supervised by the board.
    c. The vigilance committee, if the bylaws provide for one, is composed of three to fifteen shareholders and is appointed by the shareholders. The vigilance committee has broad powers and, bylaws permitting, may elect the directors and assume the authority of the syndics who may then be dispensed with.
    d. The syndics are elected by the shareholders.

8. More extensive regulatory control is exercised by a government regulatory body (Inspección General de Personas Jurídicas) over sociedades anónimas that—
   a. offer their shares to the public;
   b. have a capital exceeding 5,000,000 pesos;
   c. have mixed state and private capital or are companies in which the government holds the majority of shares;
   d. carry out investment or savings operations or in any manner solicit money or securities from the public with the promise of future services or benefits;
   e. operate concessions or public services; or
   f. are affiliates of another company subject to this supervision.
9. Financial statements of a sociedad anónima and the report of the board of directors, duly reported upon by the syndics, must be submitted to a shareholders' meeting and to the Inspección General de Personas Jurídicas each year. All sociedades anónimas must have these financial statements reported upon by a national public accountant (contador público nacional or CPN), as much all other businesses formed in the Federal District whose capital is in excess of 5,000 pesos or whose income is over 10,000 pesos.

Each individual province has differing requirements. Condensed financial statements must be published in the official bulletin. When complete statements are published, the report of the CPN is also published.

Sociedad de Responsabilidad Limitada (S.R.L.)

The limited liability company is a partnership in which each partner's liability is limited to the capital subscribed by him. The following are its main characteristics:

1. It cannot have less than two nor more than fifty partners.
2. Stock companies (sociedades anónimas and sociedades en comandita por acciones) may not be partners. An S.R.L. may be a partner in another S.R.L.
3. Capital is divided into quotas (shares) of equal value; they should be 10 pesos or multiples thereof.
4. Capital must be fully subscribed and at least 50 percent paid in (if payment is to be made in cash) at the time the company is created, and fully paid within two years thereafter. If payment is to be made in assets, capital must be fully paid upon organization.

5. Administration is in charge of one or more managers, who do not have to be partners. They have the same rights and obligations as directors in a sociedad anónima.
6. Supervising bodies (syndics or vigilance committees) must be set up when the S.R.L. has 20 or more partners and are optional when it has less. These bodies are ruled by the applicable portions of regulations for sociedades anónimas.

Branch of Foreign Corporation

A branch may perform all of the acts that its head office authorizes it to perform. Registration is a relatively simple matter and depending on the amount of assigned capital may be relatively inexpensive. In order to register a branch of a foreign corporation, it is necessary to prove that the parent company's government extends reciprocity to Argentina, otherwise a special authorization of the executive power is necessary.

The certified financial statement of a branch must be submitted annually to the Inspección General de Personas Jurídicas and must be published in the official bulletin in the same manner as required for sociedades anónimas.

Sociedad Colectiva

This type of organization is formed by two or more persons, jointly and severally liable, who combine to do business in common under a firm name.

Sociedad en Comandita

In this type of partnership, there are two classes of partners, general partners (socios solidarios), who have joint and several liability for partnership debts and management, and silent or limited partners (socios comanditarios), whose liability is limited to the amount which they contribute or promise to contribute. A limited partner who takes part in the management of the sociedad en comandita risks incurring unlimited liability.

Sociedad en Comandita por Acciones

This type of organization differs from the sociedad en comandita in that the interests of limited partners are represented by shares. It is subject, with certain exceptions, to the rules governing sociedades anónimas.

Sociedad de Capital e Industria

This type of organization is formed when one or more persons supply funds for a business or a specific commercial transaction, and where one or more other persons enter into the association but contribute their personal services only.

Sociedad Cooperativa

This is a company organized for mutual benefit and to promote a common interest through an exchange of mutual services by the company for its members and by the members for the company. Profits are usually distributed to members in proportion to their usage of offered services.

Business Records

All businesses must maintain accounting records, the design of which may vary according to the preferences of management and needs of the business, except that two books are mandatory, a daily journal and an inventory book, both of which must be bound and have prenumbered pages. Such books and continuing supplements thereto must be presented to a local commercial court to be signed and marked as required by law. The commercial judge may authorize the use of modern mechanized devices to supplement the registered books or to partially replace the daily journal. A special book to record minutes of the company meetings (i.e., board of directors, shareholders, and so forth) must also be maintained.

Law No. 19,550 also provides that business records shall be prescribed in detail by regulations to be issued.

Syndics (Statutory Examiners)

Except where a vigilance committee exists and has assumed the functions of syndics, syndics must be appointed for sociedades anónimas and sociedades en comandita por acciones but are not required for any other forms of organization. Their main functions are to protect the interests of the shareholders, and they are unlimitedly and jointly responsible to them and to third parties for the performance of their duties.

The syndic's duties are, in addition to those established by the company's bylaws, as follows:

1. To oversee the administration of the company. To this end they may examine the accounting and other company records and docu-

mentation whenever deemed necessary and must do so at least every three months.

2. To count cash and securities.

3. To attend the meetings of boards of directors, executive committees, and shareholders.

4. To prepare and submit to the shareholders a report on the company's economic and financial situation. The report should cover the annual report of the board of directors to the shareholders as well as the company's financial statements.

5. To see generally that the directors comply with all laws, bylaws, regulations, and statutes affecting the company.

Syndics must be elected by the shareholders, be lawyers or public accountants, and be currently domiciled in the country. They cannot be employers, managers, or directors of the company or of another controlled by it or which controls it, nor be relatives of such directors and general managers. They may be elected for any term not exceeding three fiscal years and may be reelected. Where a vigilance committee exists, the appointment of a syndic is not mandatory since such a committee has parallel functions and duties.

Since the financial statements of larger corporations, as submitted to the Inspección General de Personas Jurídicas, must be certified by a national public accountant (CPN), it is customary for such a CPN also to be appointed as syndic. In the opinion of most CPNs such appointments do not violate their independent status, and the Consejo Profesional (professional council) of Buenos Aires has so ruled to this effect. It is estimated that currently more than half of the syndics are CPNs.

It is apparent that the syndic is not, either by education, training, or objectives, necessarily equivalent to the U.S. CPA nor to the U.K. CA. Unless the syndic also functions as a CPN, his approval of the financial statements of a company does not, and is not intended to, give the same assurance regarding financial statements as would that of a professional independent auditor.

Inspección General de Personas Jurídicas

In addition to the control exercised by the syndics, the Argentine government exercises control over companies by the use of government inspectors who may attend shareholders' meetings and sign the minutes thereof. They also review the financial statements prior to presentation to the shareholders and have a right to inspect the books and accounts.

They can require changes to be made in the financial statements if those statements are not prepared in accordance with existing regulations. Their responsibility is to see that the corporation is complying with Argentine law. Although these inspectors are considered to be qualified persons, their effectiveness is limited because of the small number of inspectors compared with the large number of companies to be examined.

Branches of foreign corporations are also controlled by the Inspección General de Personas Jurídicas.

Extensive control is exercised over those corporations described in paragraph 8 under the heading "Sociedad Anónima (S.A.)." Limited control is applied to all other corporations and generally covers only the formation (bylaws, statutes, and so forth) and subsequent changes therein, and changes in capital.

The Accounting Profession

Although the national public accountant degree (contador publico nacional—CPN) has been established for almost 50 years, it was not until 1945 that Decree-Law No. 5103/45 was passed to regulate the economic sciences (economics, actuarial studies, and accountancy). Professional practice is limited to those with degrees; however, persons in practice at the time the law was passed were permitted to register and continue their professional activities.

Requirements for Degree of Contador Público Nacional (CPN)

Matriculation in an Argentine national university follows 12 years of elementary and high school. "Contador público national" is a degree conferred by Argentine national universities upon completion of a five-year course. The prescribed curriculum is generally comparable to that required in U.S. universities. The candidate is also required to pass a final examination when he graduates from a private university. There is no specific experience requirement.

Up to 1971, the course included four specialized subjects: economics, accounting, actuarial science, and business administration. Most students now concentrate on two of these subjects. Since 1971 the business administration degree has been a prerequisite to obtaining the CPN degree.

Duties of Contador Público Nacional (CPN)

The duties of the CPN prescribed by law include the following:

1. To act in legal matters when a public accountant is required.

2. To advise businessmen on accounting matters.
3. To certify financial statements and accounting entries.
4. To certify financial statements for presentation to official entities.

Consejo Profesional de Ciencias Económicas

Decree-Law No. 5103/45 provided that each province and the Federal District be empowered to create a professional council (Consejo Profesional de Ciencias Económicas) which includes economists, actuaries, and accountants. Among others, the duties of these councils are to—

1. Create and maintain a register of qualified professionals. An accountant must be registered before commencing practice.
2. Prepare codes of ethics.
3. Propose minimum fees.
4. Advise the government on all questions pertaining to the professions.
5. Take disciplinary action for violations of professional ethics or for charging fees lower than the minimum prescribed. Disciplinary action may include suspension or rescission of registration.

As part of the first duty listed above, each council must also prepare and maintain a "registro especial de no graduados" (register of nongraduates). This register includes those persons who at the time of passage of the decree-law were engaged in the practice of the profession without having graduated from the university. A registered nongraduate may not use the title contador público nacional.

Other Professional Accounting Organizations

The accountants of the several provinces and the Federal District of Buenos Aires have organized their own accounting associations or institutes (Colegios de Graduados en Ciencias Económicas) and some of such institutes have been in existence for more than 50 years. They are private organizations and membership is limited to legally qualified accountants. In the Federal District there are about nine thousand registered CPNs, the province of Buenos Aires has some five thousand, and the province of Santa Fe about four thousand; other jurisdictions have smaller numbers.

Instituto Técnico de Contadores Públicos
(Technical Institute of Public Accountants)

In 1969, the Instituto Técnico de Contadores Públicos was formed by action of the Federación Argentina de Colegios de Graduados en Ciencias

Económicas with the stated objective of "serving the profession in all technical-scientific matters associated with its practice." The Institute has created five permanent study commissions (1) accounting principles, (2) standards for preparation of financial statements, (3) auditing standards and procedures, (4) standards of opinions of the public accountant, and (5) professional practice and responsibilities. Projects are assigned to the study commissions, whose findings and conclusions are submitted to the Institute's board for its further action. The recommendations and opinions of the Institute must first be approved by a majority of the board and must then be submitted to the governing board of the Federación for final approval or rejection, and must be published within 30 days after approval.

Recommendations of the Institute will reflect its position on accounting matters and will constitute a basis for future opinions. The opinions of the Institute, once approved by the Federación "are specifications of standards which serve as guidelines for the public accountants in their professional practice." Furthermore, "the principles or standards contained in the opinions . . . are considered as generally accepted" and "when a public accountant makes reference in his opinion to generally accepted principles or standards, it will be interpreted that these include the principles or standards contained in the opinions of the governing board of the Federación."

Ethics

A code of ethics was prepared and approved by the Consejo Profesional of Buenos Aires for application to economists, actuaries, and accountants, and includes in summary form the following rules of conduct.

The practitioner—

1. will maintain professional dignity and honesty and will strictly comply with all verbal and written commitments;
2. must maintain absolute independence;
3. will not slander another professional;
4. may not serve both parties in a controversy;
5. must act in good faith and will not act professionally to support or facilitate acts which are incorrect or contrary to the public interest;
6. must report and express opinions, either verbally or in writing, in a manner that corresponds to the facts and is clear, precise, objective, and complete;
7. must not seek or attempt to attract clients of other professionals, but may render services when these are requested;

8. must not sign documents relating to his professional activities which have not been prepared or reviewed personally or under his direct supervision;
9. must maintain client relationships with absolute discretion and confidence and may not divulge any matters without a client's express authorization;
10. has the obligation to charge fees that are not less than those fixed by the consejo.

Similar codes have been approved in the provinces and all are policed by permanent committees of each consejo, which normally act on complaint of a member or upon complaint of a third party. Penalties usually range from admonition to temporary suspension; permanent prohibition from practice can be imposed but seldom is so.

Auditing Standards

General Standards

The Seventh National Convention of Graduates in Economic Sciences, held in Avellaneda in 1969, approved a resolution recommending the following definition of "generally accepted auditing standards," which are similar to the auditing standards prescribed in Statement on Auditing Standards No. 1 of the AICPA.

Auditing standards are classified as general standards, which include personal and field work standards, and standards of reporting.

As to personal standards, the auditor must (1) be a person with a professional or university degree which is officially recognized or have the corresponding authorization and have technical training and professional capacity for practicing the audit function; (2) perform his work and prepare his report with professional care and diligence; and (3) keep himself in an independent position in order to warrant the impartiality and objectivity of his judgments.

As to field work standards, the audit work must include (1) adequate planning and supervision of assistants; (2) adequate study and evaluation of the internal control system, in order to determine the nature, scope, and timing of the audit procedures to be applied; and (3) obtaining, through auditing procedures, valid and sufficient evidence. These procedures will include the following:

1. Comparison of the financial statements with the accounting records, including selective tests of such records with the supporting documentation to the extent considered necessary on the basis of the

results of the study and evaluation of the internal control system.

2. Physical tests and counts of significant assets (cash, inventories, fixed assets, and so forth) and insuring that all liabilities are reflected in the financial statements.
3. Direct confirmation with outsiders (banks, customers, suppliers, and so forth) to the extent necessary in each circumstance.
4. Examination of important documents and authorizations, i.e., records of organization and meetings of the entity being audited, bylaws, minute books, contracts, and representations from clients' officers as required for an opinion.

The Technical Institute of Public Accountants has issued recommendations Nos. 3 and 4 dealing with a general definition of auditing standards and specific personal standards, respectively. The contents of such recommendations are in line with the above resolution of the Seventh National Convention of Graduates.

Standards of Reporting

The resolution on "generally accepted auditing standards" approved by the Seventh National Convention includes a broad definition of standards of reporting which are similar to those included in Statement on Auditing Standards No. 1 of the AICPA. In addition it includes specific standards of reporting as follows:

1. Whenever the name of a CPN is associated professionally with financial statements, he should (a) examine the financial statements in accordance with generally accepted auditing standards and issue an opinion on such statements in conformity with such standards or (b) otherwise state that the financial statements were not audited and, accordingly, are presented without opinion.
2. The opinion covering financial statements is the written report by which a public accountant, based on his examination in accordance with generally accepted auditing standards, expresses his opinion or states that he disclaims an opinion on such statements, in accordance with these standards.
3. The opinion should carry the title "Auditor's Opinion" and should be addressed to the persons or entities that contracted his professional services or otherwise as directed by the contracting party. He should clearly identify the statements examined, the complete name of the entity whose statements were examined, and the date of and period covered by such statements. The CPN should state that the examination was made in accordance with generally ac-

cepted auditing standards and should express or disclaim an opinion based on such standards. The opinion should indicate the place and date of issue and should be signed manually with a description and registration number of the professional title following the signature.

4. In relation to the financial statements taken as a whole or statements considered individually, the public accountant should express an opinion that they fairly present, or do not fairly present, the financial position and results of operations in accordance with generally accepted accounting principles, or if unable to express a favorable or adverse opinion, the public accountant must disclaim an opinion. The qualification of a favorable opinion does not alter its general character to the extent that materiality does not justify an adverse opinion or disclaimer of opinion.

5. In addition, the opinion must state whether generally accepted accounting principles were applied on a basis consistent with that of the preceding year.

6. Any limitation of scope which does not permit an unqualified opinion should be clearly indicated, including the reason for such limitation. However, if it is not reasonable or practicable to apply some recommended auditing procedure and the auditor has satisfied himself by means of other valid and sufficient procedures, it is not necessary to mention the omission of the recommended procedures.

7. Any exception relating to generally accepted accounting principles should be clearly stated and should describe the item in question, the nature of the exception, and the amount. The text of an exception should indicate whether it involves a discrepancy relating to a matter of evaluation or disclosure, or results from a lack of necessary elements of judgment or because the determination of an amount is subject to future events, the probability of which cannot be reasonably estimated.

8. All exceptions relating to consistency should be specifically stated, indicating the items affected, the nature of the changes, and the amounts involved.

9. A disclaimer of opinion should clearly indicate whether it is based on limitations in scope or whether the opinion on the statements taken as a whole is subject to future events, the probabilities of which cannot be reasonably estimated. When limitations of scope are sufficiently important as to imply that an examination was not made in accordance with generally accepted auditing standards, re-

porting standards applicable to unaudited financial statements should be applied.

10. It is necessary to consider events subsequent to the balance sheet date to the extent that they significantly influence the financial statements. Subsequent events include those that directly affect financial position or results of operations or those that are sufficiently significant as to deserve mention in the financial statements, generally in a footnote, even though they may not directly affect financial position.

11. Accordingly, the public accountant must examine events subsequent to the balance sheet date in order to weigh their effect on such statements. The date of the opinion, which is normally the day on which the audit work is completed, terminates the responsibility of the public accountant as to the disclosure of subsequent events.

12. When a public accountant's name is associated with financial statements that have not been examined in accordance with generally accepted auditing standards, each page of the statement should clearly and visibly indicate the words "financial statements not audited and without opinion of the public accountant."

Opinion No. 1 of the Technical Institute of Public Accountants adopted specific standards of reporting very similar to those of the Seventh National Convention mentioned above.

There is no standard form of auditor's report prescribed for the CPN in Argentina. However, the Technical Institute developed several models of reports similar to those used in the United States. The CPN who certifies the accounts of a corporation should assure himself as to compliance with the instructions stated in section 75 of the regulations to the general law on accounting activities (Decree-Law No. 5103/45), which were approved by Decree-Law No. 4460/46 published in the official bulletin of August 16, 1946. This section states the following:

> The certificate . . . shall be the consequence of an analytical study of the items forming the Balance Sheet and the Profit and Loss Account. It must reflect the clear, precise and objective opinion on the position being certified, and shall at the same time state the source from which the data has been obtained—books, vouchers, controls, etc., the samples taken for the analysis of the various items requiring such analysis and the other means employed for performing the job.

The certificate shall guarantee that the figures in the statements of assets, liabilities, and profit and loss accounts, agree with the amounts in the books of account, carried in accordance with legal requirements, and supported by the corresponding vouchers; it shall also assure that in determining the values and operating results a technically correct criterion has been followed.

Two resolutions adopted by the professional council of the federal capital dated June 25 and December 30, 1969, in effect, further regulate the General Law on Accounting Activities. These resolutions require that a professional opinion be expressed on financial statements of companies whose revenues exceed 3,000,000 pesos or whose capital account is at least 1,500,000 pesos and that there shall be applied as a minimum the generally accepted auditing standards sanctioned by the Seventh Inter-American Accounting Conference of 1965 and approved by the Seventh National Convention of 1969, including the specific standards relating to auditors' reports. These standards were attached to and made a part of these resolutions. Furthermore, the Buenos Aires Stock Exchange requires auditors' reports subject to its jurisdiction to specifically state that these standards have been met.

Accounting Principles and Practices

The accounting rules and practices in Argentina do not differ materially from those in the United States since they are based predominantly on textbook material, articles, and so forth, which utilize U.S. sources to some extent. Two of the most important differences are that income tax allocation and equity method are acceptable but not at present generally used in Argentina. There are also certain differences because of the requirements of the Commercial Code and because tax law requirements are sometimes followed in company accounts.

So far, the profession in Argentina has issued no statements on accounting practices and principles that are considered in the business community to be mandatory. However, the Sixth National Convention of the Colleges of Graduates in Economic Sciences in 1962 specifically approved certain accounting principles for financial reporting purposes, and the Seventh National Convention in 1969 approved papers on "Generally Accepted Principles for the Preparation of Financial Statements" and "Form and Content of Financial Statements for Commercial and Industrial Enterprises." Furthermore, the Seventh National Convention resolved that the Technical Institute thoroughly review the matter of generally accepted accounting principles so that a uniform set may be applied.

Form and Content of Financial Statements

The Argentine government, through Law No. 19,550, passed on April 3,

1972, issued the General Law of Business Associations which became effective on October 23, 1972. This law establishes specific accounting and reporting requirements for corporations, and limited liability companies with more than 19 members, as follows:

1. The financial statements (balance sheet, profit and loss statement, and complementary notes and statements) and the board of directors' and the syndic's statutory reports must be filed with the court of registry (where the company's legal file is maintained) and with the applicable regulatory agency; such documentation must be available to shareholders during the 15 days prior to their meeting to consider it (article 67).

2. The content of financial statements is specified in articles 62 to 66 (discussed below); in addition, significant items not specifically included in the statutory contents must be disclosed.

3. Certain companies (specified in article 299, which include companies offering their securities to the public) can be required to file, in addition to statutory financial statements, a source and application of funds statement.

4. Article 63 deals with the balance sheet; it specifies the classification of assets, liabilities, and capital and requires the segregation of current assets and current liabilities.

5. Article 64 deals with the profit and loss statement; it classifies items into sales, cost of sales, expenses, extraordinary items, and prior year adjustments; expenses include the following classifications:

   a. Compensation of administrators, directors, and syndics.

   b. Fees for services rendered.

   c. Remunerations (salaries and wages) and related contributions.

   d. Research expenses.

   e. Royalties and fees for technical services.

   f. Advertising expenses.

   g. Taxes, segregating interest, fines, and surcharges.

   h. Interest, segregating suppliers, financial institutions, and controlled, controlling, and related companies.

   i. Depreciation and other provisions.

6. The profit and loss statement must be complemented with an analysis of accumulated earnings indicating beginning balance, profit or loss for the year, and ending balance.

7. Article 65 deals with information that must be disclosed either through notes to the financial statements or as complementary notes and statements; required notes include, but are not limited to, the following:

   a. Restricted assets.

   b. Liens on property.

   c. Inventory valuation method.

   d. Revaluation and devaluation of assets.

   e. Changes in accounting.

   f. Effect of subsequent events on the financial statements.

   g. Result of transactions with controlled, controlling, or related companies.

   h. Restrictions on the distribution of profits.

   i. Contingent liabilities, including those of guarantor of third-party obligations.

8. Required complementary statements include, but are not limited to, the following:

   a. Fixed assets, showing additions, retirements, and depreciation.

   b. Intangible assets, showing transactions and depreciation.

   c. Investments in securities; in the case of those involving 50 percent or more of the capital of the investor or the issuer, the latter's financial statements must be included; for any such investment between 5 and 50 percent, information on result of operations and financial position of the issuer must be included.

   d. Other investments.

   e. Reserves and provisions.

   f. Analysis of cost of sales.

   g. Foreign currency position.

9. Article 66 deals with the statutory report required of administrators (board of directors in the case of corporations) who must address themselves to the following:

   a. Reasons for significant variations in the assets and liabilities.

   b. Adequate explanation of expenses, extraordinary income, and adjustments to prior years' results.

   c. Reasons for the reserves that are proposed.

d. Reasons for the proposal of distributing profits or paying dividends other than in cash.

e. Expectations for company operations.

f. Relations with controlling, controlled, and related companies and variations in the respective participations and in amounts receivable and payable.

10. Statements of changes in financial position may be required by governmental authorities in the case of corporations.

Resolution No. 1 of the Inspección General de Personas Jurídicas

As a result of the adoption of Law No. 19,550, the Inspección General de Personas Jurídicas has issued Resolution No. 1 of January 31, 1973, which establishes the form and content to be used by domestic corporations in the preparation of financial statements. In addition to the forms prescribed, the resolution also contains general rules for the preparation of financial statements, in accordance with the requirements stated in articles 62 through 66 of Law No. 19,550.

The heading for the financial statements must include the name of organization, legal domicile, principal object, date of registration with the Public Register of Commerce, changes in statutes (bylaws), fiscal year, and identification of share capital (common and preferred stock) with description of subscribed and paid-in capital.

Inventories

Almost any inventory method which is consistently applied is acceptable in Argentina. The pricing of inventories at the lower of cost or market is widely used in practice.

Investments in Securities

Investments in securities are generally reported by Argentine companies at cost, or at cost plus the par value of stock dividends received. Some companies make provisions for permanent diminution in the value of investments, while others do not. The Inspección General de Personas Jurídicas has issued no regulations dealing specifically with the valuation of investments or the accounting for stock dividends, although assets as a general rule may not be stated above cost. The equity method of accounting for investments in equity securities is not generally used in Argentina at the present time.

Fixed Assets

Due to the devaluation of Argentine currency, three laws (Laws Nos. 15,252, 17,335 and 19,742) were passed in 1960, 1967, and 1972 respectively which enabled business enterprises to revalue their long-term tangible assets for both tax and accounting purposes.

In contrast to the first two laws under which asset revaluation was optional, Law No. 19,742 makes revaluation mandatory for all companies with paid-in capital exceeding 5,000,000 pesos that have issued stock to the public, that are in joint ventures with the government, or that utilize public concessions or services. In addition, the latest law allows the government to increase the range of companies subject to revaluation.

Revaluation requires the application of published coefficients to the residual value (acquisition cost plus installation expenses, less depreciation) of the assets revalued.

The amount of the revaluation adjustment is the difference between the computed value and the original cost less depreciation.

Under Law No. 19,742 half of the amount of the revaluation adjustment may be capitalized; the other half must be credited to a reserve to cover future losses. The allowable amount may be capitalized in installments of not more than 10 percent of the paid-in capital per year. Contrary to the earlier revaluation laws, Law No. 19,742 does not require special authorization to revalue.

There are certain differences in the rules regarding revaluation for book purposes as compared with tax purposes. The two valuations are quite independent and either one can be made without the other.

Goodwill

Accounting authorities recommend that goodwill be recorded only if purchased. It should be amortized on a reasonable basis and should be written off immediately if found to have lost its value. The amortization of goodwill is not an allowable tax deduction.

Provision for Severance Liability

Under Law No. 11,729, certain indemnities are payable in the event of an employee's death or in case of dismissal not justified by law. This may be insured against but would usually be rather expensive. There is no requirement in the law that a provision for this contingency be created. The company may elect to do so, in which case an annual provision equal to 2 percent of salaries and wages is allowed as a deductible expense for tax purposes.

For book purposes, since the company is not liable when an employee resigns voluntarily or is pensioned, a reserve of from 35 to 50 percent of the theoretical total liability at balance sheet date is considered reasonable.

Reserves From Revaluation of Fixed Assets

The increase in fixed assets resulting from revaluation for book purposes is recorded in a restricted reserve account, which may be used for (1) absorbing past or future losses, provided such losses are the net result of the operations of one commercial year (or shorter period in certain exceptional cases) or (2) increasing the capital of the company.

For corporations, either use must be approved by the shareholders; if a capital increase is approved, a stock dividend of an equivalent amount is distributed. For other than corporations, either use requires the decision of a partners' meeting.

Legal Reserve

The sociedad anónima and the sociedad de responsabilidad limitada must appropriate 5 percent of annual net profits into a legal reserve until an amount equal to 20 percent of the par value of subscribed capital stock is accumulated. This reserve may be used to absorb accumulated losses, but no distribution of subsequent profits may be made until the reserve has been restored. Any balance remaining in this reserve is distributable to stockholders upon liquidation of the company.

Statement of Income

Stock Dividends. Stock dividends received are treated as income and recorded at the par value of stock by both the recipient and the issuer.

Depreciation. Any depreciation method is acceptable so long as it is consistently applied. The straight-line method is most prevalent.

Consolidated Financial Statements

Consolidated financial statements are infrequently prepared. There is no government requirement that consolidated statements be prepared.

Requirements for Listing Securities on the Stock Exchange and Public Sale of Securities

The Argentine Securities Commission (Comisión de Valores) approves applications for registration on the stock exchanges. Applicants must meet certain basic requirements, as follows:

1. Have a subscribed and paid-up capital of not less than 200,000 pesos

with a par value for all shares of 10 pesos or multiple of 10 pesos each.

2. Have financial and management arrangements satisfactory to the commission.

3. Have statutes (i.e., charters, provisions, or bylaws) conforming to the requirements of the commission.

   These include the following:

   a. Voting rights—no series or class of ordinary shares may be deprived of its voting rights.

   b. Directors—qualification for the post of director may not be restricted to election by a certain class of stock. (Since Law No. 19,550 provides that where different classes of stock exist each class may elect one or more directors, it is probable that this rule will soon be changed.) Total remuneration to directors can be no more than 25 percent of total income for the fiscal year.

   c. Shareholders must have preemptive rights to subscribe for subsequent issues.

Applicants must also furnish copies of their bylaws and financial statements for five years. When an issue is to be offered publicly, a prospectus must be issued containing the following information:

1. Brief history of company.

2. Composition of authorized and issued share capital and details relating to issues during previous ten years.

3. Description of, and details relating to, forthcoming issues (within 12 months).

4. A list of board members and statutory examiners.

5. Summary of royalties paid for previous three years.

6. Balance sheets and profit and loss accounts for the previous three fiscal years; when the results shown in the latter statements are not strictly comparable, the pertinent additional information must be shown in a specially prescribed form. All the statements and supplementary information must be certified by a CPN in a form established by the Argentine Securities Commission.

7. Details of distribution of profits during the last previous three years and of all fees and remunerations paid to directors during

the same period, split between fees arising from distribution of profits and remunerations charged to expenses.

8. Details, supported by financial statements, of investments in other enterprises where the holdings of the applicant are in excess of 20 percent of the share capital of the issuing corporation.

9. Details of real estate, and of any revaluations made thereof, and rates of amortization for these and other fixed assets and intangibles.

10. Details of any debentures, mortgages, and compositions with creditors.

11. Summarized analyses of payables and of all receivables.

12. Information about acquired companies, if any, including a comparison of net book value and estimated market value of such assets acquired within the last five years, with the price paid; if this comparison indicates an excess of price paid over book or market value, the reasons for this excess must be stated.

13. Insurance coverage.

The prospectus also must state that the results of operations for the period have been stated in the same manner as those for the preceding year.

When an issue is not to be offered publicly, a "reseña" (summary of information) of the information otherwise contained in a prospectus must be submitted to the Argentine Securities Commission and published in the stock exchange bulletin for all issues of shares of registered companies.

There are also additional rules regulating investment corporations.

The specified form for the certificate mentioned under paragraph 6 above may be translated as follows:

> We have verified that the figures contained in the preceding balance sheets and profit and loss accounts are in agreement with the corresponding entries in the principal books of account of the corporation and that the entries in these books agree with those in the auxiliary books and supporting vouchers.
>
> On the basis of the analysis referred to in the preceding paragraph and from the information and explanations which have been furnished to us at our request, we certify that the figures reflect faithfully the assets and liabilities of the enterprise in each of the financial periods included in the period under review.
>
> We are also of the opinion that the adjustments made to the profit and loss accounts published in the company's annual reports and

> corresponding to the financial periods under consideration, establish figures which are homogeneous and representative of the net profits obtained by the enterprise in carrying on their usual business during said financial periods.

(In addition, a brief general explanation should be inserted regarding the basis of the adjustments to the profit and loss accounts, and the procedure followed in computing the provision for staff dismissal indemnity.)

Registered companies are required to submit financial statements quarterly and annually, duly certified by a CPN and in the form prescribed by the regulations, to the Argentine Securities Commission and to the stock exchange.

The examinations made of the quarterly financial statements vary quite widely in scope, ranging from a mere comparison with the books to a review with procedures approaching an annual audit. The report accompanying such quarterly review would vary according to the type of examination made.

Subsequent issues of shares require similar registration, except that if shares are registered within two years of the original registration, a brief supplementary report may be filed.

Australia

Australia

As of December 1972

Significant developments since the preparation of this chapter are presented, by chapter, in the section entitled Addenda.

Forms of Business Organization

Businesses in Australia are carried on by individuals, partnerships, companies, trusts and estates, churches, and other institutions and governments. The first three types are dealt with below.

Individuals

If an individual wishes to carry on business as a sole proprietorship he may do so either in his own legal name or under a different business name. In the latter case he must comply with the requirements for registration of business names.

Partnerships

Partnerships are formed under the laws of the several states. If the name of the partnership differs from the legal names of the partners the name must be registered under the Business Names Acts of the states and territories in which it operates. Australian partnerships are very much like those found in the United States and England. Partners have unlimited liability. They are jointly and severally liable for the partnership debts. The number of partners is limited to 20 except in the case of professional partnerships, which usually may have 50 partners; however, an accountancy partnership may have 100 members.

Companies

There is no national company law in Australia. Therefore companies are incorporated under the laws of the six states and the several federally administered territories. Generally, these laws resemble each other, but differences do exist, and therefore, the reader is directed to the legislation of the particular state in which he is interested. The following notes deal only with the limited company because unlimited companies are rare, being largely confined to a few mutual funds. The liability of a shareholder of a limited company is limited to the amount not paid up on his shares.

Companies are divided into six classes: (a) public companies, (b) no-liability companies (another type of public company), (c) proprietary companies, (d) exempt proprietary companies, (e) companies limited by guarantee, and (f) foreign companies. The following requirements are common to all types except companies limited by guarantee and foreign companies, which are dealt with separately.

1. A company must have a minimum number of members—five for public and no-liability companies, two for proprietary and exempt proprietary companies, and one for a proprietary company wholly owned by a public company. Shareholders need not be residents of Australia.
2. A company must have an authorized capital divided into shares each having a nominal (par) value. Shares of no par value are not permitted. There is no minimum requirement regarding issued shares and part of the nominal (authorized) capital may remain unissued. Shares may be issued at par or at a premium, but not at a discount except with court approval. Bearer shares are not permitted. Shares may be ordinary, or may be preferred as to dividend and return of capital on dissolution. A company may not deal in or repurchase its own shares except in special and unusual circumstances.
3. A company must have a memorandum of association and articles of association, which are printed and are generally bound together. The memorandum sets out the name, objects, and authorized capital of the company. The original members of the company formally sign the memorandum and apply for shares. The articles are the

regulations which govern the management of the company, the powers of its directors, the conduct of its meetings, and so forth. It is possible for a company to adopt the standard articles prescribed by the state in which it wishes to incorporate.

4. Companies must have a minimum number of directors—three for a public company (two of whom must be individuals residing in Australia) and two for both classes of proprietary companies (one of whom must be an individual resident in Australia). A company may be a director of another company.

   The management of a company is vested in the directors who are elected by the members. The actions of directors are subject to the provisions of the Companies Legislation, the memorandum and articles of association, and the law generally. In practice it is usual for directors of substantial companies to delegate day-to-day management to employees of the company.

5. Companies must have one or more secretaries each of whom must be an individual and one of whom must be a resident of the state or territory of incorporation. The secretary is appointed by the directors and is generally a full-time employee or a professional person. The secretary is responsible for the statutory records and is frequently also the principal accounting officer and public officer for taxation purposes. (A "public officer" is a person appointed to represent the company on income tax matters and be responsible for observance of its obligations under the income tax legislation.)

6. Companies must issue annual financial statements which are subject to the approval of the annual meeting of members. Unless the Commissioner of Corporate Affairs grants an extension of time, the financial statements must be made up as of a date not more than six months prior to the date of the annual meeting. These statements must be accompanied by a statement and report by directors, a statement by the principal accounting officer (or until recently a declaration by the secretary), and, where there are auditors, the auditors' report.

7. Companies must file an annual return with the Commissioner of Corporate Affairs in the place of incorporation giving details of authorized and issued capital, names of directors and other officers, etc. Except in case of an exempt proprietary company, the financial statements and reports referred to in the preceding paragraph must be filed with the annual return. Companies must also file returns dealing with changes, as they occur, in directors, managers and secretaries, authorized and issued capital, memorandum of association, articles, and so forth.

8. A company must have a registered office in the state or territory in which it is incorporated. This does not have to be the company's place of business, and lawyers' and accountants' offices are often used by companies as registered offices. If the registers of members and debenture holders are kept elsewhere, notice of this must be filed with the Commissioner of Corporate Affairs, as must any change in the location of the registered office.

Principal characteristics of the six categories of limited companies are briefly described, as follows:

1. *Public Company*. This form closely resembles the publicly held U.S. corporation. Its name must contain the word, "Limited," or the abbreviation, "Ltd." With few exceptions the stocks listed on Australian stock exchanges are the issued shares of public companies. There are public companies whose shares are not listed. Public companies must issue a prospectus containing specified information and reports when raising equity capital or loans from the public.

   The Companies Legislation contains extensive provisions dealing with the takeover of companies.
2. *No-Liabilitv Company*. This type of public company may only be used as the formal structure of oil and mining companies. (However, it should be noted that many oil and mining companies are ordinary public companies.) Its distinctive feature is that a shareholder has no legal liability with regard to the amount not paid up on shares, i.e., he is free to forfeit his shares, which are then sold at auction by the company. Such a company must include in its name the words, "No Liability," or the abbreviation, "N.L."
3. *Proprietary (or Private) Company*. This form of corporate organization is most commonly used by foreign investors and corresponds to the U.S. closely held corporation. A proprietary company is one which, by its constitution, restricts the right to transfer its shares, limits the number ot shareholders to 50 (exclusive of employees and former employees), and prohibits invitations to the public to subscribe for its shares or debentures or to deposit money with it. The name must be followed by the words, "Proprietary Limited" or the abbreviation, "Pty. Ltd."
4. *Exempt Proprietary Company*. This type of company is normally available for use only by family businesses and small groups of individuals. An exempt proprietary company is a proprietary company in which no share is deemed to be owned by a public company. (For this particular purpose an overseas private company may be "deemed" to be a "public company.") Generally, the company may dispense with the appointment of an auditor pro-

vided it receives the consent of all its members annually. In some states, the company which does not appoint an auditor must file its annual financial statements with the Commissioner for Corporate Affairs, unless it becomes an unlimited company. This form of company is permitted to make loans to its directors, a practice denied public and proprietary companies.

5. *Company Limited by Guarantee.* This company is formed on the basis that the liability of its members is limited by its memorandum to the amount that they undertake to contribute to the assets of the company in the event of its liquidation. Such companies are usually charities or clubs.

6. *Foreign Company (Branch or Subsidiary of "Foreign" Corporation).* Because there is no federal company legislation, each state and territory regards a company incorporated outside its borders as a "foreign company," e.g., in relation to Western Australia, a New York company and a South Australian company are both "foreign companies" and both must register as foreign companies in Western Australia if they carry on business or establish a place of business there. Foreign companies must register within one month of carrying on business in another state.

   Registration formalities include (a) filing of certified copies of the company's certificate of incorporation and the memorandum and articles of association, certain declarations and particulars of directors, (b) payment of registration fees (which are based on the authorized capital of the foreign company), and (c) the appointment of an agent in the state.

   Foreign companies have the same rights, powers, and privileges as a company incorporated in the state. Generally the company's agent must file each year a copy of the company's annual financial statements. The agent must give notice of any change in the company's board of directors and in the location of its registered office in its place of incorporation.

   Because the cost of initial registration can be substantial in the case of a large foreign company, most overseas corporations prefer to trade in Australia by means of subsidiary proprietary companies rather than branches. (It should be noted that a branch may offer tax advantages in certain circumstances.)

Business Records

The Companies Legislation provides the following:

1. A company shall—
   a. keep such accounting records as correctly record and explain the transactions and financial position of the company;

   b. keep its accounting records in such a manner as will enable true and fair accounts of the company to be prepared from time to time; and
   c. keep its accounting records in such a manner as will enable the accounts of the company to be conveniently and properly audited.

2. A company shall retain the accounting records for a period of seven years after the completion of the transactions to which they relate.
3. The company shall keep the accounting records at such place or places as its directors think fit.
4. If any accounting records of a company are kept at a place outside the state the company shall keep at a place within the state, determined by the directors, such statements and records with respect to the matters dealt with in the records kept outside the state as will enable true and fair accounts, and any documents required by the legislation to be attached to the accounts, to be prepared.
5. The accounting records of the company are to be kept in written or printed form in the English language or in such manner as will permit ready accessibility and conversion into written or printed form in the English language.
6. A company is required to give to the Commissioner of Corporate Affairs notice of the place in the state where its records are kept unless the records are kept at the registered office of the company.

Other books required to be kept, in addition to accounting records, are minute books, register of members, register of directors, managers, and secretaries, register of charges, register of substantial shareholders, register of debenture holders, register of shareholdings of directors, and so forth. The legislation sets out in detail the information to be included in each.

The Accounting Profession

During the early development of Australia, professional accounting was carried out by men who had been trained in England, and so English accounting practices had a prominent influence on the profession in Australia. Increasingly of later years, especially with the growth of international accounting affiliations and partnerships, the Australian accountant has also drawn on the experience of his counterpart in the United States and other countries.

The first organization of accountants in Australia was formed in

Adelaide, South Australia, in 1885 and during the following years similar bodies were constituted in other states.

The development of the profession of public accounting has been guided by The Institute of Chartered Accountants in Australia and the Australian Society of Accountants. These organizations have their own bylaws and codes of ethics, conduct their own examinations and professional development courses, produce their own publications and bulletins, and are continually engaged in accounting research and improving the status of the profession. Joint activities are carried out by the two organizations in a number of fields including professional development and accounting research.

The Institute of Chartered Accountants in Australia

The Institute is the only body of accountants in the British Commonwealth outside the United Kingdom to operate under a Royal Charter; the Charter was granted in 1928 when the Institute was formed.

At June 30, 1972, membership totaled 6,317, of whom 3,188 were in public practice, 1,439 were employed by members in public practice, and 1,690 were engaged outside the profession.

A member cannot undertake any public accountancy services for remuneration until he is issued a practicing certificate. Holders of a practicing certificate have an additional vote in Institute affairs.

A member of the Institute may describe himself as a chartered accountant. A member who is a fellow (associate) may use after his name the initials "FCA" ("ACA") or the words "Fellow (Associate) of The Institute of Chartered Accountants in Australia." A member is eligible to be admitted as a fellow if he has been an associate of the Institute in public practice for at least three consecutive years prior to his requested change in status.

To be eligible for admission to membership, a person must be 21, have passed the prescribed examinations, and have completed five years (or three years in the case of graduates from an approved university or college of advanced education) in the service of a member in practice or of a member of an approved body of accountants.

Special admissions may be made if the Council of the Institute considers a person has appropriate educational qualifications and experience in the practice or teaching of accountancy, but such a member will not be granted a practicing certificate until he completes such service in the practice of accountancy as the Council prescribes.

The basic qualification for registration as an examination candidate of the Institute is that of university entry standard. After completion of an approved university or equivalent tertiary course, which includes a coverage in accounting, the candidate undertakes a professional qualifying year. The main emphasis of this year is placed on participation in planned activities of a combined professional and educational character, designed to integrate previously acquired academic knowledge with practical applications likely to face members of the profession. At the end of the year an "open book" examination is held to test the candidate's ability to apply individual knowledge to situations faced by practitioners.

The Institute is providing an alternative course of five years duration until tertiary educational facilities are available to meet the needs of all who wish to seek entry to the profession.

A member's handbook is issued and includes the Royal Charter and bylaws, rulings on professional conduct, statements on auditing and accounting practice, and an outline of the Institute's educational policy.

The work of the chartered accountant in Australia is similar to that of the chartered accountant in England and, accordingly, he engages in certain activities such as administration of companies in liquidation, company secretarial work, and share registrar work, none of which is customary for professional accountants in the United States.

Australian Society of Accountants

The Society was formed in 1952, as a result of a merger between the old established Commonwealth Institute of Accountants and The Federal Institute of Accountants. The Society later admitted members of the Australian Association of Accountants, and in 1966 amalgamation was made with the Australian Institute of Cost Accountants.

At June 30, 1972, membership totaled 36,109, of whom it is estimated that 15 percent were in public practice, 15 percent in government, and the balance in commerce, industry, and education. Some of the members are also members of The Institute of Chartered Accountants in Australia. Members in public practice provide services similar to chartered accountants. The Society is active in raising the standards and status of the commercial accountant.

A member of the Society may use after his name in the case of a fellow the words "Fellow of the Australian Society of Accountants" or the letters "FASA"; in the case of a senior associate the words "Senior Associate of the Australian Society of Accountants" or the letters and word "AASA (Senior)"; in the case of an associate the words "Associate of the Australian Society of Accountants" or the letters "AASA"; and in the case of a provisional member the words "Provisional Member of the Australian Society of Accountants."

A person seeking to become a member of the Society is required to have completed a recognized course of study in a university or college of advanced education and have passed (unless exempted from examination) the subjects of the Society's qualifying examination. The standard of the qualifying examination is equivalent to that of the final year examinations for a three-year full-time tertiary course in accounting. A candidate for the qualifying examination is not required to complete a period of practical experience in accountancy before attempting the examination, but the Society attaches considerable importance to practical experience in accountancy as a qualification for full membership. An applicant for membership must have a minimum of three years experience to become an associate. Applicants with the necessary academic qualifications who have not obtained this experience are eligible for admission as provisional members. In order for a member to advance to the rank of senior associate he must obtain specialized experience and pass further examinations in a particular area, for example, management accounting.

Professional Conduct

The Institute of Chartered Accountants in Australia and the Australian Society of Accountants have strict rules of professional conduct.

Although the Institute has codified rulings on questions of ethics, there is no formal written code of conduct as it is believed that ethical conduct in the profession derives from an attitude of mind rather than from compliance with specific rules. From time to time pronouncements on particular matters are made and members may obtain guidance or seek specific rulings from the Council. Codified rulings have been made on superseding another public accountant, publicity, membership description, remuneration, inconsistent businesses, activities through companies, prospectuses and estimates, specialist services, referrals, and independence. Members should not carry out work that should be performed by legal practitioners nor permit their names to be used on certificates of estimated future profits.

The Society's codification of professional conduct covers such matters as practicing in the name of a member, advertising, nomination in opposition to another member, solicitation of business, and the prohibition of fees shared with a solicitor and fees on a commission or contingency basis.

The need for a company auditor to be independent is recognized in company legislation which provides that, if a person does not comply with specific conditions, that person is precluded from acting as auditor of a company. The Institute's ruling on independence states that neither a member, nor a firm of which he is a partner, should express an opinion on financial statements of any enterprise unless he and his firm are in fact independent with respect to such enterprise. In addition to the statutory exceptions, a member will be considered not independent with respect to any enterprise if he or one of his partners or their wives or minor children had or was committed to acquire any material financial interest in the enterprise either by way of shareholding, loan, or other means or was connected with the enterprise as a promoter, underwriter, or in some position carrying voting rights with it in respect of a material financial interest. A "material financial interest" will be said to exist where the extent of such interest might provide an opportunity for an allegation, however unjustified, that the member's professional judgment was or could be impaired, or that information obtained in professional confidence was being or could be turned to private advantage.

Professional Development (Continuing Education)

Members of the accountancy profession in Australia are provided with a wide range of professional development activities in annual programs arranged by both The Institute of Chartered Accountants in Australia and the Australian Society of Accountants.

These activities are coordinated on a national basis and provide a range of activities from one-day seminars to three- or four-day courses. The programs of the Institute are directed mainly at areas of interest to the accountant in public practice. The courses of the Society are more of interest to the accountant in commerce. In some fields, programs are jointly arranged by the Institute and the Society.

Appointment of Auditors

All companies, other than exempt proprietary companies in certain circumstances, must appoint auditors. Members usually appoint the auditors but the first auditor must be appointed by the directors within one month after the company is incorporated unless the appointment has already been made by the members at a general meeting. In the case of the first auditor's being appointed by the directors, he retires immediately before the next annual general meeting but is eligible for reappointment. Once appointed by the members no specific reappointment resolution from year to year is required and the appointment of the auditor continues until termination by death, removal, or resignation, with the exception that, where a company becomes a subsidiary of another company, the subsidiary's auditor is deemed to retire immediately before the next annual general meeting but is eligible for reelection. The continuous appointment is meant to secure a substantial degree of independence for the auditor.

The legislation provides formal procedures for the nomination of the auditor and his consent to act. The auditor can be removed only by resolution, of which special notice has been given. An auditor may retire or resign only after giving his reasons to the Companies Auditors Board and with its consent.

Registered Company Auditor

The Companies Legislation provides for the appointment of a Companies Auditors Board, one of whose functions is to effect and control the registration or licensing of company auditors and liquidators. A person or a firm may not act as an auditor of a company unless he is, or all members of the firm residing in Australia are, registered with the Companies Auditors Board as company auditors. A person may register as a company auditor if, in addition to presenting proof of general good conduct and character to the Companies Auditors Board, he meets its professional requirements. Normally in practice these requirements are satisfied by membership in The Institute of Chartered Accountants in Australia, the Australian Society of Accountants, or any accounting body outside Australia recognized by the board. A separate application is required to register as a liquidator, and evidence of the applicant's experience in liquidation work and procedures is required. Registrations of both company auditors and liquidators are renewable annually. The board may impose disciplinary action, including cancellation of registration, on any registered company auditor found to have been guilty of discreditable conduct.

Auditing Standards

Standards of auditing in Australia were initially patterned on English practice. Many accounting firms now have U.S. as well as English affiliates and accordingly North American standards have considerable influence.

General Standards and Standards of Field Work

The codification of general auditing standards is in the process of revision (December 31, 1972). The profession's current general standards are reflected in the following extracts from the Institute's "Statement on General Principles of Professional Auditing Practice":

> The scope and character of each audit depends on the exercise of professional skill and judgement and the auditor has no defence if he curtails his audit when in his judgement he honestly believes it should have been extended.
>
> Auditors have their own independent responsibilities to form and express their opinion on the accounts to be presented by the directors to the shareholders. Their opinion must be soundly based, and the fundamental auditing principles to which they subscribe must be those which are recognised and accepted. Furthermore, the auditors'

> unqualified opinion can be expressed only if (a) the accounts themselves are drawn up in accordance with sound accounting principles, (b) such accounting principles have been applied on a basis consistent from one year to another or adequate disclosure is made of the effect of any change in basis, and (c) adequate disclosure is made of all material and abnormal items on which a fair presentation rests.
>
> The efficiency of the professional audit and the value of the auditors' opinion expressed in their report on the accounts depend on the auditors' personal and technical standards—integrity, impartialty and independence and on the exercise of their professional skill and judgement which is the essence of good auditing.

Great emphasis is placed on the necessity for making a proper evaluation of accounting and internal control as the basis on which the character and scope of all audits depend. Confirmation of receivables and the observation of physical inventories are general practice and considerable significance is placed on the adequate documentation of the processes of evaluating accounting and internal control, the need to acquaint management of deficiencies in it and the consequent audit steps taken to reach an opinion.

Reporting Requirements and Standards

The auditor of a company is required by law to report along the following lines:

1. Whether the accounts and, if the company is a holding company for which group accounts are required, the group accounts are in his opinion properly drawn up so as to give a true and fair view of the profit (or loss) of the company/group for the period and the state of affairs of the company/group as at the end of the period and are in accordance with the provisions of the act.
2. Whether the accounting records and other records and the registers required by law to be kept by the company, and, if it is a holding company, by the subsidiaries other than those of which he has not acted as auditor, have been, in his opinion, properly kept in accordance with the provisions of the legislation.

In the case of group accounts the auditor is required to state the following:

1. The names of the subsidiaries (if any) of which he has not acted as auditor.
2. Whether he has examined the accounts and auditors' reports of all subsidiaries of which he has not acted as auditor, being accounts

that are included (whether separately or consolidated with other accounts) in the group accounts.

3. Whether he is satisfied that the accounts of the subsidiaries that are to be consolidated with other accounts are in form and content appropriate and proper for the purposes of the preparation of the consolidated accounts, and whether he has received satisfactory information and explanations as required by him for that purpose.
4. Whether the auditor's report on the accounts of any subsidiary was made subject to any qualification, or vital comment, and, if so, particulars of the qualification or comment.

The Companies Legislation obliges the auditor to form an opinion on each of the following matters:

1. Whether he has obtained all the information and explanations that he required.
2. Whether proper accounting records and other records (including registers) have been kept by the company as required by law.
3. Whether the returns received from branch offices of the company are adequate.
4. Whether the procedures and methods used by a holding company or a subsidiary in arriving at the amounts taken into any consolidated accounts were appropriate to the circumstances of the consolidation.
5. Where group accounts are prepared otherwise than as one set of consolidated accounts for the group—whether he agrees with the reasons for preparing them in the form in which they are prepared, as given by the directors in the accounts.

The auditor is also required to state in his report particulars of any deficiency, failure, or shortcoming in respect of any of these matters.

Reference in the auditor's report to adherence to generally accepted accounting principles or to auditing standards is not usual and reports do not normally contain a scope paragraph.

The Institute's statements on qualifications in audit reports and on audit reports on group accounts give guidance and examples of practical application on occasions where the accounts present a true and fair view subject to reservation; where the auditor is unable to form an opinion; where the accounts do not present a true and fair view; and on the nature and extent of enquiries which have to be made by an auditor to form an opinion on the accounts of a subsidiary audited by another auditor but requiring to be consolidated in the group accounts.

Directors' Report

Companies Legislation prescribes minimum contents of financial statements of companies and also certain responsibilities of directors for reporting financial information. The stock exchanges in Australia also have disclosure requirements which must be complied with by listed companies.

The legislation also prescribes that directors submit audited financial statements to an annual general meeting of shareholders at least once in every calendar year. It is required that the statements give a true and fair view of the results for the period being reported upon and of the state of affairs at the close of that period. There is no prescription of the accounting principles to be adopted in the preparation of accounts but there is an overriding requirement that accounts should present a "true and fair view"; and it is generally agreed that if accounts are presented in accordance with generally accepted accounting principles as set out in the Institute's "Statement on Accounting Principles," they will present a "true and fair view."

The directors' report, which must form part of the accounts submitted to shareholders, is to be signed by not less than two directors pursuant to a resolution of the board. Specific statements are to be made in relation to a number of matters, which include the following:

1. The names of the directors.
2. The principal activities of the company.
3. The net amount of profit or loss of the company for the financial year after provision for income tax.
4. The amounts and particulars of any material transfers to or from reserves.
5. The details, purpose, and terms of issues of shares and debentures.
6. Dividends declared and/or paid and dividends proposed.
7. Whether the directors took reasonable steps to ascertain the adequacy of bad debt write-offs.
8. Whether the directors took reasonable steps to ascertain whether any current assets were unlikely to realize their book value in the ordinary course of business.
9. Whether at the date of the report the directors are aware of any circumstances which would render the values attributed to current assets misleading.

10. Details of charges over the assets of the company which have arisen since the end of the financial year (security given over assets).
11. Whether at the date of the report the directors are aware of any circumstances which would render any amount stated in the accounts misleading.
12. Whether the results of the company's operations during the financial year were in the opinion of the directors substantially affected by any item, transaction, or event of a material or unusual nature.
13. Details of options granted during the financial year or since the end thereof and particulars of shares issued by virtue of the exercise of an option and details of the number and classes of unissued shares under option at the date of the report.

The legislation requires the directors of a holding company, instead of submitting the preceding report, to cause to be attached to all group accounts a directors' report in similar terms in relation to the affairs of the group of companies.

It is also required that in addition to the directors' report, there shall be attached to the accounts (and/or group accounts) the following:

1. A statement by the directors made in accordance with a resolution of the directors, as to whether the accounts (and/or group accounts) are drawn up so as to give a true and fair view of the profit or loss for the relevant period and of the state of affairs at the end of that period.
2. A statement by the principal accounting officer of the company as to whether to the best of his knowledge and belief the accounts (and/or group accounts) give a true and fair view of the matters required to be dealt with in the accounts.

Accounting Principles and Practices

Form and Content of Financial Statements — Legal Requirements

There are no statutory requirements as to the form of financial statements, although it generally follows English practice. It is usual for the balance sheet to show assets on the right hand side and liabilities on the left, with the capital account being shown first. However, a particular form is quite often adopted to highlight important information. The minimum content of financial statements of companies is prescribed by company law and is set out in the legislation.

Special provisions are established by law in relation to group accounts (the accounts of a holding company and its subsidiaries). In this context, companies are deemed to be subsidiaries not only by virtue of share ownership, but also by reason of board control.

The alternatives available for presenting group accounts are as follows:

1. One set of consolidated accounts covering the group.
2. Two or more sets of consolidated accounts together covering the group.
3. Separate accounts for each corporation in the group.
4. A combination of one or more sets of consolidated accounts and one or more separate accounts together covering the group.

The alternative used must result in the presentation of true and fair consolidated accounts.

The directors of the holding company must ensure that the financial year of the holding company and the financial year of its subsidiaries coincide and, in the case of a new subsidiary with a different financial year, that the financial year of the latter is brought into line with the financial year of the holding company within 12 months from when it became a subsidiary. Once the financial years of the holding company and all its subsidiaries are uniform, no change may be made, unless it is to apply to all companies in the group. A holding company that is a foreign company is exempted from these requirements. The directors of a holding company that is not a foreign company may apply to the Commissioner of Corporate Affairs for relief from the requirement for coinciding financial years in respect of any subsidiary and, if circumstances warrant it, the commissioner may grant relief. Group accounts are not required if the holding company at the end of the financial year is itself a wholly owned subsidiary of another corporation incorporated in Australia.

Special provisions also exist in relation to disclosure of accounting information for prescribed types of companies, which are as follows:

- Investment Companies
- Borrowing or Guarantor Corporations
- Banking Corporations
- Life Insurance Corporations

Accounting Recommendations

The following statements have been issued by The Institute of Chartered Accountants in Australia which relate to form and content of financial statements.

Recommendations

D1.1 Presentation of the balance sheet.

D1.2 Profit and loss statements (net profit, prior period adjustments, and extraordinary items).

D2 Treatment of stock in trade and work in progress in financial accounts.

D4 Treatment of income tax in the accounts of companies.

D5 Depreciation, depletion, and amortization of fixed assets.

D6 Trust accounts (the form and content of the accounts of estates of deceased persons and similar trusts).

D7 The interpretation of "material" in relation to accounts.

D9 Treatment of investments in the balance sheets of trading companies.

Technical Bulletin

F1 Statement of source and application of funds.
This statement does not form part of the legal requirement for presentation to members but is frequently presented by companies with stock exchange listing. There is no requirement for it to be audited.

In addition, draft statements are currently being prepared on the following topics:

- Accounting for goodwill
- Accounting problems of the extractive industries
- Accounting for leases by lessees
- Accounting for leases by lessors
- Disclosure of, and changes in, accounting policies
- Equity accounting
- Expenditure carried forward to future accounting periods
- Post balance date events
- Revaluation of assets
- The materiality concept
- Treatment of deferred income
- Treatment of stock in trade and work in progress in financial statements

Some of these matters are already referred to in existing recommendations, but the draft statements will treat the subjects in extended form, and in the light of more recent developments in accounting practice. It is anticipated that the above statements, when issued, will also be endorsed by the Australian Society of Accountants.

Comment on Certain Accounting Practices

Deferred Charges. Preliminary expenses and costs of raising capital, classified generally as "intangibles," are usually written off by a charge against profits.

Depreciation. Depreciation of buildings, which are neither an integral part of plant nor structural improvements for primary production, is not generally allowed as a deduction for income tax purposes. However, The Institute of Chartered Accountants in Australia has issued a recommendation that depreciation of buildings be recorded as a charge against profits.

Equity Accounting. Equity accounting is still in an early stage of development with only a small number of companies using this concept in their presented information. The matter of equity accounting is receiving attention by way of an exposure draft in preparation by The Institute of Chartered Accountants in Australia and one issued by the Australian Society of Accountants.

Fixed Assets. It is not uncommon for companies to revalue fixed assets and investments upward and record the resulting credit as a "capital revaluation reserve." This reserve can then be used for the issuance of so-called "bonus shares" which are deemed to have the same "par value" as the shares with respect to which they are issued.

Goodwill. Purchased goodwill has customarily been carried forward indefinitely as an intangible. However, this practice is undergoing change, and it is gradually becoming accepted that it should be written off against realized profits over the period on which the goodwill assessment was based.

Price Level Accounting. Accounting for the effect of fluctuating price levels does not form part of standard reporting practice.

Sales and Cost of Sales. Present legislation does not require the disclosure of sales and cost of sales in the income statement and this information is not generally disclosed.

Tax-Effect Accounting. In accounting for income tax as an expense, it is accepted practice to recognize deferred tax liabilities and prepaid income tax expense where a company's operations are such that material differences exist between the income subject to tax and the pretax income reflected in the financial statements. Such companies include those engaged in mining, primary production, land development, and finance leasing.

Pooling of Interests. Accounting for acquisitions on a "pooling of interests" basis is not accepted practice.

Requirements for Public Sale of Securities

The Companies Legislation provides that no person shall issue, circulate, or distribute to the public any form of application for shares in, or debentures of a company unless such form of application is accompanied by a prospectus, a copy of which has been filed with the Corporate Affairs Commission.

Legislation prescribes the various matters to be stated in a prospectus. These matters include a report by a registered company auditor (who shall be named in the prospectus but need not be the company's usual auditor) with respect to the following:

1. Profits and losses of the company and of any guarantor referred to in the prospectus in respect of the five financial years immediately preceding the last date to which the accounts of the company or the guarantor were made up.
2. The assets and liabilities of the company and of the guarantor referred to in the prospectus at the last date to which the accounts of the company and of the guarantor were made up.
3. The rates of dividends paid by the company in respect of each class of shares in each of the five financial years immediately preceding the issue of the prospectus giving particulars of each class of shares on which the dividends have been paid.

If no accounts have been made up in respect of any part of the period of five years ending on a date three months before the issue of the prospectus, this must be stated.

In no case shall the accounts be as of a date which is more than nine months before the issue of the prospectus unless the commission has consented in writing to a longer period. Where a company or any guarantor company has subsidiaries, the report must also deal with the profits or losses and assets and liabilities of the subsidiaries either separately, as a group of subsidiaries, or combined with the company.

Should the prospectus relate to shares in, or debentures of, a borrowing corporation (that is, a company which borrows money from the public by invitation), it is necessary for the report to state separately estimates of the amounts of moneys owing to and payable by the company (a) not later than two years, (b) later than two years but not later than five years, and (c) later than five years calculated from the last day to which the accounts of the company were made up.

If the proceeds or any part of the proceeds of an issue are to be applied directly or indirectly in the purchase of a business or the acquisition of shares in another company, the report by the auditor must also deal with the profits or losses and assets and liabilities of the business or company to be acquired. In relation to the acquisition of shares in another corporation the report must deal with certain specified matters.

The legislation also requires the prospectus to include a report by the directors as to whether since the date of the last financial accounts—

1. The business has been satisfactorily maintained.
2. There have arisen any circumstances adversely affecting the company's trading or the value of assets.
3. Current assets appear in the books at values believed to be realizable in the ordinary course of business.
4. There are any contingent liabilities by reason of any guarantees given by the company or its subsidiaries.
5. There are any changes in published reserves or any unusual factors affecting the profits since the last annual report.

It should be noted that a prospectus including a statement made by an expert should not be issued unless the expert has given his written consent to its issue.

Requirements for Listing Securities on the Stock Exchange

Any company which desires to issue its shares or debentures to the public must issue a prospectus, or, in certain circumstances, a memorandum of sale which must comply with the legislation in the place in which the company is incorporated. In addition, if the company desires to seek listing for its shares or fixed interest securities on a member exchange of the Australian Associated Stock Exchange, it must satisfy their official listing requirements. These requirements are uniform throughout Australia and are contained in the publicly available *Listing Manual.*

The exchanges have set minimum capital requirements for new companies of $300,000 of paid-up share capital (including premium on issue) for the one class of shares and also require a minimum of 300 holders of those shares. If a company has a paid-up capital of under $2,000,000 at least $70,000 or 25 percent of the capital of the one class of shares must be held by members of the public. For companies with capital in excess of $2,000,000 at least $500,000 or 15 percent of such capital of the one class must be held by the public. Vendors' shares in new mining companies are restricted from listing for a period of 12 months from the date of quotation of the public shares.

The exchanges have laid down numerous requirements to be included in Company Articles of Association. For example, it is provided that there shall be no restriction on the transfer of shares which are fully paid, except where precluded by law. There are also extensive provisions relating to a prospectus issued by a company wishing to raise new capital or borrowings.

The type of securities normally listed for public dealing includes shares, stock units, share options, convertible notes, debentures, unsecured notes, property trust units, and government and semigovernment bonds and securities.

Once admission to the official list is obtained, companies must then comply with a comprehensive set of requirements, specifically designed for full and timely disclosure of their activities.

Listing manuals may be obtained from any of the six member exchanges of the Australian Associated Stock Exchange.

Australia

Illustrative Financial Statements

ILLUSTRATIVE FINANCIAL STATEMENTS—AUSTRALIA

Consolidated Balance Sheet

as at _____________ and at _____________

	Current Year	Prior Year
SHARE CAPITAL AND RESERVES, AND LIABILITIES		
Authorized capital $_____________		
_____________ ordinary shares of __ each fully paid		
Issued capital		
_____________ ordinary shares __ each fully paid	....	....
Capital reserves	....	....
Retained earnings	....	....
SHARE CAPITAL AND RESERVES	....	....
Investment and building grants	....	....
Long-term debt	....	....
Provision for deferred income tax	....	....
CURRENT LIABILITIES		
Bank overdraft	....	....
Short-term borrowings	....	....
Creditors and accruals	....	....
Provision for taxation	....	....
Provision for dividend	....	....
Provision for long service leave	....	....
	....	....
Total share capital and reserves, and liabilities	....	....
ASSETS		
FIXED ASSETS		
Land	....	....
Buildings	....	....
Plant	....	....
Capital works in progress	....	....
INVESTMENTS	....	....
CURRENT ASSETS		
Short-term deposits	....	....
Trade debtors	....	....
Other debtors and prepayments	....	....
Amount owing by associated company	....	....
Contracts in progress	....	....
Stocks	....	....
Total assets	....	....

ILLUSTRATIVE PROFIT AND LOSS STATEMENT—AUSTRALIA

Years Ended ____________ and ____________

	Consolidated	
	Current Year	Prior Year
SALES AND REVENUE	....	....
OPERATING PROFIT	....	....
Add income from investments	....	....
Less interest to other persons	....	....
Pretax profit	....	....
Less provision for income tax	....	....
NET PROFIT BEFORE EXTRAORDINARY ITEMS	....	....
Extraordinary items	....	....
NET PROFIT AFTER EXTRAORDINARY ITEMS	....	....
Unappropriated profits, previous year	....	....
Prior year adjustments	....	....
Transfer from general reserve	....	....
Available for appropriation	....	....
Dividends	....	....
Transfer to general reserve	....	....
Transfer to capital profits reserve	....	....
Unappropriated profits, end of year	....	....

Belgium

Belgium

As of May 1973

Note: Although Belgium is a bilingual country, terminology in the text is given only in French (with English translation) in order to avoid burdening the reader with excessive use of foreign words and phrases. However, the Flemish equivalents of the terms used may be found in a glossary appended to this chapter.

Forms of Business Organization

The forms of business organization in Belgium have points of similarity with those in France, since Belgian commercial laws were originally derived from those of France. The principal form of business organization in Belgium is the "société anonyme" (corporation). In addition, business may be carried out as a "société en commandite par actions" (an organization which has both limited liability shareholders and general partners), "société de personnes à responsabilité limitée" (private limited liability company), "société en commandite simple" (limited partnership), "société en nom collectif" (general partnership), and "société cooperative" (cooperative). All business enterprises must register with the Register of Commerce.

Business may also be carried on through a branch of a foreign corporation.

Société Anonyme (S.A.)

The Belgian corporation must have not less than seven shareholders; the maximum life of a corporation is 30 years, which is renewable for additional 30-year periods.

Various types of stock may be issued, for example, "actions ordinaires" (common stock), "actions privilégiées" (preferred stock), and "parts de fondateurs" (founders' shares). There are also "actions de dividende" (dividend stocks), which normally share in earnings but not in capital distributions on liquidation, and "actions de jouissance" (shares that, although the original capital investment has been repaid, retain the right to super dividends, but normally do not share in capital distributions on liquidation). Shares may be in bearer or registered form and need not have a par value. All shares must be subscribed prior to formation; there is no provision for "authorized but unissued stock." Bearer shares must be fully paid before being issued. Registered shares to be paid for in cash may be issued when 20 percent of the price is paid. If such shares are to be paid for in kind, they must be fully paid before issue.

If the number of shareholders falls below seven and such condition persists for more than six months, any interested party may demand dissolution of the company. Should the number of shareholders of a corporation become less than two, the corporation is considered to be dissolved by operation of law.

The management of the corporation is in the hands of a board of directors, of which there must be at least three members, but who need not be shareholders. They are elected by the shareholders for a term of up to six years and must deposit or have deposited for them a specified number of nominal shares to guarantee performance of their duties.

The Belgian Commercial Code requires that every société anonyme must elect, for a term of up to six years, one or more statutory examiners (commissaires réviseurs), who have an unlimited right of surveillance and control over all operations undertaken by the corporation. The examiners must deposit or have deposited on their behalf guarantees of at least one share each. (Statutory examiners are described more fully under a separate heading.) One of the shareholders, especially in small family companies, is sometimes elected "commissaire."

Corporations must publish their annual financial statements in the official gazette *(Moniteur Belge)*, accompanied by a list of the directors and statutory examiners, the names and addresses of partly paid-up shareholders together with the amount remaining unpaid, and a statement showing the distribution of the profits.

Société en Commandite par Actions

This is a type of company having characteristics of both corporation and general partnership. The firm's name, preceded or followed by the words "Société en Commandite par Actions," may only include the names of the general partners. The liability of the general partners for the company debts is joint and several while the liability of the limited shareholders is limited to their share of the capital contribution. The regulations governing a corporation are applicable to this type of organization. Such a société must have at least three commissaires.

Société de Personnes à Responsabilité Limitée (S.P.R.L.)

This form of company is widely used by the small family business attracted by the advantages of limited liability. The liability of the members is limited to the amount of their share subscriptions.

The company may consist of not less than two nor more than fifty members, and corporate bodies are excluded from membership. The shares are not freely transferable; Belgian company law requires the assent of at least half of the members, holding 75 percent of the capital, to any share transfer other than to an existing member or close relatives of members. Moreover, the company statutes may impose transfer restrictions more stringent than this. The issued and paid-up capital may not be less than 250,000 Belgian francs. Shares may not have a nominal value of less than 1,000 francs.

The form of an S.P.R.L. cannot be adopted for the business of insurance, savings banks, building societies (mortgage loans), or stock exchange brokers. Bonds and debentures cannot be issued, nor can the shares be quoted on a stock exchange.

An S.P.R.L. can be administered by one or more managers who need not be members. If the number of partners (shareholders) exceeds five, a commissaire must be elected.

Under the provisions of a Royal Decree of November 4, 1963, an S.P.R.L. having not more than ten members and a capital of not more than 3,000,000 Belgian francs may elect to be taxed either under the laws applicable to corporations or under those applicable to individuals. All others are treated in the same way as corporations.

The name of the company must appear in legal and other documents preceded or followed by the words "Société de Personnes à Responsabilité Limitée," and an indication of the address of the registered office. The financial statements must be deposited with the commercial court, but not necessarily published.

The duration of an S.P.R.L. is 30 years, renewable for additional 30-year periods.

Branch of a Foreign Corporation

Foreign corporations establishing Belgian branches must apply for a Register of Commerce number authorizing them to trade in the country after producing evidence of publication of the foreign corporation's statutes in the official gazette (*Moniteur Belge*), and the filing of such statutes with the Register of Commerce. The annual financial statements of the foreign corporation (not of the branch) must also be published in the official gazette. A responsible representative domiciled in Belgium, who may be a bank, a Belgian corporation, or a private person must be appointed for the purpose of insuring the payment of taxes.

Société en Commandite Simple

This is a form of partnership with both general and limited partners. The name of the firm consists of the name(s) of the general partners and may not contain the name of a limited partner. Limited partners may take no part in the management; if one of them does so, his liability becomes unlimited with respect to the matters in which he has participated, or if he habitually undertakes managerial duties, he becomes an unlimited partner.

Société en Nom Collectif

This is in substance a general partnership, all the partners of which are jointly and severally responsible for the company's liabilities. The partnership name must consist of the names of one or more of the partners.

Business Records

The Commercial Code requires that all enterprises keep an official inventory book, an official journal, and a copy of all correspondence. The official books must be legalized by a judge, which is done by affixing the court's seal to the books in question before any inscriptions are made therein.

The law requires an annual "inventory" of assets and liabilities to be recorded in the inventory book. This requirement is usually met by inserting a copy of the year-end financial statement or trial balance. The journal must contain either in detail or in total the monthly entries posted from the subsidiary account books to the general ledger.

The share register must be kept at the company's registered office.

In addition to the books mentioned above, value-added tax and labor legislation require that sales and purchase journals must be kept in accordance with strict regulations, and a personnel register must be kept up-to-date.

In order to comply with the direct taxation authorities' minimum requirements for information, it is invariably necessary to keep the usual books of account such as the general ledger, cost of sales records, expense analyses, and so forth.

Commissaire Réviseur (Statutory Examiner)

As required in the Commercial Code, shareholders must elect one or more commissaires for a period of not more than six years. The commissaires have unlimited rights of surveillance and examination over all the transactions of the company. They need not be of Belgian nationality, reside in Belgium, nor have an accounting background. The directors of a corporation must submit to the commissaires a statement of assets and liabilities every six months and a report of the board of directors at least one month before the annual general meeting, and, in turn, the commissaires must present to the annual general meeting a report of their surveillance and any proposals that they consider appropriate. The duties of the statutory examiners are similar to, but in some respects exceed, those of the directors in that the role of the commissaires is to observe and, if necessary, to call the attention of the shareholders to the acts of the management, as well as to report on the accounts. Company law (article 65) states that the report of the commissaire must include "the propositions they think convenient or necessary to be put to the shareholders' meeting, and they must also record the method by which they controlled the inventories" (inventory of assets and liabilities).

The following is the form of a typical report of a statutory examiner:

> In accordance with clause ______________ of the statutes, we have examined the balance sheet at __________ as well as the profit and loss account for the year __________ and confirm that they are in agreement with the books of account. We have satisfied ourselves as to the existence of cash at banks and investments, and received such information as we required concerning the other items in the accounts.
>
> Our examination having been completed to our satisfaction, we propose that the balance sheet and profit and loss account as submitted by the Board of Directors be adopted by the stockholders.

The report of the usual commissaire, who is not required to have accounting training, cannot be expected to give the same assurance as to fairness of presentation of financial statements as would that of a professionally trained and independent auditor.

Publicly held companies must appoint among their commissaires at least one who is a member of the Institut de Réviseurs d'Entreprises.

Provided they are free to carry out the work in accordance with the auditing standards of their respective institutes, international accounting firms practicing in Belgium generally allow their members to be appointed as commissaires; the report of the statutory examiner is sometimes modified to include a reference to the fact that the commissaires have been assisted by the international accounting firm to which they belong.

The Accounting Profession

There are two recognized groups of independent auditors in Belgium, the réviseurs de banque and the réviseurs d'entreprises, whose titles are protected by law.

Réviseurs de Banque

The members of the Institut des Réviseurs de Banque (formed in 1935) perform specialized services for banks. Admission to membership is by appointment of the Banking Commission and requires a first-class university standard of education as well as many years' experience in financial enterprises. There are 25 members at present (1972), and they are considered the ranking class of independent accountants in Belgium.

While the réviseur de banque is a highly qualified professional in his field, his work is usually of a specialized character relating to banking and finance and does not comprise that which is ordinarily undertaken by an independent public accountant. A member of this Institut may, however, be appointed a réviseur d'entreprises.

Réviseurs d'Entreprises

Since the law that created the Institut des Réviseurs d'Entreprises requires that corporations whose shares are sold publicly must appoint at least one réviseur among its examiners (commissaires), the work of this class of accountants is largely that of the examination of the financial statements of these companies. When a company issues shares for other than cash, the equivalent value given for the shares must be approved by a réviseur d'entreprises.

The réviseur may also perform many of the services undertaken by the expert comptable (see page 62), except that he may not participate in the management of enterprises nor may he be an employee. Any services performed by him outside of his legal function as auditor are rendered privately and separately from his work as réviseur.

Institut des Réviseurs d'Entreprises

The Institut des Réviseurs d'Entreprises was formed by law in 1953, in an attempt to organize the profession, but it has not been very successful since the regulations of the Institut severely restrict the activities of its members. Conditions for admission to the Institut are to some extent similar to those of the Collège National des Experts Comptables (see page 62), but are much more restrictive. A large number of réviseurs are also members of the Collège.

Ethics (Reviseurs d'Entreprises)

A Royal Decree, dated March 16, 1957, proposed by the Minister of Economic Affairs, established a code of ethics for regulating the profession of réviseurs d'entreprises, which accordingly has the force of law. Its provisions are summarized as follows:

1. Members must practice under their own names.
2. All publicity is forbidden.
3. They may not participate in the management of any business concerns, even family ones, and may not be involved in any commercial activities.
4. They must respect the rules of professional procedure in relations with their fellow members of the Institut.
5. They must not limit their activities in such a way as to become dependent upon any particular group or authority.
6. They may not accept any missions that are not within the scope of their profession.
7. Members may be assisted only by their partners, their trainees, and their employees, or by other members of the Institut. In certain cases the Institut can give special authority for departure from this rule.
8. Members may not sign a report upon accounts that have not been verified by them or their partners or staff. In the case of accounts prepared abroad, such accounts may be accepted if they have been examined by someone abroad with an equivalent degree, and reference to this must be made in the member's report.
9. When members give an opinion on accounts they offend the rules of the profession—
    a. If they omit mentioning an important fact of which they have knowledge and which is not revealed or is insufficiently revealed in the accounts, or whose disclosure is of a nature that could affect the judgment of the reader.
    b. If they attach to the opinion that they express qualifications of such a nature that they destroy the value or bearing of the opinion.

Disciplinary procedures are entrusted under the decree to the Council of the Institut and the procedures and sanctions are detailed in chapter II of the decree.

There are other rules contained in letters from, or statements made by, the Institut that are designed to maintain the standing of the profession or to safeguard the members' independence. For example, the réviseur d'entreprises—

1. May not be an employee or sign an employment contract.
2. May not be a member of the board of directors or be a manager, proxy holder, or signing clerk in a commercial company.
3. Before being able to accept the function of commissaire réviseur in a company, must first obtain permission and authorization from the Institut des Réviseurs d'Entreprises and their agreement to the amount of his remuneration.
4. May not do any form of trading nor accept any duties that belong to other professions, for example, he—
    a. May not hold accounts.
    b. May not establish documents relating to the application of social laws.
    c. May not be an insurance broker.
    d. May not give expert opinions or advice on the valuation of real estate, or be an intermediary agent.

Expert Comptable

The designation "expert comptable" (accountant) is not protected by law, and anyone may use it. There are a number of expert accountants in Belgium, not members of the Institut des Réviseurs d'Entreprises, who perform professional accounting services and who may or may not be members of the Collège National des Experts Comptables.

Collège National des Experts Comptables

The Collège was formed in 1950, by grouping some twenty-four representative associations existing in Belgium. Its membership comprises about fifteen hundred accountants of whom about one-third are in public practice (active members); the others are called "agreed members" and are employed in private enterprises or by accounting firms.

Candidates for membership must pass an examination composed of eight parts covering accounting technique, law, administrative organization, general economics, managerial economics, mathematics and statistics, composition, and ethics. The graduates of any of the courses given by any of the institutions specifically approved by the Collège or university graduates in economics, financial or actuary courses, are exempted from these examinations. These candidates must also pass an examination on practical applications of accounting and must have had a five-year training period as an employee of an accountant who is a member of the Collège.

The Collège publishes a monthly journal in both French and Flemish.

The services to be performed by members of the Collège in Belgium have been outlined by a commission established by the Collège National des Experts Comptables. Some of the areas of interest include the following:

1. Advice in the capacity of an expert.
2. Periodic or incidental judgment regarding the state of affairs of companies.
3. Examination of annual accounts.
4. Examination and preparation of cost-price calculations.
5. Advice on the formation, administration, and liquidation of companies.
6. Assistance in the management of enterprises.
7. Advice relative to the transfer and combination of companies.

Ethics (Collège National des Experts Comptables)

The Collège has issued a code of ethics that, in ten chapters, discusses such topics as professional secrets, independence, incompatible occupations, advertising, relations with brother professionals and clients, fees, and so forth. The position taken is generally similar to that prevailing in other countries; independence is recommended both in letter and spirit, but there is no specific prohibition against having a financial interest in a client.

Other Organizations of Accountants

Of the remaining organizations of accountants in Belgium, the more important are the Société Royale Chambre Belge des Comptables and the Association Nationale des Comptables de Belgique (ANCB).

The Société Royale Chambre Belge des Comptables was formed at the turn of the century. Membership is gained by examination extending over a period of approximately seven years, depending upon the ability of the candidate and the time he has available for study, and a diploma is granted on attaining membership. There are no conditions relating to apprenticeship or service with a public accountant, but the vast majority of the candidates do have accounting employment.

The Association Nationale des Comptables de Belgique was formed in 1958, under the sponsorship of the Collège National des Experts Comptables, to represent the majority of accountants employed in commerce and in industry who do not qualify for membership in the Collège.

Auditing Standards

The accounting profession in Belgium has not as yet issued any recommendations on auditing standards and accounting principles similar to those issued by the profession in the United States and United Kingdom. However, the Collège National des Experts Comptables has had in preparation for some years a statement setting forth recommended auditing procedures.

General Standards

Adequate public accounting service is not generally available, except possibly from the most progressive experts comptables and the réviseurs d'entreprises. Except in the case of the réviseur, the Belgian auditor is permitted to have financial interests, direct or indirect, in the enterprise which he audits.

Standards of Field Work

1. Field work is frequently limited to comparison of the trial balance with the general ledger accounts, examination of the bank statements, and inspection of the documents of title to securities.
2. Payment by check is rare in Belgium, and paid checks are not returned by the banks. Cusomary practice is to make payments by bank transfer orders, i.e., payment instructions are mailed or delivered directly to the bank. Daily statements are mailed to customers, however, and under these arrangements direct confirmations of bank balances are not always considered necessary.
3. It is unusual to request direct confirmation of accounts-receivable balances from the debtors, although the practice is spreading.
4. Physical inventories are not always observed.
5. The auditor is not required to review the system of internal control and, hence, his program of audit is not based on the results of such review.

Standards of Reporting

The typical audit report issued by the accounting profession in Belgium, apart from the standard report of the commissaire shown elsewhere in this section, is a discussion in long form of the composition of the various headings of the balance sheet and earnings statement. It is addressed to the directors of the company and, unlike U.S. practice, usually does not terminate with a final paragraph stating a formal opinion on the financial statements.

The reason for this practice is that the criterion of the so-called minimum position is still generally accepted even by the réviseurs d'entreprises (but not by the réviseurs de banque who, however, not being called upon to audit corporations other than banks, do not greatly influence the prevailing standards of practice). Providing that the financial position of a company is at least as good as that shown by the accounts, the accounting profession in Belgium is expected to condone the creation and the withdrawal for use of hidden reserves. As a result, the profession in general is often unable to give a clear-cut opinion as to whether the financial statements fairly present the company's position and results of operations.

Another example of the difficulties facing the profession in Belgium is demonstrated by the treatment of depreciation in published or official accounts. In the absence of adequate profits, depreciation is sometimes not charged because it is considered essentially an instrument of financial policy. Tax law is also responsible for this tendency.

The omission of adequate depreciation from the accounts is generally mentioned in a typical commissaire's report but would rarely, if ever, give rise to a qualification of the fair view or correctness of the financial statements.

Accounting Principles and Practices

Form and Content of Financial Statements

The Commercial Code places the entire responsibility for the valuation of assets and estimate of liabilities on the directors, although it requires that the balance sheet will show fixed assets, current assets, capital, reserves and surplus, debentures, secured liabilities, and unsecured liabilities separately. The code does not list any further requirements in relation to the form and content of the income statement.

The balance sheet of a company, as approved by the shareholders, need not and usually does not conform in important particulars with the balance sheet as finally approved by the tax controller. Such approved statements are, however, binding on the taxpayer.

Consolidated Financial Statements. The practice of preparing consolidated statements is not customarily followed in Belgium.

Pooling of Interests

This method of accounting for business combinations is not followed.

Inventories

Basically, inventories for management purposes are stated at cost, but usually with a generous factor of safety. The Lifo method is not permitted, but tax authorities permit the valuation of raw materials, which are subject to considerable fluctuation in market prices, to be based on such market prices.

In practice, the inventories are priced at cost on the Fifo basis or at market value, whichever is lower.

Restatement of Fixed Assets

By special legislation passed in 1947, companies were enabled, under certain conditions, to restate those fixed assets acquired prior to World War II and still in possession at the end of the war, and to compute depreciation on the increased values. The increases arising from the restatements were credited to a reserve that could be subsequently capitalized.

Statutory Reserve

The law requires corporations to set aside into a legal reserve 5 percent of their annual profits, until this reserve equals 10 percent of the corporation's outstanding capital stock. Generally, the statutory reserve may be used only in case of losses or liquidation.

When there are no remaining undistributed profits, the statutory reserve may be used to increase the capital account; if by reason of usage for this or other proper purposes the reserve falls below 10 percent of the capital, the annual appropriations of 5 percent of each year's profit must be resumed.

Secret Reserves

Directors are not subject to penalties if they allocate profits to an official or hidden reserve, but are liable if they distribute nonexisting profits. The statutory examiner, for example, would report to the shareholders if he believed the inventory valuation was too high, but he would not feel it necessary to report if he believed it to be too low.

Accordingly, many Belgian companies provide reserves that are considered conservative in amount in Belgium but would be considered excessive by U.S. standards.

Liability for Severance Payments

Persons dismissed from service with a company are entitled to varying periods of notice, from three months to more than two years, and, in theory, serve out the time of notice. In practice, a lump-sum settlement is often made in lieu of notice, but since such liabilities cannot be foreseen, it is customary to account for them on a payment, rather than an accrual basis.

Statement of Income

Tax-Effect Accounting. Where there are significant differences between accounting for book and for tax purposes, it is not the general practice to provide for the tax effects of the differences.

Payments to Directors. Payments to directors for fees, services, or commissions are charged to profit and loss. It is quite customary, however, for bylaws to provide that, after the statutory reserve and dividends, a percentage of the remaining profits be allocated to the board of directors to be distributed among the members as they may agree. These latter payments are regarded as appropriations of profit, voted by the shareholders similar to dividends, and not as costs to be charged to profit and loss.

Requirements for Public Sale of Securities

The following is a summary of the principal requirements to be met by companies wishing to sell securities to the public:

1. Company promoters or management are required to submit to the Banking Commission, at least fifteen days before issue, an information file complying with the latter's requirements.

2. Publication of the intention to make a public issue must be made in the official gazette at least ten days preceding commencement of the offer. The following information is required by the Commercial Code:

   a. Date of act of constitution.
   b. Objects clause.
   c. Present capital structure.
   d. Particulars of unpaid capital.
   e. Description and value of assets to be brought in as consideration for issue.
   f. Composition of board of directors.
   g. Most recent balance sheet and profit and loss account.

3. The dossier of information presented to the Banking Commission usually comprises the following:
   a. Copy of proposed preliminary publication in the official gazette referred to above.
   b. Schedule of liabilities and contingent liabilities.
   c. Purpose of issue.
   d. Details of underwriting arrangements.
   e. Particulars of shares held by the promoters and underwriters.

4. The Banking Commission may complete its examination of the file by issuing a questionnaire followed by conferences. No inspection of records or audit is requested or undertaken, but penal sanctions are imposed in respect to false information. It is not clear how the latter would normally be established in the absence of reports by independent accountants.

5. Examination of prospectus and other forms of publicity by the Banking Commission with a view to establishing adequacy and accuracy as far as this can be determined without recourse to independent audit reports.

Requirements for Listing Securities on the Stock Exchange

The principal stock exchange in Belgium is located in Brussels. There is also an exchange in Antwerp, and some transactions take place on minor exchanges in Ghent and Liège.

Domestic companies in Belgium applying for listing on stock exchanges must have a minimum fund of 10,000,000 Belgian francs, capital and reserves, and the balance sheets for the last two years must have been published in the official gazette. Foreign companies, in addition, must obtain a permit from the Ministry of Finance and from the Foreign

Exchange Control Authority. The bonds of a company may not be listed unless its shares are also listed. The securities must be listed in the country of origin, and the companies must furnish the names of banks responsible for their financial service in Belgium. In regard to both domestic and foreign companies, the Stock Exchange Committee must obtain the formal approval of the listing from the Banking Commission.

Glossary

French Terms and Their Flemish Equivalents

French	Flemish
Société anonyme (S.A.)	Naamloze vennootschap (N.V.)
Société en commandite par actions	Vennootschap bij wijze van geldschieting op aandelen
Société de personnes à responsabilité limitée (S.P.R.L.)	Personenvennootschap met beperkte aansprakelijkheid (P.V.B.A.)
Société en commandite simple	Vennootschap bij wijze van eenvoudige geldschieting
Société en nom collectif	Vennootschap in gemeenschappelijke naam
Société cooperative	Samenwerkende vennootschap
Actions ordinaires	Gewone aandelen
Actions privilégiées	Bevoorrechte aandelen
Parts de fondateurs	Stichtersaandelen
Actions de dividende	Dividendaandelen
Actions de jouissance	Genotsaandelen
Commissaire	Commissaris
Moniteur Belge	Belgisch Staatsblad
Registre du Commerce	Handelsregister
Institut des Réviseurs d'Entreprises	Instituut der Bedrijfsrevisoren
Réviseurs de Banque	Bankrevisoren
Institut des Réviseurs de Banque	Instituut der Bankrevisoren
Expert comptable	Accountant
Collège National des Experts Comptables de Belgique	Nationaal College der Accountants van Belgie
Commissaire réviseur	Commissaris-revisor
Société Royale Chambre Belge des Comptables (CBC)	Koninklijke Maatschappij Belgische Kamer der Rekenplichtigen (BKR)
Association Nationale des Comptables de Belgique (ANCB)	Nationale Associatie der Boekhouders van Belgie (NABB)

Brazil

Brazil

As of March 1973

Forms of Business Organization

Brazilian business laws are promulgated by the federal government and recognize the common forms of business enterprises found in other countries in which commercial legislation was originally derived from the Napoleonic Code. All business organizations are governed by the Commercial Code promulgated in 1850, as amended. The organization and operation of corporations are specifically regulated under the Corporation Law of 1940 and the Capital Markets Law of 1965, which created and which now regulates authorized capital companies. Limited liability companies are governed by a law promulgated in 1919.

Foreigners, depending on their requirements in each particular case, may adopt any of the following forms of doing business in Brazil:

- Brazilian corporation (sociedade anônima)
- Limited liability company (sociedade por quotas de responsabilidade limitada)
- Branch of foreign corporation

Sociedade Anônima (S.A.)

The sociedade anônima is the form that most closely resembles the U.S. corporation. It is designated by a corporate name that indicates its purpose, followed by the words "Sociedade Anônima" or its abbreviation "S.A.," e.g., Indústria de Alumínio XYZ Brasileira S.A.

In addition to the ordinary form of S.A., there are two specialized forms, the sociedade anônima de capital autorizado (stock company with authorized capital) and the sociedade anônima de capital aberto (open capital company).

The Brazilian Securities Act of 1965, called the Capital Markets Law, liberalized the 1940 Corporation Law to allow for greater flexibility in the capital structure of corporations. The 1965 act authorizes the creation of "authorized capital companies" (sociedades anônimas de capital autorizado) in which the capital need not initially be fully subscribed; however, the National Monetary Council prescribes the minimum amount (15 percent of the capital as of this writing) which must be paid in. The capital of companies other than authorized capital companies must be fully subscribed at inception, although only 10 percent need be paid in.

Every corporation must have a minimum of seven shareholders, but no minimum capital is required. Shares, both common and preferred, must have the same par value and may be issued only at or above par value. Shares may be nominative (registered), nominative endorsable, or bearer, with some exceptions. For example, real estate companies, authorized capital companies, and companies which by law must have a minimum proportion of Brazilian shareholders may issue only nominative shares; banks may issue preferred, nonvoting bearer shares as well as nominative shares. Bearer shares are permitted in the case of ordinary industrial and commercial concerns, but are issued only when paid up.

An authorized capital company may acquire its own shares to hold as nonvoting treasury stock. The reissue price of such shares must be at or above par value.

Authorized capital companies may not issue participating shares (partes beneficiárias) to founders, stockholders, or third parties as remuneration for services rendered to the corporation. Corporations other than authorized capital companies sometimes issue participating shares, but these can not be capitalized. Participating shares have no par value but may participate in annual profits to a maximum of 10 percent. These shares are always callable for redemption or for conversion into stock, provided a special reserve has been created for this purpose.

The shareholders of every corporation must annually elect a "conselho fiscal" (fiscal council) composed of three or more members and an equal number of alternates, all of whom may be reelected. The functions of the fiscal council are described hereafter.

An annual report of the directors accompanied by a balance sheet and profit and loss statement, together with the report of the fiscal council, must be published in the *Diário Oficial* (official gazette) and in a local newspaper, not later than five days before the date of the annual shareholders' meeting. The requirements of Brazilian law with respect to the contents of financial statements are described in a later section.

A corporation organized either as a "sociedade anônima" or as a "sociedade de capital autorizado" is eligible to open its capital to the public. Tentatively outlined in Law No. 4506 (1964) and later in Law No. 4728 and Central Bank Resolution No. 16 (1966), the open capital company program was fully articulated in Central Bank Resolution No. 106 (1968). To qualify for open capital status, a company must meet requirements established by the Central Bank and obtain a certificate of eligibility renewable every two years. Once the company complies with the requirements, the law grants benefits both (a) to the company itself and (b) to its existing shareholders and new shareholders who acquire its shares.

The basic requirement for qualifying for open capital status is that a company distribute at least 20 percent of its capital to the public. To maintain this status, additional amounts equivalent to 10 percent of the publicly owned capital must be distributed after every two-year period until 49 percent of the capital is publicly owned. The requirements for maintaining open capital status are not onerous since a firm may take 18 years to distribute 49 percent ownership of the capital. A company can obtain and maintain open capital status either by raising new capital from the public or by a gradual transfer of shares from the controlling group to the public.

Of the 49 percent share of capital eventually to be owned by the public, only the initial 20 percent must be in the form of common voting shares; the additional 29 percent may be in the form of preferred, nonvoting full participation shares.

To insure wide distribution of shares in the public market, the law requires that open capital companies based in the states of Guanabara and São Paulo with capital of more than 1,000,000 cruzeiros must have a minimum of 500 shareholders, each holding a minimum of 100 shares equivalent to no more than one percent of the company's voting capital. Furthermore, open capital companies must register for listing with the stock exchange so that company shares may be traded on the exchange.

Tax benefits granted under the open capital company program have (a) reduced the cost to the company of the distribution of dividends to its shareholders and (b) raised the effective after-tax return to the stockholders.

Sociedade por Quotas de Responsabilidade Limitada

The limited liability company has attributes of both corporation and partnership. It is similar to a partnership with respect to the absence of formalities and publicity attending its organization and operation. An attendant disadvantage, however, is that any changes in the partnership agreement, or any transfer of "quotas" by a partner requires the consent of at least a majority of its members.

Formation of limited liability companies is regulated by Decree-Law No. 3708 of January 10, 1919. Such companies may be organized by not less than two persons; foreign corporations or nonresidents may be partners ("quota" holders), provided a suitable power of attorney is held by a resident of Brazil to enable him to sign the partnership agreement and to vote the "quotas" held by the nonresident. The partnership interests are represented by "quotas," each having a fixed unit value as specified in the partnership agreement, but no certificates are issued. Its members are liable to the amount of their respective capital subscriptions and are also jointly liable to the amount not paid in by another member. The company is designated by the names of one or more of its members or by the description of its purpose, adding in each case the word "Limitada" or its abbreviation "Ltda."

It need not appoint a conselho fiscal, provide a statutory reserve, or publish financial statements or minutes in the official gazette or a newspaper.

Branch of Foreign Corporation

It is necessary to obtain permission from the federal government to establish a branch of a foreign corporation, and governmental approval must be obtained in the event of any reorganization of a branch. In order for a foreign corporation to maintain a branch, the branch manager must have unrestricted authority to conduct business, and the branch must operate in Brazilian territory under the name of its head office, adding the words "do Brasil" or "para o Brasil" if it wishes. As do Brazilian corporations, foreign branches must publish their annual statements in the official gazette.

Sociedade em Nome Coletivo

Ordinary partnerships are known as "sociedade em nome coletivo" and require the association of two or more partners all having unlimited liability.

Sociedade em Comandita

The "sociedade em comandita" is composed of one or more partners with unlimited liability, who manage the company, and one or more silent partners, whose liability is limited to their capital contributions. (If the capital contributed by the silent partners is represented by shares, then its title is "sociedade em comandita por ações" and it is subject to the law covering corporations; but this form is rarely seen in practice.)

Sociedade de Capital e Indústria

When one or more of the partners contribute only their personal services and are not personally liable with respect to the obligations of the partnership, the designation is "sociedade de capital e indústria."

Business Records

There is a very extensive list of books of account required by both federal and state laws to be kept by commercial and industrial enterprises. The following books are the most common:

1. Journal (Diário).
2. Register of "duplicatas" (customers' notes) (no longer compulsory if details are recorded in some other book of accounts).
3. Inventory register.
4. Register of goods received (for sales and value-added taxes).
5. Register of goods shipped (for sales and value-added taxes).
6. Value-added tax register (Imposto sôbre circulacão de mercadorias).
7. Sales tax register (Imposto sôbre produtos industrializados).
8. Production and inventory control register.

In addition, corporations are required to register minute books of stockholders' meetings, directors' meetings, and fiscal council actions, also stock registers, stock transfer books, and so forth.

The books mentioned above must be bound, except the inventory register and the register of goods received and shipped, which may be computerized or mechanized with prior approval of state and federal fiscal authorities. The production and inventory control register may be mechanized or kept on "Kardex." Prior to being used, all must be registered with the Department of Commerce as well as appropriate state or federal tax departments.

The first page of each register on computer run must contain the name and registered number of the company, as well as a statement of the total number of pages and how they are numbered. Many companies use a series of numbered pages authenticated by the Department of Commerce in their recording system.

Conselho Fiscal (Fiscal Council)

The members of the fiscal council are elected annually at the general shareholders' meeting; they may be, but need not be, shareholders, and must be residents of the country. Their remuneration is fixed at the time of their election. Dissenting shareholders representing one-fifth or more of the corporation's capital, and holders of preferred stock are entitled to elect, separately, one of the members of the council and the respective alternate. There are no specific educational or experience requirements, but employees of the corporation and relatives of directors up to the third degree cannot be elected to the committee.

The most significant duties of the fiscal council, specified in the Law of 1940, are to—

1. Examine at any time, but at least quarterly, the accounting records, cash, and investments of the corporation. The directors are obliged to make all the required information available to them.
2. Record in the "Minute Book and Report of the Fiscal Council" the results of the periodic examinations.
3. Submit to the annual shareholders' meeting an opinion (parecer) on the operations of the corporation, based on the statements issued by its board of directors.
4. Report errors, frauds, or criminal acts which they may discover and suggest the appropriate corrective measures to the corporation.

Since the members of the committee may not be professionally qualified to make the required examinations, the Corporation Law permits them to use the services of a legally qualified accountant in performing their duties.

Corporations sometimes arrange for representatives of their auditors to serve on the fiscal council. Resolution No. 220, promulgated in May 1972, specifically states that the appointment of one auditing representative to the conselho fiscal does not legally compromise the independent position of his firm as auditors, but the question may arise as to whether the report issued as a member of the committee (which may be in condensed form) is incompatible with that issued by his firm as auditors. The policies of accounting firms regarding the acceptance of such appointments differ.

There is no fixed standard form of the report (parecer) which the fiscal council issues relating to the annual financial statements of a corporation. However, the following is a typical example:

> The below-signed members of the fiscal council of the XYZ Corporation, having proceeded with the required examination of the balance sheet and the profit and loss account, as well as the other accounts and written accounting documents pertaining to the period ended December 31, 19........, declare that all is in perfect order, and are of the opinion that the statements are in full agreement with the situation of the corporation and should thus be approved by the stockholders in general assembly.

It is evident that the report of the members of the conselho fiscal, who are not required to be competent in accounting and auditing, nor to be independent, does not, and is not intended to, give the same degree of assurance as to the fairness of presentation of financial statements as would that of an independent certified public accountant.

The Accounting Profession

General

The designation "contabilista" was first legally established in 1931 and 1932. It is a general one, embracing all those engaged in accounting and bookkeeping; it includes the "técnico em contabilidade" (known previously as "guarda-livros" (bookkeeper) and the "contador," who may offer his services as an independent accountant. The educational requirements and the areas of activity of each group were established by Decree-Law No. 9295 of 1946, which created the "Conselho Federal de Contabilidade" (Federal Council of Accountancy) and the Regional Councils of Accountancy where both "técnicos" and "contadores" must be registered in the location where they practice.

There is no statutory or other governmental regulation which requires corporations in the private sector, other than those publicly held companies registered with the Central Bank, to have their financial statements examined and reported upon by an independent public accountant. However, financial statements and other accounting documents of closed corporations, limited liability companies, and partnerships must be signed by accountants or bookkeepers legally registered, and the respective registration numbers of the signers given.

Income tax legislation requires that corporate income tax returns be accompanied by a certificate issued by the competent Regional Council of Accountancy to the effect that the "contador" or the "técnico" signing the financial statement is duly registered.

Técnico em Contabilidade
(Bookkeeper)

The "técnico" must be a graduate of a recognized "escola técnica de comércio," which is substantially the equivalent of the U.S. commercial high school. Because of the limited requirements of these schools, their graduates are numerous. At the end of a three-year accounting course, which does not include auditing, the "escolas" issue a diploma "técnico em contabilidade."

The duties of the "técnicos" are limited to general bookkeeping and accounting services, and to the signing, in their capacity as company accountants but not as auditors, of the financial statements which corporations are required to publish annually. In addition, the "técnico" can sign the corporation's tax return. They are not allowed to perform judicial examinations, financial statement audits, or assist the fiscal council. These latter functions, as well as those others specifically mentioned by law, are only to be performed by "contadores."

Contador
(Accountant)

The "contador" must be a graduate of a recognized university offering an approved four-year curriculum. Entrance to the university requires the diploma either of a high school or that of "técnico em contabilidade" (see above) and the passing of an examination before an examining board. No practical experience is required for one to be registered as a "contador" in the Regional Council of Accountancy.

A number of universities in Brazil offer business courses leading to a diploma of "Bacharel em Ciências Contábeis" (Bachelor of Accounting Sciences). The accounting curriculum includes, in the first two years, subjects common to all students majoring in accounting, i.e., economics, actuarial science, and business administration; a two-year accounting specialization course follows, which includes financial mathematics, statistics, specialized accounting, advanced accounting, auditing, civil, business, and fiscal legislation, finance, production administration, and so forth.

Independent Auditor

The services provided to his clients by the independent auditor are intended to be similar to those of the U.S. CPA. He may be selected by management, directors, or stockholders to examine and report upon financial statements, act as a member of the fiscal council or assist the members of the council in their functions, give tax advice, prepare tax returns, and do special accounting work in connection with lawsuits.

The independent auditor must hold a bachelor's degree in accounting sciences, or its legal equivalent. To become accredited by the Central Bank for the audits of publicly held companies, the auditor must be registered at the level of "contador" for at least three years with the Regional Council of Accountancy, and be registered at the level of auditor under terms put forth by the Federal Council of Accountancy.

Central Bank Circular No. 178 (1972) requires that the auditor seeking registration present documentary proof that he has practiced as an auditor in Brazil for at least five years, or has equivalent experience. In lieu of documentary proof, the law permits the Institute of Independent Auditors of Brazil to certify that the auditor seeking registration is a qualified member of that group and fulfills the conditions put forth in Circular No. 178.

The auditing firm seeking Central Bank registration is subject to similar requirements (registration for at least five years with the Regional Council of Accountancy and registration as an independent auditor under terms put forth by the Federal Council of Accountancy). Furthermore, those partners, directors, and other responsible officers who have power to sign technical reports and opinions must be individually registered as independent auditors at the Central Bank.

Brazilian public accounting firms are usually organized in the form of civil partnerships, although some operate as limited liability companies.

Federal Council of Accountancy

The official bodies representing the accounting profession in Brazil are the Federal Council of Accountancy and the regional councils, which represent both "técnicos em contabilidade" and the "contadores."

The Federal Council of Accountancy is composed of 15 members, the president being appointed by the federal government; the rest of the membership is composed of "contadores" (two-thirds) and "técnicos" (one-third). The essential functions of the regional councils are to register those qualified to act in either of the two mentioned capacities and to impose sanctions on members in certain cases (see discussion under "Ethics"). The Federal Council of Accountancy annually publishes a list of registered accountants and hears appeals from sanctions imposed by regional councils.

Professional accounting firms formed for the purpose of rendering accounting and auditing services in Brazil must comply with the following requirements:

1. The firm itself must be registered with the Regional Council of Accountancy, and such registration be evidenced by a fixed number given to the firm.
2. One of the partners of the firm must also be a registered accountant with his own registered number.

Instituto dos Auditores Independentes do Brasil
(Institute of Independent Auditors of Brazil)

In December 1971 the Institute of Public Accountants of Brazil and the Brazilian Institute merged to form the Institute of Independent Auditors of Brazil (IAI), a professional organization committed to standardizing accounting practices, especially with regard to the auditing of open capital companies. Although the IAI is an unofficial body, it has been recognized by the Federal Council of Accountancy and the Central Bank. With the support of these two organizations, the Institute undertook the task of drafting a set of auditing standards to be followed by independent auditors. In April 1972 the Federal Council of Accountancy passed Resolution No. 321/72 approving the draft submitted by the Institute. Many of the suggestions made by the IAI have been incorporated into Resolution No. 220 and Circulars Nos. 178 and 179, promulgated by the Central Bank in May 1972.

The Institute is subdivided into regional committees which operate independently and report to the national board.

Sindicato dos Contabilistas

Nearly every state has its own "sindicato," which is the association of both accountants and bookkeepers who practice in each state. It may be described as a union and is under the supervision of the Department of Labor. Any locally qualified professional must be registered with the respective regional council in order to practice, but he need not be a member of the sindicato.

Ethics

The code of ethics approved by Resolution No. 290/70 of the Federal Council of Accountancy established the rules of ethics to which the professional accountants and bookkeepers should adhere. Among these, the following apply when the "contador" is reporting upon an examination of financial statements:

1. He should not fail to mention any comments regarding facts known to him, the omission of which would make misleading the financial statements he is examining.
2. He should only express opinions which are adequate and properly supported.
3. He should clearly explain any false interpretation or any deviation in the application of general accounting principles.
4. He should not express an opinion on the financial statements of any enterprise where he has a family relationship up to the third degree with a member of its top management.

This last principle is the only one which deals with the concept of independence. The importance of an independent mental attitude on the part of public accountants, as it is understood in the United States, is just beginning to be recognized in Brazil. Resolution No. 220, which obliges corporations resorting to the capital markets to be externally audited by an independent auditor, characterizes "independence" in the following manner: the auditor or the auditing firm (in this case its partners or responsible accountants) (1) cannot participate in an executive or consultative body of the company being audited; (2) cannot be related to the second degree to any director or member of the conselho fiscal or any other administrative or consultative council of the company or its affiliates; (3) cannot receive from the company being audited income which represents a substantial percentage of his global income. The first two prohibitions are, of course, subject to the exception mentioned in the section dealing with the conselho fiscal which permits one member of the conselho to be an independent auditor.

The law that created the Federal Council of Accountancy established sanctions applicable under specific circumstances, which include the following:

1. Suspension of those professionals who, within the scope of their work and their technical capacity, are responsible for any falsification of documents signed by them and for irregularities in the accounting records committed for the purpose of evading taxes.
2. Suspension for a period of six months to one year of any professional who shows technical inability in performing his functions, at the discretion of the Regional Council of Accountancy to which he is subject.

The federal or regional councils do not have the necessary organization or facilities to effectively police the code except when complaints are made to them.

Auditing Standards

General Standards

General criteria governing corporate accounting and auditing procedures were standardized by Resolution No. 321/72 of the Federal Council of Accountancy, and by Central Bank Circular No. 179, issued on May 11, 1972. The two regulations are consistent, although compliance with the Central Bank norms is obligatory only for publicly held corporations. The more important provisions of the Central Bank code state the following:

1. Audits must be performed by individuals or firms qualified to per-

form audits in accordance with instructions issued by the Central Bank.

2. In performing audit work, the system of accounting and internal control of the company must be reviewed to determine the reliability of accounting records and the nature and extent of the audit procedure to be employed.
3. If exceptions are taken, the auditor must describe the nature of the exception, the reasons for taking it, and the possible effect on the statements audited. The auditor's opinion must also take exception for changes in the application of accounting principles which, although not materially affecting the results of operations of the period in which they occur, may substantially affect results in the subsequent year.
4. Whenever the auditor is unable to obtain sufficient evidence on which to base an opinion, he should submit a report on the facts of the situation.
5. Audit procedures will be applied based on criteria established by the Institute of Independent Auditors of Brazil consistent with standards issued by the Central Bank.

Standards of Field Work

The following items apply with respect to auditing procedures of Brazilian local practitioners:

1. Prior to 1972, it was not customary to make an annual investigation of internal control by written questionnaire, but in that year the Federal Council of Accountancy, under Resolution No. 321/72, recommended that internal control be investigated as part of audit procedure.
2. A fairly extensive detailed check of individual transactions is customary.
3. Since some banks do not return paid checks, disbursements are substantiated by inspecting the supporting documents and comparing the information shown in bank statements (number of check and amount) with the client's records. Bank confirmations are not generally obtained.
4. A large portion of the audit time is devoted to the checking of "duplicatas," which are the instruments representing amounts due from customers. Confirmation of "duplicatas" is sometimes practiced.

5. The observation of physical inventories is accepted as a desirable technique, but has not become common practice.
6. Written representations of management are not generally obtained.

Standards of Reporting

According to Central Bank Circular No. 179 (1972), and Resolution No. 321/72 of the Federal Council of Accountancy, the audit report must contain the following:

1. The date and periods covered by the accounting records examined.
2. A statement that the examination was conducted according to accepted auditing standards and with the application of such auditing procedures as were considered necessary under the circumstances.
3. A statement that the records examined present fairly the financial position of the company at the date of the balance sheet and the results of the company's operations for the period audited, in accordance with generally accepted accounting principles applied on a basis consistent with that of the previous year.
4. The limitations, if any, placed on the extent of the audit.
5. The place and date of the opinion.
6. The auditor's signature, professional classification, and registration number with the regional council.
7. In the case of open capital companies, a statement that the audit was performed in accordance with Central Bank requirements.

Accounting Principles and Practices

Form and Content of Financial Statements

Uniform systems of accounts have been prescribed for public utility companies, banks, insurance companies, and certain other industries. The objective is to provide uniformity in presentation of financial statements and, to some extent, to establish certain accounting principles for these enterprises.

Statement Presentation–Balance Sheet

Except for Central Bank Resolution No. 220 (1972) and Circulars Nos. 178 and 179 (which regulate publicly held corporations), the only authoritative sources of general corporate accounting principles in Brazil are the tax law and the Corporation Law of 1940, which laid down the rules governing valuation of assets and liabilities and the presentation of annual financial statements.

For privately held corporations, it is generally accepted that the balance sheet shall be presented in the following fashion:

1. Assets shall be grouped under the headings of fixed assets; investments in and advances to associated companies; liquid assets; realizable assets—current and long-term; deferred charges; memorandum accounts.
2. Liabilities shall be grouped under the headings of capital; legal and statutory reserves; liabilities—current and long-term; deferred income or credits; memorandum accounts.
3. The caption "sundry accounts" shown in the balance sheet either as an asset or as a liability shall not amount to more than 10 percent of the corporation's capital.
4. Investments in and advances to affiliates and subsidiaries should be shown separately in the balance sheet.

Brazilian financial statements have tended to show all accounts "broad"; that is, accumulated depreciation is not deducted from fixed assets. Instead, accumulated depreciation is shown in the "equity" section of the balance sheet as a "reserve for depreciation." Similarly, the provision for bad debts is not usually deducted from accounts receivable, but shown in the "equity" section of the balance sheet as a reserve for bad debts.

Publicly held corporations, under Resolution No. 220, are now required to show accumulated depreciation and provision for bad debts as deductions from the respective asset accounts. Standardized formats for the balance sheets of open-capital companies are presented in the appendix at the end of this chapter.

The classification of assets and liabilities between current and long-term is normally made on the basis of 180 days. Amounts having a term of more than 180 days will be considered as long-term. Under Circular No. 179, the company may disregard this norm in order to conform with its operating cycle, if the definition used in classifying the assets and liabilities is expressly stated in the notes accompanying the financial statements together with such further explanations as may be necessary.

Memorandum Accounts

Since most Brazilian financial statements in the past have not included notes or any explanatory comments (other than in the directors' report) and the structure of the balance sheet emphasizes only what is due and owned, a third group of accounts evolved, i.e., the compensating accounts.

These accounts show items included above in the balance sheet which are not physically in the possession of the company and assets of third parties which are in the possession of the company. Listed below are explanations of the more usual compensating accounts:

1. Deposits of the executive board. This item represents the deposits required by the Corporation Law as a pledge of guarantee made by each director.
2. Bank deposit account. This account shows the amount of trade notes (duplicatas) held by banks as collateral.
3. Bank collection account. This balance represents the amount of trade notes (duplicatas) held by the banks for collection.
4. Portfolio account. Trade notes still on hand at balance sheet date.
5. Contingent liabilities.

Statement Presentation–Profit and Loss and Surplus

The conventional Brazilian form of profit and loss statement combines the earned surplus and the income statements and follows the account form, i.e., gross profit, income from capital not employed in company's operations, other income, and the beginning surplus balance are shown on the credit side; expenses and profit distribution are on the debit side. This form of presentation does not normally show net profit and there has been very little effort made to distinguish between earnings for the period and earned surplus.

According to regulations outlined in Central Bank Resolution No. 220, publicly held companies must present a standardized statement, which is also a statement of profit and loss and surplus. The format required by the Central Bank is presented in the appendix at the end of this chapter.

Comparative Financial Statements

One of the most difficult aspects—and perhaps the most significant—of analyzing Brazilian comparative financial statements is judging the effect of inflation on their contents. Comparative statements can be very misleading if this factor is overlooked.

Consolidated Financial Statements

Until recently, it has not been common for corporations to present consolidated financial statements, and they are not acceptable for income tax purposes. However, Central Bank Circular No. 179 allows consolidated financial statements to be presented when appropriate.

Inventories

Inventories must be carried at the lower of cost or market and individual values adjusted accordingly. Lifo and direct costing are not acceptable methods of pricing inventories for tax purposes.

Bad Debts

A reserve for bad debts up to a maximum of 3 percent of the accounts receivable balance is generally acceptable for income tax purposes, with larger reserves permitted in the case of debtors in bankruptcy or receivership. It is common practice to provide the maximum allowance, regardless of the actual requirements of the company.

Fixed Assets

The Corporation Law states that property will be valued at cost. However, due to inflation, all legal entities, except public utilities whose profit does not exceed 12 percent of capital, sole proprietorships, and some classes of partnerships and "mixed economy" enterprises, must revalue fixed assets annually according to government-approved coefficients. Revaluation is based on the cost at time of acquisition or the value at time of takeover if acquired by means other than a purchase.

Circular No. 179 of the Central Bank (1972) requires publicly held corporations to disclose assets at historical cost and to show the revaluation (monetary correction) separately in determining the value of fixed assets. Although other entities are not required to disclose restatements in published financial statements, they must carry separate accounts on the books.

In the case of publicly held corporations, depreciation must be charged each period and accumulated until provision has been made for the full cost of the asset. Cost is increased by amounts corresponding to monetary corrections and the increase recorded in the books. This increase is subject to amortization on the same basis as depreciation. For other corporations, provision for depreciation is not compulsory, although it is usual.

Disposition of Increase From Restatement of Fixed Assets

The credit arising from the increase in fixed assets within the limits of official coefficients is charged with an amount corresponding to the unrealized exchange losses on foreign currency loans used to acquire fixed assets and monetary adjustments of local currency loans used for the same purpose, any excess being available to absorb accumulated losses and then for eventual capitalization through an issue of capital stock pro rata to shareholders.

Organization Expenses

The law permits organization expenses to be carried as an asset up to a limit of 10 percent of the corporation's capital. Public companies must write off such expenses over a period not exceeding five years, and for other companies the tax law requires them to be written off over a minimum of five years. Organization expenses may also be written off immediately, but this procedure might not be recognized for tax purposes.

Severance Payments

Brazilian law requires that employees discharged without just cause, legally proven, be paid an indemnity of one month's pay for each year of service. When an employee achieves ten years of service he obtains legal tenure, and if discharged, he receives two months' pay for each year of service. No indemnity is payable upon death or voluntary withdrawal or retirement. Indemnities paid are tax deductible.

Since January 1967 employers have been obliged to deposit monthly in blocked bank accounts an amount equal to 8 percent of employees' gross remuneration. The bank account, in the name of an opting employee, remains blocked until termination of employment. If dismissal is without just cause, or the employer and the employee are considered to be mutually at fault, the employee has free use of the balance in his account. The employer's monthly contribution is a deductible expense for income tax purposes.

Statement of Income

Sales and Cost of Sales. The Corporation Law of 1940 does not require sales and cost of sales to be shown in the published profit and loss statement, and in the case of privately held corporations, these figures are rarely given. Gross profit is required to be shown separately for each of the various sources or groups of related activities, but generally only one figure of gross profit actually appears in published statements.

Circular No. 179 (1972) of the Central Bank requires publicly held industrial and commercial corporations to present a standardized income statement showing sales (sales tax included), related sales taxes, net sales, cost of goods sold, selling expenses, general expenses, and depreciation in arriving at operating profit.

Depreciation. Income tax regulations do not establish depreciation rates, but depreciation of buildings at 2 percent per year, of machinery and equipment at 10 percent per year, and of vehicles at 20 percent per year is generally accepted. On machinery and equipment used during more than the normal eight-hour shift, accelerated rates are permitted.

Depreciation on assets acquired at any time during the accounting period is computed on a monthly basis at their applicable rates.

While straight-line depreciation is the normal case, income tax legislation provides that the executive power may establish a coefficient for acceleration of depreciation, independent of actual physical wastage, with a view to stimulating renewal and renovation of plants.

Income Tax. It has not been customary for Brazilian-owned corporations to accrue income tax in the year the income is earned, but rather to charge the actual payment to operations in the year of payment. However, publicly held corporations are now required by Circular No. 179 (1972) to establish a provision for income tax payable at the close of the year the income is earned, on an accrual basis.

Stock Dividends. Stock dividends received must be recorded in the books at par and, in accordance with the income tax regulations, are normally free of tax. Such dividends may be recorded as income but are often credited directly to a capital reserve account. In the case of publicly held corporations, stock dividends received from subsidiaries must be recorded directly as a capital reserve when the dividends are the result of revaluation of fixed assets.

Maintenance of Purchasing Power of Working Capital. A tax deduction, limited to 20 percent of taxable income, is allowed for an amount equal to the currency depreciation of working capital. It is the normal practice, therefore, for companies to set up a reserve for this amount in order to obtain the tax benefit.

Exchange Losses. Until 1972, unrealized foreign exchange losses had not been allowed as a deduction from income for tax purposes. Under new legislation passed in 1972, unrealized exchange losses relating to debts incurred for financing working capital are recognizable as an expense of the period and are tax deductible; but if the debt was incurred for the purpose of financing the acquisition of fixed assets, the unrealized exchange loss is still not deductible from income for tax purposes.

Exchange losses incurred in the acquisition of fixed assets are capitalized as part of the cost of acquisition to the extent that such losses exceed the monetary correction restatement of the related assets.

Credits may be taken for favorable exchange differences only when the receivable or payable giving rise to the gain is liquidated.

Fiscal Incentives. In an effort to stimulate economic development of certain geographical areas of Brazil, and certain industries (such as tourism), the Brazilian government has granted a series of fiscal incentives which can effectively lower the corporate income tax rate from 30 percent to 22.5 percent. Priority areas are (1) SUDENE—the Northeast section of Brazil, (2) SUDAM—the Amazon region, (3) SUDEPE—the fishing industry, (4) EMBRATUR—the tourism industry, and (5) REFLORESTAMENTO—projects to develop hard-wood forest reserves.

The corporation must deposit the full amount of fiscal benefit with the Banco do Brasil, which controls and frees the deposits for use in the projects selected by the corporation. The corporation then receives shares in the project (usually organized as an authorized capital company).

Thus, the corporation in Brazil opting for various fiscal incentives will have two balance sheet items which represent tax incentive investments: (1) deposits for fiscal incentive projects and (2) investments in fiscal incentive projects. Valuation of these assets presents a difficult problem, as most projects involve a long period of organization and development before production can begin.

Legal Reserve

The Corporation Law provides that 5 percent of the annual net profits of corporations (sociedades anônimas) should be set aside until the reserve equals 20 percent of the issued capital. This statutory or legal reserve is classified as surplus. Although not described as restricted surplus, it is generally understood that it is not distributable.

Surplus

Any increase in reserves (excluding legal reserve) or earned surplus of a corporation which brings the total of such accounts to an amount in excess of paid-in capital is subject to a withholding tax of 15 percent. This effectively forces a distribution of earnings; however, a transfer from reserves or earned surplus to capital through distribution of a stock dividend provides a means of accumulating earnings and, at the same time, avoiding the full impact of this tax.

Goodwill

In the case of public companies, goodwill may be recorded as an asset only when it has been purchased, and at a value not exceeding the amount paid. Such amount must be amortized over a period not exceeding five years.

Foreign Participation in Capital, Profits, and Dividends

The Profits Remittance Law and certain income tax regulations require that companies which operate in Brazil and whose capital is partly or wholly owned by a foreign entity must show in its annual accounts the division of the following, as between Brazilian and foreign shareholders or partners:

- Capital
- Undistributed profits and dividends paid
- Income and expenses

This law also requires that "credits to persons domiciled or residing abroad" be shown separately in the balance sheet when such credits are registered with the Central Bank.

There is no restriction on remittances, but additional taxes are payable on net dividends in excess of 36 percent of registered foreign capital, remitted in any period of three consecutive years.

Requirements for Public Sale of Securities

Under Central Bank Resolution No. 88 (1968), all public offerings require prior government registration with GEMAC, the Capital Markets Agency of the Central Bank. The following documents must be submitted by the company wishing to "go public":

1. Financial information covering the last three years.
2. Copies of the minutes of the shareholders' meeting at which a capital increase by public offering was authorized.
3. Copies of the charter and bylaws of the company.
4. Prospectus and other soliciting material.
5. Statement of the amount and purpose of the offering.
6. Data relevant to the issue, such as underwriter, date of issue, and issue price.
7. An auditor's report from a registered independent auditor.

Requirements for Listing Securities on the Stock Exchange

The two principal stock exchanges in Brazil are in Rio de Janeiro and São Paulo, are privately owned, and are supervised by the Central Bank. All open capital companies must register on one of the stock exchanges.

Listed companies must submit semiannual financial reports to the stock exchange on which they are listed within 30 days after the close of the companies' accounting period. Moreover, listed companies must submit copies of the minutes of the annual and extraordinary shareholders' meetings no more than 15 days after these meetings.

Brazil

Illustrative Financial Statements

ILLUSTRATIVE BALANCE SHEET OF A BRAZILIAN COMPANY

BALANÇO GERAL EM 31 DE DEZEMBRO DE 19__
(Balance Sheet at December 31, 19__)

ANEXO AO REGULAMENTO BAIXADO PELA CIRCULAR No. 179, DE 11.5.1972 (Circular 179)

ATIVO (Assets)

1. DISPONÍVEL (Liquid Assets)
   - 1.1 Bens numerários (Cash) ....
   - 1.2 Depositos bancários a vista (Demand deposits in banks) ....
   - 1.3 Títulos vinculados ao mercado aberto (Marketable securities) ....

2. REALIZÁVEL A CURTO PRAZO (Current Assets)
   - 2.1 Estoques (Inventories)
     - 2.1.1 Produtos acabados (Finished products) ....
     - 2.1.2 Produtos em elaboração (Work in process) ....
     - 2.1.3 Matérias primas (Raw materials) ....
   - 2.2 Créditos (Receivables)
     - 2.2.1 Contas a receber de clientes (Accounts receivable trade) ....
       - (–) Valores descontados (Less: Discounted) ....
       - (–) Provisão para devedores duvidosos (Less: Provision for doubtful accounts) ....
       - ....
     - 2.2.2 De empresas subsidiárias ou coligadas (Subsidiary or associated companies) ....
   - 2.3 Valores e bens (Securities and property)
     - 2.3.1 Títulos e valores mobiliários (Securities) ....
     - 2.3.2 Bens não destinados a uso (Property not for use) ....

   ATIVO CIRCULANTE (Current Assets) ....

PASSIVO (Liabilities)

1. EXIGÍVEL A CURTO PRAZO (Current Liabilities)			
1.1 Fornecedores (Suppliers)	....		
1.2 Empresas subsidiárias ou coligadas (Subsidiary or associated companies)	....		
1.4 Instituições financeiras (Financial institutions)	....		
1.5 Provisões (Inclusive para pagamento do impôsto de renda) (Provisions (including income tax))	....	....	
2. EXIGÍVEL A LONGO PRAZO (Long-Term Liabilities)			
2.1 Fornecedores (Suppliers)	....		
2.2 Empresas subsidiárias ou coligadas (Subsidiary or associated companies)	....		
2.4 Instituições financeiras (Financial institutions)	....		
2.5 Debêntures e debêntures conversiveis em circulação (Outstanding debentures and convertible debentures)	....	....	....
3. NÃO EXIGIVEL (Equity)			
3.1 Capital subscrito (Subscribed capital)		....	
(–) Capital a realizar (Less: Capital not paid in)		....	
3.2 Capital excedente (Capital surplus)		....	
3.3 Correção monetária do ativo imobolizado (Monetary correction of fixed assets)		....	
3.4 Reservas legais (Legal reserves)			
3.4.1 Reserva legal (DL 2627) (Legal reserve DL 2627)	....		
3.4.2 Reserva para manutenção do capital de giro (Reserve for maintenance of working capital)	....		
3.4.3 Outras reservas legais, (discriminar) (Other legal reserves (specify))	....	....	

ILLUSTRATIVE BALANCE SHEET OF A BRAZILIAN COMPANY

BALANÇO GERAL EM 31 DE DEZEMBRO DE 19__ (Balance Sheet at December 31, 19__)

ANEXO AO REGULAMENTO BAIXADO PELA CIRCULAR No. 179, DE 11.5.1972 (Circular 179)

ATIVO (Assets)

3. REALIZÁVEL A LONGO PRAZO (Long-Term Receivables)			
3.1 Créditos de clientes (Trade accounts)		....	
3.2 Créditos de empresas subsidiárias ou coligadas (Subsidiary or associated companies)		....	....
4. IMOBILIZADO (Fixed Assets)			
4.1 Imobilizações técnicas (Productive assets)			
Valor histórico (Historic cost)	....		
(+) Correção monetária (Add: Monetary correction)	....		
(=) Valor corrigido (Equals: Restated value)	....		
(−) Depreciações Acumuladas (Less: Accumulated depreciation)	....	....	
4.2 Imobilizações financeiras (Financial assets)			
4.2.1 Participações em empresas subsidiárias ou coligadas (Investments in subsidiaries or associated companies)	....		
4.2.2. Aplicações por incentivos fiscais (Fiscal incentives deposits and investments)	....	....	....
ATIVO REAL (Tangible)			....
5. RESULTADO PENDENTE (Deferred Expenses)			....
Subtotal (Subtotal)			....
6. CONTAS DE COMPENSAÇÃO (Memorandum Accounts)			....
TOTAL (Total)			....

NOTE: Certain details of asset and liability classifications prescribed by Circular 179 as promulgated by the Central Bank (of Brazil), have been omitted because of limitations of space.

PASSIVO (Liabilities)

3.5 Reservas estatuárias (Discriminar) (Statutory reserves (specify))		....	
3.6 Reservas livres (Discriminar) (Free reserves (specify))		....	
3.7 Provisões (discriminar) (Provisions (specify))		....	
3.7.1........			
3.7.2........			
3.8 Lucros suspensos (Retained earnings)	....		
3.9 Prejuizos acumulados (deduzir) (Accumulated deficit (deduct))	....	....	....
4. PENDENTE (Deferred Liabilities)			....
Subtotal (Subtotal)			....
5. CONTAS DE COMPENSAÇÃO (Memorandum Accounts)			....
TOTAL (Total)			....

ILLUSTRATIVE INCOME STATEMENT OF A BRAZILIAN COMPANY (INDUSTRIAL)

DEMONSTRATIVO DE RESULTADOS (Empresa Industrial) (Statement of Profit and Loss) (Industrial Companies)

1. Renda operacional bruta (Gross operating income)		....
1.1 Venda dos productos (Sales of goods)	....	
1.2 Prestação de serviços (Sales of services)	....	....
2. Imposto faturado (Taxes)		....
3. Renda operacional liquida (1-2) Net operating income (1 minus 2))		....
4. Custo dos productos vendidos (Cost of goods sold)		....
5. Lucro bruto (3-4) (Gross profit (3 minus 4))		....
6. Despesas com vendas (Selling expenses)		....
6.1 Comissões sobre vendas (Sales commissions)	....	
6.2 Propaganda e publicidade (Advertising and publicity)	....	
6.3 Imposto de circulação de mercadorias—ICM (Merchandise circulation tax (ICM))	....	
6.4 Provisão para devedores duvidosos (Provision for doubtful accounts)	....	
7. Gastos gerais (General expenses)		....
7.1 Honorários da diretoria (Directors' fees)	....	
7.2 Despesas administrativas (Administrative expenses)	....	
7.4 Despesas financeiras (Financial expenses	....	
8. Depreciações e amortizações (Depreciation and amortization)		....
9. Lucro operacional (5) – (6 a 8) (Operating profit (5 minus (6 through 8))		....
10. Rendas não operacionais (Non-operating revenue)		....
11. Despesas não operacionais (Non-operating expenses)		....
12. Lucro liquido antes do imposto de renda (9 + 10 – 11) (Profit before income tax (9 plus 10 minus 11))		....
13. Imposto de renda pago no período (Income tax paid during the period (note 8))		....
14. Lucro liquido . . . do imposto de renda (nota n° 9) (Profit . . . income tax)		....
15. Lucro suspenso ou saldo anterior (Retained earnings at beginning of period)		....

16. Reversão de provisões, provisões reservas (Reversal of provisions and reserves) ....
17. Gratificações (Employee bonuses) ....
18. Partes beneficiárias (Participation of founders shares) ....
19. Provisão para imposto de renda (Provision for income tax) ....
20. Outras provisões (Other provisions) ....
21. Resultados a distribuir (14+15+16−17−18−19−20) (Distributable profit (14+15+16 minus (17 through 20)) ....
    - 21.1 Dividendos e bonificacões (Dividends and stock bonuses) ....
    - 21.2 Provisões e reservas (Provisions and reserves) ....
    - 21.3 Lucro suspenso ou saldo atual (Retained earnings at end of period) ....

OBS: Para efeito de publicação, os valores que compõem o item 6 poderão ser apresentados englobadamente.
(Remark: For purposes of publication, amounts included in item 6 may be shown as a lump sum.)

NOTE: Certain details of the captioned classifications, required by Circular 179 to be shown, have been omitted because of limitations of space. The foregoing form of income statement is that prescribed by Circular 179 for industrial companies. A different form, which is not shown but the main captions in which (sales, cost of sales, selling expenses, and so forth) are identical to those shown above, is prescribed for commercial (merchandising and service) companies.

Canada

Canada

As of October 1973

Significant developments since the preparation of this chapter are presented, by country, in the section entitled Addenda.

Forms of Business Organization

Canadians carry on business in much the same forms of organization as those prevalent in the United States. Foreign corporations wishing to do business in Canada may establish branches in any of the provinces and are subject to their laws. Depending upon the province, the foreign corporation may be required to comply with any or all of the following:

1. Register as an extraprovincial corporation.
2. Obtain a license as an extraprovincial corporation.
3. Establish an office address.
4. Pay an initial fee, usually called a filing fee, or a license fee.
5. Furnish to authorities prescribed information by filing statements or copies of incorporation documents.

There are restrictions in Canadian law as to the type of business that can be carried on by foreign corporations or by corporations that are foreign owned, particularly in the areas of banking, finance, and communications.

The Corporation

Canadian limited liability companies can be created, as a legal entity distinct from the shareholders, in one of the following three ways:

1. By letters patent granted under the Canada Corporations Act.
2. By letters patent, registration, or filing articles of incorporation under the companies act of one of the provinces.
3. By special act of the federal parliament or of the legislature of one of the provinces. (Such corporations as banks, savings and loan corporations, trust companies, railways, and so forth, are normally incorporated by special act.)

In most cases, the liability of a shareholder is limited to the unpaid amount on shares for which he has subscribed. Certain acts provide that a shareholder's liability to creditors can be created by the redemption, or reduction, of issued capital. Except in Ontario or Quebec, where the word "Incorporated" (or "Inc.") may be used, the word "Limited" (or "Ltd.") must be included in most companies' names. Exceptions are provided for certain nonprofit organizations and certain companies incorporated under special acts. In addition, in some provinces, a company can have two official names, one in English and one in French.

The "letters patent" system of incorporation used by four of the provincial companies acts is similar to that of the federal system. Ontario business corporations are incorporated by the filing of "articles of incorporation." Under the "registration" system used by all other provinces, the Northwest Territories, and the Yukon, there are two types of shareholder-liability companies in addition to the conventional limited-liability form: one in which the shareholder is limited to the amount that he has agreed to contribute in the event of insolvency or dissolution, and one in which, similar to a general partnership, the liability of the shareholder is not limited.

Corporations may be created under either federal or provincial laws, the latter varying in the degree of control exercised over corporations. The federal law distinguishes between a public and a private limited liability company, as do most of the provinces. Such a distinction is not made by Ontario, Quebec, Nova Scotia, or Newfoundland, but in those provinces special rules do exist for companies not offering their securities to the public.

A "private" company may have no more than 50 shareholders (excluding present or former employees), its shares or other securities may not be offered to the public, and the right to transfer its shares is restricted. Both the "private" company and "companies not offering their securities to the public" have greater latitude in permitted transactions with their shareholders and directors, and, with certain exceptions, are not required to make their financial statements public. A federal "private" company is required to file its financial statements and auditor's reports with the Department of Consumer and Corporate Affairs, if it meets either of the following conditions:

1. The total assets or gross revenues of the company exceed $5,000,000 or $10,000,000 respectively.

2. The total assets or gross revenues of the company when aggregated with the total assets and gross revenues of every affiliate (world-wide) exceed $5,000,000 or $10,000,000 respectively.

A federal private company that does not meet condition (1) but does meet condition (2) need not file its financial statement and auditor's report if the top company is incorporated under this act and files consolidated statements that include every affiliate (world-wide). Such filing has the effect of making these documents available to the public.

The "public" company "offering its securities to the public" corresponds quite closely to its U.S. counterpart. Depending upon the jurisdiction under which it is incorporated, it may be formed by a minimum of one to five persons, and may have an unlimited number of shareholders, who may freely transfer their shares if "calls" are fully paid.

A company incorporated under the laws of a province, with certain exceptions, must file a prospectus or a detailed registration statement before offering its securities for sale to the public. All provinces, excluding Nova Scotia and Prince Edward Island, have agreed upon the procedures to clear a prospectus in more than one province. Generally, the securities law of Ontario is the most stringent and when, as in most cases, it is expected that sales will be made in that province, the prospectus must comply with Ontario's requirements. The same prospectus will generally meet the requirements of the other provinces. If incorporated as a federal company, a prospectus which complies with the requirements of the Canada Corporations Act must also be filed with the Minister of Consumer and Corporate Affairs.

Under the Canada Corporations Act, shareholders of companies must appoint auditors who, except in the case of private companies that are exempt from the requirement to file their financial statements with the Department of Consumer and Corporate Affairs, may not be or include an officer, director, or employee of the company, nor any partner, employer, or employee of any such persons. Some provincial acts waive the requirements to appoint auditors, with the consent of all the shareholders, for "private" companies and certain companies "not issuing their shares to the public." In addition, some provinces that allow the auditor of a private company to be an officer, director, or employee of the company, or a partner, employer, or employee of such person, require disclosure of such appointment in the auditor's report. The auditors examine and report upon the financial statements of the company, which are required to be submitted to the annual meeting of shareholders by the directors.

A copy of the financial statements and reports of federal public companies and certain private companies must be filed with the Department of Consumer and Corporate Affairs. Provincial acts require "public" companies and companies that "offer their securities to the public" to file their financial statements and reports with provincial government departments. The provisions of the various stock exchanges require similar filings if a company is listed on one of the exchanges.

Most public and private companies are required to file annual reports with the Chief Statistician of Canada, unless exempted under certain provisions of the Corporations and Labor Unions Returns Act. Specifically exempt are companies that, together with any related companies, have Canadian assets less than $250,000 and have Canadian gross revenues less than $500,000.

Information about capitalization, shareholders, officers, and directors is required as section A information and is available to the public. All other information, classed as section B information, is confidential and includes financial statements, together with the auditor's report thereon, and amounts paid to nonresidents of Canada for dividends, interest, rents, royalties, insurance, advertising, research and development, management fees, payments to officers and directors, professional fees, and the like.

Business Records

The Canada Corporations Act and acts of the several provinces contain similar provisions relating to books of account. In general, proper books of account are required to be kept at the company's head office or any other location in Canada specified by the board of directors. A federal company may keep its books of account outside of Canada provided the bylaws so authorize and the consent of the various taxing authorities is obtained, but they must be made available to the proper authorities on request. Generally speaking, the provincial companies acts require books of account to be kept in the province of incorporation, although, as a matter of fact, these provisions are not strictly enforced. A company must also maintain corporate records, such as letters of patent, bylaws, capital stock records, and so forth, of which, at least, copies usually must be kept at the head office in Canada.

The Sole Proprietor

Any person, resident or nonresident, may engage in business in Canada as a sole proprietor if he has the legal capacity to enter into a contract in

Canada. If he wishes to do business under a style other than his own name or to use the words "and Company," he must file a statement in accordance with the laws of the province in which he does business in the same way as must general partnerships.

Partnerships

A group of persons may conduct business in the form of a partnership, and, in most cases, Canadian partnerships can be classed as general or limited. General partnerships are those in which all partners are jointly and severally liable for partnership debts.

The limited partnership consists of general partners who manage the business and have the same liability as the partners of a general partnership, and of limited partners who contribute capital but who may not participate in the management, and whose liability is limited to the amount of their capital contributions. A few of the provinces limit the number of persons who may join in a partnership, but in general the differences in legislation affecting partnerships between the provinces are minor.

In some cases, partnerships are required to register in the province of their domicile and to furnish information which discloses the names of the partners, their respective interests, and whether general or limited, as well as other descriptive material.

In Quebec, however, general partnerships are divided between "commercial" and "civil" forms. The former are those carrying on a trade or business of a commercial nature; all others, including those of lawyers, accountants, and other professional people, are civil partnerships.

The Accounting Profession

The accounting profession in Canada is over 90 years old. Its development has been influenced in part by the tradition of the pioneering practitioners of English and Scottish origins during the later part of the nineteenth century and in part by the United States due to its proximity and economic ties with that country. The enlarged scope and influence of accountants in the broad scheme of business expansion since World War II have contributed substantially to the numerical growth of those in the profession.

While its development has been influenced by both U.K. and U.S. practices, the Canadian profession has retained a strong sense of independence and has not copied other systems nor relied on others' solutions. The practice of accounting in Canada has reached a high level of standards and competence.

Canadian Institute of Chartered Accountants

The Canadian Institute of Chartered Accountants (CICA) is the largest professional accounting organization in Canada with some twenty thousand members, of whom about half are in public practice. Incorporated in 1902 by an act of the Parliament of Canada, its role as a national coordinator for greater uniformity of standards among the provincial institutes was established in 1910. Membership in a provincial institute automatically carries with it membership in the CICA.

The Institute has four major programs – research, publications, professional development, and annual conferences to help all chartered accountants improve themselves professionally. These programs result in the release of accounting and auditing research recommendations; publication of research studies, audit technique studies, and the monthly journal, *The Canadian Chartered Accountant;* the development of both seminar and in-depth courses to provide a well-rounded program of continuing education for all members of the profession; and a three-day annual conference held on a rotation basis in major centers across the country. In addition, the Institute administers the uniform final examinations, maintains liaison with the federal legislature, coordinates the work of the provincial institutes, and has other programs to protect, assist, and inform the public.

The Provincial Institutes of Chartered Accountants

There is no federal act governing the use of the designation "chartered accountant" in Canada; the legislation involving accountants is a provincial responsibility. The first provincial institute of chartered accountants in Canada was incorporated in Quebec in 1880, followed by Ontario in 1883 and Manitoba in 1886. Institutes have now been organized in all ten of the provinces.

The requirements to attain the designation of chartered accountant vary slightly under each provincial institute's regulations. Generally, the candidate must—

1. Meet the institute's entrance requirements by being a graduate of a recognized Canadian university or of a foreign university that meets the institute's standards.

2. Complete a prescribed series of university credit courses (advanced credit will be given for corresponding university courses taken in either a graduate or undergraduate program).

3. Qualify to write uniform final examinations in accordance with the standards established by the Interprovincial Education Committee.

4. Pass the uniform final examinations.
5. Obtain the required period of practical experience through employment with a practicing firm of chartered accountants. (This will vary, depending upon the university program the candidate has taken. In Ontario, for example, all university graduates must complete three years of practical experience. However, this period is reduced to two years for all M.B.A. graduates of recognized universities and for those graduates of such universities who have at least 39 of the 45 semester hours of university studies when they enroll with the institute.)

Chartered accountants in Canada have developed and maintained a unique professional arrangement allowing interprovincial membership reciprocity. This situation is possible because of the coordinating role of the CICA.

Professional Conduct

Although the CICA has proposed a uniform code of ethics, this has not been adopted by all of the provincial institutes. However, careful consideration is given by the provincial institutes to any amendments to their respective rules of professional conduct to ascertain that these would generally conform to the proposed uniform code of ethics.

The rules of professional conduct adopted by the provincial institutes establish the minimum standard of a chartered accountant's responsibilities to those he serves, to the public, and to his colleagues. Some of the more important provisions prohibit the practice of public accounting by a corporation, soliciting clients through improper advertising, and fees based on results of professional service. They also deal with the confidential character of information received in the course of work, competitive bidding, and relations with retiring auditors.

The Ontario Institute's rules and explanatory notes and opinions clearly define independence and further state that—

> a member acting as an auditor shall be deemed not to be independent in relation to any organization in circumstances where he or his partner(s) or his or their immediate families have any interest in the organization or any affiliate thereof which in view of a reasonable observer might have the effect of impairing his independence.

In dealing with the rendering of an opinion on financial statements examined by a member of the Ontario Institute, its provisions specifically state that—

In expressing an opinion on financial statements examined by him no member shall

(a) fail to reveal a material fact known to him which is not disclosed in the financial statements but the omission of which renders the financial statements misleading; or

(b) fail to report any material misstatement known to him to appear in the financial statements.

No member shall express an opinion on financial statements examined by him, if he fails to obtain sufficient information to warrant an expression of opinion, or if his exceptions are sufficiently material to nullify the expression of an opinion.

The Ontario Institute took a step forward in releasing to its members, in May 1972, an exposure draft of revised rules of conduct to be put to formal vote at the annual meeting in 1973. These revisions were the result of committee work which examined the philosophy underlying the rules of conduct to ensure that they were in keeping with present-day conditions. Undoubtedly, this exposure draft will serve as a model for other provincial institutes which may be considering amendments to their rules of professional conduct.

The Practice of the Chartered Accountant

The practice of the Canadian chartered accountant generally parallels that of his U.S. counterpart, including examinations of financial statements leading to his opinion thereon, preparation of and advice with respect to tax returns, and various types of services to management. The Canada Corporations Act as well as the provincial companies acts require auditors to be appointed by the shareholders and to report to them upon the annual financial statements submitted by the directors. While there is no specific provision in corporation laws that the auditor must be a chartered accountant, the majority of companies, including practically all large publicly owned companies, appoint chartered accountants as auditors.

Under the Federal Bankruptcy Act, which governs bankruptcy proceedings in all provinces, the Superintendent of Bankruptcy appoints licensed trustees with powers to act in bankruptcy matters in various provinces. Most of the larger firms of chartered accountants have at least one partner in each province so licensed, and the great majority of licensed trustees are chartered accountants.

Licensing

Until after World War II, there was no legislation restricting the practice of accounting in Canada. Three of the provinces, Quebec,

Prince Edward Island, and Ontario, now have legislation requiring a license to practice public accounting in their jurisdictions. Conditions under which licenses were issued in the three provinces have changed from time to time, but the general rule now is that only chartered accountants will be granted licenses.

Other Organizations of Accountants

Of the other accounting organizations in Canada, two of the most prominent are The Society of Industrial Accountants of Canada and the Certified General Accountants Association. The former issues the designation RIA and the latter CGA upon completion of a required course of studies and passing uniform examinations. Both of these organizations are in the management accounting field and are national in scope.

The governing bodies of The Society of Industrial Accountants of Ontario and the Certified General Accountants Association of Ontario gave approval in 1972 to the holding of formal talks aimed at a merger plan to join the two organizations. The outcome of these negotiations will likely influence other provincial organizations to follow suit.

Auditing Standards

In Canada, the federal government and each of the provinces have enacted legislation setting out the procedures relating to the incorporation, conduct, and administration of all limited companies. All companies (except those engaged in specialized industries such as banking, insurance, or railways which fall under separate or special acts) must be incorporated under the federal or one of the provincial acts. Since the legislation is not uniform from jurisdiction to jurisdiction, there may be exceptions to any general statements made in respect of statutory audit requirements.

However, under the federal act and most provincial acts, every limited company is required to have an annual audit and to present audited financial statements to its shareholders at its annual meeting. Further, the statutes set out the procedures for appointing or dismissing the auditor, and prescribe who may act as auditor and his powers and obligations. This might be said to be the framework of auditing standards.

The principal public accounting bodies, the Canadian Institute of Chartered Accountants, and the ten-member provincial institutes, function within this somewhat generalized statutory framework. The degree of specificity in which auditing standards are codified in the United States is not matched in Canada; however, standards are referred to throughout the official pronouncements of the various institutes. These standards are found partly in the bylaws and rules of conduct of the provincial institutes covering such matters as independence, educational requirements, training and supervision of students, professional competence, and maintenance of professional standards. In addition, the Accounting and Auditing Research Committee of the Canadian Institute of Chartered Accountants has from time to time issued pronouncements on specific auditing matters such as the requirements for circularization of accounts receivable, observation of physical inventories, and form and content of the audit report (the recommended form is similar to that of the United States, except that it does not refer to "generally accepted auditing standards").

Accounting Principles and Practices

Accounting principles applied in the presentation of financial statements are generally similar to those current in the United States. The Accounting and Auditing Research Committee of the Canadian Institute of Chartered Accountants issues bulletins from time to time setting out recommended treatment of various types of accounting problems. Their pronouncements, however, thus far cover a much smaller area than that covered by the Financial Accounting Standards Board and the predecessor accounting standards setting bodies of the AICPA and consequently there is greater exercise of pure judgment in the presentation of financial statements than in the United States.

Form and Content of Financial Statements

The form and content of financial statements are governed to some extent by the statute under which a company is incorporated as well as by recommendations of the CICA research committee. As stated previously, a company may be incorporated federally or in any one of the provinces, and, consequently, statutory requirements vary. It would be an exhaustive exercise to list all variations, but, as an illustration, some of the provisions of the federal legislation, the Canada Corporations Act of 1971, might be cited.

The act provides that the directors of a company shall place before the shareholders at the annual meeting a financial statement in comparative form consisting of the following:

1. An income statement.
2. A statement of surplus.
3. A statement of source and application of funds.

4. A balance sheet.
5. The auditors' report.

The act permits the omission of comparative amounts and the statement of source and application of funds if the reason for such omission is stated by footnote.

The act goes on to set out in some detail the minimum disclosures required in each statement. These do not differ significantly from normal professional reporting standards. For example, the required disclosures for the income statement are—

1. Sales or gross revenue.
2. Income from investments in subsidiaries not consolidated.
3. Income from investments in affiliated companies other than subsidiaries.
4. Income from other investments.
5. Nonrecurring profits or losses of significant amount.
6. Provision for depreciation and depletion.
7. Amortization of goodwill or other intangibles.
8. Interest on indebtedness originally incurred for a term of more than one year.
9. Taxes on income.
10. Net profit or loss for the period.

The content of the other elements of the financial statement is similarly stipulated.

The following additional information is required to be set out by footnote or otherwise:

1. Basis of conversion of amounts originating in foreign currency.
2. Foreign currency restrictions affecting assets of the company.
3. Commitments.
4. Contingent liabilities.
5. Liabilities secured by lien on assets of the company.
6. Any default by the company on its securities.
7. Arrears of dividends on any class of shares.

8. Outstanding options to purchase shares in the company.
9. Shares of parent held by a subsidiary.
10. Loans to officers or directors.
11. Restrictions on payment of dividends.
12. Events or transactions subsequent to the date of the financial statement having a material consequence.
13. Past service liability under a pension plan.
14. Gross revenue by class of business.
15. Remuneration of officers and directors—
    a. Number of directors and their aggregate remuneration as directors.
    b. Number of officers and their aggregate remuneration as officers.
    c. Number of officers who are also directors.
16. Any change in accounting principle or practice.

Where a company has subsidiaries, the act contemplates the issuance of the financial statement in consolidated form. Where such practice is not followed, the following disclosures must be made:

1. The reason why consolidated statements are not issued.
2. The parent company's proportion of current period profits or losses of subsidiaries.
3. The income from subsidiaries included in the income statement of the parent.
4. The parent's share of the undistributed income of the subsidiaries since acquisition.
5. Any qualification in the report of the auditors with respect to the subsidiaries.

Public companies registered with the securities commissions of the various provinces are required by regulations (varying somewhat by province) to publish quarterly unaudited financial statements.

The disclosure requirements of the Business Corporations Act of 1970 of the province of Ontario parallel the federal act in most respects, and other provinces have followed or will probably follow the pattern.

The Canadian Institute of Chartered Accountants handbook sets out recommended standards of disclosure which preceded the revisions of the Canada Corporations Act of 1971 (federal) and the Business Corporations Act of 1970 (Ontario).

Business Combinations—Pooling of Interests

Until the present time (1972) there has been no pronouncement in Canada on pooling of interests treatment, although some published financial statements have been presented in this manner. Since there is also no requirement for the amortization of goodwill, the issue has not been as urgent as in the United States and purchase treatment of acquisitions is the one commonly applied. However, it is anticipated that mandatory amortization of goodwill will be introduced coupled with exceedingly narrow criteria under which poolings may be carried out. The accounting for what would be termed in the United States a "statutory merger" (a merger under certain of the companies acts) is almost identical with the pooling treatment.

Diversified Operations

The Canada Corporations Act provides that where a company has conducted business of two or more classes that, in the opinion of its directors, differ substantially from each other, the sales or gross revenue from each shall be disclosed by footnote. The Institute pronouncement on this point goes further and recommends that profitability of the segments be also disclosed.

Inventory Valuation

The Lifo method has been determined unacceptable for income tax purposes and consequently is rarely used.

Long-Term Investments

Recent recommendations of the CICA research committee cover the accounting treatment for long-term investments in other corporations. Generally, the recommendations follow the principles outlined by the U.S. Accounting Principles Board (APB) except that in cases involving less than 50 percent ownership, the recommendations refer to "effectively controlled companies" whereas the APB uses the term "significantly influence." In practice these terms have been construed to have substantially the same meaning.

Requirements for Public Sale of Securities

The Canada Corporations Act prescribes the information required for prospectuses in connection with the public issue of securities of companies incorporated under that act. The act requires that the prospectus be signed and filed with the Department of Consumer and Corporate Affairs. In almost all cases, however, if a prospectus is approved by any province or by any foreign country wherein it is a legal requirement that a prospectus be filed, the mere filing of the approved prospectus with the Department of Consumer and Corporate Affairs in accordance with local requirements is sufficient for purposes of complying with the act.

The provinces of Ontario, Alberta, Saskatchewan, Quebec, British Columbia, and Manitoba have set up securities commissions to administer and enforce the regulations under which securities may be offered for sale in these provinces; the remaining provinces operate through registrars who perform the same function under the provincial secretary as the securities commissions in the named provinces.

The requirements of these six provinces are almost uniform. Because most public companies wish to sell at least some of their securities in Ontario, the majority of prospectuses conform to the requirements of that province's securities act. The Ontario Securities Commission requires not only that the prospectus conform with the securities act under which the company was incorporated, but also with the standards of disclosure promulgated by the commission itself. Such standards are substantially the same as those set out in the Accounting and Auditing Handbook of the Canadian Institute of Chartered Accountants. Typically, a preliminary prospectus is filed with the appropriate commission or registrar after which a "deficiency letter" will be returned, the stated shortcomings will be discussed or amended, and a final prospectus will be filed.

There must be presented an audited balance sheet (consolidated, if appropriate) and, where possible, five-year consolidated statements of profit and loss and surplus, on which the company's auditors have rendered an opinion. Where the audited year-end statements are for a period ended more than 120 days prior to the date of receipt for filing of the preliminary prospectus, an unaudited balance sheet and related statements of profit and loss and surplus as of a date not more than 90 days prior to the date of such receipt are required. Mining or industrial companies in the promotion, exploration, or development stage must submit a consolidated statement of source and application of funds or a statement of cash receipts and disbursements.

Pro forma financial statements indicating the effect upon the balance sheet of the application of the proceeds of the proposed issue may be required.

As to the auditor's report, the commission assumes the following:

1. That the auditor is satisfied that the company's financial statements are in agreement with the accounting records (subject to such amendments as may be disclosed in the case of pro forma statements, and to such adjustments between years as may be deemed necessary in the case of statements of earnings and surplus).
2. That the company's financial statements are in accordance with the requirements of the commission and those of the companies act to which the company is subject.
3. That proper accounting records have been maintained so far as appears from the auditor's examination.

If the auditor is reporting on a balance sheet of a company which does not consolidate one or more subsidiaries and such subsidiary or subsidiaries in the aggregate had an excess of net losses and dividends over net profits since the acquisition of the shares by the company and such excess has not been provided for in the accounts of the company, then the auditor's report will state such amount or additional amount as may be necessary, in his opinion, to make provision for the company's portion of such excess.

Requirements for Listing Securities on the Toronto Stock Exchange

(The Principal Exchange in Canada)

Minimum Financial Requirements

1. Where the company is an industrial, investment, or real estate company with a record of earnings, it should have net tangible assets of at least $1,000,000, adequate net working capital, net income after taxes of at least $100,000 in the last fiscal year preceding the listing application, and a minimum average net income after taxes of at least $100,000 for three of the last five fiscal years.

   If an industrial, investment, or real estate company has no record of earnings, it must have net tangible assets of at least $1,500,000 and adequate net working capital. It must have a satisfactory over-the-counter market experience for at least one year, unless it is a subsidiary or an associate of a substantial existing and successful enterprise and can provide evidence of profitability.

2. A minimum of 200,000 of the issued shares shall be held by at least 300 public shareholders, each holding a board lot or more, although consideration will be given to applications where there are between 200 and 300 public shareholders, each holding a board lot or more, if there is a total of 450 or more public shareholders.
3. The market value of issued shares in the hands of the public must not be less than $1,000,000.
4. In determining whether or not a listing application will be granted, the management and sponsorship of the company will be an important factor.

Minimum requirements similar to the above apply to computer, mining, and oil and gas companies but with varying minimum levels.

Listing Application

A listing application must be filed with the exchange, which includes the following accounting information and documents:

1. Companies whose principal business is mining or the production of oil or natural gas must furnish certain documents including—
    a. One copy of each of the annual reports for the past three years (if such were issued).
    b. Two copies of a statement of assets and liabilities and of profit and loss, revenue and expenditure, or receipts and disbursements accounts covering, where possible, at least the last three yearly periods, duly certified by a chartered, public, or certified accountant.
    c. Two copies of an up-to-date financial statement (including a balance sheet and profit and loss, or revenue and expenditure, account) in the customary form, reported on by a chartered, public, or certified accountant and approved by the board of directors.
2. Industrial and investment companies must furnish—
    a. The name, address, and qualification of the company's auditors.
    b. Two copies of financial statements, certified by a chartered, public, or certified accountant and consisting of a balance sheet of a recent date not more than 120 days prior to the date of application and a detailed statement of profit and loss for each of the preceding five years, if possible, tabulated in comparative form.
    c. Two copies of annual reports of the last three years, if any

were published, in the form in which such reports were distributed to shareholders.

General

1. Section 19.12 of the Toronto Stock Exchange bylaws requires that every company whose shares are posted for trading shall forward yearly to each of its shareholders and shall submit to the exchange an annual report containing a financial statement (including a balance sheet and a statement of profit and loss) in the customary form, reported upon by a chartered, public, or certified accountant and approved by the board of directors. This statement will also contain a record of its activities, if any, during the period covered, such report to be provided within six months from the close of the fiscal year or other period covered. The shares of a company which fails to forward and submit such report shall be removed from the trading list, provided, however, that the exchange may, in its discretion, relieve any company or companies from this penalty. In addition, the board of governors of the exchange may at any time require a company to submit a financial statement in the customary form and such further particulars of its activities as the board shall prescribe.
2. Section 19.07 requires that every company whose shares are posted for trading shall file a copy of semiannual or interim financial statements required by statutes or by the exchange.
3. Section 19.08 of the bylaws requires quarterly reports to be filed within 60 days after the end of each quarter by each company whose shares are posted for trading. The report must include a statement of sales or gross operating revenue, extraordinary items of income or expense, and net profit or loss. A mining company or oil and gas company is not required to file quarterly reports if its gross annual revenue is less than $100,000. The exchange may exempt a company or a class of companies from the quarterly filing requirements.
4. Section 19.13 requires that companies whose shares are posted for trading shall file an annual questionnaire in the period and form prescribed by the board of governors. Failure to comply in providing up-to-date information about the activities of the company may result in its shares being removed from the trading list.
5. Under section 19.09, prompt notice must be given by every company, whose shares are posted for trading, of each proposed material change in the business or affairs of the company. Considered material are changes in the nature of the business of the company

or the personnel on the board of directors; the acquisition or disposition by the company of any mining or oil property or interest, or securities in another company, for a consideration payable otherwise than in shares of the company; the entering into of any management contract; and a change in the beneficial or registered share ownership of the company which is sufficient to materially affect control.

Canada

Illustrative Financial Statements

ILLUSTRATIVE BALANCE SHEET OF A CANADIAN COMPANY
(Incorporated under the laws of Canada)
December 31, 19__

ASSETS

CURRENT ASSETS			
Cash			....
Marketable securities, at cost (market value 19— ....)			....
Accounts receivable			....
Inventories, at the lower of cost and market—			
Raw materials		....	
Work in process		....	
Finished goods		....	....
Prepaid expenses			....
TOTAL CURRENT ASSETS			....
INVESTMENTS (at cost)			....
FIXED	Cost	Accumulated depreciation and amortization	
Land	....		
Buildings	....	....	
Machinery and equipment	....	....	
Leasehold improvements	....	....	
	....	....	....
OTHER			
Cash surrender value of life insurance on officers			....
Patents, at cost less amortization			....
Unamortized bond discount			....
			....
			....

ILLUSTRATIVE BALANCE SHEET OF A CANADIAN COMPANY
(Incorporated under the laws of Canada)
December 31, 19__

LIABILITIES AND SHAREHOLDERS' EQUITY

CURRENT LIABILITIES	
Bank indebtedness (against which accounts receivable are pledged as collateral)	....
Accounts payable and accrued charges	....
Income and other taxes payable	....
First mortgage bonds maturing within one year	....
TOTAL CURRENT LIABILITIES	....
LONG-TERM DEBT	
X% note payable in U.S. funds (U.S. ....) due March 31, 19__	....
X% first mortgage bonds, due .... annually March 15, 19__ to 19__	....
	....
Less installment included as current liability	....
	....
DEFERRED INCOME TAXES	....
SHAREHOLDERS' EQUITY	
Capital stock—	
X% cumulative preferred shares of .... par value each, redeemable at ....:	
Authorized less redeemed — .... shares	
Issued and outstanding — .... shares	....
Common shares of no par value:	
Authorized and issued .... shares	....
Contributed surplus	....
Retained earnings	....
TOTAL SHAREHOLDERS' EQUITY	....
	....

On behalf of the Board:

Director

Director

ILLUSTRATIVE INCOME STATEMENT OF A CANADIAN COMPANY

STATEMENT OF INCOME

Year ended December 31, 19——

SALES AND OTHER INCOME	
Sales	....
Royalties	....
	....
EXPENSES	
Cost of sales	....
Selling expenses	....
General and administrative	....
Interest on long-term debt	....
Other interest	....
	....
INCOME BEFORE INCOME TAXES	....
INCOME TAXES	
Current	....
Deferred	....
	....
NET INCOME	....
PER SHARE OF COMMON STOCK (after deducting preferred share dividends)	....

Note:

The following depreciation and amortization charges have been deducted in the above statement:

Depreciation	....
Amortization — Bond discount	....
— Patents	....
— Leasehold improvements	....
	....

(See accompanying notes to the financial statements)

Chile

Chile

As of January 1973

Forms of Business Organization

The corporate form of business organization as well as the several forms of partnerships in Chile are similar to those of other South American countries and are not unlike those of the United States. A U.S. corporation may obtain authorization from the Superintendencia de Sociedades Anónimas (Superintendency of Corporations) to engage in business in Chile by establishing a branch, or by organizing a Chilean subsidiary company to carry on its business in that country, after complying with certain formalities in each case.

A company in Chile may be either civil or commercial. A commercial company is one whose business consists of performing commercial acts; all others are civil companies. There are certain legal differences in their obligations. The discussion that follows deals only with commercial companies.

Sociedad Anónima (S.A.)

This corporate form closely resembles those existing in the United States. Shareholders are liable for the debts of the corporation only to the extent of their subscribed capital.

A Chilean government agency, the Superintendencia de Sociedades Anónimas, exercises supervision and control over sociedades anónimas.

In order to organize a corporation, two or more persons must submit to the superintendencia, for approval, the "estatutos" (charter and bylaws) in the form of a public instrument. The "estatutos" must fix the share capital and must define the rules for internal organization of the corporation. The share capital must be nominative shares, as the issuance of bearer shares is no longer allowed.

The superintendencia also has the right to audit the operations of an S.A., but this right is usually exercised only upon complaint or for some specific purpose and is not a routine procedure.

Shareholders must approve the annual accounts and proposals for distribution of dividends at a general meeting called for that purpose. The annual accounts, together with the report to shareholders, must be presented to the superintendencia, published in a newspaper, and be signed by the company's general manager, its accountant, and two "inspectores de cuentas" (see page 134, "Account Inspectors").

Sociedad de Responsabilidad Limitada (S.R.L.)

The sociedad de responsabilidad limitada has characteristics of both a partnership and a corporation. The right of management extends to all partners, and their rights are neither negotiable nor represented by any transferable document. The liability of the members is limited, however, to the amount of their contribution to capital, or possibly to a larger amount if specified in the instrument of organization.

The firm name must contain the name of one or more partners followed by the word "Limitada" (Ltda.). There may be no more than 50 partners. A partner may not transfer his interest to an outsider without the unanimous consent of all other partners. An S.R.L. is constituted by a notarial instrument containing the same information as that required for the sociedad colectiva (see below), plus a statement as to the agreed liability of partners. An extract must be inscribed in the Commercial Register (including a statement as to the limitation of liability of partners), and the extract must be published in the *Diario Oficial* (official gazette).

Sociedad Colectiva (S.C.)

The general commercial partnership is similar to its counterpart in the United States. The partners are jointly and severally liable for its debts. A partner may not transfer his interest in the partnership to an outsider without the unanimous consent of the other partners. A general partnership is organized by a notarial public instrument that must contain certain information, such as names and addresses of partners, name and domicile of firm, capital contributed, form in which contributed and basis of its valuation, basis of allocation of profits and losses among partners, and allowable drawing accounts.

The notarial instrument constituting both the sociedad de responsabilidad limitada and the sociedad colectiva does not require the approval of the superintendencia, but an extract must be inscribed in the Commercial Register and published in the *Diario Oficial.*

Sociedad en Comandita Simple (S.C.S.)

This type of partnership is comprised of both general partners (gestores) and limited partners (comanditarios). The general partners, who supply capital or services or both, have the same liability as in a general partnership and have exclusive right to management. Limited partners who supply capital have limited liability to the extent of their capital contribution to the enterprise and may not participate in the management. The sociedad en comandita simple is formed in the same manner as the sociedad colectiva, except that the names of the comanditarios can not be included in the firm name, nor are they stated in the extract of the constitutive document.

Sociedad en Comandita por Acciones (S.C. por A.)

This form differs from the sociedad en comandita simple only in that the interests of the comanditarios may be represented by shares. The capital of the S.C. por A., if less than 50 escudos, may not be divided into shares of a value less than 0.10 escudos each; if the capital is more than 50 escudos, each share may not be valued at less than 0.50 escudos.

Both forms of "comandita" have fallen into disuse and are now seldom encountered.

Asociación o Cuentas en Participación

Two or more persons may contract to enter into one or several commercial operations to be performed by one of them under his own name and credit. Such a venture has no legal standing and does not have to comply with the formalities required of corporations or partnerships in connection with its organization. The managing partner's obligation is to render an accounting to his associates and to divide the profits and losses in the proportion agreed upon. He is also responsible for the tax obligations and should withhold from distribution the amounts of income tax applicable to the other partners' participation in profits.

Business Records

The principal books required to be kept are the ledger, journal, cash book, and the "inventory and balance book," and these must be stamped by the local treasury (tesoreria comunal) of the location where the entity is established. The Stamp Act Law requires that each page bear a fixed stamp of 0.65 escudos. All official subsidiary records must also be stamped.

Special permission may be obtained to use loose-leaf or card records as part of the legal books.

Inspectores de Cuentas (Account Inspectors)

The regulations governing sociedades anónimas require that their bylaws provide for the appointment every year, at their general shareholders' meeting, of either two account inspectors or two auditors to observe the company's operations, examine the accounting records, inventories and balance sheet, and report their conclusions to the next general shareholders' meeting. The report of the account inspectors or auditors must be given in writing to the company at least 15 days before the shareholders' meeting. The account inspectors should preferably be accountants, professionals, or university technicians. The auditors must be duly qualified accountants (professionals registered in the Colegio de Contadores and having their license fee paid up to date).

The Superintendencia de Sociedades Anónimas is empowered to require the sociedades anónimas to appoint auditors instead of account inspectors in case it is justified by the amount of capital, volume of operations, number of shareholders, or other reasons. The superintendencia has not exercised the power mentioned up to date, and there are no guidelines. The auditors must be inscribed in the register prepared by the superintendencia, and their reports must be issued in accordance with auditing standards generally accepted by the profession.

The Accounting Profession

The practice of public accounting in Chile dates from the latter part of the nineteenth century, when the first British chartered accountant opened an office in Valparaiso. Later, other English and American firms established offices in the country. There are now about ten Chilean firms operating as auditors.

In addition, there are numerous individual practitioners whose practice consists mainly of serving small businesses by writing up books on a monthly basis and preparing financial statements and tax returns.

University Courses

The following universities have faculties of economics and/or business administration in Chile:

1. University of Chile (Santiago, Arica, Iquique, and Valparaiso)
2. Universidad Católica de Chile (Santiago)
3. Universidad Católica de Valparaiso
4. Universidad del Norte (Antofagasta and Arica)
5. Universidad de Concepción
6. Universidad Técnica del Estado (Santiago, Temuco, Concepción, and Punta Arenas)

The curricula include courses such as administration, statistical sciences, industrial management, marketing, accounting and computer system analysis, finance, cost accounting, financial and operational auditing, advanced mathematics, labor, commercial and tax legislation, economics, behavioral sciences, and so forth.

The degrees offered are contador público or contador auditor (public accountant—three-and-a-half to four-and-a-half-year course), bachelor in business administration, bachelor in finance, and commercial engineer (all five-year courses).

Colegio de Contadores

In 1958, an institution known as the "Colegio de Contadores" (College of Accountants) was created by law. This institution is the successor to the former Register of Accountants and its stated purpose is—

> . . . to watch over the progress, prestige, and prerogatives of the accounting profession and its regular and correct practice, to maintain professional discipline and to afford protection to accountants.

Its members consist of those persons holding the title of "accountant" issued by a commercial school, a university, or a private educational institution recognized by the state. An accountant is considered to be in practice if he has registered his title in the Colegio de Contadores and has paid the required yearly dues.

The Colegio is governed by a General Council, domiciled in Santiago, with provincial councils in various cities. It has the duty to inscribe its members on its rolls; to collect an annual license fee; to establish and maintain publications of professional interest; to impose precepts of professional ethics; to dictate rules (standards) relative to professional practice; to establish, with the consent of two-thirds of its members, the scale of professional fees; to maintain contact with other bodies of accountants; and to organize conventions, studies, or assemblies. Only those properly inscribed in the Colegio and the special register of their domicile may practice the profession of accountant. Persons practicing accountancy who are not entitled to do so are subject to fines and imprisonment.

The provincial councils may impose certain sanctions upon an accountant who, upon complaint, is adjudged to have acted unethically or not in accordance with professional dignity or standards. Appeal may be made to the General Council of the Colegio, and from that to the Supreme Court.

Sociedad Nacional de Contadores

The "Sociedad Nacional de Contadores" (National Society of Accountants), formed in 1935 through the merger of existing professional accounting associations, worked for, and obtained legal recognition of, the profession through the enactment of legislation that first created the Register of Accountants and later its successor, the Colegio de Contadores.

The Sociedad Nacional de Contadores is a member of the Inter-American Conferences on Accounting and, in 1957, was the host of the Fourth Inter-American Conference on Accounting held in Santiago.

Instituto de Contadores Profesionales Auditores (INCPA)

This Institute was organized in 1962 and received legal recognition by government decree in April of that year. Its members are qualified accountants engaged in auditing. Its objectives are the development of the (public) accounting profession and of auditing standards and techniques to which its members agree to conform. The INCPA is not a very active organization and its members are, in practice, developing their activities through the Colegio de Contadores.

Other Accounting Organizations

Other accounting organizations in existence are the Asociación de Contadores de la Universidad Católica de Valparaiso, the Asociación de Contadores Auditores de la Universidad de Chile (members qualified at these universities), the Asociación de Contadores del Estado, and the Asociación de Contadores Independientes.

The activities of these organizations are limited to professional development and social welfare.

Ethics

The Colegio de Contadores has adopted a code of ethics that, inasmuch as it is applicable to all of its members, is not specifically directed to those in the independent practice of public accountancy. The code emphasizes the duty of the accountant to observe ethical and moral standards, to maintain the dignity of the profession, to observe proper relations with his colleagues and his employer, and similar matters.

It is stated that the accountant has the responsibility that his work, and his opinions and reports thereon, be clothed with complete independence and conform to the truth and to strict accounting technique.

The Instituto de Contadores Profesionales Auditores issued a code of professional ethics in 1962, which was applicable to the independent public accounting profession, modeled on the code of professional ethics of the American Institute of Certified Public Accountants and the Members' Handbook of the United Kingdom Institute of Chartered Accountants in England and Wales. The rules cover members' professional activities, relations among members, professional conduct, and solicitation of clients and advertising.

Auditing Standards

The Sociedad Nacional de Contadores held a National Congress of Accountants in Chile in 1955. This congress published a statement of auditing standards (normas de auditoria), which, in substance, was ratified at the Fourth Inter-American Conference held in Santiago in 1957. The standards covered were those of statement preparation, auditing procedures, and the auditor's report. While summarized in form, the statement provided for most of the concepts laid down by the pronouncements of the American Institute of CPAs, such as basis of stating assets, presence at taking of physical inventories, confirmation of receivables, and, without prescribing the exact language, stated that the auditor's report should state his opinion upon the fairness of presentation of the financial statements examined, and that they were prepared on the basis of generally accepted principles, consistently applied, in accordance with generally accepted auditing standards and techniques.

To date, the Colegio has not, however, actively enforced the standards recommended in this publication. The Colegio de Contadores has created a committee on internal and external auditing, which will define the role of the auditor and endeavor to set specific guidelines for attaining professional excellence in these areas.

Auditors' Reports

The Chilean delegation to the Fourth Inter-American Conference on Accounting (1957) proposed a form of auditors' report generally similar to that in use in the United States. There is no present requirement in Chilean law or custom for a particular form of auditors' report.

Independence

While, as indicated previously, the code of ethics of the Colegio makes reference to the desirability of an independent attitude of the accountant toward his work, it does not specify the rules of conduct that might promote such an attitude. While some firms of independent auditors in Chile generally adhere to the rules of independence as understood in the United States, ownership of a financial interest in a client's business by partners and staff is not always considered a detriment to independence.

Consistency

Some firms of independent accountants in Chile recognize the importance of consistency in the application of accounting principles, but such recognition is not common among all practitioners. However, tax authorities consider consistency of treatment over a period of years a strong argument in favor of approval of a particular method.

Accounting Principles and Practices

Until recently, there had been no official statement of accounting principles by any of the organizations of accountants in Chile, but the teaching in the universities and the practice of some firms were based largely on U.S. rules and procedures. However, the Accounting Principles Board of the Colegio de Contadores de Chile issued, in January 1973, Technical Bulletin No. 1, which deals with the implications and substance of the expression "in accordance with generally accepted principles and standards of accounting." The Bulletin outlines the basic objectives of accounting and the characteristics of financial data from the theoretical viewpoint and expounds 18 fundamental accounting principles. It classifies accounting standards into two groups, general and specific, and defines general standards as those that guide the selection, measurement, and explanation of the facts of financial accounting, and specific standards as those that govern the application of general standards in particular situations. (For example, the use of Lifo in costing inventories is a specific application of the general standard relating to the determination of the valuation and measurement of an asset.) General standards require, among other things, that income be identified with the period in which realized, and expenses and charges, with the revenue that they produce; that appropriate provisions for depreciation, amortization, and depletion be made; that extraordinary gains and losses be identified and segregated in financial statements; and that accounting principles be consistently applied, failing which the effect of deviation must be described in the financial statements. As a whole, the principles and standards set forth in the Bulletin are not dissimilar to those prevailing in the United States. The pronouncements in the Bulletin are binding on all members of the Colegio.

Form and Content of Financial Statements

Statement Presentation. The Superintendencia de Sociedades Anónimas has prescribed a form of annual report (memoria), balance sheet, and income statement for sociedades anónimas (the statement of changes in financial position is not considered a basic financial statement in Chile although it is prepared by a limited number of large corporations). The balance sheet includes the following:

Assets

- Cash and banks
- Marketable securities
- Inventories
- Short-term receivables (less reserve for bad debts)
- Long-term receivables
- Deferred assets (includes prepayments, interim dividends paid, and others)
- Fixed assets
- Intangible assets and deferred costs

Liabilities

- Long-term
- Short-term
- Deferred income

Net worth

- Capital and revenue reserves, the latter including a statutory legal reserve and revaluation reserves (see below), according to local legislation.

The basis of valuation of inventories, investments, and fixed assets should be disclosed in the balance sheet or in footnotes.

"Memo accounts" (cuentas de orden), for such items as contingent liabilities, guarantee and custodian deposits, and directors' guarantee deposits, and so forth, are also provided (corresponding assets and liabilities offset each other).

The income statement is in the "Account" form as follows:

Debits

Total depreciation, amortization, depletion, write offs, and/or provision for bad debts.

General and administrative expenses.

Interest, discounts, commissions, and exchange losses.

Real estate, licenses, and social security taxes.

Provision for income tax, legal bonuses, profit sharing of management and staff, and so forth.

Directors' remuneration.

Appropriation of net income in accordance with the invested capital revaluation law (see below).

Credits

Income of the business (generally, sales less cost of goods sold).

Income of nonbusiness operations (rent, dividends, commissions, interest, and exchange gains).

The superintendencia also requires full disclosure in the footnotes to the financial statements of purchases and sales of company's shares by its directors during the year.

Consolidated Financial Statements. Consolidated financial statements are of rare occurrence in Chile, because (1) the practice of operating through subsidiaries is uncommon and (2) each individual company is obliged to publish its own individual statements and file same with the Internal Revenue Service. When subsidiaries exist, it is considered good practice to show intercompany accounts separately on the balance sheet.

Inventories

The form of balance sheet prescribed by the superintendencia includes inventories in the "current assets" section and requires them to be valued at cost. The tax code permits the application of any "adequate accounting practices," but the Tax Bureau objects to the Lifo method and tends to recommend using average cost as a basis of valuation.

Allowance for Bad and Doubtful Accounts

The tax authorities allow, as a deduction from taxable income, bad debts written off on the books provided reasonable methods of collection have been exhausted. While some companies provide allowances for doubtful accounts based upon probable collectibility of the accounts receivable as a whole, many others do not.

Revaluations

Law No. 13305, modified by an income tax law having effect from January 1, 1964, provides for the annual compulsory revaluation of invested capital by a percentage equal to the increase in the consumer price index. Invested capital for this purpose is deemed to be (with certain adjustments in respect of investments in marketable securities and savings and loan associations and intangible assets) paid-up capital, capital reserves, and surplus. The amount of the revaluation so determined is applied to increase, by the same percentage as referred to above, the book value of fixed assets net of depreciation (less any charges thereto in respect of year-end exchange adjustments) and the remainder, if any, is a tax-deductible charge to operations, limited to 20 percent of the taxable income.

Increase in capital computed in this manner is credited to a capital reserve; a corporation may issue free (bonus) shares against this reserve but no dividends may be paid out of this reserve.

Investments

Investments in securities are required to be shown at quoted market, if any, at the balance sheet date; if the resulting adjustment represents an increase, it is credited to a "Fluctuation Fund." If the revaluation represents a decrease, it may be written off immediately or carried as a deferred charge if the decline is considered temporary.

Statutory Reserve

Each sociedad anónima must, by law, provide a statutory reserve not lower than 5 percent or higher than 40 percent of annual profits until the total equals 20 percent of capital. This reserve is included in the stockholders' equity caption of the balance sheet.

Income Statement

Following are the most important considerations regarding the form of income statement prescribed by the superintendencia.

Depreciation. The tax authorities prescribe rates of depreciation, based on the years of useful life, that are generally followed in a company's accounts for the different groups of depreciable property. Special rates will usually be allowed, provided it is shown in an application submitted for this purpose, that the prescribed rates are inadequate. Depreciation is calculated on the book amount of property, plant, and equipment, which includes the revaluation and exchange adjustment increases previously discussed.

Amounts Paid to President and Directors. The regulations of the superintendencia require that all amounts paid to the president and directors of a sociedad anónima be shown separately in the income statement.

Income Distribution and Surplus. The law establishes that the balance of annual profits, after providing for the statutory reserve, be distributed pro rata to the shareholders as a dividend. As a result, the balance sheet concept known as "surplus" or "retained earnings" does not exist in Chile. If a corporation does not resolve to distribute that part of its profits that it is entitled to pay as a dividend, then such amount as exceeds the appropriated portion is transferred to an account called "Fondo de Futuros Dividendos" (Future Dividend Fund). This can be distributed at some future date but in practice is more frequently capitalized.

Tax-Effect Accounting

Tax-effect accounting is generally not adopted in Chile.

Requirements for Public Sale of Securities

The public sale of securities must be approved by the Superintendencia de Sociedades Anónimas, which will require information covering all aspects including financial data.

Requirements for Listing Securities on the Stock Exchange

An application for listing on the "bolsa de comercio" (stock exchange) must include copies of the latest balance sheet and income statement, and the company must agree to file with the stock exchange copies of its balance sheet and annual report every year. These financial statements need not be examined or reported upon by independent public accountants.

Colombia

Colombia

As of August 1973

Forms of Business Organization

Business organizations in Colombia include the "sociedad anónima" (S.A.) (similar to the U.S. corporation) and several forms of partnerships.

Foreign corporations may register to do business in Colombia by forming a branch under the provisions of Colombian law, which include the assignment of a specific amount of capital. The more usual procedure is to form a sociedad anónima as a subsidiary.

Sociedad Anónima (S.A.)

A sociedad anónima must have at least five shareholders at the time of organization and thereafter. The liability of the stockholders is limited to the amount of their investment. The sociedad anónima is organized by means of a registered public instrument (estatutos), which must state, among other things, the number of shares and value of the authorized and subscribed capital of the corporation. Upon formation, the company must have 50 percent of its authorized capital subscribed and one-third of the subscribed capital must be paid. The registered public instrument must also state the powers and duties of the revisor fiscal (statutory auditor); the first statutory auditor and his alternate must be named.

No minimum capital is required; the capital may be increased or decreased by approval of all of the shareholders or by approval of a majority of shareholders if prescribed in the bylaws. However, authorization by the Superintendency of Corporations is necessary in either case.

At least once a year every corporation must submit financial statements, signed by the statutory auditor, to the Superintendency of Corporations and publish the balance sheet in the bulletin of the local Chamber of Commerce of their domicile. Corporations that have issued bearer shares or whose shares are traded on a stock exchange must publish annual financial statements in a major newspaper circulated in the city or cities where the corporation's shares are traded.

The Superintendency of Corporations supervises corporations and verifies that they are complying with the articles of incorporation and Colombian law.

Sociedad de Responsabilidad Limitada (S.R.L.)

This is a form of partnership in which the liability of the partners is limited generally to their capital contributions. There may be no more than 25 partners. There must be a partnership agreement in the form of a public instrument, executed before a notary, stating the contributed capital, type of business, formula for allocation of profits and losses, and so forth. The capital of an S.R.L. must be divided into equal parts, each partner having as many votes as he has parts in the company. Any partner wishing to transfer or sell an interest must first offer the interest pro rata to the other partners. Any transfer requires approval of 70 percent of the partnership interests since this constitutes an amendment of the articles.

The name of an S.R.L. must be followed by the word "Limitada" or the abbreviation "Ltda."; if this is not done, the partners become jointly and severally liable for the partnership's obligations.

The Superintendency of Corporations has jurisdiction over S.R.L. partnerships in which legal entities already subject to the control of the superintendency have an interest of 20 percent or more.

Sociedad Colectiva

This is the common form of partnership, composed of two or more partners who are jointly and severally liable for the obligations of the partnership. Initially, the organizational requirements are the same as those for an S.R.L.

Sociedad en Comandita Simple

In this form of partnership there are two classes of partners: active (gestores) and limited (comanditarios). Active partners have unlimited liability and exclusive administrative powers. The liability of limited partners cannot exceed their capital contributions, and they may not take any part in administration except for special limited powers granted by active partners. The organizational requirements are the same as those for an S.R.L.

Sociedad en Comandita por Acciones

This partnership must consist of at least five partners, active and limited as defined immediately above, and it must have capital which is represented by shares of stock.

Business Records

All companies must maintain accounting records which contain a clear, complete, and accurate record of their business transactions. This general descriptive requirement is subject to regulations to be issued by the government. The only specific requirements at present are that the financial records must be maintained in Spanish and be recorded in double entry form in registered books (see below). The registered books can include removable pages or cards provided they are numbered.

Accounting records, stock record books, and minute books of the shareholders' and board of directors' meetings must be registered with the local government commercial office, "cámara de comercio." Each page or card is initialed and a certificate stating the number of pages and the use of the book is affixed. All vouchers, journal entries, and correspondence must be properly maintained and available for government inspection. All books and papers must be preserved for ten years and can be destroyed thereafter only if some acceptable system of reproduction is used and the reproduction is authenticated by the local government commercial office. It is prohibited to change the order or date of the documents of original entry, leave blank spaces in them, or make corrections or erasures, it being required that each error or omission be corrected by another entry. It is also prohibited to remove pages, change their order, or mutilate the books.

Revisor Fiscal (Statutory Auditor)

Colombian commercial law requires that corporations and branches of foreign companies have a statutory auditor (revisor fiscal) and the Superintendency of Corporations requires that an alternate be designated, both being public accountants. Other companies may have statutory auditors either because of legal requirements or their own desire. The statutory auditor may not be a shareholder of the company or retain any other duty in the company, its parent, affiliates, or subsidiaries, nor may there be close family ties between him and the company's management, cashiers, and accountants.

By law, he is required to determine that the transactions are in accordance with the articles of incorporation, decisions of the shareholders and board of directors, and legal requirements; give due notice of any irregularities encountered; cooperate with qualified governmental entities; determine that the accounting and minute books are up-to-date and that the correspondence and original entries are safeguarded; inspect the assets and assure that they are kept under control; sign financial statements; call special meetings of the shareholders; and comply with any other applicable requirements in Colombian law and the articles of incorporation.

The statutory auditor is responsible to the shareholders, to the company, and to third parties for damage caused by negligence in carrying out his duties. Statutory auditors who knowingly express an opinion on fraudulent financial statements may be prosecuted under the penal code.

Upon signing a balance sheet, the statutory auditor must state the following in his report:

1. Whether or not he has obtained all the information necessary for the performance of his duties.
2. Whether he has carried out recommended auditing procedures.
3. Whether or not he considers that the accounts are kept in accordance with legal requirements and sound standards of accounting, and whether the recorded transactions comply with the statutes and the decisions of the shareholders or directors.
4. Whether or not the financial statements have been properly taken from the books; whether or not, in his opinion, the balance sheet and statement of profit and loss present fairly, in accordance with generally accepted accounting principles, the financial position of the company at the end of the period under examination and the results of operations for the period then ended.
5. Whether or not he has any reservations as to the fairness of presentation of the financial statements.
6. Whether the acts of the administrators are in accordance with decisions of the shareholders and board of directors.
7. Whether the correspondence, original accounting entries, and minute books are prepared and safeguarded.

8. Whether there is internal control and whether it is adequate to safeguard the assets of the company or those of third parties in the custody of the company.

The statutory auditor's representations on the matters referred to in items 6, 7, and 8 above (an added requirement in the new Commercial Code, effective January 1, 1972) may be the subject of a separate report or may be combined with his report on the financial statements themselves. An illustration of dual report treatment follows:

Auditor's Report on Financial Statements

(Omitting reference to items 6, 7, and 8 above)

To the Shareholders and Board of Directors
Company XXX, S.A.
Location, Colombia

I have examined the balance sheet of Company XXX, S.A. as of .... and the related statements of income, undistributed branch earnings, and changes in financial position for the year then ended. My examination was made in accordance with generally accepted auditing standards, and accordingly included such tests of the accounting records, obtainment of the information necessary to comply with my functions, and such other auditing procedures as I considered necessary in the circumstances. I previously made a similar examination of the financial statements for the preceding year.

In my opinion, the aforementioned statements have been truthfully taken from the books and accounts and present fairly the financial position of Company XXX, S.A. at ...., and the results of its operations, changes in equity, and changes in financial position for the year then ended, in conformity with generally accepted accounting principles applied on a basis consistent with that of the preceding year; and the accounting conforms to the Statutes and was carried out in accordance with applicable legal requirements, and with the decisions of the Annual Meeting of the Shareholders, and the Board of Directors of Company XXX, S.A.

(Signed)

Location, Colombia
Date

Auditor's Report to the Shareholders and Board of Directors

(Including reference to items 6, 7, and 8 above)

To the Shareholders and Board of Directors
Company XXX, S.A.
Location, Colombia

The audited financial statements of Company XXX, S.A. and my report thereon are included hereinbefore. In addition, I have performed the procedures which I considered necessary to comply with the requirements of Article 209 of the Commercial Code. The Statutes were reviewed and the minutes of the Annual Meeting of the Shareholders and the Board of Directors were read. Journal vouchers and correspondence files were examined. As part of my examination of the aforementioned financial statements, the system of internal control was reviewed and tested, in accordance with generally accepted auditing standards.

Based upon the procedures followed during my examination of the financial statements, and those described above, it is my opinion that during the year ended .... the acts of the Administrators of the Company XXX, S.A. conformed to the requirements of the Statutes and to the decisions of the Annual Meeting of the Shareholders; the journal vouchers, and the correspondence files were properly maintained; and there were adequate measures of internal control for the custody and safekeeping of the company's assets.

(Signed)

Location, Colombia
Date

Notwithstanding the law, some reports have been presented in abbreviated form; often only the written signature of the statutory auditor appears on the statements themselves. However, the new Commercial Code, generally effective January 1, 1972, prescribes in detail what must be in the reports and presumably practices will change. While the duties of the statutory auditor still contain elements more properly attributable to an internal auditor, the present code is a great improvement over its predecessor. The code limits the service of a statutory auditor to five companies and, presumably, this also applies to alternates.

The Accounting Profession

As in many Latin American countries, public accounting is a relatively new profession in Colombia; prior to 1950 there were few accountants in public practice and there was little demand for their services. Statutory auditors were appointed to comply with legal requirements, and as a rule they were full-time employees carrying out routine internal audit functions. There were no regulations setting forth the professional requirements for this position.

The National Institute of Public Accountants (Instituto Nacional de Contadores Públicos) was formed in 1952 by a group of accounting students and professionals for the purpose of promoting their common aspirations, foremost of which was the promotion of regulatory legislation on professional practice. This group actively participated in drafting a public accounting bill which was channeled through lawyers and others to appropriate government officials. Legislative committees were appointed from time to time to study the draft and make modifications, but there were no open hearings or discussions. This process continued until Decree No. 2373 was promulgated in September 1956, which established the Central Board of Accountants (Junta Central de Contadores).

This decree was the first of two measures adopted to regulate the accounting profession. It is important because it laid down the ground rules for the profession and because of the relatively large number of nonpublic accountants who, during the initial period of its existence, were permitted to register as enrolled accountants (contadores inscritos) and public accountants (contadores públicos) and who, under a later law, were able to register as authorized public accountants.

Junta Central de Contadores
(The Central Board of Accountants)

In December 1960, Law No. 145 was enacted to govern the practice of public accounting; all previous laws on the subject were automatically revoked. The Central Board of Accountants was continued as the body to pass upon and authorize the registration of public accountants.

Law No. 145 provides that, while there shall be only one class of public accountants, there shall be two subclassifications, the one designated as certified (titulado) and the other as authorized (autorizado), as the case may be.

The Central Board of Accountants is now composed of six persons representing the Minister of Education, the Superintendency of Corporations, the Association of Universities, the Director of the Department of Accounting of the National University, the Contadores Públicos Titulados, and the Contadores Públicos Autorizados. Its present functions are to process applications for registration of contadores públicos titulados and contadores públicos autorizados, to keep a register of those approved, to prepare and publish a code of ethics, and to impose legal penalties.

The Central Board of Accountants has approved approximately sixty-five hundred persons as authorized public accountants (contadores públicos autorizados and contadores públicos titulados). The board has initiated the registration (conformidad) of accounting firms, including foreign firms.

Contador Público
(Public Accountant)

The basic requirements for registration as a public accountant with either title ("titulado" or "autorizado") are (a) to be a Colombian citizen, or to be a foreigner either domiciled in Colombia for at least three years or who has passed an examination in Colombian tax, labor, and commercial law; (b) to be a person of good repute; and (c) not to have been subject to a penalty resulting from violation of professional ethics. Beginning February 1963, only applications for registration as certified (titulado) accountants have been accepted. The law prohibits registration of persons who have been found guilty of breach of confidence, breach of ethics, or of a criminal act.

Contador Público Titulado. In addition to the above stated basic requirements to be a public accountant, the candidate for registration as a contador público titulado must have a diploma in accounting from a recognized Colombian university, a university in a country with which Colombia has reciprocity, or a university which has been approved by the Association of Colombian Universities. Failing this, he must pass an examination regulated by the Ministry of Education. A holder of a degree in economics issued prior to the passage of the law also may be so registered. The candidate must have one year's experience in practical accounting, gained either in public or private work. There are now about seven hundred fifty registered CPTs.

Contador Público Autorizado. In addition to the basic requirements, the CPA must have either (a) received a license as an "inscribed" or "public" accountant under the 1956 decree, (b) held a diploma or license issued under a 1931 law or by the Central Board of Accountants prior to the enactment of the present law, or (c) applied for and obtained registration within two years of the passage of Law No. 145 based on four years' experience as an accountant or bookkeeper in an organization of recognized importance. The number of CPAs is approximately fifty-eight hundred.

Educational Requirements. As previously stated, it is specified that the applicant for current registration (now limited to contadores públicos titulados) as a public accountant must hold a university degree in accounting. There are 17 colleges in Colombia now giving courses leading to a degree in accountancy; however, only about ten have had graduating classes. The precise number of students studying accounting in universities is not available, but it is estimated that there are approximately five thousand. To date, the number of students actually graduated is small.

To enter a university the candidate must have graduated from high school. The university term is five years. Textbooks are largely Spanish translations of U.S. texts. On completion of the university courses, the student must submit a thesis on an accounting subject.

Functions of the Public Accountant. The services of a *public* accountant are necessary in the following cases:

1. To act as a statutory auditor as previously indicated.
2. To act as an expert witness in technical accounting controversies.
3. To act as goodwill evaluators in certain cases.
4. To certify accounting information in insurance claims over 300,000 pesos.
5. To certify financial statements of corporations or partnerships in liquidation where the capital is in excess of 300,000 pesos.
6. To certify balance sheets of companies in bankruptcy and the trustees' accounting.
7. To certify financial statements of decentralized public enterprises or establishments.

Instituto Nacional de Contadores Públicos
(National Institute of Public Accountants)

This organization was described in a preceding paragraph. At present it has approximately three hundred fifty members, and the requirements for membership are as follows:

1. Applicants are to be registered as contadores públicos titulados or as contadores públicos autorizados with the Central Board of Accountants and have one year of experience.
2. Qualified foreign accountants, principally from the United States (CPAs), Canada (CAs) or England (CAs), can associate themselves with the Instituto and most have done so.

Academia Nacional de Contadores Públicos Titulados

(National Academy of Titled Public Accountants)

The membership in this organization is restricted to those public accountants who have a university degree.

Unión Nacional de Contadores

(National Union of Accountants)

The basic requirement for membership is apparently any document proving expectations of obtaining registration with the Central Board of Accountants.

Federación de Contadores de Colombia

(Colombian Federation of Accountants)

This organization is composed of members in about twenty-five regional organizations. Requirements for membership are similar to those for the Unión Nacional de Contadores.

Federación de Contadores Públicos de Antioquia

(Federation of Public Accountants of the State of Antioquia)

It is reported that this organization has a membership of approximately two hundred seventy, composed of public accountants in the state of Antioquia (Medellín). Requirements for membership are similar to those for the Instituto Nacional.

National Association of Accountants (NAA)

At present two international chapters of the NAA have been formed in Bogotá and Medellín. The combined chapters publish a quarterly bulletin in Spanish consisting of translations of U.S. articles from the NAA magazine and of original articles contributed by members, and so forth. In all other respects, the local chapters operate the same as a U.S. chapter.

Ethics

The present code of ethics was issued by the Central Board of Accountants in 1967. The code contains sixteen prohibitions, four obligations, five rules relating to third parties, seven general rules, and six articles covering sanctions. The code is quite broad and complete. There is a prohibition against advertising, except that specialties can be indicated. Generally, the code is ample and very similar to that of the AICPA with certain exceptions that are related to local laws and customs.

Violation of the code is punishable by the Central Board of Accountants by registration suspension for up to one year or, in serious cases, by its cancellation. There have been a few sanctions applied under this code or other disciplinary articles in Law No. 145 of 1960.

The Second Congress of Revisores Fiscales (statutory auditors) adopted the code of ethics recommended by the Second Inter-American Accounting Conference. This has moral, but not legal force.

Auditing Standards

General Standards

There has been no official statement defining auditing standards in Colombia, although some firms follow U.S. or British standards and practices. The educational standards in the field of accounting are improving steadily.

The National Institute of Public Accountants in 1968 published 15 bulletins covering responsibilities of the auditor, auditing standards, principles of accounting, consistency, footnote disclosures, opinions or disclaimer thereof, unaudited financial statements, and working papers. While adapted to local needs and requirements, these bulletins (issued by the Auditing Standards Committee) are not too different in their content from related pronouncements of the AICPA. These bulletins have only moral force but were adopted by the Second Congress of Revisores Fiscales (statutory auditors).

Independence. The code of ethics published by the Central Board of Accountants states, in effect, that the public accountant may not act in a controversy if he is related by blood or marriage to either or any of the parties involved, has a common interest in the business, or if he is involved in any other circumstances which might impair his judgment.

Standards of Reporting

The reporting standards of the public accountant are governed mainly by the regulations in the new Commercial Code concerning the duties of the statutory auditor. The minimum contents of the statutory auditor's opinion have been described previously.

Consistency. The National Institute of Public Accountants has issued a bulletin which calls for an opinion on the consistency of accounting principles employed. There has been no official governmental pronouncement on this subject.

Materiality. There have been no official pronouncements on the concept of materiality and its effect on the auditor's work and on his opinion on the financial statements examined.

Disclosure of Subsequent Events. It is not common practice for companies to disclose subsequent events which might have a material effect on a proper evaluation of the financial statements.

Accounting Principles and Practices

The basic accounting practices in Colombia are similar to those followed in the United States. However, because of the special requirements of the Superintendency of Corporations and the Colombian tax law, marked differences do exist in certain areas, the more important of which are discussed below.

Form and Content of Financial Statements

The Superintendencia de Sociedades (Superintendency of Corporations) prescribes the forms of financial statements to be used by corporations.

Financial statements consist of a balance sheet and a profit and loss statement, with supporting schedules for investments, fixed assets, depreciation, deferred and prepaid expenses, and reserves (including surplus). Financial statements are required to be filed 30 days after the annual meeting of shareholders at which the financial statements are approved, generally in the first quarter of the year. The forms of financial statements are now under study for revision and it is expected that reporting requirements will be amended. For Colombian tax and regulatory requirements, only the calendar year is recognized no matter when a company closes its books for internal reporting purposes.

Consolidated financial statements are prepared by some companies, but there is no government requirement that consolidated statements be presented.

Footnote disclosure is seldom used although the National Institute of Public Accountants has adopted rules requiring adequate disclosure.

Allowance for Doubtful Accounts

A mathematical formula for the computation of the allowance for doubtful accounts, or an annual provision against individual receivables over one year old up to 33⅓ percent annually of their balance, is provided for in the tax law. The result is that the amount allowable for tax purposes, which must be recorded in the books in order to be deductible, may be greater or less than that reasonably required for financial statement purposes.

Inventories

Inventories must be stated at cost for Colombian tax purposes. However, write-downs of obsolete, damaged, and so forth, materials are often reflected in the accounts by creating a reserve for this purpose. Special permission must be obtained to determine cost other than on a specific, average, or first-in first-out basis.

Revaluation of Land, Buildings, and Investments

A periodic appraisal of land and buildings is required to be made for the purpose of computing the municipal tax assessment. (Annual registration fees to be paid to the Superintendency of Corporations are also affected by this appraisal.) Companies must record on their books the differences between cost and appraised value of land as well as between depreciated cost and appraised value of buildings. The revaluation is in memorandum form only and, although the resulting credit is included in the capital section of the balance sheet as prescribed by the Superintendency of Corporations, it may not be capitalized or distributed nor may the appreciation be depreciated.

Similarly, the market value of investments as of the date of the balance sheet is required to be compared with the net book amount; if the latter exceeds market, the difference is written off against income; and if market exceeds the net book amount, an appropriate entry is made in a revaluation surplus account, which is reflected in the balance sheet as prescribed by the Superintendency of Corporations.

The appraised value of land and buildings and the market value of investments, regardless of the cost of these assets, are included in the base used in the computation of excess profits taxes; the higher the base, the lower the exposure to excess profits taxes.

Goodwill

Purchased goodwill is amortizable on a reasonable basis. Amortization, generally over five or more years, is an allowable tax deduction.

In addition, the tax law provides for an official valuation of existing goodwill. In order to request this valuation, a company should have abnormally high profits for at least five years which must be caused by operating efficiency rather than by tariff protection or exploitation of labor. This goodwill is recorded in a memorandum account and is included in the capital base resulting in a reduction of excess profits taxes. After five years, application for revision of the original valuation may be made.

Interest Charges and Exchange Losses

In some instances, capitalization of interest charges has been accepted by the Superintendency of Corporations. As to exchange losses on loans or debts, other than for importation of raw materials or trading stock, the current preference of the Superintendency of Corporations is that they should be deferred and amortized over the payment period, but there is no objection to charging such losses to current operations. This creates controversy since the tax authorities generally disallow exchange losses resulting from working capital loans, but the losses related to loans for importations of raw materials, trading stock, and equipment are deductible or can be capitalized according to the particular situation. Generally, if losses related to the purchase of equipment are capitalized, the depreciation thereof is accepted; but if such losses are deferred as exchange losses, the amortization is almost always disallowed as a deduction by the tax authorities.

Liability for Severance Pay

Under Colombian labor legislation, employers must pay severance pay equal to one month's salary for each year of service upon separation of employment except for certain stated reasons such as dishonesty, failure to obey orders, and so forth. However, the payment is generally made in all cases (including retirement on a pension) since the labor courts tend to favor employees. It is, therefore, a normal practice to accrue the full amount of this liability. Such accruals are deductible for tax purposes if they have been recorded as specific liabilities (rather than as reserves), and full details of individual balances are submitted with the tax return. The employee can draw against severance compensation for certain purposes.

Also required under Colombian labor law are payments for unjust discharge, and although there are 14 specific causes for justifiable discharge, it is doubtful that such payments can be avoided whatever may be the circumstances. The cash basis is usually employed in accounting for these indemnification payments. After ten years of service, the labor courts can order the reinstatement of any employee unjustly discharged if he so requests.

Liability for Pensions

As of January 1, 1967, the Colombian Institute of Social Security (ICSS) generally assumed the responsibility for old age pensions. Any employee with less than ten years service at that date is covered by ICSS. Those with more than ten years service are divided into three categories, viz., those with ten to fifteen years service; those with fifteen to twenty years service; and those with over twenty years service. The liability of the employer for payment of pensions in the first two categories varies with circumstances, but in the case of employees having more than twenty years service the employer is fully liable for the entire amount.

The Colombian labor code provides that companies with net worth of over 800,000 pesos are liable for old age pensions to employees, who have at least twenty years of service and have reached 50 years of age, if female, and age 55 if male. Accruals for pensions are tax deductible if based upon an approved actuarial study. The actuarial liability, computed annually, can be deducted for income tax purposes at a cumulative rate of 15 percent per year (i.e., at the end of the second year 30 percent of the liability, less the amount deducted the previous year, is deductible). In the seventh and subsequent years, the unprovided balance of the actuarial calculation is deductible. The manner of calculating the actuarial liability using an interest factor of 18 percent, is specified by law. The liability need not be funded. Payments to persons already pensioned can be deducted as paid or included in the actuarial calculation and amortized as above.

Under the new rules relating to pensions, many companies are recognizing their liability and setting up accruals since it helps their cash flow significantly. A decree still effective requires the employer to post a guarantee of payment of pensions to persons now pensioned by submitting a bank or insurance company guarantee. To date, these institutions have refused to issue such guarantees and such guarantees are usually met by pledging property.

Statement of Income and Surplus

A combined statement is not generally used. However, one of the supporting schedules for the financial statements presented to the Superintendency of Corporations calls for an analysis of the changes in all the surplus (superavit) accounts including undistributed earnings from the end of the previous year.

Depreciation. Depreciation rates are prescribed for tax purposes (and usually adopted for book purposes) for each class of asset and must be calculated on a straight-line basis unless prior permission has been given by the National Tax Division to employ some other generally accepted method. These rates are generally 5 percent or less for buildings, 10 percent for machinery and equipment, and 20 percent for vehicles. It is possible to obtain permission to use special rates which are different from the above. Upon application and submission of the required documentation proving that machinery is used over ten hours a day, for example, accelerated depreciation (double straight-line) will be approved. Depreciation is generally based on 90 percent of cost, salvage value being considered as 10 percent. If there is no salvage value after 90 percent of the cost has been depreciated, the undepreciated balance may then be depreciated.

Stock Dividends. For tax purposes, stock dividends received are treated as income calculated in one of the following manners in order of preference: market value if quoted on a stock exchange, at value fixed by the Superintendency of Corporations, or at nominal or par value failing one of the two preceding methods.

Reserve for Replacement of Fixed Assets

Under Colombian tax law, a reserve may be created equal to the cost of machinery and equipment acquired prior to June 1, 1957, and on hand at that date. Annual additions to the reserve are limited to the lower of 15 percent of net profits for the preceding year or 15 percent of the cost of machinery and equipment held as of June 1, 1957, until a reserve equal to the total cost of such items is accumulated. This reserve must be appropriated by the shareholders in a general meeting. The annual addition to the reserve is an allowable tax deduction of the current year and will be taxed if distributed as dividends.

Reserve for Economic Development

Under the tax law, any legal entity subject to control by the Superintendency of Corporations can appropriate up to 5 percent annually of the year's net income (after taxes) to a reserve for economic development, the appropriation being deductible in computing taxable income. A sum equivalent to the appropriation must be invested in approved companies, or in fixed assets or deferred charges of the company by December 31 of the following year. The provision allowing such appropriations is effective through 1973; any prior appropriations may continue to be carried as such after 1973.

Legal Reserve

Corporations, limited partnerships, share-issuing partnerships and any foreign legal entity must create a legal reserve by appropriating at least 10 percent of annual net income until a minimum of 50 percent of the par value of subscribed capital stock has been accumulated. Net losses may be offset against the legal reserve, but the reserve cannot otherwise be disposed of prior to the liquidation of the company. The addition to the legal reserve is computed based on net income for the period and is recorded in the following period after the shareholders' approval.

Requirements for Listing Securities on the Stock Exchange

Formal application and acceptance is required to trade a corporation's stock on either of the country's two stock exchanges: the Bogotá Stock Exchange (Bolsa de Bogotá, S.A.) or the Medellín Stock Exchange (Bolsa de Medellín, S.A.). The application forms are similar and basically require the following documents:

1. Two copies of the corporate bylaws.
2. Copies of financial statements, including projected appropriations of earnings, for the previous two years signed by the manager, accountant, and statutory auditor.
3. Copy of the resolution of the Superintendency of Corporations authorizing the company to do business.
4. Number of shareholders and their shareholdings.
5. The names of members of the board of directors and their alternates, manager, secretary, accountant, and statutory auditor and his alternate. The statutory auditor must submit proof that he is a public accountant.
6. Sample of the stock certificate to be issued.

There are no additional requirements for filing financial statements with the exchange. All listed companies must publish financial statements annually in a newspaper of major importance in the city or cities in which the stock is traded.

Denmark

Denmark

As of June 1973

Significant developments since the preparation of this chapter are presented, by country, in the section entitled Addenda.

Forms of Business Organization

The forms of business organizations in Denmark are the corporation (joint-stock company), the limited partnership company, the partnership, and the sole proprietorship. Also, the operation of a trade or business through a Danish branch of a foreign corporation is a legally recognized form of doing business in Denmark.

Aktieselskab
(Joint-Stock Company)

Under Danish Companies Act No. 123 of April 15, 1930 (as amended), a joint-stock company is defined as any company carrying on a trade or business (i.e., the object of the company shall be to earn financial profit) in which none of the shareholders are personally liable for the obligations of the company over the amount of share capital contributed by them. This is similar to the usual form of corporate entity found in other countries. The name of the company must contain the word "Aktieselskab" (joint-stock company) or an approved abbreviation thereof, such as "A/S."

A corporation may be formed by three or more persons. The majority of the founders, but at least three, must be residents of Denmark and Danish citizens or have been residents of Denmark for the preceding five years. All founders must subscribe for at least one share and usually in the amount of at least 500 kroner. Unless specifically authorized otherwise, corporations are required to have a minimum share capital of 10,000 kroner. At least 10 percent of the share capital (a minimum of 5,000 kroner) must be paid in at the time of registration, the remainder to be paid within one year. Special rules apply to banks and insurance companies.

In a Danish joint-stock company, there must be a minimum of three shareholders unless the total amount of shares in the company is owned by the Danish State, a municipality, a Danish joint-stock company, or a limited partnership company.

The board of directors must consist of at least three members. If the firm name includes the name of a place in Denmark or national designation, the entire board must be residents of Denmark and Danish citizens or have been residents of Denmark for the previous five years. For other companies, only the majority of the board must satisfy the above residency and citizenship requirements. The Danish Companies Act does not specify where the board must hold its meetings.

One or more executive managers may be appointed by the board of directors to conduct the day-to-day business, and, in companies with a share capital exceeding 100,000 kroner, there must be at least one executive manager. The executive managers shall have their residence in Denmark and be either Danish citizens or residents of the country for the previous two years. These provisions do not apply to executive managers of branches abroad. Foreign managers of subsidiaries of foreign corporations may obtain exemption from the above-mentioned residency and citizenship requirements.

Companies must be audited annually by independent auditors chosen at a general shareholders' meeting. If the company's shares are quoted on a stock exchange, there must be more than one auditor and at least one must be a state-authorized public accountant. If a company's shares are not listed, owners of one-third of the share capital represented at the shareholders general meeting may require auditing by a state-authorized public accountant. The shareholders' general meeting shall be held in Denmark once a year, at which the annual accounts are to be presented.

Kommandit Aktieselskab

(Limited Partnership Company)

This is a partnership between one or more individuals (general partners) and a joint-stock company (limited partner). The individual general partners cannot be shareholders in the corporate partner. The liability of the corporate partner is restricted to the amount of his investment, whereas that of the individual general partners is unlimited. The limited partnership company must be identified as such, in its name, by the words "Kommandit Aktieselskab." There are few limited partnership companies in existence in Denmark.

Branch of a Foreign Corporation

A foreign corporation may do business in Denmark through a branch located in Denmark provided this same right is accorded Danish corporations by the country of domicile of the foreign corporation. In registering a Danish branch of a foreign corporation, the name of the branch must indicate its nationality and that it is a foreign joint-stock company. The manager of the Danish branch must be given power of attorney and must be responsible for compliance with Danish law. He must satisfy the same qualifications as to residence and citizenship as the executive managers of Danish corporations, but an exemption may readily be obtained.

Partnership and Sole Proprietorship

These forms of business enterprise are generally similar to those commonly found in other countries. Partnerships as such are not subject to taxation. The partners are taxed individually on their proportionate share of the partnership revenue and capital.

Kommanditselskab
(Limited Partnership)

This is an entity consisting of one or more general partners who usually participate in the management of the business and have joint and several liability for its obligations; and one or more limited partners who usually do not participate in management and whose liability is limited to their investment in the enterprise. Joint-stock companies may be partners. This form is frequently employed for investment in small vessels but otherwise is not in general use.

Shipping Partnership

This historical partnership variant differs from the other partnerships by the fact that every partner is fully liable but only in proportion to his contribution, not jointly and severally.

Cooperative Societies and Foundations

Cooperative societies are particularly important in agriculture and affiliated industries. Foundations, endowments, and independent institutions are similar to corresponding entities in other European countries.

Business Records

The Bookkeeping Act of June 5, 1959 (as amended), prescribes that practically every one carrying on trade or business in any form of organization shall keep books.

The Danish Companies Act and other laws concerning specific enterprises prescribe certain records to be kept in accordance with that law. For example, limited companies are required by law to keep the following:

1. Status book—contains the annual balance sheet and income statement signed by management not later than six months after the end of the financial year.
2. Minute book—contains proceedings of stockholders' and directors' meetings.
3. Audit notebook—contains a report by the auditors after each examination.
4. Share register—must be authorized by the registrar of companies.
5. Register of share transactions by directors and executive managers.

The official accounts of the company must be filed with the registrar of companies and the tax authorities. All the books, vouchers, documents, and so forth (with minor exceptions), must be kept for a period of at least five years.

Qualified Auditor

The Danish Companies Act sets out certain regulations concerning the audit of a joint-stock company. Generally, any joint-stock company shall be audited by one or more qualified auditors who may, or may not, be state-authorized public accountants. A qualified auditor, according to section 52 of the Companies Act of April 15, 1930 (as amended), is anyone who is of age, of good repute, and not divested of the management of his estate. Qualified auditors must not be in the service of the company; be members of the board of directors or board of management; be in the employ (in any form) of any member of the board of directors, board of management, bookkeeper, or cashier; be related by blood or marriage in the ascending or descending line or as brothers or sisters to any of the above parties.

Furthermore, the regulations specifically state that appointed auditors must have access to all the books and accounts of the company and be entitled to examine the cash in hand and holdings of securities and inventories. The board of directors and the management are obliged to give the auditors any information they might demand for the verification of the correctness of the accounts.

As previously mentioned, the Companies Act provides that certain designated companies must be audited by one or more qualified auditors and, in specified cases, one must be a state-authorized public accountant. In practice, qualified auditors are generally state-authorized public accountants.

The Accounting Profession

General

Professional auditors, as such, were unknown in Denmark until the close of the nineteenth century when a few accounting and auditing firms were organized. Early in the 1900's, the larger business enterprises began to utilize the corporate form of doing business, that, in turn, led to a demand for professional accounting services. On May 14, 1909, the King signed Denmark's first law concerning authorized auditors.

The transition of the larger enterprises into joint-stock companies necessitated the enactment of regulations that were embodied in several companies acts. The one currently in effect is the Companies Act of April 15, 1930 (as amended), which requires certain designated companies to have their financial statements examined by one or more qualified auditors, one of whom must be state-authorized if the companies' shares are included in the official stock exchange list. State-authorized public accountants are also required in the case of banks, insurance companies, credit societies lending on mortgages, and in several other cases.

Statsautoriseret Revisor
(State-Authorized Public Accountant)

The State-Authorized Public Accountants Act No. 68 of March 15, 1967, and the Ministry of Commerce Order No. 293 of June 28, 1967, prescribe the regulations concerning state-authorized public accountants.

The license to practice as a state-authorized public accountant is granted by the Ministry of Commerce to any person who fulfills all of the following requirements:

1. Is a Danish subject.
2. Is a resident in Denmark.
3. Has completed his twenty-fifth year.
4. Has not been declared incapable of managing his own affairs, has not been placed under guardianship, and against whom proceedings in bankruptcy have not been taken.
5. Has passed a special examination.
6. Has, for at least three years after having completed his eighteenth year, been employed in an office of a state-authorized public accountant, and performed normal accountancy functions.
7. Has, to the extent of at least 100,000 kroner, insured against or given security for any financial liability he may incur during his performance of the duties of a state-authorized public accountant.

The Minister of Commerce may grant a license to any person who proves that he has received such training abroad as may be deemed to be equal to the training referred to in clauses 5 and 6, and who, in other respects, fulfills the previously mentioned conditions. Moreover, under special circumstances the Minister of Commerce may permit foreign accountants to perform duties that under existing law are to be performed by a state-authorized public accountant. Any license issued under a special exemption granted by the Minister of Commerce in pursuance of this act may be subject to restrictions and conditions.

Examination for State-Authorized Public Accountants

The latest regulations are given in the Examination Order of January 25, 1971. Regulations theretofore in effect continue in force during a transitional period, but under the most recent regulations the prerequisites for the final examination are as follows:

1. Bachelor's degree in economics.
2. Master's degree in auditing.
3. Three years' practical experience in the office of a state-authorized public accountant, during which the candidate also attends lectures in the following:
   a. Propaedeutics (foreign languages, bookkeeping, mathematics)
   b. The humanities
   c. Economics (macro- and micro-, including accountancy and information theory, and so forth)

d. Statistics
e. Auditing theory
f. Civil law and company law
g. Taxation (theory of taxation, fiscal policy, legislation, and practice)
h. Bankruptcy

The examination is conducted by a state examination board consisting of nine members. The chairman is a professor in economics, three members are practicing state-authorized public accountants, two members represent commerce, two are specialists in tax and bankruptcy laws, and one is a specialist in economics. The examination is prepared by public accountants who are also in charge of the oral examinations.

After passing the required examination, the candidate must sign a solemn declaration that he will diligently and faithfully perform the work entrusted to him and that he will conscientiously fulfill all the duties of a state-authorized public accountant.

Professional Activities, Duties, and Liabilities of a State-Authorized Public Accountant

The State-Authorized Public Accountants Act and the Ministry of Commerce Order set out certain regulations concerning professional activities, duties, and liabilities of state-authorized public accountants. These regulations provide that, among other things, a state-authorized public accountant—

1. Must not be employed in or associated with any business other than accounting and auditing.
2. Must not be a member of management or on the board of directors of a trade or industrial enterprise.
3. Must not participate in a trade or industrial company.
4. Must not be related to the client either directly or through employees in a position of trust with the client.
5. Must not reveal anything with which he has become acquainted in the course of his business.
6. Must not enter into partnership with, or be employed by, auditors who are not state-authorized.
7. Must not carry on a joint business venture with attorneys-at-law.
8. May form a joint-stock company of accountants provided that the

management (or, if a management has not been appointed, a majority of the members of the board of directors) are state-authorized public accountants.

9. May hold the position as professor at a university or a school of business administration, likewise he may be employed at a scientific institution.

The act also provides that a state-authorized public accountant may employ any number of state-authorized accountants or assistants who have had three years experience with a state-authorized accountant and may hire up to three inexperienced assistants for each state-authorized accountant in his employ. Registered assistants (including both the experienced and inexperienced assistants just mentioned) must be at least 18 years of age and employed in the profession of accounting. In August 1972, about twenty-seven hundred assistants were employed by 904 practicing accountants. There were an additional 112 state-authorized accountants not in public practice.

When more than one auditor is required to audit a particular company and one must be state-authorized, the other elected auditor cannot be on the staff of the elected state-authorized auditor, be in the same auditing company, or be in the same partnership of auditors.

Foreningen af Statsautoriserede Revisorer
(Institute of State-Authorized Public Accountants)

The Institute was founded on January 12, 1912, and is subject to the bylaws of the organization, which were adopted at the first general meeting on the founding date and thereafter amended periodically, most recently in 1970. The objects of the Institute are as follows:

1. To bring together state-authorized public accountants in all matters affecting their common professional interest.

2. To protect the professional and general interest of accountants in external as well as internal affairs.

3. To supervise and contribute to the fulfilling of the general and special duties of accountants and to enhance the reputation and ability of the profession.

The advisory committee of the Institute is frequently employed by the courts and authorities to give expert opinions on accountancy matters and these opinions, together with the work of the research committee, are analogous to the American Institute's statements on auditing standards and accounting principles, although few have been issued to date.

Membership in the Institute is limited to state-authorized public accountants (with certain exceptions for honorary members). Members are entitled to use the initials "FSR" and the stamp of the Institute. A state-authorized accountant who ceases to practice will be entitled to retain his membership unless his business or position is in conflict with the status of membership.

Generally, the advisory committee on behalf of the Institute will deliver opinions on matters concerning accountancy and auditing submitted to the Institute by one or more of its members, the legislature, the executive authorities, or the courts. Decisive opinions on these matters require the agreement of a majority of the members of the committee. The opinions are published in the members' internal publication *Idebat.* Besides *Idebat* the Institute publishes an official periodical *Revision og Regnskabsvaesen* (Auditing and Accountancy), which, among other things, contains the most important of the aforementioned opinions.

Ethics

At an extraordinary general meeting on June 14, 1954, the Institute adopted a code of professional ethics that is deemed to form part of the bylaws of the Institute.

Members of the Institute are bound to observe the following rules as set out by the code of professional ethics:

1. Members will act in accordance with the best professional standards and comply with the rules and regulations of the Institute.
2. Advertising will be permitted in connection with the commencement of a practice, a change in address, the taking over of a practice, or the joining or retiring of partners, but must be restricted to necessary information.
3. Individual press advertising is regarded as undesirable.
4. If members wish to advertise, they must be restricted to name, occupation, address, telephone numbers, and office hours.
5. There are various other restrictions on advertising.
6. An audit must not be performed gratuitously or for an unreasonably low fee except where warranted.
7. Agreements must not be made where the amount of the fee is related to the results obtained.
8. Members must neither receive nor pay commissions on client transactions.

9. Any member succeeding a state-authorized accountant on an engagement must ascertain why his predecessor discontinued the engagement.

10. A member must not offer employment to an employee of a colleague. This does not apply to advertisements or unsolicited applications.

11. Members must not criticize the work of a colleague unless the colleague has first been advised of the criticism.

Complaints of infringement of these rules are to be submitted to an arbitration committee of the Institute, consisting of five members, which will hear the complaints and attempt to settle the dispute.

Functions of the State-Authorized Public Accountant

Under Danish law, state-authorized accountants are required to be employed as auditors of corporations listed on the stock exchange as well as banks, certain insurance societies, and other institutions governed by statute.

For the purposes of law suits, public authorities may avail themselves of the services of state-authorized public accountants to obtain information about questions pertaining to accounting. State-authorized public accountants may likewise be appointed "regnskabskyndig tillidsmand" (skilled and reliable person) under section 79 of the Arrangements Outside the Law of Bankruptcy Act. Any state-authorized public accountant may, without special authorization, act as a trustee skilled in accounting under section 2 of the Bankruptcy Act but must not take part in negotiating creditor compositions.

The assistance of a state-authorized accountant is usually required for purposes of preparing declarations on applications for loans, for financing programs, and on work for public institutions.

In addition to the examination of financial statements for the purpose of reporting thereon the state-authorized public accountant may, among other things—

1. Act as an intermediary between directors and stockholders, between creditors and the public, and between the audited company and the public.

2. Act as an expert consultant in matters concerning EDP systems, modernizing bookkeeping systems, and preparing budgets and budgetary controls.

3. Make certain company analyses, render certain reports to management, or give a critique on company administration.

4. Assist in a price settlement dispute or make declarations to price controlling authorities (monopoly control) and to certain government agencies.

5. Prepare tax returns for clients, although he is not required to do so by law.

6. Act as independent adviser in economic and commercial relations, since obtaining many public loans and subsidies depends on the cooperation of state-authorized public accountants.

Auditing Standards

The practice of public accounting in Denmark is, in general, limited to qualified auditors previously described. The qualified auditor is usually, but not necessarily, a state-authorized public accountant; however, he must have certain qualifications. The profession of public accounting, as practiced by state-authorized public accountants, is specifically regulated as to qualifications, duties, and responsibilities by the State-Authorized Public Accountant Act and the appurtenant Ministry of Commerce Order as set out under "The Accounting Profession" section of this chapter.

General Standards

The requirements for license as a state-authorized public accountant assure adequate education, training, and proficiency through the provisions of the aforementioned act and order. The state-authorized public accountant must not give any declaration or certificate on matters of accounts without having investigated the case sufficiently so that an opinion can be formed as to the accuracy of the declaration or certificate. In this connection, the State-Authorized Public Accountant Act prescribes that—

> Any state-authorized public accountant who in the course of his business makes any incorrect written statement or certifies in writing anything of which he has no knowledge, or signs any accounts which have not been audited by him, except where this appears from the endorsement of the accounts, shall be punished with a fine or with mitigated imprisonment, except where a more severe punishment is prescribed under other statutory provisions.

Standards of Field Work

Generally, an audit notebook is kept by the state-authorized public accountant. The audit notebook can either be required by law or prescribed by the bylaws of a company, institution, society, and so forth or requested by the client (for other businesses). The audit notebook will, among other things, contain the following information:

1. What audit work has been executed and the state-authorized public accountant's observations or eventual criticism in this connection.
2. What period is covered by the audit.
3. Whether the auditor possesses the qualifications required by the law.
4. Whether he has received all information requested toward establishing the validity of the accounts.
5. Whether he considers the accounts to have been drawn up in accordance with the accounting and auditing provisions of the law and bylaws or the articles of a partnership.
6. In the event that special agreements have been made between the board, management, or the owner of an enterprise and the auditor, requiring performance by the auditor of work of a special nature, such agreements shall also be entered in the audit notebook.

Generally, a field audit by a Danish state-authorized public accountant is divided between interim and year-end work. There has been a departure from the detailed checking of accounts and underlying records toward the examination of internal control procedures, which now determines the nature and extent of audit work to be done. The primary responsibility for proper controls and procedures lies with management, but the auditors review these controls and procedures to determine that they are functioning properly.

As mentioned previously, the advisory committee of the Institute issues opinions on auditing standards and accounting principles that are used as a guide by the members.

The following audit procedures are generally applied by the state-authorized public accountant in obtaining sufficient evidential matter as a basis for forming an opinion regarding the annual accounts.

The Balance Sheet. The following is needed with respect to the balance sheet:

1. A count of cash on hand.
2. Confirmation of bank accounts.
3. A count of securities.
4. Accounts receivable are usually confirmed by sending out randomly selected statements of balances and by further tests to substantiate their accuracy and validity.

5. Observation of physical inventories is almost always made, as well as test counts of the year-end book inventory.
6. A physical examination of buildings and machinery is considered good auditing practice.
7. A determination that all known and estimated liabilities and commitments are provided for in the accounts.
8. A verification that the distribution of the yearly surplus (if any) is in accordance with the provisions of the law and bylaws, and so forth.

The Statement of Operations. Until quite recently, the auditor did not give the statement of operations much attention, the elements of this statement being considered mere details of the difference between two balance sheets on which the auditor concentrated his attention. However, this is no longer the case, and today the auditor devotes considerable time and effort to obtaining a well-founded opinion on the content and composition of the statement of operations. The method most commonly used is an auditing-procedure analysis and comparison applied to budgets, accounts of earlier periods, average trade figures, and so forth.

Standards of Reporting

The endorsement made by Danish state-authorized public accountants on the company's annual accounts is usually very brief and can vary considerably. A sample endorsement follows:

> The above Profit and Loss account and Balance Sheet that I have examined are in accordance with the books of the company.

However, in the State-Authorized Public Accountants Act of March 15, 1967, it is stated that, in the absence of any endorsement to the contrary, the signature of a state-authorized public accountant to accounts shall be deemed to indicate that such accounts have been audited by him, that they have been correctly prepared in accordance with the books, and have been made up with due regard to existing assets and liabilities and pursuant to statutory provisions governing the rendering of accounts.

Audit Records

As mentioned in the comments on standards of field work, an audit notebook is generally required to be kept by the Companies Act, by company bylaws, or by request of the client. In joint-stock companies, this notebook must be submitted to the board of directors, but the shareholders do not have access to the notebook. Therefore, if the auditor feels that his critical comments are important enough to be brought to the attention of shareholders and creditors, he must make his comments in his endorsement of the annual accounts. In addition, the audit notebook often contains comprehensive comments on the progress of the business as well as an analysis of the audit itself. These comments are designed to inform the board of directors of the auditor's view concerning the earnings of the company, whether operational analyses are kept up-to-date, whether budgets are prepared to guide the business during the year, and whether periodic reviews are made of these analyses and budgets for purposes of evaluating variances. Many Danish companies regard this notebook as a valuable aid to management and the board of directors.

Accounting Principles and Practices

The advisory committee of the Institute of State-Authorized Public Accountants is the unofficial authority for pronouncements of generally accepted accounting principles and practices in Denmark. Officially, the Companies Act of April 15, 1930 (as amended), sets out certain provisions for presentation of the accounts in the balance sheet and profit and loss statement. In addition, the Bookkeeping Act of June 5, 1959 (as amended), has also had some minor influence on accounting matters.

The Institute of State-Authorized Public Accountants has recently issued a publication concerning the form and content of the annual accounts. Accounts drawn up in accordance with the principles set forth in this publication give information beyond that required by the accounting provisions of the Danish Companies Act and the proposed new "Companies Act" pending in the Parliament.

Form and Content of Financial Statements

The presentation of the annual accounts varies considerably among companies. Two forms are suggested in the recent publication of the Institute, the one of which is being used by the majority of companies today although the other is expected to be adopted by an increasing number of companies in the future.

The Balance Sheet

The main entries in the balance sheet are shown in the Appendix. In regard to some of the items, the following supplementary information is presented.

Marketable Securities. Marketable securities that are included in the official stock exchange list must not be stated at an amount exceeding the buying rate quoted at the end of the financial year.

Stock of Merchandise (Inventory). Inventories are generally stated on the basis of the lower of cost or market, less a tax deductible reserve which may not exceed 30 percent of the initially calculated value. The amount at which the inventories are shown in the balance sheet may reflect direct deduction of the reserve, but the trend in good accounting practice is to show it separately in the "reserves" section of the balance sheet.

Fixed Assets—Write-Up. The Companies Act provides that a write-up of "fixed assets" (which includes investments in subsidiaries and other long-term items as well as machinery, equipment, and real property) will be permitted if the amount is used for writing down other fixed assets, covering operating deficits, or allocating to a special reserve that must only be used for such purposes. If the amounts written up are used to cover a deficit, this must be expressly stated in the accounts.

Treasury Shares. The rule mentioned above under the heading "Marketable Securities" applies to treasury shares as well. In connection with treasury shares, it should be noted that a joint-stock company must not acquire or receive as security its own shares in an amount exceeding 10 percent of its share capital. This limitation does not apply if the shares are acquired for the purpose of reducing share capital or received in settlement of a claim. The acquired shares must be accounted for as a special item with a statement of their par (or nominal) value.

Machinery, Equipment, and Real Property. It is an accepted practice to provide depreciation on assets even before they are placed in service. There is no general practice with respect to capitalizing indirect costs on fixed assets constructed by a company for its own use. It is normal practice to state the latest official assessment (appraised market value) of the real property.

Depreciation reserves are not customarily shown separately on the balance sheet, but are usually netted against the related assets. Hidden or secret reserves are generally not permitted except with respect to undervaluation of inventories and fixed assets (specifically buildings, machinery, and ships). As a rule, it is not permissible to charge income with provisions for reserves that are not actually required for a specific purpose, yet provision is sometimes made for depreciation on future purchases of fixed assets.

Organization Expenses and Goodwill. Organization expenses to the extent not written off immediately will be written off to profit and loss at not less than 15 percent per annum. Purchased goodwill is required to be amortized at the rate of 15 percent per annum.

Statutory Reserves. Statutory reserves are required by the Companies Act, which provides that not less than 10 percent of the annual profits remaining after provision for depreciation or for covering deficits from previous years will be set aside in a "statutory reserve" until this reserve equals one-tenth of the share capital. Thereafter, the annual provision may not be less than 5 percent of the annual profits until the reserve amounts to 25 percent of the share capital. To the extent that the reserve has not reached one-fourth of the share capital, any premium received from the issuance of stock in excess of amounts used to cover expenses incurred in the formation of the company or an increase in share capital will be added to this reserve. The statutory reserve may be used to cover a deficit only insofar as the deficit cannot be covered out of the company's reserves other than the statutory reserve. If the statutory reserve does not amount to one-tenth of the share capital, the dividend to the shareholders must not exceed 6 percent annually.

Stock Dividends. Stock dividends are accounted for by the issuing company on the basis of par (or nominal) value of the shares issued.

Commitments and Guarantees. Any mortgage and pledge created by the company and any surety or guarantee entered into and not expressly covered must be stated separately.

Statement of Operations

Presentation of the statement of operations varies considerably in Denmark, but the trend is toward more informative and uniform statements.

The Ministry of Commerce Order No. 226 of June 18, 1959, concerning the extent and content of bookkeeping, provides that income and expenditures shall be accounted for in well-arranged groups. Depreciation on buildings, ships, equipment, and similar fixed assets, as well as calculated interest on the equity, shall be accounted for separately.

A combined statement of income and earned surplus is usually included with a detailed explanation as to the disposition of the opening balance of earned surplus and net income for the year.

Bond discount and premiums are not ordinarily deferred on the balance sheet (except when arising from mortgages) but are customarily written off directly to profit and loss.

Consolidated Financial Statements

Consolidated financial statements are not ordinarily prepared in Denmark for submission in reports to shareholders, but are very often prepared for boards of directors. Investments in subsidiaries are usually recorded at cost.

Pooling of Interests

The accounting concept "pooling of interest," as applied to mergers and consolidations of corporations, is not recognized in Denmark.

Tax-Effect Accounting

The concept of tax-effect accounting is not generally applied in Denmark.

Requirements for Public Sale of Securities

A Danish company offering securities for sale to the public will usually have a prospectus, excluding financial statements, published in a financial newspaper. If the issuing company is listed on a stock exchange, the prospectus and the financial statements (audited by two auditors, one of whom must be a state-authorized public accountant) will be reviewed by the stock exchange board. These financial statements are available to prospective buyers for a small fee. If the issuing company is not listed, the financial statements may be signed by a "qualified auditor."

A prospectus must include, in addition to general information about the company, the following facts:

1. The purpose for which the capital is being raised.
2. Face value of new shares and the amount at which they are being offered for sale to the public.
3. Method of payment for new shares by subscribers.
4. Rules for over-subscription of the new issue.

Requirements for Listing Securities on the Stock Exchange

The most important requirements for companies filing a listing application are as follows:

1. The company shall be registered in the joint-stock company register.
2. Annual accounts for at least one year must be filed with the listing application. Such accounts must be audited by two auditors, one of whom must be a state-authorized public accountant.
3. The capital stock shall be at least 2,000,000 kroner.
4. The capital shall be fully paid up.
5. The annual general stockholders meeting shall be public and with admission to the press.
6. The dividends shall be published in one or more newspapers.
7. The stock exchange board shall be notified of amendments in the bylaws of the company.

The financial statements of registered joint-stock companies are filed annually with the registrar of such companies, where they are accessible to the public. Many companies publish their annual accounts in financial newspapers.

Denmark

Illustrative Financial Statements

ILLUSTRATIVE BALANCE SHEET OF A DANISH COMPANY

BALANCE PR: 31. DECEMBER 19__ (Balance Sheet as at December 31, 19__)

AKTIVER (Assets)

Ultimo 19__ (Preceding year) Kr.		Note	Kr.
....	Omsætningsaktiver (Current assets)		
....	Kasse-, bank og girobeholdninger (Liquid funds)		....
....	Obligationer (nom. kr.) (Bonds)		....
....	Veksler (Bills of exchange)		....
† .... †	Heraf diskonterede (Less discounted)		† ....
....	Varedebitorer (Accounts receivable)		....
....	Mellemværende med datterselskab (Current account, subsidiary company)		....
....	Andre tilgodehavender (Other receivables)		....
....	Varebeholdninger (Stock of merchandise)	(5)	....
....	Omsætningsaktiver (Total current assets)		....
	Anlægsaktiver (Fixed assets)		
	Værdipapirer (Securities):		
....	Aktier i datterselskaber (nom. kr.) (Shares subsidiary companies)	(6)	....
....	Aktier i andre selskaber (nom. kr.) (Shares external companies)	(7)	....
....	Lånedebitorer (Long-term receivables)		....
....	Maskiner, inventar m.v. (Machinery, equipment, etc.)	(8)	....
....	Fast ejendom (Real property)	(9)	....
....	Anlægsaktiver ialt: (Total fixed assets)		....
....	AKTIVER IALT: (Total assets)		....

Efterfølgende noter 1-11 inclusive er en integrerende del af regnskabet. (The following notes (1-11) form an integral part of the annual accounts.)

Note: The text of the "notes" is not shown, reference thereto being made only to show how footnotes are keyed into Danish financial statements.

ILLUSTRATIVE BALANCE SHEET OF A DANISH COMPANY

BALANCE PR: 31. DECEMBER 19__
(Balance Sheet as at December 31, 19__)

PASSIVER
(Liabilities, non-taxed provisions, and capital)

Ultimo 19__ (Preceding year) Kr.		Note	Kr.
	GÆLD (Liabilities)		
	Kortfristet gæld: (Short-term liabilities)		
....	Udbytte (Dividend)		....
....	Bankgæld (Bank loans)	(10)	....
....	Acceptgæld (Acceptances)		....
....	Varekreditorer (Suppliers)		....
....	Andre kreditorer (Sundry short-term liabilities)		....
....	Skyldig skat (Taxes payable)		....
....	Kortfristet gæld ialt: (Total short-term liabilities)		....
	Langfristet gæld: (Long-term liabilities)		
....	Prioritetsgæld (Mortgages on real property)		....
....	Anden gæld (Sundry long-term liabilities)		....
....	Langfristet gæld ialt: (Total long-term liabilities)		....
	GÆLD IALT: (Total)		....
	UBESKATTEDE HENLÆGGELSER (Non-taxed provisions)		
....	Lagernedskrivning (Depreciation on stock of merchandise)		....
....	Kontraktnedskrivning (Depreciation on buying contracts)		....
....	Investeringsfonds (Investment fund)		....
....	Akkumulerede merafskrivninger på driftsmidler og faste anlæg i øvright (Accumulated excessive depreciations on plants and equipment)		....
....	UBESKATTEDE HENLÆGGELSER IALT: (Total non-taxed provisions)		....

Ultimo 19__
(Preceding year)

Kr.		Note	Kr.
	EGENKAPITAL: (Capital)		
	Bunden egenkapital: (Restricted capital)		
....	Aktiekapital (Share capital)		....
....	Lovmæssig reservefond (Statutory reserve fund)		....
....	Bunden egenkapital ialt: (Total restricted capital)		....
	Fri egenkapital: (Free reserves)		
	Ekstra reservefond: (Extra reserve fund)		
....	Saldo 1. januar (Balance as at January 1st)		....
....	Overført fra disposition (Transferred according to suggested appropriation)		....
....	Fri egenkapital ialt: (Total free reserves)		....
....	EGENKAPITAL IALT: (Total capital)		....
....	PASSIVER IALT: (Total of liabilities, non-taxed provisions, and capital)		....

KAUTIONS-OG GARANTIFORPLIGTELSER - Kr.
(Commitments and guarantees)
Efterfølgende noter 1-11 inclusive er en integrerende del af regnskabet.
(The following notes (1-11) form an integral part of the annual accounts.)

Note: The purpose of the notes is to give further specifications and information as to the entries of the annual accounts.

ILLUSTRATIVE STATEMENT OF OPERATIONS OF A DANISH COMPANY

Resultatapgørelse før tiden 1. januar - 31, december 19—
(Statement of Operations concerning the period
January 1 - December 31, 19__)

Sidste år (Preceding year) Kr.		Note	Kr.	Kr.
....	Varesalg (Sales)			....
....	Vareforbrug lønninger og øvrige produktionsomkostninger (Cost of goods sold inclusive of wages, and other manufacturing costs)	(1)		....
....	BRUTTOVERSKUD (Gross profit)			....
....	Administrationsomkostninger (Administrative expenses)	(2)		....
....	DRIFTSOVERSKUD FØR AFSKRIVNINGER (Operating income before depreciation)			....
....	Afskrivninger (Depreciation)	(3)		....
....	OVERSKUD AF PRIMÆR DRIFT (Operating income)			....
....	Finansieringsomkostninger-finansieringsindtægter (Financial income and expenses)	(4)	....	
—	Realisationsavancer (Nonoperating income)		—	
—	Andre sekundære og ekstraordinære poster (Sundry extraordinary items)		—	....
....	DRIFTSRESULTAT FØR AFSLUTNINGSDISPOSITIONER OG SKAT (Net profit before final transfers and tax)			....
	Afslutningsdispositioner: (Final transactions)			
—	Forøgelse af lagernedskrivning (Increase of depreciation on stock)		....	
—	Formindskelse af kontraktnedskrivning (Decrease of depreciation on contracts)	†	....	

Sidste år (Preceding year) Kr.		Note	Kr.	Kr.
—	Henlæggelse til investeringsfond (Provision for investment fund)		....	
—	Forskudsafskrivning (Advance depreciation)		....	
....	Afskrivninger udover driftsmæssige afskrivinger (Depreciation other than operational depreciation		....	....
....	REGNSKABSMÆSSIGT OVERSKUD FOR SKAT (Net profit before tax)			....
....	Beregnet skat af årets indkomst (Calculated taxation on the profit for the year)			....
....	REGNSKABSMÆSSIGT OVERSKUD (Net profit)			....
	TIL DISPOSITION (At disposal):			
....	Ovenstående regnskabsmæssige overskud (Net profit for the year)		....	
—	Overførsel fra frie reserver (Transferred from free reserves)		—	
....	Ialt (Total):		....	
	Som foreslås fordelt således (Suggested appropriation)			
....	Udbytte (Dividend)		....	
....	Henlæggelse til frie reserver (Transferred to free reserves)		....	
....	Ialt (Total):		....	

Efterfolgende noter 1-11 er en integrerende del af regnskabet.
(The following notes (1-11) form an integral part of the annual accounts.)

France

France

As of July 1973

Forms of Business Organization

Business in France is conducted by individual proprietorships, various forms of partnerships, and several types of corporations. Foreigners wishing to do business in France may do so by establishing a branch in France, or by forming a French subsidiary company such as a "société anonyme" or a "société à responsabilité limitée."

A branch of a foreign corporation may be established in France by complying with certain legal formalities, which include translating and filing the company charter and bylaws with a French commercial court and inscription in the Register of Commerce. The branch of a foreign company is not recognized under French law as a separate legal entity, but is considered part of a foreign entity. All its rights and obligations therefore emanate from its status as a foreign company. The branch form is not often adopted by foreign interests due to unfavorable tax treatment.

A subsidiary may be organized as a French corporation, having a separate legal identity and being subject to the same legal and tax treatment as a domestic French company.

Société Anonyme (S.A.)

The usual French corporation, which is very similar to a U.S. corporation, is the société anonyme. It is a corporate entity, and must be created for a definite period of time which cannot exceed 99 years. The minimum number of shareholders is seven and the board of directors may vary in number from three to twelve. There must be a minimum capital of 100,000 French francs for this entity; if publicly held, 500,000 francs.

Société à Responsabilité Limitée (S.àR.L.)

The limited liability company (société à responsabilité limitée), which has features of both a partnership and a corporation, is suited to the requirements of a small or medium-sized business, has relatively few shareholders, and is not permitted to obtain capital from the public. It constitutes a legal entity, and the liability of shareholders is limited to the amount of capital that they have paid in. The life of the company is stated in the articles (statuts); it cannot exceed 99 years. There must be a minimum of two shareholders and a minimum capital of 20,000 francs. The shareholders appoint one or several managers (gérants), who may be shareholders, and who often have contracts which place them in a strong position.

Other Forms of Business Organization

The sole proprietorship and the general partnership (société en nom collectif) are very similar in law and custom to comparable organizations in the United States. The general partnership, under French law, constitutes a separate legal entity; even so, the partners are taxed individually, not as a partnership entity. Its name must include the name of at least one of its partners and be followed by "et Compagnie" when all partners' names are not used in the name of the partnership. It is a French enterprise even if all of the shareholders are aliens.

A partnership may include limited partners, in which case it is termed "société en commandite simple." Its general partners (commandités) with unlimited liability are similar to those of the société en nom collectif; the limited partners' (commanditaires') liabilities are limited to the amounts contributed to the firm, and they cannot participate in the management. The general and the limited partners may only transfer their interests with the unanimous approval of all partners. This form of organization is not in general use. Another form of partnership with limited partners is the "société en commandite par actions." Here the interests of the limited partners (commanditaires) are represented by transferable shares of stock.

There are also civil companies (sociétés civiles) under French law, which are used primarily for holding real estate. These companies differ from commercial companies and are subject to different laws. Under a recent amendment of the law, the company may be so constituted as to resemble professional partnerships in the United States.

There are also joint ventures (associations en participation), of which the financial syndicate (syndicat financier) and the underwriters syndicate (syndicat d'émission) are examples. Another type of joint venture is the grouping of economic interest (groupement d'intérêt économique), which is formed by an agreement between its members and has a legal identity separate from them; this type of venture requires no minimum capital.

A somewhat specialized entity is the "société à capital variable," which is used principally by cooperatives, whose purpose is similar to farm and other types of cooperatives in the United States. It may increase capital by contributions from existing or new participants, and the participants may withdraw their capital at any time.

Business Records

The basic accounting records required by the Code of Commerce are the general journal and the book of balances (livre d'inventaire). The latter is comparable to a trial balance book, in which are also recorded the annual balance sheet and profit and loss account. In addition, the Code of Labor requires a payroll journal (livre de paye). These three records must be prenumbered and stamped by a judge or mayor. There are other records which have to be maintained to conform with tax, social, commercial, customs, and other regulations. The nominative share transfer ledger is commonly used, but many other records are of limited use.

Le Plan Comptable Général, a standard chart of accounts (described later), approved by the French government, requires the maintenance of a general ledger, and recommends the use of such subsidiary journals, ledgers, and so forth, as may be necessary for a particular firm. A French company must also have records of its General Assembly meetings and board of directors' meetings in special books prenumbered and stamped by a judge or mayor.

Commissaire Aux Comptes (Statutory Examiner)

The basic Law of 1867, as amended July 24, 1966, and effective April 1, 1967, provides that all companies (sociétés anonymes, sociétés en commandite par actions, and those sociétés à responsabilité limitée with capital of more than 300,000 francs) and, in some cases, the groupement d'intérêt économique must have their accounts examined by one or more commissaires aux comptes. The commissaire aux comptes is elected by the shareholders for a term of six years in the case of the société anonyme and société en commandite par actions and three years in the case of the société à responsabilité limitée. The commissaire aux comptes must be appointed from a list drawn up by a special committee chaired by the first judge of the local court of appeal. The expert comptable (see page 199) is eligible for inclusion on this list. All sociétés anonymes and sociétés en commandite par actions with capital of at least 5,000,000 francs and any other publicly held companies issuing bonds to the public must have their accounts examined by two commissaires aux comptes.

The diploma of commissaire aux comptes is now given to persons who pass a qualifying examination in bookkeeping, accounting, mercantile and company law, and taxation, which is less stringent than that required of the expert comptable.

Possession of this diploma and a two-year articleship is a prerequisite for inclusion on the list of commissaires aux comptes.

Persons Ineligible

Since a principal qualification of the commissaire aux comptes is stated to be that of independence, relatives of directors or of persons contributing assets other than cash for capital stock, persons receiving salary or remuneration in any form from the company, spouses of these persons, and persons in certain other categories are disqualified from holding that office.

Company law forbids a director of a company to hold the position of commissaire for that same company, and during five years after the end of his term of office a commissaire is prohibited from being a director of a company for which he was the commissaire, or of any associated company.

Functions

Under French law, the commissaire aux comptes is officially responsible for the independent audit function. He may not allow another person to substitute for him, but he may act jointly with another commissaire, or he may have one or several assistants or be assisted by a firm of accountants. His duties and responsibilities are stated in the law in some detail, but not the manner in which they are to be carried out.

The commissaire aux comptes is required to report to the shareholders upon the financial statements presented to them by the board of directors at the annual meeting. He is not expected to prepare them. Such financial statements must be submitted to the commissaire at least 45 days before the annual meeting.

The commissaire has other duties prescribed by law which differ from those assigned to the U.S. or U.K. auditor. For example, he may call a general meeting of shareholders in case of emergency; he is required to report on contracts and agreements of the company, if known to him, in which directors or general managers are directly or indirectly involved; he must reveal to the public prosecutor any criminal acts of the company or its officers of which he has knowledge.

The duties and powers of the commissaire aux comptes as provided by law are such that it would appear that he is permitted, if not expected, to perform an examination of financial statements in a manner not too different from that customary in the United States, except that he does not generally observe the taking of physical inventories nor does he confirm accounts receivable by correspondence with the debtors. The commissaire aux comptes is permitted to contact third parties during the course of his examination of the financial statements. However, the minimum fee of a commissaire aux comptes as stated in article 120 of the Law of August 12, 1969, is low; that required, for example, for a commissaire for a company with a turnover of Fr. 45,000,000 might be only Fr. 2,500. It seems apparent that an examination of financial statements in the sense understood in the United States cannot be made with such fee limitations.

Reports of the Commissaire aux Comptes

There is no standard form of report prescribed for the statutory examiner in France, comparable to that of the AICPA in the United States or that required by the Companies Act in the United Kingdom.

Under the provisions of the Law of 1966, the statutory examiner submits to the annual meeting of shareholders, a general report, a special report, and a certified statement of the five or ten highest paid employees of the company.

The general report comments on whether the financial statements and the information contained therein are presented in a true and fair view (la régularité et la sincérité) and whether they have been consistently presented in comparison with the preceding year; it also comments on the fairness of the financial information contained in the board of directors' report to shareholders and certain other matters on which comments are required by company law such as equality in treatment of shareholders, number of shares deposited with the company to guarantee management by the directors, and so forth. The general report is often long-form, although in recent years there has been a tendency to adopt the "short-form" report.

The special report deals exclusively with contracts or agreements between the company and any of its directors and general managers (either directly or indirectly), and must state whether these contracts or agreements were initially approved by the board and how they affect the company.

A certified statement of the total wages of the ten highest paid employees of the société anonyme is required if the company employs more than 200 personnel. For less than 200 employees, a certified statement of the total wages of the five highest paid employees of the company is submitted.

It is apparent that the commissaire aux comptes, as such, is not required to have the training or experience in accounting and auditing which is expected of the independent auditor in the United States or the United Kingdom (although, if he is an expert comptable, he may have had such training or experience). Therefore, because of the difference in professional requirements, a representation in the report of a commissaire aux comptes as to fairness of presentation of financial statements does not necessarily have the same weight as a similar representation by a certified public or chartered accountant.

Organizations of the Commissaires aux Comptes

It has been stated that all companies must select their commissaires from a list established by a special committee headed by the first judge of a court of appeal. To appear on this list one must be 25 years of age, of good character, professionally capable, and possess the diploma of commissaire aux comptes. Any individual not possessing the diploma may still be included on this list if he meets any one of the following qualifications: is a holder of the state diploma of expert comptable; has been an employee of an expert comptable or of his firm for 15 years or more; has obtained 15 or more years of financial accounting and legal experience in public or private industry (the time period is reduced to 10 years if the candidate is a licensed graduate of a government technical school).

The profession of commissaires aux comptes was organized by Decree 69810 of August 12, 1969, into the Compagnie Nationale des Commissaires aux Comptes. This organization is composed of one national and many regional councils. Its aim is to safeguard the honor, independence, and moral and monetary interests of its members.

There has also been organized the Fédération des Associations de Commissaires des Sociétés Inscrits par les Cours d'Appel (Federation of Associations of Commissaires of Companies Registered by the Courts of Appeal).

The Accounting Profession

There are now two main classes of professional accountants in France, the expert comptable and the comptable agréé, each of which has different educational and training qualifications and different fields of practice. These classes were created under the Decree of September 19, 1945, as

L'Ordre des Experts Comptables et des Comptables Agréés with the object of "assuring the defense of the honor and the independence of the profession which it represents." Subsequent modifications of the decree in 1968 and 1970 will lead to the gradual elimination of the comptable agréé as a class.

The Expert Comptable

The decree, as amended in November 1968, defines the expert comptable as one who is "engaged" in the profession of reviewing and appraising any business enterprise of which he is not an employee. He is also permitted to attest to the trueness and fairness of the financial statements. It also states that "the expert comptable may also organize the accounting and analyze, by means of accounting technique, the position and functioning of enterprises under their different economic, legal, and financial aspects. He reports on his verifications, conclusions, and suggestions."

An expert comptable must be registered as a member of the Order, he must be a French citizen, of good character, 25 years of age, and have obtained the diploma of "expertise comptable" issued by the National Minister of Education. Even though he has obtained this diploma, he cannot be inscribed on the roll of the Order unless he is engaged in the practice of public accounting as a principal. If he takes a salaried position which is not in the office of another expert comptable, he ceases to be a member of the Order. In addition, the law allows various individuals with certain background and experience to become members of the Order.

Foreigners with accepted qualifications may practice in France as experts comptables provided a convention or agreement has been concluded between France and the country concerned. The only country to date to have concluded a convention with France is Switzerland although negotiations are under way with the United Kingdom.

Education and Training

The first step towards obtaining the diploma of "expertise comptable" is the passing of a series of examinations leading to the diplôme d'études comptables supérieures (advanced accounting studies) which may not be taken before the year in which the candidate reaches 19 years of age. The diploma requires the possession of certificates indicating passing of examinations in études comptables (accounting studies), études économiques (economic studies), and études juridiques (legal studies). Prior to sitting for this diploma, the candidate must have passed an examination given by members of L'Ordre des Experts Comptables et des Comptables Agréés and other qualified persons designated by the Minister of National Education. The examination (examen probatoire) covers accounting, economics, and law. Candidates possessing a diploma from a higher technical school or a business school are exempt from taking the examination as well as one or two of the above three certificates constituting the diplôme d'études comptables supérieures.

Having obtained the diploma of études comptables supérieures, or at least the accounting studies section of it, the candidate may become articled and during a period of three years is under the supervision of a monitor (contrôleur de stage). In certain instances the period may be reduced by one year for persons with extensive practical experience or for one possessing advanced degrees, subject to the approval of the Superior Council of the Order.

With the agreement of the Superior Council of the Order, the three-year term of articleship may be served as follows:

1. In the office of an expert comptable.
2. With an official of the Ministry of Economic and Financial Affairs designated to control the economic and financial interests belonging to the state.
3. Up to one year with a comptable agréé, or with a foreign practitioner authorized to practice as an expert comptable or comptable agréé.
4. Up to one year with a commercial enterprise in which the accounting is controlled by a member of the Order.
5. Up to one year with the Conseil National de la Comptabilité.
6. Up to one year abroad, with the agreement of the Superior Council of the Order, either with a foreign practitioner of a standing comparable to that of an expert comptable or of a French firm of accountants or with one or several private enterprises whose accounting is controlled by the said practitioners.

During the articled period, the progress of the candidate is supervised by his monitor to whom the candidate is required to report his progress at least every six months. The monitor in turn calls the candidate to an annual meeting at which time his professional activities and experience for the period are reviewed. At the end of the articled period, the monitor decides, usually affirmatively, whether the candidate is ready to sit for the examination of higher auditing (revision comptable).

Prior to taking the examination leading to le certificat supérieur de revision comptable (higher auditing), the candidate must also have obtained one of the following certificates:

1. Le certificat supérieur juridique et fiscal (certificate of advanced law and tax law).

2. Le certificat supérieur d'organisation et de gestion des entreprises (higher certificate of business organization and management).
3. Le certificat supérieur des relations économiques Européennes et internationales (certificate in advanced study of European and international economic relations).
4. Le certificat du traitement des données (electronic data processing).

Each of the certificates involves a written and an oral examination.

In addition, as a last requirement, a thesis must be presented to the examining board. The subject of the thesis, which is the last obligation of the candidate, must be submitted to the examining board for approval six months before the thesis is presented. An oral examination on the thesis submitted must be passed within a period of five years beginning January 1 of the year following receipt of the second certificate. When the thesis is accepted, all other requirements having been met, the diploma is issued to the candidate. He is then accepted into membership of L'Ordre des Experts Comptables et des Comptables Agréés provided he practices as a public accountant.

Functions

The expert comptable, as such, is not primarily concerned with auditing. Since France is essentially a country of small companies, closely or family held, the practice of the expert comptable deals very largely with the problems of small and medium-sized business firms. He functions mainly as a business advisor from a management and controllership standpoint, rather than as an independent auditor giving an opinion upon the fairness of financial statements. An important function is to advise his clients with respect to accounting and reporting methods which affect tax liabilities.

The tradition of French business is that of secrecy in business matters. While this viewpoint is being eroded, it undoubtedly has affected the practice of the expert comptable in France in that he has been limited in his work to those areas specifically authorized by management except when he functions as a commissaire aux comptes.

A barrier to the development of French accounting and auditing practice is the rule of the Order that each member may not utilize the services of more than ten salaried accountants, exclusive of experts comptables apprentices (Decree of February 19, 1970). This requirement effectively impedes if not prevents the development of firms of experts comptables on a scale necessary to conduct examinations of financial statements of large companies in accordance with the standards and procedures common in the United States and the United Kingdom.

Training of auditors in such methods is impeded because the apprentices may spend only one year of their required experience with U.S.- or U.K.-oriented firms of accountants, and, as noted above, if an expert comptable accepts a salaried position with such a firm, he may no longer be inscribed on the rolls of the Order unless the firm is recognized by the Order.

Independence

The Decree of 1945 as amended in 1968, establishing L'Ordre des Experts Comptables et des Comptables Agréés, provides in article 22 that the functions of members of the Order are incompatible with any occupation or any act, the nature of which would affect their independence, and in particular—

1. A member may not enter into any business transaction or act as a business intermediary.
2. A member may not perform any function in any commercial enterprise.
3. A member is forbidden to act as a commercial intermediary, to draw up contracts, to represent persons in courts or his clients before public administrations, or do any accounting work in enterprises in which he possesses, either directly or indirectly, a participation estimated as being substantial.
4. A member is forbidden to work for a company if he and/or persons employed by him are retained as commissaire aux comptes of that company.
5. Finally, a member of the Order is not allowed to devote the major part of his activity for the benefit of only one enterprise or one financial group of companies.
6. The foregoing interdictions or restrictions also apply to the member's spouse, his salaried employees, and any person acting on his behalf.

When an expert comptable accepts appointment as commissaire aux comptes of a company, it is understood that he will, in the course of his duties, give advice on tax matters, management, law, and so forth. He should not, however, as an expert comptable functioning as commissaire aux comptes, accept a definite and independent assignment to do such work. For this reason, partners and staff of French offices of U.K. and U.S. firms usually prefer not to accept such an appointment, except in the case of companies very closely held.

The Comptable Agréé

As defined in the Decree of September 19, 1945, as amended, the comptable agréé is one who "is considered as the technician who engages in the usual profession of keeping, centralizing, opening, closing, supervising, and correcting accounting and accounts of companies of which he is not an employee." He is permitted to attest to the trueness and fairness of the financial statements of business enterprises for which he maintains the accounts.

He must be a French citizen, of good character, and at least 25 years of age. He must have obtained the diploma of études comptables supérieures (advanced accounting studies) issued by the National Minister of Education and have had two years of professional practice, approved as sufficient by the Superior Council of the Order, acquired with an expert comptable or a comptable agréé or in a public or private enterprise. He must also become a member of L'Ordre des Experts Comptables et des Comptables Agréés, thus becoming subject to its rules and disciplinary authority.

The diploma of études comptables supérieures requires the possession of certificates indicating passing of examinations in études comptables (accounting studies), études économiques (economic studies), and études juridiques (legal studies).

The work of the comptable agréé is somewhat comparable to that of bookkeepers or accountants in commerce and industry; he does not perform independent auditing functions in the sense understood in the United States or United Kingdom.

The Law of October 31, 1968, will substantially eliminate the professional title of comptable agréé. Its stated aim is to "unify the two professions (expert comptable and comptable agréé) by gradually eliminating the latter." No further inscription as a comptable agréé will be accepted by L'Ordre des Experts Comptables et des Comptables Agréés after December 31, 1972. For a period of five years beginning February 23, 1970, those comptables agréés with ten years' experience in the profession will be permitted to become inscribed in the Order as experts comptable providing these individuals possess a graduate degree (Licence en Droit or Licence en Sciences Economiques) or obtain the certificates of higher auditing (revision comptable) and one of the following: certificate of advanced law and tax law (le certificat supérieur juridique et fiscal); higher certificate of business organization and management (le certificat supérieur d'organisation et de gestion des enterprises); certificate in advanced study of European and international economic relations (le certificat supérieur des relations économiques Européennes et internationales).

The law also permits comptables agréé to be inscribed as experts comptables in the Order during the five-year period beginning at the date of the publication of the law (October 31, 1968) if they are inscribed on the official court list of commissaire aux comptes and are in possession of one of the above certificates.

Organization of Accounting Firms in France

For the most part, public accounting in France is carried on by one expert comptable with one or more assistants. The practice of the profession in the form of a partnership, limited liability companies, civil companies, or a société à responsabilité limitée is also permitted, provided certain conditions are fulfilled.

Organizations of Accountants

The organization of accountants in France corresponding most closely to the American Institute of CPAs is L'Ordre des Experts Comptables et des Comptables Agréés, instituted in 1942, and formalized by decree in September 1945, which law also governs its administration and discipline. Its members are those who have received the diploma of expert comptable or have fulfilled the requirements to become a comptable agréé. Initially, many practicing accountants were given their diplomas or admitted to the Order without passing an examination. Its approximately twenty regional branches are each administered by a local council and, in turn, are under the control of a national council.

An important feature relating to L'Ordre des Experts Comptables et des Comptables Agréés is that a government official (commissaire du gouvernement) is present at sessions of the Order and he has the power to bring decisions of the Order before the court.

In addition to the foregoing, there are various organizations of accountants in France whose membership or purposes are more specialized. Recently, the Institut Français des Experts Comptables Diplômés par l'Etat was formed by the merger of the following three organizations: Chambre Nationale des Experts Comptables Diplômés par l'Etat; Compagnie Nationale des Experts Comptables; and the Union Professionelle des Sociétés Fiduciaries d'Expertise Comptable.

The first aim of the Institute is to tighten relations between its members and to safeguard their monetary and moral interests together with the diplomas and title of expert comptable.

There is also the Société des Experts Comptables Français. Essentially of a cultural nature, it arranges the French participation in the various European conferences of public accountants held under the sponsorship of the Union Européenne des Experts Comptables Economiques et Financiers (UEC) (European Union of Accountants).

In addition, the Société de Comptabilité de France is an association which is concerned with the training of professionals practicing as assistant accountants, accountants, chief accountants, and public accountants. There is also the Compagnie des Chefs de Comptabilité (chief accountants).

Ethics

The Superior Council of the Order has adopted a "Code des Devoirs Professionnels" (ethics) which, in 34 articles, discusses the duties of the members as individuals in the exercise of their profession. Also discussed are members' relations with other members, their clients, the Order itself, government representatives, and their articled clerks. The provisions of some of these articles, such as those dealing with employment of assistants and those dealing with independence, have been mentioned under previous headings of this section. Other provisions of general interest are paraphrased as follows:

1. Personal advertising is forbidden.
2. Use of titles, decorations, and diplomas is regulated.
3. Members may not speak ill of another member; they may not accept an engagement previously held by another member without first conferring with such member.
4. The members must fulfill conscientiously and devotedly the duties entrusted to them by clients.
5. Members have the right to minimize by proper means taxes payable by clients, but they must not participate in any deceit of the fiscal authorities.
6. The fact that one member recommends another does not authorize division of the fee.
7. Fees may not be based on the financial results (gross sales, and so forth) of the client.

Members of the Order take the following oath:

> I swear to exercise my profession with conscience and honesty, to respect and make others respect the laws in connection with my work.

There are provisions for various penalties to be imposed, after due process, upon members who act in contradiction of the code, which acts are interpreted to be a violation of the above oath.

Auditing Standards

The accounting profession in France does not have as a guide for its work a statement of auditing standards in a form such as that published by the AICPA as Statement on Auditing Standards No. 1. As previously stated, both the commissaire aux comptes and the expert comptable are expected to maintain an independent mental attitude towards their work.

Since 1963, the Order has issued a series of publications dealing with various aspects of accounting and auditing with a view towards provoking discussion among the Order's members. These publications are comprehensive in dealing with the subject under discussion but are not an official guide to the French practitioner on how to do his work. Rather, they are used in practice as reference material.

The Ordre des Experts Comptables et des Comptables Agréés has also issued a series of recommendations dealing with auditing standards (Normes de Revision Comptable), auditing inventory and work-in-process (Contrôle des Stocks et Travaux-en-Cours), and direct confirmation with third parties (Procédure de Confirmation Directe). However, the expert comptable is not bound to follow these recommendations nor is the statutory examiner (commissaire aux comptes) who may or may not be an expert comptable; but if the expert comptable fails to do so, he would have to explain why and justify his position.

The Compagnie Nationale des Commissaires aux Comptes has also issued a series of recommendations regarding the conduct of the statutory audit. The statutory examiner (commissaire aux comptes) is not, however, bound to follow these recommendations although he would have to justify the selection of alternative procedures in the case of a law suit.

General Standards

The expert comptable and commissaire aux comptes, as previously described, undergo scholastic and apprenticeship training which purports to adequately prepare them for their work. The code des devoirs of the expert comptable refers to the necessity for conscientious and devoted attention to the client's affairs, and French law holds a commissaire aux comptes responsible when he does not carry out his duties with due care.

Standards of Field Work

The Ordre des Experts Comptables et des Comptables Agréés has issued to its members a statement of auditing standards regarding the conduct of an audit (Normes de Revision Comptable). The statement defines standards of field work in terms of adequacy of planning and competence of evidential matter.

It is not customary, although recommended by the Order, to confirm accounts receivable by correspondence nor to observe the taking of physical inventories.

There are references in the statement to the need for an auditor (reviseur) to have knowledge of the quality and weakness of the system of internal control of the enterprise being audited.

Standards of Reporting

The statement referred to above (Normes de Revision Comptable) also lists the following requirements regarding the form and content of the report of the auditor (reviseur):

1. The report shall state whether the financial statements are presented in accordance with generally recognized accounting principles.
2. The report shall state whether such principles have been consistently observed from period to period.
3. The report must contain a reference to the financial statements examined (balance sheet, statement of income, and any annexed documents or exhibits).
4. The report must contain a description of the examination performed and indicate that the examination has been performed in accordance with generally accepted auditing standards (Normes de Revision Comptable).
5. The report shall contain an expression of opinion on the "trueness and fairness" of the financial statements.

Accounting Principles and Practices

The "Plan Comptable Général" (see page 208) and the French tax law are the most influential factors in shaping the accounting principles applied in the preparation and presentation of financial statements in France.

The influence of the accounting profession, to date, apparently has not been as great as that of the profession in the United States and the United Kingdom. The basic framework of French accounting is similar to that in other countries, but there are certain dissimilarities of which the reader of French financial statements should be aware. The principal differences are discussed herein.

Form and Content of Financial Statements

In general, the French balance sheet as prescribed by the "Plan Comptable Général" follows those of U.S. public utility companies: the assets on the left, beginning with fixed assets and ending with current assets; the liabilities and capital on the right, beginning with capital and surplus, then long-term debt, and ending with current liabilities.

There is no combined statement of income and earned surplus, as known in the United States. Instead, the statement of operating profit and loss (similar to the nineteenth-century "trading account") includes sales, purchases, inventories, costs, other income, and so forth. The balance of "operating profit" is carried to a "statement of income and profit and loss" which includes income taxes, prior years' adjustments, nonrecurring items, profit or loss on disposal of assets, and nonoperating profit or loss.

Another variation from U.S. practice is that the financial statements presented by the directors to the annual meeting of shareholders, and that are reported upon by the commissaire aux comptes, are not what would be considered the "final" figures in the United States. The purpose is to present to the shareholders a statement showing the amount of income for the year available for distribution as dividends to shareholders, as tantième (bonus) to directors, and for appropriation for various reserves. The shareholders then approve the various distributions and appropriations. The financial statements customarily printed and distributed are those that are presented to shareholders; sometimes an additional balance sheet is circulated showing the disposition of net income as approved by the shareholders.

The "Plan Comptable Général"

The desirability of reasonable comparability of financial data by company and industry has long been recognized by the government as well as by accountants in France, and French accounting thought has favored the establishment of a uniform chart of accounts adaptable to all industries.

To this end in April 1946, the government established a Commission for Accounting Standardization (Commission de Normalisation des Comptabilités), since disbanded, which developed a standard accounting system under the name "Plan Comptable Général." The Plan was approved by order of the Minister of National Economic Affairs. At the same time there was created the Conseil National de la Comptabilité, a consultative body under the Minister of Economic Affairs, composed of representatives from different ministries, L'Ordre National des Experts Comptables, the Société de Comptabilité de France, different professional groups, and certain staff members from the profession. The duties of this commission are to provide a continuing review of the Plan and to suggest revisions when deemed necessary. Such revisions were made in 1950 and 1957. The latter revision is now in current use.

However, the Plan is currently undergoing further revision and it is expected that it will be completely revised and presented to the government for approval in 1973. The Plan or a modified version of it (Plan Particulier) has been in universal use since December 31, 1969.

The stated objectives of the Plan are to provide more precise accounting data which will—

1. Promote more reliable national economic and fiscal policies.
2. Assist in eliminating fiscal inequalities.
3. Minimize social misunderstandings by informing the public of the true distribution of national wealth.
4. Provide data for the study of market trends.
5. Improve healthy competition.
6. Aid in the development of fairer taxation.
7. Provide shareholders, suppliers, and bankers with an opportunity to exercise their judgment more satisfactorily.
8. Aid governmental authorities in exercising controls.
9. Provide a clear and prompt view of financial results.
10. Permit analysis and comparison of manufacturing costs.

The "Plan Comptable Général" includes the following:

1. A detailed chart of accounts, numbered on a decimal system, from which the periodical financial statements may readily be prepared. (Title I, chapters 1 and 2.)
2. The general rules, definitions and functions of the accounts included in class 1 through 8. (Title II, chapters 1-4.)
3. A portion which is analogous to the text material in the United States Utility, Railroad, and so forth, classifications.
4. A discussion of the cost accounting procedures provided in class 9 of the Plan. (Title III, chapters 1-7.)

Throughout these sections of the Plan (Titles I, II, and III) are placed a number of model financial statements and statistical reports. The last section of the Plan includes the texts of various pronouncements and decrees relating to the preparation and implementation of the Plan, the latest bearing the date of December 28, 1959. While a detailed discussion of the Plan is not contemplated here, the following summary of the main groups of accounts will indicate the general scheme of the Plan:

Group I	Capital stock, surplus, surplus reserves, donated surplus, reserves for liabilities, long-term liabilities, inter-company, and branch accounts.
Group II	Fixed assets: organization expenses, property, plant and equipment, construction work in progress, property subject to war damage claims, long-term loans receivable, investments and related reserves for loss in value, and guarantee deposits.
Group III	Inventories: goods for resale, raw materials, materials and supplies, salvage stock, semifinished products, finished goods, work in process, packing materials, and related reserves for loss in value.
Group IV	Accounts receivable and payable: accounts payable, suppliers; accounts receivable, customers; employee accounts, accounts with the state, accounts with shareholders and partners, subsidiaries or parent company, miscellaneous receivables and payables, accrued liabilities, prepaid expenses and deferred credits, suspense accounts.
Group V	Financial accounts: short-term borrowings, short-term loans to others, bills and notes payable, bills and notes receivable, checks and coupons receivable, miscellaneous investments and government securities, cash on deposit, cash on hand, internal cash transfers.
Group VI	Operating expenses: purchases, payroll, taxes, subcontractors' costs, transportation and traveling, administrative and selling expenses, interest, depreciation.
Group VII	Operating income: sales, sales of scrap and returnable containers, allowances on sales, allowances and rebates received, miscellaneous income, financial income.
Group VIII	Profit and loss: results of operation, prior years' adjustments, extraordinary gains or losses, appropriations to reserves (nontrading or exceptional), income taxes, results of period awaiting appropriation, opening and closing balance sheet accounts.
Group IX	Cost accounts.
Group X	Special accounts: contingent assets and contingent liabilities.

Offsetting of Accounts

The "Plan Comptable Général" provides that group IV include both accounts receivable and payable; in group V are included both short-term borrowings and lending, as well as notes payable and receivable. While these groups are usually properly classified as assets or liabilities on published balance sheets, it is not always certain that complete segregation has been made. Reserves (see below) provided by approval of shareholders at the annual meeting are sometimes deducted from a related asset rather than classified according to the provisions of the "Plan Comptable Général."

Consolidated Financial Statements

There is at present no requirement in France that consolidated or group accounts be prepared or published, although they are sometimes prepared for internal purposes. It is also not required nor is it customary that parent company statements be accompanied by the financial statements of unconsolidated subsidiaries, by information comparing parent company investment with underlying net assets of such companies, or a comparison of dividends received by the parent with profits or losses of unconsolidated subsidiaries for the period.

Pooling of Interests

The "pooling of interests" concept is not known in France. The French law concerning mergers of corporations is complicated and not within the scope of this discussion.

Investments

Investments in stocks or other companies are valued at cost or net realizable value, whichever is lower.

Inventories

The general basis for stating inventories under French law is cost. (There is no provision for the use of Lifo.) Cost may be reduced to market (should this be lower than cost) for raw materials having known quotations. Cost or market may also be reduced when the items concerned are known to have deteriorated, to have changed in style, or to be slow moving, in which cases they are valued at estimated realizable prices.

The reductions from the cost or market basis are set up in appropriate reserve accounts as suggested in the "Plan Comptable Général." Such reserves are shown on French balance sheets as a reduction from the related asset, the basis of valuation of which is not stated since it is generally understood that cost or market is used.

Various methods have been permitted for revaluation of inventories in order to eliminate the effects of inflation on taxable income. The Tax Reform Law of December 28, 1959, provided for the discontinuance of all previous legislation in this respect with the exception of the "provision pour fluctuations des cours" (provision for price variations), which is only utilized by enterprises having inventories of raw materials the prices of which are influenced by international markets and the franc value of foreign currency. Other valuation reserves permitted prior to 1960 are the subject of comment under the caption "Surplus Reserves."

The aforementioned Law of 1959 further permitted the setting up of a reserve for increase in prices ("provision pour hausse des prix") of over 10 percent on products other than those included in the price variation reserve referred to above. The tax exemption in this case, however, is merely postponed for a period of six years.

The reserves provided for (a) price variations and (b) replacement are shown on the liability side of the balance sheet.

Fixed Assets

It is not customary to show the basis of stating fixed assets even though the basis is frequently not historical cost.

Inflation of currency in France since 1920, and especially since 1945, has forced various government-sponsored methods designed to cushion its effect upon business. Various decrees, the last in 1959, permitted companies to revalue their fixed assets based on the price-index principle, the resulting write-up being credited to a revaluation reserve. All companies whose average sales for the three accounting periods ending before December 29, 1959, exceeded 5,000,000 francs were obliged to revalue their fixed assets to the maximum extent. Companies with lesser average sales had the option to revalue all or part of their fixed assets, but most companies took full advantage of the permission to revalue to the maximum permitted.

Earlier decrees dealing with revaluation of fixed assets exempted revaluation reserves from tax; tax law of December 1959 imposed a special tax of 3 percent on revaluation reserves, but freed them from any future liability to income tax and, as before, left them distributable as (1) stock dividends (subject to the registration tax in the circumstances described below) and (2) cash dividends (subject to withholding tax) to the extent that such reserves may be considered realized. The meaning of the word "realized" is not, however, defined in French law. The reserves were permitted to be capitalized without payment of the 12 percent registration tax if effected before April 1, 1972. In practice most companies have capitalized these reserves.

The depreciation reserve is restated by formula at the same time and by application of the same indices as the plant, and the resulting increase is charged to the revaluation reserve. Thereafter, annual depreciation provisions are calculated on the net increased plant values.

Surplus Reserves

Included under this general heading are items such as premium on capital stock, legal reserve, optional reserves, reserve for replacement of inventories, special revaluation reserve, grants from state or public institutions, and reserve for acquisitions of fixed assets.

Each year, all companies (S.A. or S.àR.L.) are required to set aside as a legal reserve 5 percent of net profits, less tax, until the total reaches 10 percent of the nominal capital. The legal reserve may be used to compensate for an accumulated loss, in which case the company must rebuild the reserve by making appropriations in the prescribed manner out of future profits.

During the period from World War II through 1959, various methods were permitted for periodic revaluation of inventories, with the objective of eliminating the effects of inflation of taxable income. The resulting increases were credited to reserve accounts entitled "réserve de renouvellement des stocks," "réserve pour stock indispensable," or "réserve de dotation sur stocks" until the Law of December 28, 1959, instituted a tax on these reserves at a reduced rate. Thereafter these reserves were available for distribution as dividends. Since then they have to a large extent disappeared from French company balance sheets.

The "optional reserves" are those which the shareholders at the annual meeting decide should be appropriated out of that year's profits. An example is the reserve resulting from revaluations of fixed assets discussed above.

An enterprise may set up during a fiscal year a reserve for acquisition of fixed assets in an amount equal to the sums allocated to its "special participation reserve." The latter reserve is set up annually in accordance with the state mandatory profit-sharing system for the benefit of the employees out of a portion of the profits of the enterprise. If used within a year for the acquisition of fixed assets, this reserve, like the special participation reserve, is deductible in arriving at taxable profits.

Included under the headings "surplus reserves" is the "balance of profit and loss account brought forward." In public companies, most of the year's profit is customarily distributed as dividends to stockholders, bonus (tantième) to directors, or appropriated to some reserve. Consequently, the balance carried forward is usually a minor amount, and there is no significant amount which could be described as "earned surplus." Therefore, that term has no equivalent in French accounting.

Liability Reserves

Although covered by group I in the general scheme of the "Plan Comptable Général," these reserves are not included in the "capital and surplus reserves" section of the balance sheet. They are provided by charges to income to cover liabilities and losses.

Among them are provisions for risks, such as litigation, guarantees of product, self-insurance, losses on purchases for future delivery, fines and penalties, exchange losses; provision for restoration or reconditioning of rented premises at expiration of lease; provision for expenses to be spread over several periods; and provision for pensions to employees.

Contingent Liabilities

Generally notes receivable are discounted before the due date, and the resulting contingent liability is disclosed. It is also customary to disclose guarantees and liens on assets.

Capital Stock and Stock Dividends

All capital shares of French companies (with an unimportant exception) have a nominal or par value. No-par stock is unknown in France.

Capital may be increased by a vote of the shareholders at extraordinary general meetings by issuing additional shares or by increasing the par value of existing shares. At such time an amount equal to the par value of the additional shares, or the increase in par value, is transferred from reserves (unappropriated surplus) to capital. Since in all such cases the par value is the measure of the amount transferred, and not the market value as is the case in the United States with respect to stock dividends, it is not necessary in France to distinguish between a "stock split" and a "stock dividend."

The Statement of Income

Sales and Cost of Sales. Sales and cost of sales are not required to be reported in the financial statements, but "turnover" figures are usually given in the director's report.

Depreciation. Prior to 1960, the straight-line method of depreciation was the method used for both book and tax purposes. It was then supplemented with a variety of special depreciation methods, generally as a modification of the straight-line method.

Under the Law of December 28, 1959 (amended), the declining-balance method of computing depreciation is permitted, applicable to machinery and equipment purchased or produced after December 31,

1959, such as equipment and tooling used in manufacturing, transforming, or transport operations; handling equipment; water or air cleaning installations; steam, heat, or energy-producing installations; safety installations or installations of a medico-social nature; office machines, except typewriters; equipment and tooling used in scientific or technical research; warehousing and storing installations, with the exception of related premises, and buildings and equipment of hotel enterprises.

Specifically excluded from the application of the declining-balance method are items acquired secondhand or whose normal service life is less than three years; private lodgings, industrial sites, professional premises and buildings (other than hotels); and generally any item which does not specifically fall into one of the above-listed categories.

Assets acquired or constructed prior to 1960, and those listed above as not being eligible for the declining-balance method, continue to be depreciated by the straight-line method.

Depreciation rates normally accepted for tax purposes are as follows:

Types of Assets	*Depreciation Rate*
Industrial buildings (factories, warehouses, etc.)	5 percent
Commercial buildings, such as offices	2-5 percent
Dwellings	2-4 percent
Plant equipment (machines) and tools	10-20 percent
Office furniture	10 percent
Autos and trucks	20-25 percent

When demonstrated to the satisfaction of the tax authorities, higher rates may be allowed when necessary to reflect abnormal wear and tear or obsolescence. Upon abandonment of an asset, the undepreciated balance may be charged off.

The declining-balance rates prescribed vary from 1.5 to 2.5 times the straight-line rates, depending on the estimated length of the service life, as follows:

Estimated Useful Life	*Multiple Applied to Straight-Line Rate*
Three or four years	1.5
Five or six years	2.0
Over six years	2.5

When the declining-balance method produces an amount for a year less than the amount obtained by dividing the residual balance by the remaining years of life (a straight-line method), the latter method may be used.

To qualify as a tax deduction, depreciation must be recorded on the books. If, however, a loss for the year is shown before deducting depreciation, such depreciation need not be deducted but may be carried forward to the first subsequent profitable year; and if there is a profit for the year not sufficient to cover the entire provision for depreciation, the excess depreciation may likewise be deferred and deducted in subsequent years under special rules. Current depreciation is deducted before applying any of the deferred depreciation.

Tantième (Bonus) Paid to Directors. Tantième (bonus) paid to unsalaried directors is considered as a distribution of profits, and is not a tax deduction to the paying company. No director other than the "president directeur général" and the "directeur général adjoint" may be a salaried employee.

Tax-Effect Accounting. In France, there are no significant differences between book deductions from income and tax deductions. Depreciation deducted for tax purposes must be similarly recorded on the books. Accordingly, the problem does not normally arise of giving tax effect in the books to tax return deductions which are charged to income on the books in another period. Exceptions may arise when (a) excessive depreciation has been provided in prior years and (b) provision has been made for vacation pay costs currently, but which may be deducted for tax purposes only when paid.

Requirements for Public Sale of Securities

Underwritings of public issues are handled in France through banks. There are no official specifications as to form and content of financial statements to be furnished the prospective investor, nor for any report upon them by an independent auditor.

Requirements for Listing Securities on the Stock Exchange

A corporation seeking to list its securities for trading on the Paris Stock Exchange (Bourse) must comply with two sets of requirements, those of the Compagnie des Agents de Change and those of the Commission des Operations de Bourse (C.O.B.) In most respects the information required is similar or identical. The Compagnie des Agents de Change, an organization of stockbrokers which functions similarly to the Stock List Department of the New York Stock Exchange, requires the filing and publication of a prospectus which contains basic data and technical information about the securities to be listed. The Commission des Operations de Bourse (C.O.B.), a regulatory agency similar to the Securities and Exchange Commission in the United States, requires that a corporation (société anonyme or société en commandite par actions) prepare an application for registration of its securities which is filed with the commission. The decision to admit securities for trading lies with the commission after approval by the Compagnie des Agents de Change.

The points of interest from an accounting standpoint are the following:

1. An undertaking to publish quarterly, essential information concerning the activities of the enterprise, particularly the sales figures.
2. A detailed memorandum on the industrial or commercial activities of the firm, accompanied by a comparative balance sheet based on the last three balance sheets, together with an explanation of the variation of the principal items from one fiscal period to another.
3. A memorandum stating plans for investment.
4. A list of subsidiaries and their holdings, with reference to their activity, showing their capital and percentages of stock held.
5. A statement of dividends distributed.
6. A balance sheet, a profit and loss statement, directors' report, minutes of meetings of the shareholders for the last ten fiscal periods with supporting documents for the last five fiscal periods.

The Compagnie des Agents de Change also requires the filing of the Commissaire aux Comptes report on the corporation for the last ten years. The commission requires the corporation to undergo financial examination ("revision comptable") by a independent examiner appointed by the company seeking listing and approved by the commission.

France

Illustrative Financial Statements

ILLUSTRATIVE BALANCE SHEET OF A FRENCH COMPANY

BILAN AU 31 DÉCEMBRE, 19____
(Balance Sheet—December 31, 19____)

ACTIF (Assets)	Montants bruts (Gross amounts)	Amortissements ou provisions pour dépréciation (Depreciation or reserves)	Montants nets (Net amounts)	Totaux partiels (Subtotals)
FRAIS D'ETABLISSEMENT (Organization Expenses)	....	....	....	....
IMMOBILISATIONS (Fixed Assets)				
Terrains (Land)	....		....	
Constructions (Buildings)	....	....	....	
Matériel et outillage (Machinery and equipment)	....	....	....	
Matériel de transport (Vehicles)	....	....	....	
Mobilier, agencements et installations (Furniture and fixtures)	....	....	....	
Immobilisations incorporelles (Goodwill, patents, etc.)	....	....	....	
Immobilisations en cours (Construction in progress)	....	....	....	
	....	....	....	....
AUTRES VALEURS IMMOBILISEES (Other Non-Current Assets)				
Prêts à plus d'un an (Long-term loans)	....	....	....	

Titres de participation (Investments)	....	....	....	
Dépôts et cautionnements (Deposits)	....	....	....	
	....	....	....	....
VALEURS D'EXPLOITATION (Inventories)				
Matières premières (Raw materials)	....		....	
Produits semi-ouvrés (Work-in-process)	....		....	
Produits finis (Finished goods)	....		....	
Emballages commerciaux (Packing materials)	....		....	
	....		....	....
VALEURS REALISABLES A COURT TERME OU DISPONIBLES (Current Assets)				
Clients (Trade accounts receivable)	....	....	....	
Autres débiteurs (Other accounts receivable)	....	....	....	
Comptes de régularisation—Actif (Prepaid charges)	....		....	
Prêts à moins d'un an (Short-term loans)	....	....	....	
Effets à recevoir (Notes receivable)	....	....	....	
Titres de placement (Marketable securities)	....	....	....	
Banques et caisses (Cash in bank and on hand)	....		....	
	....	....	....	....
RESULTATS (Results of Operations)				
Perte de l'exercice (Net loss for the period)			....	....
Total de l'actif (Total assets)				....
MONTANT DES ENGAGEMENTS RECUS (Commitments)				....

ILLUSTRATIVE BALANCE SHEET OF A FRENCH COMPANY

BILAN AU 31 DÉCEMBRE, 19____

(Balance Sheet as at December 31, 19__)

PASSIF (Liabilities)	Montants (Amounts)	Totaux partiels (Subtotals)
CAPITAL PROPRE ET RESERVES (Capital stock, surplus, and reserves)		
Capital social (Capital stock)	....	
Prime d'émission d'actions (Issuance premium)	....	
Réserve légale (Legal reserve)	....	
Réserve générale (General reserve)	....	
Plus-values à long terme (Long-term capital gains)	....	
Provisions spéciales constituées en franchise d'impôts (Special non-tax-free reserves)	....	
	....	....
REPORT A NOUVEAU (Unallocated earnings)		
Situation nette avant résultats de l'exercice (Net worth before income (loss) for the period)		....
SUBVENTIONS D'EQUIPEMENT (Investment subsidies)	....	
Moins- Subventions inscrites à pertes et profits (Less- Subsidies credited to profit and loss)	....	
	....	....

PROVISIONS POUR PERTES ET CHARGES (Provisions for losses)	....	....
DETTES A LONG ET MOYEN TERME (Long- and medium-term debts)		
Obligations et bons à plus d'un an (Debentures)	....	
Autres dettes à plus d'un an (Other long-term loans)	....	
	....	....
DETTES A COURT TERME (Current liabilities)		
Fournisseurs (Trade accounts payable)	....	
Autres créanicers (Other accounts payable)	....	
Comptes de régularisation–Passif (Accrued charges)	....	
Emprunts à moins d'un an (Short-term debt)	....	
Effets à payer (Notes payable)	....	
Banques (Bank overdraft)	....	
	....	....
RESULTATS (Results of operations)		
Bénéfice de l'exercice (Net income for the period)	....	....
Total du passif (Total liabilities)		....
MONTANT DES ENGAGEMENTS DONNES (Commitments)		....

ILLUSTRATIVE INCOME STATEMENT OF A FRENCH COMPANY

Compte de pertes et profits pour l'exercice clos le 31 Décembre 19__ (Profit and loss statement for the period ended December 31, 19____)

DEBIT	Montants (Amounts)
PERTE D'EXPLOITATION DE L'EXERCICE (Operating Loss for the Period)	
PERTES SUR EXERCICES ANTERIEURS (Prior Years Losses)	
PERTES EXCEPTIONNELLES (Extraordinary Losses)	
DOTATION DE L'EXERCICE AUX COMPTES DE PROVISIONS HORS EXPLOITATION (Non-Operating Provisions)	
IMPOTS SUR LES BENEFICES (Provision for Income Tax)	
BENEFICE NET TOTAL (Net Income)	

CREDIT	Montants (Amounts)
BENEFICE D'EXPLOITATION DE L'EXERCICE (Operating Income for the Period)	
PROFITS SUR EXERCICES ANTERIEURS (Prior Years Gains)	
PROFITS EXCEPTIONNELLES (Extraordinary Gains)	
PERTES SUR EXERCICES ANTERIEURS ET PERTES EXCEPTIONNELLES COUVERTES PAR DES PROVISIONS (Prior Years and Extraordinary Losses Covered by Provisions)	
PERTE NETTE TOTALE (Net Loss)	

ILLUSTRATIVE INCOME STATEMENT OF A FRENCH COMPANY

Compte d'exploitation générale exercice clos le 31 Décembre 19____ (General operating statement for the period ended December 31, 19____)

DEBIT	Montants (Amounts)
STOCK AU DEBUT DE L'EXERCICE (Inventory–Beginning of the period)	
ACHATS DE MATIERES ET MARCHANDISES (Purchases)	
FRAIS DE PERSONNEL (Salaries and related charges)	
IMPOTS ET TAXES (Taxes except income tax)	
TRAVAUX, FOURNITURES ET SERVICES EXTERIEURS (Supplies and outside services)	
TRANSPORTS ET DEPLACEMENTS (Transport and travel)	
FRAIS DIVERS DE GESTION (General administrative expenses)	
FRAIS FINANCIERS (Bank charges and interests)	
DOTATION DE L'EXERCICE AUX COMPTES D'AMORTISSEMENTS (Provision for depreciation)	
DOTATION DE L'EXERCICE AUX COMPTES DE PROVISIONS (Other provisions)	
SOLDE CREDITEUR (Credit balance)	
	______

CREDIT	Montants (Amounts)
STOCK EN FIN D'EXERCICE (Inventory–End of period)	
VENTES DE MARCHANDISES ET PRODUITS FINIS (Sales)	
RISTOURNES, RABAIS ET REMISES OBTENUS (Discounts and allowances received)	
PRODUITS FINANCIERS (Interest income)	
TRAVAUX FAITS PAR L'ENTREPRISE POUR ELLE-MEME (Self-constructed assets)	
SOLDE DEBITEUR (Debit balance)	

Greece

Greece

As of January 1974

Forms of Business Organization

Business in Greece is commonly carried on through four different types of organization—the single proprietorship, the partnership, the limited liability company, and the corporation, all of which are very similar to their counterparts in other European countries.

The Corporation

A Greek corporation has the same general attributes as similar organizations in other countries. The liability of its shareholders is limited to the amount of capital contributed by each. A corporation may be formed by two or more persons under a notarial document, the "katastatikon" (memorandum of association). This document is signed by each subscriber, and sets forth (among other things) the number of shares subscribed by each, the name of the company (which must be derived from the character of its business and must include the words "Anonymos Etairia" or the abbreviation "A.E."), the registered office, and the purposes of the company. The katastatikon is filed with the Ministry of

Commerce, and is published together with the ministry's approval in the government gazette.

The minimum capital requirement is 5,000,000 drachmas, and in any case, at least that amount must be paid in. Subject to this minimum, when higher amounts of capital are subscribed, 25 percent of the subscriptions must be paid upon incorporation and the balance within ten years, as provided by the articles. If any part of the capital is to be obtained by public subscription, the minimum capital requirement is 10,000,000 drachmas, all of which must be paid up in full. Public subscription may be effected only through a bank, and the shares of the company must be listed on the Athens Stock Exchange after compliance with the respective legal requirements. Shares of a Greek corporation may be either registered shares (nominal) or bearer shares, except that partially paid shares must be registered.

A Greek corporation may be established by one or more foreign individuals or legal entities irrespective of their nationality; such a corporation must have its registered office in Greece and will have the same status as any other Greek corporation. There are no special corporation laws relating to foreign-owned Greek corporations but there are a number of provisions in Greek law intended to encourage foreign investment in companies designed to promote national production and to contribute to national progress.

A copy of the balance sheet, the directors' report, and the auditors' report (the latter being that of a certified public accountant of Greece when required) are to be submitted to the Ministry of Commerce at least 20 days before the date of the general meeting. They are also published in the government gazette as well as in one financial paper and one daily newspaper. Within 20 days after adoption by the general meeting, a copy of the balance sheet is submitted to the Ministry of Commerce.

Branch of a Foreign Corporation

A foreign corporation wishing to operate in Greece can either form a branch office, after complying with certain formalities (there is a ruling that no foreign corporation may establish a branch office in Greece unless the capitalization of the parent corporation is at least equal to the minimum capitalization requirement for Greek corporations, i.e., 5,000,000 drachmas), or establish a Greek corporation.

A branch office has no legal entity of its own, but, for all practical purposes, it is considered a projection of the foreign corporation which established it. This means that a branch office has neither corporate capital of its own nor a board of directors in Greece, but it is represented by one or more individuals who are issued special powers of attorney and by a special attorney (solicitor) appointed to accept service of documents. Branch offices in Greece are required to file copies of the balance sheets of their "head offices" within three months after such balance sheets are approved and also annual financial statements of the branches themselves.

The Limited Liability Company

This form corresponds to the British "private company" or to the French "société à responsibilité limitée" and is intended for smaller organizations with limited capital and few participants. The name of the company must include the name of one or more of the members, or an indication of the purpose of the enterprise, and the words "Etairia Periorismenis Efthynis," abbreviated "E.P.E." It may be formed by two or more persons all of whom can be foreigners, using the same initial documents as required for the corporation. The attested copy, however, is filed with the secretariat of the Court of First Instance, and a summary is published in the government gazette.

The minimum capital is 200,000 drachmas, which must be fully paid by the time the contract of association is concluded; at least one-half must be in cash. The minimum amount of each share of capital must be for 10,000 drachmas or its multiple. The member's liability cannot exceed the amount of his share contribution.

A balance sheet is required to be published in the government gazette and in certain specified newspapers at least 20 days before the general meeting. The limited liability company's affairs are managed by one or more individuals (either shareholders or any third party) who are appointed by the shareholders' meeting and who are called administrators.

The Partnership

The general partnership ("omorrythmos etairia," abbreviated "O.E.") is formed by two or more persons by a written agreement filed with the secretariat of the Court of First Instance. The name of the company must be formed from the names of the partners. The partners are jointly and severally liable for the debts of the partnership.

The limited partnership, from whose members' names the name of the company is derived, is governed by a memorandum of association and is composed of general partners, who are jointly and severally liable for partnership debts, and limited partners (whose names may not appear in the firm name), whose liability is limited to the amount of their contributions.

Business Records

Legislative Decree No. 4/1968 effective January 1, 1969, revised the requirements of the previously effective Tax Records Code.

For Tax Records Code purposes, companies are categorized according to size. There are now two categories—

Category A: Income up to 6,500,000 drachmas
Category B: Income exceeding 6,500,000 drachmas

Greek corporations and limited liability companies, foreign companies, and foreign insurance enterprises are classified under the second bookkeeping category as of the date that their operations commence.

"Category A" enterprises are obliged to maintain a cash receipts and disbursements book wherein, in columnar form, are recorded (a) income from sales of merchandise, (b) income from rendering of services, (c) income from sundry sources, and (d) all expenses paid. Independent professionals fall into "Category A" regardless of volume of income from services rendered.

The books and/or records listed below are required to be maintained by "Category B" enterprises. Except for item 3, the books and records are authenticated (perforated, rubberstamped, or both) by the district director of Inland Revenue before any entries are recorded therein.

1. Journal for all transactions accompanied by explanations or, in lieu thereof, the serial numbers of authenticated records (invoices, receipts, and so forth). Separate journals may be kept for different groups of transactions such as cash, sales, and so forth.
2. General ledger that includes a minimum specified number of asset, liability, net worth, and profit and loss accounts.
3. Subsidiary ledgers for any accounts whose detail does not appear either in an original book of entry column or in the respective general ledger account itself.
4. Closing trial balance, stock inventory, and balance sheet book.
5. Perpetual inventory books, if the yearly gross sales (with some exceptions and qualifications) aggregate at least 10,000,000 drachmas.
6. Production book and cost analysis (unless cost records are integrated with the general accounting system).
7. Receiving and shipping records.
8. Bills of exchange and notes payable or receivable registers.

The laws also prescribe strict time schedules for recording transactions (generally, for updating books of original entry, one or two days following issuance or receipt of the document that shows the value of the transaction, and, for general ledger, within the next calendar month). All accounting books must be kept according to the double-entry bookkeeping method and in the Greek language, except that foreign enterprises operating in Greece may keep their accounts both in Greek and their own language.

Corporations and limited liability companies are obliged to maintain, in addition to the aforementioned, other records such as minute books for shareholders' and directors' meetings.

The Accounting Profession

The 1920 Corporation Act required that limited liability companies have their annual statements of account audited by two "auditors" appointed by the General Meeting of Shareholders, but there was no specification of the qualifications for such appointment nor of the kind of examination to be made. Hence, the statements were not subjected to the scrutiny and challenge involved in an "audit" as the term is used today.

At present, the accounting profession in Greece comprises three groups of practitioners:

1. "Soma Horkiton Logiston" (literally, the Institute of Sworn-In Accountants, but the usual English translation is the Institute of Certified Public Accountants of Greece).
2. Greek independent practitioners and a small number of Greek firms, a group of which organized the Institute of Incorporated Public Accountants of Greece in 1968.
3. Foreign public accounting firms.

Operations of all these groups in Greece are of comparatively recent origin.

Soma Horkiton Logiston (SOL)

(Institute of Certified Public Accountants of Greece)

After World War II, the British and, later, the American Economic Missions required reliable information about the financial and economic situation in Greece. In 1949 there was established the "British Accounting Advisors to Greece"; one of their responsibilities being "to assist in the establishment of a Greek institute and profession of audit accounting." After many discussions, Law No. 3329 was passed in 1955 establishing the foundation of an accounting profession in Greece by setting up the "Soma Horkiton Logiston," or Institute of Sworn-In Accountants of Greece (SOL); it is the only officially recognized professional accountants' organization in Greece.

The function of SOL was to create a regulated and controlled body of professional accountants who might ultimately constitute the nucleus of an independent public accounting profession in Greece.

The literally translated name of this organization, Institute of Sworn-In Accountants, derives from the fact that all members, after admission, must take the following oath:

> I solemnly swear that I shall be faithful to my country, to the Constitution, and to all the laws of the country and shall honestly and conscientiously fulfill my duty.

Only 25 members are known as a "horkotos logistis" (sworn-in accountant), the usual English translation of which is "certified public accountant of Greece" (CPAG).

A 1960 amendment to Law No. 3329/55 establishing SOL provides that ". . . the date and all the terms and details of establishment of independent offices of CPAGs as well as the manner in which these offices will render their services to the public may be regulated by royal decree issued upon the advice of the Supervisory Council [hereinafter defined] and at the instance of the Ministers of Coordination and Commerce." To date, no such decree has been issued.

Supervisory Council. Originally SOL was governed by a supervisory council consisting of a chairman and eight members; however, the effect of a law passed in 1967 by decree has been the reduction of the memberships of all committees of non-private entities–i.e., governmental or public institutions–to five members. Therefore, today the Supervisory Council consists of the chairman and four members who are—

1. A professor of the Graduate School of Commercial and Economic Studies.
2. A member of the Supreme Fiscal and Audit Court of Greece.
3. The elected president of SOL.
4. Two other prominent officials, or individuals having special knowledge and experience (these may be members of SOL).

The main functions of the Supervisory Council comprise the following:

1. Appoint CPAGs, assistant CPAGs, and articled clerks.
2. Regulate examinations.

3. Compile operating procedures.
4. Fix fees.
5. Enforce disciplinary provisions.
6. Fix rates of emolument for professional and administrative personnel.

Administrative Committee. Pursuant to article 8 of Law No. 3329/55, the Supervisory Council could gradually transfer some of its specific functions to an administrative committee with the approval of certain ministers. Although such approval has not been issued, the Administrative Committee presently does discharge some of the council's functions by virtue of delegated authority. The committee consists of the president of SOL, three other CPAGs, and one assistant CPAG.

Professional Organization. Initially the Supervisory Council selected ten individuals from a group of applicants for appointment to the post of certified public accountant of Greece (CPAG). The status of CPAGs is that of obligated, accredited professional members of SOL (if they leave SOL, they may no longer use the title CPAG) and, by law, the only persons in Greece who can serve "obligatory" clients as defined by law. (For example, Greek banks refuse to confirm clients' financial data to non-CPAG auditors even though the clients request it because only CPAGs are authorized by law to receive such information.) Subsequently, there have been two additional appointments from candidates outside of SOL as well as promotions from within.

The law provided that in the first year the number of CPAGs should be ten; it might be increased to twenty-five after two years, and thereafter the number would be determined by royal decree. Each CPAG may employ no more than three assistant CPAGs and ten articled clerks.

All appointments to the posts of assistant CPAG and articled clerks have been made from applicants who hold the equivalent of a Bachelor of Science in Economics, and who have passed certain written and oral examinations.

In 1963 there were 111 members of SOL. At present there are 200 members consisting of 25 CPAGs, 75 assistant CPAGs, and 100 articled clerks.

Advancement to Certified Public Accountant of Greece. The original appointments to the posts of assistant CPAG and articled clerks were made after written examinations were given by the professors of the Graduate School of Commercial and Economic Studies. Oral examinations were held by a panel consisting of accounting and law professors and members of the Supervisory Council of SOL.

Promotion from one grade to the next is made when the workload of SOL requires it. The persons considered for promotion to the next rank must have completed the following periods of service for each grade: articled clerk B, three years; articled clerk A, five years; and assistant CPAG, three years. So far no written examinations have been required for promotion which has been based on personnel reports compiled annually on SOL personnel and on a report of a subcommittee to the Supervisory Council.

Recruitment of Articled Clerks. Candidates for entry into the profession must possess the degree equivalent to Bachelor of Science in Economics, and must pass a written examination covering accounting, commercial law, and taxation and an oral examination on accounting and foreign languages.

Sixteen such examinations have been held in the last 18 years. In addition, beginning in September 1971, an in-house professional training program for articled clerks B was instituted; this program involves about one hundred hours per year over a three-year period. Performance in this program is a factor to be considered for later promotion.

Compulsory and Optional Use of SOL's Services. The law establishing SOL defines the kinds of engagements which *must* be performed by CPAGs and the kinds of engagements which *may* be performed by CPAGs.

1. Compulsory engagements—
    a. To report upon subjects of a financial and administrative nature which require knowledge of accountancy.
    b. To conduct audits of public institutions other than municipalities.
    c. To make examinations required by law courts, tax courts, or the Supreme Fiscal and Audit Court of Greece.
    d. To conduct audits of corporations listed on the stock exchange and, when authorized by the Minister of Commerce, of corporations in which the government has an interest.
    e. To audit insurance companies' accounts when required by the Minister of Trade.
2. Optional engagements—
    a. To act as "auditor" of a corporation (not listed on the stock exchange) as prescribed by the Corporation Act of 1920. If a company makes such appointment, there need be but one auditor instead of two.

b. To make special examinations by appointment by the Currency Committee of the Bank of Greece.

c. To make examinations of corporations or other companies on request of banks or other lending institutions when a loan of over 200,000 drachmas is involved.

In addition, the members may engage in furnishing tax and finance advisory services, conducting investigations of proposed acquisitions of business and similar activities.

Operations of SOL. The operations of SOL are unique as compared with the corresponding institutes and associations of accountants in other countries. At the time of its inception, there were few Greeks with a high standard of experience in auditing, and the organization and training of a body of professional accountants were considered important tasks of SOL. It was therefore created by law and was granted certain subsidies by the government for its initial development.

CPAGs cannot practice as independent professionals since accounting and auditing work is performed by members of SOL under their direction, much as though SOL itself constituted a firm of public accountants as is understood in other countries. The CPAGs have offices and staff assigned to them within the premises of SOL according to the resolutions of the Supervisory Council. Once assigned, the staff usually remains with the designated CPAG. SOL has a central administration and common facilities for typing, communications, and so forth.

Under the law, all requests for audits or other professional work are submitted to the Supervisory Council which, at the suggestion of the Administrative Committee, then appoints a CPAG to carry out the required work. This central control is to ensure an even flow and spread of work throughout the various offices of the CPAGs. Except when fees are fixed by government agencies or by the courts authorizing the work, fees for work done are assessed by the Supervisory Council on recommendation of the Administrative Committee. The CPAGs, the assistant CPAGs, and articled clerks receive monthly salaries based on rank, period of service, merit, and similar considerations.

All reports and statements of opinion for regular audit and accounting work are signed by the CPAG responsible for the work, and are submitted to the client through the Supervisory Council. The covering letters are then signed by the chairman of the Supervisory Council.

CPAGs are not considered to be civil servants, but they do exercise a public function. They are by law required to be independent during the performance of their work and any interference with their work is expressly prohibited. They are permitted to read and examine all official records of the company under audit, and the law provides for penalties for refusal to furnish CPAGs with such documents or information as they may request.

Ethics. SOL adopted a code (standards) of ethics in 1961, which compares favorably with similar codes of other countries. Among the more important provisions governing the activities of the CPAG are the following:

1. He will not engage in any business or activity incompatible or inconsistent with his professional work. (The act itself lists the following as incompatible occupations: merchant, civil servant, judge, or notary; employment by a private or public enterprise; administrative managing director or an accountant of any company; and the pursuit of any other profession.)
2. He will not be a partner of or engage the services of a person not approved by the Institute.
3. He will not advertise his services or attainments.
4. He will not enter into competitive bidding for professional work nor solicit clients in a manner not warranted by personal relations with such clients.
5. If approached by a prospective client to supplant a previous auditor, he will communicate with the latter before accepting the engagement.
6. He may be held guilty of an act discreditable to the profession if—
    a. He is materially negligent in performing his work.
    b. He fails to disclose a material fact known to him which would make the financial statements on which he is stating an opinion misleading.
    c. He fails to obtain the information and explanations necessary to express an unqualified opinion, but nevertheless does so.
    d. He fails to disclose in his opinion any deviation from prescribed auditing standards.
    e. He violates the confidential relationship between himself and his client.

Independence. The code of ethics also provides that a CPAG will not audit the accounts of a concern if—

1. He is an official or employee of the concern.
2. He has a financial interest in the concern which is material in relation to either the capital of the concern or his family wealth.

3. He purchases shares or other securities of the concern while he is acting as its auditor.

4. He has any financial relationship with officers or employees of his client such as lending or borrowing.

In addition, the standards of auditing (see below) state that the auditor should conduct his work with impartiality, that he should not accept gifts or favors directly or indirectly from his client, that he should not have any financial relationship with his client, and that in maintaining an attitude of independence, he will be guided by the standards of ethics established by SOL.

The statement of standards also indicates that the independence of the auditor would not necessarily be impaired by the fact that he has designed or participated in the design of the accounting system of the organization which he is auditing.

Auditing Standards of SOL. Under the direction of the technical advisor to the Supervisory Council of SOL, a Statement of Auditing Standards, which was adopted on January 30, 1961, was prepared. In addition to the standards of ethics and reference to impartiality previously discussed, auditing standards are described under three headings: basic standards, standards of performance, and standards of reporting. These standards have remained as adopted in 1961 and have not been updated or amended since then, although a special committee was elected by the CPAGs during 1973 to reexamine and update them.

Basic standards—These standards comprise the requirements that are imposed by SOL. In conducting his work, the CPAG is responsible for selection (within the limit of assigned assistants), instruction, and supervision of his assistants and must bring reasonable skill and diligence to bear on his work. The matter of impartiality is also covered.

Standards of performance—The importance of the CPAG's basing his work on a thorough evaluation of internal control procedures and consideration of the factor of materiality in planning an audit program are stressed. The audit procedures should be selected so as to form a logical basis for his opinion on the financial statements, and his working papers should provide evidence that his work has been performed in accordance with the prescribed standards. Confirmation of assets by correspondence with responsible third parties is recommended. Although confirmation of accounts receivable by this method is not specifically mentioned, it is generally considered to be mandatory. Provided adequate tests have been made of the accuracy of the stated amounts of physical assets, statements of responsible officials may be accepted, but physical inspection of some of the assets is required.

The importance of inquiries as to events which have occurred subsequent to the balance sheet date, and which might reflect a material change in the fairness of presentation, is especially referred to. Specifically, the possible effects of post balance-sheet events on the valuation of inventories and receivables are given as examples.

Standards of reporting—It is stated that the ultimate objective of an auditor's examination of financial statements is to express an opinion as to the fairness thereof, except in cases where, due to absence of material evidence, the auditor is unable to express an opinion on the financial statements. In such cases, he should state the following in his report:

1. Whether or not, in his opinion, the statements and any notes forming an integral part thereof fairly present the financial position and the results of the period covered, in conformity with accepted accounting principles.
2. Whether or not the principles of accounting used by the concern under audit were consistent with those of the previous period.
3. Whether or not his examination was made in accordance with the standards of auditing accepted by SOL.
4. Whether or not the concern under audit had kept the books of account prescribed by law.
5. Whether or not the financial statements were in agreement with those books of account.
6. Any material disclosures that are not shown on the financial statements.

In further explanation of the application of these reporting requirements, it is stated that the auditor must express his opinion in clear and generally understood terms, and must furnish the reader with information complete in all material respects. If, because of the absence of material evidence, he is unable to satisfy himself as to the fairness of the financial statements, he must state such inability and his reasons therefor. If absence of evidence or inability to carry out certain audit procedures are not so material as to require denial of opinion, the auditor may qualify his opinion, stating clearly the extent of his exception.

If financial data is to be prepared without audit by a CPAG, and if his name is to be associated with such data, he must state clearly on the statements that they have been prepared from data without audit. The CPAG must not associate his name with forecasts of profits or financial position in such a manner that may lead the reader to believe that he vouches for their accuracy.

The following is the English version of the unqualified form of audit opinion used by a CPAG:

> In my opinion, based upon my examination, the accompanying financial statements (with their notes) fairly present the financial position of ______________________ at December 31, 19...., and the results of its operations for the year then ended in conformity with legal requirements and accepted accounting principles applied on a basis consistent with that of the previous year.
>
> My examination was made in accordance with the requirements of article 37 of the Companies Act of Greece (No. 2190) and also in conformity with the standards of auditing accepted by the Institute of Certified Public Accountants of Greece and accordingly included such tests of accounting records and other auditing procedures as I considered to be necessary in the circumstances. I obtained all the information and explanations (including statements of all branch operations) which I needed for the purpose of my audit.
>
> I have found that the books of account (and production cost books) as required by existing laws have been kept by your company, and that the accompanying financial statements are in agreement therewith.
>
> ______________________
> (signed)

Other Pronouncements of SOL. In addition to the "standards" discussed above, SOL has published a series of "technical notes" for the guidance of its members. These include questionnaires on internal control for various types of business, audit program guides, standardized working papers, guides to reporting and statement presentation, and so forth.

Institute of Incorporated Public Accountants of Greece (IPA)

A few years ago, a movement was begun to establish an independent public accounting profession in Greece. In addition to the basic advantages of an independent self-regulating profession, other factors have contributed to the momentum of this movement, particularly the Common Market Agreement which became effective on November 1, 1962, and which provides for "the free circulation of working people and the removal of restrictions on services and on the movement of capital by the end of the 12-year transition period." The end of the agreed upon period is 1974, and, although interpretations as to this provision's effects on the profession differ, the Greek government has initiated public discussion of the subject of an independent profession within the framework of governmental, industrial, and professional circles. A high Greek government official and former under-secretary of the Ministry of National Economy has been given charge of the project of studying, researching, and recommending ways to implement the establishment of an independent public accounting profession.

Organization. The membership of the Institute of Incorporated Public Accountants of Greece (IPA) was 40 persons in 1968. At present, its membership consists of 115 dues-paying members, 32 of whom are in public practice offering management advisory services and tax services. A few of them offer auditing services. The balance (83) hold high-level positions in private industry. Some members of IPA are U.S. CPAs or British CAs.

IPA was recently admitted to membership in the Union Européenne des Experts Compatables Economiques et Financiers (U.E.C.) as a correspondent member, and has, since its inception, organized and sponsored many lectures for members as well as nonmembers. The IPA has also been involved in inviting officials of other countries' independent professions to come to Greece and help enlighten the public and the government on the merits of an independent profession. IPA members have been actively seeking government recognition for their institute.

Purposes and certain particulars of the IPA are indicated in the following excerpts from the English-language publication *Bylaws* of the Institute of Incorporated Public Accountants of Greece (Athens, 1968).

Objectives (Article 3)

1. The objectives of IPA Institute shall be to develop accounting and auditing practices in Greece by establishing and securing high ethical, scientific, and professional standards within the public accountant's profession.

2. In particular, the Institute's objectives shall be—

   a. To establish and secure high ethical and professional standards and to improve the professional education of its members who render auditing, accounting, and business consulting services.

   b. To develop cooperation with similar organizations in other countries.

   c. To develop cooperation with Greek business institutions.

   d. To develop accounting, costing, and management information systems as well as auditing standards and techniques.

   e. To perform scientific research in the field of auditing and accounting.

   f. To assist in the improvement of the legislative, educational, administrative, and financing conditions and institutions concerning business activity in Greece.

g. To publish periodicals dealing with accounting and auditing problems and subjects.

h. To promote and safeguard the interests of its members.

Members of the Institute and Their Professional Services (Article 4)

1. Eligible for membership are university graduates [who have] attended faculties in law, economics, and business sciences, provided they possess satisfactory professional knowledge, experience, and ability to render accounting, auditing, [and] business consulting services and administer the financial matters of third parties.

2. In particular, members of the Institute shall be—

   a. Members on the date of incorporation.

   b. Persons who shall be admitted as members after the date of incorporation of the Institute in accordance with the procedures described under [subsequent articles].

3. The professional services rendered by the members especially include—

   a. The general audit; i.e., the verification, through examination of data and systems, and application of the existing legislation and business principles, of the financial position of an undertaking presented by its balance sheet and its profit and loss or revenue account.

   b. Special investigations; i.e., the ascertainment and appraisal, through investigation of financial data and application of the existing legislation and business principles, of specific questions especially with relation to the verification of accounts, claims and obligations, invoicing and costing, and the detection of errors or frauds.

   c. Valuation of an undertaking especially for transfer or credit purposes.

   d. Investigations in connection with taxation liabilities as well as advice on taxation affairs and administration thereof.

   e. Preparation and implementation of studies concerning the establishment, expansion, programming, reorganization, amalgamation, dissolution, liquidation, or bankruptcy of enterprises.

   f. Analysis of financial data.

   g. Preparation and implementation of appropriate accounting, costing, internal control, budgeting, and financial reporting systems and/or supervision of the operation of such systems.

   h. Preparation of balance sheets, profit and loss accounts, or other financial statements.

i. The administration of accounting, costing, auditing, or financial operations in general, of business enterprises.

j. Administration or supervision of financial affairs of third parties.

Professional Ethics—General Rules (Article 6)

1. The reliance of clients, employers, and third parties on the public accountant's services for establishing decisions on business and investment affairs, imposes on the members of the Institute an obligation to maintain high scientific competence, morality, and integrity standards.
2. Members are required to perform their duties with full conscience, responsibility, and objectivity and on the basis of the pertinent scientific rules and legislative provisions. Members are, in particular, required to observe the ethical, scientific, and professional standards of the Institute and its pertinent decisions in this respect.
3. Members are required to hold the affairs of their clients in strict confidence.
4. Members are required to assist in the accomplishment of the Institute's objectives and to comply with the provisions of its bylaws and the decisions of its governing bodies.
5. Members' professional services to third parties are rendered either on a salary or on a fee basis.
6. Members may practice under a firm established either by members of the Institute or by members and other professionals whose activity is relative to the services described under article 4, paragraph 3. Whenever members are practicing under such a firm, this firm may describe itself as [a] member of the Institute and may sign certificates and statements only if all its partners are members of IPA and as long as such certificates or statements have been prepared under the responsibility of members of the Institute.

Professional Ethics—Special Prohibitions (Article 7)

1. Members of the Institute shall not express an opinion on the financial affairs of an undertaking if, at the time when such opinions were expressed or at the time to which these opinions refer, the members themselves or their partners were administratively dependent on the undertaking or had a financial interest in it.
2. A member shall in no case agree to offer services on a fee which shall be contingent upon the findings or results of such services.
3. A member shall not express an opinion on questions unless such questions have been previously investigated either by him or by

other members of the Institute or by members of similar professional organizations of other countries.

4. A member shall not advertise his professional services or attainments. The details regarding the observance of this rule shall be determined by the council.
5. A member shall not participate in a competitive bid for professional engagement.
6. A member shall not pay any commission for securing assignments related to the public accountant's profession.
7. A member shall not receive any commission for merely assisting his client to hire persons or purchase articles in connection with the performance of his services without the consent of his client.
8. A member shall not encroach upon the practice of another member. In case he is invited by a client to offer his services in replacement of another member, he is required to deny such services unless he has been previously convinced that such replacement is justified and the member concerned has received all fees due to him.
9. Direct or indirect offer of employment shall not be made by a member to an employee of another member.

Professional Ethics—Special Obligations and Responsibilities (Article 8)

1. In expressing an opinion on matters which he has investigated, a member may be held guilty of an act discreditable to the profession if—
   a. He fails to disclose material facts known to him, the nondisclosure of which makes the expressed opinion misleading.
   b. He fails to acquire sufficient information to warrant expression of an opinion in accordance with the auditing, accounting, and legislative rules.
   c. He fails to justify and to prove, to those to whom the duty is owed and before the courts, the extent and depth of his work as well as the methods that he employed in performing an audit or other investigations.
   d. His opinion is not warranted by material facts and documents.
2. A member shall certify and warrant the truth of financial statements, and so forth, in an explicit manner only.
3. Opinions expressed by a member shall always bear his signature and underneath it the indication: "Member of IPA Institute."
4. A member shall not extend his services beyond the scope of his assignment without the client's consent.

5. Members are required to promptly pay the registration and subscription fees.

Operations of the IPA are conducted and governed by the general assembly (of members); the board of the general assembly; the Council; the auditor (of the IPA); and the Trial Board. The principal duty of the Council is to ensure the observance by members of the IPA's bylaws and to execute the decisions of the general assembly. The principal duty of the Trial Board is to determine whether a member is liable to expulsion for specified violations of the rules of the organization.

Auditing Standards of IPA. The April 1972 edition of the IPA's auditing standards numbers seven pages and states that, as prototypes for these, the U.S., British, and German professions' standards have been used (adapted in some respects to conform to requirements of Greek laws). The standards include the following:

- *Personal–Professional Standards*–Very similar to the three general standards of the AICPA.
- *Standards of Work*–Very similar to the three standards of field work of the AICPA, with the standard added that a member of IPA cannot have more than six assistants under his supervision.
- *Standards of Reporting*–Very similar to those of the AICPA in addition to which an IPA member's report has to include a paragraph, when applicable, to the effect that the entity audited complied with the requirements of applicable laws (e.g., the Corporation Act).

Foreign Public Accounting Firms

These are about ten in number with total professional staff of about one hundred twenty persons. The clientele of these firms necessarily consists of clients not required by law to retain SOL. Except for the top administrative posts of these firms, 90 percent of their staff consists of Greeks who have received their professional training from these firms.

Accounting Principles and Practices Imposed by the Corporation Act of 1920

(As codified by Legislative Decree 174, in 1963)

Neither IPA nor SOL have yet published pronouncements specifically relating to accounting principles or rules. Such published rules as are available are contained in the Corporation Act of 1920 of which the more significant are described below.

Accounting Principles

The Corporation Act states certain "principles of valuation" which must be followed. The following are examples:

1. Inventories and securities are to be stated at the lower of cost or market.
2. Investments in the following shall be shown at cost:
   a. Bonds of the Greek government and its instrumentalities.
   b. Debentures issued by Greek corporations.
   c. Debentures issued by the National Bank of Greece.
   d. Greek corporation bonds secured by a mortgage, collateral, and so forth.
3. Fixed assets will be shown at cost, including cost of improvements, less accumulated depreciation, which is to be provided in proportion to the wear and tear of the company's assets and the probable duration of their use.
4. Uncollectible claims (accounts receivable) are to be written off and doubtful claims shown at their estimated realizable value.
5. Debentures issued by the company are to be shown as liabilities at their redemption price; the difference between this price and the issue price may be deferred and written off over the life of the debentures.

Form and Content of Financial Statements

The act prescribes the form of financial statements in some detail. A summary of these requirements is as follows:

Balance Sheet

Assets Side:

Fixed assets

Stated by main captions, including intangibles, investments, and long-term receivables

Current assets

Inventories (by main classifications)

Circulating assets-current receivables, securities, prepaid expenses

Available assets

Cash in banks and on hand

Accumulated deficit from operations

Liabilities Side:

Capital and reserves

Stated by main captions, including surplus from revaluation, provisions for possible decline in value of assets not shown as deductions from the appropriate items, and provisions for contingent liabilities

Obligations

Stated by main captions, e.g., long-term debt (maturing after one year), short-term debt, dividends payable, and income of the following year

Retained earnings

Contingent assets and liabilities

Profit and Loss ("Results of the Year"). This statement must follow the balance sheet, be complete and clear, and show the actual profits and losses sustained. The items to be shown separately are stated hereunder:

Gross profit after deducting cost of goods sold

Less

Administrative expenses

Finance charges

Selling expenses of goods and services

Profit from normal operations of the company

Add or deduct

Income from other businesses

Interest payable

Abnormal benefits or profits

Balance

Less

Abnormal charges

Losses or provisions not includible in cost of sales

Balance

Less income tax

Profit and loss for the year ("Results of the Year")

Losses accruing during the year must be charged to profit and loss of that year, and must be estimated if not exactly known. Special losses, by permission of the Ministry of Commerce, may be deferred and written off in amounts equivalent to one-third of the succeeding annual profits. During the period of write-off, dividends may not exceed 5 percent on the paid-up share capital, and if the period of write-off extends beyond five years, dividend payments will not be continued.

The act then states that the account "Results of the Year" (profit and loss account) will be followed by a schedule showing the way net profits were appropriated. There should appear therein the balance of undistributed profits or losses of preceding years as an addition to or reduction from the aggregate of the net profits for the closing year.

The above requirements as to statement presentation are effective beginning with the year 1963.

Other Provisions Affecting Statement Presentation

1. The balance sheet and results of the year are to be prepared in comparative form.
2. Liens on fixed assets are to be described as to nature and extent.
3. Amounts due from shareholders on account of subscriptions to capital stock, and amounts due from directors, are to be shown separately.
4. Account titles in financial statements must clearly indicate their contents; the accounts must contain only like items, and asset and liability items, whether alike or not, may not be offset one against the other.
5. The accounts representing accumulated depreciation of fixed assets or long-term obligations will be deducted from the related items.
6. Administration expenses will not be shown as assets on the balance sheet, except that research expenses and organization expenses may be so treated if, by company statute or resolution of the general meeting, they are to be amortized over a period not exceeding ten years.
7. If a company has issued no par value or founders' shares, this fact must be stated on the balance sheet.
8. There are special requirements as to items to be shown in the financial statements of insurance companies.
9. Banks, commercial and similar enterprises may arrange their assets on the balance sheet in order of liquidity.
10. A public company with branches must prepare combined financial statements after adjustment for intra-company balances.

Consolidated Financial Statements

There is no requirement under Greek company law to prepare consolidated financial statements of a parent company and its subsidiary companies.

Statutory Reserve

Article 44 of the Corporation Act provides that at least one-twentieth of the net profits should be deducted annually for the formation of a statutory reserve, until such reserve equals at least one-third of the share capital. This reserve may only be used to absorb a deficit in the profit and loss account prior to the payment of any dividends. This applies to both corporations and limited liability companies.

Requirements for Listing Securities on the Stock Exchange and Public Sale of Securities

While there are requirements for financial statements to be furnished in connection with stock exchange listings and prospectuses, the provisions of the law are general in scope. For the convenience of its members, SOL has issued "technical notes" on this subject, which lists items that it believes should be dealt with in reports for this purpose.

India

India

As of December 1972

Significant developments since the preparation of this chapter are presented by country, in the section entitled Addenda.

Forms of Business Organization

Business in India may be carried on in any of the forms of organization generally found in other countries: the sole proprietorship, the partnership, the private company, the public company, and the branch of a company incorporated abroad. Many government-owned enterprises operate as limited companies. Company legislation is fundamentally based on British law, but there are important differences and, in general, the Indian Companies Act of 1956 is far more restrictive and comprehensive.

There are specific regulations that apply to banks, insurance companies, cooperative societies, and electric utilities.

Foreign investors, with the approval of the Indian government, may organize an Indian company or participate in an existing one, or may open a branch. In the case of a new enterprise, the prospective investors must first obtain approval for the project in accordance with the requirements established by the Industries (Development and Regulation) Act of 1951. The establishment of an industrial undertaking in India may also involve obtaining (a) approval of the Reserve Bank of India under the Foreign Exchange Regulation Act of 1947, (b) an approval of the central government under the Monopolies and Restrictive Trade Practices

Act of 1969, (c) a certificate of incorporation under the Indian Companies Act of 1956, (d) permission of the Controller of Capital Issues for the issue of capital, and (e) a license for the import of capital equipment and machinery under the Imports and Exports (Control) Act of 1947.

Companies—General

Companies may be unlimited, limited by guarantee, or limited by shares.

A company having the liability of its members limited by the memorandum (articles of incorporation) to such amounts as the members may respectively undertake to contribute in the event of liquidation is a company limited by guarantee.

Companies limited by shares are those in which the liability of the members is limited by the memorandum to the amount of the shares subscribed, and may be private or public, depending on the limitations on the number of shareholders and on the sale of its shares, as hereinafter explained. In the case of companies limited by shares or by guarantee, the name of the company must end with the word "Limited" or with the abbreviation "Ltd.," except where the central government permits otherwise. In the case of private companies, the word "Private" must also be used before "Ltd."

In order to obtain a certificate of incorporation, all companies must submit to the registrar of the corresponding state copies of the memorandum and articles of association (bylaws) and a declaration by an advocate, attorney, pleader, chartered accountant, director, manager, or secretary of the company that all requirements of the Companies Act of 1956, have been complied with. A public company has to comply with certain other formalities before it obtains a certificate for commencement of business.

The capital may be represented by common and preferred shares, called "equity shares" and "preference shares," respectively. A company may issue shares at a discount only under certain conditions, including the following: (a) the shares must be of a class already issued and (b) the amount of the discount (not to exceed 10 percent) must be authorized by a resolution passed at a general stockholders' meeting and be approved by the court. The central government, however, may permit a higher rate in certain cases.

The board of directors must appoint the auditors within one month of the date of registration of the company, failing which, the company in a general meeting may make the first appointment. The same or other auditors must be appointed at every annual general meeting thereafter. If this requirement is not fulfilled, the central government may appoint a person to fill the vacancy. When a company changes its auditor, the new auditor is required to inform the registrar within 30 days as to whether or not he accepts the appointment.

The remuneration of the auditors is fixed by the authority appointing them, that is, the board of directors, the shareholders, or the central government, as the case may be. The shareholders of some companies at the annual general meeting authorize the directors to fix the remuneration of the auditors.

Within 60 days from the annual general meeting, the company must file with the registrar its annual return containing the particulars specified in Schedule V of the Companies Act of 1956, and signed by a director and the manager or the secretary. If there is no manager or secretary, then it must be signed by two directors including the managing director, if any. The particulars specified in Schedule V include the following:

1. The address of the company's registered office.
2. Situation of foreign registers of members and debenture holders, if any.
3. Summary of share capital and debentures.
4. Particulars of indebtedness.
5. List of past and present members and debenture holders.
6. Particulars of past and present directors, managers, and secretaries.

The return must be accompanied by a certificate signed by the same two persons, affirming, in part, that—

1. The return states the facts as they stood on the date of the annual general meeting.
2. Since the date of the last return, all issues and transfers of shares and debentures have been properly recorded.
3. In the case of a private company, no invitations to the public for subscription of shares or debentures have been extended and, where its members are more than 50, the excess is represented by employees or former employee members.

The financial statements, the auditor's report, and the board's report must be filed within 30 days of the annual general meeting.

In the case of a private company, copies of the balance sheet must be filed separately from the copies of the profit and loss account, since the law establishes that no person other than a member of the company concerned will be entitled to inspect or obtain copies of the profit and loss account of private companies.

For public companies, a shareholders' meeting must be held within a period beginning not less than one month and ending not more than six months from the date of commencement of business, which is called the "statutory meeting." A "statutory report" must be delivered to every shareholder not later than 21 days before the date of the meeting, containing, among other information, the status of the capital issued and paid; an abstract of receipts and disbursements up to a date within seven days of the date of the report; and the names, addresses, and occupations of the directors and the auditors, and of the manager and the secretary, if any.

Annual general meetings must be held every year. The first annual general meeting may be held at any time within eighteen months of incorporation and also within nine months of the close of the first financial period. Subsequent meetings must be held within fifteen months of each other and also within six months of the close of the financial year, unless an extension is granted by the registrar.

Any director of a company who is concerned or has an interest directly or indirectly in any contract or arrangement entered or to be entered into by that company must disclose the nature of his interests at a meeting of the board of directors. Such contracts must be entered in a "Register of Contracts."

Permission by the board of directors is also required for certain types of contracts in which a director has an interest.

Private Companies

The number of members of a private company must be at least two but is limited to fifty (excluding employees and former employees who became members while in the employment of the company), and there must be at least two directors. The articles of association must restrict the rights of members to transfer their shares and prohibit any invitation to the public to subscribe for any shares or debentures of the company. Apart from these restrictions, the Companies Act requires that, to retain the privileges of a private company, the shareholdings in its paid-up capital, by one or more bodies corporate, shall not exceed 25 percent. There are certain exceptions to this rule, the more important of which are as follows:

1. If the entire share capital is held by one or more foreign bodies corporate (a body corporate includes domestic as well as foreign corporations while the term "company" refers only to Indian companies).
2. If the entire share capital is held by a single (Indian) private company and one nominee.
3. If each of the companies holding shares is itself a private company with no body-corporate members, provided the total number of the

individual shareholders of the private company and its shareholding companies is not more than 50.

Private companies other than subsidiaries of public companies enjoy certain privileges, and fewer formalities are required than those applicable to public companies. The distinctions between private and public companies in India are similar to those existing between the corresponding entities in the United Kingdom.

Public Companies

A public company does not have the limitations of a private company and may be formed by seven or more persons and must have at least three directors. The Companies Act of 1956, permits the company to fix the term of appointment of up to one-third of the total number of its directors, subject to the other provisions of the act. The remaining two-thirds must be persons who, in order of seniority, will retire by rotation at each annual general meeting.

The act establishes the overall managerial remuneration payable to directors, managing directors, and managers of public companies at 11 percent of its net profits (as computed under the statute), exclusive of the fees paid to directors for attendance at board meetings. A minimum remuneration up to 50,000 rupees may be allowed by the government in any loss year or whenever profits are inadequate. The central government may authorize an increase of this minimum where satisfactory evidence is furnished that the amount is insufficient for the effective management of the business.

There are smaller limits of remuneration for each of the categories of management personnel within the overall limit of 11 percent. In the case of directors, additional remuneration may be sanctioned by a special resolution of the company with respect to nonmanagerial services, but no such resolution is required for appointment as a legal or technical adviser.

The Companies Act has placed several restrictions on public companies in granting loans to their directors and associates and in making intercorporate loans and intercorporate investments. Such companies are required to obtain the previous approval of the central government before—

1. Making loans to a director of the company or of its holding company or any of the director's relatives or partners, or giving any guarantee, or providing any security in connection with a loan made by any other person to, or to any other person by, a director of the company or of its holding company or any of the director's relatives or partners.

2. Making loans to a private company in which a director is a director

or member or to a company at least 25 percent of whose voting power is controlled by the directors of the lending company.

3. Making other intercorporate loans and intercorporate investments beyond certain prescribed limits.

Exceptions from these restrictions are the loans or investments made by a banking company or by a holding company to or in its subsidiary.

Branch of a Foreign Corporation

The foreign corporation must first obtain approval of the central government and file, with the Registrar of Joint-Stock Companies at New Delhi and the registrar of the state where its principal office will be located, duly legalized copies of the certificate of incorporation and bylaws, a complete list of its directors, and the name and address of one or more persons resident in the country who have been authorized to represent the corporation. Copies of the annual financial statements of the head office, as well as of the branch, must be submitted to the registrar together with the reports required of public companies in accordance with the act, but the central government may waive this requirement or modify it upon request of the branch. Such waivers have been granted in very few cases. Foreign corporations with major business activities confined to India are, however, permitted to file the annual financial statements (of their head office) recast in the "Indian" form (as given in Schedule VI of the Companies Act) instead of their Indian branch accounts. Several provisions of the act do not relate to branches of foreign corporations, and the act is far less stringent with regard to such branches.

Partnerships

The Companies Act of 1956, provides that a partnership that is organized for the purpose of profits and has more than twenty partners must register as a company under the act. If the partnership is in the banking business, it must register if the number of partners exceeds ten.

Business Records

The Companies Act of 1956 states that every company must keep proper accounting records with respect to (1) all sums of money received and expended, (2) all sales and purchases, including inventory records, and (3) the assets and liabilities. They must also keep minute books, shareholders' registers, and so forth. The books must be maintained adequately in order to give a true and fair view of the affairs of the company and must be retained for a period of not less than eight years; however, for income tax purposes, the period of assessment can be extended up to seventeen years in certain circumstances.

Under the act, the government has the power to direct any class of companies engaged in production, processing, manufacturing, or mining activities to keep prescribed details of utilization of material and labor and other items of cost, and the power to require that accounts of such costs be audited in addition to, and independently of, the company's regular audit.

Such details have been prescribed for several classes of companies, for example, those engaged in the production of tires and tubes, cement, and so forth.

The Accounting Profession

The Chartered Accountant

The chartered accountant in India is the equivalent of the U.S. CPA. The Companies Act of 1956 establishes that every company, private and public, must appoint auditors and that only chartered accountants within the meaning of the Chartered Accountants Act of 1949 can qualify for such appointment. The Companies Act specifically disqualifies the following persons as auditors:

1. A body corporate.
2. An officer or employee of the company.
3. A partner or any person in the employment of an officer or employee of the company.
4. A person indebted to the company or guaranteeing or securing others' indebtedness to the company in excess of 1,000 rupees.
5. Anyone who has been disqualified on the basis of any of the above circumstances, as auditor of a company or body corporate, which is that company's subsidiary or holding company or subsidiary of that company's holding company.

The Chartered Accountants Act of 1949 provides for the registration of all accountants who have passed the required examinations, which are three in number—the preliminary, the intermediate, and the final; and who have completed the apprenticeship period, either as an articled clerk or as an audit clerk, of four and six years, respectively. Reduction of one year in the prescribed period of training is granted to the persons who pass the intermediate examination held by the Institute of Chartered Accountants of India at their first appearance and had previously secured a minimum grade of 50 percent at their first appearance in a degree examination (a person who passes a degree examination is called a graduate) with accountancy and auditing as subjects, or 60 percent in any other degree examination, or 50 percent in a postgraduate degree examination, having earlier passed the degree examination with accountancy and auditing as subjects. A person who passes the intermediate examination at the first appearance with a grade of 60 percent is also eligible for a reduction of one year in the prescribed period of training. A person may serve his period of training partly as an audit clerk and partly as an articled clerk. An articled or audit clerk may serve a part or the whole of the last year of the prescribed period of practical training in a financial, commercial, or industrial undertaking whose total assets are not less than 5,000,000 rupees. A person who has been granted remission of one year in the prescribed period of training may undergo such training for six months only in the last year of training.

To be admitted to the preliminary examination of the Institute, the applicant must have passed the intermediate examination at any of the prescribed universities or an examination recognized by the central government as an equivalent. A graduate or a candidate who has passed the national diploma in commerce examination held by the All India Council for Technical Education or a person who has secured a minimum grade of 50 percent in all the papers at one sitting in the diploma in rural services examination conducted by the National Council of Rural Higher Education is exempted from passing the preliminary examination. To qualify for admission to the intermediate examination, the candidate must have passed, or been exempted from passing, the preliminary examination and, in addition, must have completed 18 months of service under articles or 24 months of service as an audit clerk. A candidate who has secured the required marks in his degree examination, which may make him eligible for reduction of one year in the prescribed period of training, may take the intermediate examination six months earlier with permission of the Institute. Every candidate must produce a certificate from the head of the coaching organization (described later). The final examination may be taken not less than nine months after passing the intermediate examination and the candidate must be serving his last 12 months as an articled or audit clerk and have obtained a certificate from the head of the coaching organization.

The professional coaching course offered by the Institute of Chartered Accountants of India has been patterned after the correspondence courses used in other countries and especially those in the United States. The entire program presently consists of about sixty test papers, including the following subjects: accounting, cost accounting, statistics, taxation, auditing, company law, mercantile law, general commercial knowledge, and economics. Attempts to consolidate the courses offered at the universities and the Institute's course have not as yet been successful.

The preliminary examination covers English, bookkeeping, elements of economics and modern administration, commercial arithmetic, and commercial geography. The intermediate examination covers accounting, statistics, cost accounting, auditing, mercantile and company law, and general commercial knowledge. The final examination is divided into two groups comprising papers on advanced accounting, auditing, taxation, cost accounting, management accounting, law, and economics. The passing grade in the examinations is 40 percent in each paper, with an average of 50 percent for all papers. A student can appear in or pass the two groups of the final examination separately, taking one group at a time.

To be an articled clerk or an audit clerk, the individual must be 16 years of age and be either a graduate (a person who has passed any degree examination in science, arts, or commerce), hold the National Diploma of Commerce, or have passed the preliminary examination of the Institute of Chartered Accountants of India. He must register as a student for the course given by the Institute. No premium is payable by him to his principal for being admitted as an articled or audit clerk.

The chartered accountants' regulations provide that only associate and fellow members of the Institute who are in practice may engage articled clerks. The number of articled clerks, which a chartered accountant in practice may engage, varies according to the number of years of his practice as shown below:

	Number of articled clerks that can be engaged*
An associate in practice for three years	1
A fellow in practice for five years	2
A fellow in practice for seven years	3
A fellow in practice for ten years	4
A fellow in practice for fifteen years	5

* Plus an additional articled clerk who has secured marks of at least 60 percent in a degree examination.

The privilege of taking one articled clerk has also been extended to some other members of the Institute who should be full-time employees or partners of a chartered accountant in practice entitled to take an articled clerk or of a firm in which such chartered accountant is a partner.

The whole system of articleship and training, together with the syllabus of the examinations, is currently being reviewed by the Council of the Institute of Chartered Accountants of India. Proposals for raising the standards for entry into the profession are also being considered.

The Institute has also been conducting a postgraduate course on management accountancy to equip its members with specialized knowledge about management accounting techniques. The course is optional for qualified chartered accountants and is divided into two parts: Part I (Theoretical Test) and Part II (Practical Training). In the theoretical test, candidates have to sit for four papers covering management accounting, management and organization structure, and economic and management policies. In the practical part, the candidates have to undergo training for two years in an organization approved by the Council and, on completion of the training, submit a thesis on an approved subject. Finally the candidates have to appear for an interview on the thesis. Candidates are entitled to use the letters "DMA" after their names on passing both parts.

Functions of the Chartered Accountant

The chartered accountant examines and reports upon financial statements of business enterprises. Under the Companies Act of 1956, every company, private and public, formed under its provisions must appoint an auditor who is a member of the Institute of Chartered Accountants of India.

The chartered accountant advises clients on tax matters, prepares returns, and represents clients before the tax authorities.

He provides management services of various kinds for his clients and undertakes special investigations for specific purposes on behalf of managements or for government departments. He may act as liquidator of a company. He may do the work of the secretary of a company, act as registrar and transfer agent of its shares and debentures, and establish valuations for shares, especially of private companies for estate duty, for sale and other purposes.

The Institute of Chartered Accountants

The Institute was organized in 1949 by the Chartered Accountants Act of that year, and the Chartered Accountants Regulations were subsequently issued. Previously, only persons holding certificates issued by the government in accordance with the regulations of the Indian Accounting Board of 1932 were authorized to do audits of public companies. The 1949 act gave complete autonomy to the profession and placed its entire regulation and supervision in the hands of the Institute, which was made an accrediting body as well as a professional society. However, the central government made two reservations (1) it would have representation in the Council of the Institute, which was created under the act to manage the affairs of the Institute and exercise control over it and (2) would keep also for itself the final approval of any regulations of the Council. The Council is composed of twenty-one fellow chartered accountants and six other persons nominated by the central government.

The Institute is formed by two classes of members: associates and fellows, referred to as associate chartered accountants (ACA) and fellow chartered accountants (FCA). Both are entitled to vote in the elections of the Council, but only fellows may be elected. A fellow is a member who has been in public practice for at least five years.

The membership of the Institute is about fourteen thousand chartered accountants. *The Chartered Accountant* is the monthly journal published by the Institute. Membership in the chartered institutes in the United Kingdom will, in certain circumstances, confer the right of election to membership in the Institute of Chartered Accountants in India, since the Indian qualification is recognized in the United Kingdom, and members of the Institute may practice in the United Kingdom after obtaining specific approval of the Board of Trade.

The Chartered Accountants' Act of 1949 provides that, unless similar reciprocity is granted to members of the Indian Institute to practice in another country, members of institutes in that country may not become members of the Indian Institute or practice in India.

Code of Ethics

The Institute of Chartered Accountants of India has issued a code of conduct and the Chartered Accountants Act of 1949 also cites various acts or omissions as "professional misconduct," which may provoke an inquiry by the disciplinary committee and the Council of the Institute. The reports of the committee, findings of the Council, and judgments of the high courts are published in the Institute's journal under the section "Disciplinary Matters."

Some of the more important acts mentioned in the Chartered Accountants Act as constituting professional misconduct are (condensed) as follows:

1. Payment of commission or brokerage to any person other than a member of the Institute, or acceptance of part of profits of the professional work of a lawyer, auctioneer, broker, or other agent who is not a member of the Institute.
2. Securing professional business in an unethical manner, by solicitation, or improper advertising.
3. Accepting appointment as auditor, previously held by another chartered accountant, without first communicating with the latter in writing.
4. Accepting professional fees that are contingent upon the results of his employment.

5. Engaging in any business or occupation not compatible with the profession of chartered accountant, except that of director of a company of which neither he nor any of his partners is the auditor.
6. Permitting a person not a member of the Institute or a member other than his partner to sign on his behalf or on behalf of his firm any report upon financial statements.

The Companies Act provides for the imposition of a maximum fine of 1,000 rupees upon any auditor who, either in his report or in any document signed by him, willfully defaults on his duties as established by the act in section 227 (Powers and Duties of Auditors) and section 229 (Signature of Audit Report).

Institute of Cost and Works Accountants

The Institute of Cost and Works Accountants was organized as a company in 1944 by a group of industrial accountants. Later, by the Cost and Works Accountants Act of 1959, the company was replaced by the Institute as it stands at present. It has its own correspondence course and examinations, which necessarily only partially overlap with those of the Institute of Chartered Accountants.

Auditing Standards

The British influence on the Indian accounting profession is predominant. The Institute of Chartered Accountants has published A Statement on Auditing Practices, "A Guide to Company Audit," and various other statements and recommendations on matters of professional interest. The statement on auditing practices attempts to set out the practices considered to be appropriate for audit of manufacturing and trading companies. However, this statement does not attempt to prescribe either the maximum or the minimum amount of work to be performed in an audit, which will have to be decided by the auditor on the facts and circumstances of each case. "A Guide to Company Audit" also discusses, in some detail, satisfactory auditing procedures for limited companies.

General Standards

The profession in India, through its requirements for membership in the Institute and its technical assistance offered to members, advocates the same type of general standards as to training and proficiency and due care on the part of the auditor that are recognized in the United Kingdom.

Independence

The need for independence in mental attitude is recognized by the Companies Act in its list of matters that disqualify a person for appointment as an auditor. It is not considered improper for an auditor to have a financial interest (not representing a substantial interest) in a company upon which he reports.

Standards of Field Work

The standards of field work as to planning and supervision, obtaining competent evidential matter, and study and evaluation of internal control are similar to those of the United Kingdom. Although until recently the confirmation of receivables and observation of physical inventory taking were not considered generally accepted auditing procedures, the Institute of Chartered Accountants of India has recommended to the members the adoption of these practices and most of the large firms follow them.

Standards of Reporting

The requirements of reporting have been established by the Companies Act, which states that the auditor must make a report to the members of the company on every balance sheet and profit and loss account and on every other document annexed thereto. This report will state whether, in his opinion and to the best of his information and according to the explanations given to him, the said accounts give a true and fair view of the state of affairs of the company at the end of the financial year and of its profit or loss for the period then ended, and whether the accounts comply with the requirements set forth in Parts I and II of Schedule VI of the act, which relate to the form and content of the balance sheet and of the profit and loss account.

The auditor's report must also state (a) whether he has obtained all the information and explanations that, to the best of his knowledge and belief, were necessary for the purposes of his audit; (b) whether, in his opinion, proper books of account as required by law have been kept by the company so far as appears from his examination of those books, and proper returns (financial statements) adequate for the purposes of his audit have been received from branches not visited by him; (c) whether the report on the accounts of any branch office audited under section 228 by a person other than the company's auditor has been forwarded to him as required by that section and how he has dealt with the same in preparing the auditor's report; and (d) whether the company's balance sheet and profit and loss account dealt with by the report are in agreement with the books of account and returns (financial statements).

Where certain of the matters just referred to are reported in the negative or with a qualification, the auditor's report will state the reason for such negative statement or qualification.

Section 228 of the Companies Act of 1956, requires the accounts of a branch office of a company to be audited. It lays down the qualifications and powers of branch auditors and empowers the central government to make rules for exempting any branch office from the requirements of compulsory audit.

Report of Board of Directors

The Companies Act specifically requires the report of the board of directors to cover the following: (1) the state of the company's affairs (in addition to the financial statements, the current practice is to narrate the significant aspects of the company's operations during the period under review); (2) the amounts, if any, that it proposes to carry to any reserves in the balance sheet; (3) the amount of dividends recommended to be paid; and (4) any material changes and commitments affecting the financial position of the company that have occurred between the date of the balance sheet and the date of the report.

The directors must include comments on any material changes that took place during the period if they consider that such comments will not be harmful to the business of the company or its subsidiaries. These comments would refer to changes in the following: (a) the nature of the company's business or of its subsidiaries and (b) the industry or trade in which the company operates.

The report should contain adequate explanations regarding every reservation, qualification, or adverse remark contained in the auditor's report.

A copy of the balance sheet, together with the profit and loss account, the auditors' report, and every other document required by law to be attached to the balance sheet, must be sent to every holder of shares or debentures not less than 21 days before the date of the annual general meeting or, in the case of private nonsubsidiary companies, the notice period specified in the company's articles.

Accounting Principles and Practices

Form and Content of Financial Statements

The Companies Act prescribes the form and contents of the balance sheet and the contents of the profit and loss account. The principle of extensive disclosure is always present in the rules of statement presentation set forth in Schedule VI of the act, which applies to all companies excepting insurance companies, banks, and electric utilities, which are governed by special acts. The central government may exempt any company from compliance with any of these requirements if the exemption is necessary in the "public interest"; very few companies have been so exempted.

The footnotes to the financial statements are considered to be part of the financial statements, and the principle of extensive disclosure can be satisfied either by giving the required information in the body of the financial statements or in a separate schedule to form part of the financial statements.

A statement of source and application of funds is not considered to be a basic financial statement and is not required to be included by the auditor in his report. Only a few companies publish this statement for the information of their shareholders.

Statement Presentation. The balance sheet presentation is the usual type followed by British companies showing capital and liabilities on the left side and fixed assets, investments, and current assets, in that order, on the right side. Provision has been made in the Companies Act according to which a company can prepare its balance sheet in any form approved by the government, and a number of companies have obtained government approval for preparing their balance sheets in vertical form. Footnotes disclosing claims against the company, uncalled liability on shares partly paid for and held by the company, fixed dividends in arrears, estimated amount of unexecuted contracts, and other amounts for which the company is contingently liable must be appended to the balance sheet.

Comparative Financial Statements. The Companies Act states that the balance sheet and the profit and loss statement must show the corresponding figures for the preceding period.

Consolidated Financial Statements. Consolidated financial statements are not generally prepared, but the Companies Act requires that the balance sheet of the holding company must be accompanied by the financial statements, the boards' report and the auditors' report of each of its subsidiaries, all prepared in accordance with the requirements of the act. Also, a statement must be attached showing the extent of the parent's interest in each subsidiary and the profits or losses not included in the parent's accounts. The lapse of time between the balance sheet dates of the holding company and the subsidiaries cannot exceed six months. When the financial years do not coincide, the following information must be shown in respect of each subsidiary:

1. Whether, during that lapse of time, there has been any change in the holding company's interest in the subsidiary.

2. Whether, during the same period, any material changes have occurred in respect of fixed assets, investments, or loans of the subsidiary.

Current Assets, Loans, and Advances

Current assets include interest accrued on investments, stores and spare parts, loose tools, stock-in-trade, works in progress, sundry debtors (secured, unsecured, and doubtful; the provision for bad debts must be deducted and any excess provision shown as reserve or surplus) and cash and bank balances (current, call, and deposit accounts must be segregated). Loans and advances must be broken down as to the following: advances and loans to subsidiaries, bills of exchange, advances receivable in cash or in kind or for value to be received (taxes, insurance, and so forth), balances with customs authorities, and so forth. Amounts due from the directors or other officers of the company and other companies under the same management have to be separately stated.

If, in the opinion of the directors, any of the current assets do not have a value on realization in the ordinary course of business equal to the book value, the fact should be stated.

Investments

These must be properly segregated and the basis of valuation described. Additions to and deductions from investments must be disclosed, except in the case of investment companies. A list of investments should be attached to the balance sheet showing the names of the issuers, stating separately the total investment in companies in the same group. If the shares are quoted on a stock exchange, the market value of such shares on the date of the balance sheet must also be stated.

Fixed Assets

The following captions must be shown separately: goodwill, land, buildings, leaseholds, railway sidings, plant and machinery, furniture and fixtures, development of property, patents, trademarks and designs, livestock, and vehicles. Fixed assets must be stated at cost (except as stated in the following paragraph), and current additions and deductions must be shown as well as the accrued (accumulated) depreciation. It is established that when the original cost (at the promulgation of the act) could not be ascertained without unreasonable expense and delay, the valuation shown by the books, less the accumulated depreciation, could be used, and the proceeds of any subsequent sales shown as a deduction.

Restatement of fixed assets is permitted, and the credit is recorded in a capital reserve account. Depreciation on the restatement is not allowed for tax purposes. Any restatements of fixed assets must be disclosed in the financial statements for the succeeding five years.

Deferred Charges

These include—to the extent not written off—preliminary expenses, commissions, discounts, and other share and debenture issue expenses; interest paid during construction; unadjusted development expenditures; and other items.

Liabilities and Capital

The following captions must be shown separately:

1. Share capital, describing the amounts authorized, issued, subscribed, and called, for each class of shares.
2. Reserves and surplus, including premium account and profits on issue of shares. Current additions and deductions must be shown for each account. A debit balance in the profit and loss account, if any, must be deducted from the uncommitted reserves. The act provides that when preference shares are redeemed the amount equivalent to their par value must be transferred to the capital redemption reserve fund out of profit and loss account or uncommitted reserves.
3. Capital and revenue reserves have to be shown separately. A capital reserve is defined as one not available for distribution through the profit and loss account. A revenue reserve means any reserve other than a capital reserve, e.g., general reserve.
4. Secured loans, including interest accrued and due. Outstanding debentures, and loans and advances from banks, subsidiaries, directors, and so forth, must be shown separately and the nature of the security must be specified in each case.
5. Unsecured loans, including interest accrued and due, have the same disclosure requirements as secured loans.

Current Liabilities and Provisions

Current liabilities comprise acceptances, sundry creditors, amounts payable to subsidiaries, advance payments received, unclaimed dividends, interest accrued but not due on loans, and so forth. Provisions include tax provisions, proposed dividends, employees' pensions, insurance, and so forth.

Provisions vs. Reserves

The difference between a reserve and a provision has a special significance under the Companies Act. The expression "provision" means any amount written off or retained by way of providing for depreciation, renewals or diminution in value of assets, or retained by way of providing for any known liability, the amount of which cannot be determined with substantial accuracy. The expression "reserve" relates to an appropriation or earmarking of profits for purposes other than "provisions" or for known liability. Examples of reserves are general reserve, dividend reserve, and so forth.

Statement of Profit and Loss

The act does not specify any form in which the profit and loss account must be presented. However, the profit and loss account must disclose every material item, including receipts and expenses in respect of non-recurring transactions or transactions of an exceptional nature, as well as any material effect of changes in the bases of accounting. The following, among other items, must always be disclosed:

1. The turnover (i.e., the aggregate amount of net sales).
2. Commission paid to sole or other selling agents.
3. Brokerage and discount on sales, other than the usual trade discount.
4. In the case of manufacturing concerns, the purchases of raw materials and the opening and closing of inventories of goods produced. Also in respect of each class of goods manufactured, detailed quantitative information in regard to the following:
    a. The licensed capacity.
    b. The installed capacity.
    c. The actual production.
    d. Raw materials purchased or acquired.
    e. The opening and closing stock of goods produced.
5. In the case of other concerns, the gross income derived from the different operations.
6. In the case of all concerns having work in progress, the value of work completed at the beginning and at the end of the accounting period.
7. The amounts provided for depreciation, renewals, or diminution in value of fixed assets.

8. The amount of interest on the company's debentures and other fixed loans, showing separately any interest paid to managing director and manager.
9. Income tax provision.
10. The amounts provided for repayment of shares and debentures.
11. The aggregate, if material, of amounts set or proposed to be set aside to reserves but not including provisions made to meet any specific liability, contingency, or commitment known at the date of the balance sheet.
12. The aggregate, if material, of any amounts drawn from such reserves.
13. Provisions for specific liabilities, contingencies, or commitments and the amounts withdrawn from such provisions as are no longer required.
14. Expenses in connection with stores and spare parts; power and fuel; rent; repairs; salaries, wages, and bonuses; and number of employees of the company who are in receipt of 2,000 rupees or more per month; contributions to provident and other funds (a provident fund is a retirement benefit fund, the benefits being paid to the employee in one lump sum on retirement); workmen and staff welfare expenses; insurance; taxes other than on income; and miscellaneous expenses.
15. Income from other sources, such as trade investments; other investments and interest must be segregated.
16. Detailed information of payments made to various categories of managerial personnel, i.e., directors and managers.
17. Dividends from subsidiary companies.
18. Payments to auditors, as for professional services, expenses or any other capacity separately.

Depreciation

The Companies Act requires a company to provide a minimum amount of depreciation in the accounts before any dividends can be declared. This minimum can be computed either by applying rates allowable for tax purposes to the book value of each depreciable asset or by reference to the number of years for which depreciation allowances are given for tax purposes before a specific residual value is reached.

Tax-Effect Accounting

Tax-effect accounting is not used in India. The amount charged in the statement of profit and loss as income tax provision represents the amount actually payable as income tax for the period.

Requirements for Public Sale of Securities

Public sale of shares or debentures must be accompanied by a prospectus. The contents of the prospectus are listed in Schedule II of the act, and include a report prepared by the auditors of the company in respect to the following:

1. Profits and losses for each of the five annual periods preceding the issue of the prospectus, distinguishing items of a nonrecurring nature. If the company has subsidiaries, in addition to this information, similar information individually as to each subsidiary or with the combined profits and losses of the subsidiaries.
2. Assets and liabilities as of the last day to which the accounts were prepared. In the case of subsidiaries, the report must be presented in any of the forms referred to above.
3. Dividends paid by the company for each class of share during the five preceding years. If no dividends were paid, this fact should be stated.

If the date of the last completed accounting period happens to be more than six months earlier than the date of the prospectus, then the prospectus must also be accompanied by an audited statement of the accounts of the period from the date of the last completed accounting period to a date within six months of the date of the issue of the prospectus showing the interim results of operations and the assets and liabilities at the end of the period.

If the proceeds of the sale of shares or debentures are to be used in the acquisition of another company, a profit and loss statement for the five preceding years and a balance sheet of the company to be acquired, of a date not prior to four months before the date of the prospectus, must be annexed. If the prospective acquisition is that of a body corporate, in addition to the aforementioned information, the report must include a statement showing the effect of the acquisition on the shareholders' equity. If the body corporate has subsidiary companies, the information referred to in (1) and (2) above must also be submitted.

A statement of the auditor's consent as expert must be made a part of the prospectus.

Requirements for Listing Securities on the Stock Exchange

There are eight stock exchanges recognized by the government under the Securities Contracts (Regulation) Act of 1956, which regulate the stock market in India. The listing regulations of all the recognized stock exchanges are now uniform, and a company that wishes to list securities for trading on any of the recognized stock exchanges must fulfill the following conditions:

1. The subscription list inviting applications for the securities offered for sale must have been kept open for at least three days.
2. The prospectus will have been advertised in the newspapers and at least 60 percent of the total issue must have been offered to the public. However, this requirement may be relaxed with the prior approval of the central government.
3. The articles must contain the following provisions prescribed by the Securities Contracts (Regulation) Act of 1956, and the rules framed thereunder:
   a. That the company shall use a common form of transfer.
   b. That the fully paid shares will be free from all lien.
   c. That there will be no forfeiture of unclaimed dividends before the claim becomes barred by law.
   d. That the option, or right to call of shares, will be exercised only by the company in general meeting.
   e. That amount paid up in advance of calls on any share may carry interest, but shall not entitle the holder to participate in a dividend subsequently declared.
4. The company must execute a listing agreement.

The listing agreement must be accompanied by a number of documents, of which the following are of interest to accountants: (a) the prospectus and (b) the directors' reports and audited accounts for the last five years or such shorter period for which accounts have been made up.

Israel

Israel

As of October 1973

Forms of Business Organization

The forms of business organization in Israel are the company, the partnership, the cooperative society, and the sole proprietorship.

Overseas corporations may operate in Israel through branches registered as foreign companies in terms of the Companies Ordinance or through local subsidiary companies.

Companies (General)

The "company" is comparable to the U.S. corporation, although the characteristics of the two are not strictly parallel. In terms of the 1929 Companies Ordinance, as amended, two forms of companies are defined, public and private companies. The liability of shareholders may be limited by shares, limited by guarantee, or unlimited. The most common form found, almost to the complete exclusion of the others, is that of the company with liability limited by shares.

In a company limited by shares, the liability of the shareholder is limited to the par value of the subscribed shares (the no-par-value share does not exist in Israel), but the shareholder is fully liable to the company for any unpaid portion of his subscription.

A company cannot commence operations before registration with the Registrar of Companies. Together with the application for registration, there must be lodged, among other things, the memorandum and articles of association of the company.

The requirement for the appointment of an auditor is of general scope, binding both public and private companies; all companies are also bound to lay before the shareholders audited annual financial statements.

The Public Company. A public company must have at least seven shareholders. Transfer of shares is entirely unlimited, unless otherwise provided in the company's articles. There must be at least two directors.

The articles of many companies, especially those that have issued securities to the public, provide for all or some of the following bodies, and define their spheres of authority: the board of directors, chairman of the board, executive committee, managing director, general manager, secretary, and similar officials. A director need hold no shares, unless so required by the company's articles.

A public company is required to submit balance sheets to the Registrar of Companies.

Companies that have issued securities to the public are bound by the 1968 Securities Act, in addition to the requirements of the Companies Ordinance (apart from certain of its provisions, which do not apply to such companies).

The Private Company. The number of shareholders in a private company may be from two to fifty. However, employees holding shares are not taken into account in ascertaining the maximum number of shareholders.

The number of directors is prescribed by the company's articles; there may be a single director.

In addition to the limitation on the number of members, a private company must include, in its articles, provisions (1) limiting the right to transfer its shares and (2) forbidding any invitation to the public to subscribe to shares or debentures of the company.

The advantages of the private company, which is popular both among local business interests and with overseas investors in Israel, derive in part from the minimal legal requirements laid down in the Companies Ordinance. The company need not submit its financial statements to the Registrar of Companies.

Partnerships

The 1930 Partnerships Ordinance requires the registration of commercial partnerships. The number of partners is limited to ten. In addition to general partnerships, the Partnerships Ordinance permits the registration of limited partnerships (in which some of the partners may have limited liability). The Partnerships Ordinance has no requirements as to financial statements.

Cooperative Societies

There are many cooperative societies of agriculturalists and consumers, as well as in transportation, finance, and other fields of endeavor. The 1933 Cooperative Societies Ordinance, as amended, calls for the annual preparation of financial statements, audited by a certified public accountant or by special supervisory societies having as their object the audit of cooperative societies. In practice most of these supervisory societies are managed by CPAs. A new Cooperative Societies Law is in advanced stages of preparation.

Business Records

All companies and cooperative societies are bound by the relevant laws to keep proper books of account.

Regulations under the income tax and other fiscal laws require the keeping of accounts by a wide range of sole proprietorships and partnerships, such as wholesalers, building contractors, and others.

The Accounting Profession

General

The profession has been in existence in Israel for some fifty years. In 1931, a professional association was founded, which developed into the Institute of Certified Public Accountants in Israel.

In 1955, the Auditors' Law was promulgated, regulating and broadening the legal basis of the profession.

The law provides that only a person licensed as a CPA may engage in auditing practice. In accordance with the law, an Auditors' Council was established, responsible for the licensing of CPAs. The requirements for the obtaining of a license are a minimum age of 23 years, satisfying the examination requirements of the Auditors' Council (or obtaining exemption therefrom), and serving articles for two years.

The examinations held are the intermediate examinations, in two stages, and the final examinations, also in two stages.

In practice, most of those entering the profession study at universities or colleges. Study facilities for the profession exist at the Tel Aviv, Bar Ilan, and Haifa Universities, as well as other institutions. The university courses lead to the B.A. degree, while preparations are being made for the extension of studies to the masters level. University graduates obtain partial exemption from the examinations conducted by the council.

The Institute of Certified Public Accountants in Israel

The Institute, which is the sole professional body, comprises some 90 percent of the CPAs in Israel. During the last ten years, membership of the Institute has trebled, from 429 at the end of 1962, to 1,359 in August 1972.

The president and the central committee are chosen annually by the members in general meeting.

Heading the professional work of the Institute, which is carried out almost entirely voluntarily, is the Accounting and Auditing Board, with 17 members (in terms of the articles the minimum is 15). There are several professional committees (the committee on accounting principles and financial reporting, the committee on auditing standards and procedures, the tax committee, and others); liaison committees with the economic and commercial authorities and other bodies; and other ad hoc committees for specific professional affairs. Of late, the Institute has commenced the commissioning of special research studies on matters connected with the profession. Drafts of statements of opinion and recommendations are brought before the Board for discussion and decision.

Professional publications already produced, include the following:

1. Auditing Standards
2. Guidelines for Audit Procedures
3. Statement Concerning Qualifications and Disclaimers in the Auditor's Report
4. Principles of Financial Reporting
5. Recommendations Concerning Accounting Treatment and the Presentation in Financial Statements of Linked Accounts and Accounts in Foreign Currency
6. Statement Regarding the Accounting Treatment of Investment Grants
7. Statement Regarding the Accounting Treatment of Building Construction for Purposes of Sale and Contracting Work
8. Illustrative Financial Statements (for several types of undertakings)

The Institute publishes a monthly journal in Hebrew, containing publications of the Institute and articles on subjects of professional interest such as auditing, accounting, taxation, management, and related matters. An annual and certain professional publications have appeared in English.

In 1970, the Institute amended its bylaws to permit the admission of international associate members. International associateship is open to members in good standing of certain recognized accountancy organizations outside Israel. By August 1972, there were some two hundred members of this class. International associates are entitled to receive all the services provided by the Institute to its local members and may attend seminars and general meetings of the Institute, but are not entitled to vote or participate in elections.

Functions of the Certified Public Accountant

Auditing, being the examination of financial statements and the expression of an opinion thereon, is naturally the major function of the CPA. However, in addition, many CPAs in Israel give their clients other services related to the profession.

In 1965, the Institute published a list of these additional services including, among others, taxation services, financial and managerial consultancy, secretaryship of corporate bodies, evaluation of shares, trusteeship, receiving of property, and the winding-up of companies.

The income tax law requires that all annual returns filed by companies, partnerships, and cooperative societies be certified by a CPA as to their correctness under the income tax law and other statutes.

Ethics

In 1941, the Institute published rules of professional ethics, which were revised and amplified from time to time in the light of experience (latest review—1968).

The Auditors' Council, in 1965, published regulations concerning conduct unbecoming to the honor of the profession.

Following are some of the subjects of rules appearing in the Auditors' Law of 1955, or in the regulations mentioned above, and, usually in more amplified form, in the Institute's publication:

1. Independence
2. Observance of the standards, rules, and procedures accepted by the profession
3. Expression of opinion solely on the basis of personal examination by the public accountant, by his partner, by his employee, or by another public accountant
4. Observance of secrecy

5. Prohibition of partnership in auditing with any person not qualified as a public accountant
6. Prohibition of activity in commerce or as an agent therein
7. Prohibition of advertising

The Institute publishes its opinion from time to time on such questions of ethics as may arise.

Appointment of Auditors

The auditor of a company is appointed by the shareholders at their annual general meeting; the appointment falls for renewal annually.

The first auditor of a company may be temporarily appointed by the directors, in which case the appointment holds good until the first general meeting of the shareholders, who may then decide as to the continuation of the appointment.

Regarding the change of an auditor, there are provisions to be found in the Companies Ordinance, in the regulations under the Auditors' Law of 1955, and in the rules of professional conduct laid down by the Institute. The Companies Ordinance requires that notice of intention to propose a change in auditor reach the shareholders and the incumbent auditor a specified period before the general meeting.

The regulations and rules mentioned provide that the giving of services to the client of another auditor in any matter with which such other auditor has already commenced to deal requires prior consent of that auditor, unless such consent be unreasonably withheld.

Auditing Standards

The Institute published standards for auditing in 1971, replacing an earlier publication in 1963.

Other major publications relating to this field are—

1. Guidelines for Audit Procedures (1964) (a revised edition is under review)
2. Statement Concerning Qualifications and Disclaimers in the Auditor's Report (1968)

It is the government's intention, in consultation with the Institute, to issue standards for auditing and reporting, similar to those laid down in the Institute's publications. Government regulation in this matter, in terms of the Auditors' Law, would bind also that minority of CPAs who are not members of the Institute.

General Standards and Standards of Performance

The standards are similar to those of the AICPA, on which they were modeled.

Standards of Reporting

The accepted wording of the auditor's report in Israel is as follows:

> We have examined the Balance Sheet of .... as of .... and the Statement of Profit and Loss for the year ended on that date. Our examination was made in accordance with generally accepted auditing standards, and accordingly we have applied such auditing procedures as we considered necessary in the circumstances.
>
> In our opinion the Balance Sheet and Statement of Profit and Loss present fairly, in conformity with generally accepted accounting principles, the financial position of the Company as of .... and the results of its operations for the year ended on that date.

A third and final paragraph varies, for those companies to which the Securities Act applies, from that for other companies. In each case the paragraph refers to the relevant provisions of the law applicable.

The report does not mention the principle of consistency; however, one of the standards for reporting sets forth the following:

> The financial report will be considered to have been prepared on the basis of consistent application of accounting principles in the period reviewed as compared with that precedent thereto, unless otherwise specifically stated in the auditor's report, excluding those cases in which the auditor sanctions the change and proper disclosure of such change and its effects is made.

Qualifications and Disclaimers in Reports

The types of opinion in terms of the Institute's statement may be—

1. An unqualified opinion
2. A qualified opinion
3. A partial disclaimer of opinion
4. A general disclaimer of opinion
5. A negative opinion

In regard to the partial disclaimer, the statement reads, in part, as follows:

> Partial disclaimer is permissible where the items as to which the auditor considers it correct to disclaim opinion are not so many or so material as to cast doubt on the position presented by the financial statement taken as a whole.

Guidelines for Auditing Procedures

These guidelines, published by the Institute in 1964, cover the following subjects, among others:

1. Working papers
2. Extent of examination
3. Reporting procedures relating to accepted accounting principles
4. Proper books of account
5. Cash and banks
6. Stocks
7. Debtors and creditors
8. Fixed assets
9. Reserves and provisions
10. Profit and loss account

The above guidelines deal also with the presence of the auditor at physical inventory counts and the obtaining of confirmations from debtors and creditors.

Accounting Principles and Practices

The Institute has published guidelines for financial reporting, statements, and recommendations regarding various accounting matters, and illustrative financial statements for a number of types of enterprises.

Governmental authorities, in conjunction with the Institute, have also published guidelines for financial reporting, binding on certain types of companies, as follows:

1. Regulations concerning the presentation of financial statements in terms of the Securities Act.

2. Regulations for financial reporting by the controllers of banking and of insurance.
3. Principles for annual financial reporting by cooperative societies, in terms of the Cooperative Societies Ordinance.
4. Principles of financial reporting for government-owned companies, published by a joint committee of the Institute and the Governmental Companies Authority.
5. Regulations for financial reporting by recognized provident and pension funds.

Form and Content of Financial Statements

The currently accepted form for financial statements was developed by the Institute in the light of Israeli conditions, considerably influenced by the forms of statement used in the United States and the United Kingdom.

The two-sided form for the balance sheet is more widely used than the one-sided form. The one-sided form for the profit and loss statement, however, has become almost universal.

Assets are grouped as follows:

- Fixed assets
- Investments and long-term receivables
- Current assets
- Other assets and deferred charges

Equity and liabilities are grouped as follows:

- Capital, reserves, and surplus
- Provisions
- Long-term liabilities
- Current liabilities
- Contingent liabilities (not included in balance sheet total; normally stated in note)

The alternative presentation, in descending order of liquidity, is used by those undertakings where liquidity is significant (commerce, banks, and insurance companies) and also, to a certain extent, by manufacturing concerns.

The detail of the balance sheet groups required in terms of the Institute's rules for financial reporting, is similar to that common in the United States.

Some of the items that have to be separately shown include the following:

1. Loans to directors and employees
2. Loans to shareholders
3. Goodwill, patents, trademarks, and so forth
4. Deferred charges, by categories
5. Share capital—authorized, issued, called up and paid—by types of shares (share capital in Israel is always stated at par value)
6. Capital reserves—detailed
7. Distributable reserves and surpluses
8. Provisions—detailed (for instance, for severance compensation, future taxation, and so forth)
9. Indebtedness to banks
10. Dividends proposed or declared

Details must be given of secured debts and liabilities in foreign currency or linked thereto, or to any other basis.

The profit and loss statement must show the results of normal operations and, separately, the results of nonrecurring or extraordinary operations, as well as income and expenditure items deriving from the operations of previous years.

Items that have to be shown separately in the profit and loss statement, include the following:

- Operating turnover (sales)
- Cost of sales
- Gross profit
- Selling and general expenses
- Profit before financing expenses
- Financing expenses
- Profit after financing expenses
- Salaries and emoluments to directors
- Depreciation
- Income from investments
- Amortizations of intangible assets and deferred expenditure
- Provisions for taxes on income
- Transfers to and from the reserves of the company
- Dividends proposed or declared
- Profits earmarked for distribution of stock dividends

In regard to provisions for taxes, there must be differentiated amounts relating to previous years and transfers to provision for future taxation.

The Institute's rules for financial reporting include also directions for proper disclosure of various other items and matters.

The Companies Ordinance has a minimal number of provisions relating to the form and content of the financial statements. It may be presumed that this state of affairs will change radically with the projected new legislation for a revised companies law.

The regulations for the preparation of financial statements in terms of the Securities Act oblige issuing companies to make extensive disclosure relating to many items: investments in subsidiaries and affiliates, transactions with subsidiaries and interested parties, hidden reserves, and other matters.

The presentation of comparative figures for the preceding year is an accepted practice in Israel for the preparation of financial statements.

Although the Companies Ordinance does not require the preparation of consolidated financial statements, the practice of their preparation is encouraged by CPAs. The Institute has under discussion draft recommendations relating to consolidated financial statements.

Regulations in terms of the Securities Act require the publication of annual consolidated accounts in addition to the regular statements. In terms of these regulations, those subsidiaries must be consolidated in which the company holds over 50 percent of the issued nominal share capital or of the voting rights. However, a minority of the voting rights, or a minority of the issued share capital, are among the causes cited to justify non-consolidation of a subsidiary, subject to the prior sanction of the Securities Authority.

Pooling of Interests

The concept of "pooling of interests" is not in use in Israel.

Marketable Securities

Where marketable securities are held as current assets, they are customarily presented at lower of cost or market value, with the higher value noted.

Inventories

Inventories are presented at lower of cost or market value. The acceptable methods of determining cost are "Fifo," average and others. The "Lifo" method is not permitted for income tax purposes and is in practice, therefore, not in use, the majority of companies preferring their financial statements to be drawn up as far as possible in conformity with income tax requirements.

Allowance for Doubtful Receivables

As a general rule, this item is presented separately in the balance sheet, as a deduction from receivables. This is in accordance with the illustrative balance sheets published by the Institute.

The regulations in terms of the Securities Act provide that the amount of the allowance charged to the profit and loss statement must be disclosed; if the allowance does not relate to specific debts but is general, the method by which the amount has been arrived at must be stated.

Fixed Assets and Appraisal Surplus

The method of ascertaining cost is usually conservative. Inclusion of the interest during periods of construction and installation is permissible, provided suitable disclosure is made.

Reappraisal of fixed assets is acceptable in Israel. The main methods used are the following:

1. Revaluation by an independent appraiser on the basis of market value.
2. Adjustment of assets costs (where purchased in foreign currency) at new rates of exchange, after devaluation.
3. Adjustment of costs of buildings as per the index of building costs, and of costs of equipment locally manufactured at the general price index or some other appropriate index.

Details should be given in the financial statements as to the method used for revaluing property, the maker of the appraisal, and other relevant details.

It is customary to create a provision for future taxation applicable to the revaluation increment, depreciation on which would not normally be recognized for purposes of taxation. This provision is computed as a suitable proportion of the amount of the revaluation increment. The balance of the increment after deduction of the provision for future taxation, is shown as a capital reserve in the grouping "capital, reserves and surplus."

Severance Pay and Pension Liability

The liability is shown under provisions. The Institute has recommended that there be noted in the financial statements details of the liability for severance pay, the manner in which this has been computed, details of any arrangements with a pension fund scheme or insurance company and the amounts accumulated thereunder. The liability for severance pay, which in Israel is a legal obligation, is computed by multiplying the last monthly salary by the number of years of service.

The Securities Act regulations contain requirements which are in the main similar.

Unearned Income

It is customary to present the full amount of income received in advance in the grouping for current liabilities, either as a separate item or together with sundry balances.

Separate presentation outside that for current liabilities is made only in special cases, where the item is substantial or the period for which the income has been received is a lengthy one, and similar cases.

Hidden Reserves

The Securities Act regulations require disclosure in the financial statement of various types of hidden reserves as follows:

1. Superfluous provisions for losses or liabilities.
2. Excess depreciation of assets inconsonant with accepted methods and rates of depreciation calculation.
3. Inclusion of reserves or income in liability items.

Disclosure required includes details of the amounts added or deducted during the course of the year, balances at year end, and explanations of the circumstances.

Investment Grants

In terms of the Law for the Encouragement of Capital Investments (amendment of 1967) approved enterprises are entitled to a government grant in respect of investments in certain types of assets. The grant is computed at differing percentages of the cost of the assets. An enterprise receiving such grant has to undertake as a general rule the exporting of a certain proportion of its output, as well as to meet with certain other requirements. Depreciation allowable for income tax purposes is based on asset costs less grants received.

Accounting treatment of investment grants, as recommended by the Institute, is in the main as follows:

1. The cost of the assets acquired is reflected in the balance sheet without deduction of the grant.
2. The grant is brought into account on the accrual basis, parallel to the making of the investments on account of which grant is receivable.
3. The grant itself is to be shown separately in the balance sheet after the grouping "capital, reserves and surplus" and before the group-

ing "provisions," subject to the deduction therefrom of an amount to be transferred to provision for future taxation (in respect of the difference in future depreciation between that in the financial statements and that allowable for income tax).

4. After complete compliance with the conditions attaching to it, the balance of the grant is transferable to the grouping "capital, reserves and surplus."

Long-Term Construction Contracts

Two main methods of recording profits arising on such contracts are acceptable, namely, on the basis of the percentage of completion method or on the basis of the completed contract method, provided that consistency is maintained in the application of the method chosen. The Institute's 1971 statement laid down no preference for the one method over the other.

In regard to losses, full provision is to be made at the time of their determination, irrespective of the method of profit recognition used by the contractor.

Stock Dividends

The distribution of stock dividends is a common practice in Israel. Accounting for the issuing company is based usually on the par value. In the books of the recipient, according to the Institute's recommendations, no money value should be entered in respect of the stock dividends.

Depreciation

The straight-line method of depreciation is used in practice almost exclusively, as it is the basic method recognized for income tax purposes.

Tax-Effect Accounting

It is an accepted practice to give expression in the financial statements to future tax effects, as regards timing differences resulting from accelerated depreciation for tax purposes, provisions for severance payment which will be taken for a deduction in the future, and other similar matters. Securities Act regulations call for the use of the liabilities method in ascertaining the provision for future taxation.

In regard to permanent differences, transfers to a provision for future taxation are customary, as, for example, the following:

1. Where a government investment grant is received, the Institute's statement of opinion calls for part of the grant to be transferred to

a provision for future taxation. This is because, for tax purposes, depreciation will be allowed only on the cost as reduced by the grant, whereas in the financial statements depreciation will be charged on original cost.

2. Where assets are reappraised, it is usual to transfer part of the reappraisal increment to the provision for future taxation.

   As to depreciable assets, the amount of transfer is computed so as to cover the future taxes on the differences between the depreciation to figure in future financial statements on the enhanced value of the assets, and the depreciation on cost available for tax purposes.

   As to nondepreciable assets, the amount of the transfer is computed so as to cover the tax differences (land betterment tax, and so forth) arising on sale of the asset, when profit for tax will be computed on cost of assets.

Requirements for Public Sale of Securities

The offering of securities to the public is regulated by the Securities Act of 1968 and by the regulations promulgated thereunder in 1969, in regard to the details to be given in a prospectus, the form of the prospectus, and its content.

Offering of securities to the public is permitted only in terms of a prospectus whose publication has been assented to by the Securities Authority. A company applying to the Authority for its assent has to submit a draft prospectus, other material as provided by the law and additional material as called for by the Authority.

The following financial statements of the issuer have to be given in the prospectus:

1. Audited financial statements drawn up to a date not earlier than 14 months prior to the date of the prospectus.

   The profit and loss statement must give, in addition to those of the last year reported, comparative figures for the preceding three years, to be included in the scope of the auditor's opinion.

2. Where the above financial statements are drawn up to a date earlier than eight months prior to the date of the prospectus, the prospectus must include also interim financial statements (which may be unaudited) to a date six months later than the annual financial statements.

There is also required an adjustment statement to the profit and loss statements of the four years, wherever there has been a change in the application of accepted accounting principles, or the profit and loss statements for the years mentioned or some of them have included items of income and expenditure relating to previous years.

A holding company is required to include consolidated accounts in the prospectus, in addition to its regular financial statements.

There are special requirements in relation to subsidiary companies, affiliates, the investments to be made with the proceeds of the issue and other matters.

Requirements for Listing Securities on the Stock Exchange

The regulations of the Tel Aviv Stock Exchange, the sole exchange in Israel, require as one of the conditions for the listing of securities the existence of a prospectus as provided by the law. Where the prospectus has been issued earlier than 12 months before the submission of the request for listing, further material relating to the issuer and to the securities must be published as called for by the board of directors of the stock exchange.

The regulations detail the documents that have to be attached to the request for listing, and enable the stock exchange to request additional documents and information.

The issuing company is required, among other things, to publish annual financial statements and a directors' report, at least ten days before the date of the annual general meeting, and not later than six months subsequent to the date to which the financial statements are drawn up.

Italy

Italy

As of July 1973

Significant developments since the preparation of this chapter are presented, by country, in the section entitled Addenda.

Forms of Business Organization

The various forms of business organization are regulated by the provisions of the Civil Code and are classified into imprese individuali (sole proprietorships) and società (partnerships and companies).

Foreign investors usually establish an Italian subsidiary corporation (società per azioni) but occasionally operate as a branch of a foreign corporation.

The Italian government has established certain fields of activity in which foreign investment is subject to specific authorization, viz: shipyards, aircraft manufacture, airline operations, banks, and insurance companies.

Società per Azioni (S.p.A.)

This is the form of business organization that most closely resembles the American corporation. It must have a minimum capital of 1,000,000 lire, which must be fully subscribed, and at least three-tenths of the cash proceeds from the subscription must be deposited in the Banca d'Italia before registration. Once the registration has been completed, the deposit is returned to the corporation. Capital and bond issues over 500,-000,000 lire are also subject to the approval of the Treasury Department.

The Civil Code authorizes four different classes of shares: common (ordinarie), preferred (privilegiate), benefit (di godimento), and employees' shares (azioni a favore dei prestatori di lavoro). Preferred shares may not exceed 50 percent of the total capital stock. When employees' shares are issued, the capital stock must be increased by the stated value of such shares. Shares may not be issued for less than par value and must be registered. "Bearer" shares are not permitted except in Sicily, Sardinia, and in certain other cases. Upon formation, an Italian corporation must have at least two shareholders. Subsequently, the corporation may have only one shareholder, but in such a case the sole shareholder assumes unlimited liability for debts of the corporation from the date upon which he became the sole shareholder.

With certain exceptions, debentures outstanding may not exceed the par value of paid-up capital stock.

Neither shareholders nor directors need be Italian nationals or residents. There is no provision in the law regarding the number of directors. Every corporation must have a statutory board of auditors, whose functions are described later.

The directors are required to submit annual financial statements, together with their report, to the board of auditors at least 30 days before the date set for the shareholders' meeting which should take place not later than four months (in particular cases, six months) after the close of the annual operating period. Such documents and the transcript of the shareholders' approval thereof must be filed with the Registrar of Enterprises within 30 days.

The Civil Code provides that if a corporation sustains losses which are in excess of one-third of its capital, and if the losses in excess of one-third of the capital are not recovered in the succeeding year, the company must reduce its capital proportionately. If by reason of such losses, the capital is reduced below the statutory minimum (currently 1,000,000 lire), it must be brought back to that minimum or the legal form of organization must be changed.

Branch of a Foreign Corporation

As in the case of other forms of business organization, duly legalized copies of the articles of incorporation and the bylaws as well as the board of directors' resolution authorizing the branch must be filed with the Registrar of Enterprises of the corresponding district (under some circumstances with the court having jurisdiction over the foreign corporation's principal office in Italy), together with the names of the persons who will represent the foreign corporation in Italy. Thereafter, the branch must register with the Chamber of Commerce, which will assign a registration number, generally appearing on the business stationery of the company. A copy of its annual financial statements must be filed with the registrar, subject to the same rules that apply to Italian corporations. The branch form is not usually adopted by foreign investors mainly because there are no substantial advantages as compared to the organization of an Italian corporation and also because of the problem in allocating costs to the branch for tax purposes.

Società in Nome Collettivo

This is the equivalent of the unlimited partnership, in which all partners are jointly and severally liable. The association is not dissolved upon the death of a partner unless the articles of partnership so provide.

Società in Accomandita Semplice

This is a limited partnership in which the general partners are jointly and severally liable, while the limited or silent partners are liable up to the amounts of their contributions. A partner's equity may be fully transferred if partners representing a majority of the capital so agree. When the partnership's equity is represented by shares, it is called "società in accomandita per azioni," which is a legal entity.

Società a Responsabilità Limitata

This is a legal entity similar to a limited liability partnership in which the firm is liable only to the extent of its own assets, and each member is liable up to the limit of his capital contribution, which cannot be represented by shares, although the partners' interests may be easily transferred. The required minimum capital is 50,000 lire, and this type of partnership may not issue bonds.

Business Records

The Civil Code prescribes that all commercial enterprises must keep a journal (in which all transactions are recorded in chronological order), and an inventory book (in which the annual financial statements must be transcribed). These are considered official records, and before they are put into use they must be numbered and authenticated by a public notary or by the court. Corporations must also keep certain other books such as minutes of directors' and shareholders' meetings, a stock register, minutes of the board of auditors' meetings, and so forth. The following are among other books which are required by tax and labor laws.

1. Record of fixed asset additions, retirements, and depreciation.
2. Chronological record of certain payments to third parties (individuals) for commissions, fees, interest, and so forth.
3. Raw materials, goods in process, and so forth, used in the production process (yearly summary of inventory movement).
4. Payrolls and personnel records.
5. Chart of accounts with notes of basis adopted for valuing assets.

All the books and documents must be kept for a period of at least ten years.

Collegio Sindacale (The Board of Auditors)

The Civil Code provides that corporations must have a board of auditors ("sindaci") to control the management, audit the accounts, check compliance with the provisions of the Code and, in general, safeguard the interests of the stockholders. The board is composed of three or five auditors and two alternates, who need not be shareholders, are elected for a period of three years, and may be reelected. All corporations must select at least one of the active auditors and one alternate from the official list of auditors ("ruolo dei revisori ufficiali dei conti"—see discussion later in this section) and, in the case of corporations with capital stock of 50,000,000 lire or more and having a board of five auditors, not less than two members must be appointed from the official list. The chairman of the board of auditors must be chosen from those selected from the official list. Relatives of the directors by blood or marriage within the fourth degree, and persons connected with the corporation or its subsidiaries by a continuous relationship involving remunerated work (employee status) may not be appointed auditors.

The board of auditors must meet at least once every quarter and make obligatory examinations of cash and securities. The examinations performed by the auditors must be recorded in the minute book of the meetings and resolutions of the board of auditors.

Auditors must attend meetings of the board of directors and shareholders and are jointly liable with the directors for the latters' acts and omissions whenever injury would not have occurred if the auditors had exercised due vigilance.

A typical report of the board of auditors may read as follows:

> The balance sheet and income statement at .... which the board of directors presents to you, closes with a profit of lire .... and appears to us, following a close examination, [to have been] prepared on the basis of the accounting results and

in accordance with legal provisions, whose criteria for the valuation of the assets have been observed.

In view of the fact that the accounting, the records, the cash, and the securities, on the basis of our periodic examination, have been found to be kept correctly, we conclude, recommending for your approval the balance sheet, the income statement, and the proposal of the board of directors to distribute the profit.

We thank you for the faith with which you have honored us.

The duties of the statutory auditor are prescribed by the Civil Code, but no auditing methods are suggested or recommended. In addition, the chairman of the board of auditors must sign the income tax returns filed by the company (which include the official financial statements).

As indicated above, one (or in some cases, two) member(s) of the board of auditors must be a person whose name appears on the "official list of auditors," and all of them may be capable of giving good commercial, legal, or tax advice to management. Nevertheless, they do not claim to, nor are they expected to make an examination of the financial statements such as would be required of an independent chartered or certified public accountant in order to give an expert and informed opinion upon the fairness of presentation of such financial statements.

Foreign accounting firms sometimes allow their members to accept appointments as sindaci, where the concerned corporations are audited by such accounting firms in accordance with generally accepted standards in the United States or Great Britain.

The Accounting Profession

The accounting profession in Italy is not organized in a form similar to the profession in the United States or the United Kingdom; its development has been mainly governed by the regulations of the Ministry of Justice, which has established the purposes, duties, and fees to be charged, and the rules pertaining to the conduct of the profession. The provisions of the Civil Code concerning the functions and composition of the board of auditors of corporations have also contributed to the development of the accounting profession.

There are two categories of professional accountants in Italy: the "dottore commercialista" (doctor of commerce) and the "ragioniere e perito commerciale" (accountant and commercial expert). The activities of each body are governed by two separate laws both passed by the Italian Parliament on October 27, 1953. There are differences in the educational and professional backgrounds of each, and the law specifies the activities each may undertake, but, in practice, little distinction is made.

Upon fulfilling the prescribed conditions, both categories of accountants may be registered in the respective official lists (albi professionali), described later.

There are very few large local accounting firms in Italy; most of the work is done by individual practitioners, who, for the most part, do bookkeeping work, act as tax advisors, prepare official financial statements of companies, and do detailed auditing work limited to certain accounts. They are sometimes organized in corporate form.

Dottore Commercialista
(Doctor of Commerce)

This is a designation which may be obtained by admission to membership in the Ordine dei Dottori Commercialisti (Order of Doctors of Commerce). Membership in the Order is available to graduates of a four-year university course leading to the degree of Dottore in Scienze Economiche e Commerciale (Doctor of Economic and Commercial Science). In general, the course covers economics, accounting, banking and public, civic, and commercial law. The university graduate must present a doctoral thesis on a subject which must be accepted by the Ministry of Education, and he must pass an oral examination by a board of professors appointed by the state. To become a member of the Order, he must also pass a special state examination, which may be taken immediately after completing his university studies. There is no requirement for practical experience.

Most persons studying for the dottore degree are graduates of the ragioniere (accountant) schools and thus also possess the ragioniere's diploma (see below).

Ordine dei Dottori Commercialisti

The Order has a national society, which is divided into local societies to which qualified university graduates may be admitted upon passing the necessary state examinations. A member must be an Italian citizen or a citizen of a foreign country granting reciprocal arrangements. Foreign degrees or diplomas may be recognized as the equivalent of Italian diplomas.

The Order comprises two categories: (1) those in public practice, who may also register in the "official list" and (2) those who are not in public practice. It is organized in every district with at least 15 dottori commercialisti and is governed by a local and national council.

A member of the Ordine dei Dottori Commercialisti is empowered to deal with the following:

1. Administration and liquidation of business concerns, of personal estates, and of specific assets.

2. Appraisals and surveys and technical advice.
3. Administrative inspections and audits.
4. Verification of and all other enquiries concerning the reliability of financial statements, of accounting entries, and all accounting documents of business concerns.
5. Settlement and liquidation of damages.
6. Statutory audits of trading companies.
7. Tax advice and representing clients before tax authorities.

Ragioniere e Perito Commerciale
(Accountant and Commercial Expert)

To obtain this diploma, the student must have completed five years of elementary school and three years of junior high school, and have graduated from a five-year business high school (which includes courses in accounting, mathematics, business law, and so forth, but not auditing), and have passed a government-controlled examination. This diploma in itself does not entitle the holder to membership in the Collegio dei Ragionieri nor to be inscribed on the "official list" of auditors.

Collegio dei Ragionieri e Periti Commerciali
(College of Accountants and Commercial Experts)

The Collegio is organized in a manner similar to that of the Ordine dei Dottori Commercialisti, with local "collegi" having their local councils which elect the National Council (Consiglio Nazionale).

The qualifications for membership in the Collegio dei Ragionieri are the following:

1. Italian citizenship.
2. Diploma as a ragioniere.
3. Two years practical experience in the office of a member of the Collegio dei Ragionieri, or of a member of the Ordine dei Dottori Commercialisti in public practice.
4. Successful completion of a state-controlled written and oral examination concerning the provisions and procedures contained in the Civil Code, and on tax and accounting problems.

The principal activities of the Collegio dei Ragionieri are the following:

1. The administration of the admission of new members including the verification of prerequisites and conducting the examinations.

2. The enforcement of laws limiting the professional activities of members and reporting infringements by nonmembers on activities reserved for members only.
3. Acting as lobbyists for the profession.
4. Ruling on members' fees disputed by clients; if approval of the Collegio is granted, it is possible to obtain rapid collection by special legal process. Most of the fees are set by law which either provides fixed rates or gives minimums and maximums.

It is the responsibility of the Collegio dei Ragionieri to see that new members meet the requirements prescribed by law.

A member of the Ragionieri e Periti Commerciali body is empowered to undertake the following:

1. Administration and liquidation of business concerns, of personal estates, and of specific assets.
2. Appraisals, surveys, and technical advice.
3. Auditing of books of account of business concerns and all enquiries concerning financial statements, accounts, accounting entries, and accounting documents of business concerns.
4. Settlement and liquidation of marine losses.
5. Statutory audits of trading companies and other bodies.
6. Distribution of personal estates, preparation of the relative projects, and plans of liquidation in judicial cases.
7. Preparation of systems of account for private and public concerns, reorganization of accounting systems.
8. Calculation of production costs for industrial enterprises and preparation of data on accounting and administrative matters.
9. Tax advice and representing clients before tax authorities.

It is evident that there is little distinction between the defined activities of the dottore and the ragioniere and, in practice, little is made.

Ethics

While no official code of ethics has been issued, it is generally held that neither the dottore nor the ragioniere may carry on an industrial or commercial business, nor serve as director of a company where he also acts as auditor, or divulge the affairs of the client.

Ruolo dei Revisori Ufficiali dei Conti
(Official Register of Auditors)

Membership in either the Ordine dei Dottori Commercialisti or the Ordine dei Ragionieri e Periti Commerciali does not automatically provide registration in the appropriate professional official lists (albi professionali), but such registration can be obtained by any person who is of Italian nationality and has been admitted to a local organization (collegio) of the Ragionieri e Periti Commerciali body or a local organization (ordine) of the Dottori Commercialisti body.

As previously stated, at least one active member of the board of auditors of a company whose capital is less than 50,000,000 lire must be a person so registered. In the case of companies with a capital of 50,000,000 lire or more, at least one of the active members (two, if there are five active members) must be selected from the official list of auditors (ruolo dei revisori ufficiali dei conti).

Persons seeking registration on this list are required—

1. To be of Italian nationality.
2. To have served for at least five years as an active statutory auditor, a director, or administrative or accounting officer (dirigente) of a limited company having a capital stock of not less than 50,000,000 lire, or to have satisfactorily performed other similar duties.

The above term of five years is reduced either to three years in the case of persons previously included for at least five years in the roll of the dottori commercialisti or to four years in the case of persons previously included for at least six years in the roll of ragionieri e periti commerciali. In case the persons are not members of the roll of dottori or of ragionieri, the above period of five years is increased to ten years.

It will be noted that the official list contains persons who are not required to have professional experience in the examination of and reporting upon financial statements in the sense understood in the United States and the United Kingdom.

Società Fiduciarie e di Revisione
(Fiduciary and Auditing Company)

This type of organization is common in Switzerland, and there are several subsidiaries of Swiss companies in Italy. It is defined by law as being any enterprise which (1) administers property of third parties, (2) performs audits of businesses or management services, and (3) represents shareholders and bondholders. The enterprise cannot serve as a member of the board of auditors of a corporation, act as a trustee in bankruptcy, or serve in any capacity which is created as the result of a personal appointment with personal responsibility. The società fiduciarie e di revisione may take the form of a corporation or a partnership. They are under the surveillance of the Ministry of Industry and Commerce with whom they must file annual financial statements. One-half of the capital must be invested in government securities, or securities guaranteed by the state, up to a maximum amount of 500,000 lire.

The international auditing firms with offices in Italy are regulated by the laws pertaining to società fiduciarie e di revisione.

Auditing Standards

Since audits by independent public accountants are not customary with Italian business firms, and the accounting profession has not been organized as an institute or other self-regulating body usually present in most countries, there is very little that may be said with reference to standards of auditing. International accounting firms practicing in Italy use, in general, the standards of their countries of origin.

Independence

The only reference to the independence concept is found in the Civil Code, which mentions the circumstances precluding the appointment of persons to the board of auditors. There is no prohibition against holding a financial interest in the enterprise subject to the auditor's examination.

Standards of Field Work

The Italian practitioner does not generally perform the following auditing procedures:

1. Review internal control.
2. Obtain direct confirmation from banks. (It is not a common practice of banks to return paid checks.)
3. Confirm receivables and payables.
4. Observe physical inventories.
5. Make detailed test of transactions.
6. Review subsequent events.

Standards of Reporting

Since most of the audit services performed by the Italian practitioner are in connection with his appointment as a member of the board of auditors, the accounting profession has not developed a typical form of audit report other than the report of the statutory auditors previously referred to.

As has been explained before, the prescribed content and accounting basis of financial statements in Italy are those listed in the Civil Code and those enforced in tax regulations, and there is no significance attached to their consistent application. The standards of disclosure are limited to those applicable under the same circumstances.

Accounting Principles and Practices

The accounting profession in Italy has not issued any recommendations regarding accounting principles. The Civil Code, however, prescribes the contents of the balance sheet and the principles of valuation of assets and liabilities. In addition, rules of valuation and disclosure are frequently enforced through tax regulations.

Form and Content of Financial Statements

The balance sheet follows the traditional form of assets on the left side and liabilities on the right side. The Civil Code prescribes that items shall be classified under the following heads:

Assets

Stock subscriptions owing by shareholders
Land and buildings
Machinery and equipment
Furniture and fixtures
Patents and copyrights
Trademarks and goodwill
Inventories of raw materials and merchandise
Cash on hand
Cash at banks
Fixed revenue securities
Investments
Treasury stock
Accounts receivable—customers
Accounts receivable from affiliated companies

Other receivables

Memorandum accounts (per contra)

Note: Although not mentioned in the above classification, prepaid and deferred expenses are usually shown separately, with an appropriate description. The Civil Code recognizes the principle of apportioning certain charges over more than one year.

Liabilities

Capital stock

Statutory (legal) reserve

Other reserves

Reserve for amortization and depreciation of fixed assets

Reserve for severance indemnities

Liabilities for which collateral security given

Trade accounts payable

Amounts owing to bankers and other lenders

Amounts owing to affiliated companies

Bonds issued

Other liabilities

Memorandum accounts (per contra)

The offsetting of accounts in the balance sheet is not permitted. Notes to financial statements, such as those disclosing contingent liabilities, material lease commitments, and material subsequent events are rarely, if ever, appended.

In the subsequent paragraphs, the bases of valuation prescribed in the Civil Code for certain assets are given. If special reasons make it necessary to depart from such prescribed bases, the directors and the board of auditors are required to state them, justifying each individual case when reporting to shareholders on the accounts.

Consolidated Financial Statements

Consolidated financial statements are not generally prepared. Investments in affiliates are shown at or below cost, and it is not customary to present a comparison of underlying net assets nor to compare parent company income from dividends of affiliates with related net income of such affiliates.

Pooling of Interests

The method of accounting for certain types of mergers or consolidations of companies on the basis of pooling of interests is not often followed in Italy.

Accounts Receivable

Although the Civil Code calls for stating accounts receivable at net realizable values, tax legislation does not allow provisions for bad debts. Specific accounts must be proved to be uncollectible.

Inventories

Inventories must be valued at cost or market, whichever is lower; however, the basis of valuation is not generally disclosed in the balance sheet. An ultraconservative view of market value is not uncommon.

Securities

Securities must be appraised, taking into account their current market values; investments in affiliates must not be valued in excess of their underlying book values.

Fixed Assets

Fixed assets must not be stated at more than cost. Reserves must be shown on the liabilities side.

Financing costs during initial construction of a plant are generally capitalized; after commencement of operations, further costs of such nature are generally charged to expense but are frequently disallowed for income tax purposes. Extraordinary repairs and maintenance are capitalized and amortized over a period of years, the annual amortizations being tax deductible.

Restatement of Fixed Assets and Related Reserves

In past years, up to 1953, several laws were enacted permitting the restatement of fixed assets to partially compensate for the decline in the purchasing power of the lira.

In 1952, a restatement in terms of post-World War II monetary values was authorized for plant, equipment, related reserves, investments, and so forth, and, in certain circumstances, inventories. At the same time, stockholders' equity accounts were required to be revalued, but not restated on the books, by applying coefficients to each year's increase. Any excess of asset revaluations over the increase in stockholder's equity revaluation was taxable under certain circumstances. As a result, most companies limited the amount of asset revaluations to the amount which was nontaxable.

The restatement law called for a segregation of the restatement reserves as to (1) an amount equal to the restatement of capital stock and the statutory reserve and (2) the excess, if any.

Goodwill and Other Intangibles

Goodwill may be recorded only when purchased and must be written off within a reasonable number of years, based on the prudent judgment of the directors and with the approval of the board of auditors.

Intangibles must be stated at cost as reduced by appropriate amounts of annual amortization.

Bond Discount and Other Deferred Charges

Bond discount must be written off in accordance with the corresponding amortization schedules.

Preliminary expenses deferred must be written off in a period not exceeding five years.

Treasury Stock

Treasury stock must be shown separately.

Statutory Reserve

Corporations are required to segregate into a special reserve at least 5 percent of their annual net profits until the reserve has reached 20 percent of the capital issued. This reserve may be used to absorb losses, but must thereafter be restored to the minimum required.

Secret Reserves

Both Italian jurisprudence and tax laws make frequent reference to secret reserves, which historically have been more or less condoned. However, in 1954, special authority was given to disclose these reserves on the books without incurring tax liability, unless the reserves were utilized by transfer to capital or distributed. Many companies have taken advantage of this.

Taxed Reserves

Sometimes this caption is used to reflect the counterpart of items disallowed by tax authorities and then capitalized in the books.

Surplus

Financial statements consist of a balance sheet and a profit and loss statement; the surplus statement is practically never presented.

The Statement of Income

The Civil Code does not prescribe any specific form or content for the income statement, which is usually presented in account form; that is, income on the credit side and expenses on the debit side. A typical income statement is generally quite condensed and usually starts with the gross profit, although there is a trend among larger companies toward furnishing more information.

Cost and Inventory Accounting. Many corporations accumulate costs and expenses in production accounts, and only at the end of the year is the closing inventory recorded. Practice varies considerably regarding overhead allocation to the ending inventories. Standard cost techniques are gaining wider acceptance. Italian fiscal law requires that issues of raw materials and supplies be charged to production on a last-in, first-out basis.

Depreciation. The provision for depreciation in any year is generally based on the normal maximum rates allowed by the tax authorities. It is usually provided at the maximum rates, however, only in years when a profit is shown. Losses on disposition of fixed assets are deductible for income tax purposes.

In addition to normal depreciation, Italian tax law recognizes provisions for accelerated depreciation up to 15 percent per annum, but not aggregating more than 40 percent of cost in the first four years from the date of acquisition of depreciable plant and equipment.

Income Tax Expense. The larger companies provide for income tax liability on the accrual basis. In some cases, such provision represents a general appropriation unrelated to the taxable income of the current year; or it may represent a charge to income for taxes paid on a cash basis, to which may be added a provision for final or estimated official assessments received during the year for current or prior years' income taxes.

Bonuses to Directors

When the bylaws of a corporation stipulate that a percentage of profits is distributable to directors, the amount so distributed is generally charged to earned surplus.

Requirements for Public Sale of Securities

The Civil Code prescribes that a corporation may be financed through public subscription on the basis of a prospectus describing its purposes, capital, status of subscribed shares, principal provisions of the certificate of incorporation, promoters' share in profits, and so forth. The prospectus carrying the signatures of the promoters must be deposited with a public notary prior to its release and distribution, after the requirements of the Civil Code have been complied with.

The promoters are entitled to reserve 10 percent of the annual net profits of the corporation on their own behalf for a period not exceeding five years.

There are no specific regulations concerning data which must be furnished for a prospective investor.

Requirements for Listing Securities on the Stock Exchange

Stock exchanges in Italy are managed by the local chamber of commerce and are subject to the supervision of the Treasury Department.

The requirements for the first registration are mainly that the provisions of the Civil Code have been fulfilled, that operations for the two preceding years have been profitable, and that evidence be presented that the shareholders have approved the financial statements of those two years; there should be no dividend or interest payments in arrears. A company must have a minimum capital of one billion lire in order to have its securities listed on the Milan exchange. Foreign companies must publish their balance sheets for the two preceding years in the official gazette.

When an additional issue is being listed, the only requirement is that the Treasury Department authorize the issue when the capital is in excess of 500,000,000 lire.

Japan

Japan

As of December 1972

Significant developments since the preparation of this chapter are presented, by country, in the section entitled Addenda.

Forms of Business Organization

The basic statutory law governing the organization of business enterprises is the Commercial Code of Japan, as amended. The types of business organizations permissible under the provisions of this code are the single entrepreneur or merchant, partnerships, and stock corporations. With the exception of the single entrepreneur, all business organizations are classified as "kaisha" or company, which is defined as an association for the purpose of engaging in commercial activities.

A kaisha can be a partnership, of which there are three variations, or a "kabushiki kaisha," which is the most common form of business organization for large and organized businesses and closely resembles a U.S. corporation. Corporations are identified by an abbreviated designation such as K.K. (abbreviation of kabushiki kaisha); & Co., Ltd.; or Co., Inc. after the company name.

Kabushiki Kaisha
(Stock Corporation)

The formation of a corporation requires at least seven promoters who prepare, sign, have notarized, and register the articles of incorporation.

There is no stipulation in the Commercial Code as to the qualifications of the promoters or their nationalities.

Included among the provisions of the Commercial Code dealing with corporations are the following:

1. The number of shares to be issued at the time of incorporation must not be less than one-fourth of the total shares authorized.
2. Registration of incorporation must be made within two weeks after an inspector, appointed by the court, has completed his specified investigations in cases where the promoters have underwritten all the shares issued or within two weeks after the completion of the general organization meeting of promoters and the share subscribers in cases where the promoters have not subscribed for all the shares.
3. The directors and the statutory examiner (kansa yaku) must be elected by the promoters in cases where the promoters have underwritten all the shares issued or at the general organization meeting mentioned above, and at subsequent general meetings of shareholders. At least three directors must be elected. The maximum term of a director is two years except that the first term following incorporation is limited to one year; and the maximum term of a kansa yaku is one year. However, there is no specific limitation on reelection.

The Commercial Code also covers such corporate matters as duties of directors; boards of directors, its meetings and minutes of such meetings; appointment of a representative director (a director who represents the corporation before third parties and is authorized to perform all juridical and extrajuridical acts relating to the business of the corporation); duties of the statutory examiner; issuance of shares and debentures; keeping of records and accounts; alteration of articles of incorporation; reorganization; and dissolution and liquidation.

The following matters related to corporations in Japan are of interest.

Directors and Officers. There is no distinction between directors and officers as those terms are used in connection with U.S. corporations. In most cases, directors are, at the same time, officers active in company affairs, although there are some exceptions.

Kabushiki (Stock). In predominant cases, stock has a par value, the most common denomination being 50 yen. However, since shortly after World War II, the Commercial Code has required that the denomination of par value stock be at least 500 yen for companies newly organized. Dividends are now generally stated in number of yen per share but are also sometimes expressed as a percentage of par value. No-par value stock may also be issued.

Shihonkin (Capital). "Shihonkin" (referring to stated or paid-in capital) is the common word used in describing the size of a corporation in Japan.

Capital increases are frequently made through a combination of new issues and stock dividends with additional capital paid in by subscribers for new issues and transfers from earned surplus; capital can also be increased by transfer from profit reserve and capital reserve.

Often, capital stock increases are made by offering subscription rights to existing stockholders at par value, or at less than par value if the company has available a capital reserve, a profit reserve, or a revaluation reserve which may be transferred to capital in the amount of the difference between par and the offering price. (See also the heading, "Fixed Asset Revaluation.")

The word "shihonkin" is used often in establishing criteria for certain requirements or privileges or as a basis of comparison. Growth of corporations is expressed as an increase in stated capital as well as in sales volume or in profits.

Shasai (Debentures). The Commercial Code provides that debentures cannot be issued in an amount in excess of the combined total of the stated capital and reserves, or of the net worth at the latest balance sheet date in case such net worth is less than the combined total of the stated capital and reserves; new debentures cannot be issued until the subscription payment for prior debentures is completed.

The code also provides for serial debentures and convertible debentures.

Partnerships

The Commercial Code provides for two, and the Yugen Kaisha (limited company) Law provides for a third type of partnership organization.

"Gomei kaisha," a general or unlimited partnership, is created after the charter (partnership agreement) is drawn up and is registered in a local registration office; it is a juridical person. The partnership is dissolved by charter provision, agreement by all company members (partners), a merger, decrease in the number of members to one, bankruptcy, and by court order. The code also prescribes the liquidation procedures.

"Goshi kaisha" is a combined limited and unlimited partnership consisting of partners in both categories. As the word "goshi" (joint capital) indicates, this form of partnership permits a capital contribution by inactive partners whose liability and authority would be limited. Under certain circumstances where limited partners no longer exist, a goshi kaisha can become a gomei kaisha through a simple procedure.

"Yugen kaisha" (limited company) is governed by the Yugen Kaisha Law. It is a limited partnership having some of the characteristics of a corporation. The number of members is limited to 50 persons, each with a share representing his investment. Directors are chosen, usually but not necessarily, from among the members. Public offering of shares is not authorized. The law provides for mergers and change of organization into a corporation. This form of business organization is not very common.

Other forms of partnerships, similar to U.S. partnerships, are governed by the Civil Code of Japan (articles 667 through 688, "Partnerships").

Branches and Subsidiaries of Foreign Enterprises

Branches of foreign enterprises are subject to the same provisions of the Commercial Code as are companies formed in Japan. A foreign company which intends to engage in commercial transactions on a continual basis must appoint a representative in Japan and establish an office there.

A foreign corporation may also operate through a domestic subsidiary (kabushiki kaisha).

Business Records

The Commercial Code of Japan requires that every business maintain its books of account and periodically prepare a balance sheet and a detailed listing of assets and liabilities. The books of account and important documents must be kept for ten years.

Kansa Yaku (Statutory Examiner)

The Commercial Code provides that a statutory examiner (kansa yaku), who is elected by the shareholders, will examine and report upon financial statements that the directors propose to submit to a general meeting of shareholders. The code prescribes the right of the examiner to review or make copies of books and records of account, request a report on accounting from directors, or, when necessary, investigate affairs of the company and the state of its property.

There is no legal requirement that the statutory examiner be a professional accountant or auditor. In most cases, the statutory examiner does not have an audit staff. His function as an auditor is not comparable to that of either an internal or an independent auditor.

Zeirishi (Tax Agents)

Under the Tax Agent Law (Zeirishi Ho), the main functions of a zeirishi are to represent clients in tax matters, prepare tax returns, and provide advice on tax matters. The principal requirement is to pass the tax agent examination or to have qualifications evaluated by and to register with the Japan Federation of Tax Agents Association. Tax agents are not allowed to engage in audits. Both lawyers and CPAs may engage in tax practice after registration.

The Accounting Profession

The origin of the public accounting profession is said to date back to 1907, although no legal basis existed until 1927, when the former Public Accountant Law (Keirishi Ho) was promulgated. This law was repealed in 1948, when the present CPA Law was enacted. Under the former law, the title of public accountant (keirishi) was granted to anyone graduating from a college or professional school with a major in accounting. The practice of a public accountant consisted primarily of services to small businesses in bookkeeping, preparation of financial statements, and, after special registration, tax work. The audit of corporations by independent public accountants, in general, was rare until the enactment of the Securities and Exchange Law and Certified Public Accountant Law in 1948, as amended.

The Securities and Exchange Law and related ordinances require corporations, whose securities are listed or publicly held, to present, to the Minister of Finance, prescribed financial statements together with an audit report prepared by an independent certified public accountant, or "kansa hojin" (audit corporation).

The present law established a CPA system comparable to that of the United States, setting forth qualifications, examination requirements, registration, duties, and penal provisions. Public accountants registered under the former law were allowed to re-register and to continue their practice as registered public accountants (keirishi).

Another group of professional accountants is composed of foreign CPAs.

Forms of Practice

Prior to 1966, public accounting was practiced solely by individual CPAs, because there were no legal provisions for practice by a partnership.

The present CPA Law, as amended in 1966, provides for practice by kansa hojin (audit corporation), hereinafter described.

Konin Kaikeishi
(Certified Public Accountant)

Qualifications. Other than the usual exclusion of minors, adjudicated incompetents, persons with certain criminal records, and those whose licenses have been suspended or revoked, the basic qualifications are the passing of the three separate CPA examinations. These examinations are conducted by the CPA examination committee (konin kaikeishi shinsakai) appointed by the Minister of Finance.

Preliminary Examination. This examination covers the Japanese language, mathematics, and the writing of an essay on a given subject in social science. College graduates and those who have fulfilled certain minimum requirements are exempted from the preliminary examination.

Intermediate Examination. Only those who have passed the preliminary examination, or those who have been exempted, may apply for the intermediate examination which covers accounting theory, accounting practice, cost accounting, auditing, the Commercial Code, economics, and business management. The purpose of the intermediate examination is to measure the applicant's knowledge of the above subjects which are necessary to perform duties as a junior CPA (kaikeishi ho). The status of a junior CPA is similar to non-CPA assistants engaged by CPAs in the United States, except that certain formal recognition is given and the title (kaikeishi ho) is registered. College professors, assistant professors, and holders of doctorate degrees are exempted from the intermediate examination in their fields of specialization.

Final Examination. The purpose of the final examination, written and oral, is to measure the applicant's capability to apply specialized knowledge, and includes advanced accounting, auditing practice, financial analysis, tax accounting, and preparation of a thesis on a given subject. In order to be admitted to the final examination, the applicant must be or have the qualification of a junior CPA with one year's practice under a CPA or in a kansa hojin or other organization designated by the Ministry of Finance, and two additional years of practice, after having obtained junior CPA status, under a CPA or kansa hojin. The law accepts certain general accounting experience, specifically defined, in lieu of practice under a CPA or kansa hojin. The final examination is held twice a year.

In order to practice as a CPA, the qualified accountant must be entered in the CPA Register maintained by the Japanese Institute of Certified Public Accountants.

Kansa Hojin
(Audit Corporation)

CPAs (including foreign CPAs) may establish a kansa hojin to practice public accounting. A kansa hojin must use in its name the title "Kansa Hojin."

The organization of a kansa hojin must have five or more CPAs as partners, with unlimited joint liability; such partners must not include one whose license as a CPA has been suspended. Establishment of a kansa hojin must be approved by the Minister of Finance and registered with the District Legal Affairs Bureau.

Gaikoku Konin Kaikeishi
(Foreign CPA)

Article 16-2 of the CPA Law provides for registration as a foreign CPA. A person who has met requirements in a foreign country corresponding to the Japanese CPA qualifications and has sufficient knowledge of Japanese laws and ordinances relating to accounting (as determined by examination) must be entered in the Foreign CPA Register maintained by the Japanese Institute of CPAs to practice under the title of foreign CPA. Thirty-six foreign CPAs are registered as at August 1972. The last examination was given in April 1970.

Kaikeishi Ho
(Junior CPA)

Junior CPA (kaikeishi ho) is sometimes referred to as an "assistant accountant," but the Japanese Institute of CPAs uses the term "junior CPA."

Those who have passed the intermediate CPA examination or have equivalent qualifications must be entered in the Junior CPA Register maintained by the Japanese Institute of CPAs to practice public accounting as junior CPAs. As at August 1972, about eleven hundred junior CPAs were registered. In practice, most junior CPAs are engaged by CPAs, but there are some independent practitioners. Except for audit certification of financial statements and tax practice, junior CPAs can, as independent practitioners, perform the same public accounting acts as CPAs do, that is, the preparation of financial statements, the review or the planning related to financial matters, and consultations regarding financial matters.

Keirishi
(Registered Public Accountant)

Those who were registered with the Ministry of Finance as at March 31, 1967, under the old law (repealed in 1948) are permitted to continue practicing public accounting as registered public accountants except for the audit and certification of financial statements under the requirements of the Securities and Exchange Law.

Konin Kaikeishi Shinsa Kai
(CPA Examination Committee)

The committee is an adjunct organization under the Ministry of Finance organized to investigate and study matters of importance relating to the CPA system, its administration, and examinations. The members consist of not more than ten persons appointed by the Minister of Finance from among officials of the government offices concerned and other prominent persons who possess knowledge of the CPA profession. The term of a committee member is two years. The committee has 15 or less sub-committee members who conduct CPA examinations each year.

Professional Accounting Organizations

The Japanese Institute of CPAs, initially organized in 1949 and reorganized in 1966 in accordance with the provision of the CPA Law, as amended in 1966, is the only CPA organization in Japan. As of August 1972, the Institute had 12 regional chapters, more than 20 standing or special committees and approximately forty-four hundred CPA members, 29 kansa hojin members, and 700 associate members. The legal functions of the Institute are to provide guidance for liaison among CPAs and supervision over members, and to take charge of registration of CPAs, foreign CPAs, and junior CPAs, all for the purpose of maintaining the integrity of CPAs and improving professional practice. CPAs, foreign CPAs, and "kansa hojin" (audit corporations) become members of the Institute as a matter of course. Junior CPAs may become associate members of the Institute. The Institute publishes a periodical *(JICPA News)*, edits a periodical *(The Accounting Journal)*, operates a junior CPA training center, conducts or sponsors research, cooperates with the Ministry of Finance in developing sound audit procedures and accounting principles, and represents Japanese CPAs in international relations.

The Institute promulgated for its members the standard audit engagement contract format and provisions, and fee schedules. The model contract was developed jointly with the Japan Federation of Business Organizations (Keizai Dantai Rengokai), which is a federation of trade associations and large businesses.

Other professional organizations are the Japan Registered Public Accountants Association and the Japan Federation of Tax Agents Association. Both the national federation and regional associations of the tax agents are established under the Tax Agent Law. Regional associations are established on the basis of one for each National Tax Bureau district.

Responsibility of the CPA and the Kansa Hojin Under the Securities and Exchange Law

The Securities and Exchange Law, as amended in 1971, provides among other things, that if financial statements incorporated in a registration statement (yuka shoken todokeidesho) or a securities report (yuka shoken hokokusho) contained false information or lacked information on significant items and investors, misled by the yuka shoken todokeidesho or yuka shoken hokokusho, incurred a loss, then the CPA or kansa hojin who audited the financial statements must compensate them for the loss, unless it is proved that the CPA or kansa hojin did not know and was unable to know of such falsehood or omission in spite of the exercise of due professional care.

Code of Ethics

The Japanese Institute of CPAs has published rules of professional ethics, which include, among others, the following:

1. A member shall not engage in any business or occupation, concurrently with that of CPA, which is incompatible or inconsistent therewith.
2. A member shall not express his opinion on financial statements unless such statements have been examined by him or his employees. When, in expressing his opinion, he uses audit reports of other qualified independent auditors, he shall so state in his opinion.
3. A member shall not solicit clients, shall not compete against other members on the amount of fee, nor render service for a fee based upon the results of such work.
4. A member shall not injure the practice of other members, nor make an offer of employment to an employee of another member.

Summary of Legal and Professional Requirements Affecting the Accounting Profession and Practice

Administering Body	*Legal*
Ministry of Justice, Court	Civil Code
Ministry of Justice	Commercial Code
	Regulations concerning balance sheet and income statement of kabushiki kaisha

Administering Body	*Legal*
Ministry of Finance	CPA Law and related government ordinance
	Ministry of Finance regulations relating to CPA Law
	Ministry of Finance regulations relating to issues or sales of securities under the Securities and Exchange Law
	Ministry of Finance regulations relating to preparation of financial statements for reporting under the Securities and Exchange Law
	Ministry of Finance regulations relating to the examination and certification of financial statements under the Securities and Exchange Law
	Securities and Exchange Law and related government ordinance
	Tax laws and related ordinances and regulations
Ministry of Finance and other ministries	Regulations relating to specific industries

Administering Body	*Professional*
Business Accounting Council (Kigyo Kaikei Shingi Kai) Appointed by Minister of Finance	Auditing Standards
	Business Accounting Principles (generally accepted accounting principles)—Kigyo Kaikei Gensoku
	Cost Accounting Standards
	Opinion on consolidated financial statements

Administering Body	*Professional*
Business Accounting Council (Kigyo Kaikei Shingi Kai) Appointed by Minister of Finance	Opinion on differences between tax laws and business accounting Series of opinions on differences between Business Accounting Principles and related laws and regulations Series of opinions on individual subjects of business accounting Working rules for conduct of audits Working rules for preparing financial statements—Zaimu Sho Hyo Junsoku Working rules for preparing the audit report
Japanese Institute of CPAs	Audit engagement contract standards Audit fee schedule Bylaws of the Japanese Institute of Certified Public Accountants Code of Ethics Series of bulletins on auditing

Auditing Standards

Audits of large corporate businesses by independent auditors did not become common practice until the enactment of the Securities and Exchange Law and the CPA Law in 1948. Prior to that time, auditing was limited to internal auditing and to the audits of governmental and institutional organizations.

Financial statements of corporations incorporated into certain reports (discussed later) filed with the Ministry of Finance under the Securities and Exchange Law and related government ordinances and Ministry of Finance regulations must now be accompanied by an audit report, which has been prepared by an independent CPA or "kansa hojin" (audit corporation). In addition, where it is considered necessary for the protection of public interest and investors, the Ministry of Finance may also require the auditors to submit certain reports or data as reference material.

The Business Accounting Council, under the Ministry of Finance, has published auditing standards, working rules for conduct of audits and working rules for preparing the audit report. In this connection, the council stated that "these standards and rules are a summarization of principles developed among various auditing practices and considered fair and reasonable, and while they bind no one legally, they are the standards every professional auditor should abide by." Thus, these standards and rules may be considered as codified generally accepted auditing and reporting standards.

The Japanese Institute of CPAs has also published a series of notes and guidelines covering subjects such as audit reports, depreciation, allowance for bad debts, allowance for inventory fluctuation, foreign exchange, retirement allowances, and certain auditing procedures, and so forth.

Auditing Standards and Working Rules Established by the Business Accounting Council

Auditing standards consist of three categories: general standards, field work standards, and reporting standards.

General standards comprise, in broad terms, comments on auditors' qualifications, independence, exercise of due professional care, and the confidential nature of the work.

Field work standards include comments on adequacy of planning, timeliness and orderliness, training and supervision of assistants, determination of scope based on evaluation of internal control, and sufficiency of evidential matter with consideration of materiality and degree of risk.

Reporting standards include the following requirements:

1. In the audit reports which accompany publicly issued financial statements, work performed by the auditor and the auditor's opinion on the financial statements should be stated clearly.
2. The auditor's opinion should be expressed as to whether the financial statements present fairly the financial position and the results of operations.
3. Those matters which do not affect financial statements for the current period but which may materially affect the financial statements for subsequent periods should be disclosed in the audit report.

Auditing procedures are classified into (1) "normal auditing procedures," which must be followed by the independent auditor where practicable and reasonable and (2) "other auditing procedures," which are to be followed when considered necessary in the circumstances.

The "normal auditing procedures" prescribe the entire audit work from general preliminary examination to audit procedures for specific statement items. Generally, the procedures prescribed in the working rules are similar to those in the United States. Some exceptions noted are as follows:

1. As to balances of deposits with banks, examination of the banks' certificates of balances (obtained by the companies), and bank passbooks or deposit certificates is required, but independent confirmation from banks need not necessarily be obtained.
2. As to loans payable, examination of creditors' certificates of balances (obtained by the company) is permitted as an alternative for independent confirmation to be obtained from the creditors.
3. Independent confirmation of notes receivable and accounts payable is required only when considered necessary.

The working rules for preparing the audit report include the following requirements:

1. The report should contain an outline of the work the auditor has performed and his opinion on the financial statements. It should be dated, signed, and sealed with the auditor's name.
2. The outline of the work must include the following information:
    a. Identification of the financial statements audited.
    b. Whether the audit was conducted in accordance with the "auditing standards."
    c. Whether the "normal auditing procedures" and other procedures determined to be necessary under the circumstances were employed. Where a material portion of the "normal auditing procedures" was omitted, the fact of such omission and the reason therefor should be stated.
3. Opinion on the financial statements—
    a. Should express whether the financial statements present fairly the financial position and the results of operations. In order to render such an opinion, the following must be stated:
        (1) Whether the company's accounting principles are in conformity with the "business accounting principles."
        (2) Whether the above principles and procedures are applied on a basis consistent with that of the preceding period.
        (3) Whether the company's financial statements conform to the format and rules, which are generally accepted, or those

specifically established by the government ministries involved.

Material exceptions to the foregoing, if any, should be clearly stated together with their effect on the financial statements.

b. Should state, where the effect of exceptions to the financial statements is especially material, that the financial statements do not present fairly the financial position of the company and the results of its operations together with the reasons therefor.

4. Disclaimer of opinion on the financial statements—If the auditor could not obtain competent evidential matter sufficient to support his opinion because important auditing procedures were not performed, or for other reasons, and accordingly is unable to express an opinion on the financial statements, he should make a statement to that effect together with the reasons therefor.

5. Subsequent events—Material events, such as a merger, acquisition, or disaster, and so forth, having a significant effect on the financial statements for subsequent periods, which occurred subsequent to the balance sheet date and became known to the auditor before the issuance of his report, must be disclosed in the audit report.

Ministry of Finance Regulations for Audit Certification of Financial Statements for Securities and Exchange Law Purposes

The above regulations state that the audit certification is to be made by means of an audit report and that the audit report must be prepared based on the results of the audit conducted in accordance with the audit practices generally recognized as fair and reasonable, "which shall be the audit standards and working rules issued by the Business Accounting Council."

Some of the provisions noted are as follows:

1. Accounting practices which deviate from the provisions of the Commercial Code or other special laws are not considered to be in conformity with generally accepted accounting principles.

2. Where treatment of any significant item in the financial statements was inconsistent with the preceding period and the change in treatment is not determined to be justifiable, a statement to that effect, the reason why the change is not justifiable, and the effect of the change on the financial statements should be incorporated in the audit report. If the change is justifiable, only a statement to that effect is to be made in the audit report.

3. Items of loss or expense allowed under the tax law, though they may not necessarily be in conformity with the accounting principles generally considered fair and reasonable, may be regarded as being in conformity with accounting principles generally considered fair and reasonable.
4. Significant deviations from the format of financial statements prescribed in the Ministry of Finance regulations must be so noted and differences shown.
5. If the CPA or kansa hojin could not obtain competent evidential matter sufficient to support their opinion because important auditing procedures have not been applied, or for some other reason, they must indicate non-expression of their opinion giving the reason therefor in their report.

The regulations also call for a separate report called "kansa gaiyosho" which must be submitted by the CPA to the Ministry of Finance. This report contains an itemized checklist type record of audit work performed.

An example of an unqualified report of a Japanese CPA for Securities and Exchange Law purposes is shown below:

Audit Report

To the President,
XYZ Company

Date:
Auditor:
Name of Office:
Address:

______________________________ CPA
(Signature)

I have examined the financial statements, viz., balance sheet, income statement, surplus statement, statement of appropriation of surplus, and schedules of XYZ Company for the period December 1, 19...., through May 31, 19....., which are incorporated in this Yuka Shoken Hokokusho, in relation to the required audit under Article 193-2 of the Securities and Exchange Law.

My examination was made in accordance with generally accepted auditing standards, and accordingly included normal auditing procedures and such other auditing procedures as I considered necessary in the circumstances.

In my opinion, based upon my examination, the accounting principles and procedures of the company are in conformity with generally accepted accounting principles, and were applied on a basis consistent with that of the preceding fiscal period, and the presentations of the financial statements are in conformity with the rules and forms prescribed by the Ministry of Finance regulations relating to preparation of financial statements.

Therefore, in my opinion, the above-mentioned financial statements present fairly the financial position of XYZ Company as of May 31, 19...., and the results of its operations for the period then ended.

I have no interests in the company.

Independence

In connection with the requirement to be "independent," engagement as a CPA or kansa hojin for certification of financial statements for Securities and Exchange Law purposes is prohibited under certain circumstances which are outlined below.

1. Where the CPA or his spouse or his assistant is currently, or was within the past year, an officer of, or the equivalent, or in a position of responsibility in financial affairs, or an employee in, the company.
2. Where the CPA or his spouse or his other close relatives or his assistants have currently a material interest in the company. Material interest includes stockholdings of over certain amounts, creditor-debtor relationship, business relationships, and other indications of substantial interest.
3. Where the CPA, within the past two years, was closely associated with the company as a public servant (local or national government official), through duties of his office.
4. Similar provisions as above are set forth with respect to kansa hojin, its partners, and its employees.

There is a requirement that a statement by the CPA or kansa hojin regarding their relationship with the company being audited, in the light of these restrictions, must be included in the audit report submitted to the Ministry of Finance.

Accounting Principles and Practices

In general, the accounting principles and practices in Japan do not differ materially from those in the United States, although some practices in the United States, such as tax-effect accounting, the equity method of accounting for investments in common stock, and disclosure of earnings per share on the face of financial statements, have not been generally followed in

Japan. Also, a statement of changes in financial position is not considered in Japan to be one of the basic financial statements. The business accounting principles, series of opinions on various subjects of accounting, and the working rules for preparing financial statements, published by the Business Accounting Council, may be regarded, in the absence of legal compulsion, as equivalent to generally accepted accounting principles and procedures. However, this does not necessarily mean that these principles, opinions, and rules were developed out of general practice over a period of time. Business accounting principles were established to improve Japanese accounting practices of presentation of financial statements of business enterprises in order to protect investors and thus aid in the development of Japanese industries. The members of the Business Accounting Council consist of government officials, professors, practitioners, and businessmen appointed by the Minister of Finance.

Today, the business accounting principles, opinions, and working rules for preparing financial statements, published by the Business Accounting Council, are regarded as "the accounting principles and practices generally accepted as fair and reasonable," and are incorporated to a large extent into the laws and regulations which affect business accounting and financial reporting. However, it should be noted that the accounting principles and reporting standards published by the Business Accounting Council are based on the "current performance theory," while those prescribed by the Commercial Code of Japan are based on the "all-inclusive theory." All kabushiki kaisha (stock corporation) must prepare their financial statements, to be submitted to shareholders for their approval, in accordance with the provisions of the Commercial Code. On the other hand, those stock corporations, which are required to present to the Minister of Finance prescribed financial statements under the Securities and Exchange Law, must prepare such financial statements based on the accounting principles published by the Business Accounting Council. That is, it is not unusual that a stock corporation has to prepare two different sets of financial statements for different purposes. Therefore, it cannot be said which theory governs or is predominant in practice.

With a relatively centralized authority in and around the Ministry of Finance, increasingly effective steps have been taken to eliminate differences among the Commercial Code and other legal and administrative requirements, tax laws, and generally accepted accounting principles. In an effort to achieve this objective, the Business Accounting Council has issued reports such as "Opinion on Differences Between Tax Laws and Business Accounting."

General Form and Content of Financial Statements

General principles or postulates contained in business accounting principles include the principles of distinction between capital surplus and earned surplus, disclosure, clarity, consistency, conservatism, and basic uniformity as to source and correctness among statements prepared for various purposes, for example, for shareholders, creditors and tax.

Business accounting principles include the concept of matching revenue with cost, accrual basis accounting, operating income as distinguished from nonoperating, realization basis, elimination of intracompany profits, and so forth. Sales on installments are required to be accounted for by the "installment method," but recognizing income or loss in long-term construction projects is essentially similar to the U.S. practices.

Statement Presentation. Generally, the form of statement presentation as indicated by the three categories below is similar to that customary in the United States. Many Japanese companies adopt a fiscal year beginning April 1, as does the government, and report on a semiannual basis. Others report annually and some on a calendar-year basis.

1. Under the working rules for preparing financial statements, financial statements are generally considered to consist of—

    Balance sheet

    Income statement

    Statement of cost of goods manufactured (if applicable)

    Statement of earned surplus and capital surplus

    Statement of appropriation of earned surplus

    Schedules supporting financial statements

    The "statement of appropriation of earned surplus" is usually presented as follows:

Earned surplus, at end of period		xxx
Appropriations:		
Legal reserve	xxx	
Dividends	xxx	
Bonuses to directors	xxx	
Voluntary reserves	xxx	
Earned surplus, carried forward		xxx

2. Under the Securities and Exchange Law and related regulations, financial statements and supporting schedules (for the latest two fiscal periods) required for submission are—

    Balance sheet

    Income statement

Statement of earned surplus (may be combined with income statement)

Statement of appropriation of earned surplus

Schedule of securities held

Schedule of tangible fixed assets

Schedule of intangible fixed assets

Schedule of securities of affiliated companies held

Schedule of capital contribution to affiliated companies

Schedule of loans to affiliated companies

Schedule of debentures

Schedule of long-term loans

Schedule of loans from affiliated companies

Schedule of capital

Schedule of capital surplus

Schedule of profit reserve and voluntary reserve

Schedule of depreciation

Schedule of allowances

The concept of materiality is stated in various disclosure or classification requirements.

3. Under the Commercial Code, financial statements required for approval by the shareholders are—

Balance sheet

Income statement

Proposals relating to appropriation of earned surplus. (Please refer to example under "Statement Presentation." "Proposals relating to appropriation of earned surplus" is, in effect, a draft of "statement of appropriation of earned surplus," pending approval at the shareholders' meeting.)

In addition, schedules are required which show the details of the financial statements, particularly changes in capital stock and reserves, transactions with directors, statutory examiners or shareholders, and remuneration paid to directors and statutory examiners.

Consolidated Financial Statements. Preparation of consolidated financial statements has not been common in Japan, except for those companies which sold their stock or debentures in foreign countries and which prepare annual reports incorporating consolidated financial statements. However, the Securities and Exchange Law and related regulations, as amended in 1971, require that the "yuka shoken hokokusho" (securities report) of a company be accompanied by (1) a balance sheet and an income statement of each of the company's significant subsidiaries or, alternatively, (2) the company's consolidated financial statements. Such individual financial statements or consolidated financial statements need not be audited. Preparation of consolidated financial statements is guided by "Opinion on Consolidated Financial Statements," which was issued by the Business Accounting Council. The principles and procedures suggested by this opinion are substantially the same as those prevailing in the United States, except that the equity method of accounting for investments in unconsolidated subsidiaries and affiliates is not referred to in this opinion.

Assets

Current Assets. The "one-year" rule for current assets is incorporated in business accounting principles.

Marketable securities held for a temporary period and inventories should, in principle, be stated at cost; however, where market is much less than cost and recovery does not appear to be possible, they should be valued at market. Valuation at lower of cost or market is also permitted.

Fixed Asset Revaluation. Because of severe currency inflation experienced in the period immediately following World War II, the government enacted a Fixed Assets Revaluation Law in 1950 (subsequently amended) for an across-the-board revaluation of assets using stipulated adjustment factors. In the books of the companies, a credit entry was made to fixed asset revaluation reserve account under the capital surplus section, with a debit to the asset account. A fixed asset revaluation tax of generally under 6 percent was levied on the amount of write-up; depreciation thereafter was based on the restated values. In general, most of the assets as valued under the Fixed Assets Revaluation Law have now been fully depreciated.

In connection with the revaluation, additional laws were enacted to provide for buildup of stated capital by transfer of portions of the revaluation reserve with or without public offering of new shares; the balance, if any, of the revaluation reserve account at the end of the fiscal year beginning on or before March 31, 1973, and ending on or after that date, shall be deemed to have been transferred to capital reserve as of the day following such fiscal year end.

Other than the special asset revaluation, business accounting principles stipulate cost basis for all fixed assets.

Intangible Assets and Deferred Charges. Intangible assets must be amortized on a fixed basis, and shown net after deduction of amortization on the balance sheet. Detailed schedules showing accumulated amortization are required.

The Commercial Code specifies amortization for various classes of intangibles and deferred charges. Some of the more important are—

1. Goodwill, organization expense, and research and development cost —within five years.
2. Debenture issue expense within three years, or over the life of the debentures, whichever is shorter.
3. Stock issue expense within three years.

Losses of an unusually large magnitude, such as those due to natural disasters or war, incurred on fixed assets or other assets required for business operation (loss of capital nature), when larger than earned surplus and when special statutes are enacted, can be deferred and amortized by charges against earned surplus in future periods. In practice, the use of this procedure is rare.

Included in the deferred charges classification is the so-called "construction interest" which is paid to stockholders until the company's operation produces profits. To encourage investment, the Commercial Code (article 291) provides for payment of such special interest to stockholders when, due to the nature of business, a corporation does not commence its business until two years or more after its incorporation. This interest covers a specific period prior to the commencement of business and is computed at a certain rate. Inclusion of this provision in the charter of incorporation requires the approval of a court. The law further provides that such costs may be carried on the asset side of the balance sheet and amortized.

Liabilities

Provision for Retirement Allowance. Japanese companies normally have two bases for computing retirement allowances. Broadly speaking, one basis is for those retiring voluntarily and the other is for those retiring at retirement age or at the request of the company. For tax purposes, the company may only deduct 50 percent of the total liability computed on what is called the voluntary basis, and many companies accrue only this tax-deductible portion which may vary significantly from the liability computed on the involuntary basis. Under the present practice in Japan, generally speaking, this may or may not require qualification of the CPA's opinion, depending on the CPA and the purpose of the report.

Affiliated Company Loans. Loans to and from affiliated companies are to be shown separately from those involving nonaffiliated companies.

Overdue Liabilities. Liabilities, due dates for which have already passed, must be disclosed.

Capital

Financial statement presentation of capital items is somewhat rigidly prescribed by the Commercial Code, the Securities and Exchange Law, and other regulations. Clear distinction is made among capital stock items, capital surplus items, and earned surplus items. If the loss for the period exceeds the amount of earned surplus, the excess may be charged to capital surplus. Approval of shareholders is generally required. Disclosure by footnote is required in this case.

Treasury Stock. The Commercial Code prohibits acquisition of a company's own shares except in certain limited cases, usually for temporary holding and disposition, and requires the stock to be separately listed under "other current assets." The Business Accounting Council recommends treatment of treasury stock as a reduction in capital (either cost or face value), and gains or losses from treasury stock transactions as capital surplus increase or decrease.

Legal and Other Reserves of Corporations. Legal reserves consist of "profit reserve" and "capital reserve." The Commercial Code provides that a company must transfer an amount equal to at least 10 percent of cash dividends paid to a legal reserve until the amount so transferred reaches one-fourth of the stated capital of the company. This is referred to as "profit reserve" (rieki jumbikin). In addition, certain specified capital surplus items, consisting of (1) premium on stock issues, (2) credits arising from amalgamations and mergers, and (3) credits arising from reduction of capital, are included in the legal reserve required by the Commercial Code and are referred to as "capital reserve" (shihon jumbikin).

The profit reserve is shown on the balance sheet as a separate item under earned surplus. The capital reserve portion of the legal reserve is shown separately under the capital surplus section.

Based on the articles of incorporation or on a resolution at shareholders' meetings, corporations may set aside from earned surplus an amount as a "voluntary reserve." Such a reserve is set up for any purpose, such as expansion of the business and dividend equalization, and so forth, or without any specific purpose. The reserve may be used for the purposes specified by the articles of incorporation or by shareholders' meetings, upon authorization by resolution of the Board of Directors. Changes in the purposes, or reversals to unappropriated earned surplus, of the voluntary reserve can be made by changes in the articles of incorporation or by a resolution at the shareholders' meetings.

Surplus

"Surplus," as an all-inclusive concept, is defined as the excess of net worth over the legal capital.

Capital Surplus. This caption, in addition to the items classified as the capital portion of the legal reserve (above), includes such items as increases in surplus resulting from acquisitions of subsidiaries, mergers, and so forth; contributions resulting from forgiveness of debt; excess of insurance proceeds over book amount of insured property (originally from fluctuation in monetary value); and gains on disposal of treasury stock.

Earned Surplus. Represents accumulated unappropriated profits and losses from operations.

Allowances for Tax Purposes. A special tax law prescribes the procedure for deducting provisions for special depreciation on fixed assets (allowance for special depreciation) and for losses due to price declines in inventories and marketable securities (allowance for price fluctuation), and so forth. The Business Accounting Council's published opinion regards these allowances as earmarked earned surplus rather than asset valuation accounts.

Income and Surplus Statements

Intracompany Sales and Profits. Under business accounting principles, it is expected that elimination be made of corresponding purchase and sale and of intracompany profit from the inventory at the end of the period. On the other hand, if elimination of purchases and sales is not practicable, it is considered acceptable to eliminate only profit from the ending-period inventory.

Directors' Bonuses. Directors' bonuses are treated as appropriations of surplus and are not deductible for tax purposes.

Depreciation. Methods used are generally similar to those in the United States. Declining-balance methods are often used in Japan. The basis of an asset is the cost or revalued amount, the latter being the amount arrived at under the special legislation, the Fixed Assets Revaluation Law. Depreciation is deductible for tax purposes at specified rates only to the extent recorded in the books. Few companies record depreciation in excess of the amounts deductible for tax purposes. Accelerated depreciation is provided in special instances.

Nonoperating Items. Nonoperating income and expense are separated from operating income and expense, but unusual bad debt losses are included in nonoperating expense. Special discounts, such as those resulting from early payment in lieu of notes on sales or purchases, are included in the nonoperating section. Ordinary allowances, trade discounts, returns, and so forth, are offset against sales or purchases. Gain or loss on sales of fixed assets, extraordinary loss, and corrections of prior year's income and expense are, if material, shown in the surplus statement. Under the Commercial Code, however, such items should be shown in the income statement as special charges or credits.

Tax-Effect Accounting

Financial accounting in Japan tends to follow the rules laid down in the tax laws and regulations, but still there could be some differences between book and taxable income which might require allocation of income tax charges between years. However, tax-effect accounting has not been generally practiced in Japan.

Foreign Exchange Translation

In December 1971, the Business Accounting Council issued "Opinion on Accounting Treatment of Foreign Assets, and so forth, Under the Existing Foreign Exchange System." The basic principles of foreign exchange translation recommended by the opinion may be summarized as follows:

1. Foreign currency items in the balance sheet—
    a. Cash, short-term receivables, and short-term payables should be translated at the exchange rate prevailing at the balance sheet date. However, where justifiable, translation of such receivables and payables at historical rates is acceptable.
    b. Long-term receivables and payables should be translated at historical rates.
2. Revenue and expenses arising from transactions in foreign currencies should be translated at the exchange rates prevailing at the time of the transactions.

3. Translation of financial statements of foreign branches—
   a. The translation should be based on the monetary/non-monetary approach, except that long-term receivables and long-term payables should be translated at historical rates. However, translation of all items in the financial statements at the current rate is also acceptable.
   b. Translation gain or loss should be recognized currently.

Requirements for Public Sale of Securities

The Securities and Exchange Law and the related government ordinances and Ministry of Finance regulations require submission by corporations publicly offering their shares of stock or debentures (generally those making offerings of over 100,000,000 yen in the total issuing value or sales value) of a registration statement (yuka shoken todokeidesho), including a prospectus, and subsequent submission of periodic reports (yuka shoken hokokusho) for each accounting period. The law and the related ordinances and regulations, as amended in 1971, also require those corporations whose securities are listed on the stock exchanges or whose securities are traded over the counter (as defined) to submit the yuka shoken hokokusho for each accounting period, regardless of whether or not such corporations previously filed a yuka shoken todokeidesho.

The registration statement (yuka shoken todokeidesho) should include: (1) information on the new issue or sale of securities, (2) general information, (3) information on major lines of business, (4) information on current operations, (5) information on major facilities, and (6) financial information.

The periodic report (yuka shoken hokokusho) should disclose: (1) general information, (2) information on major lines of business, (3) information on current operations, (4) information on major facilities, and (5) financial information.

The financial information should include: (1) balance sheet, (2) an income statement, (3) a surplus statement, (4) a statement on the appropriation of earned surplus, and (5) schedules showing details of major items on the balance sheet and income statement.

The law requires that this financial information, which is incorporated into the yuka shoken todokeidesho or yuka shoken hokokusho, be accompanied with an audit report by a CPA or a kansa hojin (audit corporation) independent of the registrant.

Where those corporations which file yuka shoken hokokusho close their accounts annually, the Securities and Exchange Law and related regulations, which were revised in 1971, require such corporations to submit to the Ministry of Finance a semiannual report of business (hanki hokokusho) which includes semiannual financial statements in summarized form. Such semiannual financial statements need not be audited. However, as a matter of practice, there are many cases where the stock exchanges require, based on the listing agreements with individual corporations, submission of semiannual financial statements audited by a CPA or kansa hojin.

The existing Securities and Exchange Law and related regulations also prescribe that, under certain circumstances, those corporations which file the yuka shoken hokokusho are required to file a temporary report (rinji hokokusho) with the Ministry of Finance. This report does not include financial statements.

In addition, under the existing regulations, all issues of securities to nonresidents, except for those sold on stock exchanges, must be approved by the Ministry of Finance. The issuing corporation must also file a temporary report (rinji hokokusho) with the Ministry of Finance, setting forth the outline of the issue.

Requirements for Listing Securities on the Stock Exchange

There are eight stock exchanges in Japan: Tokyo, Osaka, Nagoya, Kyoto, Hiroshima, Fukuoka, Niigata, and Sapporo. Since 1961, so-called "second market" sections (dai ni shijo) were opened in the Tokyo, Osaka, and Nagoya exchanges, respectively, permitting the listing of securities which did not qualify for listing on the principal exchanges ("first market" sections). At the stock exchanges where the "second market" sections have been opened, all securities are initially listed on the second market sections, and subsequently transferred to the "first market" sections if certain requirements (discussed later) are met.

Stock exchanges are maintained and operated by member securities companies (corporations) under the Securities and Exchange Law.

Outline of Criteria for Listing on Stock Exchanges

(Effective July 1, 1972, with some probation periods)

Requirements for listing on the Tokyo Exchange are set forth below. The other stock exchanges have similar requirements.

A. Paid-in capital

1. Three hundred million yen or over if principal office of company applying for listing is located in or around Tokyo

2. Six million yen or over if principal office is located elsewhere

B. Number of shares listed

1. Six million shares or over after public offering
2. Six hundred thousand shares if par value of stock is 500 yen or more

C. Distribution of shares (after public offering)

1. Number of trading shareholders—anticipated to be 1,000 or more, each owning between 499 and 50 thousand shares
2. Number of floating shares—total owned by shareholders holding between 499 and 50 thousand each anticipated to be two million shares or more and equal to at least 15 percent of total shares listed

D. Number of years of operation—five years of continuous operation since inception

E. Net assets—eight hundred million yen or over

F. Income before income taxes for the latest three years

1. Amount

a. First year—100 million yen or over

b. Second year—150 million yen or over

c. Latest year—250 million yen or over

2. Ratio to capital stock

a. With respect to each fiscal period in latest three years—ratio of income before income taxes to average capital stock must be 30 percent or more per annum.

b. Ratio of income before income taxes for the latest year to capital stock at end of such year must be 40 percent or more.

G. Dividends

1. Dividends must have been paid during the latest two years and dividend rate on par value of capital stock for each fiscal period during the latest one year should have been 10 percent per annum or greater.

2. Continuation of the dividend rate of 10 percent per annum after the listing is anticipated.

H. Financial statements presentation

1. There were no false presentations on financial statements for each fiscal period during the latest three years.
2. Audit opinion on financial statements for each fiscal period (six months) during the latest one year was unqualified.

Outline of Criteria for Designation on the "First Market" Section

A. Paid-in capital—one billion yen or over

B. Distribution of shares (after public offering)

1. Number of trading shareholders—must be at least 2,800
2. Number of floating shares must meet one of the following conditions:
    a. Three million shares plus 15 percent of total shares listed or more
    b. Fifteen million shares or over representing 8 percent or more of total shares listed
    c. Twenty million shares or over representing 5 percent or more of total shares listed

C. Record of trading

1. Monthly average number of shares traded at the Tokyo, Osaka, and Nagoya stock exchanges for the last three months and for the preceding three months are as follows:
    a. Listing on one exchange—200,000 or over
    b. Listing on two exchanges—200,000 or over in one exchange or total of 250,000 or over in two exchanges
    c. Listing on three exchanges—200,000 or over in one exchange, or total of 300,000 or over in three exchanges

D. Dividend rate

1. Ten percent per annum or more per share on par value for each period ended during the last two years

2. A good prospect of this percentage being maintained

E. False presentation of financial statements—no false presentations of financial statements for any period ended during the last five years.

F. Delisting or transfer

1. Stocks listed in the second market section may be transferred to the first market section when the latter's requirements are met.

2. Reversal of this transfer or delisting can be made by the stock exchange with some probational periods.

Japan

Illustrative Financial Statements

ILLUSTRATIVE BALANCE SHEET OF A JAPANESE COMPANY

ABC Company
Balance Sheet
December 31, 19__

ASSETS

I. CURRENT ASSETS			
Cash and Deposits		....	
Notes Receivable	....		
Allowance for bad debts	....	....	
Accounts Receivable	....		
Allowance for bad debts	....	....	
Notes and Accounts Receivable From Affiliates	....		
Allowance for bad debts	....	....	
Securities		....	
Finished Goods		....	
Partly Finished Goods		....	
Raw Materials		....	
Work in Process		....	
Supplies		....	
Prepayments		....	
Prepaid Expenses		....	
Accrued Revenues		....	
Short-Term Loans to Stockholders, Officers & Employees		....	
Short-Term Loans	....		
Allowance for bad debts	....	....	
Sum of Current Assets			....
II. FIXED ASSETS			
1. Tangible Fixed Assets			
Buildings	....		
Accumulated depreciation	....	....	
Structures	....		
Accumulated depreciation	....	....	
Machinery and Equipment	....		
Accumulated depreciation	....	....	
Vehicles and Delivery	....		
Accumulated depreciation	....	....	
Tools and Fixtures	....		
Accumulated depreciation	....	....	

Land		....	
Construction in Progress		....	
Subtotal		....	
2. Intangible Fixed Assets			
Goodwill		....	
Mining Right		....	
Other Intangible Fixed Assets		....	
Subtotal		....	
3. Investments			
Investments in Securities		....	
Stocks of Affiliates		....	
Bonds of Affiliates		....	
Investments (other than securities)		....	
Investments in Affiliates (other than securities)		....	
Long-Term Loans	....		
Allowance for bad debts	....	....	
Long-Term Loans to Stockholders, Officers & Employees	....		
Allowance for bad debts	....	....	
Long-Term Loans to Affiliates	....		
Allowance for bad debts	....	....	
Investments in Real Estate	....		
Accumulated depreciation	....	....	
Subtotal		....	
Sum of Fixed Assets			....
III. DEFERRED CHARGES			
Long-Term Prepaid Expenses		....	
Organization Expenses		....	
New Share Issuing Expenses		....	
Bond Issuing Expenses		....	
Bond Discount		....	
Development Expenses		....	
Research Expenses		....	
Sum of Deferred Charges			....
Total of Assets			....

ILLUSTRATIVE BALANCE SHEET OF A JAPANESE COMPANY

ABC Company
Balance Sheet
December 31, 19....

LIABILITIES

I. CURRENT LIABILITIES			
Notes Payable		....	
Accounts Payable		....	
Accounts Payable to Affiliates		....	
Short-Term Borrowings		....	
Accrued Expenses		....	
Advances Received		....	
Deposits Received		....	
Deferred Revenues		....	
Provision			
Provision for repairs	....		
Provision for bonuses	....	....	
Short-Term Borrowings from Stockholders, Officers & Employees		....	
Deposits Received from Employees		....	
Sum of Current Liabilities			....
II. FIXED LIABILITIES			
Bonds		....	
Long-Term Borrowings		....	
Long-Term Borrowings from Affiliates		....	
Long-Term Borrowings from Stockholders, Officers & Employees		....	
Provisions for Employees' Retirement		....	
Sum of Fixed Liabilities			....
Total of Liabilities			....

CAPITAL

I. CAPITAL STOCK			....
II. CAPITAL SURPLUS			
1. Paid-In Surplus		....	
2. Other Capital Surplus		....	
Sum of Capital Surplus			....
III. EARNED SURPLUS			
1. Legal Reserve		....	
2. Voluntary Reserve			
Reserve for Equalizing Dividend	....		
Reserve for Construction	....		
Reserve for Plant Extension	....		
Other Appropriated Reserves	....	....	
3. Unappropriated Earned Surplus			
Ending Balance of Earned Surplus (before crediting net profit for the period)	....		
Net Profit for the Period	....	....	....
Sum of Earned Surplus			....
Total Capital			....
Total Liabilities and Capital			....

ILLUSTRATIVE INCOME STATEMENT OF A JAPANESE COMPANY

ABC Company
Income Statement
Year Ended December 31, 19....

I. SALES		
Gross Sales	....	
Sales Returns and Allowances	....	....
II. COST OF GOODS SOLD		
1. Opening Inventory	....	
2. Cost of Goods Manufactured	....	
Subtotal	....	
3. Closing Inventory*	....	....
Gross Profit on Sales	....	....
III. SELLING AND GENERAL ADMINISTRATIVE EXPENSES		
Salesmen's Salaries and Allowances	....	
Salesmen's Traveling Expenses	....	
Advertising Expenses	....	
Delivery Expenses	....	
Bad Debts Written Off	....	
Officers' Salaries and Allowances	....	
Other Employees' Salaries and Allowances	....	
Depreciation Expenses	....	
Land and House Rents	....	
Repairs	....	
Office Supplies Used	....	

Communication Charges	....	
Miscellaneous Expenses	....	....
Operating Income	....	....
IV. NONOPERATING REVENUES		....
Interest Income	....	
Interest on Securities	....	
Dividend Received	....	
Profit on Securities Sold	....	
Purchase Discount	....	....
Gross Profit for the Period	....	....
V. NONOPERATING EXPENSES		....
Interest Expense	....	
Interest on Bonds	....	
Amortization of Bond Discount	....	
Sales Discount	....	
Loss on Securities Sold	....	....
Net Profit for the Period	....	....
* Inventory valuation is based on FIFO		....

Lebanon

Lebanon

As of May 1973

Forms of Business Organization

The types of business organization found in Lebanon are the single proprietorship, various forms of partnership, and certain types of limited liability company. Basically, Lebanese law in this respect is derived from the legal system of France.

A foreign corporation wishing to establish a branch in Lebanon may do so after complying with certain formalities, or it may form a subsidiary under Lebanese law which will then be subject to the prevailing regulations governing similar Lebanese enterprises.

A subsidiary may be organized as a Lebanese corporation, such as a "société anonyme libanaise" (S.A.L.) or a "société à responsabilité limitée (S.àR.L.) having a separate legal entity and being subject to the same legal and tax treatment as a Lebanese-owned company.

There are some restrictions in Lebanon on foreign ownership of local enterprises in insurance, banking, mining, and real estate, and in the case of public services and airlines at least one-third of the capital must be held by Lebanese.

Société Anonyme Libanaise (S.A.L.)

The usual Lebanese corporation, which is similar to a U.S. corporation, is the "société anonyme." It is a corporate entity and is customarily created for a definite period of time, usually not beyond 99 years. First, the articles of incorporation (statuts) must be prepared, which include provisions similar to those of both the charter (articles) and the bylaws of a U.S. corporation; then, capital stock is issued and the first shareholders' meeting is held. The majority of the board of directors must be of Lebanese nationality, and there must also be a minimum capital of 300,000 Lebanese pounds fully subscribed (75,000 pounds to be paid in upon subscription) for commercial enterprises and 3,000,000 pounds for banks.

From the accounting standpoint, the important action of the first shareholders' meeting is the appointment (for one year) of the statutory auditor (commissaire aux comptes statutaire); subsequently, he is reappointed for one year. The duties of the statutory auditor are discussed below.

Branch of a Foreign Corporation

A foreign corporation may establish a branch in Lebanon provided approval by the Ministry of National Economy is first obtained. The required procedure involves submitting an application to the ministry which shall include the name of the foreign corporation, location of its head office, and its capital. Such application must be accompanied by a certified copy of the charter or articles of the foreign corporation; a certified statement of the capital of the foreign corporation if this information is not shown by its charter; a certified copy of the resolution of the board of directors authorizing the establishment of the branch in Lebanon; and a power of attorney executed in favor of the foreign corporation's representative in Lebanon appointing him to act on behalf of the company in the establishment of the branch in Lebanon. These supporting documents must be certified by the board of directors, authenticated by the appropriate authorities, and legalized by the Lebanese consul in the country of incorporation. They must then be translated into Arabic by accredited translators and attested to before a notary public in Lebanon. If the branch is to carry on commercial, industrial, or financial operations in Lebanon, it must also be registered in the Register of Commerce. Foreign corporations frequently register in Lebanon as a non-trading branch or a representative office; both of these forms of business organization are tax exempt.

Société à Responsabilité Limitée (S.àR.L.)

The limited liability company (société à responsabilité limitée) which has features of both a partnership and a corporation has recently been instituted in Lebanon. It is permitted to engage in any commercial enterprise other than insurance, regular air transport, banking, and investments for third parties. It is suited to the requirements of a small or medium-sized business and has relatively few partners. The limited liability company is not permitted to obtain capital from the public. It constitutes a legal entity, and the liability of partners is limited to the amount of capital which they have paid in. The life of the company is stated in its articles or partnership agreement (statuts); if it is unlimited, any partner may dissolve the company at will. There must be a minimum of three partners and generally not more than twenty, and there must be a minimum capital of 50,000 Lebanese pounds. The partners appoint a manager (gérant) who may be one of them, and who often has a separate contract that places him in a strong position.

From the accounting standpoint, the limited liability company (S.àR.L.) is not required to retain auditors except under any of the following conditions:

1. If the number of partners exceeds 20 (which may result if a deceased partner's estate is divided among family members).
2. If the company's capital exceeds 500,000 Lebanese pounds.
3. If one partner, or several partners together, representing one-fifth of the capital, request the appointment of an auditor.

Other Forms of Business Organization

The sole proprietorship and the general partnership (société en nom collectif) are very similar in law and custom to comparable organizations in the United States. The general partnership, under Lebanese law, constitutes a separate legal entity; even so, the partners are taxed individually, at corporate rates, not as a partnership entity. Its name must include the name of at least one of its partners, and, if only one name is used, it must be followed by "et Compagnie."

A partnership may include limited partners, in which case it is termed "société en commandite simple." Its general partners (commandites) with unlimited liability are similar to those of the société en nom collectif; the limited partners' (commanditaires) liability is limited to the amounts contributed to the firm, and they cannot participate in the management. The general and the limited partners may only transfer their interests with the unanimous approval of all partners. This form of organization is not in general use. Another form of partnership with limited partners is the "société en commandite par actions." Here the interests of the limited partners (commanditaires) are represented by transferable shares of stock.

Business Records

The basic records required by the Code of Commerce for companies trading in Lebanon are the general journal and a book of balances (livre d'inventaire). The latter is comparable to a trial balance book in which are also recorded the annual balance sheet, profit and loss accounts, and inventories. The general journal and balance book must have prenumbered pages and be stamped by the appropriate authority. Non-trading branches of foreign corporations are required to keep only a salary book.

Company management, in practice, determines the extent and use of supplementary ledgers and journals, and ultimately the presentation of the financial statements. French managers tend to adopt a modified version of Le Plan Comptable Général, a government-promulgated accounting manual widely used in France. Anglo-Saxon managers and Lebanese nationals trained at the American University in Beirut and abroad generally maintain records similar to those found in England and in the United States.

However, as the Lebanese government does not endorse any one standard accounting system, the management is at liberty to utilize supplementary business records as it deems necessary.

Commissaires Aux Comptes (Statutory and Court-Appointed Auditors)

The Code of Commerce, as amended, provides that all companies (sociétés anonymes) must have their accounts examined by two commissaires aux comptes, one (statutory auditor) appointed by the shareholders for one year at the first meeting and subject to reappointment annually thereafter, and the other (court-appointed auditor) appointed for a one year period by the Tribunal de Commerce from a list drawn up by the court's special committee. The court-appointed auditor is also subject to reappointment annually by the court.

There are no specific qualifications required of the statutory auditor other than he not be specifically disqualified (see p. 359). In practice, he is generally selected from local and foreign accounting firms. Qualifications for inclusion on the Tribunal de Commerce list of potential court-appointed auditors include a minimum age requirement of 25, Lebanese nationality, good character, five years of banking or business experience, and he should not be a civil servant. Candidates seeking inclusion on this list must also present their academic credentials to the special committee.

Persons Disqualified

Since a principal qualification of the auditor is stated to be that of independence, relatives of directors or of persons contributing assets other than cash for capital stock, persons receiving salary or remuneration in any form from the company, or spouses of these persons, are disqualified from holding that office. This applies to both the statutory and the court-appointed auditor.

Functions

Under Lebanese law, both the statutory and court-appointed auditors are officially responsible for the independent audit function. In practice, however, the statutory auditor tends to perform the financial examination and the court-appointed auditor's role is frequently a perfunctory one. Neither auditor may permit another person to substitute for him. Their duties and responsibilities are stated in the law in some detail but not the manner in which they are to be carried out.

The auditors are required to report to the shareholders at the general annual meeting upon the financial statements presented to them by the board of directors. They are not expected to prepare the statements although the statutory auditor frequently prepares the notes. Such financial statements must be submitted to the auditors at least 50 days before the annual meeting.

The auditors have other duties prescribed by law which differ from those assigned to the U.S. or U.K. auditor. For example, they are required to report on contracts and agreements of the company, if known to them, in which directors are directly or indirectly involved; they are also required to call a shareholders' meeting when shareholders representing one-fifth of the company's capital request it.

Examining Procedures

The duties and powers of the statutory auditor and the court-appointed auditor, as provided by law, suggest that an examination should be conducted in a manner similar to U.S. and U.K. practice. However, as mentioned above, the statutory auditor in practice is largely responsible for the financial statement examination. His conduct of the examination can range from a level comparable to that of the chartered and certified public accountant in the United Kingdom and United States to a brief bookkeeping review of the company statements. The quality of the financial statement examination and the reliance placed thereon are often determined by the statutory auditor's level of competence.

Report of the Auditors

There is no standard form of report prescribed for the statutory and court-appointed auditors in Lebanon comparable to that of the AICPA in the United States or that required by the Companies Act in the United Kingdom, with the notable exception of banks. Recently instituted regulations stipulate the form and content the latter's financial reports must take.

Under the provisions of the Code of Commerce, which governs business enterprise, the statutory and court-appointed auditors submit a general report to the annual meeting of stockholders. The report must be signed by both auditors and generally includes a reference to the principles of verification followed as well as an opinion on the financial statements presented.

It is apparent that the auditors, as such, are not required to have the training or experience which is expected of the independent auditor in the United States or the United Kingdom. A report issued by the auditors need not give the same assurance as to the fairness of presentation of financial statements as would that of the independent certified or chartered accountant although in some instances it may. The report and the reliance thereon depends entirely on the quality of the auditors who have performed the examination.

The Accounting Profession in Lebanon

The accounting profession is not organized to the extent of the profession in the United Kingdom and the United States. The government, however, has recently taken measures which will permit university students to follow courses leading to a diploma with a major in accounting (Diplôme de Technicien Supérieur). It is expected that future legislation will stipulate that the court-appointed auditor will have followed and completed the university accounting program; and it is believed this course of action will involve the court-appointed auditor more deeply in the examination of the financial statements than heretofore.

Education

The Diplôme de Technicien Supérieur with a major in professional accounting is now offered at the university level in Lebanon upon completion of four years of university studies in the following areas: mathematics, finance, statistics, auditing, law, accounting, tax, management, and business organization. The candidate is required to take examinations each year in the above subjects and pass a state examination for the diplôme at the conclusion of four years of studies.

Lebanese students, seeking a career in professional accounting, often go to France or England to obtain the "expert comptable" degree or become chartered accountants. Upon returning to Lebanon, they frequently obtain positions with the international accounting firms operating out of Beirut.

Organization of Accounting Firms in Lebanon

Public accounting in Lebanon is carried out by local and foreign firms. The firms are generally organized in the form of a partnership or single proprietorship.

Organizations of Accountants

There are two organizations of accountants in Lebanon, the Syndicat des Propriétaires des Bureaux de Comptabilité et de Revision and the Middle East Society of Associated Accountants. The former limits its members to owners (propriétaires) of local accounting and auditing firms. Eligibility for full membership to the latter is contingent upon passing two sets of examinations. However, members of U.S.- and U.K.- recognized bodies of accountants are accepted by the Middle East Society of Accountants as full members without examinations.

The primary purpose of both of these organizations is to strengthen relations between its members and to safeguard their monetary and moral interests as well as to develop and organize the accounting profession. In recent years, the Middle East Society of Associated Accountants has attempted to emulate the accounting profession as it is known in the United Kingdom and the United States by encouraging its members to adhere to Anglo-Saxon accounting practices and principles. Neither of these organizations, however, binds its members to its pronouncements on accounting matters.

Auditing Standards

The accounting profession in Lebanon does not have as a guide for its work a statement of auditing standards in a form such as that published by the AICPA as Statements on Auditing Standards.

The statutory and court-appointed auditors are permitted to choose the methods and means they deem necessary to assure themselves of the regularity and correctness of the accounts. In practice, the French or Anglo-Saxon methods tend to be followed.

With regard to banks, recently instituted government regulations stipulate standards to be followed in conducting a bank audit. This is, however, beyond the scope of the present discussion.

Accounting Principles and Practices

Modified versions of the French Plan Général Comptable, Anglo-Saxon practices, and Lebanese tax law are the most influential factors in shaping the accounting principles applied in the preparation and presentation of financial statements in Lebanon. Business entities are permitted, in the absence of defined legal requirements, to adopt such reporting practices as they choose.

Consolidated Financial Statements and Statement of Changes in Financial Position

There is no requirement in Lebanon that consolidated or group accounts be prepared or published although they are sometimes prepared for internal purposes. The statement of changes in financial position is not considered to be one of the basic financial statements in Lebanon and so far it has not been used.

Inventories

Inventories are generally stated on the balance sheet at cost or market, whichever is lower. The basis of valuation is not generally disclosed in the balance sheet. Cost or market may also be reduced when the items concerned are obsolete or deteriorated, in which cases they are valued at estimated realizable prices.

Fixed Assets

Fixed assets are generally stated at cost. Depreciation is normally provided in the accounts at the rate allowed for tax purposes.

Reserves

Included under this general heading are items such as premium on capital stock, legal reserve, and other reserves. Each year all companies are required to set aside as a legal reserve 10 percent of net profits after tax, until the total reserve reaches one-third (one-half in the case of the S.àR.L.) of the nominative capital. The other reserves are those which the shareholders at the annual shareholders' meeting decide should be appropriated out of that year's profits.

Provisions

These reserves are provided by charges to expense for book purposes. They are not tax deductible, however, until the losses against which they are provided are actually sustained. Among these reserves are provisions for risk, such as litigation, guarantees of product, self insurance, losses on purchases for future delivery, fines and penalties, and exchange losses.

Contingent Liabilities

While it is customary in Lebanon to discount notes receivable, generally only Anglo-Saxon oriented companies mention the resulting contingent liability. This is also the practice regarding disclosure of guarantees and liens on assets.

Capital Stock and Stock Dividends

All capital shares of Lebanese companies have a nominal or par value and must be issued. No-par stock is unknown in Lebanon.

Capital may be increased by a vote of shareholders at an extraordinary general meeting, by issuing additional shares or by increasing the par value of existing shares. An amount equal to the par value of the additional shares, or the increase in par value, is transferred from reserves. In all cases, the par value is the measure of the amount transferred and not the market value as in the case of stock dividends in the United States.

The Statement of Income

Sales and Cost of Sales. Sales and cost of sales are required to be reported in the financial statements.

Depreciation. The straight-line method of depreciation is used for both book and tax purposes, the amounts being computed at the rates stipulated in Decree No. 2716 of April 5, 1949, as amended. The rates appear to be low in comparision to those in use in the United States and the United Kingdom but may reflect the tendency prevalent in some countries to keep facilities in use longer than is customary in the more highly industrialized countries. Durable equipment rates vary from 2 percent to about 8 percent; light or perishable equipment rates run from 5 percent to 20 percent; rates on buildings vary from 2 percent to 10 percent depending on the nature of the trade or industry and the use to which they are put. Transportation equipment rates vary from 5 percent (railways and trains) to 25 percent (aircraft).

Fees Paid to Unsalaried Directors

Fees paid to unsalaried directors are tax deductible to the paying company.

Tax-Effect Accounting

In Lebanon there are generally no significant differences between book deductions from income and those allowable for tax purposes.

Requirements for Listing Securities on the Stock Exchange

The Beirut Stock Exchange (Bourse) admits securities to trading through action by its committee upon the filing of a series of documents (similar to the prospectus in the United States and United Kingdom) that contain basic data and technical information about the securities to be listed. Audited financial statements must be presented for the current and prior two financial periods and signed by the statutory and court-appointed auditors. In practice, there are few listings on the exchange and an inconsequential amount of trading.

Mexico

Mexico

As of November 1972

Significant developments since the preparation of this chapter are presented, by country, in the section entitled Addenda.

Forms of Business Organization

The common forms of sole proprietorship and partnership, and various corporate forms of business organization are found in Mexico and may be organized with either fixed or variable capital. A foreign corporation may, on approval of the Mexican government, establish a branch office in Mexico; but tax and other considerations usually favor operating through a subsidiary rather than as a branch.

All corporations are subject to the laws governing local companies in general, there being no special legislation limiting the operations of foreign corporations. However, permits from the Ministry of Foreign Relations are necessary for foreigners to organize or acquire control of business entities in Mexico, and the ministry may require that control remain in the hands of Mexican citizens in the case of certain industries. Ownership in petroleum, electric utilities, and railroads is reserved exclusively for government agencies; a number of other industries are required to be 100 percent of majority-owned by Mexican citizens.

Sociedad Anónima (S.A.)

This type of business organization is similar to the American corporation, with stockholders' liability being limited to payment for their shares subscribed. The requirements for establishing this type of corporation are as follows:

1. A minimum of five stockholders, each one subscribing to at least one share.
2. Capital of at least 25,000 pesos, fully subscribed.
3. Down payment of at least 20 percent of each subscription payable in cash.

Sociedad Anónima de Capital Variable (S.A.deC.V.)

This type of corporation is the same as the "sociedad anónima" with the exception that its capital may be increased through subsequent capital contributions by the stockholders or by admitting new stockholders, and may be decreased by a total or partial withdrawal of paid-in capital, without observing certain formalities that might be required of an ordinary sociedad anónima.

Sociedad de Responsabilidad Limitada (S.deR.L.)

This type of organization is constituted among partners whose liability is limited to their paid-in capital. Partners' interests may not be represented by negotiable certificates issued to order or bearer, since they are only transferable in the cases and under the conditions prescribed by law. The company's name must include that of one or more of its partners who may not exceed 25 in number. Partners' invested capital may never be less than 5,000 pesos, divided into shares that may be unequal in value or category, but which, in any case, must have a nominal value of at least 100 pesos or multiples thereof.

Sociedad en Nombre Colectivo

This type of organization is in substance a general partnership in which all partners are jointly and severally liable for the firm's debts. No partner can transfer his interest in the company nor can new partners be admitted without the consent of the other partners, unless, in either case, the partnership contract provides that a simple majority vote will suffice.

Sociedad en Comandita Simple

This is a form of partnership that is comprised of one or several general or active partners who are jointly and severally liable for the firm's debts and one or several limited or inactive partners who are liable only to the extent of their paid-in capital. The limited partner or partners cannot participate in any administrative activities even as attorney of the general partners, but authorization and surveillance given or exerted by the limited partners, within the terms of the partnership contract will not be considered to be administrative acts.

Sociedad en Comandita por Acciones

This type of organization is somewhat similar in structure to the "sociedad en comandita simple" and consists of one or several general or active partners who are jointly and severally liable for the firm's debts and of one or several limited or inactive partners whose liability is limited to the amount of their required capital contributions. However, interests in the company are represented by shares, which in the case of the active partners must be registered and may not be transferred without the consent of the inactive partners and two-thirds of the active partners. In other respects the sociedad en comandita por acciones is governed generally by the law pertaining to the sociedad anónima.

Business Records

The Commerce Code, and the income tax law and its regulations require all merchants or industrial companies, whether they are individuals or corporations, to keep records of their operations in at least three books: general ledger, general journal, and a ledger prepared annually and containing the final trial balance and a summary of inventory categories. These three books must be authorized by the tax authorities in the taxpayer's district.

It is also necessary for corporations to maintain minute books for board of directors' and stockholders' meetings.

Comisario (Statutory Examiner)

The comisario is appointed by the stockholders to act as their representative to review the operations of the company and report directly to them. The comisario's duties may be performed by one or several examiners whose appointments are temporary and revocable. They may be stockholders or persons otherwise not associated with the corporation; but persons legally forbidden to own businesses may not act as comisarios, nor, due to lack of independence, may employees of the corporation and close relatives of administrators.

Among the functions and obligations of statutory examiners are the following:

1. To review the corporation's charter.
2. To obtain from the administrators a monthly statement including all affected operations and to participate in the formulation and review of the annual financial statement.
3. To summon ordinary and extraordinary stockholders' meetings.
4. To attend, without vote, all the meetings of the board of directors.
5. To attend, without vote, stockholders' meetings.
6. Generally, to review without any limit and time, the operations of the corporation.

Any stockholder may notify the examiners of anything he considers to be irregular in the administration, and the examiners must mention these alleged irregularities in their reports to the general stockholders' meeting, recommending the considerations and propositions they believe to be appropriate.

Although the examiners must endorse the financial statements submitted to the stockholders, they do not, acting as statutory examiners, "examine" such statements as would a "contador público" (professional public accountant) nor are they required nor necessarily qualified to do so; however, in some cases the contador público and the examiner may be the same person in which event there may be some overlapping of their respective functions.

Both the S.A. and the S.A.deC.V. are required by law to have comisarios who may be one or more in number. Other kinds of business entities have "vigilance officers" or "boards of vigilance" which perform the same duties as comisarios. A minority of shareholders owning 25 percent or more of the voting stock has the right to elect one of the comisarios.

The Accounting Profession

In Mexico there are two classes of accountants that serve the public: the noncertified accountants (contadores privados) and the public accountants (contadores públicos).

Contador Privado
(Private Accountant)

The contador privado is a person who, having some accounting education or experience, holds himself out to provide bookkeeping, tax, and other accounting services to the public. He is not recognized by the government as a professional accountant (contador público) and is not organized either in a college (colegio) or in an institute. These persons may not perform those duties which by law are restricted to licensed "contadores públicos" (public accountants).

Contador Público (CP)
(Public Accountant)

The candidate for the CP degree must have met specified educational requirements and have passed all examinations.

In order to be admitted to most institutions of graduate business administration study, leading to the degree of "public accountant," the candidate must first complete six years of elementary school, three years of junior high school, and a three-year university course to obtain the bachelor degree.

Once this degree is obtained, the holder is eligible to enter certain educational institutions which offer the degree of contador público. A five-year course, composed of ten semesters, is normally required, covering subjects that compare favorably with those of typical American universities.

The student is then required to undergo a professional examination which involves preparation of a thesis and interrogation by a group of three examiners on the thesis and other subjects related to the functions of the public accountant, with the examiners determining the nature of the topics on which the candidate will be interrogated.

Upon satisfactorily completing these requirements, the certificate of CP is issued to him by the university authorities, or by those other schools authorized to issue these certificates, which in turn leads to the granting of a license to practice by Dirección General de Profesiones (Directorate General of Professions).

School hours are usually from seven to nine or ten A.M. and four to nine P.M., and most higher level accounting students work for certified public accountants or business concerns outside of school hours.

Legal Requirements for Practice

Article 25 of the Professional Law prescribes the following requirements for the practice of public accountancy or any other regulated profession by an individual in Mexico:

1. He must be Mexican by birth or naturalization, and enjoying and exercising his civil rights.
2. He must hold a legally issued and duly registered professional degree.

3. He must obtain a license from the Directorate General of Professions.

One peculiarity of the profession in Mexico is that firms arising from the association of two or more contadores públicos are no more than "de facto" partnerships with no formal recognition in the law, unless a form of partnership (sociedad civil) is organized under the Civil Code of the applicable state. Very few contadores públicos adopt this form of partnership since, in any event, professional law places all responsibility on the individual signing the specific report and not on the partnership.

Functions of the Contador Público

The services provided to his clients by the Mexican CP are very similar to those of the CPA in the United States. He may be selected by management, directors, or stockholders to examine and report upon financial statements of corporations or other business entities; prepare tax returns; represent taxpayers before the tax department and give tax advice; and may advise with respect to or supervise the installation of accounting systems.

Various laws of Mexico require that financial statements of certain companies be certified by a CP. All credit institutions are required to file their annual financial statements certified by a CP. The Law of Titles and Credit Operations requires that when a company wishes to issue bonds or debentures, its financial statements must be certified by a public accountant. The Mexican Companies Act requires that the financial statements of branches of foreign corporations operating in Mexico be examined and reported upon by a CP and be published. Banking laws require banks to obtain similarly certified financial statements from credit applicants where the amount involved is material and the collateral offered is less than the minimum necessary to obtain exemption from the requirement to submit certified statements. Banking laws require that corporations issuing bonds quoted on the market publish financial statements certified by a CP. The law establishing the Bank of Mexico states that the shareholders will appoint expert accountants (who must be CPs) to review the balance sheet.

In support of their income tax returns, taxpayers may file a report of a contador público registered in the Special Register of Auditors for Tax Purposes. Such a report should contain an opinion on the financial statements under generally accepted auditing standards, and the accountant's opinion as to the manner in which his client complied with all of the federal tax obligations applicable during the fiscal year. Reports filed for the first time must contain brief descriptions of the taxpayer's main legal, financial, and administrative characteristics as well as principal features of internal control as applied to cash and inventories; subsequent reports need only mention changes. The public accountant's report is subject to review, in lieu of the taxpayer's records, as the basis for approval by taxing authorities of the corresponding tax returns. Authorities may, at their discretion, supplement their review with the following:

1. Oral and written explanations from the contador público.
2. Examination of his working papers.
3. Inspection of the taxpayer's records.

Organization of the Accounting Profession

The public accounting profession in Mexico has had a long history of gradual growth during the present century, based on steady improvement in educational opportunities and in the work of its professional societies.

Colegio de Contadores Públicos. In 1946, a law was enacted to regulate the various professions in Mexico. This law restricted practice of the professions to Mexican citizens, except in the case of persons established in Mexico before that year. It further required members of the public accounting profession to become associated in organizations known as "colleges" in order to bring themselves under its provisions; whereupon the Colegio de Contadores Públicos de Mexico, A.C., Mexico City and, eventually, 21 colleges located throughout the country were organized. Holders of the certificate of "contador público" must belong to one of these colleges depending upon the location of the practice. There are about forty-three hundred members of the various colleges, all of whom automatically belong to the Instituto Mexicano de Contadores Públicos, A.C., once they are admitted to membership in the corresponding college.

In order to be admitted to a college, the candidates must include with their applications photostatic copies of their title and license to practice, as well as a copy of their professional thesis together with a statement of their educational curriculum and professional background. References are furnished by the applicant, and his application is sponsored by two college members. Names of applicants are listed twice in the colleges' weekly bulletin to enable other members to submit confidential objections to membership during a 30-day period.

Instituto Mexicano de Contadores Públicos. The present Instituto Mexicano de Contadores Públicos had its origin in the Mexican Association of Public Accountants (1917), which in 1923 became the Mexican Institute of Public Accountants.

The Institute functions in a manner similar to the American Institute of CPAs. It has several committees, the most important of which are as follows:

1. Accounting principles
2. Guidance and professional practice
3. Training and professional development
4. Consulting in business administration
5. Auditing procedures
6. Professional ethics

The auditing procedures committee has published a series of bulletins covering substantially all the areas of inquiry and investigation commonly encountered in a normal audit.

Since the Institute represents the various colleges, it serves the accounting profession at the local level and organizes the activities that are carried on nationally by the Institute. The main objectives of the Institute and the colleges are the following:

1. To preserve the national unity of the entire accounting profession.
2. To promote the prestige of public accountancy.
3. To advance the making of laws, rules, and standards of the profession.
4. To foster the professional interests of the members.
5. To represent the profession before the local and federal authorities, as well as abroad.

Special Register of Auditors for Tax Purposes

This Registry of Auditors is maintained by the Federal Treasury Department and includes any public accountant who applies and can meet the following requirements:

1. He must be a Mexican citizen.
2. He must have a recognized degree as a public accountant that is registered with the Directorate General of Professions.
3. He must be a member of a college recognized by the Directorate General of Professions.

4. He must not belong to a firm, office, or association that has in its firm name or management the names of persons not having a recognized degree.

Public accountants who wish to file tax certificates on behalf of clients must be enrolled in this special register.

Ethics

The Instituto Mexicano de Contadores Públicos has issued a code of professional ethics and a pamphlet, "The Indepedent Auditor's Report and His Responsibilities." The latter covers much the same ground as that of the American Institute's committee on auditing procedure in a booklet entitled Statement on Auditing Standards No. 1, "Codification of Auditing Standards and Procedures."

The code of ethics states that the public accountant is not considered independent or impartial if he has a financial interest in the firm under examination that is large enough to affect his opinion on the financial statements.

In order to administer these rules, there has been established a board of honor, composed of former presidents of the Institute, which is in charge of handling all complaints made by parties concerned. It is a matter of personal honor to comply with all rules of the code and in some cases the board may punish a member by expelling him from his college and the Institute and informing all members by special bulletin of the results of the case.

Auditing Standards

Auditing standards in Mexico are practically identical to those prescribed in the United States, and are classified into the following groups:

1. Personal standards
2. Performance standards
3. Reporting standards

The requirements to confirm accounts receivable and observe physical inventory taking are covered in bulletins on auditing procedures and are similar to those described in the American Institute's SAS No. 1.

The standard short-form auditor's report used in Mexico is a translation of the one used in the United States, with the same references to generally accepted auditing standards, conformity of financial statements with generally accepted accounting principles, and consistency of application of these standards and principles.

The auditor's short-form report for tax purposes includes a third paragraph containing the public accountant's opinion as to the fulfillment of the federal fiscal obligations of his client.

Because of certain characteristics of Mexican law and business practices, there are some auditing procedures which are different from or additional to those employed in the United States, for example:

1. Since purchase invoices must show certain information in order for the related expenditures to be deductible for income tax purposes, when reviewing purchases the auditor must examine the corresponding invoices to determine that statutory requirements are met.

2. The banks in Mexico do not return canceled checks, consequently other documentary evidence must be examined to support cash disbursements.

3. In Mexico, sales invoices are the documents that establish ownership of merchandise and, therefore, they are examined more extensively than in the United States. Further, copies of such invoices in the hands of vendors may, if an adequate system of internal control exists, constitute valuable evidence of the existence of the related accounts receivable; and auditing programs may require an examination of sales invoices as an alternative auditing procedure when the results of circularization are not satisfactory, still a very common situation in Mexico.

Accounting Principles and Practices

The accounting principles committee of the Instituto Mexicano de Contadores Públicos has issued, since September 1969, the following nine bulletins that are now in the process of review preliminary to final approval:

1. Scheme of basic theory of accounting
2. Revaluation of fixed assets
3. Fixed assets
4. Inventories
5. Contingencies and commitments
6. Accounts receivable

7. Permanent investments in subsidiary companies; consolidated and combined financial statements

8. Cash

9. Liabilities

Accounting principles are generally similar to those employed in the United States, with some exceptions as noted in subsequent paragraphs.

Form and Content of Financial Statements

Statement Presentation. Arrangement and content of financial statements are generally the same as in the United States. Depreciation and amortization are sometimes shown separately below gross profit, or in a note to the financial statements.

Consolidated Financial Statements. It is not customary to prepare consolidated financial statements nor to publish separate parent and subsidiary company statements.

Pooling of Interests

The accounting technique known in the United States as a "pooling of interests," applicable in certain circumstances when one company is acquired by or merged into another company, is not followed in Mexico.

Inventories

While, for accounting purposes, inventories are required to be and generally are stated on the basis of "lower of cost or market," there are some differences from U.S. practice resulting from the requirement of Mexican income tax law that inventories may not be valued below cost. Since most companies prefer to follow tax accounting in their books, there is some reluctance to write down inventories to salvage or market values, although many companies do provide nondeductible inventory reserves. It is possible to obtain permission for proper writedowns, and this is sometimes done.

There is no specific provision in tax law for "standard" costing as there is for "Lifo," "Fifo," average, and unit cost. In specific instances, permission may be given by the tax authorities to change to the standard cost method.

Revaluation of Fixed Assets

Although revaluation of fixed assets has been permitted in Mexico in the past, this is no longer the case and (at this writing) there is no legislation extant permitting revaluation or recognizing it for income tax purposes. However, inflation and the impact of devaluation of the U.S. dollar (which automatically caused devaluation of the peso in the same proportion) has revived interest in revaluation, and consideration has been given by the Institute's committee on accounting principles to recognizing it as an acceptable accounting practice.

Liability for Indemnities

Business enterprises in Mexico are subject to a contingent liability because of indemnities that, according to federal labor law, must be paid to workers in case of unjustified dismissal.

Usually, expenditures in this category are recorded in the period in which they are actually made.

Pensions

Reserves for pensions may be created, but, in order for provisions therefor to be deductible for tax purposes, the federal income tax law requires that they be based on actuarial computations and that the amounts thereof be invested in a special fund that must comply with certain requirements stipulated by the aforementioned law.

Compulsory Profit Sharing

Mexican labor law provides that employees are entitled to share in the profits of their employers beginning with the 1963 year. The regulations for computation of the amount of profit sharing, published in December 1963, provide for an amount of 20 percent of net distributable profit, as defined in the regulations. These regulations, according to the law, were changed in 1973. The amount of profit sharing is not deductible for income tax purposes.

Exchange Gains and Losses

Exchange gains and losses are recognized as realized for income tax purposes only in the period in which devaluation occurs. Consequently, reserves for exchange losses are not common.

The Mexican income tax law requires that all foreign currency assets and liabilities be translated into Mexican pesos at the closing rate of exchange at the end of each fiscal period.

Reserves

Sociedades anónimas are required to set aside each year 5 percent of book net income as a legal reserve until the total is 20 percent of the "capital."

Stock Dividends

Stock dividends are not taxable to corporate recipients although they must be recorded at the per-share average cost of all shares held previous to the issuance of the stock dividend.

Goodwill

The amortization of goodwill is not deductible for income tax purposes, even when the goodwill has been purchased.

Other

Mexican tax definitions make it difficult for the taxpayer to use his discretion in expensing deferred charges such as organization and preoperation costs, as well as tooling costs in manufacturing. Accordingly, these items are frequently found on balance sheets, even in nominal amounts, as assets subject to twenty-year amortization or ten-year depreciation.

Requirements for Listing Securities on the Stock Exchange

The first step in registering securities on the Mexican stock exchange is the filing of a written application addressed to the board of directors of the exchange, enclosing the following:

1. Financial statements of the company with the opinion of a Mexican CP.
2. Balance sheet and income statement for the last five years.
3. Statement of changes in stockholders' equity from inception, including dividends declared.
4. Various documents such as the company charter, board of directors' minutes, and so forth.

On approval of this data by the board of directors, the company must then submit to the Comisión Nacional de Valores certain other information, including—

1. A balance sheet and profit and loss statement with the opinion of a Mexican CP related to the last fiscal year prior to the request for

registration (providing this request is filed within six months after the date of the financial statements). If the request is filed more than six months after the date of the financial statements, then the financial statements should be those for the six months ending after the date of the last fiscal year.

2. Information covering the previous five fiscal years (or since the company's incorporation if the company has been in operation for a period of less than five years) showing for each year:

   a. Net profit
   b. Dividends paid
   c. Capital reserves and other reserves
   d. Securities issued during the five-year period showing the amount, term, interest rate, guarantees, and so forth
   e. Volume and value of the production
   f. Items included under current assets
   g. Details of fixed assets stating the depreciation methods followed and the annual depreciation charges.

If the request for registration relates to securities issued in a foreign country, in addition to the above requirements, the following conditions (among others) should be met:

1. The securities must be represented by deposit certificates issued by a Mexican banking institution.
2. The banking institution must agree to furnish reports in Spanish to the Mexican Stock Exchange, including all the information relating to the securities.
3. The banking institution must have been appointed by the issuer as its agent in Mexico for the purpose of the payment of dividends relating to the securities issued.

However, Comisión Nacional de Valores has officially stated that not all of the additional conditions required in the case of shares issued in foreign countries will be mandatory providing that (a) the foreign company has installations in Mexico representing a basic industry, (b) the securities are issued to finance such industry, and (c) the foreign company has representatives and offices in the Mexican Republic.

The companies whose securities have been registered with the Mexican Stock Exchange and Comisión Nacional de Valores, must furnish annually, within four months after the close of the fiscal year, the following information:

1. Balance sheet and statement of profit and loss with the opinion of a Mexican CP together with annual report to the stockholders.
2. Statement showing proposed distribution of profits, dividends to be declared, and method of payment.
3. Statement of investments in securities, details of issues of debentures, bonds, and so forth.
4. Volume and value of production.

There are no regulations covering information to be given prospective purchasers of securities offered privately or other than through the facilities of the Mexican Stock Exchange.

Mexico

Illustrative Financial Statements

ILLUSTRATIVE BALANCE SHEET OF A MEXICAN COMPANY

BALANCE GENERAL 31 DE DICIEMBRE DE 19__ (BALANCE SHEET DECEMBER 31, 19__)

ACTIVO (Assets)

CIRCULANTE (Current Assets)		
Efectivo en caja y bancos (Cash on hand and in banks)		....
Documentos y cuentas por cobrar: (Notes and accounts receivable)		
Documentos por cobrar (Notes receivable)	....	
Menos: Documentos descontados (Less: Notes discounted)	....	....
Clientes (Customers accounts)		....
Funcionarios y empleados (Officers and employees)		....
Deudores diversos (Sundry debtors)		....
Menos: Estimación para adeudos de cobro dudoso (Less: Reserve for doubtful receivables)		....
		....
Inventarios: (Inventories)		
Almacén de materias primas y materiales (Raw materials and supplies)		....
Producción en proceso (Work in process)		....
Almacén de productos terminados (Finished goods)		....
Mercancías en tránsito (Merchandise in transit)		....
		....
Menos: Estimación para fluctuaciones en inventarios (Less: Reserve for inventory fluctuations)		....
		....
Anticipos a proveedores (Advances to suppliers)		....
Suma (Total)		....
OTRO ACTIVO (Other assets)		
Inversiones en valores (Investments in securities)	....	
Menos: Estimación para baja de valores (Less: Reserve for price declines)	....	....
Depósitos en garantía (Guaranty deposits)		....
Cuentas corrientes (Current accounts—other)		....
Suma (Total)		....
FIJO (Fixed assets)		
Terrenos (Land)		....
Edificios, construcciones e instalaciones (Building, structures, and installations)		....

Maquinaria y equipo de producción (Machinery and production equipment)	....
Mobiliario y equipo de oficina (Office furniture and equipment)	....
Equipo de transporte (Transportation equipment)	....
	....
Menos: Depreciación acumulada (Accumulated depreciation)	....
	....

PAGOS ANTICIPADOS Y GASTOS POR AMORTIZAR (Advance payments and deferred charges)	
Pagos anticipados: (Advance payments)	
Pagos provisionales de impuesto sobre la renta (Provisional income tax payments)	....
Seguros y fianzas pagados por anticipado (Prepaid insurance and guaranty deposits)	....
Intereses pagados por anticipado (Prepaid interest)	....
Rentas pagadas por anticipado (Prepaid rentals)	....
Otros gastos pagados por anticipado (Other prepaid expenses)	....
	....
Gastos por amortizar: (Amortizable expenses)	
Gastos de organización (Organization expenses)	....
Gastos de instalación (Installation expenses)	....
Otros gastos amorizables (Other amortizable expenses)	....
	....
Menos: Amortización acumulada (Less: Accumulated amortization)	
	....
SUMA EL ACTIVO (Total assets)	....
	....

ILLUSTRATIVE BALANCE SHEET OF A MEXICAN COMPANY

BALANCE GENERAL 31 DE DICIEMBRE DE 19__
(BALANCE SHEET DECEMBER 31, 19__)

PASIVO (Liabilities)

CIRCULANTE (Current Liabilities)		
Documentos y cuentas por pagar a plazo menor de un año: (Notes and accounts payable in less than one year)		
Documentos por pagar a corto plazo (Notes payable—short-term)	....	
Proveedores (Suppliers)	....	
Impuestos y cuotas por pagar (Taxes and dues payable)	....	
Acreedores diversos (Sundry creditors)	....	
Anticipos de clientes (Customers advances)	....	
Sueldos y salarios por pagar (Wages and salaries payable)	....	....
Provisiones: (Provisions)		
Participación de utilidades al personal (Employees' profit-sharing)	....	
Provisión para gratificaciones (Provision for bonuses)	....	
Provisión para indeminizaciones (Provision for indemnities)	....	....
Suma (Total)		....
FIJO (Long-term liabilities)		
(Long-term notes payable)		....
COBROS ANTICIPADOS (Deferred income)		
Intereses cobrados por anticipado (Interest collected in advance)	....	
Rentas cobrados por anticipado (Rents collected in advance)	....	....
Suma (Total)		....
CAPITAL CONTABLE (Net worth)		
Capital exhibido: (Paid-up capital)		
Capital social (Capital stock)	....	
Menos: Accionistas (Less: Due from shareholders)	....	....
Reservas de capital: (Capital reserves)		
Reserva legal (Legal (statutory) reserve)	....	
Reserva da reinversión (Reinvestment reserve)	....	....
Resultados: (Results—operating)		
Resultados de ejercicios anteriores (Prior periods)	....	
Resultados del ejercicio (Current period)	....	....
Suma (Total)		
SUMA EL PASIVO (Total liabilities and net worth)		....

ILLUSTRATIVE INCOME STATEMENT OF A MEXICAN COMPANY

ESTADO DE RESULTADOS
(Results of operations)

DEL 1 DE ENERO AL 31 DE DICIEMBRE DE 19__
(From 1 January to 31 December 19__)

Ventas totales (Total sales)			....
Menos: (Less:)			
Descuentos sobre ventas (Discounts on sales)		....	
Devoluciones sobre ventas (Sales returns)		....	....
Ventas netas (Net sales)			....
Menos: Costo de ventas (Less: Cost of sales)			....
UTILIDAD BRUTA (Gross profit)			....
Menos: Gastos de operación: (Less: Operating expenses)			
Gastos de venta (Selling expenses)		....	
Gastos de administración (Administrative expenses)		....	
Gastos financieros (Financial expenses)	....		
Menos: Productos financieros (Financial income)	....	....	....
Menos: Otros gastos y productos:			
(Less: Other expenses and income)			
Otros gastos (Other expenses)		....	
Menos: Otros ingresos (Less: Other income)		....	....
UTILIDAD (PERDIDA) ANTES DE IMPUESTO Y PARTICIPACION (Profit (loss) before taxes and employees' profit sharing)			....
Impuesto sobre la renta (Income tax)		....	
Participación de utilidates al personal (Employees' profit sharing)		....	....
UTILIDAD (PERDIDA) NETA (Net profit (Loss))			....

The Netherlands

The Netherlands

As of June 1973

Significant developments since the preparation of this chapter are presented, by country, in the section entitled Addenda.

Forms of Business Organization

Forms of business organization in The Netherlands include the corporate form, the general partnership, and the sole proprietorship. In 1971, Dutch company law was extensively revised and thereafter the corporate form has been represented by two different types of limited liability companies, the naamloze vennootschap (N.V.) and the besloten vennootschap (B.V.). The former now has the status of a public company while the latter is deemed a private or closed company. Because of their similarity in so many important respects, the two are dealt with together in this text.

Naamloze Vennootschap (N.V.) and Besloten Vennootschap (B.V.)

Both forms have much in common, such as limited liability, capital structure (divided into shares with par value), shareholders' meetings, managing directors, and supervisory directors, the latter by choice in smaller companies and obligatory in the larger companies. The articles of incorporation have to be drawn up by a notary public and require the approval of the Ministry of Justice. No difference exists between the N.V. and the B.V. from the standpoint of taxation.

The distinguishing feature of the B.V. is that it is a closed company and, for this reason, no bearer shares are permitted. The transfer of shares to other than close relatives is restricted and is effected in either of the following ways, depending on the provisions of the company's statutes:

(a) with the consent of a person or persons designated by the company for this purpose in the statutes or

(b) after first offering the shares to other shareholders.

A permit from The Netherlands Bank is required for the formation of all enterprises (subsidiaries, branches, joint ventures, and so forth) by nonresidents. In addition, a permit from the Ministry of Economic Affairs is necessary for the formation or takeover of industrial enterprises by nonresidents. Once both approvals have been obtained, no legal difference exists between a foreign-owned company and a Dutch-owned company. There is no restriction on the appointment of foreigners as directors or supervisory directors.

Special rules apply to large companies (either N.V.s or B.V.s) that together with their subsidiaries have—

(a) a net equity (capital and reserves) of at least 10,000,000 florins,

(b) the legal obligation to establish a works council, and

(c) at least 100 employees in The Netherlands.

Such companies must have a board of supervisory directors comprised of at least three persons. The maximum age for a supervisory director is 72. The term of board members is at most four years; appointment is effected by other members of the board. The shareholders or works council can veto the appointment of a supervisory director, but such veto is subject to being overruled by the Social Economic Council (S.E.R.).

Supervisory directors may not be—

(a) employees of the company;

(b) employees of companies in which the company has a direct or indirect interest of 50 percent or more; or

(c) board members or employees of labor organizations that are involved in fixing the working conditions of the company's employees.

When nominating a person for appointment as supervisory director, details must be furnished as to the nominee's age, profession, shareholdings in the company, and occupations insofar as they may be significant in considering the appointment and the names of other companies in which he is a supervisory director.

The board of supervisory directors in these large companies has considerable power—

1. They appoint their own successors, although recommendations can be made by the shareholders, the directors, or the works council.

2. They appoint and dismiss the directors.

3. They approve the annual accounts prepared by company management.

4. They give prior approval to actions concerning a number of important matters specified in the Code of Commerce.

For Dutch subsidiaries that would normally fall under the classification for large companies but are members of a group of companies with its main center of operations outside The Netherlands, items 2 and 3 above do not apply.

It is the duty of the supervisory directors to protect the interests not only of the company but also of other parties concerned.

Publication of Annual Accounts. The main purpose for creating a special legal corporate form for privately owned companies (B.V.s) was to exempt them from the publication requirements applicable to public companies (N.V.s). As part of the harmonization of company legislation within the European Economic Community, public companies are now obliged to file their annual accounts with the Office of the Commercial Trade Register. This requirement generally does not apply to B.V.s.

Annual accounts comprise the balance sheet, the profit and loss account, and the explanatory notes. They must show the corresponding figures of the preceding year. The accounts of all N.V.s and of certain larger B.V.s must be audited. The auditor must be a registeraccountant (the recognized Dutch qualification for a public accountant) or an accountant who "by a revocable permission based on a proof of competence acquired abroad, has been admitted (to practice) by the Minister of Economic Affairs."

Since 1971 the annual accounts of all N.V.s and all B.V.s must be drawn up in accordance with the requirements of the Act on Annual Accounts of Enterprises. (See "Accounting Principles and Practices.")

The filing requirements for the annual accounts apply to all N.V.s and to those B.V.s that are in the banking or insurance business or that have bearer notes outstanding. In addition, the larger B.V.s (having total assets of 8,000,000 florins or more and having 100 or more employees in The Netherlands, alone or together with their at-least-50-percent-owned subsidiaries) must file their balance sheet (but not the profit and loss account) and the notes thereto.

An auditor's report is required with the filing of annual accounts or a balance sheet and notes, as the case may be, and must accompany such documents. In addition, all B.V.s with an issued capital of 500,000 florins or more have to be audited, regardless of whether or not their balance sheets and notes have to be filed. Certain exemptions from filing and auditing requirements apply to N.V.s and B.V.s that are subsidiaries of companies which themselves have to comply with the requirements.

Works Councils. Organizations having 100 or more persons in employment at any given location are required by a 1971 law to have a works council. Members of the council consist of the company's managing director or his representative who, in terms of the act, is the chairman of the council, and employees (the number of whom depends on the size of the unit) who are elected by their colleagues.

The council discusses, at least twice yearly, the general course of the business of the enterprise. If the publication of annual accounts is obligatory, they (or a summarized version of the balance sheet) must be presented to the council.

The council must approve proposals concerning pension schemes, employees' working hours, and other labor regulations. The council's prior advice must be solicited for important decisions regarding the continuation of the enterprise in its entirety or in part in consequence of mergers, takeovers, or substantial disposals of operations.

Merger Code. Specific rules have been established for mergers by the Social Economic Council (S.E.R.) that, at an early stage of negotiations and, in any case, before a definite decision has been reached or a public offering has been made, information concerning the intended merger must be given to the S.E.R., the shareholders, the works council, and the trade unions actively involved in matters pertaining to employees of the parties in the merger.

Partnerships

Business is also conducted in two forms of partnerships, the "vennootschap onder firma" or general partnership and the "commanditaire vennootschap" or limited partnership. The latter is distinguished from the general partnership by having two classes of partners—managing partners whose liability is unlimited and limited partners whose liability is limited to their capital contributions but who may not participate in the management of the enterprise. There is a variant of the limited partnership, the "commanditaire vennootschap op aandelen" in which the capital of the limited partners is represented by shares. Professional men such as auditors and lawyers practice in partnerships called maatschappen.

Business Records

Businesses must maintain such records as may be necessary to determine their assets and liabilities when required.

The Accounting Profession

The Netherlands Institute of Registeraccountants

The Dutch Registeraccountants Act took effect on March 6, 1967. At that time all Dutch accountants of a recognized professional level became members of an organization, an entity under public law, called the "Nederlands Instituut van Registeraccountants" (Netherlands Institute of Registeraccountants or NIvRA).

The NIvRA is responsible for the regulation of professional activities, the administration of internal discipline, and the education of the members of the profession and administration of the related examinations.

Virtually all members of the "Nederlands Instituut van Accountants" (NIvA) and of the "Vereniging van Academisch Gevermde Accountants" (Association of University-Trained Accountants), together with a few hundred other colleagues, joined the NIvRA in March 1967; at that time the names of more than 2,400 accountants were entered in the newly established Register of Accountants. (At September 30, 1972, there were 3,200 registered accountants).

The register legally limits the use of the title "registeraccountant" to those enrolled therein. Only the names of those who passed the accountant's examination either at one of the universities or under the auspices of the NIvRA may be entered in the register.

Concurrently with the passage of the 1971 Act on Annual Accounts of Enterprises, the concept of compulsory statutory audits was introduced into the Commercial Code. As prescribed in the code, the performance of compulsory audits is restricted to registeraccountants or accountants who, by revocable permission based on a proof of competence acquired abroad, are allowed by the Minister of Economic Affairs to perform such audits.

The Registeraccountants Act and the related rules of professional ethics did not materially change the principles underlying the practice of the accountancy profession in The Netherlands.

Rules of professional ethics were first laid down by the NIvA in 1910, and, with subsequent modifications and amplifications, they still form the basis for professional ethics today. The rules are currently under revision; interim changes have made possible associations with foreign accountants which, until recently, have been prohibited.

Disciplinary Function

The disciplinary bodies of the NIvRA supervise the professional activities of registeraccountants. The disciplinary functions rest with the Disciplinary Board and the Board of Appeal, both independent of the Institute's Council.

The Disciplinary Board examines alleged contraventions of the act or bylaws, negligence in the execution of professional duties, and actions alleged to be detrimental to the professional status of registeraccountants. If not satisfied with a decision of the Disciplinary Board, an appeal may be lodged with the Board of Appeal by the Institute's Council, the complainant, or the respondent.

Educational Function

The NIvRA is responsible for training accountants and organizing examinations for prospective accountants. The examination program is updated regularly. Secondary and grammar school graduates attend the preliminary NIvRA course one working day per week instead of evenings and weekends. This first stage takes two years.

The organization of the second and third stages of the courses has been under review and may, by the time of publication of this book, have been revised. The rule has been that such courses require six years to complete and are pursued outside normal working hours.

University graduates in economics can complete their studies in accountancy by following special courses organized by five universities. Examinations are in civil law, social economics, mathematics, business economics, tax law, accounting principles and procedures, and auditing. The NIvRA organizes post-graduate courses and study conferences semi-annually for the benefit of its members.

Statutory Audit

Auditors are appointed by the shareholders, the board of supervisory directors, or the board of directors.

Statutory audits by a registeraccountant or an accountant who, by revocable permission based on a proof of competence acquired abroad has been authorized by the Minister of Economic Affairs to carry out audits, were first required for public companies (N.V.s) in their financial year during which December 29, 1972, fell.

The following private companies (B.V.s) were required to have statutory audits for the first time in their financial year during which December 29, 1973, fell:

1. Banks and insurance companies, and companies that have bearer bonds outstanding.
2. Companies whose assets, according to their balance sheets aggregate at least 8,000,000 florins and which have more than 100 employees.
3. Companies with an issued share capital of 500,000 florins or more.

Certain institutions, such as pension funds and savings funds, are also required to be audited.

Ethics

The present rules of professional ethics of registeraccountants, currently under consideration for revision, include the following:

1. A registeraccountant's report on annual accounts also covers the explanatory notes forming part of those accounts.
2. A registeraccountant who practices under a joint name, in partnership with another registeraccountant, with the assistance of a registeraccountant employed by him or, by virtue of a dispensation from the Council of the Institute, under a joint name or in partnership with another accountant who is not a registeraccountant, is obliged to take whatever measures are necessary to permit him to conclude that this accountant performs his duties and issues his reports in compliance with these rules.
3. A registeraccountant is prohibited from acting in a promoter's capacity
4. A registeraccountant in public practice may not report on the following:
   a. Financial statements prepared by himself, either alone or in conjunction with others.
   b. Financial statements of persons or legal entities with whom he or his wife have employment contracts or other contracts that would impair his independence.

5. Since December 1971, the Council of the Institute has had the authority to grant to a registeraccountant dispensation from the prohibition of practicing under a joint name or in partnership with one or more accountants who are not registeraccountants. The Council may place restrictions and conditions upon such dispensation.

6. A registeraccountant cannot—

   a. offer his services, nor cause or allow his services to be offered, unless he is personally asked to do so;

   b. advertise or permit advertising on his behalf;

   c. pay a fee for procuring assignments; or

   d. accept remuneration other than that to which he is entitled by reference to the scope, nature, and import of the work.

Sundry Information

The NIvRA publishes an official magazine called *De Accountant.*

For the information of English-speaking colleagues, the NIvRA has made available translations of the text of the Registeraccountants Act, the Rules on Professional Ethics, and the Examination Regulations.

Other Organizations of Accountants

A bill governing the profession of the accountant-administratieconsulent (administration consultants) is presently before Parliament, which will regulate organizations and individuals engaged in accountants' activities outside the attest function. Their activities will be basically restricted to setting up bookkeeping systems, reviewing bookkeeping methods, preparing financial statements, and performing various clerical services for smaller enterprises. The accountant-administratieconsulent, whose title will be protected by law, will not be allowed to carry out statutory audits nor to audit financial statements or other financial presentations.

Eventually only registeraccountants, accountants who, by a revocable permission based on a proof of competence acquired abroad, have been authorized by the Minister of Economic Affairs to carry out statutory audits, and accountants-administratieconsulents will be entitled to use a designation in which the word "accountant" appears.

Auditing Standards

The auditing standards to be observed in The Netherlands are not defined in the same manner as in the Statements on Auditing Standards of the AICPA. However, the Institute's rules on professional ethics and those standards generally regarded as essential to good professional practice (although not codified in official rules) cover essentially the same ground.

The present rules on professional ethics became effective simultaneously with the Registeraccountants Act in 1967, as a temporary measure anticipating the drafting of new professional rules by the newly founded Institute.

In July 1972, a first draft of ethical and professional rules for registeraccountants, including elaborate explanatory information, was presented to the members of the Institute. The rules are expected to become effective by the end of 1973.

Unless otherwise stated, the following observations are based on the 1967 rules.

General Standards

The principal objective of the rules on professional ethics is to preserve the integrity, impartiality, and independence required of registeraccountants in their work. The requirement of impartiality and independence is detailed in article 20, which states that members engaged in public practice may not perform a service for a person, corporate body, or institution if they have any interest therein which could affect their impartiality. Such interest would be represented by a substantial financial interest in, employment with, or directorship of the enterprise under examination.

Standards of Field Work

The standards of field work as laid down by the American Institute of Certified Public Accountants in its Statements on Auditing Standards No. 1, namely, planning of work and supervision of assistants, study and evaluation of internal control, and obtaining of sufficient competent evidential matter, are not codified as such by the Dutch Institute in its rules on professional ethics, but are nevertheless recognized as standards to be observed by the profession in The Netherlands.

According to the 1967 rules, registeraccountants are required to satisfy themselves that their partners and other registeraccountants whose work they utilize or with whom they are associated comply with the rules in performing their duties. In certain cases, a review of work programs, files, and so forth may be necessary. The rules also state that members must conduct their examination in such a way as to provide a reliable basis for the resultant opinion expressed.

The study and evaluation of internal control is not specifically mentioned in the rules; however, a proper study and evaluation of internal control is regarded as an important, if not essential, part of the audit.

Particular emphasis is placed on source and disposition of funds and inventories and on analytically reviewing the financial information from a business-economic viewpoint.

Attendance at physical stocktaking is regarded as an essential audit procedure. Confirming accounts receivable and payable balances is not as usual a practice as in the United States. In most cases the auditor verifies the subsequent collection or payment of the accounts.

Standards of Reporting

The registeraccountant's reporting responsibilities are stated in the 1967 rules and may be summarized as follows:

1. The registeraccountant must formulate his reports in such a manner that they reflect correctly the results of his examinations. A report, even if it is a mere signature, or just a document without an actual report, but clearly originating from a registeraccountant, implies unrestricted concurrence with the related material unless the contrary is specifically stated in a qualification with the words "except for." The reasons for such qualification must be described with the related effect. The registeraccountant is not allowed to issue an exception to an otherwise unqualified opinion if such exception is so material that it negates or substantially affects the opinion.
2. If a document on which a registeraccountant has reported is issued together with other documents, the accountant's report is considered to apply also to the other documents to the extent that they are related to the contents of the first document.
3. Reports on annual accounts should cover the balance sheet, profit and loss account, and related explanatory notes. The 1967 rules state that unqualified reports (must) confirm that the annual accounts have been drawn up in accordance with good commercial practice, that the assets and liabilities exist as shown and that each item has been correctly valued and described. Section 8 of the Act on Annual Accounts of Enterprises requires that if the annual accounts are not in compliance with the provisions of the act, the opinion (of the accountant) should state the extent of noncompliance.
4. The registeraccountant may not issue unqualified opinions on two consecutive balance sheets without including in his second opinion the profit and loss account for the period then ended.

The auditor may give an unqualified opinion on the financial statements, qualify with clearly defined reasons, express an adverse opinion with clearly defined reasons, or disclaim an opinion when he has been unable to obtain sufficient competent evidential matter.

The adverse opinion and the disclaimer are not found in the 1967 rules. The proposed draft of new rules defines the different types of opinions. An unqualified report on financial statements according to the proposed new rules signifies that the registeraccountant is of the opinion that the statements present a true and fair view of the financial position and results.

Form of Report

The Institute has not recommended a standard wording for the auditor's report. According to the 1967 rules, a "report" means any statement by an accountant, written or oral, in which he expresses an opinion. Sometimes the report consists merely of the auditor's signature on the financial statements; it may be accompanied by the words "audited and approved" or merely "approved." There is now a trend toward a more comprehensive report, partly as a consequence of foreign accounting practice.

In March 1972, a committee of the Institute prepared an exposure draft recommending a uniform report and reading as follows:

> We have audited the annual accounts 19.... of N.V. ABC. In our opinion the balance sheet, the profit and loss account and the related notes respectively present fairly and systematically the size and the composition of the enterprise's capital as at .... 19....., and the results for the year 19.....

Although many registeraccountants would be happy with a standard form of report, the proposal is strongly opposed, due principally to its terminology.

There is general agreement that the short-form report should not state the audit procedures that were applied or omitted, because it would be considered useless and confusing to the "interested layman" who in general is not able to judge the significance of such information. A more elaborate report, containing additional financial and statistical information on the company, is sometimes submitted to the directors or to the supervisory directors.

Accounting Principles and Practices

Introduction

Official pronouncements regarding financial reporting and disclosures, comparable to the Opinions of the Accounting Principles Board issued by the American Institute of Certified Public Accountants or the Statements of Standard Accounting Practice of the United Kingdom Institutes of Chartered Accountants, have not been issued by the NIvRA.

The Dutch government has, however, enacted regulations concerning financial reporting and disclosure in the Act of September 10, 1970, prescribing Statutory Regulations for the Annual Accounts of Enterprises. This act consists of three parts. General provisions are set forth in part I; part II contains specific provisions concerning the balance sheet and explanatory notes; part III includes specific provisions concerning the profit and loss account and explanatory notes.

At the request of the Dutch government, the NIvRA together with representatives of the Dutch employers organizations and the Dutch trade unions prepared an exposure draft of their first pronouncement on the standards, which was published early in 1972. The draft covers such areas as subsidiaries, investments, inventories, and short-term and long-term liabilities.

It is not uncommon in The Netherlands to prepare separate financial statements for tax purposes, following the requirements of tax laws. Although the presentation of these statements should be in accordance with the regulations of the Act on Annual Accounts, there may be substantial deviations in valuation of assets and liabilities as found in the financial statements prepared for publication and/or the shareholders. It may have been for this reason that the influence of tax rules on accounting principles in The Netherlands is less than in certain other countries.

Form and Content of Financial Statements

Statement Presentation. No requirements or prescriptions exist as to the form of the balance sheet and the profit and loss account.

Although various forms are in use, the most common form of the balance sheet is that of U.S. public companies—assets on the left, capital and liabilities on the right. In most cases, assets are arranged with fixed assets as the first item; the remaining assets are listed in inverse order of liquidity, with cash as the last item. The right-hand side begins with capital and reserves, followed by provisions and liabilities.

Legal Requirements. The legal requirements of financial statement presentation for limited liability companies, cooperative societies, mutual insurance companies and legal entities of a cooperative nature are stated in the Act on the Annual Accounts, which came into force for annual accounts after April 30, 1971.

Part I of the act contains, among others, the following prescriptions and requirements:

1. Annual accounts consist of the balance sheet and the profit and loss account with appended explanatory notes (section 1).
2. The annual accounts provide sufficient information to permit a sound judgment to be formed on the financial position and results of the enterprise, and on its solvency and liquidity (section 2).
3. The balance sheet together with explanatory notes reflects fairly and systematically the amount and composition of the enterprise's net worth at the end of the financial year (section 3).
4. The profit and loss account together with explanatory notes reflects fairly and systematically the amount and composition of the elements comprising the enterprise's financial results for the financial year (section 3).
5. The corresponding figures for the previous year are included in the annual accounts (section 4).
6. The bases underlying the valuation of the assets and liabilities and the determination of the financial results comply with standards that are regarded as acceptable in the business environment. The notes give a commentary on these bases. Any change in the bases, which is considered significant, is described, showing its effect on the net equity and the financial results (section 5).
7. Reserves and movements therein are separately stated and explained in the annual accounts to the extent required for ensuring a fair presentation of the composition of the enterprise's financial position and results (section 6).
8. Either the profit and loss account or the explanatory notes include the appropriation of the profit or the disposition of the loss, with a reference to the relative provisions of the articles of incorporation (section 8).

According to the regulations of part II of the act, the balance sheet or explanatory notes must, as a minimum, disclose the following items:

Assets

1. Fixed assets, subdivided into business plant and premises, machinery and fittings, other durable business equipment, and fixed assets not used for business activities (section 10).
2. Intangible assets (section 11).
3. Certain details on participations and investments in other enterprises (sections 12 and 13).

4. Total amounts receivable from subsidiaries (section 12).
5. Inventories, subdivided into raw materials, supplies, semi-finished products, work in progress, finished products or merchandise (section 16).
6. Receivables, subdivided into trade debtors, installments receivable, receivables secured by a mortgage, and credits granted (section 17).
7. Discounted bills on which the enterprise still bears a risk (section 18).
8. The aggregate value of securities apart from those in (3) above or (9) below (section 18).
9. The aggregate value of securities listed on a Dutch or foreign stock exchange (section 19).
10. Cash-on-hand in banks and postal accounts (section 19).

Liabilities and Capital

1. Total equity, divided into issued share capital and reserves; details of any different categories of share capital and special rights pertaining thereto must be given (section 20).
2. Liabilities with a term exceeding one year, divided into—
   a. debenture loans and liens,
   b. amounts due to those in whose capital the enterprise participates,
   c. amounts due to those participating in the capital of the enterprise,
   d. pension liabilities, and
   e. other liabilities (section 22).
3. Current portion, remaining term and interest rate of, and security for, long-term liabilities (section 22).
4. Provisions relating to specific assets if not otherwise deducted from those assets, provision for deferred or contingent tax liabilities and provision for pension obligations (section 23).
5. Amounts payable within one year, divided into amounts due to banks, amounts due to suppliers, trading credits received and amounts payable in respect of pension and tax (section 24).

Part III of the act requires the profit and loss statement or explanatory notes to disclose the following:

1. The size of the enterprise's turnover either in absolute figures or in ratios relating to the preceding financial year (section 28).
2. The amount of wages and social charges (section 28).
3. The operating results, other income and expense, the profit or loss before taxation, and the estimated taxes on the profit (section 29).
4. Items that should be shown separately are—

   a. Depreciation of fixed assets
   b. Amortization of intangible assets
   c. Profits or losses from participations
   d. Profits or losses from investments
   e. Interest income
   f. Interest expense
   g. Extraordinary gains
   h. Extraordinary losses (section 29)

The profit and loss statement may be either in account or statement form. It sometimes includes items that, in the United States, would be shown on the statement of retained earnings. Sales and cost of sales are very rarely stated in published financial statements. Statutory reserves are not required by law but are sometimes provided for in the company's bylaws. After providing for dividends, it is customary to transfer the net profit to a general reserve which is considered freely available for distribution. "Retained earnings" is a term seldom found on Dutch balance sheets.

Special acts prescribe in detail the form and content of the annual accounts of life insurance companies, pension funds, and savings funds.

Consolidated Accounts. According to section 13 of the Act on Annual Accounts, disclosure requirements of the act apply to enterprises in more than half of whose issued share capital a company participates, either directly or indirectly. According to the act, this obligation can be met by including in the explanatory notes to the annual accounts of the participating enterprise either consolidated annual accounts or individual or combined annual accounts of the subsidiaries.

It is generally accepted in The Netherlands that consolidated accounts are essential to present fairly the state of affairs of the parent company.

Subsidiaries and Participations

Apart from the requirements mentioned above, the Act on Annual Accounts states that information should be provided as objectively as possible on the value and changes thereof during the financial year of an enterprise's participation in the issued share capital of other enterprises. Direct or indirect holding of shares constituting at least one-quarter of the issued share capital of an enterprise is considered a participation. Direct or indirect holding of shares constituting more than half of the issued share capital necessitates disclosure of all information relating to the subsidiary, which according to the Act on Annual Accounts would be included in the subsidiary's annual accounts; such disclosure can be effected either in the explanatory notes or through consolidated, individual, or combined annual accounts of the subsidiaries. If more than half of the issued share capital of an enterprise is held, its name and domicile are disclosed in the annual accounts of the participating enterprise. This rule also applies if the value of the participation is at least 15 percent of the consolidated assets of the participating enterprise and subsidiary.

"Current Value" Accounting

Due mainly to the influence of business and economic theory on the development of the Dutch accounting practice, a number of Dutch accountants prefer to charge income with the current (or replacement) costs of goods and services utilized to produce the income. This involves computing depreciation on the basis of current fixed-asset value and the computation of inventory usage at its current value, thereby approximating the Lifo basis.

Many Dutch registeraccountants subscribe to the theory that only by matching "current value" costs with the proceeds of goods sold or services rendered can true profit be computed; however, the majority of Dutch companies quoted on the stock exchange use historical cost as the basis of valuation.

Inventories

The Act on Annual Accounts does not prescribe methods of inventory valuation; it merely states that the valuation of assets should comply with standards regarded as acceptable in the business environment. The basis of valuation chosen should be applied systematically and consistently throughout the years. Various methods are used to value inventories, of which the "lower of cost or market" basis is considered the most acceptable. (The practice, however, of stating inventories at less than this amount is not uncommon.) "Lifo" and "base stock" methods are permitted for tax purposes and are also used for book purposes. A minority of Dutch enterprises (including some large international companies) apply "current value" accounting, which is considered acceptable although not permitted for tax purposes. Overheads are usually included in inventory costs but can be omitted.

Intangible Assets

According to the Act on Annual Accounts, intangible assets should be valued at an amount not exceeding their cost less accumulated amortization. Within this category the following should be stated separately: goodwill, patents, licenses, copyrights, concessions and exploitation rights, initial and starting-up expenses.

Fixed Assets

It is considered acceptable to revalue fixed assets on a current cost basis; this practice is currently followed by various companies in The Netherlands. The revaluation must be disclosed in the annual accounts and the effects on the total equity and financial results disclosed. The amount of the increase is credited to a revaluation reserve. No depreciation is allowed for tax purposes on the write-up in value.

Long-Term Liabilities and Commitments

The Act on Annual Accounts requires the disclosure, either in the balance sheet or explanatory notes of material commitments such as those relating to long-term leases, building rights, rentals, leaseholds, installment purchases, and chartering or licensing agreements. The same requirement applies to other significant obligations, such as those relating to material investments made by the enterprise.

Shares and Reserves

The Act on Annual Accounts requires disclosure of such information as the categories of shares, paid-up status, shares repurchased, and the existence of shares the holders of which are entitled to special rights.

The reserves should be divided into such categories as paid-in surplus on issued shares, revaluation reserve, and retained profits. Movements in the individual reserve accounts should be stated and explained in the annual accounts to the extent necessary for ensuring a fair picture of the enterprise's financial position and results.

Depreciation

The Act on Annual Accounts does not include specific requirements for depreciation. The general rule is that the valuation of the assets (and liabilities) and the determination of the financial results should comply with standards acceptable in the business environment.

Straight-line and declining-balance depreciation methods are commonly used. If "current value" accounting is adopted, depreciation recorded on a higher replacement valuation will exceed that permitted for tax purposes, i.e., depreciation calculated on the cost basis.

Directors' and Management Bonuses

Section 7 of the Act on Annual Accounts requires disclosure of the total amount of emoluments of the supervisory directors, divided into fixed remuneration, bonuses, and other forms. The annual accounts must state the number of supervisory directors as well as the number of them receiving no emoluments. Bonuses to directors and management are sometimes regarded as distributions of profit, especially if so described in the company's articles of incorporation; consequently, they are sometimes shown as an appropriation of net income in the statement of profit and loss. Such bonuses are, generally, deductible for tax purposes.

Requirements for Listing Securities on the Stock Exchange and Public Sale of Securities

The required contents for a prospectus offering shares or debentures to the public are listed in paragraph 15 of the regulations issued by the "Vereniging voor den Effectenhandel" (Stock Exchange Association), a semi-official body which manages the stock exchange under the supervision of the Ministry of Finance. The provisions of this paragraph relating to accounting matters include, among other things, disclosure requirements as follows:

1. For issues not previously listed on the stock exchange, an analysis of capital stock movements from the inception of the company.
2. Balance sheets, income statements, and related notes for the last two complete years and similar financial information for the current year.

The balance sheets and income statements of the company must be accompanied by an auditor's certificate except when waived by the management of the stock exchange. When an auditor's certificate is submitted, the accountant must give his written consent to its inclusion in the prospectus. An application for listing of securities must be made in writing and immediately after a prospectus is issued. It must be signed by one or more members of the Stock Exchange Association, the number depending on the circumstances. There are no accounting disclosure requirements other than that the prospectus must accompany the application. Once its securities are listed on the stock exchange, the company is obliged to publish annual accounts and, in the third and ninth month of its financial year, a statement covering the financial results of the previous six months.

The Netherlands

Illustrative Financial Statements

ILLUSTRATIVE BALANCE SHEET OF A NETHERLANDS COMPANY

BALANS PER 31 DECEMBER 19__
Balance Sheet at December 31, 19__

ACTIVA (Assets)

VASTE ACTIVA (Fixed Assets)		
Aanschafwaarde (Cost)	....	
Afschrijving op basis aanschafwaarde (Depreciation reserve—on cost)	....	....
VOORRADEN (Inventories)		....
VORDERINGEN (Receivables)		
Debiteuren op lange termijn (Long-term debits)	....	
Debiteuren op korte termijn (Short-term debits)	....	
Te ontvangen en vooruitbetaald (Accounts receivable and prepayments)	....	
		....
BELEGDE MIDDELEN (Cash at Bank and on Hand)		....
LIQUIDE MIDDELEN (Securities)		....
		....

PASSIVA (Liabilities)

AANDELENKAPITAAL (Share Capital)	....	
Waarven niet geplaatst (Less unissued)	....	
		....
RESERVES (Reserves)		
Algemene reserve (General reserve)	....	
Agioreserve (Share premium reserve)	....	
Aanvulling afschrijving vaste activa (Additional depreciation on fixed assets)	....	
		....
MINDERHEIDSBELANG IN HANDEN VAN DERDEN (Minority Shareholders)		....
VOORZIENINGEN (Provisions)		....
IN AANDELEN CONVERTEERBARE EURODOLLAR OBLIGATIELENING (Convertible Eurodollar Debenture Loan)		....
SCHULDEN OP LANGE TERMIJN (Long-Term Debts)		....
SCHULDEN OP KORTE TERMIJN (Short-Term Debts)		
Bankiers (Bank overdrafts)	....	
Handels- en andere crediteuren (Trade and other creditors)	....	
Vaste activa in bestelling (Fixed assets on order)	....	
Belastingen (Taxes)	....	
Te betalen en vooruitontvangen (Accounts payable and accrued liabilities)	....	
		....
WINST TER VERDELING (Profit Available for Distribution)		....
		....

ILLUSTRATIVE INCOME STATEMENT OF A NETHERLANDS COMPANY

WINST-EN VERLIESREKENING OVER HET BOEKJAAR 19__

Profit and Loss Account for the Year 19__

GEFACTUREERDE OMZET AAN DERDEN (Invoiced Sales to Third Parties)		....
Af: Accijns (Less: Excise taxes)		....
OMZET (Sales)		....
DIVERSE INKOMSTEN (Sundry Receipts)		....
		....
EXPLOITATIEKOSTEN ZONDER AFSCHRIJVINGEN (Operating Costs Before Depreciation)		
Salarissen en sociale lasten (Salaries, wages, and social security charges)	....	
Overige kosten (Other costs)	....	....
		....
AFSCHRIJVINGEN (Depreciation)		
Op basis aanschafwaarde (On the basis of cost)	....	
Aanvulling tot vervangingswaarde (Additional depreciation on a replacement basis)	....	....
BEDRIJFSRESULTAAT (Trading Profit)		....
INTEREST (Interest)		
Betaald (Paid)	....	
Ontvangen (Received)	....	....
		....
SALDO BIJZONDERE BATEN EN LASTEN (Balance of Sundry Profits and Losses)		....
		....
BELASTINGEN NAAR DE WINST (Taxes)		....
NETTOWINST (Net Profit)		....
GERESERVEERD (Transfer to Reserves)		....
WINST TER VERDELING (Profit Available for Distribution)		....
VOORGESTELDE WINSTVERDELING (Proposed Profit Distribution)		
Dividend (Dividend)		....
Commissarissen (Supervisory directors)		....
		....

New Zealand

New Zealand

As of July 1973

Forms of Business Organization

The principal forms of business organization are incorporated companies, partnerships, and sole traders. Almost all industrial and commercial enterprises are established as incorporated companies with limited liability.

Company Formation and Operation

Regulations governing the formation and operation of incorporated companies are contained in the New Zealand Companies Act of 1955. This act was based on, and follows closely, the 1948 United Kingdom Companies Act.

A company may be "limited by shares," "limited by guarantee," or "unlimited" and may be registered as either a "public" or a "private" company.

The registration of a company is effected by lodging with the Registrar of Companies the following documents:

1. A memorandum of association which is, in effect, its charter outlining its objects and powers, detailing its share capital, and stating that its liability is limited (if such is the case).

2. Articles of association which set out the rights and restrictions that govern the relationship between members.

These must be signed by all subscribers detailing the number of shares taken by each. The Registrar of Companies, having approved the proposed name of the company (which must conclude with the word "Limited" when that is the case) and having received the requisite fees, then issues a certificate of incorporation and entitlement to commence business.

Each year, companies are required to file with the Registrar of Companies an annual return including information to the date of its annual general meeting, as follows:

1. Address of registered office.
2. Location of register of members (which may be other than the registered office).
3. Summary of share capital and debentures.
4. Amount of registered indebtedness, i.e., mortgages and other charges given on the property of the company.
5. Particulars of directors and secretary.
6. List of members, their holdings, and changes therein since the last return.

Copies of the company's annual accounts must be filed with the Commissioner of Inland Revenue.

Public Companies

Only companies registered as "public" companies may issue a prospectus seeking share capital from the general public. Public companies closely resemble the usual U.S. corporation, and when "limited by shares," the liability of shareholders is limited to the amount unpaid, if any, on their subscriptions to capital stock. A public company must have at least seven members at all times.

The Companies Act of 1955 provides that every company shall appoint an auditor or auditors who shall make a report to the members on the financial statements examined by them and presented to the shareholders at the general meeting. The appointment of auditors is discussed in more detail in a later section. A certified copy of the relevant annual accounts together with the auditors' report thereon and the directors' report must accompany the annual return when filed with the Registrar of Companies. The minimum content of the financial accounts is set out in the eighth schedule of the Companies Act.

Private Companies

Companies which are incorporated under Part VIII of the Companies Act as private companies are not permitted to offer their shares for public subscription. However, a private company may issue debentures or obtain moneys from the public on the basis of a prospectus issued for such purpose.

Private companies are usually formed to obtain the advantages of limited liability for family businesses, small closely held businesses, and subsidiaries of other locally or overseas owned corporations. This is the more convenient form of incorporation for a subsidiary.

A private company need have only two members, but membership is restricted to 25, except where employees are also members in which case the limit is 50. The capital must be fully subscribed; that is, all shares must be allotted to members even though they need not be paid up. There need be only one director.

A private company may, in its articles of association, make provisions to give privileges or impose restrictions on its members with or without creating classes of members. For instance, the articles may restrict the transfer of shares, attach preferred voting to certain shares, and appoint some or all directors for "life."

A private company that is not a subsidiary of a public company may dispense with the requirement of being audited provided it has not borrowed moneys from the public or provided it does not come within the definition of an "overseas controlled company." This is done by the members passing a unanimous resolution annually that no auditor be appointed.

Private companies are not required to file copies of their annual accounts, directors' reports, and auditors' reports with their annual returns to the Registrar of Companies unless they have obtained loans from the public on the basis of a prospectus inviting subscription or they are an "overseas controlled company."

An "overseas controlled company" is any New Zealand incorporated company in which more than 25 percent of the effective voting power is controlled by overseas persons. A foreign corporation may form a New Zealand subsidiary or purchase an interest in an established local company subject to certain government regulations which are discussed in a later section.

Other provisions which do not apply to private companies are set forth in the ninth schedule of the Companies Act.

Companies Incorporated Overseas

Companies incorporated outside New Zealand which carry on business in New Zealand through a branch must register as overseas companies. Requirements are contained in Part XII of the Companies Act of 1955.

Within one month from the establishment of a place of business in New Zealand, these companies must deliver to the registrar a certified copy of the charter, statutes, or other instruments defining the constitution of the company, a list and particulars of the directors and secretary, and the names and addresses of one or more persons resident in New Zealand authorized to accept, on behalf of the overseas company, service of process and any notices required to be served on the company.

Every overseas company shall on all places of business, bill heads, letter paper, and notices state the name of the company, the country in which it is incorporated, and the fact that it is limited (if that is the case). Every such company is required to file such financial accounts as would be required if it had been incorporated in New Zealand with the Registrar of Companies.

Overseas insurance companies must also comply with other pertinent legislation.

Partnerships

The usual partnership with unlimited liability of partners as recognized under British and American law is also found in New Zealand.

Special partnerships may also be formed to transact business other than banking and insurance. They may have different classes of partners, some with limited liability. These special partnerships must be registered in the Supreme Court.

Business Records

The Companies Act of 1955 states that every New Zealand company must keep "full, true, and complete accounts of the affairs and transactions of the company."

If accounting records are maintained outside New Zealand, returns must be sent to New Zealand at least every six months and retained there to show with reasonable accuracy the financial position of the company. These returns must enable the company's annual accounts to be prepared in accordance with the act.

All New Zealand businesses, be they companies, partnerships, or sole traders, are required to file copies of their accounts with the taxes division of the Department of Inland Revenue. The contents of accounts and other requirements of the income tax acts do not necessarily follow those of the Companies Act of 1955.

Overseas Investment in New Zealand

Government policy is to encourage the establishment of new enterprises in New Zealand with overseas backing, particularly those which—

(a) make the greatest use of indigenous raw materials,

(b) use imported raw materials in their most basic state to enable the highest production volume in relation to overseas funds expenditure,

(c) contribute to export income,

(d) strengthen capital goods production within New Zealand, and

(e) bring with them additional technical knowledge and skills.

It is also government policy to encourage New Zealand participation in subsidiaries of overseas companies where feasible and practicable. However, because circumstances of each case vary, it is not possible to quantify the requirements of government for local equity participation. Absolute foreign ownership of individual enterprises is discouraged, but the preference for New Zealand participation does not always bar the establishment or acquisition of wholly owned subsidiaries. Each case is considered on its merits.

There are available to government three points at which it may intervene to prevent or restrict any prospective overseas participation in an established local company or in a new venture. These points of intervention, capital issues control, overseas takeover regulations, and exchange control, are subject at any time to possible change in government policy.

Capital Issues Control Regulations

Before an overseas company can register and commence business in New Zealand it must first obtain approval under the Capital Issues (Overseas) Regulations of 1965 (as amended). Consent must also be obtained under these regulations in order that an overseas company or person may raise or borrow money or, in the case of a company, issue a prospectus in New Zealand. In this case an "overseas company" is deemed to include any New Zealand incorporated company in which more than 25 percent of the effective voting power is controlled by overseas persons and any company incorporated outside New Zealand operating a New Zealand enterprise through a branch of an overseas company.

The Capital Issues Regulations also preclude any New Zealand incorporated company from borrowing or raising money outside New

Zealand without the government's consent. However, once the consent has been given for an overseas company to operate in New Zealand through a branch, no control is placed on inward remittances from the overseas parent to the branch, provided receipt of funds is through the banking system.

The regulations extend to all sources of finance within New Zealand other than bank overdraft, but bank finance is subject to both quantitative and qualitative control by the Reserve Bank of New Zealand.

Overseas Takeover Regulations

An overseas company or overseas resident seeking to gain 25 percent or more of the voting power in an existing New Zealand company is subject to the provisions of the Overseas Takeover Regulations of 1964. For the purpose of these regulations, overseas companies or persons are defined as those persons not ordinarily resident in New Zealand, companies incorporated outside New Zealand or their New Zealand subsidiaries, and New Zealand companies in which 25 percent or more of the voting power is controlled by overseas persons.

Where an overseas company, or person, makes or proposes to make, an offer which would involve yielding control of 25 percent or more of the voting power of a New Zealand company, the Minister of Finance through the Reserve Bank of New Zealand must be notified on or before the date of the offer. The information required includes selected details of the scheme and of the offeror, together with particulars of any other New Zealand shareholdings over which the offeror has any control. The Minister of Finance is bound to notify the offeror within 14 days of the lodging of the information, whether further consideration of the offer is required, and, if so, the offeror will be notified within an additional four weeks whether or not the offer is consented to.

Exchange Control

Exchange control applies to all remittances from New Zealand other than those relating to the importation of commodities. Consent of the Reserve Bank of New Zealand, the exchange control authority, must be obtained by the remitter's trading bank for all other remittances including payments of royalties, license fees, and interest, the repatriation of capital, and the remittances of profits and head office charges payable to an overseas parent company. Remittances of this nature will normally be permitted, and the remittance of dividends is not subject to exchange control. However, the prior approval of the Reserve Bank is required before a New Zealand resident may enter into any contract (other than for the importation of commodities) involving settlement in foreign exchange.

The Accounting Profession

The accounting profession in New Zealand has been regulated since the formation in 1908 of the New Zealand Society of Accountants by acts of Parliament, the most recent legislation being the 1958 Act. The Society is the recognized body of accountants, and its stated objectives are to promote the interests of accounting and to control and regulate the profession in New Zealand.

Designations

All members are designated chartered accountants and are entitled to use the letters ACA (associate) or FCA (fellow). Those members engaged in public practice are issued a certificate of public practice. Persons who have passed the examinations but who have not yet fulfilled the practical experience requirements may be admitted as provisional members. This provisional membership does not allow the use of designatory letters.

In New Zealand, only members of the Society are entitled to use the letters ACA or FCA, or describe themselves as chartered accountants.

Functions of Accountants

In addition to auditing the accounts of companies, the keeping of financial records, the preparation of annual accounts, and the filing of returns, accountants may also perform secretarial work; act as tax consultants; prepare tax returns; accept appointments as trustees; act in liquidations; provide assistance in the field of financial management; install accounting systems, cost, and budgetary controls; and act as agents for insurance companies and building societies. Accountants may also act as directors where this function does not interfere with their independence.

The New Zealand Society of Accountants

Qualifications for Membership. Membership is available to persons who have passed the Society's professional examinations and have satisfied its council that they are of good character and reputation, are not engaged in any business or occupation inconsistent with the integrity of the profession, and (since 1958) have completed five years of practical accounting experience. This experience must have been gained in the office of an approved undertaking, such as a public accountant, a government department, a bank, an insurance company, an approved local body, or other approved commercial or industrial undertaking. The period is reduced to three years for university graduates.

Membership is also available to members of certain accounting bodies in the United Kingdom, Australia, and Canada upon taking up permanent residence in New Zealand.

A prescribed academic level of education and training was established as early as 1911. The Society has always encouraged students to take a university course for a bachelor of commerce degree. Cross credits between the degree course and professional accountancy are allowed. If appropriate courses are taken in obtaining a degree, no further subjects would be necessary to comply with the Society's examination requirements.

The examination syllabus for the professional course which takes most students four years to complete is as follows:

- Accounting I
- Accounting II
- Commercial Law I
- Commercial Law II
- Economics
- Cost and Management Accounting
- Advanced Financial Accounting
- Taxation, Trustee Law, and Accounts
- Auditing
- Mathematics and Statistics

Activities of the Society. The Society has its own publication, the *Accountants' Journal*, which is published monthly and contains articles on a wide range of technical subjects including taxation, practitioners, secretarial, and student sections. It also includes pronouncements of the Society and of overseas accounting organizations.

The Society holds conventions every five years to hear papers on technical subjects. Its first residential summer school was held in 1964 to hear papers and to discuss and study these in small groups. These meetings and discussions have exerted a strong influence on the establishment and acceptance of accounting principles and auditing standards. Research lectures have been given from time to time on various accounting topics.

The Society has issued "Recommendations on Accounting Principles," which generally follow the pronouncements of the Institute of Chartered Accountants in England. New pronouncements are being prepared and the earlier ones updated.

There are branches or sub-branches of the Society in 18 towns and cities throughout New Zealand.

Ethics. The Society has adopted a written code of ethics which is strictly enforced. This code includes the following:

1. A member may not accept an engagement where the amount of remuneration is contingent upon the member's findings or results thereof.
2. A member may not prepare or certify as correct any statement which he knows to be false, incorrect, or misleading.
3. A member may not offer employment to an employee of a fellow member without prior consultation with the fellow member.
4. A client must be informed of any business connections, interests, or affiliations which might influence a member's judgment.
5. A member may not encroach upon the business of another member. If a member is approached by a client of another member to give services or advice of a special nature, he shall inform the other member of the circumstances.
6. A member may not solicit professional work.
7. A member may not have any association with an enterprise or activity of a questionable character which could bring the member, Society, or profession into disrepute.
8. A member may associate with nonmembers in management consultancy companies and computer companies.

The New Zealand Society of Accountants Rule (1958) No. 60 covers the manner and under whose name or names a member may practice. The effect of this rule is to prohibit overseas firms of accountants from practicing under their own names in New Zealand, unless they were established in the country prior to the effective date of the rule.

A recommended disclaimer statement has been issued by the Society for use on accounts prepared in an accountant's office which have not been audited.

Other Organizations of Accountants

The Practicing Accountants Association is a small group of nonqualified practitioners who are allowed to practice publicly under a designation including the term "accountant." This is a so-called "dying class" and no new members are allowed to join the Association.

Appointment of Auditors

The Companies Act of 1955 provides that every company shall have an auditor who shall be a member of the New Zealand Society of Accountants.

A private company may, however, by unanimous resolution of all shareholders, dispense with the services of an auditor. A copy of such resolution must be filed with the Registrar of Companies.

The auditor holds office from the conclusion of one annual general meeting to the conclusion of the next; a retiring auditor may be re-appointed without any resolution being passed.

If no auditor is appointed or reappointed at an annual general meeting, the Registrar of Companies may appoint one.

The following are not qualified for appointment as the auditor of a company:

1. An officer or servant of the company.
2. A person who is a partner of or in the employment of an officer or servant of the company (This does not apply to private companies).
3. A body corporate.
4. Any person who is disqualified to be an auditor of any other company in a group—be it a subsidiary or a holding company.

Auditing Standards

General Standards

The Society has from time to time, through its board of research and publications, made statements in regard to various aspects of auditing practice. These include the following:

1. General principles of auditing
2. Events after balance date
3. The auditors' responsibilities for inventories
4. Presentation of company balance sheets and profit and loss accounts

Tentative statements have also been issued in respect of the following:

1. Audit examination of debtor balances
2. Auditing standards

Chartered accountants in public practice in New Zealand have always realized the importance of maintaining high auditing standards. The general standards and standards of field work compare favorably with those in the other countries of the British Commonwealth and in the United States.

Independence. Although the code of ethics states that a client must be informed of any business connections, interests, or affiliations which might influence the judgment of a member of the Society, the chartered accountant in public practice is free to hold shares in a company being audited, so long as this does not, in his opinion, affect his independence or professional judgment. Auditors of private companies sometimes do accounting work for their own audit clients.

However, a public accountant may not act as a director of a public company being audited by his firm or by one of his partners. In the case of a private company, one partner of a firm may be a director or officer while his partner, being a public accountant, may properly be the auditor of the company.

Standards of Field Work

There is no statute which defines auditing procedures in New Zealand, nor are there any other requirements similar to those of the U.S. Securities and Exchange Commission. However, the procedures commonly in use include the following:

1. Although there is no statutory requirement that an auditor review the system of internal accounting controls, he would nonetheless examine this aspect thoroughly as part of normal audit procedures, and report on any deficiencies he may discover. He would then carry out such tests as he would deem necessary to prove that such controls are adequate and to determine the extent of his reliance on them in forming his opinion on the accounts.

2. In general the verification of balance sheet items follows the practice and procedures adopted overseas. Many of the larger firms engaged in auditing have connections with well-known international firms of accountants upon whose procedures they tend to model their own.

3. It has now become accepted practice for the auditor to witness physical stock-taking procedures. He would normally spend some time in reviewing the adequacy of the proposed procedures, would attend at some period during the physical count, and would test the pricing and arithmetical accuracy of the final listing. It is also

normal procedure to obtain a certificate from management at the appropriate level of responsibility as to the content of the inventories. In practice this is often included in a letter of representation from the client as is done in the United Kingdom and other commonwealth countries.

4. Confirmation of receivables is generally performed by a combination of the positive and negative forms of verification varied according to the nature of the business and the relative materiality of the balances involved.

5. The ownership of fixed assets would be required to be adequately evidenced according to their nature, e.g., in the case of land, certificates of title would be sighted or when mortgaged, properly certified by the mortgagee. Movements in assets are traced with documentary proof as to their purchase or disposal.

6. Likewise adequate evidence is required to support stated liabilities and enquiries made to ensure that all liabilities are indeed fully taken to account.

Standards of Reporting

There is a statutory duty under the Companies Act for the auditor to make a report to the shareholders setting out information required under the section 166, "Auditor's Report."

One form of auditors' unqualified report, which complies with the requirements of the Companies Act of 1955, is as follows:

> We have obtained all the information and explanations that we have required. In our opinion proper books of account have been kept by the company so far as appears from our examination of those books. In our opinion, according to the best of our information and the explanations given to us and as shown by the said books, the balance sheet and the profit and loss accounts are properly drawn up so as to give respectively a true and fair view of the state of the company's affairs as at .... (date) .... and the results of its business for the year ended on that date.
>
> According to such information and explanations the accounts, the balance sheet, and the profit and loss account give the information required by the Companies Act of 1955 in the manner so required.

Penalties are provided in the Act for issuing, circulating, or publishing any balance sheet without a copy of the profit and loss account and auditor's report attached thereto.

The Department of Inland Revenue does not require certified financial statements.

While it is the attitude of public accountants in New Zealand that their primary legal responsibility is to the stockholders who appoint them, they are also conscious of obligations to third parties in the carrying out of their statutory duties.

Consistency. The act states that any change in the basis of accounting which might tend to distort the accounts must be disclosed.

Materiality. The New Zealand public accountant has the same concept of materiality and its effect on his work and on his opinion relating to the financial statements as has a CPA in the United States.

Disclosure of Subsequent Events. Although footnotes are widely used, subsequent events having a material effect on the financial statements would not normally be disclosed in a footnote, although practice is moving in the direction of such disclosure. However, this information would probably be given in the directors' report.

Directors' Report

A directors' report must be attached to the balance sheet submitted to the annual general meeting of shareholders. This report must include (a) the state of the company's affairs, (b) the recommended dividend, (c) the proposed transfers to reserve accounts, and (d) any changes or proposed changes in the nature of the company's or its subsidiaries' business.

It is permissible to include in the directors' report information required by statute to be given in the accounts. If this procedure is adopted, it is an offense to issue a balance sheet unless the directors' report is attached.

Accounting Principles and Practices

The accounting rules and practices in New Zealand are based mainly on the Companies Act of 1955. The eighth schedule of this act lists the requirements which must be followed in the preparation of financial statements. The board of publications of the Society has issued (1966) a statement on the "Presentation of Company Balance Sheets and Profit and Loss Accounts."

Form and Content of Financial Statements

Statement Presentation. The general arrangement of the balance sheet in New Zealand is similar to that customary in the United Kingdom—capital and liabilities on the left side and assets on the right side. There is still a preference for the order of items used by the U.S. public utility company, i.e., fixed assets and shareholders' equity at the head of the asset and liability sides, respectively; the "account" form is used more than the "statement" form.

Under the act the financial statements of a company must give a "true and fair view" of the state of affairs of the company at the end of its financial year, and of the profit or loss for the year or other period under review.

Comparative Financial Statements. The act requires that comparative figures be presented for the immediately preceding period for all items in the balance sheet and profit and loss account. The following principles should be applied when complying with this requirement:

1. Where an item, which is required to be stated, appears in a note on the accounts or in a document annexed thereto, the corresponding amount for the immediately preceding year should be shown.
2. Where the accounts do not include an item corresponding to an item which appeared in the accounts for the immediately preceding year, the amount for that earlier year need not be shown unless the omission would cause the comparison of the two years' accounts to be misleading.
3. If items in the accounts have been regrouped, subdivided, or otherwise rearranged as compared with the accounts for the immediately preceding year, then the items for that earlier year should be rearranged similarly for the purpose of showing the comparative figures.
4. Where a change in the basis of accounting materially affects the comparability of the profit and loss account of the year with that of the preceding year, appropriate information should be included in the accounts by way of note or otherwise. This information should explain the nature of the change, and should indicate either the extent to which the accounts of the preceding year would have been affected had the revised basis been in use in that year, or, as may be appropriate, the extent to which the accounts of the current year would have been affected had no change been made.

In addition to the corresponding amounts for the preceding year, a summary covering at least the preceding five financial years of significant totals namely, capital, reserves, profit before tax, dividends and sales, is recommended.

Consolidated Financial Statements. The preparation of consolidated financial statements is covered in the act under the section dealing with accounts of holding and subsidiary companies. As a general rule, group or consolidated accounts covering a holding company and its subsidiary companies and consisting of a consolidated balance sheet and a consolidated profit and loss account are required to be prepared.

In certain cases, group accounts may be presented in a form other than a completely consolidated balance sheet and profit and loss account.

A subsidiary may be excluded from the consolidated accounts in the following cases:

1. When it is impracticable or of no real value to members of the company in view of the insignificant amounts involved.
2. When it would involve expense and delay out of proportion to the value to members of the company.
3. When it would be misleading.
4. When it would be harmful to the business of the holding company or any of its subsidiaries.
5. When the business of the subsidiary is so different from that of the holding company that they cannot be regarded as a single undertaking.

If either of the last two of these grounds for exclusion is invoked, the consent of the Governor-General by Order in Council is required. When the assets and liabilities of any one subsidiary are not brought into the consolidation, the holding company's investment in the subsidiary and any loans or advances to the subsidiary must appear as separate items.

Accounts of Overseas Company. By the Companies Amendment Act of 1971 an overseas company shall in every calendar year make out a separate balance sheet and profit and loss account of its business conducted in New Zealand as if such business were conducted by a company formed under the Companies Act of 1955. An audited copy of such accounts is required to be filed with the Registrar of Companies.

The registrar may exempt an overseas company from the preparation of such accounts where he is satisfied that the accounts of an overseas company have been prepared in accordance with the law of the place in which the overseas company is incorporated and the contents are substantially the same as required by the New Zealand Companies Act of 1955.

Pooling of Interests

The "pooling of interests" concept is recognized in New Zealand in certain and appropriate circumstances.

Assets

Current Assets. In general, current assets must be classified under headings appropriate to the company's business. If the directors of the company are of the opinion that the realizable value or current value of current assets in the ordinary course of business is less than their balance sheet value, the directors must make appropriate disclosure on the balance sheet or in a statement or report annexed thereto.

Inventories. The basis of valuation of inventories is not required to be stated in the accounts. Any departure from a basis previously used and the effect of any change if the effect is material must be clearly reported.

Investments. Investments not held for sale or for conversion into cash may be shown at market value or at cost less provision for decline in value. (Readily realizable investments held as part of the liquid resources of the company would be shown under a current assets classification).

Fixed Assets. Companies are required to indicate on their balance sheets the basis of valuation of all fixed assets. For each group of fixed assets, it is necessary to disclose the total original cost or valuation plus additions less deletions, and the aggregate depreciation provided to date. (The Companies Act of 1955 expressly provides that the book value at the commencement of the act may be treated as if it were a valuation of the assets made at that date.) Revaluation of fixed assets is permitted under the act and such write-ups are not taxed.

Deferred Charges. Preliminary expenses, share or debenture issue expenses, commissions paid in respect of shares or debentures, discounts allowed on issue of debentures, and discounts allowed on issue of shares must all be stated under separate headings until written off. Bond discount and expense are usually written off in the year incurred.

Intangibles. Write-offs or write-downs of intangible assets may be charged to reserve accounts provided full disclosure is made.

Liabilities

Secured Liabilities. The fact that a liability is secured must be stated, but the asset which secures the liability need not be disclosed.

Liabilities in Foreign Currency. Indebtedness in foreign currency is usually shown in local currency at exchange rates prevailing at the balance sheet date, and the basis of conversion is required to be stated. Normal fluctuations in exchange rates are charged or credited to income.

Debentures. In New Zealand, the term "debenture" is applied to both secured and unsecured borrowings. Debentures of the company held by a nominee or in trust for the company and the amount at which they are recorded must be shown. The balance sheet must also state the details of any redeemed debentures which the company has the power to reissue.

Contingent Liabilities. There should be footnote disclosure of any contingent liabilities, including the amount of any potential liability that may arise from assets pledged for the purpose of guaranteeing the liabilities of others. The aggregate amount or estimated amount of contracts for capital expenditures for a material amount not otherwise provided for must also be shown. Material commitments under long-term leases are not required to be disclosed.

Reserves and Provisions

There is an important difference in terminology between the United States and New Zealand in regard to reserves and provisions.

As provided in the Companies Act of 1955, in New Zealand a provision is generally an amount charged against profits or other surpluses to meet specific commitments, known contingencies, and diminution in values of assets existing as of the date of the balance sheet where the amounts involved cannot be determined with substantial accuracy.

Reserves are amounts appropriated from profits or other surpluses other than to meet known liabilities, contingencies, commitments, or diminution in value of assets. In other words, the intentions of directors in creating provisions and reserves are paramount in determining their classification. Provisions, when their existence is no longer justified, may require reclassification as reserves.

Reserves would be included with other "shareholders' funds" while provisions other than the accumulated provisions for depreciation of fixed assets would be shown with "current liabilities" usually under appropriate headings or deducted from the related current asset. The accumulated provisions for depreciation of fixed assets must be shown as a deduction from the aggregate cost or valuation of each group of fixed assets.

Reserves are further divided into capital reserves and revenue reserves. Capital reserves are those which are not regarded as being available for distribution through the profit and loss account.

Capital reserves created by the upward revaluation of fixed assets or by the issuance of shares at a premium may be utilized to issue bonus (stock dividend) shares.

The accounts must set out details of capital and revenue reserves (and any movements therein) and of certain provisions.

Secret Reserves

Provisions for depreciation, renewals, or diminution in the value of assets need not be stated under separate headings. However, where any such provision, created after September 1, 1955, is in excess of that which, in the opinion of the directors, is reasonably necessary for the purpose, then such excess shall be treated as a reserve and so disclosed.

Capital

Share Capital. The following information must be set forth either on the balance sheet or as a footnote thereto:

1. Authorized capital
2. Issued and paid-up capital
3. Amount and earliest date of redemption of any redeemable preference shares
4. Any option on unissued shares—number, description, and amount of shares affected
5. Any share capital on which interest has been paid out of capital and the rate of interest
6. Fixed cumulative dividends in arrears

Share Premium Account. This account corresponds to the paid-in surplus account in the United States. It must be shown separately as a capital reserve and may be utilized to write off preliminary expenses, commissions paid, discount allowed on issue of shares or debentures, or premiums paid in redemption of redeemable preference shares or debentures or to issue bonus shares.

Any shares issued to acquire any other business or assets should be fairly valued by the directors and the surplus credited to the share premium account. In acquiring a subsidiary company, such valuation may be the book value of such subsidiary's shareholders' funds.

Profit and Loss Account

The trend is toward the statement form of profit and loss account. While it is not mandatory for sales and cost of sales to be disclosed, such figures are being shown in the profit and loss statement with increasing frequency. Should they not be shown, the chairman of a public company frequently discloses the sales figure in his address at the annual meeting.

The profit and loss account must give a "true and fair view" of the profit or loss of the company for the financial year and must disclose any material change in the basis of accounting. Items to be shown separately are the following:

1. Income from investments distinguishing between—
   a. Government, local authority, and other public stock, debentures, or bonds.
   b. Investments in companies.
   c. Other investments.
2. Provision for normal depreciation or diminution in value of fixed assets—if no provision is made, it must be stated.
3. Provision for New Zealand taxation on income derived during the financial year.
4. Transfers to or from provisions other than for item (2) above.
5. Transfers or proposed transfers to or from reserves.
6. Extraneous, nonrecurring, and exceptional transactions unless immaterial.
7. Directors' remuneration.
8. Auditor's remuneration unless fixed by the company at the general meeting.
9. Interest paid on the company's debentures or fixed loans.
10. Amount provided for redemption of share capital and loans.
11. Dividends paid on all share capital during the year. It is usual, however, to make a provision for any proposed final dividend being recommended by the directors.

12. Details of extraordinary charges and credits. The eighth schedule of the Companies Act of 1955 provides that there will be shown in the profit and loss account, either by way of note or otherwise, any material respects in which any items shown in the profit and loss account are affected (a) by transactions of a sort not usually undertaken by the company, (b) by circumstances of an exceptional or nonrecurrent nature, or (c) by any change in the basis of accounting.

Depreciation

Most concerns, as a matter of expediency, follow the rates and procedures established for tax purposes. In general, buildings are depreciated on a straight-line basis while other assets are usually depreciated on a diminishing balance basis. Depreciation on an amount representing upward revaluation of fixed assets is not an allowable deduction for tax purposes.

Stock Dividends

Stock dividends (bonus shares) are accounted for by the issuing company on the basis of the paid-up value of the shares, without consideration being given to market or fair value thereof.

Directors' Emoluments

In New Zealand, only that portion of directors' emoluments which is classed as directors' fees need be shown in the accounts. If a director is also a full-time employee of the company, his salary need not be disclosed.

Requirements for Public Sale of Securities

The Companies Act of 1955, and the Companies Amendment Acts of 1960 and 1963, contain regulations and requirements governing (a) public issue of shares, debentures, unsecured deposits, and unsecured notes by way of prospectus or any document deemed to be a prospectus under the act and (b) take-over offers.

Prospectus Issues

The following is a brief summary of the principal matters to be specified in a prospectus as set out in the fourth schedule of the Companies Act of 1955:

1. Description of share capital and relative voting rights.
2. Details of directors and particulars of any interest they have in the promotion of the company or in any property to be acquired.
3. The minimum amount to be raised by the issue before shares are allotted.
4. Particulars of any property to be acquired out of the proceeds of the issue and the source of any other funds required.
5. The amount of any preliminary expenses, commission on sale of shares, or promotional fee to be paid.
6. A report by the auditors on the profits and losses and rates of dividend paid for each of the preceding five financial years and on the assets and liabilities at the last balance sheet date. Where the company is a holding company, group figures are to be given.
7. A report by a qualified accountant on any business or company to be acquired out of the issue, showing the profits and losses for each of the preceding five financial years and the assets and liabilities at the last balance sheet date.

A public company making an issue of shares or debentures to existing members, whether or not the "rights" are transferable to nonmembers, is relieved from complying with the foregoing, but it must file particulars of the offer with the Registrar of Companies.

While a private company is prohibited from offering its shares to the public, it may invite the public to deposit money or lend money to it, provided the act's requirements regarding prospectuses are observed.

Take-Over Offers

The following is a brief summary of the matters to be included in statements to be issued by the company making the offer ("offeror") and the company receiving it ("offeree") as required by the first and second schedules of the Companies Amendment Act of 1963. The regulations do not apply to private companies where all offerees agree in writing to waive the act's requirements, or where offers are made to not more than six members of a company.

1. In the statement by offeror, the following matters are to be specified in every offer:
   a. If offer is conditional, the minimum acceptance required, and the latest date on which the offeror can declare the offer to become unconditional.

b. Consideration, method, and period of payment.

c. Details of shares of offeree already held by offeror directly or indirectly.

2. The following additional matters are to be specified when securities are offered as consideration:

a. Description of company and its business, country of incorporation, and details of directors.

b. Statement of the profit and loss of the company for each of the preceding five financial years and the rates of dividends paid. The issued and paid-up capital, changes in capital structure over the period, and the sources of any increase in capital.

c. The paid-up value of the securities offered and whether they will be uniform in all respects with securities previously issued. If not uniform, details of differences and limitations are to be disclosed.

d. Whether stock exchange listing of the securities offered will be applied for.

e. Details of latest sale prices of the securities immediately prior to the offer, rate of dividend, and dividend yield for both offeror and offeree's securities where possible. Also, highest and lowest sale prices during each of the three years preceding the offer with explanations of variations due to alterations in capital.

f. Details of any material change in indebtedness since the last balance date and where the offer is made more than six months after the last balance date an estimate of the current trend of profit or loss.

g. A copy of the latest accounts and balance sheet and directors' report is to be attached.

Requirements for Listing Securities on the Stock Exchange

The New Zealand Stock Exchange has certain listing requirements set out in detail in a "listing manual." There are no accounting requirements or information other than those required under the Companies Act of 1955 and its amendments.

To qualify for official listing, a company must—

1. Be of sufficient magnitude and its shareholding sufficiently well distributed to ensure that there is a free market for its shares.
2. Undertake to supply promptly to the Stock Exchange Association as well as its shareholders all information called for in the listing agreement.
3. Adopt articles of association which comply with the listing requirement.

The requirements are designed—

1. To enable shareholders holding a majority in value of the issued capital to control the affairs of the company.
2. To protect minorities.
3. To ensure that reasonable information concerning the company's affairs is available to shareholders.

Norway

Norway

As of June 1973

Significant developments since the preparation of this chapter are presented, by country, in the section entitled Addenda.

Forms of Business Organization

Business operations in Norway may be carried on in the form of a joint-stock company (aksjeselskap), a "responsible" (general) partnership, a limited partnership, a limited joint-stock partnership (kommandittaksjeselskap), a silent partnership (partnership in commendam), a proprietorship, or a cooperative society. Foreigners and foreign companies may also engage in business through a branch in Norway without having to establish any separate Norwegian company, or by arranging for representation in the country without having to set up their own permanent establishment.

The type of organization of a business is not entirely a matter of free choice. The choice is limited first by the business legislation which, as regards many trades, specifies the requirements which must be satisfied in order for the business to be legally conducted on Norwegian territory. Also involved are the concession laws which regulate, for example, the right to purchase and lease real property and to buy electric power.

Aksjeselskap
(Joint-Stock Company)

The principal form of business organization in Norway is the "aksjeselskap" or joint-stock company, the legislation applicable to which is contained in the Companies Act of July 6, 1957. Norwegian legislation makes no distinction between private companies and public companies, as do the laws of some other countries. The Companies Act is applicable to all companies in which none of the participants is personally liable for the company's debts.

A joint-stock company cannot be established by less than three participants. The name of the company must contain the word "aksjeselskap" and is commonly abbreviated A/S. The minimum capital is 10,000 kroner, represented by shares not less than 50 kroner. The liability of the shareholder is limited to the par value of shares subscribed. As a rule all shares must be paid for within one year from the date of registration of the company.

Each company must have a board, which can be composed of one or more directors. If the share capital is 1,000,000 kroner or more and the company does not have a committee of shareholders' representatives, there shall be at least three directors on the board. At least half of the directors must be residents of Norway and must have lived in Norway for the last two years. The Ministry of Commerce may dispense with this rule, but such dispensation is not easily obtained.

The Companies Act itself does not require the directors to be Norwegian citizens, but the nationality of the directors is relevant under the concession legislation, the Commercial Banks Act of May 24, 1961, and the Maritime Act of July 20, 1893. The fact that the requirements of the Companies Act as to directors have been fulfilled is not always sufficient to enable the joint-stock company to carry on business. As a result of the concession and business laws, it will in many cases be necessary for the directors to be Norwegian citizens and/or domiciled in Norway to a greater extent than is required under the Companies Act. If the company operates a business which requires trading rights, one of the directors must have a trading license.

The election of directors is a matter for the general meeting. However, if the company has a committee of shareholders' representatives, it is the committee which elects the directors, unless the articles of association provide that the directors are to be elected by the general meeting.

In any joint-stock company, the board of directors is responsible for presenting annual accounts and an annual report at the end of the financial year. The annual accounts must consist of the profit and loss accounts for the financial year and the company's balance sheet at the end of the financial year. The accounts must be signed by the directors and the manager.

A joint-stock company must have one or more auditors, who may be individuals or a company engaged in auditing; and when the board has submitted the annual accounts and the annual report, the auditor(s) shall each year produce an auditor's report, which together with the annual accounts and the directors' report shall be made available to the shareholders not later than eight days before the date of the ordinary general meeting. Norwegian joint-stock companies have no general obligation to publish their annual accounts or to submit them to any public authority, except in the case of insurance companies, banks, and joint-stock companies, whose shares are quoted on the Oslo Stock Exchange.

In March 1970, a recommendation for a new Companies Act was presented. The recommendation is a result of the suggestions made in 1959-62 by the Nordic Council and the Scandinavian ministers of justice with a view to harmonizing company legislation in the Scandinavian countries. It is probable, however, that it will be some time before the recommendation results in any new act.

Branch of a Foreign Joint-Stock Company

Foreign joint-stock companies can in certain cases operate a business in Norway through a branch without establishing any Norwegian subsidiary. The foreign company is in such case liable for the branch's obligations to the full extent of its entire capital at home and abroad.

The rules contained in the Companies Act concerning Norwegian branches of foreign joint-stock companies are applicable only if the branch is placed under a separate board of directors which acts on behalf of the company and assumes liabilities toward third parties to the same extent as the directors of a Norwegian joint-stock company. The board may be composed of one or more directors. The Companies Act contains no requirement as to citizenship, residence, or qualifications of directors, hence, foreign nationals resident abroad can also be directors of the branch. The right to engage in trade, however, is normally subject to the requirement of "residence in Norway," meaning that at least half the directors of the branch must have resided in Norway for at least two years and still be resident there.

Before the branch starts to operate, its directors must notify the Company Register in accordance with the provisions of the Trade Register Act of May 17, 1890. On stationery, announcements, and other documents, the branch must always use the designation "Utenlandsk Aksjeselskap" (foreign joint-stock company) in addition to the company's name.

A foreign joint-stock company in which all the shares are issued to bearer must, within eight months after the close of the financial year, publish the company's annual accounts together with separate annual accounts for the branch, in the Norwegian official gazette.

The Companies Act does not by its terms prevent a foreign joint-stock company from establishing a branch in Norway which is not placed under a separate board of directors but is, instead, directly responsible to and managed by the foreign head office. Such branches would not come under the above-mentioned provisions of the Companies Act, but they could not engage in business which requires trading rights. If the Norwegian branch of a foreign joint-stock company has been established in accordance with the rules of the Companies Act (i.e., with a separate board of directors and registered in the Register of Companies), and at least half of the branch directors have resided in Norway for at least two years and are still residents there, the branch is considered to be a "resident of Norway," for the purpose of the Trading Act. This means that the branch has "trading rights as a merchant" on the same conditions as Norwegian joint-stock companies, and that it has such other rights as are held by Norwegian residents under the Trading Act.

Under section 10 of the Royal Decree of April 9, 1965, concerning the exploration for and exploitation of submarine petroleum deposits, a production license can be granted to a foreign company which has established a branch in Norway pursuant to the rules of the Companies Act.

Apart from the foregoing, the laws do not directly specify what kind of business a foreign company can operate through its Norwegian branch, whether it has a separate board of directors or not. However, some special laws require a joint-stock company to have its seat (principal office) in Norway in order to carry on a specified kind of business. For instance, in granting a concession for the purchase or lease of real property and electric power, the authorities will normally require the company to be established in Norway. Therefore, the only alternative for a foreign joint-stock company which intends to operate a certain kind of business in Norway may be to establish a Norwegian subsidiary.

Other Forms of Business Organization

Single proprietorship and responsible (general) partnership are similar to the corresponding entities commonly found in other countries. Partnerships as such are not subject to taxation; the partners are taxed individually on their proportional share of the partnership revenue and capital.

Cooperative societies are particularly common in agriculture and the fishing industry. In recent years cooperative societies have also become more prevalent in wholesale and retail trade.

Business Records

Norway has no particular bookkeeping act. The rules regulating the bookkeeping records are contained in special laws, such as the Companies Act of July 6, 1957, the Trade Act of March 8, 1935, and so forth.

The Accounting Profession

Public accounting is a young profession in Norway, the development of which is marked by an act from 1929 regulating the profession of certified public accountants ("statsautoriserte revisorer") and the present Act of Audit and Auditors from 1964 (effective January 1, 1965). The latter requires a license from the Ministry of Commerce for all who wish to practice as auditors and imposes compulsory audits on nearly all business enterprises specifically including those having a minimum turnover of 1,000,000 kroner per annum in the case of a person conducting trade, handicraft, manufacturing, and shipping, and those having gross commission earnings of 200,000 kroner per annum in the case of an agent. All joint-stock companies are subject to compulsory audit according to regulations in the Companies Act. The Act of Audit and Auditors of 1964 covers all auditors in the country, both the certified public accountant (statsautorisert revisor) and the registered accountant (registrert revisor).

The Norwegian Institute of Certified Public Accountants (Norges Statsautoriserte Revisorers Forening) was founded in 1930 and at present has about six hundred members.

Statsautorisert Revisor

The license to practice as a certified public accountant is granted by the Ministry of Commerce upon fulfilling specific requirements and passing two examinations, the registered accountant examination and the certified public accountant examination. To be eligible for these examinations, the candidate must be a graduate of a secondary school of commerce and economics or from an academic secondary school (general certificate of education "A" level) and hold a certificate from at least a one-year day course at a business college or secondary school of commerce and economics.

The registered accountant examination can be passed after the age of 22 and after the candidate has acquired two years of diverse practice in audit work in Norway. Having passed this examination the candidate is entitled to call himself a registered accountant and can be listed in a register of accountants in the Ministry of Commerce. In order to be listed, the candidate must have a permanent residence in Norway, have a record of honesty and integrity, be financially sound, and not have been declared legally incapacitated.

For the final certified public accountant examination, the candidate must have accumulated another three years in practice, two years of which may be gotten abroad. The ministry may waive these requirements of audit practice if it has been proven that the candidate has acquired sufficient practical experience by other means.

When an accountant, who is listed in the above-mentioned register, has passed the certified public accountant examination, the Ministry of Commerce may grant a license authorizing him to practice as a certified public accountant.

The registered accountant examination and the certified public accountant examination are set by the Audit Council. This council is a body of four members appointed by the Ministry of Commerce according to the Act of Audit and Auditors of March 14, 1964. The chairman must have the qualifications of a Supreme Court judge; one of the members is required to be a practicing certified public accountant and one of the members a practicing registered accountant. Apart from setting the examinations, the Audit Council acts in an advisory capacity to the Ministry of Commerce in its enforcement of the Act of Audit and Auditors.

The privileges that accompany registration of a certified public accountant license are revoked if the accountant ceases to have permanent residence in Norway or is declared legally incapacitated. Privileges are restored when the Ministry of Commerce determines that the reasons for the loss of privileges no longer exist. The privileges are also revoked if the accountant becomes bankrupt or comes under public composition (of debt) proceedings. If the bankruptcy or composition proceedings are not due to circumstances that render the accountant unworthy of retaining the privileges or do not damage the trust that is necessary for his position, the Ministry of Commerce on receipt of information to that effect may restore the aforementioned privileges; but otherwise, privileges will not be restored to the party concerned until he can again prove himself financially sound.

According to the Rules on Audit and Auditors issued by the Ministry of Commerce on December 8, 1964, the following groups of enterprises are required to engage certified public accountants: Norwegian corporations having share capital of more than 1,000,000 kroner or being engaged in investment banking, stockbrokerage or real estate brokerage; and Norwegian branches of foreign corporations and all forms of Norwegian partnerships (including limited partnerships) having a turnover of more than 1,000,000 kroner and share capital and liabilities (excluding mortgage debt) of more than 2,000,000 kroner or being engaged in investment banking, stockbrokerage, or real estate brokerage. In all other cases a registered auditor may be employed.

Professional Activities and the Independence of Auditors

The Act of Audit and Auditors of 1964 does not limit a certified public accountant to engaging only in audit work, but it does contain some rules regarding situations in which an accountant may not be eligible to perform audit work. The main object of the law is to preserve the independence of auditors from the company whose accounts he audits. Thus, anybody who wholly or partially acts as an employee, a member of the committee of shareholders' representatives, a director, or a manager in the company cannot act as independent auditor of the same company.

Norges Statsautoriserte Revisorers Forening

(Norwegian Institute of Certified Public Accountants)

The Institute was founded October 12, 1930, and is subject to the bylaws of the organization that were adopted at the first general meeting on the founding date and thereafter amended through 1969. The objects of the Institute are the following:

1. To raise the professional standards of the members.
2. To insure that the certified public accountants observe generally accepted auditing principles.
3. To represent the interests of the certified public accountants vis-a-vis the authorities and the public.
4. To express opinions on professional matters.
5. To promote the education of prospective auditors.

Membership in the Institute is limited to certified public accountants. All certified public accountants can be members of the Institute even if they do not practice as accountants. The advisory committee (Responsumutvalget) will on behalf of the Institute deliver opinions on matters concerning accountancy and auditing submitted to the Institute by one or more of its members, by the legislature, the executive authorities, or the courts.

Professional Etiquette

On March 13, 1962, the Council of Norges Statsautoriserte Revisorers Forening issued the present rules of professional etiquette.

According to these rules it is the duty of every member of the Institute to act in accordance with generally accepted ethical standards. Generally accepted ethical standards are those adopted and observed by conscientious and experienced certified public accountants in their behavior toward colleagues, clients, and the general public.

A member is duty-bound to treat the work of a colleague with respect and must not in reports, declarations, or other statements comment on the work of a colleague in a disparaging manner nor question his integrity or competence. In the event it is deemed necessary to direct criticism at the work of a colleague, it must be objective and unbiased. Criticism shall not be expressed until contact has been made with the colleague in question in an effort to obviate any possibility of misunderstanding.

A member is at liberty to take over assignments being undertaken by colleagues, but must not initiate steps to acquire such assignments.

Members are at liberty to enter into partnership in the form found most expedient. If the form of joint-stock company is chosen, there shall be a certified public accountant covering each assignment which the firm undertakes. The accountant must bear personal and unlimited responsibility for the assignment in addition to the responsibility borne by the firm.

A member must not accept special assignments within or outside the enterprise he audits if the special assignment places him in a position of dependency on those over whom he shall exercise control, or in any other way jeopardizes his independence.

Advertising is permitted in newspapers and periodicals and in trade directories, catalogues, and similar publications. Advertisements may be inserted by individuals or as a part of a joint advertising program in which case it must be open to all members in the area in question. Joint advertisement shall make reference to membership in the Institute. Advertisements must not be given any unusual layout and may contain only the following information:

- Name and professional title
- Address and telephone number
- Brief summary (with no descriptive adjectives) of the principal kinds of assignments the member is interested in undertaking

Letterheads on business correspondence paper may include only name and professional title, address and telephone number in ordinary print with no unusual design. The words "member of Norges Statsautoriserte Revisorers Forening" must be written in full.

Auditing Standards

General Standards

According to the Act of Audit and Auditors of 1964, and according to Rules on Audit and Auditors issued by the Ministry of Commerce on December 8, 1964, the auditor shall perform his assignment in accordance with current regulations and generally accepted auditing principles.

The rules prescribe some details of auditing procedure. Insofar as no special circumstances dictate otherwise, the auditor shall, at least twice a year, control the cash balance and bank and postal giro accounts. Further, at least once a year he shall verify the existence of securities. He shall also, at least once a year, to a reasonable extent, inspect and verify the existence of accounts receivable, inventories, and other property.

Furthermore, the auditor shall keep an audit protocol which is the property of the enterprise. The audit protocol shall be bound in cover; be holed, corded, and sealed; the pages shall be consecutively numbered and the numbers preprinted; and it must be endorsed jointly by the auditor concerned and the board of directors or responsible owner (owners). The auditor should make entries in the audit protocol regarding major control checks he has undertaken. In general he should state the date of control checks of cash balance, bank, and postal giro accounts, securities, and accounts receivable. If it can be done without impeding the efficiency of the audit procedure, he should also include the results of such control checks.

Standards of Field Work

According to the Companies Act the auditor shall—

1. Audit the current books of account.
2. Make sure that the annual accounts and, when necessary, the consolidated balance sheet are clearly presented, complete, and sufficiently detailed; that they comply with current law, articles of association, and company accounts; and that they, together with the company's annual report and other information submitted to the general meeting, give a true and fair view of the company's standing and of the operating results for the financial year.

The auditor's work is divided between interim audit and a year-end audit. It is the general view that the Norwegian auditor has both a duty to maintain a control to prevent embezzlement and other irregularities and a duty to make sure that the annual accounts are presented in accordance with laws and accepted standards. There has been a tendency to depart from detailed checking of accounts and to emphasize examination of internal control. The Rules on Audit and Auditors of Joint-Stock Companies also state that the auditor may base his work on the system of internal control executed by the staff of the company and which he finds satisfactory.

The Companies Act and the Audit and Auditors Act do not state in detail what the duties of an auditor are. The Audit and Auditors Act has a standard rule to the effect that an auditor must perform his assignments in accordance with current regulations and generally accepted auditing principles. When this act was passed in 1964, the Institute of Certified Public Accountants in Norway (Norges Statsautoriserte Revisorers Forening) acquired a legal basis for issuing recommendations or standards on auditing procedures and principles. Recommendations issued by the Norwegian Institute include the following subjects:

- General Principles of Auditing
- Examination of Internal Control
- Auditing Accounts Receivable
- Auditing Stocks

Standards of Reporting

Every year the auditor shall make a report on the annual accounts and report submitted by the directors. The report shall be addressed to the general meeting of the company.

The auditor shall make an endorsement on the annual accounts to the effect that they have been audited. If the auditor finds that the accounts ought not to be adopted, this shall appear from the endorsement. The endorsement shall be dated and shall refer to the report from the auditor to the general meeting.

The auditor's report has become more or less standardized, and its content is based on the prescriptions in Rules on Audit and Auditors. The audit report must contain statements by the auditor on the following matters:

1. Whether he has carried out his assignment in accordance with current audit regulations and generally accepted auditing principles.
2. Whether he finds that the accounts have been kept and closed in accordance with basic principles of proper accounting practice. that the annual accounts, with a written annual report from the board of directors, present a true and fair view of the financial standing of the company and of its operating results during the financial year, and that they conform with prudent and sound business practice. If secret reserves have been created or eliminated without this showing in the annual accounts or the board of directors' annual written report, the auditor shall explain this in the audit report to the extent required by generally accepted auditing principles.
3. Whether the auditor has knowledge of other facts which in his opinion may be of significance in assessing the company's financial standing or operating results as expressed in the annual accounts and the board of directors' written annual report.

4. Whether he can recommend that the submitted annual account be adopted as the accounts of the company.

If the auditor is aware of circumstances which may make members of the committee of shareholders' representatives or members of the board financially liable to the company, he must give account of this in his report. In the case of report on consolidated accounts, the auditor shall state whether he has audited other companies in the group.

The directors' annual report, which must be produced together with the annual accounts, must contain necessary information about "matters which have any bearing on the appraisal of the activities and position of the company, provided such matters are not apparent from the annual accounts." It must also give a special account of the following:

1. Valuation of the stocks of goods and raw materials.
2. Quotations which have been used for the valuation of securities and of claims and debts in foreign currencies.
3. Revaluations of assets (assets written down or written up) intended for permanent ownership or use, together with information as to the basis of the revaluation.
4. Directors' recommendation for the application of the profit.
5. Marketing conditions and price developments during the year to such extent as this information is of interest in appraising the position of the company.
6. Gross sales, total expenditure on personnel, and investments and contracts of major importance to the company, insofar as this information can be given without detriment to the company.

Accounting Principles and Practices

General

The standard requirement with respect to the profit and loss account and the balance sheet is that the annual accounts must be prepared "in such a manner that they are in all respects in conformity with proper accounting practice and with careful and sound business practice." Applying this principle, the act contains detailed rules for assessing (evaluating) items in the accounts and rules concerning specification of various assets and liabilities in the balance sheet and of income and expenditure items in the profit and loss account.

It should be noted that the provisions contained in the Companies Act concerning assessment of various items do not always correspond with the tax rules for assessment of assets and liabilities, income and expenditure items, and so forth. The tax assessment of capital and income may therefore lead to other and sometimes more onerous results for the company than those which would ensue from the rules of the Companies Act. The assessment rules of the Companies Act are primarily in the nature of maximum rules, aiming at avoiding any overstatement of the company's financial position.

Form and Content of Financial Statements

Items in the balance sheet that are to be shown separately follow:

Assets

Land and forest property

Other land areas and waterfalls

Mines, quarries, and so forth

Building and constructional installations

Machinery, transport equipment, and so forth

Ships and aircraft

Plant, ships, aircraft, and similar items in course of construction or building

Stock of raw materials and goods in process

Stock of finished products

Patents and similar rights

Claims for payment on shares

Self-owned shares of the company (treasury shares)

Shares or parts (interests) in subsidiary companies

Credits outstanding in subsidiary companies

Credits outstanding in parent company

Advances to suppliers

Securities

Bills in hand

Bank deposits and cash

Costs, and so forth that have been capitalized

Claims not included under other items of the section

Liabilities

Share capital
Legal (statutory) reserve
Other funds, separately
Mortgage debts
Long-term debt not secured by mortgage
Assessed, unpaid taxes
Accrued taxes not assessed
Debts covered by acceptances
Short-term debts not covered by acceptances

Obligations relating to surety and endorsements and similar guarantee liabilities, including pledges given for debts of third parties, shall be stated in text with a total amount, unless the same amount has been included in any liability amount.

Assets intended for permanent ownership or use by the company shall not be included in the same items as other assets. Under each item relating to such assets, it should be specifically stated how much has been added thereto and taken away in the course of the year, as well as the amount written off to profit and loss account.

In the accounts or in the directors' report, claims against members of the committee of shareholders' representatives, members of the board of directors, the business manager, staff, and workers shall be shown separately from other claims. The accounts (or the directors' report) shall show the total amount owing by the members of the committee of representatives, by the members of the board of directors and the business manager, and by the staff and workers.

The profit and loss account shall be so prepared that it gives a true and fair view of the financial results of the company's activities during the financial year, and the following items must be shown separately.

Income

Dividends on shares and participations in subsidiary companies
Dividends on shares and participations in other companies
Interest and similar capital revenues from subsidiary companies
Other interest and similar capital revenues
Profit made on the sale of assets intended for permanent ownership or used by the company
Profit earned on revaluation (writing up) of assets intended for permanent ownership or use

Other income that does not originate from the real and regular business of the company

Expenditure

Remuneration paid to members of the committee of shareholders' representatives, the board of directors, and the business manager

Interest payment to subsidiary companies

Other interest payments on debts

Taxes

Depreciation (writing down) of assets intended for permanent ownership or use

Loss on the sale of assets intended for permanent ownership or use

Other extraordinary expenditures or losses

A company need not disclose gross sales, total expenditure for personnel, and so forth, if this information can be detrimental to the company. Profit or loss transferred from the previous annual accounts shall be shown as a separate item. Any remuneration which is calculated on net profit shall be designated "commission on profits," and shall be shown in connection with the statement of profit and loss as a separate item. It shall be specifically stated how much of the "commission on profits" has accrued to the members of the committee of shareholders' representatives, the directors, and the staff.

Consolidated Financial Statements. According to the Companies Act, a "parent company" means a joint-stock company owning not less than two-thirds of the shares or the net worth of another company, or which otherwise, by virtue of owning shares or by agreement, has a controlling influence over another company and a considerable interest in its operating results. A "subsidiary company" means a company with which a parent company enjoys such relationship. For groups of companies, it is required that, in addition to the annual accounts for each company, a presentation be made of a consolidated balance sheet including all the companies of the group and showing the position of the group considered as a unit for accounting purposes.

General Rules of Valuation

The general purpose of the rules of valuation in the Companies Act is to prevent an overvaluation of assets or an understatement of liabilities. The annual accounts shall be prepared in such a manner that they in all respects are in conformity with proper accounting practice and with careful and sound business practice.

Accounts Receivable

Under no circumstances shall accounts receivable be shown in the accounts at a higher amount than can be expected to be collected. Worthless accounts must be written off, either by reducing the recorded amount of the receivables or by establishing a reserve. Reserves for doubtful claims are usually shown as a deduction from the corresponding asset. As mentioned above, claims against members of the committee of the shareholders' representatives, members of the board of directors, the business manager, staff, and employees are to be shown separately. A company must not grant loans (or guarantees) to a shareholder if its net capital is less than the share capital, or would be less should the claim not be liquidated.

Inventories

Goods for sale, raw materials, goods in process, and finished goods shall not be shown in the accounts at an amount higher than their cost, nor shall they be included at an amount higher than the selling price, after deduction of anticipated selling expenses. In principle, the basis of valuation is historical cost or market, whichever is the lower, which also is the basis recognized for tax purposes. However, the balance sheet valuation may be lower than the basic amount mentioned inasmuch as it is allowed for tax purposes to take into consideration the risk of a future fall in prices.

Fixed Assets

The amount of depreciation owing to age and wear and tear shall be at least as much as would be required under a rational plan of depreciation and other sound business practices. If the value of fixed assets is manifestly higher than the amount at which it is entered in the accounts, the carrying amount may be written up. The amount of the write-up from one annual balance sheet to the next shall in that case not exceed 20 percent of the total excess value (appreciation) unless the amount by which the asset is written up is used to offset necessary depreciation on other fixed assets or to increase the share capital of the company. In the directors' report, an account shall be given of revaluation of fixed assets, together with information as to the basis of revaluation.

Organization Expenses

Organization expense may be included as a separate item on the asset side during the first five years after establishment of the company.

Goodwill

Purchased goodwill may be included in the balance sheet as a special item on the asset side provided it is capitalized in the year in which the goodwill was acquired; this cannot be done later. The Companies Act contains no rules as to how goodwill shall be amortized. For tax purposes amortization of goodwill is generally not allowed, but deduction is allowed if goodwill is sold or if it is obvious that the goodwill no longer has any value for the company.

Bond Discounts and Premium

Discounts on long-term certificates, which are to be redeemed at a higher amount than the company has obtained for them, can be amortized over the period from inception of the obligation to maturity.

Depreciation Reserves

Norwegian companies usually present the net book value on the asset side of the balance sheet.

Premium on Capital Stock

If capital stock is sold at a premium, such premium must be added to the legal reserve.

Liabilities for Taxes

All liabilities for taxes shall be shown as debts in the balance sheet. The tax debts shall include separately accrued taxes for the year of income and the taxes that have been assessed but not paid at the end of the financial year.

Investment Fund Reserve

Business enterprises (individual and corporate) are permitted to allocate tax free a certain part of their income as a reserve for future expenditures:

1. Twenty-five percent of their taxable income for the subsequent purchase of depreciable business property. The amount must be deposited in a special, non-interest-bearing account in the Bank of Norway. The deposits are released after four years. When the enterprise purchases new business property, 85 percent of the investment reserve fund is applied against the cost and the remaining 15 percent of the released amount can be credited as income without being taxed as such.

2. Twenty percent of their taxable income to funds for market development abroad or for research which can promote the taxpayer's business. In this case, there is no definite period which must elapse before the amount can be released, but the amount has to be used within five years from the date of allocation. The amount set aside must be deposited with the Bank of Norway.

Legal (Statutory) Reserve

Every joint-stock company must accumulate a reserve fund which must equal at least one-fifth of the share capital. The fund shall not be less than 5,000 kroner, nor less than an amount which, together with the share capital, is equivalent to the debts of the company at the end of the financial year. Until the reserve fund has reached the statutory amount, at least one-tenth of the annual profit must be allocated to the fund, insofar as this profit is not required to absorb deficits from previous years. Regardless of the amount of the reserve fund, it must be credited with an amount equaling at least the amount of dividends distributed by the company each year in excess of the equivalent of 5 percent of the reserve fund plus the paid-up share capital as at the beginning of the financial year. The reserve fund can be used only to cover a deficit shown in the annual accounts which could otherwise be covered only by writing down the share capital. If the reserve fund is larger than required, however, one-fifth of the excess can be utilized each year for other purposes.

Dividends

Joint-stock companies may not pay dividends or make any other payments similar to dividends in larger amounts than are consistent with sound business practice determined with due regard to any losses which may have been incurred, or are expected to be incurred, after the balance sheet date. Apart from this, there are currently no statutory rules which limit the dividends that can be paid by a joint-stock company except those mentioned in the section on "Legal (Statutory) Reserve," above.

Requirements for Public Sale of Securities

Bonds

Raising of capital through bond loans by subscription is dependent upon recommendation from the Bank of Norway and consent from the Ministry of Commerce.

The following information shall be stated in the prospectus:

1. The exact amount of the loan.
2. The rate of interest.
3. How the loan is to be repaid.
4. Securities (collateral).
5. When the subscription has to be paid by the public.
6. The purpose of the loan.
7. Financial statements for the last five years.

Establishment of Joint-Stock Company

The promoters (at least three) must publish the prospectus in the *Norwegian Gazette* and one or more newspapers. The prospectus must give information about the following matters:

1. The nature of the business.
2. The municipality in which the company is to have its registered office.
3. The amount of share capital (minimum and maximum amount, however, may be stated in the prospectus).
4. The denomination of each share.
5. The time of opening and closing of the subscription list.
6. The price of issue if subscriptions are invited at a premium.
7. The number of shares each promoter has subscribed for or guaranteed.
8. Time and place for the statutory meeting.

Requirements for Listing Securities on the Stock Exchange

Applications for the listing of bonds or shares on the stock exchange are made in writing to the Council of the Stock Exchange by the management of the company whose securities are to be listed.

Bond issues may not be less than 2,000,000 kroner. Numbers of bonds that are allotted for repayment must be published in the *Norwegian Gazette* or daily press.

The Council of the Stock Exchange can accept listing of shares on the stock exchange, provided the company has existed for at least one year, presented annual accounts audited by a certified public accountant, and distributed dividends. The capital of the company must be at least 500,000 kroner and the new shares must be offered to the public.

Companies having shares or bonds listed on the stock exchange must send annual accounts and reports to the stock exchange. The accounts must be presented in accordance with the Companies Act.

Panama

Panama

As of May 1973

Forms of Business Organization

Financial, commercial, and industrial activities are primarily governed by the Commercial Code and by Law No. 32 of 1927, the General Corporation Law. Business operations may be carried on through the medium of a corporation (sociedad anónima), branch of a foreign (or domestic) corporation, partnership (sociedad colectiva), or sole proprietorship. In practice, most foreign entities operate in Panama through subsidiary corporations. Panamanian law makes no distinction between national and foreign companies in the requirements for formation or organization.

Sociedad Anónima

(Corporation)

Two or more persons of legal age, regardless of nationality or residence, may form a corporation for any lawful purpose. It is not necessary that the capital be even partially held by Panamanians. Although, in organizing the corporation, at least two persons must subscribe to the stock, thereafter the subscriptions may be assigned to a single individual.

The law requires a minimum of three directors and three officers: a president, a treasurer, and a secretary; however, one person may hold two offices. It is not necessary that the directors or officers be Panamanians or shareholders, but it is necessary to appoint a resident agent (whether or not the company does business in Panama) who must be a Panamanian attorney or law firm.

The articles of incorporation must include the following:

1. The name of the corporation which must include a word, phrase, or abbreviation distinguishing it from a sole proprietorship or partnership.
2. The main objects of the corporation, which may be specified in broad general terms with the normal clause of "any other legitimate business."
3. The amount of the authorized capital and the number of shares into which the capital is to be divided.
4. A statement as to whether the shares are to have no par value, in which event it is not necessary to state the amount of capital, but it is necessary to indicate the number of authorized shares.
5. The domicile of the corporation, which could be within Panama or in some other country, and the name and address of its resident agent.
6. The duration which is normally in perpetuity.
7. The names and addresses of at least three directors.

Branch of Foreign Corporation

A foreign company may qualify to do business and establish branches by filing and registering in the mercantile section of the public registry the following:

1. Proof of legalization of the charter of the foreign company or other documents relating to its organization.
2. A statement of the amount of capital to be utilized in the operations in Panama.
3. A certificate (articles of incorporation, partnership papers, and so forth) showing that it is organized and authorized to do business under the laws of the country in which it is domiciled or was organized.

Sociedad Colectiva and Sociedad de Responsabilidad Limitada

(General Partnership and Limited Liability Partnership)

The Panama Commercial Code recognizes two types of partnerships, the general partnership (sociedad colectiva) and the limited liability partnership (sociedad de responsabilidad limitada). The partnership deed must be registered in the Mercantile Registry. The general partnership, which is similar to its counterpart in the United States, is usually organized to carry on the professions of law, architecture, and accounting. Limited partnerships are normally used for joint ventures in commercial activities.

Sole Proprietorship

Any person may engage in business on his own account. However, depending on the type of business, a license may be required. Certain types of activities are reserved for Panamanian citizens or must be majority-owned by Panamanians.

Business Records

The minimum corporate and accounting books required for a Panamanian company are the following:

1. Stock register
2. Minute book
3. General journal
4. General ledger
5. Inventory and balance sheet book

All of these books must be bound and registered with the government.

The minimum accounting books required for a branch of a foreign company, a partnership or proprietorship, are a general journal, general ledger, and an inventory and balance sheet book, which must also be bound and registered.

Summary entries in the official books may substitute for detailed recordings when machine accounting or data processing is used.

The Accounting Profession

Contador Público Autorizado (CPA)

(Authorized Public Accountant)

The accounting profession in Panama was first regulated by Law No. 10 of 1935 that defined the "contador público autorizado" as an accountant capable of rendering, for a fee, certain services to other persons, specifically, the examination or verification of financial transactions, books, accounts, and registers; and the preparation, verification, or certification of the accounting of a business enterprise and the related financial statements with the purpose of publishing them or obtaining credit. The law created a board of accountancy made up of five members and five alternates, which was empowered under a special provision of the law to grant, during the first year, the CPA certificate to persons possessing certain qualifications. Thereafter, the board granted certificates to persons who passed examinations in accounting practice and theory, auditing, and business law. There were no education or nationality requirements.

In 1957, the 1935 law was superseded by Law No. 8 of that year (1957) which changed the CPA certificate to a license and recognized a new class of professional, the accountant (contador). New requirements were as follows:

1. A candidate for the license of contador was required to—
   a. hold a university degree in accounting or
   b. have a commercial high school diploma and four years' experience under the direction of a contador or a contador público autorizado.
2. A candidate for the license of contador público autorizado was required to—
   a. have a contador license;
   b. have a minimum of two years' experience after obtaining his license as a contador; and
   c. pass an examination, which had to be taken at the National University. (The board of accountancy was eliminated by this law).

Law No. 8 of 1957, as was the case of Law No. 10 of 1935, had a special provision for accountants and public accountants that were in practice at the time of its enactment, which granted the contador license to accountants in practice for at least five consecutive years and the contador público autorizado license to accountants in practice for at least seven consecutive years. A second special provision recognized all the CPA certificates issued in accordance with Law No. 10 of 1935.

Under Law No. 8 of 1957, only those persons falling into any of the categories listed below, could be considered as candidates for either of the two licenses:

1. Panamanians by birth.
2. Panamanians by naturalization.

3. Foreigners with more than five years of residence in the Republic at the time of the enactment of the law, if they were citizens of a country that accorded the same rights to Panamanians.

4. Foreigners married to Panamanians.

Law No. 8 reserved the right to perform "accounting acts" to contadores and contadores públicos autorizados. Such acts were defined to include, among others, the preparation, analysis, and interpretation of financial statements; the design, installation, or modification of accounting systems; the confirmation, verification, and examination of accounting records and the certification of their accuracy; judiciary and other governmental investigations that require an accounting report; and the preparation and certification of income tax returns.

Contadores were granted the right to perform all the "accounting acts" specified in the law, except that they were not allowed to attest or certify publicly. Contadores públicos autorizados could perform all these acts and could also attest or certify publicly.

A 1966 amendment changed the requirements for a CPA license so that at present a university graduate with a major in accounting is entitled to the license provided he also complies with the nationality requirements. The National University grants a "licenciado en comercio con especialización en contabilidad y título de contador" (in effect, a degree in business administration, with a major in accounting, plus the formal title of "accountant") after a four-year day school program or a six-year night school curriculum that includes most of the accounting courses offered by a university in the United States. The only other institution of higher learning, Universidad Santa María La Antigua, grants a "licenciado en contabilidad" for a five-year night school program of studies. A Panamanian student who has completed his education in another country is required to obtain an evaluation of his curriculum from the National University, which requires that it must meet the requirements of the "licenciado" degree obtaining the CPA license. Two of the large international firms have offices in Panama and seven are associated or represented by local firms, this situation enabling Panamanian accountants to participate in continuing education programs by attending training seminars put on by these international firms.

There are approximately two thousand contadores públicos autorizados but only about one hundred fifty are in independent public practice.

Organizations of Accountants

Colegio de Contadores Públicos Autorizados (College of Authorized Public Accountants). The Colegio de Contadores Públicos Autorizados was organized in 1957 and has a membership of approximately one hundred fifty and has 12 committees. The colegio has two types of membership: contadores públicos autorizados with a minimum of three years of practice in public or private accounting, and associate members who are foreign accountants duly qualified to practice in their countries.

Asociación de Contadores y Contadores Públicos Autorizados (Association of Accountants and Authorized Public Accountants). The Asociación de Contadores y Contadores Públicos Autorizados is the oldest accounting body in Panama, dating back to 1941. Total membership is approximately five hundred including both "contadores" and "contadores públicos autorizados."

Ethics (Colegio de Contadores Públicos Autorizados)

The Colegio de Contadores Públicos Autorizados has adopted a comprehensive set of rules of conduct to which its members are obligated to conform. These rules include the following prohibitions and definitions (summarized):

1. No member may allow the use of his name by any person who is not his partner or duly authorized representative or employee under his responsibility.
2. No member of the Colegio may pay fees to persons outside the profession for obtaining clients.
3. No member of the Colegio will dedicate himself to businesses or occupations that underrate the profession of the contador público autorizado and will perform his profession honorably and with prestige.
4. A member will be considered guilty of committing an act discreditable to the profession if, while expressing an opinion on the financial statements that he has audited—
   a. He conceals a material fact of which he has knowledge and which he does not disclose in the financial statements when the disclosure of such fact is necessary for the financial statement not to be misleading;
   b. He does not communicate any material information that is false or erroneous and which to the best of his knowledge appears in the financial statements;
   c. He is grossly negligent when performing the examination or reporting on the financial statements;
   d. He does not obtain sufficient information to justify the ex-

pression of an opinion or does not disclose that his qualifications are of sufficient importance not to express an opinion; or

e. He does not disclose a material deviation from generally accepted accounting principles or disclose any material omission of generally accepted auditing standards necessary in the circumstances.

5. The public accountant shall not violate the confidential relationships between himself and his client.
6. No member shall sign an opinion that purports to express his opinion on the result of any examination of financial statements, unless these have been examined by him, a partner or employee of his firm, a member of the Colegio or a member of a similar association in a foreign country.
7. No member shall seek the client of another contador público autorizado.
8. No member shall offer employment directly or indirectly to any employee of another public accountant without previously advising the latter.
9. No member shall offer or perform professional services for a fee that depends on his findings or the results of such services.
10. No member shall advertise his capabilities or services. However, this rule does not prohibit the publication of what is technically known as a calling card.
11. No member when rendering services as director or employee of natural or juridical persons may act as a contadore público autorizado to review, examine, audit, or certify operations of his employer or the results of these operations. These same restrictions also apply to members who perform services as directors of corporations.

While members of the Colegio are required to abide by the code, the only sanction or penalty for violation would be a reprimand from the organization and possible expulsion from its ranks.

Auditing Standards–Accounting Principles

The principal statutory audit requirement in Panama is that companies listed with the National Securities Commission must file an annual statement similar to, but not as comprehensive as, the Form 10-K filed by companies with the Securities and Exchange Commission in the United States. The National Securities Commission functions within the Ministry of Commerce and Industry and has issued regulations prescribing financial statement presentation and rules for disclosure including a requirement that the financial statements of companies listed with the National Securities Commission be examined and reported on by independent public accountants. The regulations include a definition of accounting principles to be followed. The National Securities Commission's regulations closely follow the rules set forth in Regulation S-X of the Securities and Exchange Commission in the United States.

The only other statutory audit requirement in Panama is that commercial banks operating within the Republic of Panama must publish annually certified balance sheets.

Because of the position of Panama as an international banking center, the influence of Americans and other foreigners in commercial activities and the regulations of the National Securities Commission, auditing standards and accounting principles adhere closely to those generally accepted in the United States as promulgated by the American Institute of Certified Public Accountants and the Securities and Exchange Commission.

The Commission on Accounting Principles of the Colegio de Contadores Públicos Autorizados issued Accounting Research Bulletin No. 1 in 1971, in which are set forth the basic concepts of generally accepted accounting principles. Areas covered include the following subjects:

1. Departures from opinions of the commission; disclosure.
2. Status of the commission's opinions as "substantial authoritative acceptance" (of generally accepted accounting principles).
3. Definitions of generally accepted accounting principles.
4. Basic postulates of accounting.
5. Financial statements—functions and contents.

In April 1972, the Commission on General Principles of Accounting of the Asociación de Contadores y Contadores Públicos Authorizados issued a statement on general principles of accounting that comprised, for the most part, a definition of general terms.

Form and Content of Financial Statements

With the exception of statutory requirements for publication of balance sheets of banks operating in the Republic of Panama, there are no legal requirements for published financial statements in Panama. The form and content of financial statements have generally followed reporting practices in the United States. The basic financial statements are the balance sheet, the income statement, the statement of retained earnings, and the statement of changes in financial position.

Notes disclosing information additional to the basic financial statements have become an integral part of such statements.

Perú

Perú

As of May 1973

Forms of Business Organization

General

Business organizations in Perú are governed by the Commercial Code of 1902, the Civil Code of 1936, and the Mercantile Companies Law of 1966. Specific legislation has been enacted for banking, insurance, financial, industrial, mining, fishing and petroleum enterprises, telecommunications, and public utilities. The Commercial Code and subsequent legislation regulate the different types of businesses, namely, the sole proprietorship, the partnership, the corporation, and the branch of a foreign corporation. Under the Civil Code of 1936, civil partnerships may be formed.

All types of business organizations, other than the individual proprietorship, must be officially formed by deed, executed by a notary public, and recorded in the appropriate Public Mercantile Register; subsequent changes must also be notarized and registered. Titles, agreements, and so forth, may also be registered in the Public Mercantile Register and such documents when registered have preferred acceptance in cases of legal claims.

Local operations of foreign enterprises are generally carried on in the form of a "sociedad anónima" or through a branch of the foreign entity.

Sociedad Anónima (S.A.)

This form of organization is substantially equivalent to a U.S. corporation. Its capital consists of shares subscribed by shareholders whose liability is limited to the amount of their subscriptions. The name of the corporation is generally followed by the words "Sociedad Anónima" or by the initials "S.A."

A sociedad anónima must be formed by a minimum of three (five in the case of banks) individuals or legal entities; the share capital must be issued in full and paid up to a minimum of 25 percent of its value. No minimum amount of capital is required except for banks, insurance companies, and financial enterprises. Shares issued must be nominative (registered) and cannot be issued for an amount less than their nominal value.

Sociedades anónimas with more than 50 stockholders or with a capital of 20,000,000 soles or more must have a vigilance committee unless the board of directors has been elected by the unanimous vote of the stockholders under cumulative voting rules or unless the sociedad anónima is subject to a permanent external audit. Effective for all financial years ending December 31, 1972, and thereafter, all entities whose stockholders' equity exceeds 10,000,000 soles or whose revenues exceed 50,000,000 soles, must prepare annual financial statements in accordance with the regulations of the "Comisión Nacional Supervisora de Empresas y Valores" (National Security Commission). Such financial statements must be audited by independent auditors registered with the "Colegio de Contadores Públicos" (College of Public Accountants).

There is no legal requirement that a director also be a stockholder, unless required by the bylaws. The number of directors is determined by the bylaws or by general meeting. The function of a director is personal, but in certain cases authority may be delegated if authorized in the bylaws. A sociedad anónima that does not have a vigilance committee is obliged to include in its board of directors a representative of the minority stockholders, unless the election of the board has been by unanimous vote under cumulative voting rules.

Foreign investment in the capital of enterprises domiciled in Peru is limited to certain percentages of the total capital by specific laws. Specific laws have also created workers' communities, which participate in a fixed percentage of net income as follows:

	Industry			
	Industrial	*Mining*	*Fishing*	*Telecommunications*
For acquisition of shares	15%	6%	12%	15%
For distribution in cash to employees and workmen	10%	4%	8%	10%

The percentage for acquisition of shares must be reinvested in fixed assets of the same enterprise, and capitalized in favor of the workers' community until they hold 50 percent of the capital stock of the enterprise or, if no reinvestment program has been approved by the corresponding authorities, the percentage must be used for the acquisition of shares by direct purchase from other shareholders until the 50 percent limit is reached. Shares issued to the workers' community are called "acciones comunitarias" and are nominative and nontransferable. The board of directors of enterprises that have workers' communities must include at least one workers' representative, which number must be progressively increased in proportion to the number of shares owned by the workers' community.

Branch of a Foreign Corporation

Branches of foreign corporations may be constituted in Perú, but they must have a permanent legal representative resident in Perú with sufficient powers to resolve any matters in connection with the creation and activities of the branch.

There is no legal requirement for a minimum assigned capital for branches, except those of banking enterprises. Branches regulated by the legal provisions that create workers' communities must state the amount of capital effectively invested in the country, which amount will constitute its capital for the purpose of determining the 50 percent portion that must accrue progressively to the workers' community in accordance with the procedure mentioned above for sociedades anónimas, except that the shares are called "certificados de participación," which, similar to the community shares (acciones comunitarias), are nominative and nontransferable.

Sociedad Civil de Responsabilidad Limitada (S.C.R.L.)

The "S.C.R.L." has attributes of both partnership and corporation. It is created by private agreement among its members, but the liability of its members is limited to their capital contributions. The entire capital of the concern must be paid in at inception. It is required to state on all of its forms the amount of its capital and the fact that its members have limited liability.

Sociedad Colectiva

This is the equivalent of the unlimited liability partnership, and it may be formed by two or more members. Those who contribute capital are called "socios capitalistas" whereas those who contribute services only are called "socios industriales." Capital partners have unlimited liability with regard to third parties. A partnership must do business under the name of all partners or of one or more of them followed by the words "y Compañía."

Sociedad en Comandita

This is similar to the "sociedad colectiva" except that it may have one or more partners who contribute capital only and who do not take part in the management of the business. These silent partners, called "socios comanditarios," are liable only to the extent of their capital contributions. The other partners are called "socios colectivos" and have unlimited liability with respect to third parties. The name of the partnership is followed by the initials "S.enC."

The special laws relating to foreign investment and workers' communities are also applicable to noncorporate entities.

Business Records

The Commercial Code and subsequent legislation require that every business keep the following official books: inventory and balance book, journal, and general ledger. In addition, corporations are required to keep minute books, capital stock registers, and other records specified by law.

The official books and other auxiliary records, which may be in loose-leaf form, must be legalized before use and registered at the government tax office. All records must be kept in Spanish and in Peruvian currency.

The Accounting Profession

General

In the years 1941 and 1943, and after varied legislation on the subject, the government regulated the profession of public accounting and recognized as "contadores públicos" (public accountants) the graduates of the accounting courses of Peruvian universities as well as those members of the Instituto de Contadores del Perú who, at that time, had been practicing the accounting profession for the preceding ten years.

In 1959, Law No. 13253 amended the Commercial Code by establishing that merchants (this term includes all business enterprises) must keep their accounting records with the assistance (intervención) of either "contadores públicos" or "contadores mercantiles." This law defined the functions of each and authorized those who did not have the required qualifications, but who had been signing income tax declarations for the preceding three years, to continue performing such functions. These persons are called "contadores prácticos."

Contador Público

This term corresponds to the U.S. CPA. The degree is conferred by the universities of Perú and must be registered as such in the "colegio" where the accountant is domiciled. There are several universities in Perú such as the Universidad Nacional Mayor de San Marcos, the Universidad de Arequipa, and the Universidad del Cuzco. To enroll in the accounting courses at these universities, the student must be a high school graduate and pass a general-knowledge and selective examination. The degree of "contador público" requires six years of study of subjects generally comparable to those included in similar courses at U.S. universities.

Functions. The Supreme Decree No. 28 of August 1960 organized the "Colegio de Contadores Públicos" (College of Public Accountants) and regulated the principal functions of the contador público, which were originally outlined in Law No. 13253 of 1959, and defined the most important areas of his activities. These include the examination of financial statements and the expression of an opinion thereon, the organization of accounting systems, and other matters relating to the exercise of his profession.

Organization of Auditing Firms. This decree also stated the requirements to be observed by auditing firms, as follows:

1. The partnership agreement must be created by public deed which should clearly indicate the joint and several responsibilities of its partners.
2. The audit reports which the firm issues must be signed by a contador público who represents the firm for that purpose. The contador público must be a member of the Colegio and is jointly responsible with the firm he represents for the acts arising from the discharge of his duties and authority vested.
3. The firm must be registered in the corresponding colegio.

A recent internal regulation of the Colegio has established that all partners of auditing firms must necessarily be contadores públicos duly registered with the Colegio.

Contador Mercantil

Peruvian law provides for the degree of "contador mercantil" to be conferred by the Department of Education on those who have completed a commercial course at a state school or at an officially authorized private school. This could be compared to a commercial high school in the United States.

In addition to keeping the accounting records of merchants, as permitted by the Law of 1959, a contador mercantil is authorized to sign "balances" (financial statements) for income tax purposes. He may also perform the functions of a contador público in locations where there are less than three contadores públicos.

Contador Práctico

These are the accountants who do not possess any of the educational qualifications required for either contador público or contador mercantil, but whose function of signing "balances" for income tax purposes was recognized under the Laws of 1943 and 1959. The register of contadores prácticos was closed in February 1961.

Registro Fiscal de Contadores

The "Registro Fiscal de Contadores" (Fiscal Register of Accountants) which was created by the Law of 1959, is composed of three separate sections representing each group of accountants (públicos, mercantiles, and prácticos). There is a central register in Lima and a subsidiary register in each province of the country.

Accounting Organizations

Colegio de Contadores Públicos. A "colegio de contadores públicos" may be formed in every province where ten or more public accountants practice. Their bylaws are subject to the approval of the Treasury Department. Registration of the contador público in the colegio is obligatory.

The principal functions assigned by law to the colegios are to keep a register of its members, to establish and enforce a code of professional ethics, to issue reports on technical matters as requested by public and official institutions, to establish minimum professional fees, and to sponsor an academy of professional practice for students and graduates.

At present, there are colegios functioning in Lima and in the principal provincial capitals. The Colegio in Lima was formed as a private organization in 1942 and became the official body under the Law of 1959. It now has about thirty-five hundred members. At the Second National

Convention of Public Accountants in 1961, a "federación" was created which combined all the colegios.

Instituto de Contadores del Perú. This, the first Peruvian accountants' association, was organized in 1900. The head office is located in Lima and there are offices in every province.

At present, the membership comprises mainly accountants in private industry and contadores prácticos.

Asociación de Contadores de Lima. The members of this association are mainly practical accountants (contadores prácticos). They do not engage in what would be understood as professional activities.

Code of Ethics

At the Third National Convention of Public Accountants in 1971, a code of professional ethics was approved that covers the rules of professional conduct and ethics of all contadores públicos who work for a government entity, private enterprises, and educational institutions or who are working as independent auditors and in relationship with the public in general. It also contains rules regarding disciplinary measures, sanctions, and so forth.

Auditing Standards

The auditing committee of the Colegio de Contadores Públicos has published bulletins setting out the generally accepted auditing standards to be followed by the profession in Perú. Basically, these standards are the same as those approved by the countries represented at the Seventh Interamerican Accounting Conference held in Mar del Plata, Argentina, in 1965 and are also practically identical to those generally accepted in the United States. These standards are set out under three headings which follow:

1. General and professional standards
2. Standards of field work
3. Reporting standards

It should be noted that the standards referred to above have been recently incorporated into the regulations covering the technical standards of control to be exercised by the government over state entities and all those in which the state is associated or which receive public funds. The control referred to above must be carried out by the "Contraloría General de la República," by the internal auditing departments of the entities concerned, or by external auditors.

Accounting Principles and Practices

General

There is no code, either written or unwritten, of accounting conventions similar to generally accepted accounting principles as recognized in the United States.

The following authoritative groups define and promote the application of generally accepted accounting principles:

1. Colegio de Contadores Públicos de Lima.
2. Superintendencia de Banca y Seguros (for banking, insurance, and financial enterprises).
3. Comisión Nacional Supervisora de Empresas y Valores (equivalent to the SEC). This body has published rules ("Reglamento de Auditoría y Certificación de Balances") regarding auditing and certification of financial statements of companies whose shares are quoted on the stock exchange, or which are applying for a quotation, making a public issue, and so forth, and all entities have a shareholders' equity in excess of 10,000,000 soles or revenues in excess of 50,000,000 soles. These rules are far in advance of anything previously published and include among the requirements the presentation of a statement of changes in financial position.

Form and Content of Financial Statements

As indicated above, the Comisión Nacional Supervisora de Empresas y Valores has recently published rules, which cover the form and content of financial statements. Their application has been extended to include all companies with revenue and capital above certain amounts.

Financial statements must include the following:

1. Balance sheet
2. Statement of income
3. Statement of retained earnings
4. Statement of changes in financial position

5. Notes to financial statements
6. Supplementary schedules
7. Auditors' opinion

The notes and supplementary schedules are very comprehensive and include details of all material items in the financial statements.

Summary of Accounting Practices

Accounting practices are generally the same as in the United States. Certain differences exist with regard to the accounting for, and reporting of, certain assets, liabilities, and items of revenue or expense. Some of these differences are as follows:

1. Inventory accounting and valuation procedures are generally the same as in the United States. However, for income tax reasons, there is a general reluctance to establish an allowance for obsolescence.
2. There are no significant differences with regard to the capitalization of fixed assets. However, where there are outstanding foreign currency loans for the purchase of fixed assets, the practice is to add the exchange differential arising from devaluations or settlements to the cost of the fixed asset.
3. Generally, depreciation of fixed assets is calculated on a straight-line basis using rates prescribed by the tax authorities. In special circumstances, authorization for the use of higher rates may be obtained.
4. Purchased intangible assets are normally capitalized and amortized for book and tax purposes in equal annual installments over ten years.
5. Wasting assets are normally depleted in accordance with special laws or decrees. The allowance for depletion must be reinvested by the company and is not available for distribution to the shareholders.
6. Contingency reserves are often set up, particularly where earnings are high.
7. Accounting practices for bad debts vary considerably and are primarily governed by tax considerations. The tendency is to write off bad debts rather than set up allowances.

The following are other significant accounting practices in effect in Perú which are different from those in the United States:

1. Very few companies make inter-period allocation of income taxes arising from timing differences.
2. There are no legal requirements for consolidation of subsidiary or affiliated companies. However, the Comisión Supervisora de Empresas y Valores may require that consolidated financial statements be presented.
3. It is the custom for companies such as banks and insurance companies to record contingent liabilities in memorandum accounts.
4. No standard definition or treatment exists for the presentation in financial statements of prior period adjustments or extraordinary items.

The accounting practice with regard to revaluation of fixed assets is as follows:

1. The most recent decree-law regarding revaluations was published on April 1, 1971. With certain exceptions, this decree-law requires all those entities which are required to file tax returns to revalue their fixed assets in accordance with specified percentages and procedures. The net amount of the revaluation is subject to a 10 percent tax.
2. The net amount of the revaluation is deductible for income tax purposes over the remaining useful lives of the assets concerned and the 10 percent tax thereon is deductible for income tax purposes when paid.
3. The net amount of the revaluation must be capitalized after offsetting prior year's losses. In the case of certain companies, a percentage of the tax on revaluation must be capitalized in favor of the workers' community.
4. Details of revaluations are generally disclosed in the annual reports either on the face of the balance sheet or in a footnote.
5. Auditors' opinions are not qualified because of revaluations.

The accounting practice with regard to accounting for depreciation is as follows:

1. Up to 1968, the amount of depreciation recorded and the amount claimed for tax purposes were required to be the same. Since that

date, differences have been permitted, but, if depreciation is not recorded, it can not be carried forward for tax purposes to subsequent years.

2. It is not customary to see material deviations between the depreciation recorded in the books and the amounts allowed as deductions for income tax purposes. The depreciation rates allowed for tax purposes are normally fair and reasonable.

3. Depreciation on revaluation write-ups is allowed as a deduction for income tax purposes.

Liability for Income Tax

It is customary to provide for income tax on the books in the same year in which the income is earned. The tax laws are sufficiently explicit to permit a company to compute its income tax liability, but there are areas where differences of interpretation exist. Provisions for bad debts, if reasonable and substantiated, are allowed as deductions for income tax purposes, but the amount of bad debts allowed as a deduction is not, of course, fixed by statute. Tax allocation due to timing differences is not generally recognized. Expenses paid in one year but applicable to prior years are not allowed for tax purposes. As a general rule, a provision for expense is allowed only if actual payment is made within 90 days of the financial year end.

Legal Reserve (Law No. 16123)

If net income exceeds 7 percent of issued capital, a minimum of 10 percent of net income must be set aside as a legal reserve until the reserve reaches 20 percent of issued capital. This reserve may be used to cover losses but it then must be restored out of subsequent earnings to 20 percent of issued capital.

Dividends

Dividends are usually paid in cash or in stock. There is no restriction as to the granting of foreign exchange for the payment of dividends, but the payment of cash dividends is subject to the approval of the "Banco de la Nación."

The current withholding tax on dividends is 25 percent for residents and 40 percent for nonresidents; the 40 percent withholding tax may be reduced to 30 percent under certain circumstances. The tax must be withheld and paid to the fiscal authorities within 15 days of the dividend declaration.

Stock dividends are known as "capitalización" and normally arise from the capitalization of retained earnings and/or free reserves and are subject to a 15 percent tax payable by the company. Capitalization or distribution as a dividend becomes obligatory when retained earnings and free reserves exceed 100 percent of the paid-in capital.

Liability for Separation Indemnity

The labor laws provide that an employer must pay separation indemnity to an employee whose employment is terminated except in cases of dishonesty. The amount of the indemnity for all employees is equivalent to one month's wage or salary, with certain maximum limitations for those employed subsequent to July 1962.

Employees may borrow up to 50 percent of their accumulated indemnities for the purchase of a house or for the cost of structural improvements to existing housing, subject to the prior approval of the loans by the Ministry of Labor.

Normally, the maximum amount for separation indemnities is accrued as a liability and such accruals are allowable deductions for income tax purposes. Disclosure is generally made in annual reports as to the provision for separation indemnities as well as the amount accrued. It is customary that auditors' opinions be qualified if separation indemnities are not provided for in the accounts.

Royalties and Management Fees

These are allowed as deductions for income tax purposes provided that the appropriate taxes are withheld and paid to the tax authorities and the legalized contracts have been registered with the appropriate authorities. There are no restrictions as to the granting of foreign exchange for the payment of royalties and management fees, but the payment of these items is subject to the approval of the Banco de la Nación.

Requirements for Listing Securities on the Stock Exchange and Public Sale of Securities

Companies desiring to have their shares listed for trading on the stock exchange must have previously presented to the Comisión Nacional Supervisora de Empresas y Valores financial statements prepared under the rules contained in the Reglamento de Auditoría y Certificación de Balances. They are also obliged to submit various additional documents such as incorporation papers, amendments to bylaws, and so forth. Once their shares are listed, they are required to present certain information periodically to the comisión.

Those companies which are to be established by public offering of securities must submit (a) a feasibility study and (b) forecasts for the next three years, with the opinion of an auditing firm. But the forecast period may be extended to five years under certain circumstances.

The Philippines

The Philippines

As of June 1973

Forms of Business Organization

The forms of business organization in the Philippines are similar to those found in the United States—the single proprietorship, the partnership, and the corporation. Philippine business law is generally modeled after that prevailing in the United States, although there are some concepts that were derived from Spanish law.

A foreign partnership may do business in the Philippines by filing with the office of the Philippine Securities and Exchange Commission three copies of its partnership agreement, certified by a Philippine consul, and by complying with certain other formalities. A foreign corporation may not do business in the Philippines until it has filed various documents with and has obtained a license from the Securities and Exchange Commission. Foreign partnerships and foreign corporations must obtain a written certification from the Board of Investments that the proposed business enterprises would "contribute to the sound and balanced development of the national economy on a self-sustaining basis . . ." before the Securities and Exchange Commission can issue a license to do business.

Corporations

A corporation may be organized by no less than five nor more than fifteen persons, the majority of whom must be residents of the Philippines.

The duly executed and notarized articles of incorporation must be filed with the Philippine Securities and Exchange Commission, which publishes, at the company's expense, information on the firm's assets and liabilities in a newspaper of general circulation, and issues a certificate of incorporation. The articles of incorporation include the usual information as to name, purpose, location, and duration (which normally may not exceed 50 years; amendments of articles are allowed to extend life no more than 50 years at a time); names and addresses of incorporators; number, names, and addresses of directors; number of shares and amount of capital stock (for no-par stock, only the number of shares into which the capital stock is divided need be stated); names and addresses of subscribers and amounts of their subscriptions, as well as payments made on subscriptions.

An affidavit by the treasurer elected must accompany the articles of incorporation showing that at least 20 percent of the authorized capital stock has been subscribed and at least 25 percent of the subscription price has been paid into the corporation.

A code of bylaws (which may contain among other items (a) the time, place, and manner of calling and conducting regular or special meetings of directors and of stockholders or members; (b) the number of stockholders or members necessary to constitute a quorum for the transaction of business; and (c) the qualifications, duties, and compensation of directors and officers) must also be adopted and filed with the Securities and Exchange Commission within 30 days from the date the certificate of incorporation is issued.

Control of the corporation is exercised by a board of directors elected by the members or stockholders; each director of a stock corporation must own continuously during his term at least one share which shall stand in his name on the books of the corporation, and at least two directors of all corporations organized under the Philippine Corporation Law must be residents of the Philippines.

All corporations, as well as general partnerships with a capital of 3,000 pesos or more, must register with the Securities and Exchange Commission. All businesses must register with the Bureau of Internal Revenue. Registration of business names in certain instances is made with the Bureau of Commerce, renewable usually every five years as stated in the certificate of registration.

Partnerships

The Civil Code of the Philippines governs the formation of partnerships and the obligations and rights of partners, including limited partners. It is similar to the U.S. Uniform Partnership Act and the Uniform Limited Partnership Act.

Two or more persons may form a general partnership, and the contract of any partnership having a capital of 3,000 pesos or more must be set forth in a public instrument recorded in the office of the Securities and Exchange Commission.

Limited partnerships are formed by two or more persons with one or more general partners (with unlimited liability) and one or more limited partners, whose liability is limited to the amount of capital paid in. While the code is silent on the information to be contained in a general partnership agreement, it does provide that a limited partnership agreement should contain, among other items, (a) the name of the partnership, adding thereto the word "Limited"; (b) the kind of business, duration and location of principal place of business; (c) name and residence of each limited and general partner, specifying his category; and (d) contribution and compensation of each limited partner (contribution may not be in services).

The notarized certificate containing this information must be recorded in the office of the Securities and Exchange Commission.

Business Records

Corporations are required under the Corporation Law to keep and carefully preserve a record of all business transactions, minute books for meetings of directors, members, or stockholders (which must set forth the time and place of holding the meeting, how authorized, whether regular or special; if special, its object, those present and absent, and every act done or ordered done at the meeting) and a stock and transfer book.

The records of all business transactions of the corporation and minutes of any meeting shall be open to the inspection of any director, member, or stockholder of the corporation at reasonable hours.

A regulation of the Bureau of Internal Revenue, approved by the Department of Finance, requires that all corporations, partnerships, or persons required by law to pay internal revenue taxes shall keep a journal and a ledger, or their equivalents, provided however, that those whose gross quarterly sales, earnings, or receipts do not exceed 5,000 pesos shall keep and use a simplified set of bookkeeping records duly authorized by the Secretary of Finance. Corporations, partnerships, or persons whose gross quarterly sales, earnings, or receipts exceed 25,000 pesos shall have their books of accounts audited and examined yearly by independent certified public accountants. The regulation further requires that such records and invoice and receipt forms be submitted to the bureau for approval and registration before they may be used.

The Accounting Profession

General

In the early 1900's, a few British accountants commenced limited accounting practices in Manila. The activities of these and their successors grew until accountancy was recognized as a profession in March 1923, with the passage of Act No. 3105. In August 1967, a new accountancy law, Republic Act No. 5166, was passed. This act governs the standardization of accounting education, the examination for registration of certified public accountants, and the regulation of the practice of accountancy in the Philippines. To carry out its provisions, the act created the Board of Accounting Education and the Board of Accountancy. As in the Accountancy Act of 1923, only citizens of the Philippines and citizens of foreign countries extending similar privileges to citizens of the Philippines with respect to the practice of accountancy can take the CPA examinations and therefore become CPAs qualified to practice in the country. The act also provides that the Commissioner of the Securities and Exchange Commission shall not register any corporation organized for the practice of public accountancy.

Certified Public Accountants

Requirements for the Certificate. The applicant must be a Filipino citizen (or a citizen of a foreign country granting reciprocal privileges, by law, to Filipinos with respect to the practice of accountancy), of good moral character, and at least 21 years of age. He must be a holder of a degree of Bachelor of Science in Commerce or its equivalent from any college or university recognized by the government, and be certified by such college or university as having acquired not less than one year of employment or apprenticeship experience in accountancy or a related field or, as a substitute, having completed two semesters covering 12 units of equivalent practical training through academic work.

After approval of his application, the applicant must take the scheduled examination given by the Board of Accountancy. The examination covers theory of accounts, business law, taxation, management services, auditing theory and practice, and practical accounting. Having passed this examination, he takes the "oath of the profession" administered by the board, which issues him a certificate of registration as "certified public accountant." Each CPA practicing his profession must pay an annual professional license fee to the national government.

Functions. Under the Accountancy Act of 1967, a person is deemed to be engaged in the practice of public accounting if he (condensed)—

1. Indicates to the public that he is qualified to render professional services as an accountant.
2. Renders to more than one client such services as the—
   a. audit or verification of financial transactions and accounting records;
   b. preparation or signing of reports of audits, statements to be used for publication, governmental, or credit purposes;
   c. installation and revision of accounting systems; and
   d. preparation of income tax returns (when related to accounting procedures).
3. Represents clients before governmental agencies on tax matters related to accounting.
4. Renders professional assistance in matters relating to accounting procedure and the recording and presentation of financial facts or data.

The report of an independent certified public accountant on financial statements is required in a number of instances. Stock corporations, with an authorized or paid-up capital of 50,000 pesos or more, are required to file copies of annual certified financial statements with the Securities and Exchange Commission. Branches of foreign corporations are required to file certified financial statements annually, both for the branch itself and for the company as a whole. The Internal Revenue Code provides that corporations, partnerships, or persons whose gross quarterly sales, earnings, receipts, or output exceeds 25,000 pesos must file certified financial statements with their tax returns. The return itself need not be signed by a CPA.

Other government regulatory bodies, such as the Central Bank and the Department of Public Works, Transportation and Communications, which exercise jurisdiction over banks and public utilities, respectively, also require audited financial statements for varied purposes.

The Board of Accounting Education

The Board of Accounting Education, established by Republic Act No. 5166 of August 1967, has the authority to standardize and regulate accounting education. Its functions are to prescribe—

(a) minimum requirements for the admission of candidates to the CPA examinations,

(b) requirements for one-year employment or apprenticeship experience or their academic substitutes, and

(c) collegiate courses for the degree of Bachelor of Science in Commerce or its equivalent.

The Board of Accountancy

The Board of Accountancy regulates the practice of accountancy in the Philippines. It is composed of a chairman and five other members, appointed by the President of the Philippines. Members must be certified public accountants of recognized standing, academically and morally qualified, who have been in practice for at least ten years; who are not directly or indirectly connected with any college or university granting degrees that may qualify graduates with such degrees for admission to the CPA examination; and who do not have any pecuniary interest in such school, college, or university.

The Board of Accountancy conducts the CPA examinations, evaluates the results, and issues a certificate of registration to those who have satisfactorily complied with its requirements. It sets professional standards for the practice of accountancy, promulgates rules and regulations necessary for the practice of accountancy in the Philippines, and is empowered to reprimand erring CPAs or suspend or revoke registration certificates in cases of noncompliance with ethical or professional standards and other violations or misconduct as spelled out in the Accountancy Act.

Ethics

The Board of Accountancy, under its authority to "set professional standards for the practice of accountancy" has promulgated a set of rules of professional conduct, the provisions of which are summarized as follows:

1. The CPA shall not commit any act discreditable to the profession. He shall at all times conduct himself in a manner contributing to the honor and prestige of the accounting profession.
2. He shall be guided by high ideals of personal honor in all his professional work, practicing in the spirit of fidelity to his clients and loyalty to the public. His obligation to the public dictates that he present an accurate and honest statement of facts as he finds them.
3. He shall express an opinion on financial statements only after he has examined them in accordance with generally accepted auditing standards.
4. He shall be held guilty of an act discreditable to the profession if, in expressing an opinion on representations in financial statements which he has examined, he—

a. fails to disclose a material fact known to him which is not disclosed in the financial statements but disclosure of which is necessary to make the financial statements not misleading;

b. fails to report any material misstatement known to him to appear in the financial statements;

c. is grossly negligent in the conduct of his examination or in making his report thereon;

d. fails to acquire sufficient information to warrant expression of an opinion, or his exceptions are sufficiently material to negate the expression of an opinion; or

e. fails to direct attention to any material departure from generally accepted accounting principles or to disclose any material omission of generally accepted auditing procedures applicable in the circumstances.

When he believes that the financial statements are false or misleading in any significant respect, he should require either adjustment of the accounts or adequate disclosure of the facts, as the case may be; otherwise he should not permit his name to be associated with the statements in any way.

5. He shall not allow the use of his name in conjunction with financial statements in a manner that would lead an ordinary reader of the statements to believe that he is acting as an independent public accountant unless—

   a. he expresses an unqualified opinion;

   b. he renders a qualified opinion;

   c. he gives an adverse opinion;

   d. he disclaims an opinion on the statements taken as a whole and states clearly his reasons for doing so;

   e. he expresses an opinion on specific items in the financial statements with which he is satisfied although an opinion is disclaimed or an adverse opinion is given on the financial statements taken as a whole; or

   f. when no audit has been performed, or the auditing procedures performed are insignificant under the circumstances, he discloses clearly and conspicuously on each page of the financial statements the fact that they were not audited.

6. He shall not allow his name to be associated with any estimates or forecast of earnings contingent upon future transactions, unless he makes full disclosure of the source of information used, the major

assumption made, the character of the work he has performed, and the degree of responsibility he is taking; and he states clearly that he does not vouch for the accuracy of the forecast.

7. He shall not express an opinion on financial statements of an enterprise with respect to which he is not independent.
8. He shall not divulge information or evidence about his client which has been obtained by him in his professional capacity.
9. He shall not render services for a fee which is contingent upon his findings or the outcome of the engagement.
10. He shall not advertise or cause to be advertised his professional attainments or services.
11. He shall not solicit clients, directly or indirectly, and he shall not encroach upon the practice of another CPA.
12. He shall not receive or pay commissions or share fees or profits with any individual or firm not regularly engaged or employed in the practice of public accounting as a principal occupation.
13. He shall not practice in the name of another nor shall he allow any person to practice in his name unless he is in partnership with him or in his employ.
14. He shall not engage in any business or occupation conjointly with that of public accounting which is incompatible or inconsistent with such practice.
15. He shall not offer employment, directly or indirectly, to one who is employed by another CPA unless due notice is given to the latter.

The Philippine Institute of Certified Public Accountants

In 1929, a group of CPAs organized an association called the Philippine Institute of Certified Public Accountants. This organization was largely successful in protecting the CPA certificate and in promoting the accounting profession in general, but little attention was given to developing standards of performance in the profession itself. World War II caused suspension of its activities. After the war, the Institute was revived and incorporated, and its name became the Philippine Institute of Accountants. Although the certificate of CPA is a prerequisite to membership, it was felt that the omission of "certified public" from the name would emphasize that its purpose was no longer primarily protective, but was to improve the professional standing of its members. In November 1961, the original name, Philippine Institute of Certified Public Accountants (PICPA), was adopted to avoid confusion of the Institute's initials (PIA) with other associations bearing the same initials and to make known that its members are certified public accountants.

The PICPA does not concentrate its activities in Manila and its suburbs alone. It has given active support and encouragement to the establishment of provincial chapters in order to serve members in other geographic areas as well. As of August 1972, twenty-two chapters had been organized and all are actively engaged in implementing the Institute's program in the provinces.

The Institute also encourages the formation of junior Philippine institutes of accountants in colleges and universities in order to make accounting students aware, at an early date, of the need for professional unity.

Various services are rendered by the PICPA to its members. In addition to annual conventions, monthly membership meetings are held where speakers in accounting and allied fields such as banking, finance, economics, and taxation are invited. The Institute publishes a quarterly technical journal and a monthly news bulletin which contains, among other things, tax rulings and decisions and commercial law digests. It also publishes reprints of new laws, opinions, rules of government entities, and other materials of interest to members.

As to the improvement of technical standards, the Institute's activities include the holding of professional seminars and the issuance of bulletins on accounting principles and audit standards and procedures. Since 1949, the Institute has released the following bulletins which are still in effect:

Audit Bulletins

No. 1, "Audit Procedures for Import Quota Application"

No. 2, "Audit Fees"

No. 3, "Reports and Certifications of the Independent Certified Public Accountants"

No. 5, "Audit Procedures for Accounts Receivable"

No. 6, "Audit Procedures for Inventories"

No. 8, "Audit Procedures for Property, Plant, and Equipment"

No. 9, "Audit Procedures for Liabilities"

No. 10, "Audit Procedures for Capital Stock and Surplus"

No. 11, "Audit Procedures for Income and Expenses"

No. 15, "Guides to Implementation of Generally Accepted Auditing Standards" (Replaces earlier Audit Bulletin No. 12; incorporates earlier Audit Bulletins Nos. 13 and 14)

No. 16, "Guides to Financial Statement Presentation"

No. 17, "Audit Procedures for Investments" (Replaces earlier Audit Bulletin No. 7)

No. 18, "Audit Procedures for Cash" (Replaces earlier Audit Bulletin No. 4)

Accounting Principles Bulletins

No. 1, "Basic Concepts in Accounting for Business Enterprises"

No. 2, "Accounting for Income Taxes"

No. 3, "Funds Statement for Business Enterprises"

Special Bulletins

No. 1-70, "Accounting for the Effects of the Floating Exchange Rate"

No. 2-71, "Revaluation of Fixed Assets"

The Institute has also published a code of ethics which is essentially the same as the rules on professional conduct promulgated by the Board of Accountancy.

With the enactment of the Accountancy Act of 1967, the role of the Institute in the development of the accounting profession was given formal recognition: first, by making the president of the organization a member of the Board of Accounting Education; second, by authorizing the Institute to prepare a list of names from which the president of the Philippines appoints members of the Board of Accountancy; and third, by giving the organization a voice in the promulgation by the Board of Accountancy of rules and regulations and professional standards for the practice of accountancy.

Auditing Standards

General

The generally accepted auditing standards as adopted by the membership of the Philippine Institute of Certified Public Accountants are codified in a bulletin entitled "Statement of Generally Accepted Auditing Standards," which was later amplified in a bulletin entitled "Guides to Implementation of Generally Accepted Auditing Standards." These auditing standards are similar to those prescribed by the AICPA in the United States.

Specifically, the bulletin discusses the audit standards under the following headings:

General Standards

1. Adequate technical training and proficiency of the auditor
2. Independence in the auditor's mental attitude
3. Due professional care in the performance of the auditor's work

Standards of Field Work

1. Adequate planning of field work and proper supervision of assistants
2. Proper study and evaluation of internal control
3. Sufficiency and competence of evidential matter

Standards of Reporting

1. Conformity with generally accepted accounting principles
2. Application of the consistency standard
3. Adequacy of informative disclosures
4. Expression of the auditor's opinion

Independence

Reference to the independence concept is found in section 7, article IV of the rules and regulations of the Board of Accountancy. This rule on independence has been adopted by both the Philippine Institute of Certified Public Accountants and the Bureau of Internal Revenue.

Under the rules, a CPA is prevented from expressing an opinion on financial statements of an enterprise with respect to which he is not independent. Before expressing his opinion on financial statements, the CPA has the responsibility of evaluating whether, under the circumstances, his opinion will be considered independent and unbiased by one who has knowledge of all the facts. For instance, a CPA shall not be considered independent with respect to any enterprise if—

(a) during the period of his professional engagement or at the time of expressing his opinion, he had acquired or was committed to acquire any direct financial interest or material indirect financial interest in the enterprise; or

(b) he was connected with the enterprise as a promoter, underwriter, voting trustee, director, officer or employee during the period of his professional engagement, at the time of expressing his opinion or during the period covered by the financial statements.

A firm of certified public accountants, one of the members or employees of which is actually keeping or supervising the keeping of the books of accounts of a certain client, cannot audit the said books of accounts of the latter.

Standards of Reporting

The standards of reporting, as enunciated in the bulletin issued by the Philippine Institute of Certified Public Accountants entitled "Guides to Implementation of Generally Accepted Auditing Standards," indicate the requirements for the expression of an opinion on financial statements. The standards require that the auditor's report state whether the financial statements are presented in accordance with generally accepted principles of accounting and whether such principles have been consistently observed in the current period in relation to the preceding period; and should contain an expression of opinion regarding the financial statements, taken as a whole, or an assertion to the effect that an opinion cannot be expressed. When an overall opinion cannot be expressed, the reasons therefor should be stated. In all cases where an auditor's name is associated with financial statements, the report should contain a clear-cut indication of the character of the auditor's examination, if any, and the degree of responsibility he is taking. Unless otherwise indicated in the auditor's report, informative disclosures in the financial statements are to be regarded as reasonably adequate.

The standard short-form report contains a scope paragraph, wherein is outlined the work of the auditors, and an opinion paragraph, wherein is expressed the conclusion arrived at by the auditor after performing the examination described in the scope paragraph. Where necessary, an intermediate paragraph or paragraphs are included to explain limitations, if any, on the examination, to give reasons for exceptions in the auditor's opinion, or to incorporate other explanations and comments.

The audit bulletin on generally accepted auditing standards indicates when an unqualified opinion can be expressed and gives guidelines on the expression of a qualified opinion, an adverse opinion or a disclaimer of opinion, and a piecemeal opinion, where appropriate.

The bulletin outlines the usual circumstances which require modifications of the standard short-form report. Such instances, wherein the auditor should qualify his opinion, disclaim an opinion on the financial statements taken as a whole, or render an adverse opinion, include limitations in the scope of the examination, lack of conformity with generally accepted accounting principles, non-disclosure or inadequate disclosure of a material item, lack of consistency in the application of generally accepted accounting principles, and existence of unusual uncertainties as to the effect of future developments on certain items.

Accounting Principles and Practices

General

During the period of establishment and initial growth of the public accounting profession in the Philippines, the country was an American possession. American accounting textbooks were used in teaching, and a number of Filipinos studied accounting in American universities. Many of the larger companies in the Philippines were subsidiaries or branches of American companies, and their accounting reflected United States accounting principles. Further, Title II (Income Tax) of the Philippine Internal Revenue Code was originally patterned after the United States law. For these reasons, the generally accepted accounting principles recognized in the Philippines are similar to those recognized in the United States. To keep up with certain economic changes, however, special bulletins have been issued by the Philippine Institute of Certified Public Accountants which cover matters not included in AICPA pronouncements. These include bulletins entitled "Accounting for the Effects of the Floating Exchange Rate" (issued in March 1970) and "Revaluation of Fixed Assets" (issued in November 1971).

Revaluation of Fixed Assets

In a bulletin issued by the Philippine Institute of Certified Public Accountants, which became effective for fiscal years ending on and after December 31, 1971, the acceptability of using appraised values as an alternative to the cost method of fixed-asset valuation was recognized, provided the requirements in the bulletin regarding accounting treatment and disclosures in the financial statements are followed and depreciation is based on appraised values.

A summary of the conclusions in the PICPA bulletin follows:

1. The Committee believes that recognition of the effects of changes in price levels on financial statements should be given general acceptance in accounting practice.
2. The application of price-level adjustment, as a practical matter, may be limited to fixed assets and depreciation alone. In the absence of coefficients determined specifically for asset revaluation, appraised values may be used.
3. The revalued amounts and their effect on the financial statements may be indicated as supplementary information to the financial statements or incorporated in the accounting records so as to show appraised values in the financial statements themselves.

4. Historical cost will continue to be an alternative method of valuing fixed assets and determining related depreciation charges to operations.

5. If appraised values are incorporated in the financial statements, disclosure should be made of the appraised values, accumulated depreciation on appraised values, depreciation on appraisal increment, excess of appraised values over cost and date of appraisal. Historical cost and depreciation on historical cost should be disclosed in addition. This is necessary so that a comparison of financial position and results of operations between companies using appraised values and companies using historical cost is possible.

6. If appraised values are incorporated in the accounts, depreciation should be based on appraised values; until further government action, depreciation for tax purposes will still be based on cost.

7. The excess of appraised values over cost will not be available for dividends. (This statement is merely a recommendation, since the portion of revaluation increment which has been realized through depreciation charges on appraisal increment is legally available for dividends, cash, or stock.)

8. If the revaluation of fixed assets was performed by independent appraisers and the auditor has satisfied himself as to the general fairness of the appraised values, and the statement presentation and disclosure follow the recommendations set forth in this bulletin, no reference need be made in the auditor's report relative to the valuation at appraised values. However, the guidelines relative to the application of the consistency standard of reporting should be referred to in the year the change in accounting for fixed assets is made from historical cost to appraised values.

Long-Term Foreign Currency Indebtedness

When a floating exchange rate was adopted for the Philippine peso in 1970, the exchange rate of the peso to the dollar dropped by about 67 percent as at the end of that year, thereby necessitating the restatement of obligations denominated in foreign exchange to provide for the additional pesos required to liquidate these obligations. This restatement was made by charging expenses, inventories, or fixed assets as follows:

1. If the indebtedness arose from expenses incurred or other expired costs, the additional liability was charged to operations.
2. If the indebtedness arose from purchases of inventories, the additional liability in terms of pesos was charged to the cost of such in-

ventories (if on hand at the balance sheet date) or to operations (if inventories had been sold as of the balance sheet date).

3. If the indebtedness arose from the importation of fixed assets, it was considered part of the cost of such assets.

Recent developments in accounting principles in the United States which have applicability in the Philippines have not yet been adopted in the country. These include the equity method of accounting for investments in common stock and pension costs. The equity method is acceptable and has been used by some companies but is not considered mandatory. Thus, investments in common stock may be valued either at equity or at cost. As to pension costs, there is no definite requirement that provisions for retirement benefits be based on actuarial computations. Accruals in cases where actuarial estimates are absent are based on arithmetical computations.

Form and Content of Financial Statements

The form of financial statements and the rules of disclosure follow those which prevail in the United States. Specifically, a bulletin issued by the Philippine Institute of CPAs entitled "Guides to Financial Statement Presentation" assists CPAs in financial statement presentation within the framework of generally accepted accounting principles and reporting standards. The basic financial statements, particularly the balance sheet and the statement(s) of income and retained earnings are discussed in the bulletin, with an outline of the statement presentation and disclosure requirements for each of the more important accounts included in each statement.

There are no statutory regulations requiring submission of consolidated statements in the Philippines. The Bureau of Internal Revenue, for instance, does not permit the filing of income tax returns on a consolidated basis and the Philippine Securities and Exchange Commission does not require the submission of consolidated financial statements. However, consolidated statements are prepared whenever required by management for internal use of the company or in response to a request by its parent company or foreign auditors.

Bad Debts

Provision for bad debts may be recorded in the books based on reasonable estimates of probable losses. However, only debts which are actually ascertained to be worthless and charged off within the taxable year are allowed as deductions for income tax purposes.

Depreciation

As a general rule, depreciation claimed as a tax deduction must agree with the amount recorded in the books. However, internal revenue authorities permit differences between book depreciation and depreciation for tax purposes in certain instances. Under the Philippine Investment Incentives Act, enterprises registered with the Board of Investments are allowed to depreciate fixed assets on an accelerated basis. Depreciation for tax purposes is based on historical cost without regard to appraised values.

Requirements for Public Sale of Securities

Securities must be registered with the Securities and Exchange Commission (SEC) before they can be offered to the public for sale. Procedural steps for registration of securities include the filing of a sworn registration statement; payment of the required fee; publication of the notice of hearing in two newspapers of general circulation, one in English and the other in Spanish, once a week for two consecutive weeks; the hearing; and after issuance of an order approving the application, the certificate of registration.

Among the documents and papers that must accompany the sworn registration statement of an applicant company are copies of the resolution of the board of directors authorizing the registration of the applicant's securities; curriculum vitae of officers and members of the board of directors; samples of stock certificates; balance sheet accompanied by a long-form audit report of an independent certified public accountant; a financial work program duly certified by the applicant's president or treasurer; underwriting agreement, if an underwriter to sell the securities will be engaged; and a statement by the promoter justifying the claim for promotion fee in case such fee will be paid by the corporation. In addition to the following, there are special papers required to be submitted by oil and/or mining companies.

The registration statement itself must include certain information, such as the names and addresses of the directors, executive, financial and accounting officers, and underwriters; the general character of the business to be transacted by the issuer; a statement of the capitalization of the issuer; the specific purposes for which security is offered; the remuneration paid or to be paid to directors and officers; the amount of issue of the security being offered; the price at which the security will be sold; a detailed statement showing the items of cash, property, intangible assets and other considerations for which securities have been or are to be issued in payment; and the amount of cash or of capital stock which may be paid as a promotion fee.

Requirements for Listing Securities on the Stock Exchange

There are at present two major stock exchanges operating in the Philippines, namely, the Manila and Makati Stock Exchanges. Each stock exchange has its own trading rules, but they are essentially similar in many respects.

The procedure for listing consists of filing a listing agreement and listing application, forms for which are available at said stock exchanges. Among the things to which the issuer agrees with the stock exchange in the listing agreement are to publish annually a consolidated balance sheet at the end of the year, a consolidated income statement, and analysis of consolidated surplus for the year. These statements have to be certified by a certified public accountant.

To be included in the information called for in the listing application forms are the following: the number of shares to be listed; distribution of capital stock among shareholders; nature of applicant's business; authority granting the issuance of securities; purpose of the issue and uses of proceeds therefrom; history of applicant corporation; tabulated list of subsidiaries stating date and place of incorporation; nature of business and composition of capital stock issues; amount of and other information on mortgage and other indebtedness; description of property owned (including that owned by subsidiaries); policy on depreciation; dividends paid or declared; names and addresses of directors, transfer agents and registrars; names of officers; and so forth. Additional information is required of corporations which own or operate mines.

The listing application forms must be accompanied by certain papers, among which are the registration and licensing order of the Securities and Exchange Commission of the securities to be listed and the applicant's latest balance sheet and related income statement, duly certified by an independent certified public accountant. A listing fee, the amount of which is based on authorized capital, is also paid.

Two copies of the listing application forms are filed with the Securities and Exchange Commission.

If the exchange approves the listing, it sends notice to the SEC of such approval. Listing usually becomes effective three days after receipt by the exchange of the notice of approval by the Commission.

Republic of South Africa

Republic of South Africa

As of November 1972

Significant developments since the preparation of this chapter are presented, by country, in the section entitled Addenda.

Forms of Business Organization

General

The forms of business organization in the Republic of South Africa are similar to those found in the United Kingdom, the principal ones being private and public companies with limited liability. Regulations governing their formation and operations are prescribed in the South African Companies Act of 1926, as amended. This act is similar in many respects to the British Companies Act, with special modifications for South Africa.

In addition to the two types of companies stated above, business may be carried out as a partnership or as a sole proprietorship. A partnership may not consist of more than 20 persons, however, unless registered as a company under the act or formed pursuant to some other law.

Every company, public or private, foreign or domestic, operating in South Africa must be registered with the Registrar of Companies in Pretoria, except foreign and local banks and insurance companies which must be registered with the Registrars of Banks and Insurance, respectively. By virtue of the Companies Amendment Act of 1969, any company registered in South-West Africa under a provision of the Companies Ordinance of 1928, shall be deemed to be registered under the provisions of the South African Companies Act.

On June 1, 1972, the supplementary report and draft bill by the Commission of Enquiry into the Companies Act, was tabled in Parliament. This means that a new Companies Act may come into being as early as 1973, incorporating numerous changes to the existing company law in the Republic, and comments are contained herein on certain of the proposals.

The Public Company

This form of organization most closely resembles the publicly held corporation of the United States. It must be formed by a minimum of seven shareholders, but there is no limit to the total number of shareholders. There is a requirement that a public company have at least two directors who must deliver to the Registrar of Companies written consent to act as directors. A company registered with limited liability must have "Limited" in its name.

The operations of a company are governed by the memorandum of association. The internal workings of a company must be conducted in accordance with the articles of association. When a company is registered, an original and two notarized copies of the memorandum and articles of association must be lodged with the Registrar of Companies.

Before a public company may issue shares, it must file with the Registrar of Companies a prospectus, or a statement in lieu of a prospectus where shares are not going to be issued publicly. It must obtain a certificate from the Registrar of Companies in order to commence business. A statutory report giving certain details of subscription to shares, cash received, names and addresses of directors and officers, and estimated preliminary and flotation expenses of the company must be prepared and presented to the registrar and to the shareholders of the company at a statutory meeting to be held not less than one month nor more than three months from the date that the company is entitled to commence business.

The public company is subject to compulsory annual audit and its annual balance sheet and profit and loss account, auditors' and directors' reports, as well as its annual summary pertaining to share capital are required to be filed with the registrar's office. All companies are required to hold an annual general meeting of shareholders not later than six months after the end of each financial year, at which the financial statements together with directors' and auditors' reports are tabled.

The Private Company

This type of company is formed to obtain the advantage of limited liability for family businesses, small closely held businesses, and subsidiaries of other companies. It may be formed by two or more persons and must have at least one director. The number of members is limited to 50, excluding employees and former employees. Transfer of shares of a private company is restricted, and such a company in South Africa may not issue shares or debentures publicly. A private company must add to its names the words "Proprietary" and "Limited," except that the use of the word "Incorporated" is permitted under certain special circumstances.

Although a private company is subject to compulsory annual audit, it is neither required to file its annual balance sheet and profit and loss account publicly nor to file a statutory report nor to hold a statutory meeting. It is, however, required to file an annual summary and can have one director, if authorized by its articles of association. It may commence business immediately after registration without specific authorization.

Company Taxation

Company profits, adjusted for nontaxable items, are subject to state normal tax. There is no provision at present for a tax on capital profits. Assessed losses from previous years are carried forward and deducted from profits of subsequent years. There is no carryback of tax losses. Companies with local shareholders are required to distribute a certain portion of profits as dividends provided that reserves exceed a certain limit. If no such distribution is made, the company may become liable to undistributed profits tax. Every company must appoint a public officer whose duty it is to take full responsibility for preparation and rendering of tax returns.

Branch of a Foreign Company

All banks and insurance companies are governed by special laws, whether they are incorporated in South Africa or are branches of foreign companies. Any other foreign company may establish a place of business and carry on its activities without forming a local subsidiary. It must publicly file its annual balance sheet and profit and loss account. However, registration of a local company is recommended if land is to be purchased, and most foreign companies operate through local subsidiaries in the Republic of South Africa, rather than through branches.

Other Forms of Business Organization

From two to twenty persons may form a partnership by agreement, either oral or written. Each partner is jointly and severally liable for all debts contracted by the partnership.

The Accounting Profession

Chartered Accountant (S.A.)

The accounting profession in South Africa dates from the early part of this century when societies of accountants were formed in the four provinces of the Republic. In 1927, the Parliament passed "The Chartered Accountants' Designation (Private) Act No. 13" which conferred upon the members of the four societies the sole right to the use of the designation "chartered accountant (S.A.)." The members of these societies are not all in public practice, many of them being in full-time employment in industry or otherwise. There is no distinction as to title or classification of membership whether the member is in public practice or engaged in some other capacity.

Public Accountants' and Auditors' Act of 1951, as Amended

This act was designed to govern those members of the accounting profession who are engaged in the practice of public accounting. Its administration is carried out by the "Public Accountants' and Auditors' Board" composed mainly of representatives of the provincial societies, as well as representatives of the universities and government bodies. The act specifies certain qualifications for those entitled to register under the act, and restricts the practice of public accounting to persons, resident in the Republic, who are registered in terms of the act. The board may register as nonresident accountants and auditors members of certain other professional bodies, including members of the American Institute of Certified Public Accountants.

The board's powers include—

1. Regulating the required service under articles of clerkship.
2. Conducting the final qualifying examination.
3. Prescribing what will constitute improper conduct and imposing sanctions for such actions.
4. Taking any steps which it may consider expedient for maintenance of integrity, the enhancement of the status and improvement of standards of professional qualifications.

5. Encouraging research in connection with problems relating to any matter affecting the accounting profession.

Powers and Duties of Auditors

In terms of the Public Accountants' and Auditors' Act of 1951, as amended, no person acting in the capacity of auditor to any undertaking shall without such qualification as may be appropriate in the circumstances, in pursuance of any audit carried out by him in that capacity, certify or report to the effect that any financial statements are correct or reflect a true and fair view of the matters dealt with therein, unless—

1. He has carried out such audit free of any restrictions whatsoever.
2. Proper accounting records, in one of the official languages of the Republic, have been kept in connection with the undertaking in question, so as to exhibit a true and fair view of the affairs of that undertaking and to explain all transactions thereof.
3. He has obtained all the information, vouchers, and other documents that, in his opinion, were necessary for the proper performance of his duties.
4. He has in the case of an undertaking regulated by law complied with all the requirements of that law relating to the audit.
5. He has by means of such methods as are reasonably appropriate having regard to the nature of the undertaking in question satisfied himself of the existence of all assets and liabilities shown in the financial statements.
6. He is satisfied as far as is reasonably practicable as to the correctness or truth and fairness of any such financial statements.
7. Any material irregularity (see below) had, at the date on which he so certified or reported, been adjusted to his satisfaction.

No auditor or accountant shall, when acting otherwise than in pursuance of an audit, certify or report, without such qualifications as may be appropriate in the circumstances, to the effect that any account, statement or other document relating to the business or financial affairs of any undertaking is correct or reflects a true and fair view of matters dealt with therein unless he has mutatis mutandis complied with the provisions of paragraphs (1), (3) and (6) above.

"Material irregularity" is a matter specifically dealt with by the Public Accountants' and Auditors' Act of 1951, as amended, which requires that where any person acting in the capacity of auditor to any undertaking is satisfied or has reason to believe that in the conduct of the affairs of such undertaking a material irregularity has taken place, or is taking place, which has caused, or is likely to cause, financial loss to the undertaking or to any of its members or creditors, he shall forthwith dispatch a report in writing to the person in charge of that undertaking giving particulars of the irregularity.

Unless, within 30 days after an auditor has dispatched such a report, he has been satisfied that no such irregularity has taken place or that adequate steps have been taken for the recovery or prevention of any such loss, he shall forthwith furnish the necessary details to the Public Accountants' and Auditors' Board. The board may then disclose to any attorney general or any officer in the public service or any member or creditor of the undertaking concerned any information supplied to it in terms of the above report.

Disciplinary Rules

The board is empowered to inquire into and deal with any complaint laid before it with respect to any registered accountant and auditor. These rules relate mainly to complaints concerning any assistance in the evasion of taxes, divulging confidential information to third parties, charging of fees which are in any way dependent upon results, and soliciting of professional work.

Ethics

The code of professional etiquette promulgated by the board requires that before accepting an engagement previously undertaken by another registered accountant and auditor, the latter shall be consulted by the auditor who has been approached to succeed to the engagement.

The code also covers among other things the basis for quoting fees, publishing of articles on professional subjects, criticism of other registered accountants and auditors, the recruitment of staff employed by fellow accountants and conducting of consultancy services.

The board may remove or suspend any person registered under the Public Accountants' and Auditors' Act, who is found guilty of contraventions of the act or of unprofessional conduct.

The National Council of Chartered Accountants

In 1945 the Provincial Societies and the Rhodesian Society formed what is now known as the National Council of Chartered Accountants whose main functions are as follows:

1. To act as an advisory council to the societies and to coordinate their activities more closely and effectively.
2. To deal at the request of the societies with matters affecting the profession which require consideration on a national rather than a provincial level.
3. To develop on behalf of the societies a public relations organization.
4. To promote the prestige of the profession by encouraging a high standard of professional and general education and knowledge.
5. To provide for research in South Africa in accounting, auditing, and related areas.
6. To issue statements on accounting and auditing for the guidance of members.
7. To publish a journal relating to accounting and auditing matters.

Training of Chartered Accountants

The period of clerkship under articles is five years which is reduced if the clerk holds a university degree.

South African universities provide the academic training of articled clerks. A certificate in the theory of accountancy is conferred on candidates who successfully complete five years of part-time study at these universities. Holders of university degrees obtain certain credits toward subjects included in the course. It is a requirement of the Public Accountants' and Auditors' Board that candidates for the final qualifying examination be in possession of a certificate in the theory of accountancy.

As the universities provide the academic training of clerks, accounting firms in general concentrate on practical "on-job training" supplemented by "in-house" training programs.

Functions of Chartered Accountants in Public Practice

The prime function of public accountants is to act as auditors to public and private companies. Additional services offered to clients cover a wide field relating in the main to the following:

1. Acting as consultants in the fields of financial management and management accounting.
2. Acting as tax consultants.
3. Accepting appointments as trustees, executors, and liquidators.

4. Performing secretarial and accounting services.

5. Acting as directors of companies for which they are not the auditor.

Appointment of Auditors

The Companies Act provides that every company at each annual general meeting of shareholders shall appoint auditors to act from the end of that meeting until the end of the following annual meeting. The auditors are considered to be representatives of the shareholders and, as such, are looked upon by the shareholders for an opinion as to whether the financial statements, as presented by the directors, fairly present the affairs of the company.

The act states that the auditor will have access to the books, accounts, and vouchers at all times and will have the right to obtain whatever information or explanations from the officers of the company that, in the auditor's opinion, are necessary for the performance of his duties. He is entitled to attend any general meeting of the company and may speak on matters pertaining to him as auditor.

It is obligatory that the auditor's report be read at the annual general meeting of shareholders, unless all the members present agree to the contrary. No financial statements which are laid before a company in the annual general meeting shall be issued or published without the auditor's report being attached thereto.

At any annual general meeting, a retiring auditor, however appointed, shall be deemed to be reappointed without any resolution being passed unless (a) he is not qualified for reappointment, (b) a special resolution has been passed at the meeting appointing somebody instead of him or providing expressly that he shall not be reappointed, or (c) he has given the company notice in writing of his unwillingness to be reappointed.

Where a resolution is to be passed for the removal of any auditor, special notice (not less than 28 days notice to the company, which, in turn, shall give its members not less than 21 days notice) shall be required for such a resolution. The retiring auditor is entitled to receive notice of such a resolution, and the auditor is entitled, if he so wishes, to submit representations in writing to the company. The company must indicate in its notice to members that representations have been made and must send copies of these representations to every member of the company.

General

The standards of auditing and accounting in South Africa have been developed to meet the high standards which have been set by the profession. These requirements have been influenced to a large extent by both British and American standards.

Auditing Standards

General Standards and Standards of Field Work

The National Council of Chartered Accountants has issued various statements for the guidance of members. The following is a list of statements issued up to 1972:

Statements on Auditing

1. Auditing principles and standards
2. Stock in trade and work in progress
3. Electronic data processing and the auditor
4. Unaudited accounts and statements
5. Legislation in relation to reports and certificates
6. Applications for audit certificates
7. Verification of assets and liabilities
8. The auditor's duty with regard to articles deposited in safe custody with trust companies
9. Examining and reporting on group accounts
10. Internal control

Statements on Accounting

1. Desirable features of annual accounts
2. Terms used in accounts

General Statements

1. Guide to incoming auditors following a change in appointment
2. The duties of members in respect of unlawful acts or unlawful defaults of their clients
3. Practitioners' engagement letters
4. Auditor's independence
5. An auditor's duties with regard to prospectuses
6. Reports in connection with profit forecasts
7. The retention of records

Exposure Drafts of Statements to Be Issued. In addition to the above published statements, certain exposure drafts have been issued by the "Accounting Principles Committee of the National Council of Chartered Accountants."

The aforementioned statements, both published and unpublished, cover some of the general and field work standards applicable in South Africa. They include references to independence, internal control, materiality and the auditor's responsibility for discovery of fraud.

Independence

The Companies Act provides that the following persons shall be disqualified from appointment as auditor of a company:

1. An officer (which includes a director) or servant of the company or of any other company performing secretarial work for the company.
2. A person who is a partner of, or employs or is in the employment of, an officer or servant of the company.
3. A person who, by himself, or with his partner or employee, habitually or regularly performs the duties of secretary or bookkeeper to the company (under certain circumstances, an auditor of a private company can also perform secretarial and accounting duties).
4. A body corporate.

Further guidance on the independence required of auditors is included in the statements issued by the National Council of Chartered Accountants, extracts from which include the following:

Relationships Possibly Affecting Independence

1. Dealing in shares in a client company by the auditor or members of his family.
2. The holding of substantial investments in a client company by the auditor or his family.
3. Substantial indebtedness of the auditor or members of his family to a client.
4. The participation by the auditor in management or policy decisions of his client.

5. The fact that an auditor may conduct a practice consisting solely or principally of appointments from one client.
6. The ability of the auditor to withstand undue client pressure.

Observation of Inventories

The National Council of Chartered Accountants has recommended that—

> As part of his auditing procedures as a whole, the auditor will give consideration to the desirability or otherwise of attending when physical inventories of stocks and work in progress are to be taken by the client. Although it is recognized that it might not be practical to do so in all cases, particularly as the annual accounts of many businesses are made up to similar dates, National Council recommends that auditors should seek to adopt, as a general practice, physical inspection of stocks where they are material in relation to current assets as a whole.

Confirmation of Receivables

The National Council of Chartered Accountants has recommended that—

> Requests for confirmation of selected balances should be dispatched to a number of debtors. Such confirmations can be sought either positively or negatively. The method of confirmation to be adopted would depend upon the circumstances of each case, but a combination of the two methods may be preferable.

Standards of Reporting

The standards of reporting of the auditor in the Republic of South Africa are governed mainly by the Companies Act, as amended, the Insurance, Banking, Building Societies Acts and other legislation. There is no standard form of audit report. Most practitioners choose to use the actual wording of the section of the Act in making the statements that are required to be made, followed by their opinion.

The usual form of auditor's unqualified report, which complies with the requirements of the Companies Act is as follows:

> We have examined, to the extent to which we have considered necessary, the books and accounts and vouchers of the company and have satisfied ourselves of the existence of the securities. We have obtained all the information and explanations which to the best of our knowledge and belief, were necessary for the purpose of our audit. In our opinion, proper books of account have been kept by the company, so far as appears from our examination of those books.

> The financial statements are in agreement with the books of account and in our opinion and to the best of our information and according to the explanations given to us, the said statements give the information required by the Companies Act, 1926, as amended, in the manner so required and the balance sheet gives a true and fair view of the state of the company's affairs and the income statement gives a true and fair view of the profit (or loss) for the year.

An auditor of a holding company must report on consolidated statements and must report whether they reflect a "true and fair view" of the affairs of the group from the point of view of the members of the holding company.

"True and fair view" has been replaced in the draft bill of the proposed new Companies Act by the words "fairly present" which will represent a material change in the emphasis of the auditor's report.

The Companies Act requires disclosure, by footnote or in the body of the accounts, of any inconsistent application in the basis of accounting.

Materiality

The South African Chartered Accountant has the same concept of materiality and its effect on his work and on his opinion on the financial statements as does a CPA in the United States.

Directors' Report

The Companies Act requires that the directors prepare and present a report on the state of affairs of the company at each annual general meeting of shareholders. This report is to be presented as part of the financial statements and should include a statement as to dividends paid, declared or proposed, the amount (if any) to be transferred to "reserves," and the amount of directors' remuneration recommended if it is to be determined at the annual general meeting. It must state any change during the course of the year in the nature of the company's business or in the composition of the board of directors of the company or of any of its subsidiaries. It must also disclose the particulars of material facts or circumstances which have occurred between the date of the balance sheet and the date of the report. The report must also state the details of any allotments of shares or debentures made during the period covered by the report.

Under the present act, auditors are not required to report on the contents of the directors' report. The Commission of Enquiry into the Companies Act was, however, of the opinion that auditors should be entitled and obliged to comment freely on the state of affairs of the company and accordingly recommended that the financial statements as well as the directors' report be dealt with in the auditor's report.

Accounting Principles and Practices

General

The Public Accountants' and Auditors' Board and the National Council of Chartered Accountants actively promote the application of generally accepted accounting principles. The published financial statements of companies must comply with these principles and the provisions of the Companies Act.

Form of Accounts

In terms of the Companies Act, a company must for every financial year present annual accounts at the annual general meeting. These accounts consist of a profit and loss account and a balance sheet to which is attached the directors' report and the auditor's report. Where the company has any subsidiaries, group accounts form part of the financial statements. The Companies Act provides that every balance sheet, profit and loss account, and group accounts (where applicable) shall give a true and fair view of the state of affairs of the company and of the group and that every profit and loss account of the company shall give a true and fair view of the profit and loss of the company (and of the group) for the financial year.

Presentation of Accounts

The main provisions of the Companies Act relating to statement presentation are detailed below:

Balance Sheet

1. The authorized and issued capital, liabilities, and assets shall be summarized with such particulars as are necessary to disclose the general nature of the assets and liabilities.
2. The reserves, provisions, liabilities, and fixed and current assets shall be classified under headings appropriate to the company's business.
3. The method of arriving at the amount of fixed assets shall be stated, and it shall be to take the difference between—

a. cost, or if it stands in the company's books at a valuation, the amount of the valuation; and

b. the aggregate amount provided or written off since the date of acquisition or valuation, as the case may be, for depreciation or diminution in value. This provision shall not apply to goodwill, patents and trade marks.

4. If, in the opinion of the directors, any of the current assets have not at the date of the balance sheet a value, on realization in the ordinary course of the company's business, at least equal to the amount at which they are stated, the fact that the directors are of that opinion shall be disclosed.

5. Aggregate market value of quoted investments where it differs from the amount of the investments as stated shall be shown.

6. Reserves shall be shown separately from provisions and capital reserves shall be shown separately from revenue reserves.

7. Provision is defined as any amount written off or retained by way of providing for depreciation, renewals, or diminution in value of assets or retained by way of providing for any known liability of which the amount cannot be determined with substantial accuracy. A capital reserve does not include any amount regarded as free for distribution through the profit and loss account, and a revenue reserve means any reserve other than a capital reserve.

Income Statement or Profit and Loss Account. There shall be shown separately—

1. Profits or losses on share transactions.
2. Amount of income from investments.
3. Aggregate amount of dividends paid and proposed.
4. Profits or losses on the realization of non-trading and fixed and other capital assets.
5. Amount charged to revenue by way of depreciation, renewals, or diminution in value of fixed assets.
6. The amount of interest paid on debentures and other fixed loans.
7. The amount of the interest or other consideration for other borrowed monies.
8. The estimated amount provided for taxation in respect of the

period covered by the financial statements and the amount, if any, provided in respect of any other period.

9. The amounts, if material, set aside or withdrawn from provisions or reserves.
10. Remuneration of auditors if not fixed by the company in general meeting.
11. Remuneration of directors distinguishing between emoluments for services as a director and other services.

Notes on Financial Statements. Notes on financial statements must cover—

1. Details of any option or preferential right of subscription over shares of the company.
2. Amount of any share capital which shareholders have authorized directors to issue.
3. Amount of arrears of fixed cumulative dividends.
4. Particulars of any charge on assets of the company to secure the liabilities of any other person.
5. The general nature of any contingent liabilities not provided for and where practicable, the aggregate amount or estimated amount of those liabilities if it is material.
6. Where practicable the aggregate amount or estimated amount, if it is material, of contracts for capital expenditure so far as not provided.
7. Basis on which foreign currencies have been converted into South African currency, where the amount of the assets or liabilities affected is material.
8. Except in the case of the first financial statements of the company, the comparative figures of all amounts appearing in the financial statements.
9. If depreciation or replacement of fixed assets is provided for by some method other than a depreciation charge or provision for renewals or is not provided for, as the case may be, a note must be shown to this effect.
10. If no provision for taxation has been made, a statement of that fact, the reason therefor, and the period in respect of which no provision has been made.

11. Any material respects in which items shown in an income statement are affected—
    a. by transactions of a sort not usually undertaken by the company or otherwise by circumstances of an exceptional or non-recurrent nature and
    b. by any change in the basis of accounting.

Proposed New Companies Act

The draft bill of the proposed new Companies Act incorporates certain amendments to the present requirements for the presentation of financial statements.

The major changes include the introduction of no par value shares and the inclusion in the financial statements of a source and application of funds statement for all companies. Other requirements are aimed at disclosing additional information in the following areas:

1. Fixed assets, in particular details relating to fixed property.
2. Investments.
3. Inventory including the basis of valuation.
4. Turnover.
5. Income from subsidiaries.
6. Details of intercompany charges between holding and subsidiary companies.
7. Auditor's remuneration must be disclosed in all cases (the new provision of the proposed new act concerning auditors' remuneration is that it must be agreed to between the auditors and the directors acting for the company).
8. Directors' report.
9. Accounting by groups of companies.
10. Provisional annual financial statements and interim reports.

Pooling of Interests

The "pooling of interests" concept is not recognized in South Africa.

Treasury Shares or Debentures

Companies may not deal in their own shares. They may, however, re-acquire their own debentures, and any resulting profit is usually credited to capital surplus.

Requirements for Public Sale of Securities

The Companies Act requires that a copy of every prospectus proposed to be issued by a company will be filed for registration with the Registrar of Companies. If the prospectus states that the whole or a portion of the shares or debentures offered for subscription has been underwritten, a copy of the underwriting contract and certain other documents will also be filed with the registrar.

The contents and requirements for preparation of a prospectus or offer to sell securities are included in the sixth schedule of the Companies Act, and must include the following (summarized):

1. Material and relevant particulars of the company and its subsidiaries concerning all share capital, and options thereon, any premium to be paid on shares to be issued, loans, working capital, history and prospects, agreements, directors' and vendors' interests, expenses of the issue and the purpose thereof, also the time of opening of subscription lists and the closing thereof.
2. An auditor's report covering dividend information on all types of shares issued during the previous five years, and indicating when no dividends were paid, information as to any write-up of fixed assets within three years, balance sheet at the closing date, and profit and loss account covering preceding five years, with such adjustments considered necessary.

The adjustments made and the reasons therefor must be indicated to the Registrar of Companies and to the Stock Exchange Committee, but need not otherwise be published.

Where the prospectus covers a holding company and its subsidiaries, the financial statements should include the latest statement of assets and liabilities of the holding company and its subsidiaries either on a combined or an individual basis. The profit and loss accounts for the preceding five years of the holding company and its subsidiaries either on a combined or an individual basis should be included. If the proceeds of the issue are to be used to purchase a business or acquire another corporate body which will become a subsidiary, it is necessary to submit a report by accountants who must be named in the prospectus, giving similar information in respect of such business or corporate body.

There must also be a directors' report showing any material change in the assets or liabilities of the company or any of its subsidiaries which may have taken place between the date as of which the financial statements of the company or its subsidiaries were presented and the date of the prospectus.

Requirements for Listing Securities on the Stock Exchange

The rules and regulations of the Johannesburg Stock Exchange, the only exchange in South Africa, set forth the minimum standards of disclosure and the requirements for publication of the information in prospectuses by companies seeking to have their shares listed for trading. Applicants must meet certain preliminary requirements, as follows:

1. The company must name a member of the stock exchange to act as its sponsor in all liaison work with the Stock Exchange Committee.
2. A listing fee must be paid.
3. The company must submit the memorandum and articles of association for examination. The committee insists that the articles conform to its requirements and indicate control of issue of stock securities, preemptive rights, absence of transfer restrictions, reasonable borrowing power of the board, remuneration of directors, and reporting on subsidiaries. (A company will not be listed where certain shares confer special privileges of management and control).
4. If the securities have already been issued publicly, a definite proportion must still be held by the public. This rule has been interpreted to mean holding by at least 200 persons and it is required to assure marketability of the shares.
5. A list of shareholders certified by the company's auditor must also be submitted.

The main document that must be prepared in connection with the application for listing is the "Advertised Statement," which may take the form of a prospectus provided that all the necessary information is included in full. It must be published in a Johannesburg newspaper and one other national daily newspaper.

The ending balance sheet must mark a period that ended within twelve months prior to the date of application. The auditor must also report on material changes in the accounts between the date of the last balance sheet and the application date; he must state that debtors' and creditors' accounts do not include any non-trade amounts; he must report on the adequacy of the bad debt provision; he must make a statement that the directors have certified that adequate provision has been made for obsolete, damaged, or defective goods; he must make a statement on the basis of valuation of supplies, raw materials, and work in progress; and he must make a statement as to the elimination of inter-company accounts in consolidation.

In addition, the "Supporting Statement," "General Undertaking," and "Statutory Declaration" must be presented. The supporting statement is signed by the directors and covers certain additional information. The general undertaking is a resolution by the board to supply all information required by the Stock Exchange Committee and to furnish such additional information on a continuing basis as is required. The statutory declaration is sworn to by the chairman and the secretary and also affirms certain facts. There are also numerous other documents which must be submitted plus special requirements in connection with amalgamations and the protection of minority interests in such undertakings.

Spain

Spain

As of July 1973

Forms of Business Organization

General

Commercial operations in Spain are primarily governed by the Commercial Code, which, although promulgated in 1885, still has general application. A series of laws and decrees have modified, but not changed, the basic principles laid down in this code.

Legal forms of commercial enterprises are the following:

1. Sociedad anónima (S.A.)—(joint stock corporation).
2. Sociedad de responsabilidad limitada (S.R.L.)—(limited liability company).
3. Sociedad colectiva—(partnership).
4. Sociedad en comandita—(limited partnership).
5. Sucursal extranjera—(branch of a foreign company).

All entities must be legally formed and inscribed in the Mercantile Register. Only a sole proprietorship may operate without being formed as a legal entity. The business form used by the majority of foreign investors is the joint stock corporation—tax, legal, and exchange control factors all influencing the choice.

Sociedad Anónima (S.A.)

(Joint Stock Corporation)

The establishment, operation, and dissolution of sociedades anónimas are governed by the Law of July 17, 1951. The S.A. bears a strong resemblance to its American counterpart and has the advantage of personal liability being limited to unpaid consideration for which shares were issued. An S.A. must be domiciled in Spain and may be chartered for an unlimited time, but is usually given a limited life which is renewable. The words "Sociedad Anónima" or "S.A." must appear in the firm's corporate name, which must not duplicate that of an existing firm. At least three persons are required to form an S.A.; no restrictions are placed on the nationality or domicile of its founders, but the general rule is that foreigners may own not more than 50 percent of the capital stock of a Spanish corporation although in a limited number of industrial activities foreign ownership may go up to 100 percent. At any time subsequent to its formation, the number of stockholders may be reduced to one.

Spanish law provides for two methods of formation: the simultaneous and the successive. The simultaneous method is used when the founders have sufficient capital to start operations. The successive method is employed when a public-share offering is needed to raise the capital to begin the business. In the latter case, a prospectus must be issued, the subscribers must approve the bylaws, and other formalities must be observed, after which the public contract, which must be inscribed in the Mercantile Register, can be drawn up. However, foreign investors rarely use the successive method.

Inscription in the Mercantile Register, maintained in all provincial capitals, is obligatory for corporations. For a foreign company to be registered, a certificate must be issued by the Spanish Consul in the firm's country stating that the firm is legally qualified to contract, is subject to the laws of the home country, and is registered in the Spanish consulate.

The requisite documents for inscription in the Mercantile Register are (1) a notarized copy of the constitution (charter) of the company, along with the name, purpose, and address of the company; (2) the amount of authorized and paid-in capital; (3) the names of the founders and amount of their contributions; (4) a description of the administrative structure; (5) arrangements for compensation of directors; and (6) voting provisions.

There is no minimum capital requirement, but all companies capitalized at over 50,000,000 pesetas must be formed as an S.A. Also, there can be no authorized but unissued stock; capital must be fully subscribed and a minimum of 25 percent paid in at the time of incorporation either in cash or nonmonetary assets. Shares may be registered or bearer, and cannot be issued for less than par value. A register of subscribers must be kept for registered shares, and all transfers must be recorded in this register. Bearer shares are more common; however, shares must be in registered form until they are fully paid or if required by special legal provisions. All share transfers must be through a stockbroker or a notary. Shares of the same class of stock have equal voting rights. Shares with multiple voting privileges are prohibited.

Directors, elected by the stockholders, need not be Spanish citizens, nor are they required to be stockholders. The number of directors is fixed in the bylaws, and may be limited to one person. The only distinct provision for members of boards is the requirement applicable to mining companies allowing foreigners to be members, but restricting their number in proportion to their shares (maximum—50 percent). The board of directors is the administrative organ for the corporation, but boards may delegate some functions to executives. Generally, day-to-day operations are delegated to the "consejero delegado" who would be the equivalent of the corporate president in the United States.

The incorporation costs of a Spanish corporation include the following: notary fees for documents, which vary according to the amount of authorized capital; fees for inscription in the Mercantile Register; municipal license fees; and a 2.7 percent transfer tax on stated capital.

Sociedad de Responsabilidad Limitada (S.R.L.)
(Limited Liability Company)

This entity is similar to an S.A. and is subject to the same rules. It must be domiciled in Spain, and the duration of its life is usually mentioned in the contract. The limited liability company combines features of both partnerships and corporations. It is restricted to firms which are capitalized under 50,000,000 pesetas and is therefore employed principally by small and medium-sized firms. Because of these limitations, this form is infrequently used by foreign investors. (The Law of July 17, 1953, is the source of regulations for this entity.) "S.R.L." or "Sociedad Limitada" must appear in the firm's name, which cannot duplicate that of another firm.

The company is formed by public contract, inscribed in the Mercantile Register. Participating members cannot number more than fifty or be fewer than two. Members bear no personal responsibility for the firm's debts; they are liable only for the amount of their contribution. All participants have the same rights.

The limited liability company has a fixed capital, which is not, however, evidenced by negotiable instruments and is not freely transferable. All of the capital must be paid in before the company begins operations. Since capital cannot exceed 50,000,000 pesetas, if the business requires more than that an S.A. must be formed.

Compañía or Sociedad Colectiva
(Partnership)

The Spanish Commercial Code of 1885 contains the legal provisions concerning partnerships (articles nos. 125 to 144). This entity closely resembles the general partnership employed in the United States. The partnership agreement has to be filed and registered in the Mercantile Register. Each partner has a voice in the conduct of the business and each, in turn, is responsible for the liabilities of the enterprise to the full extent of his commercial and personal property.

The name of the firm may contain either the names of all partners or the names of one or some of the partners, followed by the words "y Compañía" (and Company). The name may not include the names of individuals who are not firm members.

Sociedad en Comandita
(Limited Partnership)

This type of entity conforms to the limited partnership concept found in some other European countries. It is made up of one or more limited (silent) partners who invest capital but do not participate in the management of the firm, and one or more active partners who manage the business. The legal basis of this entity is also found in the Commercial Code of 1885 (principally in articles nos. 145 to 150).

The name of the firm may include either the names of all the active partners or the names of some of them followed by "y Compañía." The names of limited partners may not appear in the firm's name.

Sucursal Extranjera
(Branch of a Foreign Firm)

To open a branch office, a foreign company must present for recording in the Mercantile Register the following: the statutes, deeds, or acts of the constitution of the parent company; the name of a local holder of a power of attorney and a definition of his powers; and a certificate issued by the Spanish consul stating that the firm is constituted and authorized in accordance with the laws of the country where it is domiciled.

Branch offices have been infrequently used in Spain by foreign investors and then mainly in service industries and by oil companies engaged in prospecting in Spain. Branches involve several drawbacks for the foreign investor. Permission must be obtained from the Spanish Foreign Exchange Institute each time branch profits are transmitted abroad, and such permission is not automatically granted. In addition, the creditors of the branch could extend the branch's obligations to the parent company. Also, until January 1966, taxes on branch operations were based on total company profits on the basis of some relative measure such as the ratio of branch sales in Spain to worldwide sales—even if the branch itself operated at a loss. Since 1966, separate accounting for tax purposes has been permitted to branches.

Business Records

The Commercial Code requires businesses operating in Spain to keep a number of basic financial records. In general, these include the following:

1. A general ledger (libro mayor).
2. A general journal (libro diario) or auxiliary journals which serve as direct posting sources to the general ledger.
3. An inventory book or register (libro de inventarios y balances) for posting the year-end general ledger trial balance.
4. A minute book (libro de actas) for meetings of directors and shareholders.
5. A book for copies of correspondence (copiador de cartas y telegramas).

These records are considered the official books. The law requires that each book be bound, that the pages be numbered consecutively, and that they be authenticated by an official of the local commercial court before use. The code requires that entries be made on a day-to-day basis covering every single transaction with full explanation for each. Although the law does not specifically require that the records be kept in the Spanish language or in pesetas, it is advisable to maintain them in Spanish terms. The official records must be preserved for a period of 15 years from the date of the last entry.

Literal compliance with the Commercial Code would be so time-consuming with respect to accounting records that the tendency is to ignore the rather outdated requirements. Frequently, the official books will be less than useful, and the bulk of the information needed by management will be compiled separately from records that detail costs, sales, and so forth, quite independently of the official books. The cumbersome provisions of the Commercial Code have also been blamed in part for the still quite general practice of openly maintaining two sets of records. There is a marked movement toward reform in this area.

The bankruptcy of a company which has not kept its records in accordance with the law could be considered fraudulent, in which case the directors of the company would be held personally liable for the company's debts and could be sentenced to prison.

Early in 1973, the tax authorities issued a standard chart of accounts with the recommendation that it be used by all companies. Although use of the chart is optional for the time being, it may become mandatory in the near future; and it is expected that certain tax advantages will be available only to companies that do use it.

The Accounting Profession

The accounting profession in Spain is not organized in a form similar to that of the United States or the United Kingdom. This is primarily because the independent audit function has not yet developed to any significant degree.

The profession is led predominantly by members of the Instituto de Censores Jurados de Cuentas de España. The Institute was established in 1944 and comes under the control of the Ministry of Commerce. Admission to this Institute has been by way of examination open to candidates who have the degree of "profesor mercantil" with the additional conditions of nationality, age, professional competence, and possession of all civil rights. At present, the Institute has about fifteen hundred members subject to regulations passed in 1945 and amended in 1957 and 1959.

A representative member of the Instituto de Censores Jurados is a "profesor mercantil," that is, a holder of a commercial school degree, who has also specialized in accounting, taxation, statistics, or an allied field. In addition to being a member of the Institute, he would also be a member of the Colegio Oficial de Titulares Mercantiles in the province in which he resides. The Colegio Oficial de Titulares Mercantiles is an organization open to all graduates of commercial schools regardless of specialization. Members of the colegio are called "titulares mercantiles."

Ethics

The Institute has a fairly comprehensive code of professional ethics and conduct, including a strict enjoinder against its members engaging in incompatible occupations. Negligence or fraud are punished by suspension or expulsion from the Institute.

Audit Requirements

Corporations Listed on a Stock Exchange

In accordance with a regulation dated June 30, 1967, Spanish corporations with securities listed on a stock exchange are required to retain an independent auditor who must belong to the Instituto de Censores Jurados de Cuentas. The stock exchange and the Institute have agreed to limit the audit work to that required for certification that the financial statements are in agreement with the accounting records.

Corporations Not Listed on a Stock Exchange

Spanish corporations not listed on a stock exchange are not required to retain an independent auditor, but are required to submit their balance sheet, profit and loss statement, and profit distribution statement at the end of each fiscal year to a shareholder committee, which is made up of two active shareholder auditors (accionistas censores de cuentas) and two alternates.

These shareholder auditors, who cannot be directors of the company, are elected annually by the shareholders. In cases where all shareholders are directors of a company, it is not possible to comply with this legal requirement. If a minority of the shareholders (holding at least 10 percent of paid-in capital) do not agree with the majority as to the nomination of the shareholder auditors, they may elect an additional member and an alternate to the shareholder committee. This additional member cannot be a shareholder and must be a member of the Instituto de Censores Jurados de Cuentas.

The directors are required to submit the above-mentioned documentation to the shareholder committee at least 45 days before the annual shareholder meeting. The shareholder committee gives an opinion on the truth and fairness of presentation of the documents submitted for their approval. Normally the committee performs a perfunctory review.

Auditing Standards

As audits by independent accountants are not customary in Spain and as the accounting profession is in the development stage, there is very little that may be said in reference to auditing standards. Most international audit firms have offices in Spain and, generally, apply U.S. or U.K. auditing standards.

Accounting Principles and Practices

General

The accounting profession in Spain has not issued opinions or recommendations regarding accounting principles. However, certain provisions of the Commercial Code, the Corporation Law, and the Tax Law influence and affect accounting principles applied by Spanish companies.

Form and Content of Financial Statements

There is no required form for presentation of financial statements; however, the corporation law provides generally that certain accounts are to be shown. Financial statements in Spain, particularly the income statement, are considerably more concise and less informative than is the case in the United States.

In the Spanish balance sheet, assets are on the left-hand side, more or less in order of liquidity, with shareholders' equity on the right, beginning with capital and reserves, the payables, valuation reserves, and, finally, unappropriated earnings. Debits are usually on the left and credits on the right, even valuation reserves.

The Spanish income statement tends to be very condensed. The "T" form is often used.

Receivables

Trade and nontrade as well as current and noncurrent receivables are often combined. As a provision for doubtful accounts is not deductible for tax purposes, Spanish companies often do not have an allowance for anticipated losses but rather state receivables at gross amounts. Accounts are generally not written off until noncollection is certain.

Inventories

Inventories are stated at the lower of cost or market but, since a provision for obsolescence is not deductible for tax purposes, they are not generally stated at net realizable value.

Property, Plant and Equipment, and Intangible Assets

These assets are recorded at cost. Acquisition expenses, including interest where applicable, can be capitalized as a part of the cost of an asset.

Depreciation is provided annually over the estimated useful lives of the various classes of assets. The tax code sets out maximum depreciation rates, and the maximum period over which depreciation may be claimed for tax purposes; thus taxpayers are permitted to choose the depreciation rate to be used each year provided they do not exceed the maximum legal rate and period of time. Thus, within limits, the amount of depreciation taken is determined by the net income the companies wish to show rather than by applying rates based on estimated useful lives consistently from year to year.

Spanish companies frequently capitalize organization expenses and start-up costs. These should be amortized over ten years; however, it is preferable for tax purposes to amortize start-up costs over five years.

Investments

Securities quoted on a stock exchange should not be stated at a value in excess of the average market price during the last quarter of the fiscal year. If the market price is lower than cost, a valuation reserve should be established. For securities not quoted, the board of directors must assign a value which may not exceed cost.

Capital

Authorized capital is shown on the credit side of the balance sheet. If it is not fully paid, the difference between the amount subscribed and the amount paid is shown on the debit side as due from stockholders. The amounts thus shown are not actual debts of the stockholders until the unpaid balance of subscriptions has been officially called by the board of directors.

Legal Reserve

The necessity for providing this reserve arises if the profits after taxes exceed 6 percent of stated capital stock. The annual amount provided is 10 percent of total profits before income tax. This provision may be suspended when the reserve is equal to 20 percent of paid-in capital. The purpose of this reserve is to provide a margin of safety against possible losses. When losses are charged against the reserve, annual provision in succeeding profitable years must be resumed until the reserve is once again at the 20 percent level.

Other Reserves and Retained Earnings

Each year at the annual shareholders' meeting, a resolution is passed as to the distribution of earnings. A portion of the earnings may be allocated to the legal reserve, a dividend may be declared, and the remaining earnings will ordinarily be allocated to other reserves. It is not customary to leave a portion of the earnings, other than a small amount due to rounding of other allocations, unappropriated as retained earnings.

Statement of Income

Only sales (and, in some cases, only gross profit on sales), other income, and broad classes of expenses are shown.

Other Statements

Statements of shareholders' equity and changes in financial position are generally not prepared by Spanish companies.

Requirements for Listing Securities on the Stock Exchange

The three official stock exchanges in Spain are in Madrid, Barcelona, and Bilbao. Madrid is the most important of the three, handling almost one-half of all Spanish security transactions; Barcelona handles somewhat less than one-third, and Bilbao accounts for most of the rest.

There are a number of legal requirements for listing a stock on one of the three principal exchanges. However, no statement of the company's record, size, or ownership is necessary.

A request for listing on a stock exchange must describe the issue, stating the type, class, nominal value, and serial numbers, and whether the securities are registered or bearer. In addition, at least the following must be submitted with the application:

1. Charter or other document establishing the legal existence of the issuer.
2. Bylaws or other governing rules or agreements.
3. Certification from the Mercantile Register of registration.
4. Receipt of payment of transfer taxes on the proposed issue.
5. Certificate that securities can be freely traded.
6. Certified minutes of the board of directors authorizing the application for listing.
7. Certificate that interest and declared dividends on other issues are paid to date.
8. Annual reports and financial statements for the last three years approved by the shareholders. The financial statements for the most recent year must be certified by a censor jurado de cuentas.
9. Specimen security.
10. Proof that shares are currently in circulation and owners have all rights thereto.

The Stock Exchange Committee usually takes from 15 to 30 days to approve an application. Once approved, the listing must be announced in the official newspaper, *Boletín Oficial del Estado.* This approval, when presented to another exchange, is all that is required to be listed on that exchange.

Sweden

Sweden

As of March 1974

Forms of Business Organization

The forms of business organization in Sweden are the limited liability company, the partnership, the sole proprietorship, and the cooperative. The latter is of special importance in Sweden, although similar organizations are, of course, not uncommon in other countries.

Aktiebolag
(Limited Liability Corporation)

This is a corporate entity which is similar to the stock corporation found in other countries. The legislation applicable to the "aktiebolag" is contained in the Companies Act of 1944, which was effective January 1, 1948.

A minimum of three legally competent Swedish citizens, or entities resident in Sweden, may form a corporation. After incorporation, the number of shareholders may be reduced to one.

The name of the company as specified in the bylaws must contain the word "Aktiebolag," which is commonly abbreviated "AB."

The minimum capital is 50,000 Swedish kronor represented by shares of (usually) not less than 50 kronor, and, except in special instances, the shares must be registered. The liability of the shareholder is limited to the par value of shares subscribed. All shares must be paid up within two years of incorporation.

At the constituent meeting called by the incorporators, a board of directors is elected consisting of one or more members. If the maximum authorized capital exceeds 500,000 kronor, at least three directors must be elected and a managing director, who need not be a member of the board, must be appointed. The corporation is considered formed when the meeting has adopted the bylaws and voted its formation.

The shareholders must appoint one or more auditors to examine and report upon the balance sheet and income statement, and to report on the administration of the company. If the maximum authorized capital exceeds 500,000 kronor, at least two auditors must be appointed, and, if such capital is 2,000,000 kronor or more, at least one of the statutory auditors must be a Swedish authorized public accountant (APA). With the permission of the Royal Board of Trade (Kommerskollegium), a foreign citizen may act as the second auditor. The qualifications and duties of the APA are discussed in a later section.

Even in respect to minor corporations, an APA or an approved examiner of accounts (see later discussion), must be appointed at the request of shareholders holding at least one-tenth of the share capital.

The Companies Act requires that the board of directors and the managing director submit a report which includes financial statements (balance sheet at year end and income statement for the year) and the board's report on administration to the annual meeting of shareholders. The auditors must report on these documents which, after approval by the shareholders, are filed with the Royal Swedish Patent and Registration Office in Stockholm where they may be inspected by anyone. The managing director of a parent corporation must also present to the board and to the auditors (but not to the shareholders), a consolidated balance sheet or a consolidated statement of retained earnings.

Subsidiary or Branch of a Foreign Corporation

Prior to 1956, a foreign enterprise wishing to carry on business in Sweden was generally limited to doing so through a Swedish subsidiary. Under a law of 1955, most provisions of which were incorporated in a new law in 1968, a foreign corporation may establish a branch in Sweden by obtaining permission from the Royal Board of Trade, which is granted provided the applicant company is operating in the country of its origin. There are certain activities which are not permitted, such as the manufacture of war materials, domestic air transportation, or shipping in Swedish vessels. In general, the laws of Sweden are equally applicable to branches of foreign corporations doing business in Sweden. The branch must have a managing director resident in Sweden and must appoint a Swedish-authorized public accountant as auditor. The annual financial statements of the branch and the auditor's report have to be filed and made public in the same way as the corresponding documents of Swedish corporations.

Ekonomisk Förening

(Cooperatives)

This legal form of organization is reserved for cooperative enterprises and housing associations; both agricultural and consumer cooperatives are important in the Swedish economy and have between two and three million members. They are required to furnish their members with annual financial statements and usually furnish them to the public on request.

The Cooperative Societies Act of 1951 states that auditors must be appointed to examine and report upon the annual financial statements. The auditor must have such experience in bookkeeping and knowledge of economic conditions as his appointment requires, but he need not be an authorized public accountant or an approved examiner of accounts. It is customary for the larger cooperative societies to appoint an authorized public accountant.

Partnerships

The partnership form is not as common in Sweden as in other countries because the capital requirements for the corporate form are minimal and corporations are easily and inexpensively organized.

There are three forms of partnership—the simple partnership ("enkelt bolag"), the regular partnership ("handelsbolag"), and the limited partnership ("kommanditbolag"). No form of registration is required of the simple partnership, but the name under which the handelsbolag carries on business must be registered. All members of the simple and regular partnership have unlimited liability toward third persons.

The limited partnership has both active and silent partners. Active partners are jointly and severally liable for partnership debts but silent partners are liable only to the extent of their capital in the partnership.

Business Records

The Bookkeeping Law (1929) requires that certain bound books be kept —specifically, the journal in which day-to-day transactions or, to a certain extent, summaries of such transactions are recorded and the status book in which the assets and liabilities are recorded at the end of the year. Limited liability companies are required to maintain a share register. Generally, there must be kept such additional records as are necessary, depending on the size and nature of the operations.

The Accounting Profession

For many years, the bylaws of limited companies in Sweden have made provisions for audits of the accounts. The Companies Act of 1895 prescribed that the board's administration be reviewed and the company's accounts be examined by one or more auditors. These auditors were often persons with business experience, but seldom were they skilled in accounting matters. During the early twentieth century, however, development of an accounting profession began. In 1909, the Stockholm School of Economics offered a university education which was comprised of business administration (accounting and finance), economics, and business law. The profession was established by action of the Stockholm Chamber of Commerce in 1912, when it adopted its first statutes for authorization of public accountants. In Sweden, the chambers of commerce (of which there are twelve—one in each of the Swedish districts) are private organizations, authorized by the Crown. Their duty is to look after the interests of economic life, and, among other things, they report on draft bills after their consideration by the appropriate royal commissions.

After July 1, 1973, the Swedish government took over from the chambers of commerce the task of authorizing public accountants. This is now handled by the Royal Board of Trade (Kommerskollegium).

Auktoriserad Revisor

(Authorized Public Accountant)

The Royal Board of Trade may admit as an APA any Swedish man or woman who—

1. Is professionally engaged in the field of auditing.
2. Is not under any restriction as to his or her person or property.
3. Has received an economics degree (bachelor of commerce) at a Swedish university or school of economics with the special provision that the examination for that degree include economics, business administration, and law (with special emphasis on accounting, auditing, and business law), and that certain qualified grades be obtained in business administration and law.
4. Has satisfactorily worked in the auditing profession for a period not less than five years, at least three years of which must generally be with an independent authorized public accountant.

It is possible to obtain authorization without the academic degree mentioned above, by passing a special examination in the same subjects given by professors of a Swedish university or school of economics; in practice, this course is seldom followed.

Having complied with the above requirements and having been authorized as a public accountant, the applicant makes the following declaration to the chamber:

> I, ..., hereby promise on my faith and honor, as a public accountant authorized by the .... Chamber of Commerce, to carry out audits entrusted to me with honesty and zeal, carefully and to the best of my ability, to observe the secrecy incumbent upon an accountant, and otherwise in every particular to comply with the regulations laid down in respect of my office.

After this declaration has been filed, the chamber issues the accountant's certificate.

In Sweden, while there are no special professional examinations required, all authorized accountants have passed rigorous university examinations. There was no "grandfather clause" admitting practicing accountants without the qualifications specified at the time the chambers of commerce instituted the authorization.

It is stipulated that the authorized public accountant may not carry on any business as a merchant or agent, nor may he be an active partner in a business enterprise of any kind. He may not hold a salaried public or private office. He may, of course, be a partner or employee of another APA. The Board of Trade may grant exceptions from this rule, but permission is usually granted only for teaching activities. If an APA should accept a salaried position in industry, his authorization would be revoked. In Sweden, therefore, a person entitled to use the designation "authorized public accountant" is always an independent professional accountant.

The statutes provide that an APA may not undertake the audit of a business enterprise of which he is an officer or employee or is in a subordinate or dependent position in relation to persons in the administration of the enterprise; or if he has more than a negligible financial interest in the enterprise; or if there are any other special circumstances likely to raise questions about his impartiality in the performance of his duties.

As in other countries, APAs may practice as individuals, with one or more assistants (who may be APAs or approved examiners), or in partnership with several other APAs. Also, a number of Swedish auditing firms are organized as limited companies, of which the shareholders and board members must all be APAs. Regardless of the form chosen, a partnership or corporation may not be appointed as auditor of a limited liability company—the appointment is always of an individual APA.

Föreningen Auktoriserade Revisorer
(The Authorized Public Accountants Association)

This Association was founded in 1923 and it's present "statutes" were adopted in 1965. Membership is composed of those who possess the Board of Trade authorization as a public accountant and "have a reputation for integrity and are considered suitable for membership."

The objectives of the association are to maintain a high-principled and professionally skilled corps of APAs, to promote sound principles and rational methods of auditing, accounting, and business administration, to safeguard the professional interests of its members, and to foster a spirit of solidarity and mutual understanding among its members.

Ethics

The Association has included in its statutes a number of statements bearing on the ethical conduct of its members, which essentially cover the matters spelled out in the code of ethics of the American Institute of Certified Public Accountants. They are as follows (condensed):

1. A member shall carry out conscientiously and to the best of his ability the tasks entrusted to him with honesty, diligence, and care.
2. A member may not reveal information obtained in the course of his professional work or make use of it to his own or another's advantage.
3. A member may not, in addition to his accountancy work, carry on any other business that may adversely affect his independence or is otherwise incompatible with his position as an APA.
4. A member must not undertake to report upon a business firm in which he has direct or indirect interest, which includes holding one or more shares or participating rights in the firm; and he must not place himself in a position of dependence.
5. Advertising is limited to brief announcements in newspapers or periodicals not exceeding 12 in any one year.

There are other unwritten but generally observed rules of conduct. An APA who is asked to replace another person as auditor of a company should confer with his predecessor prior to accepting the engagement as to whether there may be any reason why he should decline the appointment. It is considered a breach of professional etiquette to approach a prospective client with offers of unreasonably low fees or promises of better service than is offered by other colleagues. A member of the Association may not offer employment to an employee of a colleague without first having conferred with the latter. He may not undertake an audit of a business enterprise where he or his firm has performed bookkeeping work.

Disciplinary Procedure

The statutes state that a member who in the course of his work deliberately commits a wrong or who otherwise acts dishonestly, or who in some other way disregards the duties incumbent upon him as a member, may be given a warning or a caution or may be expelled from membership in the Association, depending on the seriousness of the offense and whether there are mitigating circumstances. The resolution of the Council may be appealed by the board of the Association.

Penalties Imposed Under the Companies Act

The Companies Act prescribes penalties (in the form of fines or imprisonment) if, in an audit report or in the financial statements, an accountant intentionally or through gross negligence gives incorrect, incomplete, or misleading information or fails to criticize management although there is reason therefor. He may be fined if he disregards the regulations concerning the contents of the audit report or the certificate on the financial statements.

Functions of the Authorized Public Accountant

The APA, when appointed as one of the official auditors of a limited liability company, examines its annual financial statements as submitted by the management to the annual meeting of shareholders, and reports upon his examination of such financial statements. The Companies Act mentions certain specific duties of the auditor: to examine the books and all other accounting material; to read minutes of board and stockholder meetings; to conduct or inspect inventories of cash and other assets; to examine the company's system of internal control; to examine the annual financial statements and the annual business report.

Although not legally compelled to do so, many smaller Swedish companies appoint an APA as one of their auditors.

One of the duties of the auditor in Sweden (whether or not he is an APA) is to examine and report upon the administration of the company's affairs. This is, of course, an unusual function of the independent auditor from the professional point of view in most other countries. The purpose is to bring to the notice of stockholders any administrative acts that might affect the shareholders' decision whether or not to grant to the board its annual discharge from responsibility.

The authorized public accountant in Sweden also carries out valuations, investigations, organizational commissions, and assignments as arbitrator; occasionally he may act as administrator of property, administrator of estates, and trustee in bankruptcy.

The Swedish auditor incurs heavy responsibility for preparation of income tax returns if taxable income has been understated. Therefore, accountants usually prepare income tax returns only when they have a very detailed knowledge of the data on which the return is based, which they may have when they are also auditors for the concern. They do, however, consult with their clients on tax matters and assist in investigation of tax cases.

Godkänd Revisor

(Approved Accountant)

This classification of accountants is also recognized by the chambers of commerce. The approved accountant is expected to possess such knowledge and experience as will enable him to examine accounts and consider simple administrative questions connected with such examination.

In addition to the qualification of good character required of the APA, the approved accountant must possess good knowledge of bookkeeping, and the laws governing annual reports and taxation, and have displayed an aptitude for accountancy work. The necessary knowledge may be evidenced by an examination certificate issued by a school of commerce or a junior college of commerce, or by the nature of the practical work in which he or she has been engaged. Such practical work shall generally include five years of auditing, at least three years of which as an accountant of an APA or an approved accountant. He is required to file a declaration with the chamber of commerce identical to that filed by the authorized public accountant.

The approved accountant may be appointed auditor of a limited company, except where the Companies Act requires the appointment of an APA, or he may act as an assistant to an APA. He is permitted to carry on auditing work in addition to other employment, and often does so.

Svenska Revisorsamfundet

(The Swedish Accountants Association)

Most members of this Association are approved accountants, but the membership also includes some other accountants in Sweden, including a few APAs.

The qualifications for membership in this Association are essentially the same as those given above for the approved accountant.

Auditing Standards

Any Swedish citizen may practice accounting in Sweden, and with the exception of larger companies, as previously described, the auditors of limited companies need not be qualified accountants. The profession of independent public accounting as practiced by the authorized public accountants does have standards enunciated both in the statutes of the chambers of commerce and of the APA Association, although these are not "codified" in any one statement. However, the APA Association adopted in 1970 a basic statement of auditing standards, "Audits of the Accounts of Swedish Corporations, Their Scope and Extent" (first published in tentative form in 1967), and the Association intends to follow it up with specific recommendations on auditing procedure. A tentative statement on the audit of inventories was published in 1974.

General Standards

The requirements for admission as an APA assure adequate training and proficiency of the auditor, and the necessity for an independent attitude is stressed in the aforementioned statutes. The Association has stated that honesty, diligence, and due care are requisite in the performance of the auditor's work.

Standards of Field Work

Emphasis is laid on the review of internal control. The board of directors has primary responsibility for the maintenance of a satisfactory system, but the auditors must review it to determine whether it is functioning properly and, if not, to so report to the management.

In larger companies, a detailed audit is generally done by internal auditors, but in smaller ones the elected auditor may perform it. Most APAs now consider that, based upon a comprehensive review of internal control and upon a review of the work of the internal auditors, the work of the APA may consist of tests of the transactions during the year combined with examination of year-end balances. In smaller companies where internal control is weak and there are no internal auditors, some auditors consider it necessary to make a detailed audit of transactions for the year.

There is no specific provision for confirming accounts receivable with the debtors, though it is common practice to do so. As previously noted, the Companies Act specifies that the auditor should "conduct or inspect inventories of cash and other assets." Observation of physical inventory-taking is not obligatory, but it is often carried out.

Standards of Reporting

There are two aspects of the auditor's report in Sweden. First, the auditor must sign the balance sheet and income statement for identification; and, second, he must present a separate audit report. The signature on the financial statements shall be accompanied by a simple statement, "Reference being hereby made to the audit report, it is certified that this balance sheet is in accordance with the books."

As to the separate audit report, there is no established or fixed form of wording. The Companies Act, however, does specify the matters to be covered by such a report. The more important of these are (condensed)—

1. The results of the auditor's examination, specifically whether the auditor has any reservations regarding the company's financial statement, its bookkeeping, the safeguarding of its assets, or the administration of the company's affairs, and if there are such reservations, the reasons for them.
2. Whether the auditor recommends approval of the balance sheet; whether he recommends that the managing director and the board be discharged from responsibility for the administration for the accounting year, and whether he concurs in the management's proposals for the distribution of profit or disposition of loss for the year, including the due appropriations to legal reserves.
3. Whether there has been a writeup of fixed assets (as permitted under certain provisions of the Companies Act), or whether current assets are recorded above cost.

If the company reported upon is a parent company, certain other statements must be made in the auditor's report: (1) whether the legal rules concerning consolidated statements and preparation of a special statement on ownership of subsidiary company shares, intercompany accounts, property pledged by a subsidiary, and so forth, have been observed and (2) if a dividend is proposed, whether it is considered to be in conflict with sound business practice considering the financial position and the retained earnings of the group as a whole.

An example of the auditor's report upon a large Swedish company follows:

Statutory Audit Report Upon the Accounts of ABC Company

At December 31, 19___.

In our capacity as auditors to the ABC Company, we hereby submit the following report for the year 19___.

We have examined the Annual Report and the consolidated statements, studied the accounts, the minutes and other documents containing information as to the financial position and the management of the corporation, and made such other inquiries as we considered necessary.

The detailed checking of the records has been carried out by the Corporation's internal audit department who have reported to us on their examination.

The provisions of the Companies Act concerning shareholdings and group reporting have been complied with.

In the course of the audit there appeared no reason for remarks to be made upon the Annual Report, the bookkeeping or the verification of assets, or upon the management.

The Board of Directors and the Managing Director propose that the profits according to the balance sheet be appropriated as follows:

Transfer to Legal Reserve	SK______
Dividend to Shareholders of SK per share	SK______
Carried Forward	SK______
Kronor	

This proposal does not conflict with the provisions of the Companies Act concerning appropriations to legal reserves nor with sound business practice, considering the financial position and the retained earnings of the group.

We recommend:

that the balance sheet as at 31st December 19__, included in the Annual Report and signed by us, be adopted, that the profits be appropriated as proposed above, and that the Board of Directors and the Managing Director be granted discharge from liability for their management for the period covered by the annual report.

Stockholm,

Authorized Public Accountant | Authorized Public Accountant

No specific reference to codified auditing standards or accounting principles appears in the reports of Swedish auditors. The matter of consistency is referred to in the following section.

Report of the Board of Directors and Managing Director

This report on administration, in Swedish practice, is required for all limited companies, regardless of size and number of stockholders; it is submitted to the auditors for review and comment; it is presented at the annual meeting and filed with the registration authority, where it is open to public inspection. It is considered a part of the financial statements and is the vehicle for much of the disclosure of the company's affairs. Some of the matters which are required by the Companies Act to be disclosed in this report are the following:

1. The assessed values of real estate for tax purposes, and the fire insurance coverage of real estate, machinery, and plant.
2. The average number of workers and the average number of other employees.
3. The total amount of salaries and wages for the period covered by the financial statements, showing separately (1) manual workers, (2) board and management personnel, and (3) all other.
4. Reasons for, and amount of any writeup of fixed assets, and utilization of resulting reserve.
5. A proposal by management for the distribution of profits, including, where required, appropriations to the legal reserves.
6. When the reporting is that of a parent company, the group's total distributable profits (retained earnings) must be included.

If any current asset is carried at an amount higher than cost, but which can be justified as in accordance with generally accepted accounting principles and sound business practice, the fact must be stated and reasons therefor given.

Certain changes in accounting practices as compared with the previous year must be disclosed as follows:

1. Any change in classification of assets as to current or fixed.
2. Any change of major importance in principles of computing depreciation.
3. Undervaluation of inventories is considered to be in conformity with sound business practice, but if changes in the amount of such reserves have a material effect on net income, the details must be disclosed. (In recent years, most leading corporations have given full information about undervaluation of inventories.)

There are certain other items which shall be included in the report of the management, if it can be done "without detriment to the corporation." They are the following:

1. Net sales (if not indicated in the income statement). Other matters of importance such as changes in the activities of the corporation

by opening new branches or new sales markets, and substantial property or subsidiary acquisitions.

2. Post-balance sheet events of importance.

Accounting Principles and Practices

The Swedish Authorized Public Accountants Association has issued a series of recommendations relating to accounting principles and practices, but as they do not have legislative or other backing, they have not had quite the same influence or general acceptance that is found in like pronouncements of similar organizations in some other countries. The general principle guiding accounting practices, which is mentioned both in the National Bookkeeping Law and the Companies Act, is that they must be employed "in accordance with generally accepted accounting principles and sound business practice." As to valuation of assets the "principle of lowest value" is the one often applied.

The Swedish tax law has significant influence on accounting practices because taxable income is determined from the actual book entries of the taxpayer with certain exceptions where special rules on depreciation are followed.

The two laws in Sweden which have the greatest influence on accounting matters are the Bookkeeping Law (Bokforingslagen, 1929) and the Companies Act (effective January 1, 1948). The former applies generally to the keeping of business records, bookkeeping procedures, and the kind of information to be shown in such records. The latter deals with valuations, certain accounting practices, and prescribes standard statement classifications.

The Swedish Association of Metalworking Industries has issued a standard chart of accounts, which, while directed only to that industry, has had wide influence on accounting in general, with special reference to cost accounting.

Finally, it is considered "sound business practice" in Sweden to level out net income from year to year, and this practice is encouraged by the income tax law which allows the taxpayer (1) to undervalue inventories, (2) to over- or under-provide for depreciation, within certain limits, at company discretion, and (3) to make discretionary allocations to investment fund reserves up to 40 percent of net profit before taxes.

During the 1960's it became the standard practice of the larger Swedish companies to give full disclosure as to the effect of such accounting practices. Thus, one usually finds, in the income statements of these corporations, an amount reported as "income before year-end appropriations and taxes" which is unaffected by changes in "inventory reserve," over- or under-provision for depreciation, and so forth.

Form and Content of Financial Statements

The Companies Act prescribes in some detail the items to be shown on the financial statements. In general, the order is similar to that of public utility companies in the United States—on the assets side of the balance sheet, fixed assets first (plant and equipment, patents, goodwill, long-term investment), followed by current assets; on the liability side, capital first, followed by legal and general reserves, special reserves, depreciation reserves, long-term debt, current liabilities, and finally, unappropriated profits. The Association of APAs has recommended the order more commonly used in the United States, that is: current items first, descending to fixed assets and capital on the respective sides. Most published balance sheets of the larger companies in Sweden follow the latter form.

Consolidated Financial Statements. The managing director presents to the board and to the auditors a consolidated balance sheet or a consolidated statement of retained earnings. There is no legal requirement for these statements to be presented at the annual meeting of the parent company, but the management's report must state the amount of the group's retained earnings in order that such a meeting may take this factor into consideration.

Though there is no legal obligation to do so, practically all larger companies publish their consolidated statements (balance sheet, income statement, and often a statement of changes in financial position).

The rules of consolidation stated in the Companies Act are similar to those customary in the United States—intercompany accounts and transactions and intercompany profits in inventories are eliminated. However, goodwill arising in consolidation is usually deducted from surplus at acquisition or from free reserves; negative goodwill is treated as an undistributable reserve.

Notes to Financial Statements. "Notes to financial statements" have become quite common in the annual reports of larger corporations in the last few years, but outside this area the use of such notes is not highly developed. This is due to the fact that information required to be given (see below), as well as other types of disclosure, is more often included in the report of the management. The following is required to be disclosed and sometimes is shown on or in a note to the balance sheet:

1. The balance sheet value of pledged assets with separate amounts for mortgages on real estate, chattel mortgages, mortgages on ships, and mortgages on other movable property.
2. The total amount of contingent liabilities resulting from accomodation endorsements, guarantees, etc., and (separately) the amount of discounted notes.

3. Pension obligations, if exceeding what has been recorded as liabilities (see under the heading "Pension Costs").

Pooling of Interests

The accounting concept of "pooling of interest" as applied to mergers is not recognized in Sweden.

Current Assets

General. The general rule for valuation of current assets (including marketable securities and inventories) is that they be stated at no more than the lower of cost or market, but "good business practice" may permit a lower valuation.

Accounts Receivable. Accounts receivable are required to be stated at the amount deemed collectible and worthless accounts must be written off. Portions of accounts deemed uncollectible may be written off, either by reducing the recorded amount of the receivable or by establishing a reserve, which may be deducted from the asset. An estimated provision such as a percentage of sales or recorded amount of receivables is not permitted by tax law, except in the case of installment sale receivables. It is not common practice to show separately either the amount by which receivables have been reduced or the "reserve for bad debts."

Claims against members of the board, the managing director, or the auditors, must be shown separately if they exceed either 10,000 kronor or 2 percent of the corporation's net worth as shown by its balance sheet. Receivables from and liabilities to subsidiaries must be shown separately.

Inventories. The Companies Act prescribes the lower of cost or market as the basis for valuation of inventories. The income tax law requires inventories to be priced on the same basis, cost being calculated using the first-in, first-out method. The gross valuation thus determined may be reduced by write-downs (inventory reserves) as follows:

1. The initial inventory computation, after deducting obsolete or unsalable items, may be reduced by as much as 60 percent.
2. The 60 percent rule may be applied to the average inventory of the two preceding years. If the quantity of inventories has declined markedly in recent years, it is possible that the inventory reduction applied to the closing inventory could produce a negative closing inventory. If so, it would be shown on the credit side of the balance sheet.

3. The third method deals solely with inventories of raw materials or staple commodities. The management has the option of using the lowest market price of the current period or the lowest price of any of the nine preceding periods. This latter lowest price can then be further reduced by 30 percent. If this method is selected, it precludes the use of the second method (above), but the first method can still be used for other parts of the inventory.

Not all companies use any one of these methods, and even those that do, do not always write the inventory down to the lowest amount allowed; thus, there is a wide range of choice for inventory valuations for a Swedish company. There is also no uniformity in the balance sheet classification of the resulting inventory reductions; in some cases, they are deducted from the inventory and, in others, are shown on the liability side among the reserves. If such reserve is restored in a subsequent year, the amount so restored is subject to income tax.

Fixed Assets

Fixed assets may not be shown at more than cost (but see below as to "enduring value"). If "true value" is found to be materially lower than cost less accumulated depreciation, a special depreciation allowance must be provided unless an increase in the depreciation rate can be considered sufficient to accomplish the desired result.

Fixed assets considered to have an "enduring value" substantially in excess of the amount at which they were shown in the last preceding balance sheet may be written up to not more than such "enduring value" if the amount by which they are increased is used for (1) writing down of other fixed assets or (2) an increase of capital by the issue of bonus shares. Real estate may not be written up to an amount exceeding the latest assessed value for tax purposes.

The report of the management (which is considered a part of the financial statements) must disclose whether there has been a writeup of fixed assets, the amount thereof, and the disposition, if any, of the resulting increase.

Goodwill, Patents, and Trademarks

The purchase cost of acquiring from a third party such intangibles as trademarks, trade names, or similar items must be written off for both book and tax purposes generally over a ten-year period. Patents are amortizable over their remaining life.

Prepaid and Deferred Charges

It is not required that these items be shown separately on the balance sheet; they may be grouped with "other current claims."

Corporate organization expenses are not tax deductible and may not be capitalized. Research expenses and expenses of advertising and selling in connection with introducing a new product may be capitalized and written off over five years or longer "if justified by generally accepted accounting practices and sound business practice."

Bond Discount and Premiums

Discounts on outstanding debt may be amortized over the life of the related issue or they may be charged off directly to expense. Premiums are usually shown as a liability and amortized over the life of the related issue.

Reserves

Depreciation Reserve. The Companies Act classification allows accumulated depreciation to be recorded on the liability side of the balance sheet, while the Association recommends that depreciation be shown separately as a deduction from the related assets. However, many companies show only the net book amount on the asset side.

Investment Fund Reserve. Business corporations are permitted by the government to set aside, at their own discretion, up to 40 percent of their pretax net business income as an investment reserve for economic stabilization. The amount so set aside is deductible for both national and local taxes, but an amount equal to 46 percent thereof must be deposited in a blocked, non-interest-bearing account in the Swedish National Bank. In general, the reserve may be used and the corresponding blocked deposit released when so authorized by the authorities, for construction of buildings, acquisition of new machinery and equipment (including ships), and the development of mineral deposits. The total cost of the asset so acquired is then reduced by the amount of the investment fund set aside for the purpose; only the net balance of the asset is then subject to depreciation.

There is no ceiling on the total amount or the number of years during which the investment reserve may be set aside. There are a number of special provisions in the tax law relating to the usage of the reserve in certain circumstances.

Statutory Reserves. The Swedish Companies Act requires that companies set aside annually 10 percent of net income to provide a legal reserve until such reserve equals 20 percent of the outstanding capital stock. This can be used only to cover losses which cannot be absorbed in any other way.

If total liabilities (as defined in the act) exceed the sum of legal reserve and the capital stock, the company must provide a "supplementary legal reserve," the computation of which is specified in the act. There is also a restriction on the payment of dividends from current earnings when circumstances require provision of a supplementary reserve. The act provides for dissolution of the supplementary reserve when the total of capital stock, the legal reserve, and the supplementary legal reserve exceeds legal liabilities, and specifies to what extent the reserve may be reduced and the manner in which the reduction in such reserve may be treated.

Premium on Capital Stock

If capital stock is sold at a premium, such premium must be added to the legal reserve.

Treasury Stock

The Companies Act prohibits the purchase of a corporation's own shares either by itself or by a subsidiary.

Statement of Retained Earnings

The Swedish financial statements do not include a statement of retained earnings due to the fact that they are prepared before the annual meeting has approved the dividend and appropriations to reserves. The balance sheet shows the retained earnings at the beginning of the year, the dividends and appropriations approved during the year from that balance, and the amount available for the current year distributions as follows:

Profit on balance sheet December 31, 1971		SK 500,000
Deduct, approved at 1972 annual meeting:		
Appropriated to legal reserve	SK 50,000	
Dividend to shareholders	150,000	200,000
Unappropriated earnings from previous year		300,000
Profit for the year 1972		600,000
	Total	SK 900,000

A further statement may be added to indicate the proposed distributions for the current year:

At the disposal of the 1973 annual meeting		SK 900,000
Disposition proposed by the board:		
Appropriation to legal reserve	SK 60,000	
Dividend to shareholders	200,000	
To be carried forward	640,000	SK 900,000

Statement of Income

The Companies Act states the items to be included in the income statement, with the provision that whenever it may be considered necessary according to generally accepted accounting principles and sound business practice a further breakdown shall be given. The specific items listed are as follows:

Income

1. Income (gross profit) from the company's business operations, segregated from any independent operations which may be carried on, unless such segregation is found to be detrimental to the corporation.
2. Dividends received, showing separately dividends received from subsidiaries.
3. Interest income, showing separately interest received from subsidiaries.
4. Profits on sales of fixed assets, unless under the circumstances a different accounting is permitted by generally accepted accounting principles and sound business practice.
5. Other income, not resulting from business operations.
6. Gratuitous or other extraordinary receipts.

Expenses

1. Loss from business operations, or from operations which must be reported separately (see "Income," above).
2. Interest expense, showing separately interest paid to subsidiaries.
3. Income taxes.
4. Depreciation of fixed assets, classified in accordance with the fixed asset accounts on the balance sheet.
5. Losses on sales of fixed assets, unless under the circumstances a different accounting is permitted by generally accepted accounting principles and sound business practice.
6. General administrative expenses.
7. Extraordinary expenses and losses.
8. Net profit (loss) for the year.

Sales and Cost of Sales. The amount of sales is not required to be disclosed in the income statement; however, if not considered detrimental to the corporation, the sales figure must be included in the report of the management. Similarly, cost of sales is not required, although management must include in its report the total amount of wages and other remunerations, apportioned as to workers, the board, the managing director, and others in managerial positions, as well as other employees of the company. The income statement, therefore, often begins with the "gross profit" figure, which is arrived at after deducting selling expenses. There has, however, in later years been a trend towards reporting sales and cost of sales in the income statement.

Pension Costs

All persons gainfully employed receive pensions, the cost of which is borne by the employers. Up to a certain level, the pensions are handled by the state. In the case of white-collar employees, amounts above this level are often insured or else become the direct obligation and thus a long-term liability of the company. Actuarial computations for uninsured pensions have to be made each year. If the present value of such pension obligations exceeds what is recorded as a liability, the deficiency must be shown in a note to the balance sheet.

Tax-Effect Accounting

Since book accounting is usually almost identical with tax accounting in Sweden, the question of allocation of income taxes (deferred or "latent" taxes) seldom arises.

Depreciation

As a general rule, depreciation must be computed on cost, the annual charges being based on the estimated useful lives of the assets. The rules governing the amount of depreciation allowable for tax purposes also generally govern the amount provided in the books. These rules, which follow, usually result in fixed assets becoming fully depreciated over a period shorter than their useful lives.

Depreciation on buildings is limited to an amount based on the estimated useful life and, for tax purposes, normally ranges from 1.5 percent to 5 percent per annum.

Depreciation on machinery and equipment, however, is guided by quite liberal rules. There are two permissible methods: "book depreciation" and "planned depreciation." The rules permit changing from one method to the other in certain circumstances.

The book depreciation method provides only ceilings or maximums. The taxpayer may take less than the maximum allowable in any year, and thus postpone deductions to a later year. Most large companies use the book depreciation method. The maximum deduction in any one year is established by either of two alternatives, which may be elected by management. These are (1) the 30 percent declining-balance rule and (2) the 20 percent straight-line rule. It is not required to follow the same alternative in each successive year. Under the declining-balance method, over half (51 percent) of the cost of machinery can be written off in two years; under the straight-line method, the entire cost is written off over five years.

Under the planned depreciation method, the depreciation deducted on the tax return need not coincide with that charged on the books. Essentially, it represents a straight-line method based on estimated useful lives of the various classes of assets. It is useful when a company is reporting losses or small profits, because any planned depreciation in any year which is in excess of that amount required to reduce the taxable profit to zero can be carried forward indefinitely, until a net taxable profit is shown.

Depreciation on buildings is normally computed on cost.

There is no requirement for disclosure of the method of computing depreciation, but if a change in the method is of major importance, it must be commented upon in the management's report.

General Administrative Expense

There is no authoritative statement of expenses to be included in this classification, and there is quite a wide variety of practice in this area. However, a corporation is expected to be consistent in its treatment of this expense from year to year.

Stock Dividends

Stock dividends are accounted for at their par value by the issuer. The recipient as a rule would not adjust the cost of his investment.

Requirements for Listing Securities on the Stock Exchange and Public Sale of Securities

Sale of a limited liability company's securities to the public is ordinarily handled through a commercial bank, which determines information to be furnished to a prospective purchaser. There are no governmental regulations which prescribe requirements for the data to be furnished. Any financial data included in the data furnished prospective purchasers is submitted by the board of directors.

Applications for the listing of shares on the stock exchange are made in writing to the Council of the Stock Exchange by a member of the stock exchange or by the management of the company whose shares are to be listed, and the details are usually handled by a Swedish bank. Shares of companies whose share capital is less than 5,000,000 kronor may not be registered; neither may bonds or debentures if the nominal amount of the loan to be listed is less than 5,000,000 kronor.

In addition to the usual data as to the shares to be listed, it is required that the company's annual report and the auditor's report be submitted for the last five accounting years, although in special cases the council may permit listing when the annual report and the auditor's report cover only one year. It is not required that applications for listing of bonds and deferred or other debentures be accompanied by such reports, unless the company does not have its shares listed; in the latter case, the company's annual reports and auditors' reports for the last two accounting years must be submitted.

The general provisions regarding the auditors and their reports, previously discussed, are applicable; since the capital of a company wishing to list its shares must be at least 5,000,000 kronor, one of the statutory auditors must be an authorized public accountant.

As previously stated, all annual reports of Swedish companies and statutory audit reports are available for inspection by the public in the Royal Swedish Patent and Registration Office.

Proposed New Legislation

General

In 1971, two Swedish Royal Commissions published reports which included proposals that are likely to lead to changes in the legislation and the organizational structure described in this chapter. A short summary of these proposals is given here, but it should be noted that none has yet (as of fall 1974) reached the Riksdag (Parliament).

New Companies Act

In 1969 through 1971, government committees in Sweden, Denmark, Finland, and Norway published their proposals for new Companies Acts. These proposals represent an attempt at a far-reaching harmonization—in fact, if the laws are enacted, the four countries will get companies acts that are to a considerable extent identical.

Some of the proposed changes of the rules of the present Companies Act of Sweden are the following:

1. The present minimum for the par value per share (SK 50) shall be abolished (but shares of no-par-value will not be permitted).
2. Whereas the present law requires the appointment as auditor of a corporation to be personal, it is proposed that a properly authorized Swedish firm of accountants, organized either as a partnership or as a company, should be eligible as auditor.
3. A number of changes in the prescribed forms for the financial statements are proposed.
4. "Notes to financial statements" will be a regular feature of company annual reports. Much of the information now required to be given in the "report of the management" shall instead be included in the notes.
5. The present requirements as to appropriations to statutory reserves (legal reserve and supplementary legal reserve) out of profits shall be abolished.

Special Accounting Requirements for Large Companies; Prospectuses

According to a proposal submitted by the committee on stock exchange reform, special accounting requirements would be added to those in the Companies Act for, among others, all companies (1) whose shares are listed on the Stockholm Stock Exchange or (2) who employ more than 500 persons. These rules would (a) compel disclosure of practically all under-valuation of assets, (b) make the publication of consolidated balance sheets and income statements obligatory, and (c) make the publication of interim reports obligatory. The new rules would have little impact on corporations listed on the stock exchange since they already conform to these requirements.

The proposal also deals with prospectuses, their content and publication.

Switzerland

Switzerland

As of January 1974

Forms of Business Organization

General

The principal forms of business organization in Switzerland are the joint stock company (aktiengesellschaft or A.G.) and the private limited liability company (gesellschaft mit beschränkter haftung or G.m.b.H.). Other forms of business organization are the general partnership (kollektivgesellschaft), the limited partnership (kommanditgesellschaft), the partnership partially limited by shares (kommanditaktiengesellschaft), the cooperative society (genossenschaft), the branches of Swiss or foreign entities (zweigniederlassungen), and the single proprietorship (einzelfirma).

Aktiengesellschaft (A.G.)
(Joint Stock Company)

The prevalent form of business organization is the joint stock company, which most closely resembles the U.S. corporation. The Swiss joint stock company must be formed by at least three incorporators (individuals or bodies corporate). The articles of association are drawn up according to the federal requirements and in the language of the canton (state) in which the company is to be domiciled; there are 25 cantons. The contents of the articles of association are in general terms similar to those of other countries. The formation deed which contains the articles of association must be authenticated by a notary and filed with the cantonal Register of Commerce. Each of the 25 cantons has a Register of Commerce, which is open for inspection by the public; some cantons maintain a separate register for each district. The important entries in the Register of Commerce are published in the *Swiss Official Journal of Commerce.* The company can act as body corporate only after registration in the Register of Commerce and after the publication in the *Swiss Official Journal of Commerce.* Resolutions to change or amend the articles of association must be approved by the shareholders in a general meeting and also be authenticated by a notary and filed with the Register of Commerce.

Except when a joint stock company engages in banking, financial, or insurance activities, its annual financial statements need not be published or filed with the Register of Commerce.

Swiss law on joint companies (Aktienrecht), articles 620 to 763 of the Swiss Code of Obligations (OR), does not provide for "authorized and unissued" capital. All the shares of a Swiss joint stock company must be fully subscribed at the time of formation. A Swiss joint stock company must have a minimum capital of 50,000 Swiss francs divided into shares with a face value of at least 100 Swiss francs. "No-par-value" shares are not allowed. The issue price for each share may not be lower than its face value. One-fifth of the par value or at least 20,000 francs of the capital must be paid in prior to the incorporation meeting, and the balance is payable on call. Each share is entitled to one vote; however, since shares of differing value may be issued, each vote may not represent the same amount of capital contribution. Shares may be bearer or registered or a combination of both. Bearer shares may be issued only if they are fully paid; registered shares originally partly paid may be converted to bearer form when fully paid. A register of shareholders must be maintained in respect of registered shares.

Preferred shares may also be issued giving preference in profit distributions, preemptive rights, and special rights in the event of liquidation.

Swiss joint stock companies may restrict ownership of their shares, provided the shares are registered, e.g., to Swiss residents or entities.

Swiss joint stock companies may also issue participation certificates which entitle the holders thereof to a share in the profits and the liquidation surplus, and to exercise option rights but not voting rights. Such certificates may be issued in favor of persons who are in some way connected with the company as shareholders, former shareholders or creditors, and, if the original articles of association permit, as founders of the company. Although there is no authorizing provision in the law, companies have recently begun issuing participation certificates against payment in cash as a means of obtaining capital.

The joint stock corporation is managed by a board of directors (verwaltungsrat) or by a single director. Directors must hold qualifying shares and are elected by the shareholders. The first members of the board are named at the incorporation meeting and serve for up to three years. Thereafter, directors are elected for periods up to six years. A majority of the directors must be citizens and residents of Switzerland. If there is a single director, he must be a citizen and a resident of Switzerland. In case this requirement is not met, the company may be required to cease operations. The board may delegate to board members (delegierte), or non-board members (direktoren) the power to act in the name of the company.

The shareholders in the general meeting approve the annual accounts of the company and decide upon the application of the profits, i.e., the amounts to be distributed as a dividend, appropriated to the legal reserve, and so forth.

For some years, a revision of the Swiss law on joint stock companies (Aktienrecht) has been under consideration. The main amendments that are under discussion are in respect of—

1. The introduction of authorized and, in connection with the issue of convertible debentures, conditional capital.
2. The issue of bonus shares and participation certificates.
3. The issue of "no-par-value" shares.
4. The issue of so-called people's shares with a face value of one franc.
5. The preemptive rights.
6. The acquisition by the company of its own shares (at present, a company may not acquire its own shares).
7. The form of the annual accounts and the preparation of consolidated accounts.
8. The question of the creation and elimination of undisclosed reserves.
9. The position and duties of the statutory auditor and his independence.
10. The question of information on and the publication of the annual accounts of the company.

Such amendments as may be proposed will probably not become law for some years to come.

Gesellschaft mit beschränkter Haftung (G.m.b.H.)

(Private Limited Liability Company)

The private limited liability company must be formed by at least two incorporators (individuals or bodies corporate). The name of the company must contain the abbreviation "G.m.b.H." or in French "S.à.R.L." As in the case of a joint stock company, the formation deed, authenticated by a notary, must be filed together with the articles of association and a list of the members including their names, residence or domicile, nationality, and capital contributions, with the cantonal Register of Commerce for publication in the *Swiss Official Journal of Commerce.* A list of members with the details mentioned above and particulars of any changes must also be filed with the Register of Commerce at the end of each fiscal year.

The share capital of a private limited liability company must be at least 20,000 francs but not more than 2,000,000 francs and is divided into fixed shares of 1,000 francs or a multiple thereof; all the shares must be subscribed and at least 50 percent paid in. No certificates are issued; the shares are only inscribed in a special members' register which is maintained by the company. Transfer of shares is by a notary deed only and requires the consent of three-quarters of the members holding three-forths of the share capital.

The private limited liability company constitutes a legal entity, and the liability of its members is limited to their subscribed capital; in the event of bankruptcy, the members become jointly and severally liable directly to the creditors for any unpaid share subscriptions. Unless otherwise provided for in the articles of association, voting rights and allocation of profits and losses are normally in proportion to capital contributions.

Management of the private limited liability company follows the rules of partnership. In case the articles of association do not specifically contain a provision or the members' meeting does not decide otherwise, all members are joint managers. If a manager is appointed by the members in general meeting, he need not be a member; however, at least one of the managers (if more than one is appointed) must be resident in, but not necessarily a citizen of, Switzerland.

Depending on the articles of association, the private limited liability company may or may not appoint auditors. Except when the company engages in banking, financial, or insurance activities, its annual financial statements need not be published nor filed with the Register of Commerce.

Zweigniederlassungen

(Branches of Foreign Entities)

Branches of foreign partnerships and companies have the same legal status for Swiss purposes as the partnerships or companies have in the country of their head office or incorporation. To obtain official status in Switzerland, the basic documents (partnership agreements, articles of association) and all amendments thereto, translated where necessary into one of the official languages of Switzerland, must be filed with the Register of Commerce in the canton in which the branch will be domiciled, together with the name, nationality, and residence of partners, directors, officers, and so forth. A manager resident in, but not necessarily a citizen of, Switzerland must be appointed and registered. The registered name of the branch must contain the place of registration of the head office and a clear designation as "branch." Excerpts from the articles of association and all registration matters are published in the *Swiss Official Journal of Commerce.* The branch must maintain its own accounting records.

Kommanditgesellschaft
(Limited Partnership)

This is a business association of one or more general partners (individuals only) with unlimited liability, and one or more limited partners (individuals or bodies corporate) with liability up to a specified amount. The firm name must include the surname of at least one general partner and an indication that the organization is a partnership. Relations between partners are determined by the partnership contract or deed. The maximum amount of liability of limited partners is inscribed in the Register of Commerce and published in the *Swiss Official Journal of Commerce.* The management of the company is in the hands of the unlimited partners; limited partners do not participate in management, but have the right to obtain the annual accounts and to examine books and records or have them examined.

Kommanditaktiengesellschaft
(Partnership Partially Limited by Shares)

This is a company with a share capital, in which one or more members are jointly and severally liable to creditors, whereas the liability of the other members is limited to the amount of the shares subscribed by them. The board of directors is composed of members with unlimited liability, the names, residence or domicile, and nationality of whom must be registered with the Register of Commerce and be published in the *Swiss Official Journal of Commerce.* The members with limited liability appoint a supervisory board. In other respects, the partnership limited by shares is governed by the law relating to joint stock companies.

Kollektivgesellschaft
(General Partnership)

This is an association of two or more individuals in a business firm, each partner being jointly and severally and without limitation liable if the firm defaults. The firm name must include the surname of at least one partner with an indication that the firm is a partnership, and must be registered in the Register of Commerce. The relations between partners are determined by the partnership contract or deed.

Genossenschaft
(Cooperative Society)

This is a body corporate with fluctuating membership and consequently changing capital. The liability of its members is limited to their capital contributions; voting rights are by head and not by capital contribution or number of shares held. The organizational structure is simple, i.e., general meeting of members, board of administrators, statutory auditor.

Einzelfirma
(Single Proprietorship)

A single proprietorship must be registered with the Register of Commerce unless its annual gross turnover is less than 50,000 francs.

Business Records and Their Preservation

Those business organizations that are subject to registration in the Register of Commerce must keep proper books and records. The books and records required vary according to the character and extent of the business, but must be adequate for the type and size of operations and permit the determination of the assets and liabilities of the business and the results of its operations on an annual basis. There is no requirement that the books be officially stamped. Books may be kept in any currency, but the annual financial statements must be expressed in Swiss currency.

All books and records of the business organization must be preserved for ten years from the date of the last entry; all incoming and copies of outgoing letters, invoices, and so forth must be preserved for the same period. These documents must at all times be available in Switzerland for submission to the court in the event of litigation and submission to the tax authorities at periodical audits.

The Accounting Profession

General

There are two official organizations of accountants in Switzerland; these are the "Vereinigung Eidgenössischer Diplomierter Buchhalter" (Union of Federally Certified Bookkeepers) and the "Schweizerische Treuhand-und Revisionskammer" (Swiss Chamber of Trustees and Accountants).

The certified bookkeepers are normally employed by companies as chief accountants or controllers; they are not concerned with auditing and have had no specific audit training. Accordingly, the following discussion is limited to a description of the Schweizerische Treuhand–und Revisionskammer, the organization of professional accountants.

The accounting profession (with reference in particular to auditing) is not as formally controlled in Switzerland as it is in the United States. Anyone can act as an auditor, whether or not he has the necessary professional qualifications, except in the relatively few instances, discussed later, where the law requires an independent accountant to be appointed as auditor. However, the practice of appointing qualified members of the accountants' professional organization to perform audits is increasing.

Schweizerische Treuhand-und Revisionskammer
(Swiss Chamber of Trustees and Accountants)

The Schweizerische Treuhand–und Revisionskammer is the principal body of control of the accounting profession in Switzerland. The Chamber was formed in 1925 and is composed of three basic groups:

1. Verband Schweizerischer Bücherexperten (VSB)—(Society of Swiss Certified Accountants)
2. Vereinigung Schweizerischer Treuhand–und Revisionsgesellschaften—(Association of Fiduciary and Accounting Firms)
3. Vereinigung der Bankenrevisionsverbände—(League of Bank Audit Associations).

The purpose of the Chamber is, on the one hand, to examine candidates for the title of certified accountant (see below)and, on the other hand, to further the interests of the profession and to protect its reputation, honour, and independence.

In 1968, the Chamber formulated the following rules of professional conduct which are binding for all practicing members of the three groups of the Swiss Chamber of Trustees and Accountants:

1. The members are obliged to practice the profession in such manner as to deserve the confidence placed in them; they must carry out the assignments entrusted to them with necessary care and in accordance with the law and to the best of their knowledge and belief, and they must abstain from any activity that is inconsistent with the reputation of the profession.
2. The members must practice the profession fully independently of their clients or any third parties; they must abstain from any action which will jeopardize their independence and impartiality.
3. The members are bound to professional secrecy.
4. The members are obliged to maintain good relations with, and conduct themselves fairly towards, other members of the profession by—
   a. advertising only in a discreet and professional manner,
   b. not competing for clients in an unethical manner, and
   c. not recruiting staff from other firms belonging to one of the three groups of the Swiss Chamber of Trustees and Accountants.

A violator of these rules is brought before a professional court of honor, which may issue reprimands, impose fines, and possibly order expulsion from membership in the Chamber.

The Swiss Chamber of Trustees and Accountants has released a publication entitled "Auditing Handbook of Switzerland" (Revisions–Handbuch der Schweiz), which is specially adapted to Swiss conditions and circumstances, is intended to serve on the one hand as teaching material for the professional training and education of junior accountants and, on the other hand, as a reference book for practicing accountants. The handbook provides a conveniently organized treatment of all the facts needed for thorough understanding and considered decision on any problems in the accounting area, and its nine coordinated sections, when completed, will give an appropriate treatment of accounting systems, electronic data processing, internal control, preparation of financial statements, and auditing standards and procedures, including the auditing of automatic data processing systems.

Eidgenössische Diplomierte Bücherexperten
(Federally Certified Accountants)

The title of "eidgenössischer diplomierter bücherexperte" is obtained by passing a professional examination, which is prepared and given every two years by the Schweizerische Treuhand–und Revisionskammer under the control of the Swiss Federal Ministry of Economics. The candidates must have at least three years general commercial and administrative experience in an accounting office, a commercial or industrial enterprise, or a bank, or in a position of administrative authority or in the management of a trade association before taking the preliminary examination. After having successfully passed the preliminary examination and after three additional years of activity in the field of accounting and auditing and after having reached the age of 27, the candidates may take the final examination. Prior to taking the final examination, the candidate must write an essay on a topic which he may choose himself. The subject thereof must, however, be selected from the field of accounting and auditing and be based on the examination of the yearly financial statements of an enterprise and involve a number of special problems emanating therefrom. The purpose of the essay is to show evidence that the candidate possesses the theoretical knowledge and the practical experience to practice the profession independently, as well as the faculty of critical analytical judgment. The written and oral examination itself covers in part the same problem areas and, in addition, law and taxation. The names of the candidates who successfully complete the final examination are entered in the official register of federally certified accountants. They may join the Verband Schweizerischer Bücherexperten and are entitled to use the "Bücherexperte VSB" after their names.

The society was established in 1913 and has now about eight hundred ten members. It has also issued rules of professional conduct, which are similar to those of the Swiss Chamber of Trustees and Accountants set out above. In Switzerland, only the title "diplomierter bücherexperte" is protected, not the practicing of the profession.

Treuhand—und Revisionsgesellschaften
(Fiduciary and Accounting Firms)

The Swiss national firms of accountants are almost all organized as corporations and offer services of a fiduciary as well as of a professional accounting nature. A firm of accountants may, however, be organized in any form recognized by the law. To become a member of the Association of Fiduciary and Accounting Firms, a firm must be organized as a legal entity with a capital of at least 100,000 francs. The services which are offered by the members of the accounting and auditing firms as well as by the members of the Verband Schweizerischer Bücherexperten, who practice on their own, include the following:

- Statutory audits
- Audits of banks (provided they are members of the panel authorized to perform bank audits)
- Preparation and filing of tax returns
- Tax consulting

- Executor and trusteeships
- Management consulting
- Business organization analysis including the preparation of articles of association
- Fiscal advice
- Legal advice to business
- Court-appointed bankruptcy and fraud experts
- Industrial analysis
- Directors of companies (as long as the individual is not actually the statutory auditor)
- Formal management of companies and foundations
- Bookkeeping and accounting

Legal Requirements for the Examination of Financial Statements

General

Joint stock companies and cooperative societies must by law have their financial statements examined as set out below. Other types of business organizations may appoint statutory auditors if this requirement is set forth in the articles of association.

The following details relate to the joint stock company since it is the most important form of business organization.

There are three basic types of examination in Switzerland:

1. The examination by the statutory auditor in accordance with article 727 of the Swiss Code of Obligations (OR), et seq.
2. The examination by independent accountants in accordance with article 723 of the Swiss Code of Obligations.
3. The examination in the event of reduction of capital in accordance with article 732 of the Swiss Code of Obligations.

The Examination by the Statutory Auditor (Article 727 of the Swiss Code of Obligations, et seq.)

The statutory auditor may not be a member of the board of directors or an employee of the company being audited. Fiduciary and accounting firms may act as statutory auditors. The statutory auditor is initially elected by the founders for one year and subsequently may be reelected by the general meeting of shareholders for terms of not more than three years.

A statutory auditor named in the deed of formation of a company must file a written consent with the Register of Commerce. The statutory auditor need not have any professional qualifications or meet any legal requirements; he is not considered an independent contractor as might be the case in the United States under similar circumstances, but he does have an essential role in the corporation as its controlling authority. The power and duties of the statutory auditor are discussed below.

Financial statements must be examined by the statutory auditor before they are submitted to the annual general meeting of the shareholders. Article 728 OR describes the duties of the statutory auditor as follows:

> The auditor determines whether the balance sheet and profit and loss statement agree with the books, whether the books are properly kept, and whether the information as to the operating results and the financial position of the company complies with the requirements of the law as to valuation and with any special provisions of the articles of association of the company.

The board of directors must make the books and supporting documents available to the auditors and, if requested, furnish explanations about the inventory and its valuation principles or any other matters pertinent to the examination.

The statutory auditor attends the general meeting of shareholders and he must submit a short-form report to the meeting wherein he states the results of his examination. Article 729 OR requires that this report recommend either the acceptance of the financial statements, with or without qualifications, or their rejection by referring them back to the directors. The statutory auditor also expresses his opinion as to the propriety of the directors' proposal regarding the appropriation of the profits. The report of the statutory auditor is important because the general meeting of shareholders cannot pass any resolution concerning the financial statements unless this report has been submitted to it.

The auditor's report need not be accompanied by the financial statements, but in common practice this is done.

Any deficiency in administration or any violation of provisions laid down by law or by the articles of association which are brought to light by the auditor in the course of his examination must be reported to the superior of the responsible person and to the chairman of the board, and in serious cases even to the general meeting. The auditor may be held responsible for any loss or damage resulting from an improper discharge of his duties.

Despite the responsibility given to the auditor and the heavy demands placed upon him by law, anyone can be appointed as statutory auditor because the law, as already mentioned, has not laid down any rules concerning the qualification of the person so appointed. Very often, professional accountants, or fiduciary and accounting firms, are appointed as statutory auditors.

The Examination by Independent Accountants (Article 723 of the Swiss Code of Obligations)

Since the lawmakers were aware of the inadequacies of many persons permitted to be elected statutory auditors, they wrote into law stricter auditing requirements for stock companies over a certain size in the interest of both the public and the creditors. In accordance with article 723 OR, the board of directors of a corporation is required to appoint an independent accountant to examine their company's financial statements in case their company has a share capital of 5,000,000 francs or more, has outstanding debentures, or solicits the deposit of money by the public.

In contrast to the statutory auditor, specialized knowledge and professional experience is required; however, the independent accountant does not have to be a certified accountant. Of course, certified accountants, fiduciary and accounting firms, or other organizations that meet the professional requirements and standards of independence can be named. The law does not make clear what type of examination is required of such independent accountants, but one may assume that the principles of examination mentioned in article 728 OR are also applicable in this case and that this examination is expected to be carried out in a professional manner.

The report of the independent accountants is to be submitted to the board of directors and to the company's statutory auditor and will usually be issued in long form and include detailed information on most items in the balance sheet and profit and loss statement and often also an outline of the audit procedures followed.

The Examination in the Event of a Reduction of the Share Capital (Article 732 of the Swiss Code of Obligations)

When share capital is reduced without being concurrently offset by new fully paid-in capital, the interests of the firm's creditors may be jeopardized. The law, therefore, requires that the general meeting of shareholders may not pass a resolution to reduce the company's share capital unless an audit report is presented which states that the demands of the creditors will be fully covered by the assets even after the share capital has been reduced.

The audit report must be prepared by either a fiduciary and accounting firm or a bank audit association which must have been approved for this purpose by the Swiss Federal Council and must be appointed by the board of directors.

Bank Audits

The federal law on commercial and savings banks of March 11, 1971, requires a close examination of the financial statements of commercial and savings banks consistent with their special position in the economy. The examination is to be effected yearly by either a bank audit association or a fiduciary and accounting firm which (a) meets the very strict requirements set out in the Decree of the Federal Council enacting regulations in connection with the federal law on commercial and savings banks of March 11, 1971, (b) has been officially recognized by the Federal Banking Commission, and (c) is on the special panel of bank auditors. The bank auditors must prepare a detailed long-form report in which all the matters set out in detail in the enacting decree are dealt with.

In case the statutory auditor and the special bank auditor are identical, he is elected by the shareholders in general meeting; otherwise the statutory auditor is elected by the general meeting and the special bank auditor is appointed by the board of directors. In case a bank wishes to change its special bank auditor, it must advise the Banking Commission giving full particulars of the reasons for the proposed change in consequence of which the Banking Commission may object to the change.

Auditing Standards

General Standards

The Schweizerische Treuhand–und Revisionskammer has not yet promulgated any compilation of generally accepted auditing standards, but in the Auditing Handbook of Switzerland it deals with measurement of the quality of performance of auditing procedures and the objectives to be attained in the employment of the procedures undertaken.

Although the statutory auditor may not be a director or an employee of the company being audited, he may be a shareholder or have some other financial interest in the company. Only in the case of bank audits is the auditor required to be absolutely independent. Article 730 of the Swiss Code of Obligations states that auditors may not divulge any information obtained in carrying out their duties to individual shareholders or to third parties.

Standards of Field Work

There is no statute which defines auditing procedures in Switzerland, nor are there any other standards promulgated similar to those of the American Institute of CPAs. The following differences in auditing procedures exist in Switzerland:

1. Accepted practice does not require the Swiss auditor to request direct confirmations of bank balances, accounts receivable, and accounts payable or to observe the taking of physical inventories unless specifically asked to do so. The Swiss auditor satisfies himself as to the correctness of the bank balances, the validity of accounts receivable and payable balances, and the completeness and correct evaluation of the inventory by tests of the company's available records. In the new Auditing Handbook of Switzerland, reference is, however, made to the performance of the above procedures as parts of an adequate examination.
2. The accounting system and the system of internal control are only studied to the extent necessary to write the audit program and to determine the amount of testing required. Although the review of a system of internal control is not mandatory, the handbook points out that the effectiveness of the system of internal control is of importance in determining the scope of the examination; the handbook also contains an internal control evaluation guide.
3. The auditors will generally rely on verbal confirmations by the management that the financial statements include all the assets and liabilities of the company. The handbook recommends that the auditors request the following representation letter from the management:

> We make the following representations in connection with your examination of the yearly financial statements of our company as at ....:
>
> 1. To the best of our knowledge and belief the books and records we have submitted to you comprise all accountable transactions of the financial year ....
> 2. All accountable assets are included in the balance sheet. All recognizable losses thereon have been duly considered in their valuation.
> 3. Apart from the liabilities appearing in the balance sheet there are no other liabilities, in particular no contingent liabilities in the sense of article 670, par. 1 OR. Adequate provisions have been made for all recognizable risks.
> 4. The changes in the undisclosed reserves known to us have been reported to you in accordance with article 663, par. 3 OR.

5. We declare that to the best of our knowledge and belief we have given you all the information and explanations and that we have put at your disposal all the vouchers and documents which may be of importance for an appreciation of the economic and financial position of the company at the balance sheet date and/or at the time of the examination. These are, in particular: Bonds of security, transfers of title and encumbrances, assignments, etc., and law suits of any importance; pension commitments which are not covered by provisions or by capital funds of the foundation; events subsequent to date of financial statements.

Standards of Reporting

The standards of reporting by the statutory auditor have been established by article 729 of the Swiss Code of Obligations, which requires that the auditor certify that (a) the financial statements truly reflect the company's financial condition as shown by the books, (b) that the books have been properly kept, and (c) that the results of operations and the financial position of the company are shown in conformity with legal and statutory valuation principles.

The statutory auditor must recommend either acceptance of the financial statements with or without reservations or rejection of them by returning them to the board of directors. He must also state whether or not the recommendations made by the board of directors as to the appropriation of the available profits are in accordance with the requirements of law. In 1969, the Schweizerische Treuhand–und Revisionskammer recommended that its members use the following standard form of unqualified auditor's report:

Report of the Auditors to the General Meeting of ....
Company

As auditor(s) of your company, I (we) have examined the accounts for the year ended .... in accordance with the provisions of the law.

I (we) have come to the conclusion that
– the balance sheet and profit and loss account are in agreement with the books
– the books of accounts have been properly kept
– the financial position and the results of operations are presented in accordance with the principles of evaluation prescribed by the law and the requirements of the statutes.

Based on the result of my (our) examination. I (we) recommend that the accounts submitted to you be approved.

I (we) further confirm that the proposal(s) of the board of directors for the disposal of the available profits is (are) in agreement with the law and the statues.

Name and Signature

Enclosures:
Balance sheet
Profit and loss account
Disposal of profit

The statutory auditor who is not a professional accountant will usually submit only this report, whereas a certified accountant acting as statutory auditor will often supplement this report with a long-form report. The latter will include the discussion of his findings and an analysis of the various important balance sheet and profit and loss account items. This long-form report is only intended for the board of directors and not for the shareholders. Occasionally, the long-form report includes a description of the audit procedures followed although no rule requires this.

In the case of the report of the independent accountant acting under the provisions of article 723 OR, the audit procedures followed would often be described, since there are no generally accepted auditing standards to which reference can be made. Moreover, the report prepared under the provisions of article 723 OR must not only be presented to the board of directors, but also to the statutory auditor, when the latter is not identical with the independent accountant required by the law.

Consistency

In the application of accounting principles, consistency is not expressly required by the Swiss Code of Obligations or any other regulations. Consistency as a principle is in conflict with the accepted accounting practices in Switzerland relating to the right to set up, increase, or decrease undisclosed reserves. The law does not require disclosure in the annual accounts of the basis on which the amounts or individual items are stated; in particular, the existing amount of undisclosed reserves and the increase or decrease therein in each year need not be indicated. The statutory auditors must be informed of the variations in undisclosed reserves, but unless they are so authorized by the board, they are not allowed to refer thereto in their report to the shareholders.

Materiality

Although the principle of materiality is never expressly stated, the auditor, whether a statutory auditor or an independent accountant (or one acting in both capacities) must decide whether, giving full consideration to the surrounding circumstances, there are certain material and significant items which should be disclosed either orally, or by reference thereto in the long-form report, or by qualification of his short-form opinion.

Directors' Report (Business Report)

The directors must submit to the general meeting a written business report on the financial position, the operations, and the results of the company for the year under review.

This report should also include a proposal concerning the payment of dividends and the disposition to be made of the remaining balance of retained earnings. The business report is not subject to examination by the statutory auditors.

Accounting Principles and Practices

Form and Content of Financial Statements

The accounting rules and practices in Switzerland are based on the applicable articles of the Swiss Code of Obligations. In addition, the Schweizerische Treuhand–und Revisionskammer and the professional accounting organizations actively promote the application of generally accepted accounting principles.

Statement Presentation. All businesses required to keep books must prepare a balance sheet and a profit and loss account (supported by adequate details) within a reasonable time after the end of each financial year. The form and presentation of annual accounts is left to the discretion of those responsible except in the case of banks, mutual funds and their management companies, insurance companies, and railways.

The annual accounts must be expressed in Swiss currency, prepared in accordance with generally recognized commercial principles, and be complete, true, and clear. The usual arrangement of the financial statements is for assets to be shown on the left side and liabilities and capital on the right side. The financial statements must be signed by the proprietors, general partners, directors, or managers as the case may be.

The order of the items in the balance sheet is usually in accordance with their liquidity, as can be seen from the following:

Assets

Cash on hand and in banks

Accounts receivable

Raw materials

Finished goods and work in process

Furniture and fixtures

Machinery and equipment

Buildings

Investments

Prepaid expenses, etc.

Patents

Liabilities

Accounts payable

Accrued liabilities

Medium- and long-term liabilities

Retained earnings

Legal reserve

Special reserve

Share capital

However, the order of listing in which the asset side begins with fixed assets and the liability side with share capital is also seen frequently. It should also be noted that the valuation allowances such as for bad debts, depreciation, and the like are often included under liabilities rather than deducted from the related asset.

There is no uniform practice as to form or presentation of the profit and loss statement in Switzerland. Often sales and cost of sales are shown separately, but sometimes only the gross profit on sales is shown.

Legal Rules of Valuation. Assets may not be valued at more than their worth to the business. The law specifies valuation principles applicable only to joint stock companies, private limited liability companies, and partnerships partially limited by shares, as follows:

1. Formation and organization expenses, including stamp duty on capital, can be charged directly to profit and loss or may be deferred and amortized over a maximum of five years.
2. Fixed assets may not be valued at more than cost, less appropriate provisions for depreciation. If such items are insured against fire risks, the total sum covered by insurance must be indicated on the

balance sheet. When money is borrowed to finance the construction of new facilities, interest charges or loan discounts may be capitalized. Although, according to article 665 of the Swiss Code of Obligations, a revaluation of land and buildings and other fixed asset items is not permitted, in practice the view that exceptions from the legal maximum valuation provisions can be tolerated under the following circumstances and conditions, is considered defensible—

a. in case of an evident, material, and lasting excess value, which, for instance, in the case of land and buildings, should be confirmed by an objective and prudent appraisal of its market value;

b. the revaluation profit is shown separately in the profit and loss account;

c. the revaluation profit is used to cover a loss or to write down overvalued assets; and

d. the revaluation is explicitly mentioned in the report of the statutory auditor.

3. Intangible assets must be valued at cost less appropriate amortization.

4. The valuation of inventories (raw materials, supplies, work in process and finished goods) may not exceed cost or market, whichever is the lower. Companies which maintain complete inventory records with sufficient details of quantities and prices and basis for such prices, may value inventories for tax purposes at a minimum value of up to one-third below cost, or market, whichever is lower.

5. The maximum valuation of quoted securities is the average quoted price during the month preceding the balance sheet date; if securities are quoted only outside Switzerland, transfer and other restrictions must be taken into account.

6. Unquoted securities and investments may not be valued at more than cost adjusted for either accrued income (current interest or dividends) or diminution in value on account of losses or otherwise. The view, mentioned above, regarding the revaluation of fixed assets is also applicable in the case of investments.

7. The aggregate of redemption prices of debenture bonds must be shown as a separate item on the liability side of the balance sheet. The difference between the issue price and the amount payable on redemption may be deferred and amortized by annual installments until the date of redemption of the latest to mature. Premiums payable on equal annual redemption installments may be charged against the earnings of the year in which they are due.

Information to Be Included in Accounts

1. Unpaid capital must be shown on the balance sheet as an asset as it represents a claim of the company against the shareholders.
2. Contingent liabilities, guarantees, and assets pledged or hypothecated must be noted on the balance sheet showing the total amount for each group.
3. Provision must be made in the accounts for anticipated losses arising from guarantees, and so forth, or from the fulfillment, or inability to fulfill, sale or purchase commitments and similar transactions.
4. Important subsequent events should be disclosed in the body of the report rather than in footnotes, which are generally not used in Swiss reports.

Depreciation

Depreciation may be applied on cost less accumulated depreciation (declining balance method). On this basis, normal depreciation rates accepted by most of the cantonal and the federal tax authorities would be 20 percent for office furniture and fixtures, 25 percent for industrial machinery, and 30 percent for motor vehicles. Frequently, too, depreciation is based on cost; in which case, the rates used would be half of the above rates. The tax authorities may permit considerably higher rates of depreciation. Because of inflationary trends in the Swiss construction industry, the tax authorities may, in special cases, allow the depreciation of real property before it is placed in service. Otherwise, depreciation commences when such property is placed in service.

Pooling of Interests

The "pooling of interests" concept has no accounting significance in Switzerland. Regardless of the type of merger, the assets of the merged company are recorded in the books of the merging company in accordance with tax regulations.

Undisclosed Reserves

The valuation principles set out above only indicate upper limits for the valuation of assets. The law does not require disclosure in the annual accounts of the basis on which the amounts of individual items are stated. Company law specifically permits the board or management, at its discretion, to undervalue assets in the balance sheet or to set up hidden or secret reserves with a view to insuring the continued prosperity of the company or permitting the distribution of uniform dividends. The existence and the amounts of undisclosed reserves, and amounts set aside or released in the year, need not be reported. The statutory auditors must be informed of the variations in undisclosed reserves, but unless they are so authorized by the board, they are not allowed to refer thereto in their report to the shareholders.

Legal Reserve

Under Swiss law, companies must appropriate at least 5 percent of annual profits until the reserve is equal to 20 percent of the paid-in capital. If dividends and/or similar distributions exceed 5 percent of the paid-in capital, the equivalent of 10 percent of such excess must also be transferred from profit and loss account to legal reserve. Share premiums must be credited to the legal reserve unless they are used for depreciation or amortization of assets or for staff welfare purposes. To the extent that the legal reserve does not exceed the equivalent of one-half of the authorized capital, it can be used only to cover losses or maintain the company in times of adverse business conditions.

The requirement in respect of transfer to legal reserve of the equivalent of 10 percent of dividends in excess of 5 percent and the limitation of the use of the legal reserve are not applicable to companies whose main object is the holding of investments (holding companies).

Liability for Income Tax

The income tax system in most of the Swiss cantons is one in which the taxes due and levied in a year are determined on the basis of the prior year's income. Therefore, the amount accrued for income taxes at the end of a fiscal year in Switzerland is that based on the income of the prior year. No accrual is made for taxes based on income of the current year, since there is no legal liability for tax on that year's income at the current balance sheet date although there is a liability in the economic sense.

A determination of the tax liability is complicated in Switzerland since the Confederation and many cantons compute taxes on the average income of a two-year period preceding a two-year assessment period, and also because tax payments are deductible for purposes of federal and certain cantonal income taxes.

Publication of Annual Accounts

Only banks and insurance companies are required to publish annual accounts (in condensed form) in the *Swiss Official Journal of Com-*

merce; other companies may do so if they wish. Swiss companies with large numbers of shareholders usually have the accounts and directors' report printed and circulated.

Requirements for Listing Securities on the Stock Exchange and Public Sale of Securities

Sale of shares and debentures of a joint stock company to the public is ordinarily handled through one or a group of commercial banks. The Swiss Code of Obligations prescribes the information which must be furnished in the prospectus in connection with an offer to sell securities. Since the offer to sell new securities is usually accompanied by an application for listing such securities for trading on the stock exchange, the prospectus must also conform with the requirements of the Federal Association of Stock Exchanges. The principal Swiss international stock exchanges are in Zurich, Basel, and Geneva, and there are a number of exchanges of domestic importance in other cities of Switzerland. The exchanges are governed by the Local Association of Stock Exchange Members and supervised by the Federal Association of Stock Exchanges.

The most important requirements for the prospectus are the following:

1. Name, domicile, and purpose of the company and date of its registration in the Register of Commerce.
2. Total outstanding share capital, surplus and reserves, classes of stock outstanding and voting rights.
3. Outstanding participation certificates, if any, and the voting rights attached thereto.
4. List of directors and names of statutory auditors.
5. Last balance sheet and profit and loss account together with auditor's certificate.
6. Details of dividends paid during the preceding five years, or from the inception of the company, respectively.
7. Details of debentures issued and outstanding.
8. Details of the resolution passed to issue the new shares offered for sale and subscription, total amount of issue, purpose of issue, and terms of issue.

9. Details of existing limitations on the payment of dividends, and of any existing preferential rights.

In addition, the company must issue a statement and publish a printed report on its operations to be placed at the disposal of shareholders and bondholders at the bank or banks through which the securities are being sold.

For the application for listing the securities for trading on the stock exchange, the above information prescribed by the Swiss Code of Obligations must be supplemented by the following additional data:

1. Details of the company's most important subsidiaries with a statement of their capital and bonded debt.
2. Summary of the company's operations in case more than six months have passed since the last ordinary shareholders' meeting.

The application must be accompanied by 12 copies of the prospectus, 12 copies of the last published annual report, and 12 copies of the articles of association as well as a facsimile of the share or debenture certificates. Thereafter the company has an obligation to submit annual reports to the Stock Exchange Association Committee and to notify the committee of any changes in the articles of association.

In order for a company's securities to be admitted for trading on a stock exchange, the total par value of the securities must be at least 500,000 francs for a domestic issue and 5,000,000 francs for a foreign issue. Where debentures are to be issued, the capital must be equal to the value of the debentures to be issued if under 1,000,000 francs and if over that amount, the capital must be at least 1,000,000 francs.

The company which applies for listing of its shares must have completed one year of operations and the financial report for that year should be available. Dividends and interest must be payable, free of bank charges, at the places where the securities are listed.

United Kingdom

United Kingdom

As of July 1973

Significant developments since the preparation of this chapter are presented, by country, in the section entitled "Addenda."

Forms of Business Organization

The forms of business organization familiar to U.S. readers are also found in the United Kingdom, as U.S. laws are generally derived from the British. There are, of course, significant differences, but the sole proprietorship, the partnership, and the limited liability company (corporation) are generally similar.

Companies

With the exception of certain special types of companies—for example, companies incorporated by Royal Charter—the formation and dissolution of all companies incorporated in the United Kingdom are controlled by the provisions of the Companies Acts of 1948 and 1967. All companies must file certain documents with the Registrar of Companies, an official of the Department of Trade and Industry. Such documents include the following:

1. The memorandum of association, which gives information concerning the company's external relations, for example—
    a. The name of the company.
    b. The authorized share capital and its division thereof into shares of a fixed amount; this precludes the issue of shares of no par value.
    c. Whether the liability of the members is limited.
    d. The objects of the company.
2. The articles of association, which give information concerning its internal affairs, for example—
    a. The rights of particular classes of shares; i.e., voting rights, dividend rights, and rights in dissolution.
    b. The election, duties, and powers of directors.
    c. The procedures to be adopted at meetings.
    d. The form share transfers are to take.

    (The Companies Act of 1948 includes model articles which apply to all U.K. companies except insofar as they are excluded.)
3. Notice of the address of the company's registered office.
4. Particulars of the directors and company secretary.
5. Particulars of charges on the company's assets.
6. An annual return containing matters specified in the Companies Act of 1948, a copy of the annual accounts as laid before the members in general meeting, and a certified copy of the report of the auditors thereon and the report of the directors.

It should be noted that these and other documents are available for public inspection and that it is the Department of Trade and Industry who carry out a "watchdog" function of the companies sector.

Management of a U.K. company is vested in its board of directors, who are appointed by the company's shareholders. Every company (by action of its members) must appoint an auditor or auditors to report to the members on the annual accounts submitted at the annual general meeting. To be eligible for appointment, the auditor must either be a member of one of certain specified accounting bodies or be authorized individually by the Department of Trade and Industry. Companies may be registered as—

1. A company limited by shares, in which the liability of a member to contribute to the company's assets is limited to the amount, if any, unpaid on his shares.
2. A company limited by guarantee, in which the liability of a member is limited to the amount which he has undertaken to contribute in the event of the company's being wound up.
3. An unlimited company in which the liability of a member is unlimited.

The majority of registered companies are companies limited by shares. The Companies Acts also distinguish between a public and a private company.

Public Company

This corporate body corresponds closely to the publicly held U.S. corporation. By definition, it is simply a company which is not a private company (defined later); there is no necessity for it to be a quoted company. While it must have at least seven members, there is no upper limit to the maximum number of shareholders. It must have at least two directors.

It is usual for a prospectus to be issued by a public company prior to its offering of shares or debentures for sale to the public. The fourth schedule of the Companies Act of 1948 prescribes the contents of this document which contains provisions similar to those required under the United States Securities Act of 1933. In certain other circumstances, a public company may be required to file a "statement in lieu of prospectus" the content of which is similar to a prospectus. Copies of these documents must be filed with the Registrar of Companies, where they are available for public inspection. The object of all these documents is to provide the investor or potential investor with a source of information about the company.

Private Company

The private company is one which, while generally found in circumstances similar to those of the closely held U.S. company, is not strictly comparable in a legal sense to any form of business organization prevalent in the United States. Under section 28 of the Companies Act of

1948, a private company is a registered company which by its articles of association—

1. Restricts the right of members to transfer their shares (this is usually done by requiring the directors' consent to each transfer).
2. Limits the number of members to 50 (exclusive of employees and past employees who have continued to be members).
3. Prohibits an invitation to the public to subscribe for any of its shares or debentures (thus a prospectus will never be issued by a private company, capital being usually raised privately from friends or relatives).

Any registered company whose articles do not contain all of the above three provisions is a public company. The private company has certain privileges, among which are these: it need have no more than two shareholders nor more than one director; it can commence business immediately upon incorporation, whereas a public company must first satisfy the provisions of section 109 of the Companies Act of 1948; it need not hold a "statutory meeting" or produce a "statutory report," which impose obligations on public companies with respect to the disclosure of full information as to the results of the formation of the company. Nevertheless the private company must still send annual accounts to its members and make an annual return to the Registrar of Companies. An auditor or auditors must be appointed under the same conditions as for a public company, and the same standards of reporting are required.

Branch of a Foreign Corporation

A foreign company wishing to establish a branch in the United Kingdom must first obtain formal Treasury Department approval through the latter's agent, the Bank of England. There must then be filed with the Registrar of Companies—

(a) the name and address of the person(s) resident in the United Kingdom upon whom legal process against the company may be served,

(b) particulars of the directors of the company,

(c) a certified copy of the company's charter and bylaws (if it is not in the English language, a certified translation of it is required) and

(d) a copy of subsequent annual accounts of the foreign company complying with the provisions of the Companies Acts.

In practice, accounts drawn up in accordance with the laws and procedures of a country where the accounting standards do not differ materially from those prevailing in the United Kingdom (for example, those of the United States) are accepted by the registrar.

Partnership

The Companies Act of 1948 provides that a partnership which is organized for the purpose of profit and has more than 20 partners must register as a company under the act. In the 1967 act, exemption from the above rule was granted to partnerships of specified professions including accountants. Partnerships in general are governed by the Partnership Act of 1890.

Business Records

Section 147 of the Companies Act of 1948 requires every company to keep proper books of account with respect to—

(a) all amounts received and expended and the matters in respect of which the receipt and expenditure takes place,

(b) all sales and purchases of goods, and

(c) the assets and liabilities of the company.

It states further that proper books of account will not be deemed to to be kept "if there are not kept such books of account as are necessary to give a true and fair view of the state of the company's affairs and to explain its transactions." Records may be kept in various forms provided adequate precautions are taken for guarding against falsification and for facilitating its discovery.

Other books required to be kept include registers of members, debenture holders, directors and secretaries (corporate), substantial holdings, directors' shareholdings and charges, and minutes of directors' and shareholders' meetings.

The Accounting Profession

General

The practice of accounting as a profession, as we know it today, was born in the United Kingdom beginning in the early or middle nineteenth century, although recognition of the "professional accountant" is implied by his employ on insolvency cases arising under the Scottish Bankruptcy Act of 1696. A directory of accountants was available in Edinburgh in 1773.

As a result of many business failures in earlier years, various methods of dealing with liquidations of bankrupt estates were enacted, culminating in the Bankruptcy Act of 1869, which in effect transferred the administration of insolvent estates to professional accountants. At first, therefore, accountancy practice was largely concerned with bankruptcies, liquidations, and receiverships. However, in 1883 a new Bankruptcy Act established the office of "Official Receiver," which led to some reduction in the involvement of the professional accountant in the settlement of insolvencies.

The decline in this type of work, however, was soon offset by increased demands for accounting and auditing work. The "company" form of organization became more prevalent and business enterprises larger. Such companies needed improved accounting methods and procedures to control their operations—services the professional accountants were able to supply. In addition, their area of examination was expanded in consequence of an increasing recognition that companies which raised capital from the public should provide their shareholders with accounts reported on by their auditors. This trend was accentuated by the requirement of the Companies Act of 1879 that banks must appoint auditors. The Companies Act of 1900 extended this requirement to all limited companies.

The first Royal Charter was granted in 1854 to the Society of Accountants of Edinburgh (since merged in 1951 with other Scottish bodies to form the Institute of Chartered Accountants of Scotland). The Institute of Chartered Accountants in England and Wales was incorporated by Royal Charter in 1880. These institutes have been the model for the accountancy profession in the countries comprising the Commonwealth, and have greatly influenced the development of the profession in many other countries. Some other accounting bodies have since been organized in the United Kingdom. Admission to and control over the activities of the members of these accounting bodies are in the hands of the organizations themselves.

The Chartered Accountant

The title "chartered accountant" may be used by persons obtaining membership of the Institutes of England and Wales, of Scotland, or of Ireland. The discussion which follows indicates the requirements for membership of the Institute of England and Wales; those of Scotland and Ireland differ in minor details.

The practical experience requirement for membership in the Institute involves for graduates of U.K. universities, a period of three years and for nongraduates, four years, excluding an academic year at a polytechnic. This training period is spent in the office of a chartered accountant and is subject to a training contract (which has recently replaced the former articles of clerkship), the terms of which are subject to the rules of, and under the supervision of, the Institute. To be eligible to enter into a training contract, the student trainee must have reached the age of 17 and have met certain educational requirements. These are either a degree at a recognized university or, for a nongraduate, two passes at advanced level of the General Certificate of Education. For the nongraduate, attendance for a year at a recognized polytechnic and success in examinations giving exemption from the Institutes' Foundation Examination are also requirements. Student trainees need not be citizens of the United Kingdom. The selection of persons who wish to become student trainees (generally a maximum of four in service at any time per member) is made by the member who must be in public practice.

In addition to practical training, which is the responsibility of the member, the student trainee must pass the Foundation Examination, Professional Examination I, and Professional Examination II. Exemption is granted in respect of the Foundation Examination—

1. Where the student trainee has successfully completed a one-year foundation course at a recognized polytechnic.

2. Where a non-accounting graduate has successfully completed a 4½-month, approved full-time conversion course in accounting subjects.

3. Where the student trainee has graduated with an approved (accountancy related) degree.

The subjects covered in the examinations include bookkeeping, accounting (including management accounting and elements of financial decisions) auditing, taxation, executorship and trusteeship, costing, law, economics, statistics, and general financial knowledge.

Preparation for the examinations is the responsibility of the student trainee who is required to be a member of one of the chartered accountant student societies. These societies arrange lectures on accounting subjects and, in some cases, classes for instruction. Although the student should devote much of his out-of-office time to study, he will receive a minimum of 22, and a maximum of 26 weeks' study leave during the training contract, which is used for linked tutorial and correspondence course study and revision.

Organizations of Accountants

The Institute of Chartered Accountants in England and Wales is composed of members who, after serving as student trainees and after having passed certain examinations as outlined above, have been admitted as associates (ACA); and of those associates who have been admitted as fellows (FCA) after having either (a) been in public practice for at least five years or (b) completed ten years of membership in the Institute. However, in the future, the fellowship will be awarded only after certain optional post-qualification tests are passed. Membership may be suspended or revoked by the Disciplinary Committee of the Institute if the member is found to have violated any related provisions of the Royal Charters.

The Institute issues many publications, for example—

1. Statements of Standard Accounting Practice (a new series which is being added to and sets forth a practice generally expected to be followed by members of the Institute (see p. 611))
2. Recommendations on Accounting Principles
3. Statements on Auditing
4. Directives on "Professional Conduct"
5. A monthly magazine, *Accountancy*
6. Survey of Published Accounts—a synopsis of U.K. quoted company practice

The Institutes of Scotland and Ireland are similar to The Institute of Chartered Accountants of England and Wales in structure and in services to their members. The Scottish Institute recognizes services under articles with a member practicing as a public accountant in any part of the United Kingdom.

Admission to the Association of Certified Accountants is gained by examination after service either with a practicing accountant or in the finance and accounting department of a commercial or industrial company, in one of the nationalized industries or in local government, if that employment has been approved by the Council of the Association as providing accounting experience of adequate scope and character.

There are certain other organizations of accountants in the United Kingdom which serve specialized fields of accountancy. Examples are The Institute of Municipal Treasurers and Accountants and The Institute of Cost and Management Accountants.

Functions of the Chartered Accountant

The U.K. chartered accountant examines and reports upon financial statements of business enterprises. Every company formed under the provisions of the Companies Acts of 1948 and 1967 must appoint an auditor who is a member of an accountancy body recognized by the Department of Trade and Industry or who is individually authorized by the department as having similar qualifications obtained abroad or having experience specified in the act. The accountancy bodies so recognized are the three Chartered Institutes (England and Wales, Scotland, and Ireland) and the Association of Certified Accountants. Several hundred overseas accountants have also been individually authorized by the Department of Trade and Industry as having the requisite qualifications obtained abroad. The U.K. chartered accountant advises clients on tax matters, prepares returns, and discusses proposed changes in returns with the Inspector of Taxes. He provides management services of various kinds for his clients and undertakes special investigations for specific purposes on behalf of managements or for government departments.

There are some activities in which the U.K. chartered accountant often engages but which would not be customary for a CPA in the United States. He may act as a liquidator or receiver of a company or as a trustee in bankruptcy. He may do the work of the secretary of a company, act as a registrar and transfer agent of its shares and debentures, or as appraiser of shares (especially of private companies) for estate tax, for sale, and other purposes. He may also be required to report on statements prepared by his client to claim a government grant or in connection with a profit forecast.

Ethics

One of the primary objects of the Institute, as expressed in the Royal Charter of 1880, is to compel the observance of strict rules of conduct as a condition of membership. Rules similar to the American Institute of CPAs' code of ethics apply to members of the Institute (see later section on "Independence"). These regulations are embodied in the five fundamental rules included as clause 20 of the Supplemental Royal Charter of 1948, certain of the provisions of clause 21, and in various statements of the Council of the Institute to be found in the Members' Handbook.

The five rules of clause 20 of the charter may be briefly summarized:

1. A member will not allow a nonmember to practice in his name unless he is in partnership with that nonmember.
2. A member in practice will not share a fee with any person other than his partner, his employee, or a public accountant without the consent of his client.

3. A member in practice will not accept fees or profits of any person other than a public accountant or his employee without the consent of the client.
4. A member in employment may not carry on public accountancy work in his own name on behalf of an employer who is not a chartered accountant in practice but whose business is such as would ordinarily be performed by a member of the Institute in practice.
5. A member in practice may not carry on any business incompatible with the practice of accountancy.

Clause 21 of the charter provides for disciplinary action against a member who (condensed)—

1. Violates any fundamental rule of the Institute applicable to him.
2. Has committed a felony, misdemeanor, or fraud.
3. Has been guilty of any act or default discreditable to a public accountant or a member of the Institute.
4. Is adjudged a bankrupt, fails to satisfy a judgment, or makes an assignment for the benefit of creditors.
5. Willfully commits any breach of the bylaws of the Institute.

The Council from time to time has issued statements bearing on matters of professional ethics affecting its members. Some of the more important of these cover the following subjects: changes in appointment of auditors, contingent fees, professional designations, publicity, practice as an incorporated company, special reports, relations with other professions, professional confidence, and independence.

Appointment of Auditors

The directors of a company may appoint the auditors at any time before the first annual general meeting of the shareholders, but if this is not done, the shareholders will appoint the auditors on that occasion. If the shareholders have not appointed auditors, the Department of Trade and Industry must be notified, and that department will cause the vacancy to be filled.

The shareholders of every company have the duty, at each annual general meeting, to appoint an auditor or auditors, who will hold office from that meeting until the conclusion of the next annual general meeting. Although the auditor is technically reappointed annually, it is not necessary that a resolution to that effect be passed at each annual general meeting, provided that there have been no positive steps to the contrary, that he is duly qualified, and that he has not given notice of his unwillingness to be reappointed. Directors may fill a vacancy in the office of auditor that occurs for reasons such as the death or incapacity of the auditor.

A change in auditors may be suggested by any shareholder, provided notice of the intention to propose a resolution to that effect is given not less than 28 days before the annual general meeting. The company must, at least 21 days before the meeting, notify the shareholders and the retiring auditor of this intention. The retiring auditor has the right to make representations in writing to the company, to have them sent to the shareholders, and to be present and to be heard at the general meeting on the resolution and on any other matters which concern him as auditor. While not covered in the Companies Acts, the rules of the Institute require that the proposed auditor communicate with the retiring auditor, primarily to determine whether there is any professional reason why the proposed engagement should not be accepted.

It is considered that when a firm of auditors is appointed, the appointment is of all the constituent partners, and that each must satisfy the requirements of the acts as to eligibility.

Remuneration of Auditors

The remuneration of the auditor is fixed by the company "or in such a manner as the company in general meeting determines." In practice, the company often delegates to the directors the duty of arranging the auditors' remuneration in consultation with the company's duly appointed auditors. The remuneration must be disclosed under a separate heading in the accounts. The remuneration here referred to is that for his work in his capacity as auditor; it does not refer to other types of accounting or tax work for which arrangements are made with the directors or other company officials.

Auditing Standards

General Standards and Standards of Field Work

While the Companies Acts lay down provisions relating to company law, company accounts disclosure requirements, and the general requirement that each set of accounts shall display a true and fair view, it is basically left to the profession itself to set auditing standards.

Statements on Auditing

There are a series of statements relating to auditing practice and audit reports. In the first of these statements, "General Principles of Auditing," matters are covered which in essence are dealt with under "General Standards" and "Standards of Field Work, section 310," in the American Institute's publication, Statement on Auditing Standards No. 1. The Institute of Chartered Accountants has always emphasized the need for training of personnel, due care in the performance of work, proper planning and supervision, the importance of internal control, and the obtaining of competent evidential matter. These matters are covered in the statement referred to and in many articles and discussions by members.

Inventories and Receivables

It is regarded as normal practice for the auditor to be present at inventory taking. Recommendation U9 of the Statement on Auditing, "Attendance at Stocktaking" states, "Therefore wherever it is practicable and stock-in-trade and work-in-progress is a material factor in the business, the auditors should satisfy themselves as to the effectiveness of the application of the client's stocktaking procedures by observation on a test basis of these procedures whilst the stocktaking is in progress."

Similarly, Recommendation U7 states, ". . . In the absence of any similarly properly controlled procedure carried out by the company itself, the auditors should consider direct communication with debtors as one of the means by which they can form an opinion as to the adequacy of the system of internal control over sales and its operation in practice."

Thus both these procedures are normally carried out by U.K. auditors as part of their battery of tests. However, if such tests are not carried out, no reference would normally be made to this fact in the auditors' report.

Liability Certificates and Other Representations of Management

Two directors are required to sign, on behalf of the board of directors, the U.K. statutory accounts presented to the annual meeting of stockholders. To a certain extent, this takes the place of the full letter of representation received by auditors in the United States. It is, however, the practice of most U.K. auditors to obtain certificates from management and directors concerning such items as stock valuation, outstanding liabilities, capital commitments, and directors' emoluments.

Independence

Paragraph 6 of the Institute's Statement on Auditing U1 states that (the auditors) "must approach their work as auditors with an independent outlook and must do nothing which would impair that independence." The fact that under the Companies Act of 1948 auditors are appointed by the shareholders, and not by directors or management, contributes to the independent status of the company's auditor. The Companies Act of 1948 also provides that none of the following will be qualified for appointment as auditor of a company:

1. An officer or servant of the company.
2. A person who is a partner of or in the employment of an officer or servant of the company.
3. A body corporate.
4. Any person disqualified under (1) or (2) for appointment as auditor of that company's parent company, subsidiary, or fellow subsidiary.

It is not lawful for one of the partners in the firm which serves as auditor to be a director of a client company.

There is no prohibition against the appointment as auditor of a person who is a blood relative of an officer of the company, nor against the auditor having a financial interest in the company. Some professional firms have taken the U.S. view and prohibit all partners and staff from holding an investment in client companies. Purchases or sales based on confidential information obtained in the course of an audit of the company would be considered misconduct, and such dealings are expected to be made criminal offenses in the Companies Act, a draft of which is expected in late 1973.

It is not usually considered that the independence of a firm is impaired if staff members other than those engaged on an audit of a client write up its books.

Standards of Reporting

The content of the auditors' report upon the accounts, i.e., the balance sheet and profit and loss statements submitted to the annual general meeting of shareholders of a company, is specified in section 14 of the Companies Act of 1967. The report must state whether in the auditor's opinion (a) the accounts comply with the Companies Acts of 1948 and 1967 and (b) the accounts give a true and fair view of the state of affairs and of the profit or loss for the year. It is also the duty of the auditors to carry out such investigations as will enable them to form an opinion as to the following matters (condensed): (a) whether proper books have been kept, (b) whether proper returns adequate for their audit have been received from branches not visited by them, (c) whether the accounts are in agreement with the books of account and returns, and (d) whether they have received all the information and explanations which they required. It is their duty to report on those matters, only if, in their opinion, these requirements have not been complied with. The absence of any comment in their report is, therefore, equivalent to a positive statement by the auditors that they have investigated and satisfied themselves on all these matters. There are also specific items which the auditors must include in their report if disclosure is not made in the accounts. These items mainly concern directors' emoluments and related matters.

The Institute of Chartered Accountants has suggested in the Members' Handbook a form of auditors' report which, in the opinion of counsel, satisfies the provisions of the 1948 and 1967 acts. There are a number of variations of the form in use, and it is usual to modify it where there are subsidiaries audited by others or where consolidated statements are prepared. In the former case the Institute stresses that the phrase "The accounts of some of the subsidiaries have been audited by other firms" does not relieve the parent company auditor from the obligation of forming an opinion on those accounts, and additional inquiries may be necessary.

Although there is no requirement that specific reference be made in the report to generally accepted auditing standards or to conformity with, and consistency of application of, generally accepted accounting principles, it is evident that these are important considerations in framing the report. The Institute's series, Statements of Standard Accounting Practice, defines accounting standards in specific areas and any departure from such a standard, whether justified or not, must be referred to in the auditor's report. Secondly, in the Statement of Standard Accounting Practice, "Disclosure of Accounting Policies," it is clear that accounting policies not covered by an accounting standard must be disclosed in the accounts where they affect items which are judged material or critical in relation to interpretation of the accounts. Examples of matters for which different accounting bases are recognized and which are not yet covered by an accounting standard or an exposure draft thereof include depreciation of fixed assets, research and development expenditure, and warranties for products or services. When preparing a report upon a U.K. subsidiary of a U.S. parent company, however, the auditor would usually, if required, issue a U.S. short-form report in addition to the U.K. statutory form.

Consistency

The Companies Act of 1967 provides that the profit and loss account shall show any material effect on any item therein affected by any change in the basis of accounting. If there has been such change, the auditor must cover it in his report unless it is shown on the face of the statements or in a footnote.

Disclosure of Subsequent Events

The British view is that the financial statements are issued as at a given date and that, in general, subsequent events should not be reflected in the accounts. Later information regarding such items as the valuation of receivables or inventories may be useful in determining their proper amounts at the balance-sheet date. Disclosure of subsequent events is usually considered necessary if such events are so material that informed decisions on financial matters cannot be made by shareholders without considering the accounts in light of these events. Subsequent events, such as disposal of a substantial part of the business, would normally be disclosed in the directors' report accompanying the accounts.

Dating of Audit Reports

The date of a U.K. statutory audit report does not have the same significance as its U.S. counterpart. The U.K. report is signed and dated after the accounts have been approved by the directors. This approval is confirmed by the signing of the balance sheet by two directors.

Accounting Principles and Practices

The establishment of "generally accepted accounting principles" in the United Kingdom is left largely to the accounting profession, except as provided for in the Companies Acts. Such principles are set forth in the Statements of Standard Accounting Practice, Recommendations on Accounting Principles, other pronouncements included in the Members' Handbook published by the Institute of Chartered Accountants in England and Wales, and publications of other professional accountants' societies. Whereas the Statements of Standard Accounting Practice are expected to be applied by the members, the Institute's Recommendations are not binding on its members and depend for recognition on their being generally accepted by the business community.

The standards prescribed by the Statements of Standard Accounting Practice have the approval of the three Chartered Institutes, the Association of Certified Accountants and the Association of Cost and Management Accountants. The Council of the Institute of England and Wales, for instance, expects members of the Institute who assume responsibilities in respect of financial accounts either as directors, auditors, or reporting accountants to observe accounting standards. Significant departures in financial accounts from applicable accounting standards should be disclosed and explained. The financial effect should be estimated and disclosed unless this would be impracticable or misleading in the context of giving a true and fair view. If the financial effects of departures from those standards are not disclosed, the reasons therefor should be stated.

Statements have been issued to date (July 31, 1973) on (a) accounting for the results of associated companies, (b) disclosure of accounting policies, and (c) earnings per share; exposure drafts on a considerable number of other subjects are outstanding. Statements on accounting practice are important reading for all those dealing with U.K. accounts.

In so far as they are not replaced by Statements of Standard Accounting Practice, Recommendations on Accounting Principles will continue in effect as guidance statements and indication of best practice. They are persuasive in intent and departures do not necessarily require disclosure.

Form and Content of Financial Statements

In the United Kingdom, the balance sheet and profit and loss account are most frequently presented in a vertical form; however, the horizontal form is still used for the balance sheet. Typically, the vertical form of the balance sheet is titled "Capital Employed" or "Net Assets Employed." The most usual order of presentation of assets in the balance sheet is to show fixed assets followed by intangible assets, investments, and current assets less current liabilities.

The content of financial statements is prescribed in various sections of the Companies Acts and in the second schedule to the 1967 act. As indicated previously, the auditor must state in his report whether the financial statements give the information required by the acts in the manner prescribed. The basic requirement as stated in section 149 of the 1948 act is that the balance sheet give a true and fair view of the state of affairs of the company at the close of its financial year, and that the profit and loss account give a true and fair view of its profit or loss for the financial year.

Comparative Statements. It is a statutory requirement that the preceding year's figures be given for both balance sheet and profit and loss items. The Institute recommends that where an item appears in a note to the statements, the corresponding amount for the previous year should also be shown.

Consolidated Statements. The presentation of the financial statements of a company which has subsidiaries is dealt with in the Companies Acts by requiring, subject to certain exceptions, the preparation of "group" accounts. In general this means "consolidated" financial statements, but section 151 of the 1948 act permits the directors to authorize variations if the same or equivalent information can be made available to the shareholders in another form: for example, several sets of financial statements dealing with the company and various groups of subsidiaries.

It is required that the parent company balance sheet be given in addition to the "group" accounts. A separate profit and loss account of the parent company is not required, if the consolidated profit and loss account shows how much of the consolidated profit or loss for the year was dealt with in the accounts of the parent company.

Where there are unconsolidated subsidiaries, the accounts must show the investment in and indebtedness of or to those subsidiaries as separate items. When all a group's subsidiaries are not dealt with in group accounts there must also be shown (a) the reasons why such subsidiaries are not dealt with in group accounts; (b) the net aggregate amount of those subsidiaries' profits or losses attributable to the holding company, but not dealt with in the group's accounts, distinguishing between the profit or losses of the current year and those of earlier years since acquisition; (c) information corresponding to that shown in (b) above, in respect of the profits and losses dealt with in the group's accounts; and (d) any material qualifications in the audit reports on the accounts of those subsidiaries. Only in certain restricted circumstances laid down by the acts is a company exempted from preparing group accounts in respect of all its subsidiaries.

The major exception to the preparation of group accounts is in the case of a holding company which is itself a wholly owned subsidiary of a U.K. company. In this case, it has been provided disclosure of the subsidiaries' profits and losses will be excused, provided that a statement is annexed showing that the value of the company's investment in its subsidiaries is no less than the figure stated in its balance sheet.

Excess (or Deficiency) of Cost of Investment Over Net Assets of Subsidiary at Date of Acquisition

When the cost of an acquired subsidiary's stock exceeds its net assets at the date of acquisition, U.K. practice is to classify such excess in the consolidated balance sheet as "goodwill," "net premium on acquisition of shares in subsidiaries," "cost of control," and so forth. Such goodwill may be written off either in whole or in part or retained in full in the group accounts. When it has been determined by independent appraisal that the fixed assets of the acquired subsidiary are understated on its books, it is considered acceptable to adjust the fixed assets' valuation on the books of the subsidiary at the time of acquisition, thus reducing or eliminating the goodwill arising in consolidation. (The same result would be attained in U.S. practice in a consolidation entry.)

When there are several subsidiaries, some of which in consolidation produce positive and some negative goodwill, it is customary in the United Kingdom to offset one against the other, to produce net "goodwill" which, if negative, would be included with "capital reserves" and the amount would be disclosed.

Pooling of Interests

U.K. accounting practice recognizes that the accounting treatment accorded an "acquisition" may be different from that accorded a "merger." The accounting technique referred to in the United States as a "pooling of interests" (applicable in certain circumstances when one company is acquired by or merged into another company) has been applied in the United Kingdom on a very limited number of occasions. An exposure draft entitled "Accounting for Acquisitions and Mergers" was issued by the Accounting Standards Steering Committee in January 1971, but, after receiving comments, the issue of a Statement of Standard Accounting Practice on the subject has been delayed. The exposure draft defined a merger as occurring on the amalgamation of two or more companies when all the following conditions are met (simplified):

1. The substance of the main business of the constituent companies continues in the amalgamated undertaking.
2. The relative sizes of the constituent companies, as measured in terms of equity voting rights in the amalgamated undertaking are similar.
3. The amalgamation is a result of an offer, the consideration for which is mainly in the form of shares.

In general, the accounting treatment for a merger is similar to that of the pooling concept, except that such treatment relating to the values assigned to shares acquired and those issued and the treatment of the resulting difference may not agree with the treatment accorded in the United States. Details of the possible alternate treatment acceptable in the United Kingdom are outside the scope of this study.

In the case of an acquisition, the accounting treatment would require that no pre-acquisition profits of the acquired company be distributed by the acquiring company.

Associated Companies

The first of the series of Statements of Standard Accounting Practice was entitled "Accounting for the Results of Associated Companies." While a consolidation procedure is used for companies with subsidiaries, a modified consolidation technique is used where the investing company holds interests in associated companies.

> A company (not being a subsidiary of the investing group or company) is an associated company of the investing group or company if (a) the investing group or company's interest in the associated company is effectively that of a partner in a joint venture or consortium or (b) the investing group or company's interest in the associated company is for the long term and is substantial (i.e. not less than 20 percent of the equity voting rights) and having regard to the disposition of the other shareholdings, the investing group or company is in a position to exercise a significant influence over the associated company.
>
> In both cases it is essential that the investing group or company participates (usually through representation on the board) in commercial and financial policy decisions of the associated company, including the distribution of profits.

Subject to certain exceptions, the consolidated profit and loss account of the investing group should show its share of the profits less losses of associated companies before tax, the tax attributed to its share of profits of the associated companies, its share of extraordinary items, and its share of net profit retained by associated companies. In the consolidated balance sheet, the investment in associated companies should be shown (unless a valuation is used) at (a) the cost of the investments less any amounts written off and (b) the investing groups' share of post-acquisition retained profits and reserves of the associated company.

Full details of the treatment to be adopted will be found in the standard published by the Accounting Standards Steering Committee. It will be seen that the above is basically the equity method, and the treatment is similar to that required by APB Opinion No. 18.

Current Assets

Loans to Directors, Officers, and Employees. Except under certain conditions, loans to a director may not be made, other than advances for expenditures incurred or to be incurred by him in connection with his duties as director.

The amount of loans made to and loans repaid by a director or officer during the year must be disclosed in the financial statements, unless the loan is one made in the ordinary course of business by a company whose business includes the lending of money. Loans to employees for the purpose of purchasing fully paid shares in the company, or its holding company, should be disclosed in aggregate.

Inventories. The manner in which stock-in-trade or work-in-progress is computed should be shown if the amount is material for the understanding by the members of the company's state of affairs or profit or loss for the financial year. An exposure draft of a Statement of Standard Accounting Practice, issued for discussion purposes to members of the profession and industry, has proposed that inventories be stated at cost including fixed and variable overhead addition but not in excess of net realizable value (unless such a basis would be incompatible with the requirement that accounts show a true and fair view). The comparison of cost and net realizable value should be made in respect of each item of stock separately. Where this is impracticable, groups or categories of similar stock items may be taken together. In the case of long-term contracts, an appropriate portion of conservatively estimated profit should be added to cost. It remains to be determined whether this exposure draft will emerge unaltered as a Statement of Standard Accounting Practice.

Fixed Assets

Fixed assets should be disclosed under appropriate categories. The statement should show movements on fixed assets and state the method used to arrive at the disclosed figure.

While the Institute's Recommendation on Accounting Principles No. 15, "Accounting in Relation to Changes in the Purchasing Power of Money," continues to favor historical cost as the basis for reporting fixed assets, there is no prohibition against substituting values based on independent appraisals. The increment resulting from an upward appraisal of fixed assets is usually credited direct to reserves. There are differing legal decisions on the question whether or not a company is permitted to distribute a surplus of this kind; however, the reserve so created may be utilized for distribution of bonus shares. Subsequent depreciation should be computed and charged to income on the higher appraised values of the fixed assets and an appropriate part of reserves released to income. For tax purposes, capital allowances (depreciation) are permitted only on cost and at rates prescribed by the revenue authorities.

The Companies Acts require that the method or methods used to arrive at the amount of fixed assets under each heading will be stated.

Where fixed assets are included at a valuation, a note should show the year or years of valuation, and, for assets valued during the period covered by the accounts, the bases of valuation and the names of the valuers or their qualifications should be stated.

Interest and Overhead During Construction

Except in the case of businesses engaged in property development, "interest during construction" is rarely charged to the cost of fixed assets in the United Kingdom, and if charged, the amount is based on interest actually paid. The cost of fixed assets constructed by the company's employees usually includes overhead applicable to the work.

Goodwill and Other Intangibles

Unless circumstances indicate that these items should be written down in order to present a true and fair view of the accounts, they may either be retained in the accounts at cost or written down by a charge to the profit and loss account or to reserves. There is no standard practice for dealing with goodwill and no requirement that it be written off over a set number of years. However, whatever treatment is followed, it should be disclosed if the amount is material. If it is included in fixed assets, the basis used to arrive at the amount of goodwill is required to be shown.

Debt Discount and Expense

These items are usually written off to the profit and loss account when they are incurred, although the method of amortization over the life of the related issue is permissable. The 1948 act permits a charge to share premium account.

Organization (Preliminary) Expenses

Preliminary expenses are required by the 1948 act to be separately stated in the balance sheet "so far as they are not written off." There is no requirement for amortization of this type of deferred item, but it is usually written off over a short period or charged to share premium account if one is available.

Liabilities

Liabilities and provisions should be classified under headings appropriate to the business. Specific items for disclosure include (1) particulars of any charge on the assets of the company (usually shown by way of a note), (2) taxation, (3) the basis on which any amount set aside for taxation is computed, (4) bank loans and overdrafts, (5) borrowings with details of repayment dates, (6) intergroup indebtedness, (7) proposed dividend, (8) contingent liabilities shown by way of note, and (9) future capital expenditure—showing the estimated amounts (if material) contracted for but not provided for and authorized by the directors but not contracted for.

Liability Under Long-Term Leases

It is not usual to disclose liabilities on long-term leases in U.K. financial statements.

Pension Liability

The Institute of Chartered Accountants in England and Wales recommends that, where there is an obligation to provide pensions or other retirement benefits which are not covered by contributions to a retirement benefits plan, provision should be made for the related liability if the amount is material. Alternatively, if no such provision has been made, disclosure of the facts should be made in a footnote to the financial statements. If, at the time a pension plan is established, the cost of past service has not been provided and paid in full, the amount of such unpaid cost should be disclosed in the financial statements of each succeeding year until the total of such cost is paid or provided for.

Provisions and Reserves

The Companies Acts distinguish between balance-sheet items entitled, respectively, "provisions" and "reserves." The source of a "provision" is a charge against current income in arriving at profits; the source of a "reserve" is an appropriation of profits. A provision may either represent a valuation allowance (for bad debts, depreciation, and so forth) or an amount to provide for a known liability the amount of which "cannot be determined with substantial accuracy." If the amount could be reasonably determined, it would be classified as an accrued liability.

Reserves should be classified under headings appropriate to the company's business. The former division of reserves into revenue reserves and capital reserves no longer has any statutory basis and it is a growing practice to amalgamate these reserves under one heading. Movements in reserves stating the source of any increase and the application of any decrease should be disclosed. The following reserves must be specifically disclosed: (1) share premium account and (2) capital redemption reserve fund.

Share Premium. The Companies Acts provide that the share premium account (premium on capital stock paid in), which is a nondistributable reserve, may only be applied in the following ways: (a) paying up an issue of bonus shares (stock dividend); (b) writing off preliminary expenses or the expenses of an issue of shares or debentures; and (c) providing the premium payable on the redemption of any redeemable preference shares or debentures of the company. The share premium account is otherwise treated as part of the share capital of the company which cannot be reduced or repaid without consent of the court under an approved capital reduction scheme.

Capital Redemption Reserve Fund. The acts also provide that when redeemable preference shares are redeemed out of profits, an amount equivalent to their par value must be transferred from profit and loss to "capital redemption reserve fund." This reserve may be utilized only for the issue of "bonus shares" (stock dividend).

Redeemable preference shares may also be redeemed out of the proceeds of a new issue, in which case no transfer is made to capital redemption reserve fund. If such shares are redeemed at a premium, the premium must be charged to profit and loss, or against the existing balance of a prior share premium account.

Secret Reserves. The acts prohibit the creation of "secret reserves" by requiring disclosure of the additions to and the reductions of each reserve under individual headings. Further, the provision for depreciation, renewals, or diminution in value of assets, or provisions for any known liability which is in excess of that which, in the opinion of the directors, is reasonably necessary for the purpose, must be shown as a reserve and not as a provision.

Exemption is granted from the above restrictions to banking, discount, assurance, and certain types of shipping companies. The Department of Trade and Industry may permit companies not to disclose certain reserves if satisfied that such disclosure would be prejudicial to the company's interests. In cases where such companies maintain secret reserves, the accounts would not show a true and fair view, and the auditors' report would accordingly omit any reference to a true and fair view.

Stock Options

Stock options are sometimes granted in the United Kingdom. The Companies Acts require that, in such cases, there be disclosed in the annual accounts by a note or in a statement or report annexed thereto, the number, description, and amount of shares under option, the period during which the option is exercisable, and the price to be paid for shares under such option.

Stock Dividends

In the United Kingdom, bonus shares (stock dividends) are accounted for at par by the issuer, and the amount thereof would be charged to reserves. They are usually substantial in amount and are not issued in lieu of cash dividends. No adjustment is made in the book amount of investments when stock dividends are received by a corporation.

Foreign Currencies

The basis of translation of foreign currencies should be shown where the amount of the assets or liabilities affected is material. In the United Kingdom, the current rate method of translation is used rather than the historical rate employed in the United States.

Profit and Loss Statement

The format of a U.K. profit and loss account is similar to that of a U.S. profit and loss account, although there are certain specific differences in treatment and disclosure. The items required to be shown include the following.

Sales and Cost of Sales. It is a requirement that turnover should be shown, and that where shown, a definition of turnover should be given. Turnover need not be shown in the case of banks and discount companies or small companies which are not part of a group and whose turnover is less than 250,000 pounds. Cost of sales is rarely disclosed.

Income

1. Income from rents (if forming a substantial part of the company's revenue).
2. Income from investments distinguishing between income from quoted and unquoted investments.

Charges

1. The amount charged to revenue for depreciation, renewals, or diminution in value of fixed assets. Other disclosure requirements relating to depreciation are usually dealt with in the notes to the accounts to which the profit and loss account will be referenced. These requirements are dealt with later.
2. The amount of interest payable showing separately—
   a. Interest on bank loans, overdrafts, and loans repayable within five years.
   b. Interest on all other loans.

3. The amounts charged to revenue for hire of plant and machinery, if material.
4. The remuneration of the auditors (including reimbursed expenses).
5. Directors' emoluments should be disclosed in aggregate in the accounts or notes annexed thereto. There must be included in this figure all amounts received from the company and its subsidiaries for services, including such of their expenses as are charged and treated as emoluments for income tax purposes, together with any contributions under any pension plan scheme. These amounts must distinguish between sums received as a director and other emoluments, such as those received as a salaried officer. Other disclosure requirements relating to directors' emoluments are usually dealt with in the notes to the accounts. These requirements are covered later.

Taxation. The amounts of charges for taxation on profits and the basis on which the charge for U.K. taxation is computed should be disclosed.

Extraordinary and Prior Year Items. An exposure draft of a statement of standard accounting practice (ED 7), "Accounting for Extraordinary Items" has been issued, but the final version may well reflect changes before it receives official approval from the Institutes. The exposure draft's proposals for the definition and treatment of extraordinary items are almost identical to those adopted by APB Opinion No. 9. The proposals for prior year items, however, these being defined as "adjustments relating to previous accounting periods which could not have been quantified or reasonably foreseen at the time in question," are that they be dealt with through the profit and loss account in the year in which they are recognized and, if appropriate, disclosed as extraordinary items according to their nature. Thus the profit and loss account should show a net profit or loss after extraordinary items reflecting all profits and losses recognized in the accounts of the year other than unrealized surpluses on the revaluation of fixed assets, which should be credited to reserves.

Appropriations of Profits

1. The amounts provided for redemption of redeemable preference shares and for redemption of loans.
2. The amount set aside or proposed to be set aside to, or withdrawn from, reserves.
3. The aggregate amount of dividends paid or proposed.

Earnings Per Share. The third Statement of Standard Accounting Practice requires that the audited accounts of quoted companies should disclose, on the face of the profit and loss account, the earnings per share before extraordinary items. The basis of computing the earnings per share should also be given. Where there is a potential dilution of 5 percent or more attributable to conversion of (for example) outstanding convertible loan stock, the accounts should disclose the earnings per share giving effect to such dilution.

Directors' Emoluments. There shall also be disclosed (a) the number of directors whose emoluments (excluding pension contributions) fall in each bracket of a scale in multiples of 2,500 pounds, (b) the emoluments (excluding pension contributions) of the highest paid director if in excess of the chairman, (c) the emoluments (excluding pension contributions) of the chairman, and (d) the number of directors who have waived the right to receive emoluments and aggregate amount thereof. None of these disclosure requirements apply to a company which is neither a holding company nor a subsidiary company and the aggregate directors' emoluments of which shown in its accounts do not exceed 15,000 pounds. Items (a) and (b) do not apply to directors whose duties were wholly or mainly outside the United Kingdom.

More Highly Paid Employees. There shall be disclosed the emoluments of employees receiving more than 10,000 pounds per annum (excluding pension scheme contributions), showing in the accounts the number of employees whose emoluments fall in each bracket of a scale in multiples of 2,500 pounds starting at 10,000 pounds. There shall be excluded employees working wholly or mainly outside the United Kingdom.

Depreciation and Depletion. The straight-line method is the most common method of computing depreciation; however, the reducing balance method is also used.

The Institute recommends that if additional provisions are made for obsolescence that cannot be foreseen, or for a possible increase in cost of replacement, they should be treated as appropriations of profits to a reserve not available for distribution.

Provision for depletion of wasting assets (mines, wells, quarries, etc.), is recommended by the Institute, and if the practice of a particular company is not to make such provision, it should be made clear to the shareholders that dividends distributed to them are, in part, a return of capital.

It is a statutory requirement that if the charge for depreciation, renewals, or diminution in value of fixed assets is provided by some method other than depreciation or provision for renewals, or is not provided for, then the method used or the fact that it is not provided must be disclosed. In addition to the statutory requirement, it is generally accepted that a company's depreciation policy is one of the significant matters for which different accounting bases are recognized, and as such it will usually be disclosed following Statement of Standard Accounting Practice, "Disclosure of Accounting Policies." It is likely that an exposure draft of a Statement of Standard Accounting Practice on depreciation will be issued in the near future.

Statement of Changes in Financial Position

There is no statutory requirement that such a statement be published. This statement, usually styled "a source and application of funds statement," is rarely provided in the United Kingdom, but its use is increasing. Where the statement is presented for a U.K. company, the auditors would not normally refer to it in their report. It is anticipated, however, that the forthcoming Standard on this subject will require that all companies listed on the stock exchange provide this statement and that it will be covered by the auditor's report.

Provision for Corporation Tax

The financial year for U.K. corporation tax begins on April 1st. For each financial year a corporation tax rate is fixed, and the rates for the appropriate financial years are applied pro rata to the taxable profits of the company according to which financial year the profits of its own accounting period fall. For this purpose a straight-line basis is used.

The taxable profit need not be the same as the profit disclosed in the accounts. Examples of adjustments usually made are those in respect of capital allowance for fixed assets, nondeductible expenses, and dividends from organizations also subject to corporation tax.

The Companies Act of 1967 requires that companies disclose "the basis on which the amount, if any, set aside for U.K. corporation tax is computed." It also requires that "if an amount is set aside for the purpose of its being used to prevent undue fluctuations in charges for taxation, it shall be stated." Recommendation N. 27 of the English Institute recommends that "the liability for corporation tax on the profits of the period covered by the accounts should be disclosed either as an item of current liabilities or as a separate item with the due date for payment shown. Corporation tax for earlier periods not yet paid should normally be shown under current liabilities."

Deferred Taxation Accounts

An exposure draft has recently been issued on this subject which requires that "taxation expense be based on the profit stated in the accounts rather than on the profits assessed to taxation and should therefore include the tax effects of timing differences." The exposure draft recommends that the deferred taxation account be maintained on a modified deferral method. It is modified to the extent that it is only acceptable to set up a debit deferred tax balance if it is considered with reasonable certainty that the amount will be recovered in the foreseeable future. No proposal exists to separate the current portion of the deferred tax balance from the noncurrent as is practiced in the United States. At present, most U.K. companies maintaining a deferred taxation account do so on the liability method rejected by APB Opinion 11. The exposure draft is therefore likely to meet with much opposition.

Directors' Report

It is compulsory under the Companies Acts to attach to every balance sheet laid before the company in general meeting a report by the directors with respect to the company's affairs.

The contents of this report are specified by the Companies Act of 1948, section 147, and the Companies Act of 1967, sections 16 to 22. It should include the recommended dividend; proposed transfers to reserves; directors' names; principal activities of the company; significant changes in fixed assets; information relating to material differences in the book and market value of land and buildings held; the number of shares issued in the year, consideration received therefor, and the reason for making such issue; directors' interests in any contract with the company, in shares of the company, and their rights to acquire shares; analysis of turnover; average number of employees; aggregate remuneration of employees; political and charitable donations; exports; and any other matters so far as material for the appreciation of the company's state of affairs and not harmful to the business of the company.

Requirements for Listing Securities on the Stock Exchange and for Prospectuses Under the Companies Acts

Since in almost all cases the issuance of a prospectus in connection with an offer to sell new securities is accompanied by an application for listing such securities for trading on the stock exchange, the requirements for both are considered jointly. The prospectus must conform to the requirements of the fourth schedule of the Companies Act of 1948 and the listing application with the requirements of the stock exchange.

The requirements include the presentation of an accountant's report as to the following matters:

1. A detailed statement of profits and losses for the last five years.
2. Balance sheet at the last date to which the accounts were made up, together with a summary of balance sheets at the end of each previous accounting period reported on and at the beginning of first such period.
3. Rate of dividends for the past five years.
4. Accounting policies followed in dealing with material or critical items in determining profits or losses and net assets.
5. Other relevant matters.
6. If the accounts have not been made up and audited to a date within three months of the date of issue, the report must state this fact.

The statement of profits and losses is presented on a group basis. The latest balance sheet of both the company and the group is required, but the summary balance sheet information is presented on a group basis only.

If the proceeds of sale are to be applied to the purchase of a business or a company which will become a subsidiary, a similar report by accountants upon such business or company has to be furnished covering profits and losses, assets and liabilities, and so forth.

The five-year statement of profits and losses, while based on the statements shown in the annual accounts, may reflect adjustments as between years of the five-year period resulting from changes in the basis of accounting during such period, allocation to the proper period of subsequently arising items of income and expenditure, and other matters requiring adjustment. There must be filed with the stock exchange a statement setting forth the adjustments made and the reasons therefor in order that the statement may fairly serve the purpose for which it is prepared.

In addition to their report and statement of adjustments as mentioned above, the reporting accountants have to provide the following: (a) letter of consent to the appearance of their report in the context of the prospectus; (b) statement that they are satisfied with the evidence available that stocks and work-in-progress had been properly ascertained throughout the period under review and properly brought into account on bases and standards in accordance with accepted accounting principles consistently applied; (c) statement that proper provision for depreciation of fixed assets has been made; (d) information concerning the deferred taxation with special reference to net book values of fixed assets and tax-written-down values; and (e) statement that the accounting policies shown in arriving at the figures shown in the report are in accordance with standards approved by the accountancy bodies, or are in accordance with accepted accounting principles.

The prospectus in the United Kingdom commonly contains a statement which will not be found in one issued in the United States. This is the statement of future prospects, which is the responsibility of the directors of the company offering securities for sale. It is required that where profit forecasts appear in any document addressed to shareholders, the assumptions, including the commercial assumptions, upon which the directors have based their profit forecasts must be stated in the document. The accounting bases and calculations for the forecasts must be examined and reported on by the reporting accountants.

Before grant of quotations, all companies must sign a listing agreement that they will provide promptly certain information about their operations, including information in their annual accounts, and that they will follow certain administrative procedures. They will therefore provide half-yearly unaudited interim accounts and disclose in their annual accounts rents payable if material, a list of principal products, particulars of major currency difficulties or political uncertainties, and a table of relevant comparative figures for the past ten years. If the information provided is inadequate, the only sanction the stock exchange can effectively impose is the withdrawal of quotation.

United Kingdom

Illustrative Financial Statements

ILLUSTRATIVE BALANCE SHEET OF A UNITED KINGDOM COMPANY

Balance Sheet at 31st December, 19—

The Company 19— £	NET ASSETS EMPLOYED	The Group 19— £
	FIXED ASSETS	
....	SUBSIDIARIES	....
....	ASSOCIATED COMPANY	....
	CURRENT ASSETS	
....	Stock	....
....	Debtors and payments in advance	....
....	Short-term deposits	....
....	Bank balances and cash	....
....		....
	Deduct: CURRENT LIABILITIES	
....	Trade and other creditors	....
....	Taxation	....
....	Dividend proposed on ordinary shares	....
....		....
....	NET CURRENT ASSETS (LIABILITIES)	....
....		....
	LESS: DEFERRED LIABILITIES	
....	Corporation tax payable 1st January, 1975	....
....	Deferred taxation	....
....	NET ASSETS	....
	REPRESENTED BY	
....	Share capital	....
....	Reserves	....
....		....

________________ }
________________ } *Directors*

Note: Necessary notes to the balance sheet would appear on separate pages and would show details of various balance sheet items, bases of valuation, information with respect to subsidiaries, and so forth.

ILLUSTRATIVE INCOME STATEMENT OF A UNITED KINGDOM COMPANY

Consolidated Profit and Loss Account

Year ended 31st December, 19__

	19__
	£
GROUP TURNOVER	....
PROFIT BEFORE TAXATION AND EXTRAORDINARY ITEMS	....
Taxation based on profit of the year	....
PROFIT AFTER TAXATION AND BEFORE EXTRAORDINARY ITEMS	....
EXTRAORDINARY ITEMS	....
PROFIT ATTRIBUTABLE TO SHAREHOLDERS OF PARENT COMPANY	....
DIVIDENDS	....
PROFITS RETAINED	....
Earnings per ordinary share	....
Dividend paid per ordinary share	....

Note: Necessary notes to the consolidated profit and loss account would appear on separate pages and would show details and information pertinent thereto.

United States

United States

As of January 1973

Forms of Business Organization

The most common forms of business organization in the United States are the corporation, the partnership, and the sole proprietorship. The rules governing each form of organization are embodied in the statutes of the individual states. The legal profession has been instrumental in formulating several important uniform statutes which have been adopted by many of the states such as the Uniform Partnership Act, the Uniform Limited Partnership Act, the Uniform Commercial Code, and others. A uniform corporation law has not yet been adopted. Nevertheless, the corporation laws of most of the states are quite similar in many respects.

While corporations may be organized for profit or for charitable, educational, or religious purposes, the comments in this section apply specifically to those corporations organized for profit. Many large U.S. companies of this type were incorporated in the state of Delaware; consequently, except where otherwise indicated, the statutes referred to are those of that state and are representative of those in most states. Ordinarily, however, a corporation organized under the laws of one state may do business in another state if it registers in the other state and meets certain other requirements.

The Corporation

Under the Delaware Corporation Law, a corporation may be formed by any person for purposes of transacting any lawful business. A certificate of incorporation must be filed with the secretary of the state of Delaware setting forth various particulars including the name of the corporation (which must include a reference to "incorporated, corporation, association, etc." or an abbreviation thereof, such as "Inc."), nature of the business, classes and numbers of shares of authorized stock, par value per share (if applicable), and duration of corporate existence.

According to the Delaware Corporation Law, the business of every corporation is to be managed by a board of directors, the number of directors to be as provided in the corporate bylaws but not less than three (unless the number of stockholders is less than three). Directors need not be stockholders unless so specified in the certificate of incorporation or in the bylaws. Every corporation will have a president, a secretary, and a treasurer.

The liability of the stockholders of a corporation is generally limited to the amount of their subscribed capital, whether paid for or not. In general, stockholders can freely transfer their paid-up shares unless specifically prohibited from doing so by the corporate bylaws. No minimum amount of capital is required before a corporation can commence business in the state of Delaware.

State laws generally do not require a corporation to appoint auditors or to furnish stockholders with audited periodic financial statements. However, a corporation, intending to raise capital by offering securities for sale to the public in more than one state for an aggregate sales price in excess of a prescribed minimum must meet the requirements of the Federal Securities Act of 1933, and these requirements include the filing of appropriate financial statements, which in most cases are audited by an independent certified public accountant or an independent public accountant (see discussion later in this chapter).

Audited financial statements are also required, both with the original listing application (Form 10) and with the annual reports (Form 10-K), by the Federal Securities Exchange Act of 1934, which regulates securities exchanges and trading in securities listed for trading on such exchanges. Under the 1964 Amendments to the Act, audited financial statements are required for certain unlisted companies (see later discussions in this chapter). In addition to the above statutes, the New York Stock Exchange, in general, requires all listing applications for securities of corporations to contain financial statements examined by independent public accountants who are qualified under the laws of some state or country and requires all future annual reports published or sent to stockholders to contain similar audited financial statements. Other major stock exchanges have similar requirements.

It is customary for publicly held companies, whether listed on an exchange or not, and most other companies of any substance, to include in the published annual report a report of an independent public accountant, containing an opinion as to the fairness of presentation of the financial statements. There are certain exceptions to this general statement but they are rapidly disappearing.

The Partnership

The Uniform Partnership Act defines a partnership as "an association of two or more persons to carry on as co-owners a business for profit." The Uniform Partnership Act has been adopted by many of the states and most of the remaining states have adopted laws similar in many ways to the act. Delaware has adopted the Uniform Partnership Act but not the Uniform Limited Partnership Act. The former applies to a general partnership in which all of the partners are jointly and severally liable for partnership debts. The latter applies to a limited partnership that consists of both general partners who have the same liability as partners in a general partnership and limited partners whose liability is limted to the amount of capital contributed. All partnerships must register in the state, giving names of partners, their respective interests, whether general or limited, and other information.

The Sole Proprietorship

Any person may engage in business on his own account in any of the states or the District of Columbia, but he should first ascertain whether a license is necessary to conduct the particular type of business and whether a fee or tax must be paid before commencing business. The liability of such a sole proprietorship is not limited to the assets of the business but extends to all the personal assets of the owner.

Business Records

The representative Delaware Corporation Law contains no specific requirement that books of account (e.g., general ledger and journal) must be maintained by a corporation. But Delaware law gives stockholders the right, under certain circumstances, to inspect "the corporation's stock ledger, a list of its stockholders, and its other books and records."

The New York State Business Corporation Law specifically provides that each corporation will keep correct and complete books and records of account and minutes of the proceedings of its shareholders, board, and executive committee meetings. It must also maintain a stock ledger book and stock transfer book.

The United States Internal Revenue Code and regulations thereunder provide that every person (including business entities) subject to U.S. income taxes must keep such permanent books of account or records, including inventories, as are sufficient to establish the amount of gross income, deductions, and so forth, required to be shown in an income tax return.

The Accounting Profession

The Certified Public Accountant

The designation "certified public accountant" (CPA) is conferred in the United States by each of the 50 states, the District of Columbia, the Virgin Islands, and Puerto Rico. In these jurisdictions, individual regulations govern the practice of accountancy and the issuance of CPA certificates. CPAs in all jurisdictions of the United States were estimated to number over 150,000. New York State enacted the first CPA law in the United States in 1896, and that state has issued more certificates than any other. The regulations and requirements of New York State are among the most stringent of the 53 jurisdictions and are summarized in this section as illustrative of professional qualifications. Some significant variations in other jurisdictions are explained.

Professional Requirements. The Education Department of New York State administers the New York Education Law governing the accounting profession. This includes the issuance of the certificate of certified public accountant in New York.

The Education Law was amended on July 2, 1971, the amendment becoming effective September 1, 1971. The new rules for obtaining a CPA certificate issued by the state of New York provide generally as follows.

A candidate—

1. Is at least 21 years of age and of good moral character.
2. Has received a bachelor's or a higher degree based on a program in accounting, in accordance with the Commissioner's regulations, which provide for at least twenty-four semester hours in accounting, six in law, six in finance, and six in economics, unless fewer hours at the graduate level are approved by the Department of Education, or has graduated from college and has the equivalent of college training in accountancy as determined by the New York State Commissioner of Education, or has had at least 15 years' experience in the practice of public accounting satisfactory to the state Board for Public Accountancy.

3. Has passed the examination required by the Department of Education.
4. Has completed two years of experience (one year for a candidate who has satisfactorily completed a registered graduate curriculum in accounting) involving the diversified application of accounting principles and the diversified application of auditing procedures in the practice of public accountancy either on his own account as a licensed public accountant, as a member of a co-partnership, as an employee on the professional staff of one engaged in the practice of public accountancy, or the satisfactory equivalent thereof as determined by the Board for Public Accountancy in the exercise of its discretion.

A candidate is no longer required to be a citizen or express an intention to become a citizen, nor is residency required under the new law.

Anyone receiving the certificate of certified public accountant from the state of New York is entitled to use the designation "certified public accountant" or the letters "CPA" in connection with his name.

Each state and territory of the United States and the District of Columbia administers a uniform CPA examination prepared and graded under the supervision of a nine-member board of examiners of the American Institute of CPAs. The examination consists of four subjects: theory of accounts, commercial law, accounting problems, and auditing.

The CPA requirements vary by states as to education and experience. Several jurisdictions require a high school education only. Some states waive educational requirements if certain experience requirements are met and the converse is true in other states. Nearly all states require some form of accounting experience for various periods of time, generally from two to four years. Many states require public accounting experience while other states may accept, in lieu thereof, either private or government experience or both.

The (Noncertified) Public Accountant

Accountancy may also be practiced in the United States by individuals licensed s "public accountants" (PAs), a second public accountancy group. In most of the 53 accountancy jurisdictions, a public accountant's license is or was issued based on an application for such a license and certain broad requirements regarding the extent of an applicant's practice of accountancy. These licenses are not dependent on the successful completion of a professional examination or specified education.

In 1972, 40 of the 53 jurisdictions had laws dealing with public accountants. Several U.S. jurisdictions no longer issue licenses for public accountants. Fifteen of the 40 jurisdictions with provisions for public accountants permit new registrations, while the other 25 stipulate dates after which no new public accountants' licenses are to be issued. For example, 1961 was the terminal year for public accountants' licenses issued by the state of New York. Jurisdictions without public accountant legislation permit accountants to practice without registration.

Practice by Accountants From Other Countries

The American Institute of Certified Public Accountants recommended in 1956 a form of regulatory public accountancy bill for adoption by the several states. Section 4 of the bill, which deals with the registration of foreign accountants, together with the Institute's comment, follows:

> *Registration of Foreign Accountants.* The Board may, in its discretion, permit the registration of any person of good moral character who is the holder of a certificate, license, or degree in a foreign country constituting a recognized qualification for the practice of public accounting in such country. A person so registered shall use only the title under which he is generally known in his country, followed by the name of the country from which he received his certificate, license, or degree.
>
> *Institute's Comment*
>
> It is proposed by this section to give effect to a recommendation of the executive committee of the American Institute of Accountants made many years ago that a qualified professional accountant of a foreign country in possession of a certificate, license, or degree in his country constituting a recognized qualification for the practice of public accountancy and which is issued under acceptable professional standards be permitted to practice in this country subject to such requirements as to registration or payment of fees as may be required and be permitted to use the title under which he is registered in his own country provided the country of its origin is indicated.

The laws of about half of the jurisdictions include this provision.

Organizations of Accountants

American Institute of Certified Public Accountants. The American Institute of Certified Public Accountants and its predecessors have a history dating back to 1887, when the American Association of Public Accountants was formed. In 1916, the American Association was succeeded by the Institute of Public Accountants, at which time there was a membership of 1,150. The name was changed to the American Institute of Accountants in 1917 and remained so until 1957, when the name was again changed to the American Institute of Certified Public Accountants. The American Society of Certified Public Accountants was formed in 1921 and acted as a federation of state societies. The Society was merged into the Institute in 1936, and, at that time, the Institute agreed to restrict its future members to CPAs. The Institute's membership totals over 100,000, of which approximately 60 percent are in public practice.

The Institute currently has 150 principal committees and boards which, among other duties, deal with accounting principles, auditing standards and procedures, professional ethics, federal taxation, management services, and governmental relations.

The official publication of the Institute is the *Journal of Accountancy*, which is published monthly and currently has a circulation of over 190,000. It contains technical articles and general comments discussing matters of current interest to accountants, as well as pronouncements and actions of the important committees and the Council of the Institute.

State Societies of Certified Public Accountants. State societies of certified public accountants exist in each of the states and territories of the United States and the District of Columbia. Each society develops its own policies and conducts its own programs. Even though the American Institute exerts no control over the state societies, their policies are usually influenced by the Institute which maintains a committee on relations with state societies. Many state societies publish periodicals dealing with subjects of interest to their members and have committee structures resembling those of the Institute.

Other Organizations of Accountants. Other organizations in various fields of accounting in the United States are the following:

The National Society of Public Accountants—Members are primarily noncertified public accountants, who are licensed or registered accountants. The Society was formed in 1945, at which time it had 3,800 members. It currently has over 14,000 members, 98 percent of whom are engaged in public practice, either on a full- or part-time basis.

American Accounting Association—Members include accounting educators at the college or university level as well as many professional accountants.

The Institute of Internal Auditors—Members are typically employed by industrial and commercial companies and perform administrative or supervisory internal auditing functions.

Financial Executives Institute—Members are corporate management executives with accounting and financial responsibilities, including financial vice presidents, treasurers, and controllers.

National Association of Accountants—Members are largely accountants with industrial and commercial companies.

Federal Government Accountants Association

Ethics (American Institute of Certified Public Accountants)

The reliance of the public and business community on sound financial reporting and advice on business affairs imposes an obligation to maintain high standards of technical competence, morality, and integrity on the public accounting profession. To this end, a member or associate of the American Institute of Certified Public Accountants must maintain independence of thought and action, hold the affairs of his clients in strict confidence, strive continuously to improve his professional skills, observe generally accepted auditing standards, promote sound and informative financial reporting, uphold the dignity and honor of the accounting profession, and maintain high standards of personal conduct.

Each member of the Institute is bound by the following AICPA Rules of Conduct that were adopted by the membership and became effective March 1, 1973.

Applicability of Rules

The Institute's Code of Professional Ethics derives its authority from the bylaws of the Institute which provide that the Trial Board may, after a hearing, admonish, suspend, or expel a member who is found guilty of infringing any of the bylaws or any provisions of the Rules of Conduct.

The Rules of Conduct which follow apply to all services performed in the practice of public accounting including tax and management advisory services except (a) where the wording of the rule indicates otherwise and (b) that a member who is practicing outside the United States will not be subject to discipline for departing from any of the rules stated herein so long as his conduct is in accord with the rules of the organized accounting profession in the country in which he is practicing. However, where a member's name is associated with financial statements in such a manner as to imply that he is acting as an independent public accountant and under circumstances that would entitle the reader to assume that United States practices were followed, he must comply with the requirements of Rules 202 and 203.

A member may be held responsible for compliance with the Rules of Conduct by all persons associated with him in the practice of public accounting who are either under his supervision or are his partners or shareholders in the practice.

A member engaged in the practice of public accounting must observe all the Rules of Conduct. A member not engaged in the practice of public accounting must observe only Rules 102 and 501 since all other Rules of Conduct relate solely to the practice of public accounting.

A member shall not permit others to carry out on his behalf, either with or without compensation, acts which, if carried out by the member, would place him in violation of the Rules of Conduct.

Definitions

The following definitions of terminology are applicable wherever such terminology is used in the Rules and Interpretations.

Client. The person(s) or entity which retains a member or his firm, engaged in the practice of public accounting, for the performance of professional services.

Council. The Council of the American Institute of Certified Public Accountants.

Enterprise. Any person(s) or entity, whether organized for profit or not, for which a CPA provides services.

Firm. A proprietorship, partnership, or professional corporation or association engaged in the practice of public accounting, including individual partners or shareholders thereof.

Financial statements. Statements and footnotes related thereto that purport to show financial position which relates to a point in time or changes in financial position which relate to a period of time, and statements which use a cash or other incomplete basis of accounting. Balance sheets, statements of income, statements of retained earnings, statements of changes in financial position, and statements of changes in owners' equity are financial statements.

Incidental financial data included in management advisory services reports to support recommendations to a client, and tax returns and supporting schedules do not, for this purpose, constitute financial statements; and the statement, affidavit, or signature of preparers required on tax returns neither constitutes an opinion on financial statements nor requires a disclaimer of such opinion.

Institute. The American Institute of Certified Public Accountants.

Interpretations of Rules of Conduct. Pronouncements issued by the Division of Professional Ethics to provide guidelines as to the scope and application of the Rules of Conduct.

Member. A member, associate member or international associate of the American Institute of Certified Public Accountants.

Practice of public accounting. Holding out to be a CPA or public accountant and at the same time performing for a client one or more types of services rendered by public accountants.The term shall not be limited by a more restrictive definition which might be found in the accountancy law under which a member practices.

Professional services. One or more types of services performed in the practice of public accounting.

Independence, integrity and objectivity

Rule 101—Independence. A member or a firm of which he is a partner or shareholder shall not express an opinion on financial statements of an enterprise unless he and his firm are independent with respect to such enterprise. Independence will be considered to be impaired if, for example:

A. During the period of his professional engagement, or at the time of expressing his opinion, he or his firm
   1. Had or was committed to acquire any direct or material indirect financial interest in the enterprise; or
   2. Had any joint closely held business investment with the enterprise or any officer, director or principal stockholder thereof which was material in relation to his or his firm's net worth; or
   3. Had any loan to or from the enterprise or any officer, director or principal stockholder thereof. The latter proscription does not apply to the following loans from a financial institution when made under normal lending procedures, terms and requirements:
      (a) Loans obtained by a member or his firm which are not material in relation to the net worth of such borrower.
      (b) Home mortgages.
      (c) Other secured loans, except loans guaranteed by a member's firm which are otherwise unsecured.

B. During the period covered by the financial statements, during the period of the professional engagement or at the time of expressing an opinion, he or his firm
   1. Was connected with the enterprise as a promoter, underwriter or voting trustee, a director or officer or in any capacity equivalent to that of a member of management or of an employee; or
   2. Was a trustee of any trust or executor or administrator of any estate if such trust or estate had a direct or material indirect financial interest in the enterprise; or was a trustee for any pension or profit-sharing trust of the enterprise.

The above examples are not intended to be all-inclusive.

Rule 102—Integrity and objectivity. A member shall not knowingly misrepresent facts, and when engaged in the practice of public accounting, including the rendering of tax and management advisory services, shall not subordinate his judgment to others. In tax practice, a member may resolve doubt in favor of his client as long as there is reasonable support for his position.

Competence and technical standards

Rule 201—Competence. A member shall not undertake any engagement which he or his firm cannot reasonably expect to complete with professional competence.

Rule 202—Auditing standards. A member shall not permit his name to be associated with financial statements in such a manner as to imply that he is acting as an independent public accountant unless he has complied with the applicable generally accepted auditing standards promulgated by the Institute. Statements on Auditing Standards issued by the Institute's auditing standards executive committee are, for purposes of this rule, considered to be interpretations of the generally accepted auditing standards, and departures from such statements must be justified by those who do not follow them.

Rule 203—Accounting principles. A member shall not express an opinion that financial statements are presented in conformity with generally accepted accounting principles if such statements contain any departure from an accounting principle promulgated by the body designated by Council to establish such principles which has a material effect on the statements taken as a whole, unless the member can demonstrate that due to unusual circumstances the financial statements would otherwise have been misleading. In such cases his report must describe the departure, the approximate effects thereof, if practicable, and the reasons why compliance with the principle would result in a misleading statement.

Rule 204—Forecasts. A member shall not permit his name to be used in conjunction with any forecast of future transactions in a manner which may lead to the belief that the member vouches for the achievability of the forecast.

Responsibilities to clients

Rule 301—Confidential client information. A member shall not disclose any confidential information obtained in the course of a professional engagement except with the consent of the client.

This rule shall not be construed (a) to relieve a member of his obligation under Rules 202 and 203, (b) to affect in any way his compliance with a validly issued subpoena or summons enforceable by order of a court, (c) to prohibit review of a member's professional practices as a part of voluntary quality review under Institute authorization or (d) to preclude a member from responding to any inquiry made by the ethics division or Trial Board of the Institute, by a duly constituted investigative or disciplinary body of a state CPA society, or under state statutes.

Members of the ethics division and Trial Board of the Institute and professional practice reviewers under Institute authorization shall not disclose any confidential client information which comes to their attention from members in disciplinary proceedings or otherwise in carrying out their official responsibilities. However, this prohibition shall not restrict the exchange of information with an aforementioned duly constituted investigative or disciplinary body.

Rule 302—Contingent fees. Professional services shall not be offered or rendered under an arrangement whereby no fee will be charged unless a specified finding or result is attained, or where the fee is otherwise contingent upon the findings or results of such services. However, a member's fees may vary depending, for example, on the complexity of the service rendered.

Fees are not regarded as being contingent if fixed by courts or other public authorities or, in tax matters, if determined based on the results of judicial proceedings or the findings of governmental agencies.

Responsibilites to colleagues

Rule 401—Encroachment. A member shall not endeavor to provide a person or entity with a professional service which is currently provided by another public accountant except:

1. He may respond to a request for a proposal to render services and may furnish service to those who request it. However, if an audit client of another independent public accountant requests a member to provide professional advice on accounting or auditing matters in connection with an expression of opinion on financial statements, the member must first consult with the other accountant to ascertain that the member is aware of all the available relevant facts.

2. Where a member is required to express an opinion on combined or consolidated financial statements which include a subsidiary, branch, or other component audited by another independent public accountant, he may insist on auditing any such component which in his judgment is necessary to warrant the expression of his opinion.

A member who receives an engagement for services by referral from another public accountant shall not accept the client's request to extend his service beyond the specific engagement without first notifying the referring accountant, nor shall he seek to obtain any additional engagement from the client.

Rule 402—Offers of employment. A member in public practice shall not make a direct or indirect offer of employment to an employee of another public accountant on his own behalf or that of his client without first informing such accountant. This rule shall not apply if the employee on his own initiative or in response to a public advertisement applies for employment.

Other responsibilities and practices

Rule 501—Acts discreditable. A member shall not commit an act discreditable to the profession.

Rule 502—Solicitation and advertising. A member shall not seek to obtain clients by solicitation. Advertising is a form of solicitation and is prohibited.

Rule 503—Commission. A member shall not pay a commission to obtain a client, nor shall he accept a commission for a referral to a client of products or services of others. This rule shall not prohibit payments for the purchase of an accounting practice or retirement payments to individuals formerly engaged in the practice of public accounting or payments to their heirs or estates.

Rule 504—Incompatible occupations. A member who is engaged in the practice of public accounting shall not concurrently engage in any business or occupation which impairs his objectivity in rendering professional services or serves as a feeder to his practice.

Rule 505—Form of practice and name. A member may practice public accounting, whether as an owner or employee, only in the form of a proprietorship, a partnership, or a professional corporation whose characteristics conform to resolutions of Council.

A member shall not practice under a firm name which includes any fictitious name, indicates specialization or is misleading as to the type of organization (proprietorshp, partnership or corporation). However, names of one or more past partners or shareholders may be included in the firm name of a successor partnership or corporation. Also, a partner surviving the death or withdrawal of all other partners may continue to practice under the partnership name for up to two years after becoming a sole practitioner.

A firm may not designate itself as "Members of the American Institute of Certified Public Accountants" unless all of its partners or shareholders are members of the Institute.

Auditing Standards

The AICPA's committee on auditing standards issued Statement on Auditing Standards No. 1, "A Codification of Auditing Standards and Procedures," in 1973. This statement codifies all of the earlier pronouncements of this committee, superseding Statements on Auditing Procedure No. 33 through No. 54. It incorporates all of the substantive matters covered in those statements.

Generally Accepted Auditing Standards

Statement on Auditing Standards No. 1 defines auditing standards as differing from auditing procedures in that "procedures" relate to acts to be performed, whereas "standards" deal with measures of the quality of the performance of those acts and the objectives to be attained by the use of the procedures undertaken. Therefore, auditing standards concern themselves not only with the auditor's professional qualities, but also with the judgment exercised by him in the performance of his examination and in his report.

The generally accepted auditing standards as approved and adopted by the membership of the American Institute of Certified Public Accountants are as follows:

General Standards

1. The examination is to be performed by a person or persons having adequate technical training and proficiency as an auditor.
2. In all matters relating to the assignment, an independence in mental attitude is to be maintained by the auditor or auditors.
3. Due professional care is to be exercised in the performance of the examination and the preparation of the report.

Standards of Field Work

1. The work is to be adequately planned and assistants, if any, are to be properly supervised.
2. There is to be a proper study and evaluation of the existing internal control as a basis for reliance thereon and for the determination of the resultant extent of the tests to which auditing procedures are to be restricted.
3. Sufficient competent evidential matter is to be obtained through inspection, observation, inquiries, and confirmation to afford a reasonable basis for an opinion regarding the financial statements under examination.

Standards of Reporting

1. The report shall state whether the financial statements are presented in accordance with generally accepted principles of accounting.
2. The report shall state whether such principles have been consistently observed in the current period in relation to the preceding period.
3. Informative disclosures in the financial statements are to be regarded as reasonably adequate unless otherwise stated in the report.
4. The report shall either contain an expression of opinion regarding the financial statements, taken as a whole, or an assertion to the effect that an opinion cannot be expressed. When an overall opinion cannot be expressed, the reasons therefor should be stated. In all cases where an auditor's name is associated with financial statements the report should contain a clear-cut indication of the character of the auditor's examination, if any, and the degree of responsibility he is taking.

All members of the American Institute of Certified Public Accountants agree to observe these standards. Most bylaws or codes of professional ethics of state societies and state statutes dealing with professional conduct include similar standards.

Materiality

Statement on Auditing Standards No. 1 deals with the concept of materiality, which is inherent in the work of the auditor. In considering a question of audit procedure or of application of accounting principles, the effect of the resulting decision on the fairness of presentation of the related financial statements must be taken into consideration. If it is determined that the result of such decision is not material, the auditing procedures followed may be modified, and the strict application of a preferred accounting principle may be waived.

No criteria have been set by the American Institute as to what constitutes materiality. This is left to the judgment of the independent auditor in the particular case after he has considered all contributing factors.

Independence

The second general standard requires that the auditor be "independent"; that is, he must maintain an attitude of impartiality and be without bias with respect to the client under audit. To be recognized as independent, he is expected to be free from any obligation to or interest in the client, its management, or its owners. The auditor must not only be independent; in fact, he must avoid situations that may lead outsiders to doubt his independence.

The profession has established through the Institute's Code of Professional Ethics precepts to guard against the presumption of loss of independence. The Securities and Exchange Commission has likewise emphasized the importance of independence by adopting similar rules.

To emphasize independence from management, many corporations follow the practice of having the independent auditor appointed by the board of directors or elected by the stockholders.

Statement on Auditing Standards No. 1, section 517, provides that independence is something the auditor must decide as a matter of professional judgment. If the auditor is not independent, he should disclaim an opinion.

The recommended disclaimer of opinion, regardless of the extent of services performed is as follows:

> We are not independent with respect to XYZ Company, and the accompanying balance sheet as of December 31, 19—, and the related statement(s) of income and retained earnings for the year then ended were not audited by us; accordingly, we do not express an opinion on them.
>
> (Signature and Date)

Each page of the financial statements should clearly and conspicuously be marked "Unaudited—see accompanying disclaimer of opinion," unless the disclaimer of opinion appears thereon.

Evaluation of Internal Control

In the United States, great emphasis is placed on evaluation of the client's internal control. Internal control comprises the plan of organization and all of the coordinate methods and measures adopted within a business to safeguard its assets, check the accuracy and reliability of its accounting data, promote operational efficiency, and encourage adherence to prescribed managerial policies.

The purpose of the auditor's study and evaluation of internal control incident to his examination of financial statements is to establish a basis for reliance thereon in determining the nature, timing, and extent of audit tests to be applied. This is expressed in the second standard of field work included in the generally accepted auditing standards (Statement on Auditing Standards No. 1, section 320) adopted by the profession, as follows:

> There is to be a proper study and evaluation of the existing internal control as a basis for reliance thereon and for the determination of the resultant extent of the tests to which auditing procedures are to be restricted.

Suggestions for improvement in internal control frequently arise from audit engagements and may also arise from special engagements undertaken for that or other purposes.

Evidential Matter—Confirmation and Observation

The Institute members voted in 1939 to establish confirmation of receivables by correspondence with debtors and observation of the taking of physical inventories as generally accepted auditing procedures, where they are practicable and reasonable, and the assets concerned are material to financial position or results of operations. Statement on Auditing Standards No. 1 reaffirms the importance of these well-established auditing procedures and emphasizes that the independent auditor who issues an opinion when he has not employed them must bear in mind that he has the burden of justifying the opinion expressed.

When the auditing procedures of confirmation of receivables or the observation of the taking of inventories are not practicable or reasonable, the independent auditor may be able to satisfy himself by the application of other auditing procedures. If the independent auditor has been unable to confirm receivables or observe the client's taking of physical inventories solely because it was impracticable or impossible to do so but has satisfied himself as to receivables or inventories by means of other auditing procedures, no comment need be made in his report, although he may wish to disclose the circumstances of the engagement and describe the other procedures. The auditor should consider carefully his decision that confirmation of receivables or observation of inventories is impracticable or impossible.

When the independent auditor is unable to satisfy himself by the application of other auditing procedures, depending on the degree of materiality of the amounts involved, he should indicate clearly in the scope paragraph (or in a middle paragraph) the limitations on his work and either qualify his opinion on the financial statements taken as a whole or disclaim an opinion on them.

If either confirmation of receivables or observation of inventories is omitted because of a restriction imposed by the client, and such inventories or receivables are material, the auditor should indicate clearly in the scope paragraph (or in a middle paragraph) the limitations on his work and, generally, should disclaim an opinion on the financial statements taken as a whole.

The omission of these procedures at the beginning of the year is not required to be disclosed in situations where the independent auditor has satisfied himself by means of other auditing procedures. Nevertheless, he may wish to disclose the circumstances of the engagement and briefly describe the other procedures.

If the independent auditor has not satisfied himself by means of other auditing procedures with respect to opening inventories, he should either disclaim an opinion on the statement of income or qualify his opinion thereon, depending on the degree of materiality of the amounts involved.

Timing of Audit Work

Many audit tests can be conducted at almost any time during the year. The independent auditor makes tests of the client's records, procedures, and representations, at interim dates, and the practice of carrying out a significant part of an examination during the year is acceptable. When internal control is effective at interim and examination dates, audit procedures as of the examination date may consist mainly of comparisons of year-end balances with those at prior dates, and review and investigation of unusual transactions and significant fluctuations.

Working Papers

Working papers are the records kept by the independent auditor of the procedures he followed, the tests he performed, the information he obtained, and the conclusions he reached pertinent to his examination. Working papers, accordingly, may include work programs, analyses, memoranda, letters of confirmation and representation, abstracts of company documents, and schedules or commentaries prepared or obtained by the auditor.

Although the quantity, type and content of working papers will vary with the circumstances, they generally would include or show the following:

1. Data sufficient to demonstrate that the financial statements or other information upon which the auditor is reporting were in agreement with (or reconciled with) the client's records.
2. That the engagment had been planned, such as by use of work programs, and that the work of any assistants had been supervised and reviewed, indicating observance of the first standard of field work.
3. That the client's system of internal control had been reviewed and evaluated in determining the extent of the tests to which auditing procedures were restricted, indicating observance of the second standard of field work.
4. The auditing procedures followed and testing performed in obtaining evidential matter, indicating observance of the third standard of field work. The record in these respects may take various forms, including memoranda, checklists, work programs, and schedules and would generally permit reasonable identification of the work done by the auditor.
5. How exceptions and unusual matters, if any, disclosed by the independent auditor's procedures were resolved or treated.
6. Appropriate commentaries prepared by the auditor indicating his conclusions concerning significant aspects of the engagement.

Consistency

The independent auditor is required to state in his report whether the accounting principles applied in the period under examination are consistent with those applied in the preceding period. When a change has been made in the accounting principles employed during the year or years the independent auditor is reporting upon and the change has a material effect upon financial position or results of operations, he should refer in his opinion paragraph to a note to the financial statements which adequately describes the change and its effect, or describe adequately in his report the nature of the change and its effect. If the comparability of the statements is affected by changes in business or other conditions, fair presentation of the financial statements may require disclosure of these changes in notes to the statements.

Disclosure of Subsequent Events

The auditor is charged with considering subsequent events and requiring, as appropriate, adjustment of the accounts or disclosure of those matters essential to proper interpretation of the financial statements being presented. If subsequent information is acquired which would have been utilized had it been available at the balance sheet date, appropriate adjustments should be made in the financial statement. Examples are collection of receivables, or settlement or determination of liabilities on a substantially different basis from that previously anticipated.

Subsequent events which have no direct effect on the financial statements of the prior year, but have a material effect on how such statements should currently be interpreted, do not require retroactive adjustment, but do call for disclosure. Examples are the sale of a capital stock issue or large bond issue with restrictive covenants, purchases of businesses, or serious damage from fire, flood, or other casualty.

Subsequent events such as war, legislation, management changes, product changes, strikes, unionization, marketing agreements, and the loss of important customers do not, of course, call for any adjustment of past financial statements and, more often than not, do not even require disclosure in current financial statements in footnotes. However, in some cases, their effect may be so significant as to require disclosure.

Short-Form Report

The short-form report of the auditor is customarily used in connection with the basic financial statements. It is also often included as part of a long-form report. The usual short-form report consists of a representation as to the work performed, expressed in an opening or "scope" paragraph, and a representation as to the independent auditor's conclusions, usually in a closing or "opinion" paragraph.

The short-form report cited in the AICPA Statement on Auditing Standards No. 1 as the form which "the profession in general has adopted" is as follows:

> We have examined the balance sheet of X Company as of December 31, 19—, and the related statements of income and retained earnings and changes in financial position for the year then ended. Our examination was made in accordance with generally accepted auditing standards, and accordingly included such tests of the accounting records and such other auditing procedures as we considered necessary in the circumstances.

> In our opinion, the aforementioned financial statements present fairly the financial position of X Company at December 31, 19—, and the results of its operations and the changes in its financial position for the year then ended, in conformity with generally accepted accounting principles applied on a basis consistent with that of the preceding year.

The independent auditor may be required to deviate from the standard short-form report because of the following:

1. The scope of his examination is limited or affected—
   a. By conditions which preclude the application of auditing procedures considered necessary in the circumstances.
   b. By restrictions imposed by clients.
   c. Because part of the examination has been made by other independent auditors.
2. The financial statements do not present fairly the financial position or results of operations because of—
   a. Lack of conformity with generally accepted accounting principles.
   b. Inadequate disclosure.
3. Accounting principles are not consistently applied.
4. Unusual uncertainties exist concerning future developments, the effects of which cannot be reasonably estimated or otherwise resolved satisfactorily.

Where the independent auditor is unable to satisfy himself by the application of customary auditing procedures, he indicates clearly in the scope paragraph of his report the limitations on his work and, depending on the materiality of the amounts involved, he either qualifies his opinion or disclaims an opinion on the financial statements taken as a whole.

When an independent auditor believes that the presentation of a material item is at variance with generally accepted accounting principles, he qualifies his opinion or, if he regards the effect of such variance as sufficiently material, expresses an adverse opinion. An adverse opinion states specifically that the financial statements "*do not* present fairly" the financial position and results of operations in conformity with generally accepted accounting principles.

Long-Form Report

While the accounting profession has generally adopted the short-form report in connection with financial statements intended for publication, auditors also issue a substantial number of so-called long-form reports. In addition to the basic financial statements, these reports ordinarily include details of the items in these statements, statistical data, explanatory comments, or other informative material, some of which may be of a non-accounting nature, and sometimes a description of the scope of the auditor's examination more detailed than the description in the usual short-form reports. In some cases both a long-form report and a short-form report are issued on the same engagement, but in many cases the long-form report constitutes the only report issued.

In issuing a long-form report, the auditor is expected to state whether or not the data other than the basic financial statements included in the long-form report have been subjected to the same examination as the information contained in the basic financial statements.

Accounting Principles

Development of Accounting Principles

Generally accepted accounting principles, which are required by generally accepted auditing standards to be referred to in the independent auditor's report, have evolved over many years of professional accountancy practice in the United States. These principles are generally accepted because the business and financial communities, as well as members of the accounting profession, recognize and use them in financial statements of business enterprises. They have not been codified by a professional organization or a government agency.

Committees and boards of the AICPA lead in developing accounting principles through issuing bulletins, statements, opinions, recommendations and interpretations. In addition to the AICPA, three other organizations have a major influence on the development and adoption of accounting principles in the United States: (1) the United States Securities and Exchange Commission, (2) the New York Stock Exchange, and (3) the Internal Revenue Service of the United States Treasury Department.

American Institute of Certified Public Accountants. From 1939 to 1959, the Institute's committee on accounting procedure issued bulletins on various accounting matters. These bulletins, known as Accounting Research Bulletins or "ARBs," were the most widely accepted pronouncements on recommended accounting principles.

The Institute reorganized and expanded its research efforts in 1959, with the aim to specifically state the nature of generally accepted accounting principles and to determine appropriate practices. The Accounting Principles Board replaced the committee on accounting procedure. The status of opinions issued by the Board depended on general acceptance, the same as Accounting Research Bulletins. Operations of the Board included an expanded accounting research division of the AICPA to carry out and publish research studies authorized by the Board. The results of this formal accounting research were published as individual Accounting Research Studies for consideration by the Board, the profession as a whole, and the public. The Board issued formal opinions on the subjects of these research studies and issued additional opinions on current problems or accounting practices of general interest. The Council of the AICPA in May 1964 adopted a resolution to the effect that members of the AICPA should disclose in their reports material departures from an opinion of the Accounting Principles Board.

In response to increasing criticism from within and outside the profession, two special study groups were established in 1971 to review the objectives of financial statements and the method of operation of the Accounting Principles Board. The first group to report—Study Group on Establishment of Accounting Principles—recommended that the Board be replaced by a seven-person full-time Financial Accounting Standards Board to be independent of the AICPA. This recommendation was approved by the membership council of the AICPA in April 1972.

The Financial Accounting Foundation, the Financial Accounting Standards Board, and the Financial Accounting Standards Advisory Council were established on June 30, 1972, to perform important and distinct functions in establishing and improving standards of financial accounting and reporting. The Financial Accounting Foundation, the organization which formed the Financial Accounting Standards Board and the Financial Accounting Standards Advisory Council, was incorporated as a body separate from all existing professional organizations.

The following is a brief description of these bodies.

The Financial Accounting Foundation—The Financial Accounting Foundation is governed by a board of trustees composed of nine members. Eight of these members are elected by the board of directors of the American Institute of Certified Public Accountants for three-year terms. Four of the elected trustees are certified public accountants in public practice at the time of their election; two are, or in the judgment of the board of directors of the Institute have extensive experience as, financial executives; and the remaining two are, or in the judgment of the board of directors of the Institute, have extensive experience as, respectively, a financial analyst and an accounting educator. The ninth member of the board of trustees is the senior elected officer of the American Institute of Certified Public Accountants who is not an employee thereof, who serves as ex officio trustee during his term in such capacity with the Institute.

The primary duties of the board of trustees of the Financial Accounting Foundation are these:

1. To appoint the members of the Financial Accounting Standards Board.
2. To appoint the members of the Financial Accounting Standards Advisory Council.
3. To arrange for the financing of the organization.
4. To prepare and administer the budget of the Financial Accounting Foundation.
5. To approve the annual budget of the Financial Accounting Standards Board and the Financial Accounting Standards Advisory Council, as prepared and presented by the chairman of the FASB.
6. To review periodically the bylaws of the Financial Accounting Foundation, and the basic structure of establishing and improving standards of financial accounting and reporting.

The Financial Accounting Standards Board—The seven members of the FASB are appointed by the board of trustees of the Financial Accounting Foundation for five-year terms. Of the seven members, all of whom are fully remunerated and serve full time, only four are certified public accountants drawn from public practice or are, in the judgment of the board of trustees, principally experienced as public practitioners. The remaining three members, who need not but may be certified public accountants are, in the judgment of the board of trustees, well versed in problems of financial reporting.

The certificate of incorporation of the Financial Accounting Foundation delegates to the Financial Accounting Standards Board all authority, functions, and powers of the Foundation and its board of trustees in respect of standards of financial accounting and reporting, including the conduct of all related activities. As a result, the Financial Accounting Standards Board has responsibility, among other things, for issuing Statements of Financial Accounting Standards and Interpretations of those Statements, Interpretations of Accounting Research Bulletins of the Committee on Accounting Procedure of the American Institute of Certified Public Accountants, and Interpretations of Opinions of the Accounting Principles Board of the Institute.

The Financial Accounting Standards Advisory Council—The Financial Accounting Standards Advisory Council consists of not less than 20 persons who, in the judgment of the board of trustees of the Financial Accounting Foundation, are knowledgeable about the problems and impact of financial reporting or who possess an expertise of value to the Financial

Accounting Standards Board. It is intended that members of the advisory council be broadly representative of varied professional and occupational backgrounds with no profession or occupation predominating. Members of the advisory council are appointed for one-year terms by the board of trustees of the Financial Accounting Foundation. Membership on the advisory council is personal to the members, and functions of members and attendance at meetings may not be delegated to others.

The Financial Accounting Standards Advisory Council has an integral role in the process of establishing and improving standards of financial accounting and reporting. It is intended to be one vehicle for contact with and communication between the Financial Accounting Standards Board and interested persons and organizations. Members of the advisory council are expected to work closely with the FASB in an advisory capacity. Thus, upon the request of the chairman of the FASB (who is also chairman of the advisory council), members of the advisory council are to consult with the chairman or the FASB concerning the Board's agenda of projects and the assigning of priorities thereto, matters likely to require the attention of the FASB, the selection and organization of task forces to work on specific projects, and such other matters as may be requested. Upon request of the chairman, members are also to provide written comments in respect of the Statements of Financial Accounting Standards and Interpretations proposed to be issued by the FASB. The chairman and the Financial Accounting Standards Board are expected to consider fully and carefully all advice and comments offered by members of the advisory council, but the chairman and the FASB are not precluded from seeking advice and comments from, and consulting with, other persons and organizations.

The advisory council will meet as often as deemed necessary by the chairman of the FASB, but generally not less than quarterly, and will be advised by the chairman as to the activities and plans of the FASB. The advisory council will not vote as a body, and the advisory council and its members are not authorized to issue public communications. The minutes of meetings of the advisory council and written comments of members of the advisory council in respect of Statements of Financial Accounting Standards and Interpretations proposed for issuance will constitute part of the public record of the FASB.

The second study group issued its report on the objectives of financial statements in October 1973. The Accounting Objectives Study Group concluded that the development of objectives should be based not on the operating needs of the managers of businesses, but rather on the needs of users of financial information outside enterprises or organizations. In the development of objectives of financial statements, the study group has attempted to identify and evaluate desirable goals of the financial accounting process.

A summary of objectives of financial statements as viewed by the study group are as follows:

1. To provide information useful for making economic decisions.
2. To serve primarily those users who have limited authority, ability, or resources to obtain information and who rely on financial statements as their principal source of information about an enterprise's economic activities.
3. To provide information useful to investors and creditors for predicting, comparing, and evaluating potential cash flows to them in terms of amount, timing, and related uncertainty.
4. To provide users with information for predicting, comparing, and evaluating enterprise earning power.
5. To supply information useful in judging management's ability to utilize enterprise resources effectively in achieving the primary enterprise goal.
6. To provide factual and interpretative information about transactions and other events which is useful for predicting, comparing, and evaluating enterprise earning power. Basic underlying assumptions with respect to matters subject to interpretation, evaluation, prediction, or estimation should be disclosed.
7. To provide a statement of financial activities useful for predicting, comparing, and evaluating enterprise earning power. This statement should report mainly on factual aspects of enterprise transactions having or expected to have significant cash consequences. This statement should report data that require minimal judgment and interpretation by the preparer.
8. To provide information useful for the predictive process. Financial forecasts should be provided when they will enhance the reliability of users' predictions.
9. To provide for governmental and not-for-profit organizations, information useful for evaluating the effectiveness of the management of resources in achieving the organization's goals. Performance measures should be quantified in terms of identified goals.
10. To report on those activities of the enterprise affecting society which can be determined and described or measured and which are important to the role of the enterprise in its social environment.

Securities and Exchange Commission. The SEC was created by the Securities Exchange Act of 1934, and administers a number of securities acts and regulates the sale of corporate securities to the public and the trading of securities. The SEC is empowered to prescribe the form and content of the financial statements included in prospectuses and in the annual reports filed with it. The Commission has sweeping authority to require the application of certain accounting principles, but it has not used this authority fully or issued detailed rules on accounting methods. A series of SEC accounting releases generally endorse the accounting principles accepted by the accounting profession. The policy of the SEC is generally to cooperate with the professional accounting organizations, including the AICPA and the FASB, and support the development of accounting principles by the FASB.

New York Stock Exchange. The New York Stock Exchange also has significantly influenced the acceptance of accounting principles through its control over the financial reports issued by corporations whose shares are listed on the exchange. Special cooperating committees between the exchange and the Institute laid the groundwork for the development of accounting principles in the United States. Like the SEC, the New York Stock Exchange maintains a close liaison with the accounting profession, the AICPA, and the FASB.

The Internal Revenue Service. The Internal Revenue Code and regulations, rulings, and court decisions interpreting it influence accounting principles adopted in the United States. The "Lifo" method of pricing inventories is the only accounting method which must be used for financial accounting purposes if it is employed for income tax purposes. Tax-allowable accounting procedures and methods for other items need not be recorded in the books and thus affect financial reports to stockholders only indirectly. Many taxpayers desire to minimize differences between tax accounting and accounting underlying financial statements and consequently use an advantageous tax method for both purposes.

Accounting Practices

Financial statements represent reporting based on accounting principles, practices, and methods adopted by an individual enterprise. No attempt is made here to distinguish between principles, practices, and methods. The term "practices" is generally used to include all three. It is also used with regard to presentation, classification, and disclosure of items in financial statements.

The purpose of this section is to briefly describe the usual financial statements presented in the United States and those generally accepted accounting practices which often differ from those accepted in one or more of the other countries in this study. Part of the discussion includes recommendations of the Committee on Accounting Procedure and the Accounting Principles Board of the AICPA and of the Financial Accounting Standards Board.

Form and Content of Financial Statements

The form and content of financial statements have been developed and clarified over the years by the appropriate committees of the Institute, by writings of professional accountants and educators, and significantly, by requirements of the SEC in its Regulation S-X, which deals with the financial statements required to be filed with the Commission. The New York Stock Exchange also has particular requirements applicable to financial statements of companies whose securities are listed on this exchange.

Management has the primary responsibility for the fairness of representations made through financial statements. The independent auditor's responsibility for the statements he has examined is confined to the expression of his opinion on them. However, the independent auditor is expected to suggest form and content of presentation of financial statements.

Presentation of Statements. The basic financial statements presented in the United States are the balance sheet, the income statement, the statement of retained earnings (earned surplus), which is combined with the income statement or presented separately, and the statement of changes in financial position. In addition, supplementary information is often furnished to meet special reporting requirements or circumstances.

Customary forms of basic U.S. financial statements are described briefly in this section and illustrated in the appendix to this book.

Balance Sheet. The general balance sheet form used by commercial and industrial companies in the United States is the "statement" form, in which assets are listed on the left in order of liquidity, beginning with current assets and descending to properties, deferred charges, and intangibles. The right side begins with current liabilities, continues with long-term liabilities and deferred credits, and concludes with the stockholders equity—capital stock, capital contributed in excess of par, and retained earnings (earned surplus).

Some specific industries vary this format. As an example, regulated utilities show properties as the first assets on the left side of their balance sheets and capital accounts are presented as the first sections on the right side of their balance sheets.

Income Statement. Income statements are presented in either "single-step" or "multiple-step" form. The difference between the two forms is that the multiple-step arrangement shows a number of intermediate balances such as gross profit on sales, income from operations, income before federal income taxes, and extraordinary items, if any, whereas the single-step form consists of one grouping for revenues less a total of the expense groupings except for extraordinary items. Such items are always segregated from normal income and expense items. All income statements normally show sales, cost of sales, selling, general and administrative expenses, other income (expense), provision for federal income taxes, and net income for the period. Substantial income or expense items are segregated in the income statement.

Statements of retained earnings, whether combined with income statements or not, are essentially reconciliations of retained earnings at the beginning and end of the period.

Statement of Changes in Financial Position. When financial statements purporting to present both financial position (balance sheet) and results of operations (income statement) are issued, a statement summarizing changes in financial position must also be presented as a basic financial statement for each period for which an income statement is presented. The purpose of the statement of changes in financial position (in substance previously referred to as the statement of source and application of funds) is to summarize the financing and investing activities of the business enterprise which is essential for users of financial statements. This statement is required for all profit-oriented business entities. The statement begins with income or loss before extraordinary items, if any, and then shows expenses not requiring an outlay of working capital. The resulting total is usually called "Working capital provided from (used in) operations, exclusive of extraordinary items" or "Funds provided by operations." After showing extraordinary items, each major source of funds (primarily from changes in noncurrent assets and liabilities) is then listed. From the total of the above, each major application of funds (primarily from changes in non-current assets and liabilities) is deducted. The difference represents the net change in working capital (current assets less current liabilities). Finally, the change in each major current asset and liability is shown.

If the reporting entity does not classify its assets and liabilities as current and noncurrent, the statement usually concludes with the net change in cash for the period.

Notes to Financial Statements (Footnotes). Common practice in the United States is to disclose certain essential information in notes to financial statements including a summary of significant accounting policies.

Generally accepted accounting principles consist of pervasive principles, broad operating principles, and detailed principles. The accounting policies of a reporting entity are the specific accounting principles and the methods of applying those principles, which are selected by the management of the entity from among the various acceptable alternatives. Because of the effect that such policies can have on the financial statements of an entity, a summary of such policies is considered to be an integral part of the financial statements. The summary usually includes the basis of consolidation, depreciation methods, amortization of intangibles, inventory pricing, accounting for research and development costs (including basis for amortization), translation of foreign currencies, recognition of profit on long-term construction-type contracts, and recognition of revenue from franchising and leasing operations. Generally, the summary is shown in the first note to the financial statements.

Footnotes are an integral part of the financial statements but cannot be a substitute for proper accounting treatment or disclosure in the statements. Notes to financial statements may be classified into the following types:

1. Summary of significant accounting policies—described above.
2. Restrictions and liens—provisions of debt or preferred stock agreements restricting the payment of dividends or requiring the maintenance of specified working capital; assets pledged against loans; foreign currency not realizable in U.S. currency.
3. Commitments of an unusual nature—description of long-term leases; extraordinary commitments for plant or other expansion; compensation, stock option plans and pension plans.
4. Contingencies—descriptions of status of lawsuits, tax controversies, and assets and liabilities of uncertain amount.
5. Changes in application of accounting principles—while disclosure of a change in the application of accounting principles having a material effect on the financial statements is required in the opinion of the independent auditor, the nature and effect of the change are ordinarily described in a note referred to in the opinion or, if necessary, described in the opinion itself.
6. Events subsequent to the balance sheet date, other than those recognized in the accounts.

The SEC emphasizes the importance of notes to financial statements, and in its own reporting requirements makes clarification by footnotes mandatory in certain instances.

Comparative Financial Statements. It has become common practice that published financial statements included in reports to stockholders be shown in comparison with those of the preceding year. In many cases several years' summaries of earnings are given. The New York Stock Exchange for many years has required comparative financial statements in listing applications.

Consolidated Financial Statements. A corporation which owns or controls (control is usually presumed where more than 50 percent of the outstanding voting stock is owned) one or more other corporations usually prepares consolidated financial statements. This procedure is adopted to present the financial position and results of operations of an entire enterprise. Institute pronouncements recommend presenting consolidated statements, and both the New York Stock Exchange and the SEC generally require this practice.

In general, consolidated financial statements combine the parent company and all majority-owned subsidiaries, except in special circumstances. Intercompany balances and transactions are eliminated in preparing consolidated statements. Minority equity in subsidiary companies is presented on the credit side of the consolidated balance sheet between the liabilities and stockholders' equity sections; the amount represents proportionate shares in the subsidiaries' net assets. Minority interests in earnings are shown as a separate deduction in the consolidated income statement.

Interim Financial Reports. Interim financial information is essential to provide investors and others with timely information as to the progress of the company. The usefulness of such information rests on the relationship that it has to the annual results of operations. Accordingly, the Accounting Principles Board concluded that each interim period should be viewed as an integral part of an annual period.

Opinion 28 (a) outlines the application of generally accepted auditing standards to the determination of income when interim financial information is presented, (b) provides for the use of estimated effective income tax rates, and (c) specifies certain disclosure requirements for summarized financial information issued by publicly traded companies.

The principal objectives of Opinion 28 are to provide guidance on accounting and disclosure issues peculiar to interim reporting and to set forth minimum disclosure requirements for interim financial reports of publicly traded companies.

In general, the results for each interim period should be based on accounting principles and practices used by a company in the preparation of its latest annual financial statements unless a change in an accounting practice or policy has been adopted in the current year. However, the Board concluded that certain accounting principles and practices followed for annual reporting purposes may require modification and interim reporting dates, so that the reported results for the interim period may better relate to the results of operations for the annual period. These modifications which are necessary or desirable at interim dates in accounting principles or practices followed for annual periods are set forth in Opinion 28.

The Board defined a publicly traded company for purposes of Opinion No. 28 to include any company whose securities are traded in a public market on either (a) a stock exchange, domestic or foreign, or (b) in the over-the-counter market (including securities quoted only locally or regionally).

Current Assets

Current assets designate cash and other assets or resources which are expected to be realized in cash or sold or consumed within the normal operating cycle of the business, generally one year. The operating cycle of a business is considered to be the average time intervening between the acquisition of materials or services and the realization of cash from the sale of products or services.

Marketable Securities. Marketable securities classified as current assets exclude investments in securities or advances made for purposes of control, affiliation, or other continuing business advantage and also exclude those held for special purposes. Marketable securities are usually stated at cost with current market value disclosed. The carrying amount is generally reduced to a lower market value only when a decline in the market price seems permanent.

Receivables. Receivables not collectible within one year from the date of the balance sheet are excluded from current assets, except that long-term installment notes and accounts may be classified as current assets if they conform generally to normal trade practices and terms within the industry. Unearned carrying and interest charges on installment accounts are shown in the balance sheet as a deduction from the related receivables.

Receivables from affiliated and subsidiary companies, employees, officers, directors, stockholders, and those arising from transactions outside the ordinary course of business are separately designated. Also shown separately are deposits, advances, interest, and amounts receivable for returned purchases and claims. When receivables from other than trade debtors and other current assets are not significant, they are usually grouped in one amount described as other assets.

Allowance for Doubtful Receivables. An allowance for doubtful receivables is an appropriate expense of the period and accumulated allowances are deducted from the related receivables in the balance sheet. The amount of a current allowance is determined on the basis of collection experience and the status of outstanding receivables in order to state total receivables at the estimated realizable amount.

Inventories. The components of inventory—finished goods, work-in-process, and raw materials and supplies—are generally not shown separately in the balance sheet or in a note to the financial statements unless the statements are included in a filing with the SEC where such disclosure is required. The basis of determining the amounts disclosed and, to the extent practicable, the method of determining cost is indicated.

Chapter 4 of Accounting Research Bulletin No. 43 sets forth and discusses the various general principles applicable to accounting for inventories in the United States. The most important of ten summary statements are the following:

1. The term "inventory" is used herein to designate the aggregate of those items of tangible personal property which (a) are held for sale in the ordinary course of business, (b) are in process of production for such sale, or (c) are to be currently consumed in the production of goods or services to be available for sale.

2. The primary basis of accounting for inventories is cost, which has been defined generally as the price paid or consideration given to acquire an asset. As applied to inventories, cost means in principle the sum of the applicable expenditures and charges directly or indirectly incurred in bringing an article to its existing condition and location.

3. Cost for inventory purposes may be determined under any one of the several assumptions as to the flow of cost factors (such as first-in first-out, average, and last-in first-out); the major objective in selecting a method should be to choose the one which, under the circumstances, most clearly reflects periodic income.

4. A departure from the cost basis of pricing the inventory is required when the utility value of the goods is no longer as great as their cost. Where there is evidence that the utility value of goods, in their disposal in the ordinary course of business, will be less than cost, whether due to physical deterioration, obsolescence, changes in price levels, or other causes, the difference should be recognized as a loss of the current period. This is generally accomplished by stating such goods at a lower level commonly designated as "market."

5. As used in the phrase "lower of cost or market" (or equally acceptable "cost or market, whichever is lower"), the term "market" means current replacement cost (by purchase or by reproduction, as the case may be) except that—

a. market should not exceed the net realizable value (i.e., estimated selling price in the ordinary course of business less reasonably predicted costs of completion and disposal); and

b. market should not be less than net realizable value reduced by an allowance for an approximately normal profit margin.

Accrued net losses on firm purchase commitments for goods for inventory, measured in the same way as are inventory losses, should, if material, be recognized in the accounts and the amounts thereof separately disclosed in the income statement.

Other Current Assets. In addition to immaterial miscellaneous receivables, expenses such as insurance, interest, and taxes that are paid in advance usually are included in current assets. However, any material portion of such prepaid expenses that will not be used or absorbed within one year or within the operating cycle of the business is classified as a noncurrent asset.

Intercorporate Investments

In cases where a company does not control another company but rather has the ability to exercise significant influence over the operating and financial policies of the other company (usually presumed where more than 20 percent but less than 50 percent of the outstanding voting stock is owned), the equity method of accounting should be followed. Under the equity method, which is applicable to unconsolidated subsidiaries, corporate joint ventures and other investments which qualify for such method should be shown in the balance sheet of the company making the investment as a single amount. Also included among other things, are (a) intercompany profits and losses that have not been realized should be eliminated, (b) the difference between the cost of an investment and the amount of underlying equity in the net assets of the company invested in should be accounted for as if the company invested in was a consolidated subsidiary, and (c) the investment in common stock. The share of earnings or losses under the equity method should ordinarily be shown in the income statement as a single amount.

Where less than 20 percent of the outstanding voting stock is owned, it is usually presumed that significant influence does not exist and therefore the cost method should be used. Dividends received, in excess of earnings subsequent to the date of investment, are considered a return of investment and are recorded as reductions of cost of the investment. Where losses are sustained, provision should be made for any material impairment of the investment, unless such impairment is deemed to be temporary.

Property, Plant and Equipment

Property, plant and equipment are generally recorded at cost. Cost includes all direct expenditures necessary to purchase or construct the property and make it usable: the invoice or contract amount, materials, supplies, labor, and related overhead employed in construction or installation, preliminary engineering studies, and title costs. The inclusion in costs of interest on funds used for construction during the construction period is acceptable but is not a general practice except by certain industries, principally regulated utilities.

Nondepreciable property, such as land and idle property, is usually segregated in financial statements. The costs of all other property, plant, and equipment are charged systematically to operations over their estimated useful lives using specific methods of depreciation, depletion, and amortization. The accumulated allowances for depreciation, depletion, and amortization are deducted from the cost of properties in the balance sheet.

Depreciation. Three principal methods of depreciation are used currently in the United States: (1) straight-line, (2) declining balance, and (3) sum-of-the-years-digits. Another depreciation method used primarily in extractive industries is unit-of-production. All four are permissible for income tax purposes. Depending on individual circumstances, a company may use one method for some of its assets and another method for others. In addition, one method may be used for financial reporting purposes while another method is used for federal income tax purposes. An appropriate method is selected based on factors such as industry, type of property, and useful life of property.

Lump sum write-offs may be appropriate in special situations, such as sudden obsolescence or changes in business operations or policies.

Depletion. "Depletion," as an accounting term, is amortization of the cost of investment in natural resources by charges to operations over the period during which the quantities or units of such resources are extracted or exhausted. Generally, any one of several methods of computation is acceptable if the depletable base (cost plus certain development expense) is periodically charged to income on a systematic basis. Percentage depletion, a specific method allowed for income tax purposes, is not a generally accepted accounting practice because the amount of depletion under this method is computed as a percentage of income (as defined) from the depletable property and is not related to its cost.

Amortization. Lease-hold improvements are generally amortized to operations over the life of the lease or life of the improvement, whichever is shorter.

Intangibles and Deferred Charges

Cost is ordinarily the initial amount assigned to all types of intangibles. The cost of some intangibles, such as those acquired in exchange for securities, may be either the fair value of the consideration given or the fair value of the property or right acquired, whichever is the more clearly evident.

Intangibles with limited life (such as patents, copyrights, and franchises) are amortized by systematic charges to income over the period benefited. Intangibles with unlimited life (such as trade names) are carried in the balance sheet at cost until their lives are determined to be limited or are amortized by systematic charges to income. When reasonably evident that the life of unamortized intangibles becomes limited, their cost is amortized by systematic charges to income. It is not acceptable to make lump sum write-offs of intangibles to retained earnings immediately after acquisition or to charge the cost or amortization of intangibles to capital surplus. Prior to October 31, 1970, goodwill (purchase price in excess of net assets of acquired companies) was generally considered an intangible with unlimited life and therefore was accounted for by the method described above. However, goodwill arising since October 31, 1970, must be amortized by systematic charges to income over a period of not more than 40 years.

Deferred charges include unamortized debt discount and expense, deferred research and development costs, organization costs, and prepaid expenses which will not be used or absorbed within one year or during the operating cycle of the business.

Current Liabilities

Current liabilities include obligations for items entering into the operating cycle which result in accounts payable for materials purchased, accruals of wages, rentals, taxes, and like items. There are also included estimated or accrued amounts for known obligations payable within the year, even though the amounts can be determined only approximately or the payee is unknown at the balance sheet date.

Loans and Debt. The portion of long-term debt payable within one year is classified as a current liability unless it is clear that the amount is to be refinanced through other long-term debt. Obligations to banks, demand loans, and notes payable to others are either shown separately in the balance sheet or are combined with details disclosed in a note.

Severance Pay. Neither federal nor state statutes provide for mandatory severance pay. Many companies adopt a policy to pay extra compensation to salaried employees on severance and account for the amounts as expense when paid. Union contracts frequently provide that "supplemental employment benefits" computed on various bases be paid to separated employees; many companies provide currently for an estimated related liability.

Unearned Revenues. Unearned revenues collected in advance, such as rents, royalties, and subscriptions, are allocated to income as earned, usually based on time or performance. That portion of unearned revenues which is applicable to the next year or relates to current assets is usually included in current liabilities. The remaining portions are commonly classified as noncurrent items.

Contingency Provisions

Under U.S. accounting principles, it is deemed desirable to provide, by charges in the current income statement, properly classified, for all forseeable costs and losses applicable against current revenues, to the extent that they can be measured and allocated to fiscal periods with reasonable approximation. But it is not considered proper to permit income to be affected by reserve transactions not related to current operations.

The AICPA Committee on Accounting Procedure was of the opinion that reserves such as those created (a) for general undetermined contingencies; (b) for any indefinite possible future losses such as losses on inventories not on hand or contracted for; (c) for the purpose of reducing inventories other than to a basis which is in accordance with generally accepted accounting principles; (d) without regard to any specific loss reasonably related to the operations of the current period; or (e) in amounts not determined on the basis of any reasonable estimates of costs or losses are of such a nature that charges or credits relating to such reserves should not enter into the determination of net income.

However, reserves of this nature or for general corporate purposes may be appropriated from retained earnings. This action, of course, has no effect on current results of operations, but merely segregates retained earnings as appropriated and unappropriated in the stockholders' equity section of the balance sheet.

Accordingly, it was the opinion of the committee that if a reserve of the type described above is set up:

1. It should be created by a segregation or appropriation of retained earnings.
2. No costs or losses should be charged to it and no part of it should

be transferred to income or in any way used to affect the determination of net income for any year.

3. It should be restored to retained earnings directly when such a reserve or any part thereof is no longer considered necessary.
4. It should preferably be classified in the balance sheet as a part of shareholders' equity.

Capital Surplus

The term "capital surplus" is frequently used to describe capital in excess of par or stated value of capital stock. More precise terminology describing sources and avoiding the word "surplus" is recommended by the AICPA. Typical appropriate designations are the following:

1. Additional paid-in capital.
2. Excess of proceeds of sale over cost of treasury stock.
3. Capital in excess of par or stated values.
4. Excess of market value of stock dividend over par or stated value of shares issued.
5. Capital arising from reduction in par or stated value of capital stock.

Treasury Stock

Treasury stock is generally recorded at cost and shown separately as a reduction of total capital stock, capital surplus, and retained earnings. Treasury stock may be classified as an asset if held for a specific corporate purpose, such as stock option, stock purchase, or profit-sharing plans.

Stock Options

Options to purchase shares of common stock of companies are often granted to directors, officers, or certain key employees of such companies. Option prices are generally set to provide maximum tax benefits for the grantees, which means that the option prices are usually at or slightly above the market price at the date options are granted. Any element of compensation is generally not recorded in the accounts as long as the option price on the date of the grant is no less than the market price. On the other hand, if the option price on the date of grant is less than the market price, the total amount of the difference is an expense of the issuer and compensation to the recipient to be accounted for over the term of the option. Usual practice, when no element of compensation exists, is to record as capital the amount of cash received when options are exercised and respective shares of stock issued.

The AICPA recommends that financial statements disclose the status of options or option plans at the end of the period stating the number of shares under option, the option prices, and the number of shares for which options were exercisable. The number and option prices of shares issued for options exercised during the period covered by the financial statements should also be disclosed. The New York Stock Exchange and SEC require still further disclosure.

Stock Dividends

Under U.S. definitions, stock distributions to existing stockholders are considered "stock dividends" when the newly issued shares are less than 20 to 25 percent of the number of shares previously outstanding. If a distribution exceeds these percentages, it is considered a "stock split-up" and usually capital stock amounts are unchanged because any par or stated value may be reduced proportionately.

A publicly held company in the United States issuing a stock dividend transfers from retained earnings to capital stock and capital surplus an amount equal to the fair value of the additional shares issued. This accounting practice recognizes that many recipients regard stock dividends as distributions of corporate earnings usually in an amount equal to the fair market value of the distributed shares. A stock split-up requires transfer from retained earnings of only the amount necessary to meet legal requirements for par or stated value of total shares of stock.

Receipt of a stock dividend is not considered income in the United States. The recipient's investment is represented by an increased number of shares and the carrying amount is unchanged.

Retained Earnings

Retained earnings (earned surplus) are accumulated, undistributed earnings. Unappropriated retained earnings are normally available as a source of dividends. Negative retained earnings are called "deficits."

Capital surplus, however created, is not used to relieve the income account of charges from operations, and capital stock and capital surplus, whatever their nature, are not used to increase retained earnings.

Hidden Reserves

The term "hidden reserves" implies the existence of ownership equity concealed through the understatement or omission of assets, the overstatement of liabilities, or the inclusion of fictitious liabilities. In the

United States, it is not considered acceptable to establish hidden reserves by charges to current income with possible restoration to income in a later year or with a view to leveling out reported income over the years.

Net Income

Income statements in the United States conclude with an amount of net income (or loss) for the period. The term "income" is used to describe a conventional general concept. Amounts reported as net income are based on the concept that an enterprise is a going concern and that generally unrealized gains are not recorded but that all losses are recorded when foreseeable.

Net income includes all items of profit and loss recognized during the period except prior period adjustments, with extraordinary items net of applicable federal income taxes shown separately as an element of net income for the period. Accounting Principles Board Opinion No. 9 describes the principal advantages of the above approach as follows:

1. Inclusion of all operating items related to the current period, with segregation and disclosure of the extraordinary items.
2. A reporting of current income from operations free from distortions resulting from material items directly related to prior periods.
3. Proper retroactive reflection in comparative financial statements of material adjustments relating directly to prior periods.

Opinion No. 30 of the Accounting Principles Board states that extraordinary items are events and transactions that are distinguished by their unusual nature *and* by the infrequency of their occurrence. Thus, *both* of the following criteria should be met to classify an event or transaction as an extraordinary item:

1. Unusual nature—the underlying event or transaction should possess a high degree of abnormality and be of a type clearly unrelated to, or only incidentally related to, the ordinary and typical activities of the entity, taking into account the environment in which the entity operates.
2. Infrequency of occurrence—the underlying event or transaction should be of a type that would not reasonably be expected to recur in the foreseeable future, taking into account the environment in which the entity operates.

Certain gains and losses should not be reported as extraordinary items because they are usual in nature or may be expected to recur as a consequence of customary and continuing business activities. Examples include the following:

1. Write-down or write-off of receivables, inventories, equipment leased to others, deferred research and development costs, or other intangible assets.
2. Gains or losses from exchange or translation of foreign currencies, including those relating to major devaluations and revaluations.
3. Gains or losses on disposal of a segment of a business.
4. Other gains or losses from sale or abandonment of property, plant, or equipment used in the business.
5. Effects of a strike, including those against competitors and major suppliers.
6. Adjustment of accruals on long-term contracts.

Prior period adjustments "are limited to those material adjustments which (a) can be specifically identified with and directly related to the business activities of particular prior periods, and (b) are not attributable to economic events occurring subsequent to the date of the financial statements for the prior period, and (c) depend primarily on determinations by persons other than management, and (d) were not susceptible of reasonable estimation prior to such determination. Such adjustments are rare in modern financial accounting. Examples are material, nonrecurring adjustments or settlements of income taxes, of renegotiation proceedings or of utility revenues under rate processes. Settlements of significant amounts resulting from litigation or similar claims may also constitute prior period adjustments."

The following, however, should be excluded from the determination of net income under all circumstances:

1. Adjustments resulting from transactions in the company's own capital stock.
2. Amounts transferred to and from accounts properly designated as surplus appropriations, such as charges and credits with respect to general purpose contingency reserves.
3. Amounts deemed to represent excessive costs of fixed assets, and annual appropriations in contemplation of replacement of productive facilities at higher price levels.
4. Adjustments made pursuant to a quasi-reorganization.

Accounting Principles Board Opinion No. 20 describes the three types of accounting changes and their effect on reported net income as follows:

1. A change in accounting principle resulting from the adoption of a generally accepted accounting principle different from the one used previously for reporting purposes, for example, a change in depreciation method for previously recorded assets, such as from the double declining balance method to the straight-line method. The effect of this type of change should not be used to retroactively adjust previously issued financial statements but the cumulative effect of the change on opening retained earnings should be shown as a separate item in the income statement between the captions "extraordinary items" and "net income."

2. A change in accounting estimate, for example, allowances for uncollectible receivables, inventory obsolescence, and so forth. The effect of this type of change should be accounted for in the current period only or in the current period and future periods, if applicable.

3. A change in reporting entity, for example, presenting consolidated or combined statements in place of statements of individual companies. The effect of this type of change should be shown retroactively by restating prior period financial statements.

If an error, resulting from a mathematical mistake, a mistake in the application of an accounting principle, or an oversight or misuse of facts that existed at the time the financial statements were prepared, in previously issued financial statements is discovered, it should be treated as a prior period adjustment.

The Accounting Principles Board, in Opinion No. 30, concluded that the results from discontinued operations including gains or losses from disposal of a segment of business should be reported separately from discontinued operations but not as extraordinary items. Accordingly, operations of a segment that has been or will be discontinued should be reported separately as a component of income before extraordinary items and the accumulative effect of accounting changes (if applicable). Amounts of income taxes applicable to the results of discontinued operations and gains or losses from disposal of the segment should be disclosed on the face of income statements or related notes. Revenues applicable to the discontinued operations should be separately disclosed in the related notes.

Earnings Per Share

Because of the significance attached by investors and others to earnings per share data, together with the importance of evaluating the data in conjunction with financial statements, earnings per share or net loss per share data must be shown on the face of the income statement and must be consistent with the income statement presentation; for example, if extraordinary items are shown in the income statement, earnings per share should be presented for (a) income before extraordinary items and (b) net income.

Earnings Per Common Share or Earnings Per Common Share and Common Equivalent Share

On the face of the income statement, a company must show either one of these captions. In the simplest example, earnings per common share is arrived at by dividing earnings or losses for the period attributable to common shareholders (i.e., net income less dividends on cumulative preferred senior securities) by the weighted average number of common shares outstanding during each period. A monthly average giving retroactive recognition to stock dividends and splits and shares issued in a business combination accounted for as a pooling of interests is generally used. When shares are issued to acquire a business in a transaction accounted for as a purchase, such shares should enter into the computation from the date the acquisition takes place.

Earnings per common share and common equivalent share are used when in addition to common stock a company has potentially dilutive convertible securities, options, warrants, or other rights, considered in substance to be equivalent to common shares, that upon conversion or exercise could in the aggregate dilute (reduce in excess of 3 percent) earnings per common share.

In addition to either one of the above captions, a company may show a second pro forma presentation which reflects the dilution of earnings per share that would have occurred if all contingent issuances of common stock that would individually reduce earnings per share had taken place at the beginning of the period (or time of issuance of the security, if applicable). Thus, this caption signifies the maximum extent of potential dilution of current earnings that conversions of securities that are not common stock equivalents could create. Convertible securities, options, warrants, stock purchase contracts, participation securities, and agreements to issue stock in the future are included in the computation of fully diluted earnings per share.

It should be noted that, for all computations, common stock equivalents or other contingent issuances should not be considered if such considerations have an anti-dilutive effect on the computation.

A schedule or note relating to earnings per share data must explain the basis upon which both primary and fully diluted earnings per share are calculated.

Pension Costs

It is generally accepted that for most pension plans the entire cost of benefit payments ultimately to be made should be charged against income subsequent to the adoption or amendment of a plan and that no portion (i.e., past service costs) should be charged directly against retained earnings. Past service costs are those costs attributable to the years prior to the adoption of the plan.

The annual provision for pension cost should be based on an accounting method that uses an acceptable actuarial cost method (a rational, systematic method consistently applied that assigns a portion of current and past service costs to each accounting period resulting in reasonably stable annual charges) and results in a provision between the minimum and maximum stated below. The accounting method and the actuarial cost method should be consistently applied from year to year.

Minimum. The annual provision for pension cost should not be less than the sum of (1) current year's cost based on benefits accruing to employees for current year's service, (2) an amount equivalent to interest on any unfunded past service cost, and (3) a provision for vested benefits (defined as benefits that are not contingent on an employee's continuing in the service of the employer), if applicable. A provision for vested benefits should be made if there is an excess of actuarially computed value of vested benefits over the total set aside to pay such benefits. Generally, the provision is the lesser of such deficiency or an amount necessary to make the aggregate annual provision for pension cost equal to the total of (1) and (2) above plus amortization of past service costs.

Maximum. The annual provision for pension costs should not be greater than the amount determined above except that past service costs are amortized over a ten-year basis.

The following disclosures regarding pension plans must be made in the financial statements or notes thereto:

1. A statement that such plans exist, identifying or describing the employee groups covered.
2. A statement of the company's accounting and funding policies.
3. The provision for pension cost for the period.

4. The excess, if any, of the actuarially computed value of vested benefits over the total of the pension fund and any balance sheet pension accruals, less any pension prepayments or deferred charges.

5. Nature and effect of significant matters affecting comparability for all periods presented, such as changes in accounting methods (actuarial cost method, amortization of prior service cost, treatment of actuarial gains and losses, and so forth), changes in circumstances (actuarial assumptions, and so forth), or adoption or amendment of a plan.

Tax-Effect Accounting

Taxes are allocated when the difference between income for federal tax purposes and income for financial reporting purposes is material, thus producing a difference between the current tax obligation and the amount obtained by applying the current tax rate to accounting net income.

In general, guidelines for balance sheet and income statement presentation of the tax effects of timing differences, operating losses, and similar items as stated in Accounting Principles Board Opinion No. 11 are as follows:

1. Interperiod tax allocation is an integral part of the determination of income tax expense, and income tax expense should include the tax effects of revenue and expense transactions included in the determination of pre-tax accounting income.

2. Interperiod tax allocation procedures should follow the deferred method, both in the manner in which tax effects are initially recognized and in the manner in which deferred taxes are amortized in future periods. Under the deferred method, the tax effects of current timing differences are deferred currently and allocated to income tax expense of future periods when the timing differences reverse. The deferred taxes are determined on the basis of the tax rates in effect at the time the timing differences originate and are not adjusted for subsequent changes in tax rates or to reflect the imposition of new taxes.

3. The tax effects of operating loss carrybacks should be allocated to the loss periods. The tax effects of operating loss carryforwards usually should not be recognized until the periods of realization.

4. Tax allocation within a period should be applied to obtain fair presentation of the various components of results of operations.

5. Financial statement presentations of income tax expense and related deferred taxes should disclose (1) the composition of income tax

expense as between amounts currently payable and amounts representing tax effects allocable to the period and (2) the classification of deferred taxes into a net current amount and a net noncurrent amount.

Investment Credit

The Revenue Act of 1971 provides for restoration of an "investment credit" (under the name of Job Development Investment Credit) as an offset to income tax liability. In general, the credit equals a specified percentage of the cost of certain newly acquired depreciable assets. APB Opinion No. 4 recognizes two methods of accounting for the investment credit: (a) the credit may be reflected in net income over the productive life of the acquired property or (b) the credit may be treated as a reduction of federal income taxes for the year in which the credit arises. The Board expressed a preference for method (a). However, the United States Congress has ruled that either method is acceptable. This is the first time in the history of the United States that the Congress has ruled on accounting principles.

Long-Term Construction Contracts

Two generally accepted accounting methods commonly followed by contractors in recognizing long-term construction contract revenue are as follows:

1. The percentage-of-completion method, which recognizes as revenue the portion of estimated total revenue equal to the ratio of costs incurred to date to total estimated costs. This method recognizes revenue currently and reflects the status of uncompleted contracts, but is necessarily dependent on estimates.
2. The completed contract method, which recognizes revenue when the contract is completed. This method recognizes final results only and results of operations are not recognized currently.

When estimates of costs to complete a contract and the extent of progress toward completion are reasonably dependable, the percentage-of-completion method is preferred. Under either method, provision should be made for any anticipated losses.

International Operations and Foreign Exchange

Earnings of U.S. companies from international sources are includable in income to the extent to which they are received in the United States or represent unrestricted funds available for remittance. International earnings in excess of such amounts are included in income only after careful consideration of all the facts, and the amount is disclosed, if significant.

Whether or not foreign subsidiaries are included in consolidated statements, adequate information must be furnished concerning their assets and liabilities, income and losses, and the parent's equity therein.

Realized gain or loss from translating accounts expressed in foreign currencies should be recognized in income statements. Any unrealized losses, such as may arise from translating foreign net current assets, are charged to income. However, unrealized gains are deferred to the extent that they exceed prior provisions for unrealized losses. Deferred U.S. federal income taxes should be provided on unrestricted and unremitted international earnings to the extent that the U.S. parent company does not intend to leave such earnings permanently outside the United States.

The Financial Accounting Standards Board, in December 1973, issued its Statement of Financial Accounting Standards No. 1, "Disclosure of Foreign Currency Translation Information." The FASB concluded that certain disclosures should be made in financial statements that include amounts denominated in a foreign currency which have been translated into the currency of the reporting entity. The amounts may result from transactions, the consolidation of subsidiaries, and the equity method of accounting for investees. The following information shall be disclosed:

1. A statement of translation policies including identification of (a) the balance sheet accounts that are translated at the current rate and those translated at the historical rate, (b) the rates used to translate income statement accounts (e.g., historical rates for specified accounts and a weighted average rate for all other accounts), (c) the time of recognition of gain or loss on forward exchange contracts, and (d) the method of accounting for exchange adjustments (and if any portion of the exchange adjustment is deferred, the method of disposition of the deferred amount in future years).

2. The aggregate amount of exchange adjustments originating in the period, the amount thereof included in the determination of income and the amount thereof deferred.

3. The aggregate amount of exchange adjustments included in the determination of income for the period, regardless of when the adjustments originated.

4. The aggregate amount of deferred exchange adjustments, regardless of when the adjustments originated, included in the balance sheet (e.g., such as in a deferral or in a "reserve" account) and how this amount is classified.

5. The amount by which total long-term receivables and total long-term payables translated at historical rates would each increase or decrease at the balance sheet date if translated at current rates.

6. The amount of gain or loss which has not been recognized on unperformed forward exchange contracts at the balance sheet date.

The disclosures required by this statement are designed to provide information concerning a company's translation practices to facilitate assessment of possible implications with respect to its financial position and results of operations. This statement does not supersede, alter, or amend any APB Opinion or Accounting Research Bulletin (ARB).

Price-Level Accounting

It is not customary in the United States to record the effects of price-level changes in the accounts or in the formal published financial statements of business enterprises. The importance of the effect of price-level changes, especially on the statement of income, has long been recognized, and numerous articles and studies on the subject have been published, including bulletins of the AICPA and an AICPA research study. The Institute supports the publication, as supplementary statistical data, of financial schedules, explanations, or notes by which management may explain and illustrate the need to retain earnings because of price-level changes. This procedure is not yet common, but a few corporations have experimented with some form of reporting on price-level changes.

Business Combinations–Pooling of Interests vs. Purchase

Groups of stockholders may decide to combine their respective corporations. Two accounting bases are recognized for combinations—pooling of interests among the constituent corporations and purchase of one or more corporations by another. A combination is treated as either a pooling or a purchase. To be treated as a pooling, several specific conditions must be met.

In a pooling of interests, corporations are combined by an agreed-upon exchange of shares. No new basis of accountability arises, and the book values of each corporation are carried forward to the combined enterprise. Generally, retained earnings of the constituent companies continue as the retained earnings of the combined enterprise. The requisites to a pooling of interests specified by Opinion No. 16 of the Accounting Principles Board are as follows:

1. Attributes of the combining companies

   a. Each of the combining companies is autonomous and has not been a subsidiary or division of another corporation within two years before the plan of combination is initiated.

b. Each of the combining companies is independent of the other combining companies.

2. Manner of combining interests

a. The combination is effected in a single transaction or is completed in accordance with a specific plan within one year after the plan is initiated.

b. A corporation offers and issues only common stock with rights identical to those of the majority of its outstanding voting common stock in exchange for substantially all of the voting common stock interest of another company at the date the plan of combination is consummated.

3. Absence of planned transactions

a. The combined corporation does not agree directly or indirectly to retire or reacquire all or part of the common stock issued to effect the combination.

b. The combined corporation does not enter into other financial arrangements for the benefit of the former stockholders of a combining company, such as a guaranty of loans secured by stock issued in the combination, which in effect negates the exchange of equity securities.

c. The combined corporation does not intend or plan to dispose of a significant part of the assets of the combining companies within two years after the combination other than disposals in the ordinary course of business of the formerly separate companies and to eliminate duplicate facilities or excess capacity.

All expenses related to effecting a business combination accounted for by the pooling-of-interests method should be deducted in determining the net income of the resulting combined corporation for the period in which the expenses are incurred.

A combination of businesses may also be effected through purchase of one corporation's assets by another corporation for cash or other consideration. In a purchase, some existing stockholders' interests are eliminated, or other factors requisite to a pooling of interests are not present. Under these circumstances, a new basis of accountability is created based on the consideration paid. Assets acquired in a purchase are recorded at the consideration directly or indirectly paid to achieve the business combination. Ordinarily, such consideration is allocated to the assets acquired on the basis of their relative fair value. This accounting frequently results in recording an intangible asset called "purchase price in excess of net assets of acquired companies (goodwill)."

Interest on Receivables and Payables

Business transactions often involve the exchange of property, goods, or services for a note or similar instrument. The use of an interest rate that varies from prevailing interest rates warrants evaluation of whether the face amount and the stated interest rate of a note or obligation provide reliable evidence for properly recording the exchange and subsequent related interest. Unless the note is recorded at its present value in the circumstances, the sales price and profit to a seller in the year of the transaction and the purchase price and cost to the buyer are misstated, and the interest income and interest expense in subsequent periods are also misstated. In order to establish the present value of the note, an attempt should be made to obtain the cash value that would have been given up instead of the note or if the note is traded in an open market, the market rate of interest which would permit the market value of the note to be determined. If neither of these is available, the applicable interest rate can be approximated, using the interest rate used in normal business transactions at that point in time. The value of the note will then be the residual.

This section is applicable to all business transactions except the following:

1. Receivables and payables arising from normal trade transactions where payment is due within one year.
2. Deposits, advance payments, and so forth.
3. Transactions where interest rates are affected by the tax attributes or legal restrictions prescribed by a government agency.
4. Transactions between parent and subsidiary companies and between subsidiaries of a common parent.

Reporting of Leases in Financial Statements of Lessee

Typically, in a noncancelable lease or a lease cancelable only upon the occurrence of some remote contingency, if either of the two following conditions exist, the lease should be considered to be in substance a purchase:

1. The initial term is materially less than the useful life of the property, and the lessee has the option to renew the lease for the remaining useful life of the property at substantially less than the fair rental value; or

2. The lessee has the right, during or at the expiration of the lease, to acquire the property at a price that at the inception of the lease appears to be substantially less than the probable fair value of the property at the time or times of permitted acquisition by the lessee.

Because of the significance of the commitment involved, the Accounting Principles Board in Opinion No. 31 concluded that financial statements of the lessees should disclose sufficient information relating to noncapitalized lease commitments to enable users of the statements to assess the present and prospective effect of those commitments upon the financial position, results of operations, and change in financial position of the lessee. Accordingly, the Board specified that the information below be disclosed as an integral part of the financial statement.

Total Rental Expense. Total rental expense (reduced by rentals from subleases, with disclosure of such amounts) entering into the determination of results of operations for each period for which an income statement is presented should be disclosed. Rental payments under short-term leases for a month or less which are not expected to be renewed need not be included. Contingent rentals, such as those based upon usage or sales, should be reported separately from the basic or minimum rentals.

Minimum Rental Commitments. The minimum rental commitments under all noncancelable leases should be disclosed, as of the date of the latest balance sheet presented, in the aggregate for—

(a) each of the five succeeding fiscal years,

(b) each of the next three five-year periods, and

(c) the remainder as a single amount.

The amounts so determined should be reduced by rentals to be received from existing noncancelable subleases (with disclosure of the amounts of such rentals). The total of the amounts included in (a), (b), and (c) should also be classified by major categories of properties, such as real estate, aircraft, truck fleets, and other equipment.

Additional Disclosures. Additional disclosures should be made to report in general terms the following:

1. The basis for calculating rental payments if dependent upon factors other than the lapse of time.

2. Existence and terms of renewal or purchase options, escalation clauses, and so forth.

3. The nature and amount of related guarantees made or obligations assumed.
4. Restrictions on paying dividends, incurring additional debt, further leasing, etc.
5. Any other information necessary to assess the effect of lease commitments upon the financial position, results of operations and changes in financial position of the lessee.

Present Value of Commitments. The Board believes that disclosure of the present value of the minimum rental commitments as discussed above may be helpful in evaluating the credit capacity of the lessee and in comparing the lessee's financial position with that of other entities using other means of financing to obtain the use of property. Such disclosure, if presented, may include the following, as of the date of the latest balance sheet presented:

1. The present values of the net fixed minimum lease commitments (based on the interest rates implicit in the terms of the leases at the times of entering into the leases) in the aggregate and by major categories of properties such as real estate, aircraft, truck fleets, and other equipment.
2. Either the weighted average interest rate (based on the present values) and range of rates, or specific interest rates, for all lease commitments included in the amounts disclosed under (1) above.
3. The present value of rentals to be received from existing non-cancelable subleases of property included in (1) above (based on the interest rates implicit in the terms of the subleases at the times of entering into the subleases).

Requirements for Public Sale of Securities

With certain exceptions, companies offering securities for sale to the public must file a registration statement with the Securities and Exchange Commission under the Securities Act of 1933. The exceptions include offerings of which the aggregate offering price does not exceed $500,000, securities of governmental units, and those of certain common carriers, such as interstate railroads.

The registration statement consists of two parts—the prospectus, which must be furnished to the buyer of the registered security, and a second part containing information not required in the prospectus. The principal financial statements are contained in the prospectus, whereas certain supporting schedules appear in part II.

In general, a balance sheet is required as of a date within 90 days prior to the filing of the registration statement, or under certain conditions, within six months of such date. If this balance sheet is not certified by an independent public accountant, a certified balance sheet at the close of the fiscal year ending within one year prior to the filing date must be filed. Also, income, retained earnings and capital surplus statements, and statements of changes in financial position must be filed for the three fiscal years preceding the date of the latest certified balance sheet and must be certified; in addition, uncertified income, retained earnings and capital surplus statements, and statements of changes in financial position are required for the period from the close of the fiscal year to the date of the latest (uncertified) balance sheet filed and also for the corresponding interim period of the preceding fiscal year. In addition to certain other information, part II of the registration statement includes schedules containing details of balance sheet and income statement items, some of which must also be certified.

If the company has subsidiaries, there must be filed consolidated financial statements and schedules at the same dates and for the same periods as those for the parent company, and similar reports of independent public accountants must accompany them. When consolidated financial statements are filed, unconsolidated financial statements of the parent company may be omitted under certain specified conditions.

In practically all cases, and for many years in the past, the sale of securities to the public has been underwritten by firms of investment bankers. Even before the passage of the Securities Act of 1933, it was general custom that prospectuses contain financial statements certified by independent certified public accountants. While the SEC requires a summary of earnings for at least five years to be included in the prospectus, such summary is not required to be certified. In practice, however, underwriters usually require that the summary of earnings be certified for at least that period (usually three years) for which the more detailed income statements required by the SEC must be certified.

In addition to the requirements of the Securities and Exchange Commission, and the matters included on advice of the underwriters and their counsel, prospectuses offering securities for sale in many states must comply with the respective state statutes, known as "Blue Sky" laws. These laws have been in effect in every state except Delaware and Nevada for many years; they vary among the states and often require information differing from that required by the SEC.

Requirements for Listing Securities on the Stock Exchange

The Securities Exchange Act of 1934 governs the registration of national securities exchanges, securities listed on such exchanges, and brokers and dealers trading in the over-the-counter securities markets.

A corporation seeking to list its securities for trading on a national securities exchange must comply with two sets of requirements—those of the securities exchange and those of the SEC. In most respects, the information required is similar or identical. The SEC requires that a corporation prepare an application for registration of its securities under the 1934 act, which is filed with the securities exchange on which the corporation is to be listed, and also with the Commission. The SEC also requires the filing of annual reports by each listed company that are designed to give the public annual financial information about the company.

In addition, listed corporations must comply with listing and annual reporting requirements of the various exchanges on which they are listed, the most stringent of which are the requirements of the New York Stock Exchange.

Under the listing agreement of that exchange, the company undertakes to publish quarterly statements of earnings and annual reports, notify the exchange of changes in the company's practices, and numerous other matters. It is also required that all annual financial statements submitted to stockholders be audited by independent accountants qualified under the laws of some state or country and be accompanied by the independent accountant's opinion. Exception has been made to this requirement in the case of railroads, banks, and insurance companies, which are supervised by government agencies.

Reporting Requirements for Unlisted Companies

Under the Securities Acts Amendments of (August) 1964, many companies whose securities are not listed on a National Securities Exchange but are traded "over-the-counter" are subject to reporting requirements similar to those applicable to listed companies. The companies which are required to register with the Securities and Exchange Commission are those with total assets of over $1,000,000 and having equity securities held of record by more than 500 stockholders. Certain banks and insurance companies are exempt from these registration requirements, but must meet certain disclosure requirements of appropriate federal and state regulatory bodies.

The form for registration contains substantially the same financial information as that required for listed companies. In addition, the requirements for annual reports are the same as those for listed companies.

United States

Illustrative Financial Statements

ILLUSTRATIVE BALANCE SHEETS OF A UNITED STATES COMPANY

CONSOLIDATED BALANCE SHEETS

ASSETS	December 31, 19__	December 31, 19__
CURRENT ASSETS		
Cash	....	....
Marketable securities, at cost (market quotations $........ in 19__ and $........ in 19__)	....	....
Notes and trade accounts receivable, less allowance of $........ in 19__ and $........ in 19__, for doubtful accounts	....	....
Inventories at the lower of cost (first-in first-out) or market	....	....
Other current assets	....	....
	....	....
INVESTMENTS	....	....
DEFERRED RECEIVABLES	....	....
PROPERTY, PLANT AND EQUIPMENT, at cost		
Land	....	....
Buildings	....	....
Machinery and equipment	....	....
Leasehold improvements	....	....
Construction in progress	....	....
Less—accumulated depreciation and amortization	....	....
	....	....
OTHER ASSETS		
Purchase price in excess of net assets of acquired companies, net of amortization	....	....
Deferred research and development costs, net of amortization	....	....
Patents, trademarks, etc., at cost	....	....
Unamortized debt discount and expense	....	....
	....	....
	....	....

LIABILITIES AND STOCKHOLDERS' EQUITY

	December 31, 19__	December 31, 19__
CURRENT LIABILITIES		
Notes payable to banks	....	....
Long-term debt, due within one year	....	....
Accounts payable	....	....
Accrued liabilities	....	....
Accrued federal income taxes	....	....
Other current liabilities	....	....
LONG-TERM DEBT	....	....
First mortgage 5% bonds, due 19__	....	....
Debentures, 6½%, ... due serially to 19__	....	....
	....	....
DEFERRED FEDERAL INCOME TAXES	....	....
MINORITY EQUITY IN CONSOLIDATED SUBSIDIARIES	....	....
OTHER NONCURRENT LIABILITIES	....	....
	....	....
STOCKHOLDERS' EQUITY		
Preferred stock, $4 cumulative preferred $100 par value; authorized and outstanding .... shares in 19__ and .... shares in 19__	....	....
Common stock, $1 par value; authorized and outstanding .... shares in 19__ and .... shares in 19__	....	....
Capital surplus	....	....
Retained earnings	....	....
	....	....
	....	....

ILLUSTRATIVE CONSOLIDATED STATEMENTS OF INCOME AND RETAINED EARNINGS OF A UNITED STATES COMPANY

	For the year ended December 31,	
	19__	19__
NET SALES	....	....
COST OF SALES	....	....
Gross profit	....	....
SELLING, GENERAL, AND ADMINISTRATIVE EXPENSES	....	....
OTHER INCOME (EXPENSE)	....	....
Interest, dividends, and royalties	....	....
Minority common stockholders' investment in net income	(........)	(........)
Interest expense	(........)	(........)
Amortization of debt discount expense	(........)	(........)
Income before federal income taxes and extraordinary items	....	....
PROVISION FOR FEDERAL INCOME TAXES		
Currently payable	(........)	(........)
Deferred	(........)	(........)
Income before extraordinary items	....	....
EXTRAORDINARY ITEMS		
Gain on sale of fixed assets, net of federal income taxes	....	—
Loss on devaluations of foreign currencies, net of federal income taxes	—	(........)
	....	....
NET INCOME	....	....
RETAINED EARNINGS, beginning of year	....	....
Less dividends paid on preferred stock $7 per share in 19__ and 19__	(........)	(........)
RETAINED EARNINGS, end of year	....	....
EARNINGS PER COMMON AND COMMON EQUIVALENT SHARES		
Income before extraordinary items	....	....
Extraordinary items	....	....
Net income	....	....
EARNINGS PER COMMON SHARE— assuming full dilution		
Income before extraordinary items	....	....
Extraordinary items	....	....
NET INCOME	....	....

ILLUSTRATIVE CONSOLIDATED STATEMENTS OF CHANGES IN FINANCIAL POSITION OF A UNITED STATES COMPANY

	For the year ended December 31, 19__	19__
WORKING CAPITAL WAS PROVIDED BY		
Operations		
Income before extraordinary items	$	$ ....
Depreciation and amortization of fixed and intangible assets	....	....
Deferred federal income taxes	....	....
Deferred receivables	....	....
Funds provided by operations	....	....
Extraordinary items	....	(........)
Increase in long-term debt	....	....
Retirement of property, plant and equipment	....	....
Decrease in other assets	....	....
Proceeds from exercise of options and warrants and sale of common stock	....	....
Total funds provided	$	$ ....
WORKING CAPITAL WAS USED TO		
Purchase property, plant and equipment	$	$ ....
Retire long-term debt	....	—
Increase investments	—	....
Decrease minority equity in consolidated subsidiaries and other noncurrent liabilities	....	....
Increase (decrease) in working capital	....	(........)
Total funds applied	$	$ ....
COMPONENTS OF WORKING CAPITAL CHANGED AS FOLLOWS		
Cash	$	$(........)
Marketable securities	(........)	....
Notes and trade accounts receivable	....	(........)
Inventories	....	....
Other current assets	....	....
Notes payable and long-term debt	(........)	(........)
Accounts payable and accrued liabilities	....	....
Accrued federal income taxes	(........)	....
Other current liabilities	....	(........)
Increase (decrease)	$	$ ....

Venezuela

VENEZUELA

As of February 1975

Forms of Business Organization

The forms of business organization in Venezuela are similar to those of other Spanish-American countries and are provided for in the first ("On Commerce in General") of four sections of the Code of Commerce which was partially reformed in 1955. Other sections of the Code of Commerce deal with maritime commerce, bankruptcies and commercial jurisdiction. Certain professional organizations are regulated under the Civil Code.

The compañía anónima (or sociedad anónima) and the general partnership have their counterparts in similar forms common in the United States; there are specialized forms of limited partnerships which differ somewhat. The Code of Commerce of Venezuela does not distinguish between foreign and domestic corporations or partnerships; nevertheless, new foreign investments must have prior approval of the Superintendent of Foreign Investments. In view of the recently established rules, it is no longer practicable for a new investor to register a branch of a foreign corporation. Accordingly, a U.S. company wishing to engage in business in Venezuela, should do so by organizing a subsidiary under Venezuelan law; such subsidiary has certain other tax advantages.

The government, through various agencies (Superintendency of Banks,

Superintendency of Insurance, Superintendency of Foreign Investments, Treasury, Central Bank, Ministries of Development, Mines and Hydrocarbons, Labor, and so forth), supervises the operations of insurance, banking, oil, industrial and other concerns in which it has an interest (see Accounting and Reporting for the Oil Industry, later in this chapter), as well as those companies in which foreigners have investments, and those national companies which have royalty agreements with foreign owners of technology. Industrial enterprises have to be registered in the "Catastro de Industria" (Census of Industry), kept in the Ministry of Development, within a period of 90 days following the start of operation. In order to register in this Catastro, the companies have to submit the constitutive document, list of products to be manufactured, and so forth. Furthermore, income tax inspectors may inspect the records of any company, and regulations in regard to labor and other matters are provided in social legislation.

Compañía Anónima (C.A.) or Sociedad Anónima (S.A.)

The most common form of incorporation is the compañía or sociedad anónima which is organized by not less than two incorporators, but after initial registration has no required minimum number of stockholders. Liability of stockholders is limited to the amount of their subscriptions. All authorized shares must be fully subscribed, a minimum of 20 percent must be paid for and deposited in a bank, and shares must have a par value. If property other than cash is paid in on subscriptions, its value must be approved by all stockholders, and must be acceptable to the Registrar of Companies. The company must have a specified life, but that life can be extended prior to expiration.

The constitutive document of a Venezuelan corporation includes matters usually set forth in both the charter and bylaws of a U.S. corporation. It must be presented to the Mercantile Registry (Court of Commerce) in the district of its domicile, published in a local newspaper and inscribed in the Commercial Register. This document must state the compensation and special rights granted to promoters, if any, which may be only in the form of participation in future profits not in excess of 10 percent and for not more than five years. It must also state the number of comisarios (statutory examiners) who have an unlimited right of inspection of all operations of the corporation.

The legal reserve is provided at 5 percent of the annual profits until it equals 10 percent of the capital. This requirement may be higher if so provided in the bylaws, which may also provide other reserves.

Every six months (for banks, every year) the administrators must present financial statements to the comisarios, who must examine them and report upon them to the stockholders at the annual meeting. Ten days after approval by the stockholders, a copy of the financial statements and the report of the comisarios must be filed with the local Mercantile Registry (Court of Commerce).

Compañía (Sociedad) de Responsabilidad Limitada (C.R.L. or S.R.L.)

This entity resembles a corporation (C.A. or S.A.) in that the contributors are liable only to the amount of their subscriptions to their participation quotas, divided in units of 1,000 Venezuelan bolivars or multiples thereof. The capital subscribed must be not less than Bs 20,000 nor more than Bs 2,000,000. Comisarios must be appointed if capital exceeds Bs 500,000.

Unless the instrument of organization provides otherwise, quota-holders wishing to transfer their interest must first offer them to other partners, and in order to transfer to third parties, must have the consent of a majority of partners representing at least three-fourths of the capital. Quotas may not be represented by negotiable shares or securities.

Within a maximum of three months after the close of a fiscal period, the managers must prepare a balance sheet and profit and loss statement, and statement of proposed distribution of profits.

Other Forms of Business Organization

Compañía en Nombre Colectivo. This is the usual form of partnership in which all partners are jointly and severally liable for partnership obligations. The partnership agreement must include: the name and domicile of the partnership and of all its partners, the kind of business, and the contributions of partners and methods of sharing profits and losses.

The general partnership is not required to have comisarios.

Compañía en Comandita Simple. In this type there are two classes of partners—general (solidarios) who have joint and several liability for partnership debts, and have exclusive right to management. The liability of silent or limited partners (comanditarios) is limited to a specific amount.

Compañía en Comandita por Acciones. This differs from the above only in that the interests of the limited partners may be represented by shares. The instrument of organization must also specify the amount of capital with limited liability, and the number of comisarios.

Sociedad Anónima de Capital Autorizado (S.A.C.A.). This new type of legal entity was recently introduced by the new Capital Markets Law, with the stockholders being able to authorize increases of capital up to a stated amount through the issuance of new stock when the administrators so decide and in the amounts so decided.

Sociedad Anónima Inscrita de Capital Abierto (S.A.I.C.A.). This new type of company was also recently provided by the new Capital Markets Law, and must have a paid-in capital of not less than Bs 1,000,000, and not less than 50 percent of the capital must be owned by not less than 50 persons for each Bs 1,000,000 of capital, and no group may own more than 10 percent of the capital.

Variable Capital Corporations or Mutual Funds and Mutual Fund Management Corporations. The Capital Markets Law provides for these types of corporations but, as yet, there has been no significant activity therein.

Business Records

All businesses (including sole proprietorships) must maintain a journal, general ledger, and an "inventory book." Somewhat less elaborate records are required of retail merchants. The journal and the inventory book must be bound and the pages numbered. All other records, including the general ledger, may be maintained in any way which is to the advantage of the company. The Code of Commerce permits the summarization of transactions on a monthly basis. It is, therefore, often the practice for the journal to contain only one entry per month summarizing the total debit and credit movements of all major accounts during the month.

At the commencement of operations, the journal and the "inventory book" must be presented to the local Court of Commerce to be signed and dated on the initial page, and all pages must be stamped with the seal of the court.

Corporations and share-issuing limited partnerships must also maintain a stock-transfer book and minute books for directors' and shareholders' meetings, which must be similarly bound and stamped on each page.

Comisario (Statutory Examiner)

The Commercial Code of Venezuela states in effect that the shareholders of a corporation shall appoint one or more comisarios, who may or may not be shareholders, but not officers of the company to prepare a report for presentation at the shareholders' meeting of the following year explaining the results of the examination and the information obtained from management, reporting their observations arising from their examination, and stating their approval (or disapproval) of financial statements and other relevant matters. As mentioned above, the statutory examiners have an unlimited right of inspection of the books and records of the company. They are deemed to be the stockholders' representatives in the financial affairs of the corporation. They are probably subject to civil fraud suits from stockholders or third parties if they make false declarations.

There is no penalty if statutory examiners are not appointed although it is a common practice to appoint the comisarios at the first meeting after the constitution of a company. Any interested party may ask the commercial court to appoint the statutory examiner if one has not been appointed by the shareholders. There are no qualifications for the position of statutory examiner. There is no present requirement that the statutory examiner be a "contador público"; but a contador público must certify the comisario's report if shareholders owning 20 percent of the capital so request. In view of the recently established rules of the National Securities Commission and of the Superintendent of Foreign Investments, there clearly appears to be a tendency not to name the practicing public accountant to serve as a statutory examiner. At the same time, more and more domestic, as well as foreign corporations, are requesting examination by practicing public accountants in addition to the work carried out by the statutory examiner.

There is no prescribed form for the statutory examiner's opinion. Many comisarios utilize a report which is basically identical to the opinion normally issued by a practicing public accountant. Another form used by some comisarios states that—

- The balance sheet and profit and loss statement have been presented to him (comisario) for his opinion.
- That he has examined such financial statements.
- That he found the statements in accordance with accounting records and sufficient supporting evidence.
- That he obtained all necessary information.
- That he recommends the statements for shareholders' approval.

No mention is made either of accounting principles followed by the company or of auditing procedures used by the comisario.

Since the comisario is not required to have competence in the accounting field or to be independent, any report or opinion issued by him with respect to financial statements does not as a general rule give the same degree of assurance as to the fairness of financial statements as would that of an independent auditor.

The National Securities Commission and the Superintendent of Foreign Investments have objected to members of the auditing firm serving as comisarios. For that reason, there will most likely be a trend away from public accountants serving as comisarios for the companies which they examine. Then too, the Capital Markets Law requires the usage of two separate comisarios, with the apparent intention that the second comisario be the representative of the minority shareholders.

The Accounting Profession

In September 1973, the Venezuelan government promulgated the Law for the Practice of Public Accounting. That new law restricts the practice of public accounting to those persons who have graduated from or have been revalidated by national universities; however, provision was made to admit without examination those individuals who had practiced public accounting for seven or more years, and to admit after successful completion of an examination those nongraduates who had practiced for four or more years. All practicing public accountants are required to be members of a Colegio de Contadores Públicos.

During early 1975, the President of Venezuela decreed the regulations to clarify and interpret the Law for the Practice of Public Accounting. Those regulations clarified the right of local firms to represent international accounting firms, which had been an issue long opposed by the Federation of Colleges of Public Accountants (Federación de Colegios de Contadores Públicos). These new regulations do not in all instances coincide with the desires of the Federación and, accordingly, it appears very likely that that body and its member colegios will attempt to obtain modifications.

Broadly speaking, it could be said that there are about five hundred individuals engaged in public accounting practice in Venezuela, of which approximately three hundred work on the staff of the representatives of international public accounting firms. Of these, almost all are members of one of the leading accounting organizations referred to below. Many of the older accountants are members of the Asociación de Contadores de Venezuela (Colegio Nacional de Técnicos en Contabilidad). Whereas, most of the younger men are university graduates and are members of one of the Colegios de Contadores Públicos.

There are perhaps one hundred independent practitioners who are engaged in their own public practice either as individuals or as associates in small local firms. However, most of the professional accounting services in Venezuela are performed by the offices which were founded by the international public accounting firms.

Generally speaking, the services presently performed by the Venezuelan public accountant are somewhat the same as those performed by a smaller U.S. CPA: bookkeeping services, with some auditing and income tax assistance, and occasionally the handling of detailed administration matters such as employees' social security and income tax retentions.

Training of Accountants

Until 1946, the only business training courses available were five-year schools of commerce, which were of high school level and were operated by the government. In 1946, a school of business administration was created at the Central University of Venezuela, but it was not until 1956, that courses in public accounting were introduced.

In 1950, the first group graduated from this school, and until 1959, the graduates were given a degree as business administrator-accountant. In 1956, this school was divided into business administration and accountancy, and in 1960, the university held the first graduation of students following a separate curriculum in accounting. At present, the title granted to graduates of this school is licensee in business administration (administrador commercial), and licensee in public accountancy (licenciado en contaduria publica), respectively.

Under the Venezuelan system, admission to a university is subject to a satisfactory completion of the secondary school (five years) with majors in science or humanities. The graduates of this school have the bachelor's degree which resembles the European baccalaureate system and in the better schools can be said to be a combination of American high school and one year of college.

In the case of public accountancy, admission to the school of business administration was originally accorded, in addition to graduates of the secondary school, to graduates from the schools of commerce referred to above and to persons who had ten years' experience in accounting and were able to pass an entrance examination. This third class of admission was subsequently rescinded and in order to be candidates for the university degree, students have to complete the full secondary school (bachillerato).

The university course is a five-year course leading to a degree in business administration or public accountancy. Classes are held in the evening, usually from 6 P.M. to 10 P.M. The curriculum for the first three years is the same; the last two years are devoted to specialization in one of the two fields. The present syllabus for public accountancy includes 3,000 hours of instruction covering general, cost and advanced accounting; auditing and accounting systems; civil, commercial, labor and tax law; economics, finance, mathematics and statistics; business organization and administration, and collateral subjects.

There are five state and two private universities in Venezuela offering courses leading to a degree in business administration or public accountancy. Up to 1975, there had been approximately four thousand graduates.

Professional Accounting Organizations

Asociación de Contadores de Venezuela (Colegio Nacional de Técnicos en Contabilidad). This colegio was founded in 1942 and is the oldest accounting organization in the country and many of the older non-graduate practicing accountants are members. In view of the passage of the Law for the Practice of Public Accounting, it is believed that this colegio will henceforth be principally active in the industrial and commercial accounting areas, rather than in public accounting.

This colegio, since its foundation, has represented Venezuela in international accounting congresses and is the sponsor and official representive of Venezuela before the Interamerican Accounting Conferences. The total membership of this colegio probably amounts to around three thousand, and this colegio is well known for its long struggle for recognition of the practicing accountant.

Federación de Colegios de Contadores Públicos de Venezuela (Federation of Colleges of Public Accountants of Venezuela). This colegio is made up of graduates in public accountancy from Venezuelan universities; graduates in similar courses in foreign universities have found it quite difficult to revalidate their degrees in Venezuela. Graduates of foreign universities are almost always required to take at least two years of the university curriculum. Presently, there are possibly twenty-five hundred members. As in the previously mentioned colegio, the practicing of public accountancy is not a prerequisite for membership. As a matter of fact, the overwhelming majority of the members work either for private enterprises or government agencies.

Other Accounting Organizations. The Institute of Internal Auditors and the Systems and Procedures Association have chapters in Caracas. Their meeting programs are in line with their names, and they have no influence whatsoever either in the practice or the regulation of the accounting profession.

Ethics

Both the Asociación de Contadores de Venezuela (Colegio Nacional de Técnicos en Contabilidad) and the Federación de Colegios de Contadores Públicos de Venezuela have adopted codes of ethics which are in some ways quite similar—the great difference being that the Federación de Colegios de Contadores Públicos de Venezuela has rules which are intended to make it unethical or impossible for its members to be partners or employees of accounting firms with international connections. The general areas of the codes deal with the manner in which the members shall practice accountancy and their relations with fellow members and their clients. Specifically, it is prohibited to solicit clients through improper advertising, to base fees on the results of professional service, to accept fees or commissions from or to pay them to the laity, to engage in competitive bidding, to certify *pro forma* projections of earnings, to engage in noncompatible occupations when in the practice of public accounting, and to divulge confidential information obtained in the course of the work.

It is considered injurious to the profession if the accountant, in expressing an opinion upon financial statements which he has examined—

1. Does not include a material fact not disclosed in the statements, or the statements contain a material fact which is untrue;
2. Becomes liable for professional negligence during the process of his investigations or in the issuance of his report;
3. Failed to obtain sufficient information to allow the issuance of an unqualified opinion, or expresses an opinion when the exceptions are such as to preclude the issuance of an opinion;
4. Fails to disclose the application of accounting principles not generally accepted, or to disclose any material omission of accounting principles applicable in the circumstances.

The provisions of the Code of Ethics relating to the issuance of an opinion based on generally accepted auditing standards and to independence are given under the later heading "Auditing Standards."

Rules to Regulate the Public Accounting Profession

The proposals for a law to govern public accountancy date back to 1955 when a regulatory project was initially proposed by the Asociación de Contadores de Venezuela (Colegio Nacional de Técnicos en Contabilidad). In September 1973, the Venezuelan government promulgated the Law for the Practice of Public Accounting which was along the general lines requested by the Federación de Colegios de Contadores Públicos, except that that law was substantially less restrictive against international firms than had been requested by the Federación. Then in early 1975, the President of Venezuela decreed regulations which were intended to clarify and implement the law; however, the Federación de Colegios de Contadores Públicos de Venezuela has opposed those regulations, primarily on the grounds that they have not been sufficiently restrictive.

The present rules require that the services of a public accountant be utilized in many instances including auditing financial statements prepared for judicial usage, credit purposes, or administrative matters.

The law provides that public accountants must be graduated from or have their degrees revalidated by national universities, except that other practicing public accountants are to be admitted without examination provided that they had seven years of experience in Venezuela prior to the passage of the law, or had four years previous public experience and can pass a required examination.

There continue to be substantial unresolved differences regarding the extent to which international accounting firms can be represented in Venezuela. The Federación is not in favor of any type of representation of foreign firms; whereas, the new 1975 regulations clearly state that such representation is permitted.

Auditing Standards

General and Field Work Standards

There have been no formal pronouncements or codification of auditing standards. However, the influence of international auditing firms in Venezuela has had a significant effect on the standards of some of the Venezuelan practitioners. Auditing procedures will normally include confirmation of cash in banks and receivables, and physical observation of inventories.

Independence

A public accountant cannot establish a practice unless he assumes a personal and unlimited responsibility. He must maintain an independent and impartial judgment in examining and expressing an opinion on the financial statements; and he cannot have any economic or other connection with the corporation to be examined which might in some way affect his independence of judgment. In practice, some of the Venezuelan practitioners may not always have the same degree of independence that might be found in other countries.

Standards of Reporting

Over recent years, there has been substantial progress in developing standards of reporting. In general, the auditor's report is frequently very similar in wording to the standard auditor's report found in the United States.

The Comisión Nacional de Valores has prescribed certain rules which must be applied in relation to those companies whose shares are offered for public sale. Those rules result in disclosures very much akin to the types of information which is frequently given in the United States.

Despite the substantial progress during recent years, there are still considerable variances among the procedures followed by independent practitioners. Then too, in some instances, the reader cannot even be assured of the consistent application of accounting principles by corporations. The comisario's reports often do not include any reference to the accounting principles used in the preparation of the financial statements.

Accounting Principles and Practices

In general, accounting practices followed in Venezuela can be described as being in accordance with generally accepted accounting principles as defined in the United States. However, as indicated in the following discussion, commercial, labor, and tax legislation and regulations still influence many accountants in determining the accounting principles used.

General Form and Content of Financial Statements

Under Venezuelan income tax laws and regulations, financial statements which are a part of tax return forms—which must be signed by the accountant of the corporation in addition to the person who prepares the return and the taxpayer or his representative—are presented in a way similar to American practice: assets and liabilities are classified as current, fixed, long-term, and so forth; "valuation reserves" are shown as deductions from the related asset accounts, and so forth. In addition, supplementary schedules showing details of costs and expenses and other financial data are to be presented.

Statement Presentation. As previously mentioned, according to the Code of Commerce the administrators of the corporation should prepare every six months a "summary statement of assets and liabilities condition," which should be put in the hands of the comisarios. Furthermore, the administrators should present to the comisarios the balance sheet of the corporation, together with supporting documents, at least a month in advance of the meeting of shareholders in which such balance sheet will be discussed. The balance sheet "will show with evidence and accuracy the real profits earned and lossed incurred." Assets must be stated "at values they really have," but generally this requirement is not followed. Corporate financial statements together with the report of the statutory examiner must be filed with the Court of Commerce within ten days after approval. There is no indication that this filing is anything more than a formality and no prescribed form of presentation exists, nor is there any real penalty if the filing is not made.

Insurance companies, which are supervised by the Superintendent of Insurance, and banks, supervised by the Superintendant of Banks, are required to publish their financial statements periodically, and the form is rigidly prescribed.

Consolidated Financial Statements. There is no government requirement that consolidated statements be presented. Under the fiscal legislation, companies are treated as separate taxpayers and except for the additional fifty-fifty tax on income from petroleum and mining when consolidation is obligatory, intercompany affiliations are not recognized for tax purposes.

The National Securities Commission (created under the new Capital Markets Law hereinafter referred to) does stipulate the types of financial statements and their contents, and those rules are not substantially different from those that would be applied in the preparation of financial statements by a major corporation in the United States. It is expected that the National Securities Commission will have a growing influence on the presentation of financial statements, and current trends seem to indicate that it is the intention for the Commission to establish rules which are in keeping with good accounting practices.

Balance Sheet—Income Tax Considerations Only

Accounts Receivable. Uncollectible accounts written off to expense in the taxable year are deductible for tax purposes. Recoveries of bad debts written off are required to be taken into income of the period in which it was collected. Allowance for unspecified bad debts cannot be deducted.

Inventories. Inventories must be stated at cost for tax purposes. Cost of materials, merchandise, and so forth, purchased for resale, processing, or use in Venezuela are deductible for tax purposes as well as related transportation, insurance, normal purchases, commissions calculated as a percentage of cost, taxes, and other direct expenses. Pricing should not exceed normal pricing in the supplying market and, in any case, must be supported by vendors' invoices. "Reserves" or allowances for inventory or other losses are not deductible. When an inventory is written down to market, the writedown must be applied to the individual items so that the pricing can be scrutinized.

Fixed Assets and Depreciation. Depreciation must be taken currently for tax purposes; the taxpayer cannot defer depreciation to be charged to income in a year when he has profits. Any method of depreciation which determines the annual charges based on cost and the number of years of useful life is allowed for tax purposes. Straight-line, declining balance, and sum-of-the-years-digits are among the acceptable methods, and the unit of production method is specifically permitted. Once a method has been chosen, it may not be changed without the prior authorization of the tax authorities.

In determining the amount to be depreciated, no allowance need be made for salvage value. Maintenance and repairs are deductible expenses provided they do not appreciably prolong the life of the asset or alter its original structure.

Balance Sheet—Nontax Matters

Liability for Severance Pay. Under the Venezuela Labor Law and the Law Against Unjustified Dismissals, there are certain types of payments upon termination of employment not having a fixed duration. Irrespective of the reason for his severance, the departing employee is entitled to benefits which are roughly equal to one month's pay for each year of service; if the employee was unjustifiably dismissed, he may be entitled to double that amount. There is no requirement in the law that a provision for these indemnities be created; however, nearly all companies now accrue substantially all of the single indemnities, and some companies are beginning to accrue a portion for the double indemnities which might stem from unjustified dismissals. Those accruals are not deductible for income tax purposes; at the time that an individual payment is made, that amount is deductible.

Legal Reserve. Five percent of net profit for the year must be appropriated for a legal reserve until the reserve reaches 10 percent of subscribed capital stock. There is no precise definition as to the purpose for which the reserve may be used. It is not available for dividends and does not have to be funded.

Statement of Income—Income Tax Considerations Only

Cash vs. Accrual Basis. The accrual basis is prescribed for computing taxable income of commercial and industrial activities (including petroleum and mining, agriculture and fishing). Income derived from realty, personal property, professions, remunerations, and winnings is taxable when cash is received or available.

Profit on Construction Contracts. Profit on construction contracts that take more than a year to complete is determined by estimating the income earned and related costs at the end of the tax year. If the contract takes less than a year, the profit may be taken up in the tax year in which the work is completed.

Profit on Real Estate Development. For real estate development businesses, the cost of sales is determined by adding the cost of urbanizing to the cost of the land and dividing by the number of square meters available for sale to obtain a unit price. This unit price will be applied to the number of square meters sold to obtain the cost of sales.

Profit on Installment Sales. Profit on installment sales is recorded for tax purposes when the sale is made; it is not necessary to await the successive maturities of the installment payments. However, the law specifically permits recording real estate credit sales on a cash basis.

Capital Gains. In determining the tax basis on the sale of shares issued by another company, a domestic corporate taxpayer may add to cost the par value of shares received through the capitalization of earnings.

Other Nontax Matters

Treasury Stock. A company's own stock may be purchased only out of profits. Stockholders' approval is necessary to make such a purchase.

"*Profit for the Year.*" This does not have for some local companies the same meaning as in the United States. These companies frequently prepare a "statement of distribution of profits" in which the following appropriations of "profits" are shown: employees' bonuses, board of directors' fees, provision to maintain statutory, valuation and capital "reserves," income tax, and so forth.

Accounting and Reporting for the Oil Industry

The petroleum industry has been a very important factor in the Venezuelan economy, and has been treated separately in the Venezuelan Income Tax Law. This is a very specialized field and the rules related thereto have been changing at a very rapid pace. It presently appears that the petroleum concessions and related assets will pass to the government within a relatively short period of time, possibly within one year. In view of that, and the other rapid changes in the rules applicable to the industry, it has been deemed preferable not to attempt to go into any great detail insofar as accounting and reporting for the petroleum industry are concerned.

Andean Pact

On January 1, 1973, Venezuela became a member country of the Andean Pact. Accordingly, Venezuela, Colombia, Ecuador, Peru, Bolivia, and Chile are now attempting individually to institute rules which will result in a six-country tariff union. Among other matters, the countries are individually committed to establishing rules governing foreign investments.

New foreign investors are now required to obtain prior approval of the Superintendency of Foreign Investments whenever they wish to make a new investment in Venezuela. The Superintendency also has to approve technology agreements which are signed with foreign suppliers of technology.

Certain fields of endeavor are now reserved for nationally owned companies (over 80 percent locally owned). Some of those areas are telephone and telecommunications, electricity, vigilance and security services, television and radio, Spanish-language magazines and newspapers, internal transportation, publicity, and internal commerce. Foreign companies which were previously involved in these activities have until May 1, 1977, to offer to sell sufficient shares to bring the foreign investment down to under 20 percent.

Foreign owned companies which were involved in manufacturing at the time of Venezuela's entry into the Andean Pact are not required to divest shares unless they wish to trade with other countries within the block. Such investments, however, as with all foreign investments, are required to be registered with the Superintendency of Foreign Investments.

Prior to Venezuela's entry into the Andean Pact, there were no limitations on the remittance abroad of earnings; however, foreign investors may now receive only 14 percent net of taxes (16.47 percent pre-tax) per annum on their registered investments. In addition, there are rules governing expansion of existing foreign investments except that these may be expanded 5 percent per annum without prior approval.

There are also certain rules which now apply to loans received from abroad, and the Superintendency is developing rules which will govern the use of foreign technology.

Since the Venezuelan government is still developing its rules concerning foreign investments, any U.S. company wishing to make investments should take steps to be assured that they are complying with the rules. Generally speaking, the leading accounting firms are able to render assistance to the potential investors.

Capital Markets Law

On January 31, 1973, President Caldera signed the Capital Markets Law, which regulates public offerings of securities of medium and long term, except bonds forming part of the public debt and other securities issued pursuant to the Central Bank Law and the General Law of Banks and Other Credit Institutions.

This new law introduced certain concepts new in Venezuela, which include the following:

1. National Securities Commission and National Securities Register (Title I)
2. Convertible Bonds (Title II)
3. "Corporations of Authorized Capital" ("SACA") (Title III)
4. "Open Capital Corporations" ("SAICA") (Title III)
5. Variable Capital Corporations or Mutual Funds and Mutual Funds Management Companies (Title III)

The law also regulates stock exchanges, stockbrokers and, somewhat analogous to the Securities Act of 1933 and Securities Exchange Act of 1934 in the United States, regulates the form and content of a prospectus, and financial information (Title IV) required of a listed company. Rules extending the provisions of the Commercial Code relating to treasury stock are included in Title V; protection of minority stockholder provisions are set forth in Title VI; income tax incentives (Title VIII) and penalties (Title VIII) are also established.

Chapter I of Title II defines "securities" which are subject to the control of the National Securities Commission, and which include (article 18) shares of corporations and other documents ("títulos") issued in large numbers which possess the same characteristics and bestow the same rights within their class. A "public offering" of securities and intangible assets, for the purposes of this law, will be any offer to the public or to sectors of the public or determined groups through publicity or diffusion.

National Securities Commission and Register

Article 2 of the law establishes the National Securities Commission (NSC) as part of the Finance Ministry, consisting of a chairman and four directors with alternates. The chairman and directors are appointed by the president, the former for a four-year term and the latter for three years. The Commission will be located in Caracas and may open branches in other cities. Article 10 defines the responsibilities of the Commission which include issuance of monthly reports in relation to the capital markets trend, floating of securities, authorization of public offerings by individuals or legal entities domiciled in Venezuela and, when in the national interest, by foreign companies; authorization of the issuance of securities abroad by Venezuelan corporations; registration of securities in the National Security Register; authorization of and approval of prospectuses; authorization of public offerings of intangible property; prescription of the form and content of financial statements to be presented to the NSC to provide an investor with sufficient information to understand the financial situation. In addition, the NSC is granted power to protect investors, delist securities by cancelling authorizations, regulate exchanges and brokers, and prepare an annual report of activities to the president.

Decisions of the NSC are subject to reconsideration and may be appealed only to the Supreme Court of Justice.

Article 20 describes the information required to be submitted by an applicant for a public offering. In addition to descriptive information concerning the organization and legal characteristics of the applicant, this article specifically requires submission of the balance sheet, income statement, statement of changes in working capital and origin and application of funds (statement of changes in financial position) corresponding to the last fiscal year with the report of independent public accountants. If these statements are more than 120 days old, the subsequent trial balances must also be submitted.

The Commission is given broad powers to request additional information and to carry out inspections to determine compliance with the law.

Article 47 provides that companies which have made a public offering of securities must advise the NSC of (1) dissolution, (2) merger or change of form, (3) transfer of assets, (4) restoration, increase or reduction of capital, (5) change of purpose, and (6) modifications of bylaws related to the five changes.

Chapter II of Title I provides that the NSC will maintain a National Security Register ("NSR"). The organization and functioning of the registry will be determined by regulations to be issued. The information included in the registry will, for the most part, be open to the public.

Debentures, Mortgage Bonds, Convertible Bonds

Corporations may issue, with authorization of the NSC, debentures in amounts not exceeding capital stock, retained earnings, and unrestricted appropriations of earnings. Mortgage bonds may be issued with proper authorization if guaranteed by mortgages or assets of the issuer or by pledge of government securities, the value of which is equal to or exceeds 150 percent of the principal amount of the bonds. The law defines the corporate formalities required and information to be included in the prospectus, including the requirements of article 20 and other detailed information of the issue.

Articles 31-35 grant corporations the right to float, in a public offering, bonds convertible into stock pursuant to the terms, conditions, and price included in the offering prospectus. Restrictions for the protection of bondholders while the bonds are outstanding are included in the law, including, among others, the restriction of dividend declarations from earnings after the issuance of the convertibles and the issuance of new stock only for cash and for a price per share equal to or greater than the conversion price of the bonds into stock.

Articles 36-45 provide for the appointment of a bondholders' representative which may be a credit institution, insurance company, or an association of investors authorized by the Commission. This representative will have trustee functions.

Corporation of Authorized Capital

Corporations of authorized capital ("sociedades anónimas de capital autorizado" "S.A.C.A."), a new type of legal entity introduced by the Capital Markets Law for the first time in Venezuela, are defined in article 48 as those in which the stockholders may authorize the administrators once or more frequently to increase capital to a stated amount through the issuance of new stock whenever and in what amounts as the administrators may decide. Authorized capital may not be greater than paid-in capital. The stockholders' resolution must be registered with the NSR, and the capital increase is also subject to the registration requirements of the Code of Commerce. Articles 51-55 define certain procedures and rules for the issuance of new stock.

Any company with subscribed capital of Bs 1,000,000 or more may become a "S.A.C.A."

Open Capital Corporations

To provide for widely held public companies, the Capital Markets Law authorizes a new type of legal entity—"sociedad anónima inscrita de capital abierto" ("S.A.I.C.A."). Such companies must be registered with the NSC through the NSR, have a paid-in capital of not less than Bs 1,000,000 and, most important, not less than 50 percent of the capital will be owned by not less than 50 persons per Bs 1,000,000 of capital. Rules of constructive ownership in determining stockholdings are applied. Each stockholder must contribute at least Bs 1,000 for capital and no group within this 50 percent may own more than 10 percent of the capital. In the case of a natural person, spouse and relatives are considered as a single stockholder. The shares must be registered and will be traded on a securities exchange.

Corporations may be provisionally inscribed in the NSR if the company declares its intention to comply with the distribution rules within five years of the date of registry and submit a program of "going-public."

Rules are also established in the event that the 50 percent of widely distributed capital falls to 40 percent. The NSC may increase the percentage of widely distributed capital to 75 percent.

Variable Capital Corporations or Mutual Funds and Mutual Fund Management Corporations

The law provides for the formation of mutual funds with a capital of not less than Bs 2,000,000 which are registered in the NSR. The proceeds of the sale of shares of a mutual fund cannot be invested directly by the fund; instead this must be done through a fund management corporation, and no stock of any fund management corporation may be owned by a mutual fund. In addition, rules for the formation and regulation of mutual fund management corporations are included in the law. The funds must issue quarterly balance sheets.

Stock Exchanges

The operations of stock exchanges are to be authorized by the NSC; definition, requirements, and functions of the stock exchanges are included in Chapter V.

Accounting and Reporting Requirements

Throughout the law, there are provisions as to the accounting and reporting requirements of companies subject to this law. Article 20 of the law discussed above describes the information required to be submitted by an applicant to register a public offering. These requirements include the three basic financial statements of the last fiscal year prior to the registration, accompanied by the report of independent public accountants. Article 10, paragraph 9, gives the NSC power to determine the form and contents of financial statements.

Article 92 provides that a listed company must submit annually, within the first three months of the close of its fiscal year, the three basic financial statements and the report mentioned above. The same article provides for disclosures of adverse events, notices of shareholder and bondholder meetings, modification of the charter or bylaws, dividend declaration notices, and quarterly informative reports. These reports will be published.

Article 55 provides that capital may not be included in the issuer's balance sheet until actually subscribed to if the issuer is a S.A.C.A.

Title IV of the law is specifically designated as the financial information section.

Article 111 requires that the NSC shall prepare the rules as to form and content of financial statements and related reports indicating minimum disclosure requirements. It will also establish the principles to be followed, by companies under its control, in order to "evaluate the items in the balance sheet" (presumably to establish generally accepted Venezuelan accounting principles).

Article 112 provides that open capital corporations and companies whose securities are registered in the National Security Registry must provide the Commission with an annual report including the financial statements submitted to the annual meeting with the report of independent public accountants and legal auditor ("comisario"); these data are due within 30 days after the annual stockholders' meeting. Semi-annual reports of financial condition are due within 60 days after the semi-annual close. Other information requirements cover charter or bylaws changes, insider transactions, compensation information of directors, dividend declaration proposals, and any other information the Commission considers necessary. The annual financial statements must be published in a newspaper of national circulation.

Directors are to report on important claims against the company and submit their opinion as to its outcome. Acquisitions, mergers, or any event involving significant changes in grouping, classification, or presentation of accounts must be disclosed. Detailed information required concerning the parent's or acquirer's information in an investee is described in articles 115 and 116.

Treasury Stock

Rules concerning the acquisition of a company's own stock is included under Title V of the law. Liabilities of directors for violation of these rules are provided for. In general, the rules follow the requirements of the Code of Commerce.

Protection of Minority Stockholders

Title VI of the law grants minority stockholders of open capital corporations the right to directly elect members of the board of directors; and requires that the open capital corporation shall have two legal auditors ("comisarios") who may not be members of the board, employees, or close relatives, but who must have experience in financial matters. The election of the two are separate.

Companies whose stock is publicly owned must pay as dividends 50 percent of net income of which at least half will be in cash. Officers' and directors' special compensation should not exceed 10 percent of net income and must be approved at the stockholders' meeting and is subordinated to the dividend payments. The National Securities Commission under certain circumstances may call an annual meeting of stockholders.

Tax Incentives

To encourage public trading the law grants the National Executive after consulting with the NSC, the power to—

1. Exclude in whole or in part capital gains arising from the sale of stock in open capital corporations if reinvested in the same type of company; interest and dividends received from a S.A.I.C.A. may also be excluded.

2. Exclude up to 15 percent of tax payable on "total net income" of open capital corporations in proportion to the number of stockholders.

The terms of the exclusions may not exceed ten years.

Any company seeking tariff protection may be required to become a S.A.I.C.A. and preference will be given to these companies.

Penalties

Title VIII of the law provides for civil and criminal penalties for violation of the law. Article 138 provides that co-authors, accomplices, and instigators are subject to the penalties. (This could be interpreted to provide for directors and independent public accountants' liability beyond that described below). A five-year statute of limitation is provided. Article 146 specifies that a fine of Bs 10,000–Bs 40,000 can be imposed on—

1. Issuers of unauthorized securities;

2. Offerers of securities whose registration is cancelled or suspended;

3. Independent public accountants who, because of gross negligence or fraud, issue false reports on the financial situation of the registrant with the purpose that the latter could obtain necessary authorization for a public offering or to avoid cancellation or suspension of trading privileges.

4. Members of the Board of Open Capital Corporations who received profit participation prior to payment of dividends;

5. Companies failing to provide required financial information;

6. Directors of security exchanges for certain violations;

7. Security exchanges violating specific rules.

There are other specific acts for which lesser fines are imposed. These include, among others, issuing securities to the public without an approved prospectus.

Directors and officers of registrants who issue false information for the benefit of themselves or other persons are subject to criminal penalties.

Transitory Provisions

Corporations whose securities are publicly listed have one year to comply with the provisions of this law.

West Germany

West Germany

As of August 1973

Forms of Business Organization

Business in Germany is conducted under the usual forms of organization: single proprietorship, partnership (limited or unlimited), and several forms of corporate organization. Foreigners may freely organize new corporations or acquire control of existing corporations. A foreign corporation may also conduct its business through branch offices, which requires registration in the Commercial Register. In practice, tax and other considerations have, for the most part, led foreign corporations to operate through a subsidiary rather than a branch.

Aktiengesellschaft (A.G.)
(Stock Corporation)

The German A.G. closely resembles the U.S. public corporation. There must be at least five incorporators, and at least 25 percent of the stated or registered capital, which may not be less than 100,000 Deutsch marks (DM), must be paid in. The capital is divided into shares which can be freely transferred, the par value of which must be DM 50, DM 100, or a multiple of the latter. No-par-value shares are not permitted under German law. Either registered or bearer shares may be issued.

The law (Companies Act) regulates in considerable detail the conduct of corporate affairs, including accounting. The A.G. has two independent governing bodies—the "vorstand" (board of directors or management) and the "aufsichtsrat" (supervisory board exercising control and giving instructions to the management). These bodies act with independent personal responsibility and no one may be a member of both simultaneously. The financial statements of the A.G. must be examined by independent public accountants (wirtschaftsprüfer), filed with the local trade register, and published in the *Federal Gazette.*

Gesellschaft mit beschränkter Haftung (G.m.b.H.)
(Limited Liability Company)

There is no exact legal counterpart in the United States to the German G.m.b.H., which has certain legal attributes of both a corporation and a partnership.

The capital of a G.m.b.H. must be at least DM 20,000, of which not less than DM 5,000 must be paid in upon organization. There must be at least two organizers. Each member must subscribe at least DM 500 and additional subscriptions must be in multiples of DM 100. The liability of the members of the G.m.b.H. is limited to the amount of their subscription.

Share certificates are rarely issued. Transfer of interests may be restricted by contract so that the personal relationship between the members may be maintained. One person may acquire all the interests of the other members; in other words, a one-man G.m.b.H. is possible.

Affairs of a G.m.b.H. can be conducted with greater flexibility and informality than those of the A.G. Therefore, unless there is expectation that recourse to public financing through stock or debt issues may be had in the future, the G.m.b.H. ordinarily is the more advantageous legal form for U.S. firms operating in Germany.

Other Forms of Business Organization

Kommanditgesellschaft (K.G.) (Limited Partnership). This form of partnership has two different classes of members: the general partners who have sole responsibility and authority for the management of the business and unlimited liability for the firm's debts; and the limited partners whose liability is limited to the amount of their investment. Members may be either individuals or entities. The name of the firm must include that of at least one general partner and must be followed by the designation "Kommanditgesellschaft" or K.G.

Kommanditgesellschaft auf Aktien (K.G.A.) (Limited Partnership with Shares). This form of organization is quite similar to the K.G., having two classes of partners, the general and the limited, the first with management responsibility coupled with unlimited liability and the second having only their investment at risk. Its principal difference is that the limited partners have shares of stock evidencing their investments while the general partners usually, but not invariably, hold shares.

Offene Handelsgesellschaft (O.H.G.) (General Partnership). The O.H.G. is substantially identical with the general and common form of partnership in the United States in which all partners are jointly and severally liable for the firm's debts. The firm name must include the name of at least one partner, and if it does not include all their names it must be followed by some designation such as "O.H.G." to indicate that it is a partnership.

Publishing Requirements for Firms Other Than A.G.s

All single proprietorships, partnerships, and G.m.b.H.s are now required to prepare annually certain financial statements and, in the case of a G.m.b.H., a report of the "vorstand" (board of management), if during at least three consecutive years two of the following criteria are met:

1. Balance sheet total more than DM 125,000,000
2. Annual sales more than DM 250,000,000
3. Average number of employees more than 5,000

These annual financial statements and (if any) the report of the board of management have to be audited by independent public accountants (wirtshaftsprüfer) in accordance with the prescriptions of the Companies Act for A.G.s, and must be filed with the local trade register and published in the *Federal Gazette.*

Business Records

The Commercial Code requires that each business keep suitable records in a living language (not necessarily German) in bound form; erasures and alterations which would make the original entry illegible are forbidden.

Despite the legal requirement of bound books, loose-leaf accounting, ledgerless accounting, and electronic data processing have been sanctioned through practice and have also been accepted by the tax authorities subject to certain conditions.

The Accounting Profession

In Germany, there are two classes of accountants serving the public, "wirtschaftsprüfer" (WP) and "vereidigte buchprüfer" (VBP). In addition, there is a profession of tax advisers which is divided into two classes, the "steuerberater" (StB) and the "steuerbevollmächtigter" (St Bev). At present, the majority of the WPs and may of the VBPs hold the additional qualification of StB.

In general, professional standards of the WP and VBP are similar, but the educational requirements and scope of practice differ. The Federal Accountancy Law passed in 1961 had the effect of ultimately extinquishing the VBP class and no more VBPs will be licensed.

Wirtschaftsprüfer (WP)

The wirtschaftsprüfer closely resembles a certified public accountant in scope of services, professional standards and ethics, and educational and other entrance requirements.

To become a WP, a candidate must have certain personal and professional qualifications and must pass an examination. He must normally be of German nationality or from a foreign country that grants reciprocity to Germans, and meet the necessary educational and experience requirements.

Graduation from a university with a major in law, economics, business, or engineering is usually required. Before entering the university, students spend four years in an elementary school and nine years in a secondary school, the curriculum of which is college preparatory. Following the period of formal study, a candidate for WP is required to get six years of practical experience, of which at least four years must be served within the profession (two years with a WP). Candidates who have not graduated from a university are acceptable if they have had at least ten years' experience in the profession. As a practical matter, it is almost impossible to fulfill all requirements before the age of 30, and few persons qualify before the age of 35.

The examination covers the following areas:

1. Theory and practice of accounts and business administration.
2. Business law (more detailed knowledge is required than the mere fundamentals which are necessary in the United States).
3. Tax law (about 90 percent of the candidates for WP qualify as StB before the WP examination and thus avoid the tax law section of the WP examination).
4. Law and ethics of the profession.

5. Legal requirements and auditing practice.

The candidate must prepare a thesis and submit to a written and an oral examination. A candidate who fails must generally wait at least one year before applying again. Usually a candidate may not reapply after three failures. After passing the examination, the candidate is licensed by the government.

As of June 30, 1972, 2,752 individuals in public accounting were qualified wirtschaftsprüfer. The profession may be practiced by sole practitioners, in the form of a partnership or in corporate form, A.G. or G.m.b.H. An accounting firm is known as a "wirtschaftsprüfungsgesellschaft," abbreviated WPG.

Ethics. The Wirtschaftsprüferkammer (Chamber of Public Accountants) is authorized to issue rules for the exercise of the profession and holds disciplinary hearings on complaint of violation of the following rules:

1. Compatible occupations—The WP must practice his profession as his main occupation. Certain occupations are not compatible with the profession, such as participation in commercial or other business enterprises or in finance companies; employment by corporations, including being a member of the management of corporations other than wirtschaftsprüfungsgesellschaften; and being a government employee, except as a university teacher. Specifically mentioned as being compatible with the profession are consultation services, teaching assignments, and free-lance writing.

2. Independence—The profession in Germany recognizes independence both in the subjective and the objective sense. A WP may not accept an engagement when he is doubtful about his impartiality. But a WP also must refuse an engagement when there are reasonable grounds for an outsider to doubt his independence. As illustrations of this latter situation, it is stated that a WP is not considered independent if he has a material investment in or is indebted in a material amount to the company to be audited (or its parent or any subsidiary) or when he or his spouse is closely related to the owner, a member of the board of directors, or the managers of the enterprise audited.

   The "Institut der Wirtschaftsprüfer" issued a pronouncement that there is normally no reason to infer lack of independence from the fact that the WP (a) assisted in the preparation of the financial statements (the key word is "assisted"—a WP may not examine financial statements prepared solely by him); (b) examined financial statements of prior years; (c) acted as consultant for the client in accounting, tax, or management services; (d) represented the client in accounting or tax matters with government agencies or third parties; (e) has issued for the client advisory opinions in accounting or tax matters; (f) was a witness or expert witness in a law suit to which the client is a party; (g) examined the parent company of the client. On the other hand, a WP would not be considered independent if he exercised a management function for his client or if his activities were such that they made him the equivalent of an employee.

3. Confidential relationship with client—The prohibition against disclosure of secrets of clients is not only a professional duty, but a breach is a criminal offense subject to fine and/or imprisonment. The criminal sanction also applies to the professional staff of the WP. Matters revealed to a WP in his professional capacity are generally privileged communications in civil as well as in criminal proceedings.
4. Advertising and solicitation—There are the usual rules against advertising: e.g., announcements may be inserted only in a newspaper covering the region in which the WP is active; the size must not be larger than 2 × 3.5 inches; it must be dignified and must be restricted to establishment of practice, change of address, admission of a partner, and similar matters; circulars may be sent only to existing clients. A WP may not solicit clients; of course, he may answer requests.
5. Personal responsibility—According to the principle of personal responsibility, a WP is required to reach his own conclusions and express his own opinions. He must therefore use care in selection of assistants, assign to them only tasks which they are qualified to perform, and supervise them to the extent that he can form his own opinion. An accounting firm may not require a WP to sign an opinion if he has personal reservations. Under German law, a WP or WPG has unlimited liability to clients and third parties for knowingly having signed false statements or committed other intentional violations, whereas for negligence in connection with legal audits his liability is to his client only and is limited to DM 500,000 for each case of negligence.

   For assignments other than legal audits the unlimited liability may be reduced to a limited liability by the terms and conditions agreed upon by the parties when confirming the assignment. Each WP or WPG must provide for insurance covering at least DM 500,000 for each case of liability.
6. Conscientiousness—The WP must conduct himself so as to justify the confidence which the public has in him because of his official

status, and at all times maintain loyalty toward his clients. In the performance of his work, he must act as his conscience dictates; he must conform not only to legal requirements but also to professional ethics. He must exercise due care and give scrupulous attention to the affairs of his client. Examination procedures and extent of examination are governed by legal and professional requirements and are not subject to instructions of the client.

Functions. The legally required annual audits of an aktiengesellschaft (public corporation) must be performed by a WP, as must those of banks, insurance companies, home building and loan associations, public utilities, and business organizations which meet the criteria mentioned previously under the heading "Publishing Requirements for Firms Other Than A.G.s" regardless of the legal form in which such businesses are conducted. The WP gives advice in tax matters and represents his clients before the tax authorities. A difference from practice in most other countries is that the WP is permitted to render legal advice to his clients, provided such advice is related to business law in connection with his professional mission. As a result, many German WPs have fully qualified lawyers as members of their staffs.

Vereidigte Buchprüfer (VBP)

In consequence of the Federal Accountancy Law of 1961, the VBP is a dying class and at June 30, 1972, there were only some three hundred practicing VBPs left.

The VBP is generally subject to the same rules of ethics as the WP. He also may practice in the corporate form subject to the same restrictions. He may render the same kind of professional services as the WP except that annual audits required by law may only be performed by WPs.

Steuerberater (StB)

The StB is an expert in tax law and practice. The requirements are similar to those for a WP, including academic study, practice requirements and an examination which concentrates on tax accounting and related tax law. For that reason many WPs are also StBs and vice versa. Candidates without the academic qualifications are also admitted to practice under certain conditions.

Steuerbevollmächtigter (StBev)

The StBev is enrolled to assist clients in tax matters, generally limited to practice before local tax offices. Requirements to become a StBev are comparatively few. The German Bundestag recently passed a law providing for the merger of the StB and StBev, and so the StBev as a professional class will eventually go the way of the VBP.

Organizations of Accountants

Wirtschaftsprüferkammer (Chamber of Public Accountants). As required by the law dated July 24, 1961, concerning the professional organization of public accountants (Wirtschaftsprüferordnung), all wirtschaftsprüfer and certain other practicing accountants must be members of the Wirtschaftsprüferkammer, a public corporation. The main task of this corporation is to protect and promote the professional interests of its members and to supervise their professional activities.

Institut der Wirtschaftsprüfer (Institute of Public Accountants). Prior to the establishment of the Wirtschaftsprüferkammer, the wirtschaftsprüfer were already professionally organized in the "Institut der Wirtschaftsprüfer." While the Wirtschaftsprüferkammer is concerned with all professional matters, the activities of the Institut der Wirtschaftsprüfer are confined to technical questions, especially to the interpretation and application of legal provisions and accounting principles and to the protection and promotion of the professional interests of its members.

The Institute traces its history back to 1930. Its voluntary membership includes about 90 percent of the WPs in Germany. The remaining vereidigte buchprüfer are now also incorporated in the Institut der Wirtschaftsprüfer.

The Institute publishes a journal twice a month and bulletins and opinions on technical matters. Such technical opinions are not legally binding; however, a practitioner who deviates from them without important reasons risks liability in case of a law suit. The principal committee of the Institute dealing with professional matters is the "Accounting and Auditing Committee," which has the following subcommittees for national activities:

1. Banks
2. Insurance companies
3. Community
4. Modern accounting systems
5. Evaluation of enterprises
6. Legal and trusteeship matters
7. Tax matters

8. Business economics
9. Management consulting

For international activities, the Institute is a member of the Union Européenne des Experts Comptables Economiques et Financiers (UEC), the International Fiscal Association and of several international liaison committees.

A collection of numerous bulletins and opinions was published by the Institute in 1956 and supplemented in 1967. A new edition is under way and may have been issued by the time this book is published.

The Institute has issued a recommended form of contract between the client and auditor which is generally made part of the written contract for audits. If negligence is claimed by the client in connection with the audit of an A.G. (public corporation), the WP's liability is limited by law to DM 500,000 and the recommended form contains a similar provision.

Other Organizations. A separate organization of the VBP no longer exists but there are federal and regional organizations of StBs and StBevs, which, however, are gradually merging.

Auditing Standards

In Germany, there is no codification of generally accepted auditing standards and necessary audit procedures. However, there are in existence certain norms, based partially on provisions incorporated in the law, partially on pronouncements of the German Institute, and partially on literature and usage. Under the 1961 law, the Wirtschaftsprüferkammer (Chamber of Public Accountants) has the duty to issue professional directives, which were published in 1964.

General Standards

The equivalent of American general standards is contained in a pronouncement of the German Institute approved by the membership in 1958 and partially incorporated in the Wirtschaftsprüferordnung (Public Accountancy Law) passed in 1961. The first of the general standards corresponds to the rule on personal responsibility discussed previously under "Ethics" (paragraph no. 5), the second to the rule on independence (paragraph no. 2), and the third to the rule on conscientiousness (paragraph no. 6).

Standards of Field Work

There is no codification of standards of field work although there are several specific areas commented on in the literature and in pronouncements of the German Institute. These are discussed below in relation to their counterparts in the pronouncements of the American Institute.

1. *First standard (AICPA)*

   The second part of the first standard of field work (proper supervision of assistants) is explicitly covered above under professional ethics paragraph no. 5. The first part of this standard (adequate planning of work) has no exact counterpart in German law or official pronouncements. However, accounting literature states that only by proper planning can an audit be efficiently performed.

   The concept of iterim examinations is specifically recognized by a provision of the law but the extent of audit work which may be performed before the fiscal year's end is apparently not settled. In general, it appears that the practice is much the same as it is in the United States; that is, the individual auditor determines the scope and extent of interim work and thus the amount of detailed examination that he will have to make at and after the end of the accounting period.

2. *Second standard (AICPA)*

   The review of the system of internal control is not required as such under German law. However, it is obvious that the range of an audit depends on the efficiency of the system of internal control and that an examination of the system of internal control is a very important factor in the planning of an audit. Accounting literature and a pronouncement of the German Institute in 1967 put strong emphasis on internal control as the basis for conducting an examination. For example, in the 1968 edition of the WP handbook, there is one section devoted to a systematic explanation of the principles of internal control and how to examine the existing system. It closely follows American literature on the subject.

   At present, the examination of the system of internal control constitutes the foundation of an audit only when it will permit the extent of the respective balance sheet audit to be reduced; if, on the other hand, a complete balance sheet audit is to be performed in any event, the examination of the system of internal control is not a prerequisite.

   In one of its bulletins, the German Institute states that an ordinary audit is not designed to discover defalcations. If, however, the auditor becomes suspicious, he must notify his client of the suspicious circumstances; otherwise he may become liable to his client Liability may also arise if the auditor does not use due care in his examination and as a result does not discover or recognize circumstances which might have aroused his suspicion.

3. *Third standard (AICPA)*

The standard of competence of evidential matter is different in Germany, mainly with respect to audit procedures regarding confirmation of receivables and bank balances and observation of physical inventories.

Observation of physical inventories is not required, but is stated to be "appropriate" in the literature. Otherwise, the German auditor will inquire into the instructions given for the taking of inventories, he will inspect original inventory count sheets and trace them into the inventory compilation, and obtain an inventory certificate from the management. Equally, confirmation of receivables as well as independent confirmation of bank accounts or accounts payable is not required, but more and more practiced.

It is standard practice to request a letter of representation from the management, usually in the form suggested by the Institute. The letter contains representations that all the records submitted for examination were complete, that all assets and liabilities were set forth in the balance sheet at their proper valuation, that all con-contracts, law suits and disputes which might affect the financial statements were disclosed, and so forth.

There is no legal requirement for the management to sign the letter. There is, however, a legal requirement that the management give all information necessary for the conduct of the examination so that the auditor may elicit through specific inquiry all the information usually contained in the letter of representation. The letter is considered desirable rather than necessary.

In general, the auditor may rely on the representations of management, except when circumstances arouse his suspicions. In such case, it is his responsibility to satisfy himself by additional procedures to the extent possible. On the other hand, a representation by management can never take the place of necessary audit procedures. Representations are important in those situations where the information is not subject to audit substantiation.

Standards of Reporting

Standards of reporting, as well as the accounting principles discussed in the following section, evolved in response to the requirements of the

Companies Act. They are prescribed by law for public corporations. However, they have been made applicable by law to financial statements of other companies which are now required under certain circumstances to be examined, and in practice are generally applied to the financial statements of all other companies, although they are probably less binding and more flexible in the last case.

The wording for the accountant's report (Bestätigungsvermerk) is laid down in the Companies Act, and, furthermore, the German Institute has recommended that it be universally used. It states that "according to the audit, made in conformity with the professional duties, the accounting and the annual financial statements and the report of the board of management comply with German law and the company's statutes." Legal requirements deal generally with proper keeping of accounts and with orderly development of annual financial statements; both will be discussed later.

The accountant's report which follows the legal language contained in the Companies Act differs from American form in that it is ostensibly a statement of fact rather than of the auditor's opinion. However, accounting literature emphasizes that since the report is based on an examination which is limited, it is self-evident that the report may not reflect absolute fact but only a subjective evaluation of the evidence. The addition of the phrase "in our opinion" would not limit the responsibility of the auditor; it is implicit under the circumstances.

The law specifically mentions qualified opinions and denials of opinion. A qualification must be clearly stated and, if possible, an indication of the magnitude of the affected area should be given. Not every disagreement between the auditor and the management requires a qualification; the decision whether disclosure is sufficient, or whether a qualification or, possibly, a disclaimer is necessary depends on the magnitude and importance of the items. It is a matter of professional judgment of the auditor, but only clearly identified departures from the provisions of the law or the articles of association in the preparation of the financial statements may lead to a qualification. Some situations mentioned in the literature as requiring qualifications are the following:

1. Violation of generally accepted accounting principles.
2. Violation of—
   a. Rules relating to annual financial statements.
   b. Professional rules.
   c. Generally accepted principles relating to annual financial statements, especially regarding classification and valuation.
3. Violation of legal prescriptions regarding the report of the board of management, especially if—

a. The economic development and situation of the enterprise are not fairly stated.

b. Important facts have not been properly mentioned.

c. Comments on annual financial statements, especially regarding valuation methods, have not been stated fairly and properly and if under certain circumstances the numerous effects of changes in valuation methods have not been disclosed.

d. Certain legally required additional disclosures have not been made.

4. Violation of statutes of the company, insofar as they relate to annual financial statements.

5. Violation of management's duty to answer all requests for information as well as to supply all necessary documents and other items of substantiation.

Although neither annual financial statements nor auditor's report are required to do so, the report of the board of management must reflect the principle of consistency, since the Companies Act prescribes that changes of methods of valuation, depreciation, and amortization and, under certain circumstances, the numerous effects thereof must be disclosed in said report.

Long-Form Report

Despite the attest function of the short-form report, an additional long-form report, prescribed by law only for A.G.s and other firms whose financial statements must be audited, must be issued for use by the supervisory board (aufsichtsrat) as an aid in reaching their own conclusions on problems of management. This long-form report is generally detailed and contains not only statements of fact, but also judgments on the various items included in the balance sheet and earnings statement.

The general outline and content of the long-form report, which contains many details that in American practice would be found only in the audit working papers, are prescribed by the Companies Act for A.G.s and all other firms whose financial statements must be audited, and cover the following matters:

1. Whether accounting, annual financial statements, and the report of the board of management are in accordance with the law.
2. Whether the management has supplied all necessary documents and other items of substantiation and has responded to all requests for information.

3. Details of composition of, and comments on, items in annual financial statements.
4. Remarks on facts either jeopardizing the existence of an enterprise or inhibiting its development.
5. Major violations by the board of management of law or company statutes.

General remarks, such as those dealing with sales and production volume, capacity and utilization of facilities, work force, and so forth, mainly in comparison with the preceding year, are not required by the Companies Act, but such information is given in practice without legal prescription.

The report will normally also contain comment on major violations of principles of good internal control, but will not contain more routine suggestions for minor changes in accounting and internal control procedures.

Where examinations of financial statements are made even though not required by law, in good practice the WP's long-form report is similar to that prescribed by law for A.G.s.

Accounting Principles and Practices

Form and Content of Financial Statements

The form of financial statements is set forth in considerable detail in the Companies Act. There is frequent discussion in the literature as to how specific items are to be classified. The act specifies that the prescribed classifications must be followed unless the business requires a different classification which must be equally informative. The legal classifications are considered minimum requirements; a more detailed presentation is permissible and may, indeed, be necessary for clarity of presentation. Specifically prohibited is the offsetting of liabilities and assets.

The balance sheet is presented in the following form:

Assets	*Liabilities*
Fixed Assets	Capital Stock
Current Assets:	Reserves
Inventories	Liabilities
Securities	
Receivables	
Cash	

Contrary to U.S. practice, the written-down balances of the individual fixed asset groups at the beginning of the accounting period are shown on the face of the balance sheet together with the changes during, and the net figures at the end of, the period. Accumulated cost and accumulated depreciation are not usually shown separately on the balance sheet and in fact often cannot easily be obtained from the books.

The earnings statement was formerly presented in account form, cost and expense items being netted against revenues. However, in 1965, the Companies Act was changed with a view to making the earnings statement more informative, and, since then, a single-step earnings statement has been required for A.G.s and is being used for companies other than A.G.s.

In general, netting of cost and expense items against revenues is now prohibited with the result that total sales must now be disclosed. The sales figure is adjusted by the increase or decrease in inventories of finished and in-process products and for cost of construction by the company of fixed assets for its own use, giving the total value of the production performance of the company. From this figure, the cost of material consumed is deducted leaving a gross profit which differs from that which would be shown in U.S. income statements in the following two ways:

1. It has been adjusted by the labor and overhead elements contained in the change in inventories and in the cost of fixed assets constructed by the company for its own use.
2. Direct labor and manufacturing overhead have not been deducted.

The law specifies which items of income and expenditure must be shown separately in the income statement; those not so shown are included under "other income" and "other expenditures," captions which therefore contain a conglomeration of items not required to be shown elsewhere.

Under the Companies Act, an integral part of the annual report by management, in addition to the financial statements, is a narrative section which is subdivided into two parts, one dealing with business matters and the other with financial matters.

In the business part are covered the results of the past year and prospects for the coming year, competitive position, orders on hand, and so forth; comment would be made, for example, on the opening of new branches during the past year and plans for additional branches in the future.

The law specifically requires that post-balance-sheet events of major importance be disclosed. This requirement is especially significant because the annual report is normally issued three to five months after the end of the fiscal year. Types of major events to be reported would be significant price changes, important new contracts, acquisition of real estate, acquisition of a new business, major losses, and so forth.

The financial section is designed to supplement and explain the financial statements. Specifically, the methods of valuation and depreciation should be stated as fully as needed to give a fair view of the company's financial position and operating results. Any inconsistencies in the application of accounting principles are to be disclosed if material, e.g., a change in depreciation method.

In addition to these general provisions, the law contains a list of specific matters which must be disclosed, among them the acquisition of treasury stock, assets pledged, contingent liabilities, guarantees, and relationship with affiliates.

The financial part of the narrative section fulfills to some degree the function of footnotes in American practice. Disclosure requirements are not as firmly established and clearly developed; although in some respects the requirements go beyond those established in the United States.

The entire narrative section is subject to the auditor's examination and covered by his report which the auditor would be obliged to qualify if he deemed any of the statements therein to be incorrect or misleading.

The financial statements, together with the narrative section and the auditor's report, must be submitted to the stockholders' meeting and filed with the local trade register. The financial statements have to be published in the *Federal Gazette* and in some cases in the commercial press. They may be submitted voluntarily to banks or other interested parties.

Consolidated Financial Statements. The Companies Act of 1965 requires that under certain circumstances consolidated financial statements be prepared and published. Numerous large companies which do not meet the tests prescribed by the Companies Act prepare consolidated financial statements on a voluntary basis, some of which are even published in the press.

The Companies Act prescribes in detail the principles to be applied when consolidating financial statements. Such principles are derived from generally accepted consolidation practice but do not apply to statements which are voluntarily consolidated. Ownership of a majority of the outstanding stock is generally considered a necessary condition. Insignificant subsidiaries may be omitted from a consolidation. Foreign subsidiaries may be consolidated. Intercompany accounts and intercompany profits, e.g., in inventories, must be eliminated.

A separate narrative part must be included in the management's report in those cases where consolidated financial statements are required by the Companies Act. Domestic subsidiaries consolidated must be listed individually but foreign subsidiaries, if consolidated, may be noted but need not be listed.

The narrative part of the consolidated financial statements is twofold and deals with the performance and financial position of the group, and supplements and explains the consolidated financial statements. Events of significance which have occurred after the closing date must be reported as well as material changes in application of accounting principles.

Accounting Practices

In German theory and practice, the results of operations are determined by the net changes during the accounting period in those balance sheet items which are, in a sense, deferred for later transfer into the earnings statement. From this follows the formal principle of balance sheet continuity; i.e., the closing balance sheet of one period is necessarily the opening balance sheet of the next. However, although current assets written down at the end of the year are carried forward at the new valuation into the next year, they do not (if on hand at the end of the next year) necessarily remain at the written-down valuation but may be revalued upward within the limits of the acquisition cost or manufacturing cost. If a material revaluation is made, the amount of write-up must be disclosed. This is different from American practice where a write-down to market of an inventory item will establish the carrying value of the item for the next inventory.

The law also established the principle of completeness, i.e., the balance sheet must contain all assets and liabilities. Excepted from application of this principle are intangible assets purchased which may be capitalized or expensed when acquired. If goodwill is capitalized, the amount must be shown separately and (for financial accounting purposes) be amortized within five years. Whether or not such item is capitalized for financial accounting purposes, for purposes of taxation the acquisition value remains unchanged and no amortization is permitted. A liability for which the statute of limitations has tolled must be shown if the corporation does not intend to avail itself of its right to refuse payment; assets acquired under conditional sales contracts are to be set up and conversely the seller must record the receivable and eliminate the cost of the asset sold.

General Principles of Valuation

Acquisition cost or manufacturing cost is the maximum balance sheet value for assets whereas liablities must be carried at the amount actually payable; unrealized gains may not be reflected in the carrying amounts. Conservatism is the basic principle of valuation insofar as current assets are concerned; German law requires that current assets be written down to the lower of replacement or reproduction cost or net realizable value. Current assets may also be written down to the extent permissible for purposes of taxation. Arbitrary undervaluation of assets is not permitted; write-down or understatement of the cost of acquisition or production at which current assets generally are to be carried is allowed only within the limits set by the law.

However, the application of German tax law often leads to an understatement of assets in statutory financial statements. The chief examples are accelerated depreciation for various types of fixed assets and inventory reserves of up to 20 percent on certain imported products. Normally, advantage can be taken of these provisions of tax law only if the amounts involved are reflected in the financial statements.

In making the cost/market comparison, it is generally necessary to deal with individual items. For example, if two different securities are owned, it is not permissible to compare aggregate cost with aggregate market value and thereby offset a loss in value of one security against an increase in value of the other. Some groupings and, therefore, offsets are acceptable in the case of fungible goods or goods of a similar nature.

Basically, market value is determined as of the balance sheet date. However, losses and drop in prices between the balance sheet date and the later time of valuation should be recognized to the extent that they affect goods on hand or liabilities at the balance sheet date. For example, if a debtor goes into bankruptcy after the balance sheet date, the receivable should be reduced in value if it is considered that the debtor was already in difficulty at the balance sheet date.

Inventories

Raw material cost includes freight in, duty, and other expenditures to bring the material into place and is to be reduced by trade discounts and cash discounts.

Cost of work in process and finished goods includes material, labor, and overhead. Material cost is usually determined by the average method as this is the only method which is unconditionally accepted by the tax authorities. In preparing the statutory financial statements, all other methods recognized in generally accepted accounting principles such as Fifo, Lifo, and so forth, are permissible although they are not permitted for tax purposes. In any case, conservatism rules, and the maximum balance sheet value of inventories is the lower of cost or market. Change in the method of valuation is permitted, but if a change has a material effect on profit or loss, disclosure in the narrative section of the annual report is required by the Companies Act.

German trade and tax law requires that physical inventories be taken every year. The physical count may be made at any time within the period from three months before to two months after the balance sheet date. If the date of taking inventories is different from the balance sheet date, all changes in the aggregate value of inventories between those dates must be proved by the records.

Accounts Receivable

Uncollectible accounts should be written off. For doubtful accounts, it is necessary to provide a reserve. In general, a specific reserve is provided for individual accounts and a general reserve for the remainder of the accounts.

Long-term receivables free of interest or at a low rate of interest normally have to be carried at their discounted amount. Receivables in foreign currencies have to be translated at the current rate or the rate prevailing at the date of origin whichever is lower.

Long-Term Debt

In Germany, a long-term debt is one which matures more than four years after date of inception. Such debt must be shown in the balance sheet at the amount repayable except annuity obligations which are carried at their discounted value. Debt discount is shown separately on the asset side and is amortized over the term of the debt. Portions of long-term debt maturing within four years are included in long-term debt but mentioned in a note to the balance sheet.

Assets pledged as security should be disclosed in the narrative section of the annual report. Bonds repurchased (treasury bonds) that may be reissued are to be shown as securities on the asset side.

Legal Reserve

The Companies Act requires that a legal reserve be established for the safety of creditors. In general, 5 percent of net earnings must be set aside until the reserve reaches 10 percent (or a higher amount if so provided in the bylaws) of the capital stock. Any paid-in surplus must also be allocated to the legal reserve. The reserve may be utilized only to cover operating losses.

Capital Stock

Capital stock is shown at par value and each issue of stock with different rights is set forth separately. Disclosure of the amount of authorized capital appears not on the face of the balance sheet but in the narrative. Treasury shares and subscriptions receivable for capital stock are shown as separate asset items.

Requirements for Listing Securities on the Stock Exchange and Public Sale of Securities

At present there are eight stock exchanges in Germany, the principal ones being in Frankfurt and Düsseldorf. These are supervised through authority of the state in which the exchange is located (Börsenaufsicht). The listing of securities on an exchange is governed by the Stock Exchange Law as amended and supplemented. Application for listing of securities is made to an admissions committee of the stock exchange by a member bank or a syndicate of banks acting as brokers. The committee passes on the adequacy and completeness of the information submitted, but does not investigate and does not take responsibility for the correctness of the information, the responsibility for which rests with the bank and the issuer.

The issue of domestic bonds and debentures requires approval of the Federal Ministry of Economics but in the case of DM loans of foreign borrowers such an approval is not necessary. The issue of shares no longer requires approval.

An application for listing on an exchange must be accompanied by certain documents among which are—

1. A prospectus signed by the applicant and the participating bank(s)
2. Articles of incorporation and bylaws
3. Excerpt from the Trade Register
4. Annual reports of the company for the last three fiscal years

The prospectus includes items such as—

1. Excerpts from the articles of incorporation
2. Financial statements and notes thereto for the latest year
3. Accountants' report
4. Information as to the activities of the company
5. Comments of management on the present and future prospects of the company
6. Information on investments in other companies
7. In the case of debentures, details must also be set forth as to the conditions under which the debentures are issued

In practice, the details of disclosure are agreed upon in consultation between the issuer, the bank, and the stock exchange.

The main steps of the listing procedure are the following:

1. Filing of the application by the bank or the syndicate
2. Granting of the admission by the admission committee of the stock exchange
3. Publication of the prospectus
4. Three days after publication of the prospectus, first official quotation

Requirements for listing on an exchange are not too well defined by regulations or general practice. Disclosures, while more extensive than those supplied in the annual report, are somewhat less than those normally found in American listing applications and prospectuses.

West Germany

Illustrative Financial Statements

ILLUSTRATIVE BALANCE SHEET OF A WEST GERMAN COMPANY (AKTIENGESELLSCHAFT)

BILANZ ZUM 31, DEZEMBER 19____
(Balance Sheet at December 31, 19____)

AKTIVA (Assets)

I. AUSSTEHENDE EINLAGEN AUF DAS GRUNDKAPITAL
(Outstanding Payments on Subscribed Share Capital) ....

II. ANLAGEVERMÖGEN
(Fixed Assets and Investments)

A. Sachanlagen und Immaterielle Anlagewerte (Fixed Assets and Investments)

1. Grundstücke und grundstücksgleiche Rechte mit Geschäfts-, Fabrik- und anderen Bauten (Office, factory, and other buildings, including land and similar rights) ....
2. Grundstücke und grundstücksgleiche Rechte mit Wohnbauten (Dwelling houses, including land and similar rights) ....
3. Grundstücke und grundstücksgleiche Rechte ohne Bauten (Land and similar rights not built upon) ....
4. Bauten auf fremden Grundstücken, die nicht zu Nummer 1 oder 2 gehören (Buildings built upon foreign land, except those belonging to figure 1 or 2) ....
5. Maschinen und maschinelle Anlagen (Machinery and heavy equipment) ....
6. Betriebs- und Geschäftsausstattung (Factory and office equipment) ....
7. Anlagen im Bau und Anzahlungen auf Anlagen (Plant under construction and advance payments on account of fixed assets) ....

ILLUSTRATIVE BALANCE SHEET OF A WEST GERMAN COMPANY (AKTIENGESELLSCHAFT)

BILANZ ZUM 31, DEZEMBER 19____
(Balance Sheet at December 31, 19____)

ACTIVA (Assets)

8. Konzessionen, gewerbliche Schutzrechte und ähnliche Rechte sowie Lizenzen an solchen Rechten (Franchises, patents, licenses, trademarks, and similar rights and licenses to such rights)	....	....	
B. Finanzanlagen (Finance investments)			
1. Beteiligungen (Trade investments)	....		
2. Wertpapiere des Anlagevermögens, die nicht zu Nummer 1 gehören (Securities held as long-term investments, except belonging to figure 1)	....		
3. Ausleihungen mit einer Laufzeit von mindestens vier Jahren (Loans, contractual redeemable within four years)	....	....	....
III. UMLAUFVERMOGEN (Revolving Assets)			
A. Vorräte (Stock)			
1. Roh-, Hilfs- und Betriebsstoffe (Raw materials and supplies)	....		
2. Unfertige erzeugnisse (Unfinished products)	....		
3. Fertige Erzeugnisse, Waren (Finished goods, including merchandise)	....	....	
B. Andere Gegenstände des Umlaufvermögens (Other revolving assets)			
1. Geleistete Anzahlungen, soweit sie nicht zu IIA Nr. 7 gehören (Advances to suppliers except belonging to IIA, figure 7)	....		
2. Forderungen aus Lieferungen und Leistungen (Accounts receivable, trade) davon mit einer Restlaufzeit von mehr als einem Jahr . . . . (Of which there is payable beyond one year . . . .)	....		

3. Wechsel (Notes receivable) davon bundesbankfähig . . . . (Of which . . . . is discountable by the Federal Bank System) ....
4. Schecks (Checks) ....
5. Kassenbestand, Bundesbank- und Postscheckguthaben (Cash in hand, in federal bank and in postal check accounts) ....
6. Guthaben bei Kreditinstituten (Cash at other banks) ....
7. Wertpapiere, die nicht zu Nummer 3, 4, 8 oder 9 oder zu IIB gehören (Marketable securities, except belonging to figure 3, 4, 8 or 9 or to IIB) ....
8. Eigene Aktien unter Angabe ihres Nennbetrags (Treasury shares, nominal . . .) ....
9. Anteile an einer herrschenden oder an der Gesellschaft mit Mehrheit beteiligten Kapitalgesellschaft oder bergrechtlichen Gewerkschaft unter Angabe ihres Nennbetrages, bei Gursen der Zahl (Shares in a controlling company, nominal . . .) ....
10. Forderungen an verbundene Unternehmen (Receivables from associated companies) ....
11. Forderungen aus Krediten, die (a) unter § 89; (b) unter § 115 fallen; (Receivables from (a) managers; (b) directors) ....
12. Sonstige Vermögensgegenstände (Other receivables) ....

IV. RECHNUNGSABGRENZUNGSPOSTEN (Deferred Charges and Prepaid Expenses) ....

V. BILANZVERLUST (Accumulated Net Loss) ....

ILLUSTRATIVE BALANCE SHEET OF A WEST GERMAN COMPANY (AKTIENGESELLSCHAFT)

BILANZ ZUM 31, DEZEMBER 19____
(Balance Sheet at December 31, 19____)

PASSIVA
(Liabilities and Shareholders' Equity)

I. GRUNDKAPITAL (Share Capital—State Separately Each Class of Shares) ....

II. OFFENE RÜCKLAGEN (Open Reserves)
 1. Gesetzliche Rücklagen (Legal reserve) ....
 2. Andere Rücklagen (Free reserves) ....

III. WERTBERICHTIGUNGEN (Adjustments to Assets) ....

IV. RÜCKSTELLUNGEN (Reserves for Estimated Liabilities and Accrued Expenses)
 1. Pensionsrückstellungen (Reserves for pensions) ....
 2. Andere Rükstellungen (Other reserves) ....

V. VERBINDLICHKEITEN MIT EINER LAUFZEIT VON MINDESTENS VIER JAHREN (Liabilities, Contractual Payable Beyond Four Years)
 1. Anleihen (Loans) davon durch Grundpfandrechte gesichert . . . . (Of which . . . . secured by mortgage) ....
 2. Verbindlichkeiten gegenüber Kreditinstituten (Liabilities to banks) ....
 3. Sonstige Verbindlichkeiten (Other liabilities) ....

 Von Nummern 1 bis 3 sind vor Ablauf von vier Jahren fällig (Total of 1 to 3 payable within four years . . . .)

VI. ANDERE VERBINDLICHKEITEN (Other Liabilities)
 1. Verbindlichkeiten aus Lieferungen und Leistungen (Liabilities to suppliers) ....

2. Verbindlichkeiten aus der Annahme gezogener Wechsel und der Ausstellung eigener Wechsel (Notes payable)	....	
3. Verbindlichkeiten gegenüber Kreditinstituten, soweit sie nicht zu Nr. V gehören (Liabilities to banks, except belonging to figure V)	....	
4. Erhaltene Anzahlungen (Customers' prepayments)	....	
5. Verbindlichkeiten gegenüber verbundenen Unternehmen (Liabilities to associated companies)	....	
6. Sonstige Verbindlichkeiten (Other liabilities)	....	....
VII. RECHNUNGSABGRENZUNGSPOSTEN (Deferred Income)		....
VIII. BILANZGEWINN (Accumulated Net Profit)		....

ILLUSTRATIVE INCOME STATEMENT OF A WEST GERMAN COMPANY (AKTIENGESELLSCHAFT)

GEWINN- UND VERLUSTRECHNUNG
(Profit and Loss Account)

1.	Umsatzerlöse (Net sales)	....	
2.	Erhöhung und Verminderung des Bestandes an fertigen und unfertigen Erzeugnissen (Increase or decrease of finished and unfinished products)	....	....
3.	Andere aktivierte Eigenleistungen (Other manufacturing costs for fixed assets)		....
4.	Gesamtleistung (Total output)		....
5.	Aufwendungen für Roh-, Hilfs- und Betriebsstoffe sowie für bezogene Waren (Raw materials and supplies, purchased goods consumed in sales)		....
6.	Rohertrag/Rohaufwand (Gross profit (loss))		....
7.	Erträge aus Gewinngemeinschaften, Gewinnabführungs- und Teilgewinnabführungsverträgen (Income from profit transfer agreements)	....	
8.	Erträge aus Beteiligungen (Income from trade investments)	....	
9.	Erträge au den anderen Finanzanlagen (Income from other long-term investments)	....	
10.	Sonstige zinsen und ähnliche Erträge (Other interest and similar income)	....	
11.	Erträge aus dem Abgang von Gegenständen des anlagevermögens und aus Zuschreibungen zu Gegenständen des anlagevermögens (Income from the retirement and from the appraisal of fixed assets)	....	
12.	Erträge aus der Herabsetzung der Pauschalwertberichtigung zu Forderungen (Income from the cancellation of lump allowances)	....	

13. Erträge aus der Auflösung von Rückstellungen (Income from the cancellation of overstated reserves for estimated liabilities and accrued expenses) ....

14. Sonstige Erträge (Other income), davon auszerordentliche . . . . (of which . . . is extraordinary) ....

15. Erträge aus Verlustübernahme (Income from loss transfer agreements) ....

....

16. Löhne und Gehälter (Wages and salaries) ....

17. Soziale Abgaben (Social taxes) ....

18. Aufwendungen für Altersversorgung und Unterstützung (Expenses for pension plans and relief) ....

19. Abschreibungen und Wertberichtigungen auf Sachanlagen und Immaterielle Anlagewerte (Depreciation and amortization of fixed assets and investments) ....

20. Abschreibungen und Wertberichtigungen auf Finanzanlagen mit Ausnahme des Betrages, der in die Pauschalwertberichtigung zu Forderungen eingestellt ist (Depreciation and amortization of finance investments) ....

21. Verluste aus Wertminderungen oder dem Abgang von Gegenständen des Umlaufvermögens außer Vorräten (§ 151 Abs. 1 Aktivseite III B) und Einstellung in die Pauschalwertberichtigung zu Forderungen (Losses by deduction or on the retirement of

ILLUSTRATIVE INCOME STATEMENT OF A WEST GERMAN COMPANY (AKTIENGESELLSCHAFT)

GEWINN- UND VERLUSTRECHNUNG
(Profit and Loss Account)

	current assets other than inventories and expenses by lump—allowances)	....	
22.	Verluste aus dem Abgang von Gegenständen des Anlagevermögens (Losses on the retirement of fixed assets and investments)	....	
23.	Zinsen und ähnliche Aufwendungen (Interest and similar expenses)	....	
24.	Steuern (Taxes)		
	(a) vom Einkommen, vom Ertrag und vom Vermögen (On income and net assets)	....	
	(b) sonstige (Other)	....	
25.	Aufwendungen aus Verlustübernahme (Losses arising from loss transfer agreements)	....	
26.	Sonstige Aufwendungen (Other expenses)	....	
27.	Auf Grund einer Gewinngemeinschaft, eines Gewinnabführungs- und eines Teilgewinnabführungsvertrages abgeführte Gewinne (Profits transferred to parent company under profit transfer agreements)	....	....
28.	Jahresüberschuß/Jahresfehlbetrag (Profit or loss for the period)		....
29.	Gewinnvortrag/Verlustvortrag aus dem Vorjahr (Profit or loss brought forward from the preceding year)		....
			....
30.	Entnahmen aus offenen Rücklagen (Release of reserves)		
	(a) aus der Gesetzlichen Rücklage (Release of legal reserve)	....	
	(b) aus freien Rücklagen (Release of free reserves)	....	....
			....

31. Einstellungen aus dem Jahresüberschuß in offene Rücklagen (Amounts appropriated to reserves out of profit for the period)		
(a) in die gesetzliche Rücklage (Appropriated to legal reserve)	....	
(b) in freien Rücklagen (Appropriated to free reserves)	....	....
32. Bilanzgewinn/Bilanzverlust (Accumulated net profit/loss)		....

Addenda

Australia

Forms of Business Organization

Foreign Company

In the early part of 1974, the states of New South Wales, Queensland, and Victoria entered into an agreement and enacted laws creating an Interstate Corporate Affairs Commission, the purpose of which is to allow a company to deal with the one office within that company's state of incorporation instead of the separate participating states' Corporate Affairs Commissions in matters of reservation of names, borrowing corporations, trust deeds for investment schemes, and foreign companies. Other Australian states can participate in this arrangement by becoming parties to the agreement and passing the appropriate legislation.

Those companies incorporated in one participating state and carrying on business in another participating state are now known as "recognized companies," as to which the company law of the host state no longer requires registration of certain information which would duplicate that on record in the home state.

Auditing Standards

A revised Statement on Auditing Standards, which will replace the Statement on General Principles of Professional Auditing Practice (originally issued in 1969), has been completed for issue late in 1974. The new statement expands the details of concepts in the original statement, and recognizes the current responsibilities of the auditor under the law as well as changes and developments in accounting principles and auditing techniques which have become accepted by the profession in recent years.

Accounting Principles and Practices

Accounting Recommendations

The Institute of Chartered Accountants in Australia and The Australian Society of Accountants have issued certain revised Statements on Accounting Standards dealing with the subject matter of those identified as D1.2 and D5 in the chapter on Australia, and have completed and issued statements D10 (expenditure carried forward to subsequent accounting periods), DS7 (materiality in financial statements), and DS11 (disclosure of accounting methods used in preparing financial statements), all of which are noted as being in draft stage in the text.

Canada

Auditing Standards

In 1973 the Accounting and Auditing Standards Research Committee of the Canadian Institute of Chartered Accountants was split into two separate committees, the Accounting Research Committee and the Auditing Standards Committee. The latter committee is made up entirely of individuals in the public practice of accounting, but the Auditing Standards Committee has in its membership representatives from the academic sector, industry, finance, and other accounting bodies. Each committee has a support staff of full-time chartered accountants employed by the Canadian Institute.

These committees have undertaken a substantial number of projects since they were created in 1973. Of particular interest is the release of the Accounting Research Committee dealing with business combinations (effective for fiscal years beginning after March 31, 1974), the most significant recommendations in which are (1) mandatory amortization of goodwill over a period not to exceed 40 years and (2) a virtual ban on the pooling method of accounting for business combinations. Another recommendation of the Accounting Research Committee deals with the "statement of changes in financial position" and outlines, in some detail, the concepts and methods to be followed in the preparation of such a statement. The Committee did not make mandatory the inclusion of this statement in financial reports, although the Securities Commissions and various Companies Acts do require it.

Denmark

Since the chapter on Denmark was written, a new Companies Act has become effective as of January 1974. Significant changes in law applicable to the areas covered by the original chapter are briefly described in the following paragraphs.

Forms of Business Organization

Aktieselskab
(Joint-Stock Company)

It is now necessary that only two founders be *domiciled* in Denmark, and there is no longer any citizenship or residence requirement. Minimum capital is now 100,000 kroner, and at least 50 percent of the capital (but not less than 100,000 kroner) must be paid in at the time of registration. There is no longer any requirement that shareholders be at least three in number; one person may own all the shares.

While the rules regarding composition of the board of directors remain generally in effect, they have been modified in the case of companies having share capital of less than 400,000 kroner and employees averaging less than 50 in number for the three preceding years; such companies may now have as few as two directors with one deputy (alternate). Further, if a company has a minimum of 50 or more employees for three consecutive years, the employees as a body have the right to elect two members of the board and two deputies from their own group. Only half the board members need have Danish domicile.

Appointment of an executive manager (or managers) is now mandatory only where the share capital is 400,000 kroner or more, and managers need only be *domiciled* in Denmark.

If a company's shares are quoted on the stock exchange, owners of one-tenth of the share capital may require auditing by another state-authorized accountant or registered accountant in cooperation with the auditor already selected. The annual accounts of *any* joint-stock company are now accessible to the public.

Anpart-Selskab
(Private Company)

This is a newly authorized form of business organization which is expected to be used primarily by family enterprises and small business undertakings. It is very similar in form to the aktieselskab, but the formalities as to foundation, amendment of articles and capital, and so forth are less burdensome. One difference of substance is that the minimum capital required is only 30,000 kroner.

Qualified Auditor

Except in the case of the anpart-selskab, at least one of the qualified auditors must be a state-authorized accountant or a registered accountant.

The Accounting Profession

Registered Accountant

This is a newly created class of auditors which in various ways can obtain the title "registered accountant" by fulfilling certain requirements. Such requirements are substantially less than those for the state-authorized public accountant.

Auditing Standards

Standards of Reporting

In addition to the endorsement of the annual accounts mentioned in the chapter on Denmark, the auditor is now required to submit a report on the audit at the general shareholders' meeting. The report must contain, among other things, a declaration as to whether the annual accounts have been made up in the manner required by law and the company's articles. The auditor must also comment on any matters that may involve liability of the board of directors or the management, and may include in his report any other information that he considers appropriate to bring to the attention of the shareholders.

Accounting Principles and Practices

Form and Content of Financial Statements

In contrast to the former Companies Act, the new Companies Act contains very specific requirements as to the items that must be shown separately in the balance sheet and the profit and loss account. Apparently there will be little variation in the form of financial statements except to the extent, as permitted by the new law, that any deviation from the statutory form can be shown to be consistent with good accounting practice. The new act also requires that a great deal of special information with respect to particular items be presented, either on the face of the balance sheet and profit and loss account or in the footnotes thereto.

A summary of the statutory requirements is presented as follows:

Balance Sheet

A. ASSETS

I. *Current Assets*
(To be listed separately under this caption are cash; shares or "anparts" in other companies; work in progress for third parties; stock (inventories); and prepayment to suppliers.)

II. *Capital Assets*
(To be listed under this caption are shares or "anparts" in subsidiaries; shares or "anparts" in other companies; bonds and other securities; other receivables; prepayments to suppliers; patent and similar rights; goodwill; deferred charges; machinery, equipment and similar stock-in-trade; ships and aircraft; and real property.)

III. (There is no specific caption for this third class of assets, but the items to be listed thereunder are shareholders' subscriptions and "own shares.")

B. LIABILITIES AND NET CAPITAL

I. *Short-Term Liabilities*
(To be listed separately under this caption are notes payable; taxes payable or accrued; prepayments by clients (customers); bank and similar liabilities; and other short-term liabilities.)

II. *Dividends to the Shareholders*
(To be listed separately are previously declared but unpaid dividends; and current year dividends unpaid.)

III. *Long-Term Liabilities*
(To be listed under this caption are mortgages payable; other secured debt; convertible bonds; debentures; and other liabilities.)

IV. *Investment Funds and Other Reserves, Specified*
(This form does not show the items which would fall in this category.)

V. *Capital*
(To be shown under this caption are (a) restricted net capital, divided into share capital, legal reserve, and appreciation account and (b) free net capital, divided into free reserves (specified) and retained earnings (deficit).)

C. PLEDGED ASSETS
(Under this heading the amount of pledges secured by real property, and other pledges, individually, with the book value of the pledged assets, are to be disclosed.)

D. GUARANTEE OBLIGATIONS
(Discounted bills of exchange and securities and guarantees not specifically secured, are to be disclosed under this heading.)

Profit and Loss Account

The profit and loss account shall show the gross revenues from the company's operations, unless, due to special circumstances, disclosure thereof might be detrimental to the company. Revenues required to be shown separately include dividends on shares in subsidiaries; dividends on other shares; interest; profit on disposal of capital assets; and other extraordinary income. Expenditures to be shown separately include interest paid; depreciation and write-down of capital assets; loss on disposal of capital assets; other extraordinary expenditures; estimated amount of tax chargeable on the year's income, plus prior year adjustments; and appropriations to investment reserves.

The special information required to be furnished with respect to particular items, either in the balance sheet or profit and loss account, pertains to the following:

1. Shares or anparts in other companies (name, nominal and book value, and so forth, unless detrimental to the company).
2. Ships, aircraft, and real property (cost, revaluation adjustments, changes during the year, depreciation, and write-downs).
3. Pension commitments.
4. Convertible bonds (details of conversion rate, dates, interest rates, and so forth).
5. Share capital (details of classes of shares).
6. Share capital (changes during the year).
7. Real property (latest appraisal).
8. Current assets (variances between original cost and carrying amounts).
9. Write-up of capital assets (disposition of credit).

10. Changes in classifications in balance sheet and profit and loss accounts affecting comparability with other years' financial statements.
11. Effect on the results of the current year of changes in valuation of current assets, depreciation policies, and so forth.
12. Whether the valuation of work in hand for third parties includes any estimated profit and, if so, explanation.
13. If sale of assets at balance sheet valuation would result in taxation, disclosure of details is required unless the related tax liability is provided for.
14. Total amount of taxes paid during the accounting year.
15. Own shares or shares in parent company (if any acquired during the year, details of nominal value, percentage of total capital acquired, and purchase price).

Changes in the treatment of certain balance sheet items, required by the new act, are briefly described in the following:

Stock of Merchandise (Inventory). The new Companies Act requires that the inventory reserve be shown separately in the balance sheet rather than netted against the inventory amount.

Fixed Assets. The reserve arising from a write-up of "fixed assets" may no longer be used to cover deficits, but may be used for issuing bonus shares.

Machinery, Equipment, and Real Property. It is now compulsory to state the latest appraised value of real property.

Statutory Reserve. The statutory reserve may now be used for issuance of bonus shares, unless the company has a deficit.

Consolidated Financial Statements. Parent companies of affiliated groups are now required to prepare consolidated financial statements for each accounting year.

India

Forms of Business Organization

The present policy of the government of India (as of late 1974) is not to encourage the establishment of branches of foreign companies. Existing branches of foreign companies other than banking companies have been directed to seek approval for carrying on their business, and the government has announced that such companies will be asked to convert themselves into Indian companies. Foreign airlines and shipping companies will not, however, be required to so convert.

The Foreign Exchange Regulation Act of 1973 which came into force as of January 1974 has replaced the Foreign Exchange Regulation Act of 1947. Under the provisions of the new act permission of the Reserve Bank is required in the case of nonresident foreigners, nonresident companies other than banking companies, or Indian companies in which the nonresident interest is more than 40 percent, for various matters in connection with carrying on business in India.

Companies-General

The Companies (Amendment) Act of 1974 has made several amendments of far reaching consequences to the Companies Act of 1956. The government has not yet (as of late 1974) announced the date on which the amendments will come into force.

The Amendment Act seeks to limit the number of company audits per partner of an auditing firm. The ceiling has been fixed at twenty companies of which not more than ten should be companies having paid-up share capital of 2,500,000 rupees each.

The auditors of a company in which 51 percent or more of the shares are held by the government must be appointed by the central government.

Private Companies

The Companies (Amendment) Act of 1974 provides that, in order to retain the privileges of a private company, not only shall the shareholding in its paid-up capital by one or more bodies corporate be less than 25 percent, but its annual turnover (sales) shall be no more than 10,000,000 rupees and it shall not hold 25 percent or more of the paid-up capital of a public company.

The Accounting Profession

The Chartered Accountant

The apprenticeship period has been reduced to three years for an articled clerk or four years for an audit clerk, and no further reduction in period of training is allowable to candidates on the basis of their results at the degree examination and the intermediate examination. The preliminary examination has been renamed the "entrance examination." This examination must be passed by an applicant to become an articled or an audit clerk unless such applicant has secured a minimum grade of 50 percent in a degree examination. The apprentice period required to qualify for admission to the intermediate examination has been reduced to 12 months of service as an articled clerk or 16 months of service as an audit clerk. Under the present regulations, the final examination may be taken only after the candidate has completed his training as an articled or audit clerk.

The scope of the entrance, intermediate and final examinations has been expanded to some degree, but in general it parallels that outlined in the chapter on India, except with respect to the final examination in which the candidate is required to appear for examination in any two of the following additional subjects: corporate management; operations research and statistical analysis; managerial economics; systems analysis and data processing; production and inventory control; tax planning and tax management; or management and operational audit.

The previous rule providing for remission in the period of practical training in an industrial undertaking from twelve months to six months under certain conditions, is no longer in effect.

The number of articled clerks that can be engaged by a fellow in practice has been increased by one in each time category (five, seven, ten, and fifteen years).

Institute of Cost and Works Accountants

The Companies Act provides that if the government considers it necessary it may direct an audit of the cost accounts of a company mentioned in the section on business records. Such an audit should be carried out by a cost accountant within the meaning of the Cost and Works Accountants Act of 1959, or, until such time as the government otherwise determines, by a chartered accountant or any other person who possesses the prescribed qualifications. The qualifications prescribed for a chartered accountant are that he must be in practice and must have passed the first part of the management accountancy examination of the Institute of Chartered Accountants of India.

The audit will be in addition to the normal statutory audit, and the auditor's appointment, powers, and duties for this audit correspond to those of the company's statutory auditor in relation to the statutory audit. An audit of cost accounts must be carried out by a person other than the statutory auditor, and the cost auditor is required to submit his report to the Company Law Board of the central government and to furnish a copy thereof to the company.

Accounting Principles and Practices

Investments

Disclosure must be made of the amount of investments in the capital of a partnership.

Statement of Profit and Loss

The profit and loss account must disclose the following additional information:

1. Analysis of turnover (sales), showing amount and quantities of each class of goods sold.
2. In the case of manufacturing companies, the value of raw materials consumed, showing separately the value and quantities of important basic raw materials and all items accounting for 10 percent or more of the total value of raw materials consumed; also the quantities and values of each class of goods in the opening and closing inventories of goods produced.
3. Any item of miscellaneous expense in excess of one percent of total revenue or 5,000 rupees, whichever is higher.
4. Number and total remuneration of employees receiving in excess of 3,000 rupees per month.
5. Detailed information as to payments to auditors, whether for services as auditors, as advisers, or in any other capacity for taxation matters, company law matters, management services, or in any other areas.

Italy

Proposed Legislation

The Italian government has published details of proposed changes to certain sections of the Civil Code relating to limited liability companies. These modifications have been conceived within the framework of Article 220 of the Treaty of Rome which established the European Economic Community, but are not necessarily anticipatory of the planned standardization of legislation contemplated by the treaty.

The following principal matters included in the proposed legislation are:

1. The establishment of definitions of (a) a "controlled company" and (b) an "associated company."
2. Modification or introduction of regulations covering—
   a. Debentures and other loan stock convertible into shares.
   b. Option rights of existing shareholders in capital increases.
   c. Increases in share capital and the issue of debentures and other loan stock.
   d. Shareholders' proxies.
   e. Cross holdings of shares.
3. As to financial statements—
   a. Standardization of the information to be shown in the statement of income.
   b. Requirement that accounts (financial statements) show details of book and actual values of investments in subsidiaries and associated companies, and that copies of the accounts of subsidiaries be attached thereto.
   c. Requirement that operating results be reported semi-annually.
   d. Requirement that annual audits be made by an authorized auditing firm.
   e. Recognition of audited figures for legal purposes.

f. Establishment of a formal body to control published information relating to quoted companies.

A number of the proposed legislative changes apply only to quoted companies, but are indicative of the Italian government's desire to introduce procedures and regulations which are already operative in other parts of the western world. Enactment of the proposed legislation would result in a marked departure from traditional business customs.

Japan

In December 1973, the "Foreign Section (Gaikoku Bu)" was established in the Tokyo Stock Exchange for listing stocks of foreign companies. During 1974, the new "Law for Special Measures under the Commercial Code with Respect to Auditing, etc. of Stock Corporation" was promulgated. Brief descriptions of the principal effects of these and other changes in law and regulations applicable to the areas covered by the chapter on Japan are set forth under the captions corresponding to those of the main chapter to which they relate. (For the purpose of this addendum, the term "company" refers only to stock corporations.)

Forms of Business Organization

Kabushiki Kaisha
(Stock Corporation)

The reference to issuance of stock at less than par value, made in the paragraph on "shihonkin (capital)," is no longer appropriate.

Kansa Yaku (Statutory Examiner)

Under the new law, the auditing and reporting requirements of statutory examiners became more stringent, and in respect to some companies the examiners are now required to audit the performance of the directors in carrying out their duties, in addition to auditing the financial statements. The statutory examiners may now request reports from subsidiaries and may examine their accounts if they consider it necessary, although such requests may be denied if denial can be justified. The term of office of a statutory examiner is now two years instead of one; and he may not hold office as a director, general manager or employee of the company or any of its subsidiaries.

In respect to companies having paid-in capital of one hundred million yen or less, the statutory examiners' duties are similar to those prescribed under the old law. They are not required to audit the performance of the directors; they must, however, submit an audit report on the balance sheet, income statement, business report and proposals as to reserves and distribution of profits, within four weeks after these financial documents are received from the directors. The audit report must also cover the detail account statements which supplement the financial documents. The directors are required to submit the financial documents to the examiners five weeks, and the related detail statements three weeks, in advance of the general shareholders' meeting.

In respect to companies having paid-in capital of more than 100,000,000 but less than 500,000,000 yen, the statutory examiners' obligations are more burdensome. In addition to the requirements pertaining to companies having less than 100,000,000 yen capital, the examiners must audit the performance of the directors' duties. Their report must include an outline of the methods of audit; references to missing or false entries and discrepancies; statement as to fair presentation (or the contrary and the reasons therefor); comment on propriety of proposals with respect to reserves and distribution of profits; statement as to accuracy of the business report; disclosure of any improper acts of directors; and reasons why a proper audit could not be made, if that should be the case. The statutory examiners' report and the financial statements must be sent to the shareholders at least two weeks before the general meeting. The examiners are also required to express an opinion as to compliance of the agenda of the meeting and the documents to be submitted thereto, with the company's articles.

A public company (one which is required to be audited pursuant to the Securities and Exchange Law) having paid-in capital of 500,000,000 yen or more, and all companies having paid-in capital of one billion yen or more (whether public or not) are now required to have both statutory examiners and independent auditors. The directors are required to furnish both with sets of financial documents eight weeks, and detail account statements four weeks, in advance of the general shareholders' meeting. The independent auditors first submit their report to both the directors and the statutory examiners, and within one week thereafter the statutory examiners must present their report to the directors with copy to the independent auditors. However, in these cases the statutory examiners' report will cover only the reasonableness of proposals as to reserves and distribution of profits, the content of the business report, improper acts of the directors, reasons why a proper audit could not be made, if that should be the case; and comment on the reasonableness of the independent auditors' examination methods. The notice of the general shareholders' meeting must be accompanied by copies of both the independent auditors' and the statutory examiners' reports.

The new law also provides that non-public companies having paid-in capital of 500,000,000 yen or more, but less than one billion yen, shall be subject to audit by independent auditors, but the effective date of this provision is to be set by future legislation. The scope of such audits will be the same as that now prescribed for statutory examiners' audits of companies having capital of more than 100,000,000 yen but less than 500,000,000 yen.

The Accounting Profession

As now defined, "independent auditors (kaikei kansa nin)" must be "certified public accountants (CPAs)," "foreign certified public accountants," or an "audit corporation (kansa hojin)"; they are to be appointed, or removed, by resolution of the board of directors with the consent of a majority of the statutory examiners. Such appointment or removal must be reported to the general shareholders' meeting with, in the case of removal, a statement of the reason therefor.

A certified public accountant who is a director, statutory examiner, or employee of the company concerned, its parent or subsidiaries, or who has been suspended from practice as a CPA, cannot qualify as "independent auditor," nor can an audit corporation having a member who would be disqualified under the foregoing rule. Neither CPAs nor audit corporations which do qualify should use the services of any person who would be disqualified under the same rule.

If the independent auditors discover evidence of commission of improper acts by a director in the performance of his duty, or any violations of applicable laws or the company's articles, they must report such matters to the statutory examiners. The independent auditors are required to attend the general shareholders' meetings and present their opinions in person if requested to do so by a shareholders' resolution.

It is important to note that, under the new law and regulations, the duties and activities of the independent auditors and the statutory examiners are interdependent and to some extent commingled. Therefore, reference should be made to the preceding section captioned "Kansa Yaku (Statutory Examiner)."

Auditing Standards

Independence

The existence of certain proscribed business relationships, such as the rendering of services as tax agent to the company, or association therewith in the capacity of public servant during the preceding two years, precludes certification of financial statements for Securities and Exchange Law purposes by the CPA or audit corporation involved. The rule also applies to the CPA if the proscribed relationship exists in respect to his spouse or his assistant.

Under the new law, any "interest relationship" between the CPA (including with him his spouse, assistants, or close relatives), or between an audit corporation (including with it its partners, their spouses, assistants, and close relatives), and a company precludes the CPA or audit corporation from acting as the company's independent auditor. An "interest relationship" is deemed to exist where the CPA, or any partner of the audit corporation is a director, statutory examiner, or employee of the company being audited, its parent or subsidiary; or is receiving compensation from the company on a continuing basis for rendering services as a tax agent.

Accounting Principles and Practices

In 1974, the Business Accounting Council published a partial revision of Business Accounting Principles (BAP) which collectively constitute the basis on which CPAs express opinion on the financial statements which are audited pursuant to the Securities and Exchange Law. Important changes effected by the revision are summarized as follows:

1. As a basis for determining income, the "current performance theory" has been superseded by the "all-inclusive theory." As a result, the financial statements to be prepared under the BAP are now the statement of income, the balance sheet, the statement of appropriation of profit, and attached schedule.
2. The statement of income is now divided into three sections: the computation of operating income, ordinary income, and net income.
3. The statement of income is required to show the changes during the current period in unappropriated earned surplus account.
4. Sales on the installment basis should be recognized on a delivery basis. (Use of the "installment method" of accounting is, however, still permitted as a conservative alternative.)
5. Intracompany profit, sales, and purchases are now required to be eliminated without exception, but such elimination may be made on an estimated basis.
6. Under the new BAP, trade receivables and payables arising in the ordinary course of business are to be classified as current assets

and liabilities regardless of age or maturity. The "operating cycle concept" takes the place of the "one year rule."

7. Capital surplus items, other than those required by the Commercial Code to be accounted for as capital reserve, are to be shown as "other surplus."

The new Commercial Code prescribes that fair accounting practices should be considered in interpreting the provisions regarding business records. A detailed listing of assets and liabilities, preparation of which was required under the old Code of all business organizations is no longer necessary.

The title of the "Ministry of Justice Regulation Concerning Balance Sheet and Income Statement of Stock Corporation" has been changed to "Regulation Concerning Balance Sheet, Income Statement, and Related Detail Account Statements of Stock Corporation." The changes made in the Regulation with respect to requirements for account presentation and notes thereto are summarized as follows:

1. The monetary effect of any material accounting change must now be disclosed in a note to the balance sheet or income statement. Under the old regulation only the fact of the change had to be disclosed.
2. Detail account statements are now required to supplement the balance sheet and income statement, showing changes in capital stock and reserves; details of changes in fixed assets; details of receivables from the majority shareholder and subsidiaries; details of investments in subsidiaries; assets pledged; transactions with the directors, statutory examiners, and majority shareholder; remuneration of statutory examiners and directors; and where a reserve for specified expenditures or loss has been created, the reasons why the expenditures or loss are expected and the method of determining the amount provided during the current period.

Capital

Legal and Other Reserves of Corporations. Under the new Commercial Code, a stock corporation, the accounting period of which covers twelve months, may (subject to certain conditions) once a year pay an interim cash dividend by providing in its Articles that the shareholders registered as of a certain date during an accounting period may receive a cash distribution by resolution adopted at a directors' meeting. However, an appropriation to profit reserve of one-tenth of the amount of the interim dividend is required until the balance of the reserve reaches 25 percent of the paid-in capital.

Requirements for Public Sale of Securities

The Ministry of Finance Regulations pertaining to the issue and sale of securities under the Securities and Exchange Law and the preparation of financial statements for reporting under that Law have been revised. The requirements as to the financial statements to be included in the Registration Statement and Securities Report, which are to be submitted to the Ministry of Finance by foreign companies, have been specifically prescribed. Also, in line with the changes in business accounting principles, the "current performance theory" has been superseded by the "all-inclusive theory" as the basis for determining income for reporting under the Securities and Exchange Law. The effects of other important changes are briefly described, as follows:

1. Foreign companies whose shares are publicly offered or listed are subject to the same reporting requirements as Japanese companies. However, the *form* of registration statement and securities report to be used by foreign companies is now separately specified. When permitted by the Ministry of Finance, a foreign company may file financial statements prepared in accordance with the accounting principles and form of presentation generally accepted in its home country, although the differences in accounting practices between Japan and the home country should be explained in footnotes. Thus, it is now possible for foreign companies to file consolidated financial statements instead of parent company statement only, with the Ministry.
2. The statement of earned surplus has been eliminated.

Requirements for Listing Securities on the Stock Exchange

At the time of writing the chapter on Japan, stocks of foreign companies were not listed on any Japanese stock exchange; hence, this section in that chapter applies only to Japanese companies. In December 1973, the "Foreign Section (Gaikoku Bu)" was established in the Tokyo Stock Exchange, the requirements for listing on which are different from those applicable to Japanese companies. These requirements are summarized below:

1. Number of shares listed—
   Stock traded in units of 1,000 shares – 6,000,000 shares or more

Stocks traded in units of 100 shares – 600,000 shares or more
Stocks traded in units of 10 shares – 60,000 shares or more

2. Status of distribution in Japan—

   a. Number of "trading shareholders" anticipated to be 2,000 or more.

      (A "trading shareholder" is one who owns less than 50,000 shares, if the stock is traded in units of 1,000 shares; less than 10,000 shares, if the stock is traded in units of 100 shares; or less than 1,000 shares, if the stock is traded in units of 10 shares.)

   b. Number of floating shares owned by the trading shareholders anticipated to be 2,000,000 shares as to 1,000 share units; 200,000 shares as to 100 share units; and 20,000 shares as to 10 share units.

3. Net assets—

   Net assets at end of fiscal period immediately preceding date of listing application is two billion yen or more.

4. Income before income taxes—

   a. Income before taxes for each of the three preceding years was three billion yen or more.

   b. Ratio of pre-tax income attributable to common stock, to average of common stock outstanding, during the three preceding years was 30 percent (20 percent as to average stock in excess of one billion yen); and ratio of pre-tax income of the last preceding year attributable to common stock, to common stock outstanding at end of period preceding date of listing application, was 40 percent or more (20 percent as to stock in excess of one billion yen.)

5. Dividends—

   a. Dividends have been paid on common stock for each fiscal period during the latest two years, at a rate (for the latest year) of 10 percent or more per annum.

   b. Continuation of the dividend rate of 10 percent or more per annum after the listing is anticipated.

Mexico

Forms of Business Organization

On May 9, 1973, new legislation, the "Law to Promote Mexican Investment and Regulate Foreign Investment," became effective. This legislation imposes statutory limitations on foreign investment, many of which, however, were already imposed by administrative regulations and are generally covered in the paragraph captioned "Forms of Business Organization."

Accounting Principles and Practices

The Instituto Mexicano de Contadores Publicos has recently issued a comprehensive statement regarding accounting principles and practices and consisting of a series of bulletins divided into six groups, as follows:

- Basic Accounting Principles
- Financial Statements
- Principles Applicable to Specific Captions (of the balance sheet)
- Specific Problems in Operating Statements
- Principles Applicable to Entities of Special Characteristics
- Theory Investigation

The bulletins number more than thirty, of which nine are already mandatory of application and the remainder are in various stages of adoption.

Revaluation of Fixed Assets

Consideration of revaluation as an acceptable accounting practice has progressed to the point where the Mexican Institute's Committee on Accounting Principles has stated its position on the principles which should attend its use:

1. Revaluation must be adequately revealed in financial statements.
2. Balance sheets must show separately the original cost, accumulated depreciation, and amount of revaluation, and the revaluation reserve must be clearly disclosed.
3. Revaluation must be supported by studies and recommendations of independent technicians (appraisers).
4. The revaluation reserve should not be distributed as a dividend, but may be capitalized.

A bulletin has been issued but not yet approved, and revaluation is not considered a compulsory procedure even where it might be entirely appropriate.

Compulsory Profit Sharing

Contrary to the expectation expressed in the text of the chapter on Mexico, regulations were not changed in 1973 nor have they been to date (August 1974).

The Netherlands

The Accounting Profession

Ethics

New "Rules of Conduct and Professional Activities" were promulgated by the NIvRA in November 1973. Following is a summary of items of special interest:

1. Of the 34 specific rules, some are applicable to all registeraccountants (members of the NIvRA) irrespective of their occupations or employment; some are applicable to registeraccountants only when acting as auditors; and some are applicable only to registeraccountants when acting as public accountants.
2. A registeraccountant is considered to be acting as an *auditor* if he holds himself out to be such, examines the "fairness of accounts," or acts under a joint name with another registeraccountant-auditor. A registeraccountant *acting as an auditor* is considered to be acting as a *public accountant* if (among other things and subject to certain exceptions) he holds himself out to be such, allows publication of a report given by him, or (if employed) he gives a report to someone other than his employer or accepts an appointment outside his employment.
3. The rules applicable to all registeraccountants, irrespective of the capacity in which they act, require abstention from acts discreditable to the profession and notification of interested parties when a registeraccountant ceases to act as a public accountant; and provide that a registeraccountant is considered to have examined the "fairness of accounts" if he issues or permits issuance of a document containing accounts not rendered by himself or in his behalf, in such a manner as to give the impression that such document originated with him, unless the document bears a specific disclaimer.
4. Rules applicable only to registeraccountants acting as *auditors* cover such matters as the following:
   a. Confidentiality of information and secrecy.

b. Conditions under which opinions may be expressed.
c. Scope of reports.
d. Implications of the several forms of opinion, as follows:
   - An unqualified report implies that the registeraccountant is of the opinion that the accounts comply with the requirements relating to them.
   - Qualified approval of the accounts implies objections or uncertainties which are immaterial in effect but which are deemed to warrant disclosure, in which case the term "subject to" shall appear in the report.
   - Disapproval of accounts implies that they do not comply with the pertinent requirements, in which case the terms "not a fair view" or "incorrect" and disclosure of the nature and significance of the reasons for disapproval shall appear in the report.
   - A disclaimer of opinion is indicated by the phrase "no opinion on the fairness of .... (description of accounts . . .) taken as a whole," in which case the matters of uncertainty shall be disclosed.
e. Prohibition of use of another auditor's report unless due care has been exercised in selecting such other auditor. (Under some circumstances a review of such other auditor's work or a supplementary examination of the accounts examined by him may be required.)

5. Further rules applicable only to registeraccountants when acting as *public accountants* cover such areas as independence; permitted forms of practice; conditions of publication of reports; advertising and solicitation; replacement of other accountants; and conditions of acceptance of appointment. Of particular interest are the rules governing permissable forms of practice, which are summarized as follows:

   a. As independent practitioner, whether or not under a joint name with others. (A registeraccountant may practice under a joint name with no other than another registeraccountant, or a non-registeraccountant practicing a liberal profession (irrespective of whether as a private person or a legal entity) in respect of whom the Council of the NIvRA has issued a "statement of acceptance." The "statement of acceptance" will be issued only if it is established that the registeraccountant can bear the co-responsibility arising from practicing under a joint name.)
   b. As employee of another registeraccountant practicing as a public accountant.

c. As employee of a non-registeraccountant who is domiciled outside The Netherlands, for examinations carried out abroad.

d. In the employment of a legal entity in respect of which the Council has issued a "statement of admission." (Issuance of a "statement of admission" is subject to the condition that the legal entity must be controlled by the registeraccountant involved, or by persons qualified to practice under a joint name. Further, members of the NIvRA must be notified of the general terms of the proposed admission, and may instruct the Council regarding such terms.)

The Rules are very comprehensive and specific, and merit study in depth by anyone interested in professional practice in The Netherlands.

Other Organizations of Accountants

The act regulating the profession of Accountant-administratieconsulent (accounting consultant), briefly described in the chapter on The Netherlands, became effective on February 1, 1974. The activities permitted this professional group, as legislatively defined, are as follows:

a. Designing and efficacious accounting system, judging the manner in which accounts are being kept, or keeping a set of accounts; and

b. Giving, in an explanatory report, an analysis or interpretation of data derived from accounting documents, or giving, either orally or in writing, information about, or advice based on such data.

The accountant-administratieconsulent (A.A.C.) is expressly forbidden to express opinion on the "fairness of accounts." However, the A.A.C. may prepare reports relating to financial statements prepared by or on behalf of his employer (client); but such reports may be given to the employer only, may not be published or given to a third party by the employer, and may not be in such form as to create the impression that they are issued by someone acting in the capacity of auditor.

This act further provides that after five years from date of enactment the use of the name "accountant" by any other than registeraccountants, accountant-administratieconsulents, or foreign accountants admitted by the Ministry of Economic Affairs, shall be prohibited.

Norway

The Accounting Profession

The procedures whereby the status of registered accountant (registrert revisor) and certified public accountant (statsautorisert revisor) are attained have been modified. Although the basic requirements as to residence, honesty, financial stability, and so forth, remain unchanged, educational and procedural requirements as modified by regulations promulgated in January 1974 are now as follows:

1. To qualify as a registered accountant—
   a. District college course in auditing for 2½ years. (A "district college" appears to be similar to the "junior college" in the United States.)
   b. Examination in accounting administered by the Ministry of Commerce.
   c. Two years practical experience.
2. For a registered accountant to qualify as a certified public accountant—
   a. Two year course at the commercial university (University of Bergen).
   b. Examination in advanced accounting.
   c. Three more years of practical experience.
3. Alternative route to qualification as as certified public accountant—
   a. Four and one-half year course at the University of Bergen, graduating with degree in economics.
   b. Additional one to one and one-half year course in auditing at the same institution.
   c. Examination in advanced accounting administered by the Ministry of Commerce.
   d. Three years practical experience.

The methods described in the chapter on Norway are still in use but these outlined immediately above are now more prevalent.

Accounting Principles and Practices

Investment Fund Reserve

The comments made in the chapter on Norway with respect to the Investment Fund Reserve no longer apply.

South Africa

Forms of Business Organization

General

The new Companies Act referred to in the section captioned "Forms of Business Organization" has been enacted and consists of 443 sections with numerous supporting schedules and regulations running to more than 350 pages. The principal provisions impose considerably more responsibility on auditors and directors, require much fuller disclosure in annual financial statements, and prescribe tighter time-tables for the issuance of such statements. Time limitations and the volume of the new legislation preclude presentation of further details in this book.

United Kingdom

The Accounting Profession

Organizations of Accountants

In December 1973, The Institute of Municipal Treasurers and Accountants was changed to the Chartered Institute of Public Finance and Accountancy.

Accounting Principles and Practices

In addition to the three statements of standard accounting practice mentioned in the text of the chapter on the United Kingdom, the following statements were issued as of August 1974:

- The Accounting Treatment of Government Grants
- Accounting for Value Added Tax
- Extraordinary Items and Prior Year Adjustments
- Accounting for Changes in the Purchasing Power of Money (provisional, application not mandatory)

The last two standards are of particular interest to U.S. readers.

The definition of an extraordinary item is similar to but not so restrictive as that contained in APB Opinion 30. The standard provides that the profit and loss account should include all items of income and expense recognized in the year. The only items that may now be charged to reserves are the monetary effects of revaluations; however, adjustments relating to movements in foreign currency exchanges are specifically excluded from the standard.

Prior year adjustments resulting from changes in estimates are to be reflected in the profit and loss account; but those adjustments attributable to material changes in accounting policy or resulting from the correction of a fundamental error are to be accounted for by restating the prior year's financial statements and adjusting the opening balance of retained profits.

Because the problems of inflation are still under investigation by a government commission, the application of the last standard has not yet (August 1974) been made mandatory. The standard provides that a company listed on the Stock Exchange should submit a supplementary statement showing historic costs adjusted by application of an index of general purchasing power. The information is to be presented in summarized form as a supplement to the historical cost financial statements and is to be audited.

Statement of Changes in Financial Position

An exposure draft of an accounting standard has been issued which would require all companies to furnish a statement of source and application of funds, which statement would be required to be audited.